THE INSTITUTE FOR POLISH–JEWISH STUDIES

The Institute for Polish–Jewish Studies in Oxford and its sister organization, the American Association for Polish–Jewish Studies, which publish *Polin*, are learned societies that were established in 1984, following the International Conference on Polish–Jewish Studies, held in Oxford. The Institute is an associate institute of the Oxford Centre for Hebrew and Jewish Studies, and the American Association is linked with the Department of Near Eastern and Judaic Studies at Brandeis University.

Both the Institute and the American Association aim to promote understanding of the Polish Jewish past. They have no building or library of their own and no paid staff; they achieve their aims by encouraging scholarly research and facilitating its publication, and by creating forums for people with a scholarly interest in Polish Jewish topics, both past and present.

To this end the Institute and the American Association help organize lectures and international conferences. Venues for these activities have included Brandeis University in Waltham, Massachusetts, the Hebrew University in Jerusalem, the Institute for the Study of Human Sciences in Vienna, King's College in London, the Jagiellonian University in Kraków, the Oxford Centre for Hebrew and Jewish Studies, the University of Łódź, University College London, and the Polish Cultural Institute and the Polish embassy in London. They have encouraged academic exchanges between Israel, Poland, the United States, and western Europe. In particular they seek to help train a new generation of scholars, in Poland and elsewhere, to study the culture and history of the Jews in Poland.

Each year since 1986 the Institute has published a volume of scholarly papers in the series *Polin: Studies in Polish Jewry* under the general editorship of Professor Antony Polonsky of Brandeis University. Since 1994 the series has been published on its behalf by the Littman Library of Jewish Civilization, and since 1998 the publication has been linked with the American Association as well. In March 2000 the entire series was honoured with a National Jewish Book Award from the Jewish Book Council in the United States. More than twenty other works on Polish Jewish topics have also been published with the Institute's assistance.

Further information on the Institute for Polish–Jewish Studies can be found on its website, <www.polishjewishstudies.co.uk>. For the website of the American Association for Polish–Jewish Studies, see <www.aapjstudies.org>.

THE LITTMAN LIBRARY OF JEWISH CIVILIZATION

Dedicated to the memory of
LOUIS THOMAS SIDNEY LITTMAN
*who founded the Littman Library for the love of God
and as an act of charity in memory of his father*
JOSEPH AARON LITTMAN
and to the memory of
ROBERT JOSEPH LITTMAN
who continued what his father Louis had begun
יהא זכרם ברוך

'*Get wisdom, get understanding:
Forsake her not and she shall preserve thee*'
PROV. 4: 5

*The Littman Library of Jewish Civilization is a registered UK charity
Registered charity no.* 1000784

POLIN

STUDIES IN POLISH JEWRY

VOLUME THIRTY

Jewish Education in Eastern Europe

Edited by

ELIYANA R. ADLER

and

ANTONY POLONSKY

Published for

The Institute for Polish–Jewish Studies

and

The American Association for Polish–Jewish Studies

The Littman Library of Jewish Civilization

in association with Liverpool University Press

2018

The Littman Library of Jewish Civilization
in association with Liverpool University Press
4 Cambridge Street, Liverpool L69 7ZU, UK
www.liverpooluniversitypress.co.uk / littman
Managing Editor: Connie Webber

Distributed in North America by
Oxford University Press Inc, 198 Madison Avenue,
New York, NY 10016, USA

Catalogue records for this book are available from
the British Library and the Library of Congress

ISSN 0268 1056

ISBN 978–1–906764–50–0 (cloth)
ISBN 978–1–906764–51–7 (pbk)

Publishing co-ordinator: Janet Moth
Copy-editing: Mark Newby
Proof-reading: Andrew Kirk and Joyce Rappoport
Index: Bonnie Blackburn
Design, typesetting and production: Pete Russell, Faringdon, Oxon.

Printed in Great Britain on acid-free paper by
T J International Ltd, Padstow, Cornwall

Articles appearing in this publication are abstracted and indexed in
Historical Abstracts and *America: History and Life*

This volume is dedicated to

RYSZARD FENIGSEN

born Radom, 10 December 1924, died Waltham, 27 April 2016

*eminent cardiologist and medical ethicist, a devoted connoisseur of music,
painting, and literature, the embodiment of the best of Polish Jewish culture;
a man who read and wrote incessantly in five languages, quoted Russian
poetry at length, searched for the best in every field, and was captivated
by Piero della Francesca and Marcel Proust*

———

This volume benefited from grants from

THE MIRISCH AND LEBENHEIM CHARITABLE FOUNDATION

THE KORET FOUNDATION

THE LUCIUS N. LITTAUER FOUNDATION

Editors and Advisers

Preface

AN EMPHASIS on education has long been a salient feature of the Jewish experience. The pervasive presence of schools and teachers, books and libraries, and youth movements, even in an environment as tumultuous as that of nineteenth- and twentieth-century eastern Europe, is clear from the historical records. Historians of the early modern and modern eras frequently point to the centrality of educational institutions and pursuits within Jewish society, yet the vast majority treat them as merely a reflection of the surrounding culture. Only a small number note how schools and teachers could contribute in dynamic ways to the shaping of local communities and cultures.

This volume addresses this gap in the portrayal of the Jewish past by presenting education as an active and potent force for change. It moves beyond a narrow definition of Jewish education by treating formal and informal training in academic or practical subjects with equal attention. In so doing, it sheds light not only on schools and students, but also on informal educators, youth groups, textbooks, and numerous other devices through which the mutual relationship between education and Jewish society is played out. It also places male and female education on a par with each other, and considers with equal attention students of all ages, religious backgrounds, and social classes.

The essays in this volume span two centuries of Jewish history, from the Austrian and Russian empires to the Second Republic of Poland and the Polish People's Republic. The approach is interdisciplinary, with contributors treating their subject from fields as varied as east European cultural history, gender studies, and language politics. Collectively, they highlight the centrality of education in the vision of numerous Jewish individuals, groups, and institutions across eastern Europe, and the degree to which this vision interacted with forces within and external to Jewish society. In this way they highlight the interrelationship between Jewish educational endeavours, the Jewish community, and external economic, political, and social forces.

As in earlier volumes, the 'New Views' section we include in this volume contains articles on a range of topics: the historiography of the shtetl, antisemitic campaigns in interwar Poland, the gender perspective on the rescue of Jews in Poland during the Second World War, Julian Tuwim's self-fashioning, and a discussion on a report on the situation in Poland in mid-1941 prepared by Roman Catholic activists. Also part of the volume is an interview with David Roskies on his most recent book on Holocaust literature, conducted by Paweł Wolski.

Polin is sponsored by the Institute of Polish–Jewish Studies, which is an associated institute of the Oxford Centre for Hebrew and Jewish Studies, and by the American Association for Polish–Jewish Studies, which is linked with the Department of Near Eastern and Judaic Studies, Brandeis University. As with earlier issues, this volume could not have appeared without the untiring assistance of many individuals. In particular, we should like to express our gratitude to Professor Ron Liebowitz, president of Brandeis University, to Mrs Irene Pipes, president of the American Association for Polish–Jewish Studies, and to Andrzej Szkuta, treasurer of the Institute for Polish–Jewish Studies. These three institutions all made substantial contributions to the cost of producing the volume. A particularly important contribution was that made by the Mirisch and Lebenheim Foundation, and the volume also benefited from grants from the Koret Foundation and the Lucius N. Littauer Foundation. As was the case with earlier volumes, this one could not have been published without the constant assistance and supervision of Connie Webber, managing editor of the Littman Library, Ludo Craddock, chief executive officer, whose retirement we greatly regret, Janet Moth, publishing co-ordinator, Pete Russell, designer, and the tireless copy-editing of Mark Newby, Witold Turopolski, and Joyce Rappoport.

Plans for future volumes of *Polin* are well advanced. Volume 31 will be devoted to a comparison of the situation over the *longue durée* of Jews in Poland and Hungary, volume 32 will investigate Jewish musical life in the Polish lands, and volume 33 will examine Jewish religious life in Poland since 1750. Future volumes are planned on Jewish autonomy in the Polish lands, on Poland and Israel including the Yishuv, and on childhood, children, and childrearing in Jewish eastern Europe. We should welcome articles on these issues. We should also welcome any suggestions or criticisms. In particular, we are always grateful for assistance in extending the geographical range of our journal to Ukraine, Belarus, and Lithuania, both in the period in which these countries were part of the Polish–Lithuanian Commonwealth and subsequently.

Owing to the length of time it takes to publish reviews in an annual publication, we now post all our reviews on the website of the American Association for Polish Jewish Studies (aapjstudies.org) rather than in hard copy, enabling us to discuss new works much nearer to their date of publication. We welcome the submission of reviews of any book or books connected with the history of the Jews in Poland–Lithuania or on Polish–Jewish relations. We are happy to translate reviews submitted in Polish, Russian, Ukrainian, Lithuanian, Hebrew, or German into English. They should be sent to one of the following: Dr Władysław T. Bartoszewski, Forteczna 1A, 01-540, Warsaw, Poland (email: wt@wtbartoszewski.pl); Professor Antony Polonsky, Department of Near Eastern and Judaic Studies, Brandeis University, Waltham, Mass. 02254-9110 (email: polonsky@brandeis.edu); Professor Joshua Zimmerman, Yeshiva University, Department of History, 500 West 185th Street, New York, NY 10033-3201 (email: zimmerm@yu.edu).

We very much regret that in the article in volume 29 by Antony Polonsky, 'The POLIN Museum of the History of Polish Jews in Warsaw', the names of the historians responsible for Gallery 3, 'Paradisus Judaeorum 1508–1648', and Gallery 4, 'The Jewish Town 1648–1772', were incorrectly stated. The lead historian in both galleries was Adam Teller of Brown University. In the Paradisus Judaeorum gallery he worked closely with Igor Kąkolewski, but the overall academic conception of the gallery, its structure, and the choice of exhibits were his responsibility alone. He alone was responsible for the gallery on the Jewish town.

We note with sadness the deaths of the following major figures in our field: Elie Wiesel, the indomitable voice of the survivors of the Holocaust; Andrzej Wajda, one of the great Polish filmmakers; Halina Turska (née Paszkowska), longstanding and well-recognized sound engineer in the Polish film industry; and Zygmunt Bauman, eminent sociologist and social commentator. They will be sadly missed.

POLIN

Gentle Polin (Poland), ancient land of Torah and learning
From the day Ephraim first departed from Judah

From a *seliḥah* by Rabbi Moshe Katz Narol of the exiles of Poland, head of the Beth Din of the Holy Congregation of Metz:

We did not know, but our fathers told us how the exiles of Israel came to the land of Polin (Poland). When Israel saw how its sufferings were constantly renewed, oppression increased, persecutions multiplied, and how the evil authorities piled decree on decree and followed expulsion with expulsion, until there was no relief for Israel, they went out on the road and sought an answer from the paths of the wide world—which is the correct road to take to find rest for one's soul. Then a piece of paper fell from heaven:

Go to Polaniya (Poland)!

So they came to the land of Polin and they gave a mountain of gold to the king, and he received them with great honour. And God had mercy on them, so that they found favour with the king and the nobles. And the king gave them permission to reside in all the lands of his kingdom, to trade over its length and breadth, and to serve God according to the precepts of their religion. And the king protected them against every foe and enemy.

And Israel lived in Polin in tranquillity for a long time. They devoted themselves to trade and handicrafts. And God sent a blessing on them so that they were blessed in the land, and their name was exalted among the peoples. And they traded with the surrounding countries, and they also struck coins with inscriptions in the holy script and the language of the country. These are the coins which have on them a lion rampant from the right facing left. And on the coins are the words 'Mieszko, King of Poland' or 'Mieszko, Król Polski'. The Poles call their king 'Król'.

When they first arrived from the land of the Franks, they found a forest in the land, and on every tree a tractate of the Talmud was carved. This is the forest of Kawęczyn, which is near Lublin. And every man said to his neighbour, 'We have come to the land where our ancestors dwelt in ancient times for Torah and learning.'

And those who look for Scripture's inherent meaning say: This is why it is called Polin. For thus spoke Israel when they came to the land, 'Here rest for the night (*po lin*)'. And this means that we shall rest here until we shall merit going to the Land of Israel.

If this is the tradition, we accept it!

S. Y. AGNON

published in *Hatekufah* in 1919; trans. Gershon Bacon
used with permission of the Toby Press

POLIN
Studies in Polish Jewry

Contents

PART II
NEW VIEWS

PART III
OBITUARIES

Note on Place Names

POLITICAL connotations accrue to words, names, and spellings with an alacrity unfortunate for those who would like to maintain neutrality. It seems reasonable to honour the choices of a population on the name of its city or town, but what is one to do when the people have no consensus on their name, or when the town changes its name, and the name its spelling, again and again over time? The politician may always opt for the latest version, but the hapless historian must reckon with them all. This note, then, will be our brief reckoning

There is no problem with places that have accepted English names, such as Warsaw. But every other place name in east-central Europe raises serious problems. A good example is Wilno, Vilna, Vilnius. There are clear objections to all of these. Until 1944 the majority of the population was Polish. The city is today in Lithuania. 'Vilna', though raising the fewest problems, is an artificial construct. In this volume we have adopted the following guidelines, although we are aware that they are not wholly consistent.

1. Towns that have a form which is acceptable in English are given in that form. Some examples are Warsaw, Kiev, Moscow, St Petersburg, Munich.

2. Towns that until 1939 were clearly part of a particular state and shared the majority nationality of that state are given in a form which reflects that situation. Some examples are Breslau, Danzig, Rzeszów, Przemyśl. In Polish, Kraków has always been spelled as such. In English it has more often appeared as Cracow, but the current trend of English follows the local language as much as possible. In keeping with this trend to local determination, then, we shall maintain the Polish spelling.

3. Towns that are in mixed areas take the form in which they are known today and which reflects their present situation. Examples are Poznań, Toruń, and Kaunas. This applies also to bibliographical references. We have made one major exception to this rule, using the common English form for Vilna until its first incorporation into Lithuania in October 1939 and using Vilnius thereafter. Galicia's most diversely named city, and one of its most important, boasts four variants: the Polish Lwów, the German Lemberg, the Russian Lvov, and the Ukrainian Lviv. As this city currently lives under Ukrainian rule, and most of its current residents speak Ukrainian, we use the Ukrainian spelling unless another form is required by the context.

4. Some place names have different forms in Yiddish. Occasionally the subject matter dictates that the Yiddish place name should be the prime form, in which case the corresponding Polish (Ukrainian, Belarusian, Lithuanian) name is given in parentheses at first mention.

Note on Transliteration

HEBREW

An attempt has been made to achieve consistency in the transliteration of Hebrew words. The following are the key distinguishing features of the system that has been adopted:

1. No distinction is made between the *alef* and *ayin*; both are represented by an apostrophe, and only when they appear in an intervocalic position.

2. *Veit* is written *v*; *ḥet* is written *ḥ*; *yod* is written *y* when it functions as a consonant and *i* when it occurs as a vowel; *khaf* is written *kh*; *tsadi* is written *ts*; *kof* is written *k*.

3. The *dagesh ḥazak*, represented in some transliteration systems by doubling the letter, is not represented, except in words that have more or less acquired normative English spellings that include doublings, such as Hallel, kabbalah, Kaddish, rabbi, Sukkot, and Yom Kippur.

4. The *sheva na* is represented by an *e*.

5. Hebrew prefixes, prepositions, and conjunctions are not followed by a hyphen when they are transliterated; thus *betoledot ha'am hayehudi*.

6. In the transliteration of the titles of works published in Hebrew, only the first word is capitalized; other than in the titles of works, names of people, places, and institutions are capitalized following the conventions of the English language.

7. The names of individuals are transliterated following the above rules unless the individual concerned followed a different usage.

YIDDISH

Transliteration follows the YIVO system except for the names of people, where the spellings they themselves used have been retained.

RUSSIAN AND UKRAINIAN

The system used is that of British Standard 2979:1958, without diacritics. Except in bibliographical and other strictly rendered matter, soft and hard signs are indicated by *y* before a vowel (e.g. Ilyich) but are otherwise omitted, and word-final -й, -ий, -ый, -iй in names are simplified to -*y*.

PART I

Jewish Education in Eastern Europe

Introduction

Education for Its Own Sake

ELIYANA R. ADLER

> I had approached my studies differently from all the others—without a practical
> purpose in mind, without a materialistic goal. I studied only out of conviction.
> In a certain sense, perhaps, it could be called *lishmah*—that is, for its own sake.
>
> S. ETONIS, 1932

IN THE COURSE of S. Etonis's autobiography, submitted to the YIVO youth autobiography contest in 1932,[1] we witness his family and town buffeted by the First
World War, the Russian revolution, border and troop changes, and post-war economic and political conditions, yet all of these major events are just the backdrop
to his educational development. The real story is what S. Etonis learned in and
from the various schools, traditional and modern, he attended and how his outside
reading influenced him. Even as war and revolution led to dislocation and loss,
S. Etonis narrated the variety of schools he was able to attend and what each one
taught him.

For a young person, it would appear, the progression of teachers was of greater
import than the progression of armies and regimes. These teachers, whom he
describes as 'the grammarian', 'the mechanic', and 'the homeless former merchant
and his daughter', represented stages in his apprehension of the world of the intellect. Politics as well were filtered through his classroom experience. 'Of course,
every rumor', he informed his readers, 'makes its way to *kheyder*'.[2] He and his
classmates not only debated with one another and their teachers but were even
inspired by the times to stage a strike against one of their teachers.[3]

---

[1] YIVO called for young Jews to submit their autobiographies to competitions in 1932, 1934, and
1939. The extant autobiographies are at YIVO Archives, New York, RG 4 'Autobiographies of Jewish
Youth in Poland (1932–1939)'. There have been three anthologies published: *Awakening Lives: Autobiographies of Jewish Youth in Poland before the Holocaust*, ed. J. Shandler (New Haven, Conn., 2002);
Ostatnie pokolenie: Autobiografie polskiej młodzieży żydowskiej okresu międzywojennego, ed. A. Cała
(Warsaw, 2003); *Alilot ne'urim: otobiyografyot shel benei no'ar yehudim mipolin bein shetei milḥamot olam*,
ed. I. Bassok (Jerusalem, 2011).

[2] YIVO Archives, RG 4: Autobiography 3845, in *Awakening Lives*, 6.   [3] Ibid. 5.

Far more than politics, especially as he grew older, it was the content of his studies that animated his narrative. S. Etonis was torn between the offerings of secular and religious education. He found pleasure and frustration in both, and ultimately his mastery of *musar* (moral discipline) affected his reading of Hebrew literature:

Now, though, I read in a completely different way than I had before. I wanted to understand what I was reading. I had to make my own critique of each book, form my own impressions and judgments.[4]

By the end of the autobiography, S. Etonis had reached his twentieth year. He had completed his yeshiva studies and stood at the cusp of his future, with some experience as a teacher and unsure whether it would be possible for him to attend a gymnasium.

This, then, is the story of a life in education—a true *Bildungsroman*. And although his particular story is unique, the topic of education permeates the entire collection of autobiographies of young Polish Jews. Education was only one of a number of topics encouraged by the contest guidelines. The English version of the 1938 announcement read:

You and your family, war years, teachers, schools and what they gave you. Boyfriends, girl-friends. Youth organizations, [political] party life, and what they gave you. How you came to your occupation or how you are planning to come to your occupation. What events in your life made the greatest impression on you.[5]

Yet education, formal and informal, secular and religious, collective and self-motivated, is central to both the individual stories and the entire autobiography collection.

Each of the individual stories is powerful, captivating. Each one is also different and deserving of attention on its own. At the same time, there are recurrent themes. These young people were growing up in changing and challenging times. They wrote of the process of maturation and the uncertainty of the political, social, and economic situation around them. They wrote of their commitment to various causes as possible cures, or at least escapes, from the problems they faced. And profoundly, they wrote about education, in all of its forms: youth groups, schools, teachers, apprenticeships, books, libraries, political awakening, and religious study are all treated with the utmost honour and focus in these texts.

It is impossible to read these autobiographies without noticing the devotion to education. Perhaps it would be possible to read a single autobiography and be caught up in the drama of the individual story, but in aggregate the centrality of education is manifest. No wonder then that nearly a third of the contributors to this volume of *Polin* rely on texts from the YIVO autobiography contests to illuminate

    [4] YIVO Archives, RG 4: Autobiography 3845, in *Awakening Lives*, 16.
    [5] Cited in B. Kirshenblatt-Gimblett, M. Moseley, and M. Stanislawski, 'Introduction', in *Awakening Lives*, p. xxiii.

aspects of Jewish education during the interwar period. Although it would appear that Max Weinreich originally envisioned the contest as a means of studying young Jews, and he even succeeded in using them for that purpose,[6] the contributors to this volume have employed them in the study of education.

It is important to emphasize, however, that it is not the texts themselves, nor the time period, that ties these chapters together. Rather all of the chapters in the present volume seek to demonstrate the salience of placing education at the centre of the study of the Jewish past. This effort requires a new approach to sources, as well as a commitment to looking to the social factors within historical processes.

Historians of the east European Jewish experience frequently point to the centrality of educational institutions and pursuits within Jewish society. No history of a Jewish community in any era would be complete without a discussion of its institutions of learning. However, schools, whether traditional or modern, are often viewed as passive reflections of the surrounding culture, rather than active participants in shaping it. Whereas historians of education understand that schools and teachers have agendas and contribute in diverse and unpredictable ways to the communities in which they function, historians of the Jewish past have frequently been content to view them as simple and static. This volume will seek to undermine those assumptions by presenting education as an active and potent force for change in east European Jewish society.

Simon Dubnow (1860–1941), in many ways the father of east European Jewish historical writing, was, according to his daughter's autobiography, deeply committed to his children's education.[7] He also wrote textbooks for modern Jewish schools, as Vassili Schedrin discusses in this volume. However, his crucially important *History of the Jews in Russia and Poland* not only treats the *ḥeder* and yeshiva as petrified institutions but mostly passes over the new modern Jewish schools that blossomed during his lifetime.[8] Despite a personal passion for education and an awareness of the social forces within Jewish society, he did not see education as worthy of attention in a historical work.

Instead, it was chiefly scholars and practitioners of education who produced the most important early scholarship on schools and their effects. Zevi Scharfstein's work on the *ḥeder* and Khayim Shloyme Kazdan's study of the transition from the *ḥeder* to the modern Yiddish school are but two examples of foundational scholarship on Jewish education in eastern Europe.[9] Yet both of these men wrote primarily for other educators and scholars of education. They were not trained in history, and their work was considered marginal to historical scholarship.

More modern scholars were able to avoid this unfortunate bifurcation. Exemplary in this regard were Michael Stanislawski's integration of government schools

---

[6] Ibid., pp. xvii–xxvi.

[7] S. Dubnova-Erlich, *Bread and Matzoth*, trans. A. Shaw (Tenafly, NJ, 2005), esp. ch. 2.

[8] S. M. Dubnow, *History of the Jews in Russia and Poland* (Bergenfield, NJ, 2000).

[9] Z. Scharfstein, *Haḥeder beḥayei amenu* (Tel Aviv, 1951); K. S. Kazdan, *Fun kheyder un 'shkoles' biz 'tsysho': dos ruslendishe yidntum in gerangl far shul, shprakh, kultur* (Mexico City, 1956).

for Jewish boys into his larger study of Jewish policies and transformations under Tsar Nicholas I and Steven Zipperstein's examination of educational innovations within the context of developments in Odessa.[10] The sophisticated work of Shaul Stampfer on the yeshiva and of Mordechai Zalkin on the *ḥeder* have truly moved those institutions from objects of hagiography or hatred to legitimate objects of serious study.[11] In the Polish arena, Gershon Bacon, among others, has written about the important interface between politics, religion, and education.[12] And there is also Iris Parush's pioneering work on Jewish women's education.[13]

These are certainly not the only scholars of Jewish education in eastern Europe, but together they provide a sense of what has been achieved. Despite these important examples, much of the scholarship on east European Jewish history continues to treat education separately or as a symptom or effect rather than a cause of change and development. The chapters in this volume, spanning the nineteenth and twentieth centuries and the Austrian and Russian empires and both the Second Polish Republic and the Polish People's Republic, demonstrate that there is much more to be discovered and provide models of how to integrate the study of education into Jewish history.

This volume also seeks to move beyond a narrow definition of Jewish education. Jewish education and the education of Jews are equally valid subjects of study. Formal and informal training in academic or practical subjects for male and female students of all ages merit attention. Additionally, chapters focus not only on schools and students but also on educators, youth groups, textbooks, and other innovative methods for showcasing the complicated and mutual relationship between education and Jewish society. With ongoing scholarly consideration, this relationship, so intuitive to S. Etonis and the other young autobiographers who submitted their personal stories to YIVO in the 1930s, will provide insights into the east European Jewish past.

CONTENTS

The volume is organized in a more or less chronological fashion, with some attention to geographical and thematic coherence as well. While this section seeks to lay out the major findings of the individual chapters, the following section will

---

[10] M. Stanislawski, *Tsar Nicholas I and the Jews: The Transformation of Jewish Society in Russia 1825–1855* (Philadelphia, 1983); S. J. Zipperstein, *The Jews of Odessa: A Cultural History, 1794–1881* (Stanford, Calif., 1985).

[11] S. Stampfer, *Lithuanian Yeshivas of the Nineteenth Century: Creating a Century of Learning*, trans. L. Taylor-Guthartz (Oxford, 2012); M. Zalkin, *El heikhal hahaskalah: tahalikhei modernizatsyah baḥinukh hayehudi bemizraḥ eiropah bame'ah hatesha-esreh* (Tel Aviv, 2008).

[12] See e.g. G. Bacon, *The Politics of Tradition: Agudat Yisrael in Poland, 1916–1939* (Jerusalem, 1996).

[13] I. Parush, *Reading Jewish Women: Marginality and Modernization in Nineteenth-Century Eastern European Jewish Society*, trans. S. Sternberg (Hanover, NH, 2004).

emphasize their shared themes. For, while the chapters cover a large span of time and vastly different approaches to a variety of sources, as a group they not only highlight the importance of education but also contain complementary findings.

Geoffrey Claussen provides an in-depth analysis of an ambitious project for revitalizing Jewish education and Jewish society through exposure to intense *musar* instruction in 'Repairing Character Traits and Repairing the Jews'. Just as maskilim sought to revolutionize Jewish society through the creation of modern Jewish schools, Rabbi Simhah Zisl Ziv envisioned elevating the troubled traditionalist world around him through raising a generation of leaders committed to the work of moral perfection. The *talmud torah*s of Kelm and Grobin succeeded in training an elite group of educators who went on to introduce some of Simhah Zisl's innovations into other elite institutions. Ironically, as Claussen shows, due to outside opposition and factors intrinsic to *musar* practice, the schools that he created ended up fostering an isolationist ideology among his disciples.

In 'Rabbi Tsevi Elimelekh of Dynów's Regulations for the Support of Torah in Munkács', Levi Cooper shows a similar story of grand expectations and limited results. Tsevi Elimelekh used his authority to promulgate a set of regulations aimed at stopping modern education making inroads into Munkács. The regulations proved popular and were republished with minor changes numerous times. Cooper highlights how the nature of the changes and Tsevi Elimelekh's own interest in financial and sartorial issues rather than educational content demonstrate the concerns of individual rabbinic leaders and their communities. He also shows that there is very little evidence of the regulations having any influence on the changing educational scene in the Hungarian lands during his lifetime.

Daniel Viragh's chapter on Jewish education during the period of the dual monarchy in Hungary, 'The Narrative of Acculturation', not only extends Cooper's exploration of Hungarian educational policies and practices but also inaugurates a triptych of essays about textbooks. The books that Viragh explores were created by Jewish educators for precisely the sort of modern Hungarian Jewish schools that Tsevi Elimelekh so strenuously opposed. Viragh analyses the ways in which the books' authors sought to inculcate new and complementary ideas about both Hungarian and Jewish identities. He chronicles the developments in the books, the linguistic acculturation of the students, and the conceptions of Hungarian–Jewish symbiosis over the course of the period of study.

Attempts to reform or improve the east European Jewish community came not only from its own members but sometimes from outside as well. In 'The Reaction of the Polish Press to Baron Maurice de Hirsch's Foundation for Jewish Education in Galicia', Agnieszka Friedrich traces the response to an educational endeavour initiated by the philanthropist Baron Maurice de Hirsch for the Jews of Galicia. Despite the goal of productivization, favoured by so many social reformers, and the fact that some of the schools envisioned would serve non-Jewish as well as Jewish students, Friedrich shows that the Polish press expressed a good deal of suspicion towards the proposed gift. Her chapter highlights the important place of education in social and political debates of the time.

Like Viragh, Vassili Schedrin uses textbooks as a way of tracing both the motivations of educators and the changing mores of the times. Until fairly recently, only scholars of education studied textbooks. Historians are just beginning to recognize the wealth of information contained within these published time capsules. In 'A Story within a Story', his close reading of books written to be used in modern Jewish schools and by Jewish pupils in Russian schools, Schedrin demonstrates the panoply of messages embedded in these histories of the Jewish people, as well as their development over time. His use of book reviews and censors' reports highlights the degree to which contemporaries were aware of the subtleties of presentation and potential for indoctrination. 'The stories recounted in these histories', Schedrin informs the reader, 'shaped the national consciousness of this generation and thus also shaped Jewish life in the modern world.'

The next three articles follow Schedrin in examining aspects of Jewish education in tsarist Russia. Eliyana Adler's 'Clothes Make the Man' uses memoirs and photographs to investigate the role of the Russian secondary-school uniform in Jewish identity and society. What was at first not only novel but even provocative became fairly ubiquitous by the end of the century. Focusing on this secondary result of Jews entering Russian schools provides unexpected corroboration and elaboration of the paths of acculturation available to the Russian Jewish community.

Victoria Khiterer's and Brian Horowitz's chapters explore different facets of the interplay between official government policies and Jewish communal initiatives. In 'How Jews Gained Their Education in Kiev', Khiterer focuses on Kiev, which had a unique status and thus special residential and other laws for Jews. She shows how a ban on Jewish schools before 1901 led to a cat-and-mouse game between the authorities and local Jews who were establishing illegal institutions. At the same time, Jews from elsewhere sought to enter Kiev in order to attend the Russian schools there. This became significantly more difficult after the introduction of strict quotas on Jewish students in 1887. Throughout the tsarist period Jews continued to try to reside in and gain an education in Kiev despite the restrictions.

Horowitz exposes the ways in which these same restrictions, together with changes within the Jewish community, led to a new evaluation of the *heder* in the late tsarist period in 'The Return of the *Ḥeder* among Russian Jewish Education Experts'. Decreased access to Russian schools due to quotas and developments in Jewish politics led to increasing appreciation not only for the reform of the *heder* but even for its traditional variants. Horowitz discusses how this interest continued to develop through the early decades of the twentieth century, the civil war years, and the early Bolshevik period, which creates an ideal segue into the many chapters focusing on educational programmes to emerge from this later tumultuous era.

The following chapters proceed in close chronological order and minute detail to illuminate educational occurrences during and after the First World War in Poland. As discussed above, these chapters return frequently to the YIVO youth autobiography contests materials. Yet their approaches to the sources, as well as their conclusions, while complementary, are highly diverse. Nonetheless they underline the importance of this unique set of documents and the many uses to which it can be put.

In 'From Theory to Practice', Andrew Koss chronicles the unlikely blossoming of Yiddish and Hebrew schools in Vilna during the First World War. The problems of providing education for refugee children raised at the end of Horowitz's article became an opportunity for innovative Vilna-based educators. They even continued to thrive under German occupation. In fact, as Koss explains, their very success contributed to their decline as 'education became the tail wagging the dog of politics'.

Koss's invocation of intra-Jewish political disputes leads into the interwar period and his focus on Vilna to Jordana de Bloeme's chapter, 'Creating a New Jewish Nation'. The Vilna Education Society could only have emerged from the peculiar situation of the war and the subsequent incorporation of Vilna into Poland. Additionally, as De Bloeme demonstrates, its attempt to champion nonpartisan Jewish cultural autonomy was an outgrowth of the particular circumstances and personalities in Vilna. Eventually, despite some impressive achievements, especially its programmes for young people, the Vilna Jewish community had to adjust its goals and expectations to those of the country they were now a part of. 'Education, youth, and a preoccupation with the future of Polish Jewry', De Bloeme tells us, 'were intensely intertwined with the political and cultural rights of the Polish Jewish minority in the Second Polish Republic.'

The majority of Jewish children in interwar Poland attended state schools. In 'Between a Love of Poland, Symbolic Violence, and Antisemitism', Kamil Kijek offers a portrait of some of the paradoxical results of that situation. With sensitive reading of the YIVO autobiographies, as well as other sources, Kijek illustrates the ways in which the very successes of the state schools with regard to minority students also held the key to their failures. Jewish students overwhelmingly absorbed the patriotism and nationalist fervour that was integral to the curriculum, yet they simultaneously felt alienated from the very country they embraced. This painful relationship, which Kijek describes as one of 'unrequited love' and 'symbolic violence', obviously had repercussions on Polish–Jewish relations at the time, as well as how they were seen in retrospect.

Sean Martin's chapter, 'Between Church and State', looks at another side of Jewish attendance at Polish schools: the place of religious instruction. Martin begins by examining the apprehensions of the Jewish community and the Catholic state regarding the place of Judaism in public schools. Both the schools and the Jewish community expended resources and tried various means to seize this educational opportunity. Nevertheless, Martin's conclusion is similar to Kijek's: 'if the goal of the Polish authorities was to assimilate Jewish children, their policy on religious instruction could only undermine it'.

In '"Vos vayter?"', Adva Selzer uses the YIVO autobiographies to examine another trauma faced by Polish Jews. Despite the fact that the public schools were free, most families could not afford to keep their children out of the work force indefinitely, and leaving school became a painful rite of passage. Selzer introduces this important nexus and the way in which Jewish youth responded, including increased participation in youth organizations and self-education through intensive reading and writing. 'Their emotional crisis, an existential crisis that almost each and every one of them experienced, became a major driving force that left its mark on Jewish society and culture in interwar Poland.'

The centrality of youth movements in the lives of young Polish Jews appears as a given in many of these chapters. Ido Bassok analyses the ways in which these organizations functioned in the lives of their adherents. In 'Jewish Youth Organizations in Poland between the Wars as Heirs of the *Kehilah*', he suggests that for many they came to fill the same roles as religion had for previous generations. Bassok then goes on to analyse regional differences in the practices of the youth movements. While the other chapters on the interwar period treat Poland as a unified state, it had in fact been only recently cobbled together from the ruins of the pre-war empires. To a degree then, Bassok's geographical differentiation returns to the Hungarian, Russian, and Vilna focus of earlier chapters in the collection.

Naomi Seidman's exploration of the formation of the Bais Yaakov school system in 'A Revolution in the Name of Tradition' offers a different direction for educational development, but one very much within the same context of upheaval and innovation. Seidman is at pains to contrast Sarah Schenirer's enduring image as a simple and modest paragon of tradition with her canny reliance on the very same group-building exercises—ecstatic singing and identity-strengthening techniques—employed by secular educators such as the Vilna Educational Society. As well as quoting Schenirer's own rhetoric as proof, Seidman cites the tremendous growth of the Bais Yaakov schools among many competing options.

Katarzyna Person's '"The children ceased to be children"' presents translations and analysis of a set of documents from Emanuel Ringelblum's Oneg Shabbat Archive from the Warsaw ghetto. The products of interwar Poland's educational system, in all of their frustrations and fullness, were faced with caring for children who lacked food, clothing, hygiene, and sometimes even parents. Person's English translations show the earnest and insightful care-givers carefully describing their successes and their needs in reports sent to the agency providing funding. Her introduction discusses the historical context and educational import.

The end of the war offered new opportunities to those Jews fortunate enough to have survived but also new challenges. Just as Khiterer and Horowitz examined how Jews sought to further their education despite restrictions by the Russian government, Anna Sommer Schneider's chapter, 'The Survival of *Yidishkeyt*', looks at the efforts of the American Jewish Joint Distribution Committee to work with and around the Polish communist state after the war. All educational institutions function within legislative and political contexts, although at some times the hand of government is far heavier than at others. By making these opposing forces explicit, all of these papers highlight the frustration and creativity of Jewish educators functioning within oppressive systems. Schneider's paper traces the evolution of JDC activities to the end of the communist period.

THEMES

The chapters in this volume span two centuries, several distinct political eras, and much of eastern Europe. Whereas some volumes of *Polin* focus on a particular country or period, we have instead elected to look at a crucially important element within Jewish society in all times and places. No one questions the importance of education to the 'People of the Book', and yet the study of education in Jewish life is often marginalized. The proverbial book is placed on a shelf, as if its contents and influence were not critical to understanding Jewish society in any given period.

This collection seeks to showcase the benefits of using education to study the Jewish past. The contributors have made innovative use of sources. Chief of these are the YIVO youth autobiographies. Jeffrey Shandler's edited and translated collection of a selection of these texts, with the thoughtful introduction by Barbara Kirshenblatt-Gimblett, Marcus Moseley, and Michael Stanislawski, helped to bring these long-forgotten texts to greater attention. The introduction also highlights the many educational themes in the autobiographies. The authors in this volume take this a step further by focusing on particular issues in interwar Polish Jewish society and using the autobiographies to illustrate what these meant for people.

Textbooks, often published in large numbers and multiple editions, exist in many archival collections. Unlike autobiographical writings by students or teachers, they cannot tell us what classrooms in the past were like, but when read carefully they can tell us a great deal about the educational goals and societal expectations of their periods, especially in conjunction with other sources. Vassili Schedrin reads textbooks together with reviews and censors' reports. Daniel Viragh reads them in the context of the lives of their creators and changing societal norms. For Sean Martin, the textbooks are not his main source but one among many used to illuminate the experience of learning about Jewish religion in Polish Catholic schools. All three establish the great potential of this often overlooked resource.

Delving into educational experiences in the past requires new approaches to old sources or access to new sources. As well as the autobiographies and textbooks, contributors have used financial reports, photographs, educational plans, and newspaper editorials. Anna Sommer Schneider's analysis of the JDC's work in

Poland makes excellent use of the minutiae of funding charts to show developments over time. Eliyana Adler juxtaposes photographs, often lacking contextual-
izing documentation, with memoirs to show the visual and emotional impact of
school uniforms. Both Geoffrey Claussen and Levi Cooper prove that even when
not fully implemented, educational plans can provide vital information about
Jewish societies. Agnieszka Friedrich's paper makes a similar point about the
firestorm in the Polish press caused by a largely theoretical grant for the education
of Galician Jewry.

Notwithstanding the concentration of essays on the interwar period, this
volume highlights important trends both within and outside narrow time periods.
All of the chapters on interwar Poland see youth groups as crucial educational,
political, and cultural outlets for young Jews. Adva Selzer's chapter shows how
enthusiastically young Jews sought out such organizations as a replacement for
formal schooling. Jordana de Bloeme and Naomi Seidman make it clear that
educators were also well aware of the impact on identity and affiliation that these
groups had. Ido Bassok shows both geographical and ideological differences within
and among the youth groups. All of them highlight the importance of informal
educational institutions and activities as well as schools.

While most of the chapters in this volume focus on the educational options
afforded by the changing times, such as youth groups, modern Jewish schools, or
Jewish attendance at state schools, several look at Orthodox responses to these
innovations. Seidman most explicitly, but also Claussen and Cooper, demonstrate
how Orthodox claims of tradition and conformity were in fact undercut by their, at
times, radical educational endeavours. This fits well with recent scholarship about
Orthodoxy in modern Europe, while also drawing attention to the importance of
education in Orthodox projects.

What emerges from all of these chapters is the centrality of education in the
visions of so many Jewish individuals, groups, and institutions across eastern
Europe and the degree to which these visions were always interacting with forces
both within Jewish society and outside it. In some cases the internal Jewish factors come across most strongly. Brian Horowitz shows how the changing winds
of Jewish politics in late imperial Russia turned the Society for the Promotion of
Enlightenment among the Jews of Russia towards positive engagement with the
ḥeder. In the work of Victoria Khiterer, Kamil Kijek, and Katarzyna Person, external forces are more obvious. All of them show Jewish educators and children
struggling against conditions imposed by restrictive laws, nationalist attitudes,
or war.

Andrew Koss's chapter highlights both of these aspects. The conditions of war,
well outside the power and purview of the Jewish community, opened up certain
possibilities for educators in Vilna. Yet eventually, as stability returned, it was
internal Jewish politics that led to a splintering of the coalition and a less unified
and stable educational system. The relationships between Jewish educational

endeavours, the Jewish community, and outside economic, political, and social forces at the heart of each of these chapters are thus clearly articulated in this case.

The dynamic role of education within Jewish society informs the entire volume and will ideally spill beyond its pages into east European Jewish historiography more broadly. Regardless of the exact sources used or the particular geographical, chronological, or topical focus, the place of education in Jewish society cannot be minimized. Studying education for its own sake is thus necessary. Additionally, given that each and every generation of Jews has valued and pursued education, it should follow that understanding the Jewish past requires studying educational endeavours and experiences. By including education in their studies of the past, scholars can learn more about how Jewish society functioned, what its priorities were, and how it pursued them. And, as this volume shows, education played a role not only in internal Jewish life but also in the interactions between Jews and the societies in which they lived.

Repairing Character Traits and Repairing the Jews

The Talmud Torahs of Kelm and Grobin in the Nineteenth Century

GEOFFREY CLAUSSEN

THE *talmud torah* in Kelm (Kelmė) was a yeshiva regarded by many of its students and admirers as offering a model of education that was unique in the world. Their pride in this model is well illustrated by the story that some told about a conference of German university chancellors at which one admitted that there was an important subject that was not taught in German universities: 'the repair of human character traits'. In fact, the chancellor noted, the repair of human character traits was taught seriously in only one place in the whole world: at a Jewish school in the small Lithuanian town of Kelm.[1]

The Kelm Talmud Torah was an institution of the pietistic *musar* (moral discipline) movement that sought to convince Jews to devote themselves to 'the repair of human character traits' in unprecedented ways. One of the early leaders of the *musar* movement, Rabbi Simhah Zisl Ziv (1824–98), founded the school with hopes that its graduates and the model it offered would transform Jewish communities—and perhaps even, as the above story indicates, provoke the envy of Europe's most distinguished educators. Such hopes were never fulfilled, and yet Simhah Zisl's vision of social transformation through the *talmud torah* remains an important chapter in the history of nineteenth-century east European Jewry.

The *musar* movement emerged in Lithuania in the middle of the nineteenth century under the guidance of Simhah Zisl's teacher, Rabbi Israel Salanter, who urged his fellow Jews to engage in a range of practices that would help to bring *musar* to their souls. With its focus on virtue and the role of the emotions in moral life, the *musar* movement emerged, in part, as a reaction against the intellectualist

This chapter expands on some of the research presented in G. Claussen, *Sharing the Burden: Rabbi Simhah Zisl Ziv and the Path of Musar* (Albany, NY, 2015), ch. 1. The brief selections from that volume that appear in this chapter are reprinted by permission of SUNY Press.

[1] D. Katz, *Tenuat hamusar*, 2nd edn., 5 vols. (Tel Aviv, 1952–63), ii. 172.

culture of rabbinic circles; with its concern for piety and passionate defence of traditionalism, it was a reaction against the Jewish Enlightenment, the Haskalah.[2]

Following Salanter's vision, Simhah Zisl hoped that the *talmud torah* would be a force for reshaping rabbinic culture and for combating the Haskalah, partially through isolating his students from the broader society and sending them out as missionaries for *musar* once their basic training had been completed. At the same time, as signalled by his establishment of the *talmud torah* as the first traditionalist institution in eastern Europe to teach general studies alongside Jewish studies, Simhah Zisl hoped to forge a model of traditionalism that could somewhat accommodate the Haskalah vision.[3]

This chapter explores the *talmud torah*'s curriculum, its efforts to influence Jewish education by exporting its model of *musar* study to other yeshivas, its limited acceptance in the city of Kelm and by rabbinic authorities more generally, and its efforts to separate itself from many aspects of Jewish society while nevertheless hoping to effect social change. The *talmud torah* had limited success in directly influencing Jewish society on the whole, but it did have a significant influence on the development of traditional Jewish education in eastern Europe.

THE ESTABLISHMENT OF THE KELM TALMUD TORAH

In the 1860s, after years of study with Israel Salanter in Kovno (Kaunas) followed by years of private study, Simhah Zisl had settled in his hometown of Kelm in the region of Zamet (Žemaitija) on the western edge of the tsarist empire. For some time, he filled the role of preacher at the town's central synagogue. Following the example of Salanter, who had held a position as a public preacher in Kovno, Simhah Zisl's sermons were *musar* sermons, offering moral criticism of the city's Jewish community. As Eliezer Eliyahu Friedman, a native of Kelm who was particularly unimpressed by Simhah Zisl, put it in his memoirs:

With his sermons, he aspired to bring changes in the behaviour of the community and reforms to public institutions. These sermons did not please the leaders and elders of the community, and they stopped Rabbi Simhah Zisl's efforts in Kelm, and sought to push him aside, and they distanced him from the people in Kelm.[4]

Simhah Zisl's experience in Kelm was not dissimilar to the experience Salanter had had in Kovno. As Immanuel Etkes has argued, Salanter's preaching seems to have also included a good deal of social critique, which aroused public opposition. Salanter then seems to have turned his attention to creating a private educational

[2] On Salanter and the *musar* movement, see I. Etkes, *Rabbi Israel Salanter and the Mussar Movement: Seeking the Torah of Truth*, trans. J. Chipman (Philadelphia, 1993); H. Goldberg, *Israel Salanter. Text, Structure, Idea: The Ethics and Theology of an Early Psychologist of the Unconscious* (New York, 1982).
[3] On Simhah Zisl's thought and his place within the *musar* movement, see Claussen, *Sharing the Burden*.   [4] E. E. Friedman, *Sefer hazikhronot* (Tel Aviv, 1925), 78.

institution, a *beit midrash* for students in their teens and twenties at the Nevyozer *kloyz* in Kovno where Simhah Zisl himself had studied.[5] Simhah Zisl followed his teacher's path, moving from public preaching to private education, focusing on young students whose character could be easily moulded.[6]

Sometime during the course of the 1860s Simhah Zisl established a *talmud torah*, a primary school for boys.[7] Such schools, traditionally, did not charge for tuition, being funded by local Jewish communities for the education of orphans and children from impoverished families. While standard *talmud torah*s taught the same subjects as traditional *ḥeders*—providing some familiarity with the prayer book, Pentateuch, and talmudic literature—a number of Haskalah-influenced *talmud torah*s in the nineteenth-century tsarist empire began also to teach practical general subjects, such as Russian and mathematics. The Haskalah movement had advocated modernized, general education in Jewish schools, and bringing a general curriculum to *talmud torah*s was a major accomplishment. The change also made such schools very attractive to many parents, including those with greater financial resources. Some began to accept boys from wealthier families, so long as those families paid full tuition fees. Thus a new model of the *talmud torah* developed which offered a 'modern' education to students from a range of socio-economic backgrounds.[8]

Simhah Zisl's *talmud torah* was of this reformed variety, as it taught general studies and accepted fee-paying students. In fact, it does not seem to have received any funding from the Jewish community in Kelm. Instead, it came to depend on private donations—among its most prominent supporters was the tea merchant Kalman Ze'ev Wissotzky, who had studied alongside Simhah Zisl at the Nevyozer *kloyz*—and on tuition fees.[9] Simhah Zisl seems to have made substantial efforts to attract students from wealthy families from throughout Zamet and the region to its north, Courland. While it included poorer boys as well, the *talmud torah* developed into a boarding school that filled its beds and study hall with the sons of successful businessmen.[10] This arrangement not only provided income for the school but also

---

[5] Etkes, *Rabbi Israel Salanter*, 198–9; see Katz, *Tenuat hamusar*, i. 170.

[6] See E. E. Friedman, 'Toledot ba'alei hamusar', pt. 2, *Hamelits*, 29 May 1897, p. 6; Katz, *Tenuat hamusar*, ii. 127–9.

[7] The precise date of the establishment of the institution is not clear (see G. Claussen, 'Rabbi Simḥah Zissel Ziv: The Moral Vision of a 19th-Century Musar Master', Ph.D. thesis (Jewish Theological Seminary of America, 2011), 33 n. 68).

[8] See S. G. Rappaport, 'Jewish Education and Jewish Culture in the Russian Empire, 1880–1914', Ph.D. thesis (Stanford University, 2000), 40–1, 195–9.

[9] On Wissotzky's support, see Katz, *Tenuat hamusar*, ii. 63; H. Lifshitz, 'Gan hashem', *Halevanon*, 7 July 1875, p. 363; S. Z. Broida, 'Kelm', *Halevanon*, 25 Mar. 1874, p. 254; on Simhah Zisl's fundraising efforts, see Katz, *Tenuat hamusar*, ii. 63; Y. Mark, *Bemeḥitsatam shel gedolei hador*, trans. S. Hagai (Jerusalem, 1958), 221; M. Eidelshtein, 'Kelm', *Halevanon*, 20 Sept. 1873, p. 53; A. L. Frumkin, 'Kovno', *Halevanon*, 31 Mar. 1875, p. 62.

[10] Friedman, 'Toledot ba'alei hamusar', pt. 2, 6; id., *Sefer hazikhronot*, 81; id., *Letoledot kitat hamusaraim* (Jerusalem, 1926), 9; Mark, *Bemeḥitsatam shel gedolei hador*, 220; Y. A. Mondshein,

allowed Simhah Zisl to reach those children who would be most likely to grow up and have influence in their communities. Though Simhah Zisl was committed to aiding the poor and other marginalized Jews, he was also interested in transforming Jewish society as a whole, and so he sought to reach the children of an elite—not the rabbinic elite, who saw the *talmud torah* as dishonouring time-honoured models of Jewish education, but those businessmen whose status was rising. Rather than focusing on the parents, who were already set in their ways, Simhah Zisl focused on their children, who could be more easily persuaded to dedicate their lives to the work of *musar*.[11]

The *talmud torah* soon expanded to accommodate older students as well, eventually constituting itself as a yeshiva—a more advanced academy dedicated to the study of the Talmud—which served sixty or seventy students mostly between the ages of 10 and 17.[12] Like other Lithuanian yeshivas, the *talmud torah* devoted time to the Talmud and its commentaries, but it also set aside time for two untraditional areas of study: *musar* was studied to an unprecedented degree, and it was also the first traditional yeshiva in eastern Europe to set aside time for general studies—mathematics, geography, and Russian language, literature, and history. Both of these additions to the curriculum came at the expense of Talmud study, and most traditionalists saw Simhah Zisl as impugning the honour of the Talmud.

The *talmud torah* did not receive the support of all the Jews in Kelm. In 1878 eight of the town's residents signed a petition asking for the school to be officially licensed by the Russian government—and the school duly received a licence in 1879[13]—but others were more troubled by Simhah Zisl's efforts to reform traditional education and to critique established conventions. In 1873 a newspaper article about the school referred to efforts by its opponents to close it.[14] Later in the decade, opponents allegedly informed governmental authorities that the school was in fact a centre for fomenting rebellion against the tsar.[15]

Though Simhah Zisl was cleared of this accusation, he seems to have concluded that it was not possible to run his school in Kelm. He saw a more hospitable

---

'Warsaw', *Hatsefirah*, 10 Feb. 1885, p. 42; Katz, *Tenuat hamusar*, ii. 66; see also *Kitvei hasaba vetalmidav mikelm*, 2 vols. (Bnei Berak, 1997), i. 67; on poorer students at the Kelm Talmud Torah, see Katz, *Tenuat hamusar*, ii. 192, 207, 212.

[11] Salanter also shifted his focus to the younger generation in Kovno (see Katz, *Tenuat hamusar*, i. 170), but Simhah Zisl concentrated on much younger students than Salanter did.

[12] On the age range of students, the number of students enrolled, and the status of the institution as a yeshiva, see Claussen, 'Rabbi Simhah Zissel Ziv', 36.

[13] Kauno apskrities archyvas, Kaunas, f. J-49, ap. 1 (Mar. 1878–July 1879), b. B/26 137-78: Kovno Governorate Administration, resolution authorizing the opening of a school at the home of Simhah Ziv, 28 June 1879. I am grateful to Regina Kopilevich for locating this material.

[14] Eidelshtein, 'Kelm', 52.

[15] Katz dates this to 'roughly' 1876 (*Tenuat hamusar*, ii. 65). However, the accusations most probably occurred after the school had received its licence and perhaps in response to it. I have found no record of these accusations in the archives.

environment in Courland, a region where Jews imbibed not only Lithuanian Jewish culture but also the German culture that Simhah Zisl much admired.[16] In a later letter, he noted his admiration for what he described as the characteristically Germanic traits within Courland's non-Jewish population: 'German ways of loving order' and 'keeping their word', among others.[17] Under the influence of their German Jewish neighbours, Courland Jews may have also been more open to general education; moreover, Courland was an area where other *musar* movement leaders had previously found little opposition.[18]

The Dessler family, Courland residents whose sons had been students at the *talmud torah* in Kelm, offered to fund the re-establishment of the school in the quiet town of Grobin (Grobiņa).[19] By 1880 Simhah Zisl had reopened the *talmud torah* there.[20] The general structure of the curriculum in Grobin remained the same as in Kelm. As an 1882 newspaper article put it, the school 'was established by the government to teach Torah, wisdom, and moral decency [*derekh erets*] to the children of Israel'. 'Torah', here, refers to the traditional study of the Talmud and its commentaries; 'wisdom' refers to general studies; and 'moral decency' refers to *musar*, to Simhah Zisl's efforts to cultivate virtue among his students.[21]

THE LIMITS OF TALMUD STUDY AT THE KELM TALMUD TORAH

This division meant that, in both Kelm and Grobin, students at the *talmud torah* spent only three hours each morning studying the Talmud. Such a period of time might seem to indicate a strong commitment to Talmud study, but other yeshivas devoted many more hours to it, and the *talmud torah* developed a reputation as a school where talmudic learning was marginalized. 'They did not learn much Talmud in the yeshiva', noted the biographer Ya'akov Mark, explaining that 'the essence of the learning was *musar* and character traits'.[22] A later characterization by Menachem Glenn contends that 'at R. Simḥah Zisl's yeshiva, *musar* was the

---

[16] See Y. Maor, 'Latvia', in *Encyclopaedia Judaica*, 2nd edn., 22 vols. (Detroit, 2007), xii. 520–4; M. Bobe, 'Courland', in *Encyclopaedia Judaica*, v. 245–6.

[17] *Sefer hazikaron: beit kelm* (Bnei Berak, 2002), 267.

[18] See Etkes, *Rabbi Israel Salanter*, 190, 353 n. 64.

[19] A number of sources mention that the purchase of a tract of land and the construction of a new building were made possible through the support of (Israel) David Dessler, a merchant in Courland's major city, Libau (Liepāja) (see M. Shapira, 'Grobin', *Hatsefirah*, 5 Oct. 1881, p. 300; Mondshein, 'Warsaw', 41; I. Elyashev, 'Gerobin', pt. 1, *He'avar*, 2/1 (1918), 107). David Dessler's two sons, Reuven Dov and Hayim Gedaliah, were students at Simhah Zisl's *talmud torah*. Katz, citing the testimony of Eliyahu Eliezer Dessler, sees the financial support as having been provided by David Dessler's brother Eliezer (*Tenuat hamusar*, ii. 66).

[20] See Mondshein, 'Warsaw', 41; Elyashev, 'Gerobin', pt. 1, 107.

[21] B. T. L. Tzizling, 'Liboya', *Hatsefirah*, 12 Sept. 1882, p. 271; for similar formulations, see Katz, *Tenuat hamusar*, ii. 193–4; Elyashev, 'Gerobin', pt. 1, 109.

[22] Mark, *Bemeḥitsatam shel gedolei hador*, 220.

chief study, while the study of Talmud was only of minor importance and little time was devoted to it'.[23] Dov Katz, whose father had studied with Simhah Zisl and who became the first chronicler of the *musar* movement, notes that, to the school's credit, skills in talmudic reading mattered little in the assessments of students given by Simhah Zisl and his fellow administrators: 'At the Kelm Talmud Torah, they did not judge everyone based on their skills, as was customary at other yeshivas, but rather they first and foremost evaluated their character traits and the virtues of their souls.'[24] In other Lithuanian yeshivas, and indeed in much of Lithuanian Jewish culture, social status was correlated with understanding the complex legal dialectics of the Talmud; at his *talmud torah*, Simhah Zisl sought to create a culture where those who were most admired were those who cultivated humility, equanimity, reverence for God, and love for God's creatures.[25]

While the *talmud torah* was located in Kelm, it was clear that many in the local community were not eager to host a yeshiva that they saw as rejecting their values. Some, strikingly, seem to have viewed Simhah Zisl as imitating the efforts of the Ba'al Shem Tov and the hasidic movement to overturn Jewish society. Hasidism had limited success in Lithuania, but it seemed to some that the *musar* movement was now trying to revive its spirit. Some opponents of the movement referred to its devotees as the 'hasidim of Zamet',[26] and Ya'akov Mark describes a general suspicion among the scholars of Kelm that Simhah Zisl 'had in mind to found a new sect, a modern sort of hasidism'.[27]

Although the *musar* movement was hardly hasidic, it did seem to resemble hasidism in a number of ways: its focus on the inner life, its lengthy and often ecstatic prayer and meditation sessions, and its critiques of the idea that talmudic scholarship should be the measure of piety.[28] Eliezer Eliyahu Friedman described

---

[23] M. Glenn, *Israel Salanter, Religious-Ethical Thinker: The Story of a Religious-Ethical Current in Nineteenth-Century Judaism* (Philadelphia, 1953), 71.

[24] Katz, *Tenuat hamusar*, ii. 183; for his father's connection to Simhah Zisl, see ibid. 72. Katz himself was a student of Simhah Zisl's student Natan Tsevi Finkel and wrote a five-volume work on the *musar* movement which presents the life and thought of all of the movement's leaders based heavily on reports that he heard from their students or from others within *musar* circles. Katz generally takes a hagiographical and apologetic approach, painting the *musar* movement's leaders as saints, with Simhah Zisl among the most saintly of them all. But despite these tendencies, Katz preserves a wealth of valuable and well-referenced reports regarding Simhah Zisl's *talmud torah*s. As Shaul Stampfer points out, Katz is a valuable source especially because of his commitment to honesty and fairness (*Lithuanian Yeshivas of the Nineteenth Century: Creating a Tradition of Learning*, trans. L. Taylor-Guthartz (Oxford, 2012), 256). While Katz's writings on Simhah Zisl have not been translated into English, they are summarized in E. Ebner, 'Simha Zisl Broida (Ziff)', in L. Jung (ed.), *Guardians of our Heritage: 1724–1953* (New York, 1958), 317–36.

[25] For Simhah Zisl's stress on these various qualities, see Claussen, *Sharing the Burden*.

[26] H. T. H. Broida, 'Lakaḥat Musar Haskel', *Hamelits*, 11 June 1897, p. 2.

[27] Mark, *Bemeḥitsatam shel gedolei hador*, 219.

[28] See Etkes, *Rabbi Israel Salanter*, 197; for hasidic models, see M. Wilensky, *Hasidim umitnagdim*, 2 vols. (Jerusalem, 1970); G. Dynner, *Men of Silk: The Hasidic Conquest of Polish Jewish Society* (New York, 2006).

Simhah Zisl as a charismatic 'rebbe' who revived the spirit of hasidism especially through his efforts to downplay the importance of Talmud study:

Just as we had seen this drama when the hasidic sect began to flourish, so we saw the sect of '*musar* masters' begin to flourish. Just as . . . [the Ba'al Shem Tov] awakened the spirit of the masses to new life by preaching to the people that a person cannot acquire eternal life by Torah-learning alone . . . so too Rabbi Simhah Zisl awakened the spirit of his faction [by preaching that] even a person who is great in Torah-learning has not fulfilled his obligations if he is distant from *musar*. Quite the opposite: a person, even if he is not great in Torah-learning or hair-splitting dialectics, if he applies himself to the *musar* of the heart and purifies his soul and raises up his thoughts in contemplation, he will merit God's inheritance and stand on a level above the level of Torah scholars.[29]

Friedman thought that such rhetoric was particularly unappealing to the citizens of Kelm, who prided themselves on their learning. In Kelm, he recalled, 'all of the people of the city were scholarly, learned in Torah . . . as there was not a single uneducated person [*am ha'arets*] to be found in the city'.[30] Even middle-class householders were 'extraordinarily learned, sharp minded, and expert in the Talmud and legal codes', and the poor artisans of the town had a firm grasp of classical Jewish literature and esteemed serious scholarship.[31] According to Friedman, those who were sympathetic to Simhah Zisl were merchants who had recently settled in Kelm. These merchants were not scholarly and were not readily welcomed by the established townspeople;[32] however, they were enthusiastic supporters of Simhah Zisl's plans to establish a school that would value moral virtue over erudition.[33]

In his polemical efforts to depict the Kelm Talmud Torah as disdaining traditional scholarship, Friedman characterized Talmud study there as not only confined to a limited time but also as taught at a very low level. In the early 1870s Friedman studied at the rival yeshiva in Kelm run by Rabbi Eliezer Gordon. Gordon had studied alongside Simhah Zisl at the Nevyozer *kloyz* and was not unsympathetic to the need to encourage *musar* in the lives of his students, but he

[29] Friedman, 'Toledot ba'alei hamusar', pt. 2, p. 6; see also id., *Sefer hazikhronot*, 81.

[30] Friedman, *Sefer hazikhronot*, 9. *Am ha'arets* might also be understood as 'simple people' (see n. 32 below). Friedman's depiction of Kelm as entirely scholarly is repeated in the memorial book for Kelm (I. Markus-Karabelnik and B.-S. Levitan-Karabelnik, *Kelm: ets karut* ([Tel Aviv], 1993), 26).

[31] Friedman, 'Toledot ba'alei hamusar', pt. 2, p. 6; see id., *Sefer hazikhronot*, 9, 78. Friedman describes artisans as studying texts such as Ḥayei adam, a legal code 'which they knew almost by heart'; the medieval *musar* treatise *Menorat hama'or*; and classical Midrash, including *Ein ya'akov*, a medieval compilation of non-legal material from the Talmud.

[32] The merchants were brought to Kelm by the new opportunities arising from the completion (in around 1858) of a new highway connecting Prussia with Riga (and with St Petersburg beyond) that passed through Kelm (see Mark, *Bemeḥitsatam shel gedolei hador*, 219). Friedman refers to these merchants as 'simple people' (*anashim peshutim*): that is, without talmudic knowledge. On this characterization of Jews, see S. Stampfer, *Families, Rabbis, and Education: Traditional Jewish Society in Eastern Europe* (Oxford, 2010), 147.   [33] See Friedman, 'Toledot ba'alei hamusar', pt. 2, p. 6.

saw this as best accomplished through instruction in Talmud and he focused his yeshiva exclusively on Talmud study.[34] Friedman considered Gordon's approach wise, and he mocked the Kelm Talmud Torah for its failure to produce competent Talmud students. Friedman recounts that he and a classmate were once invited by Simhah Zisl to study at his school, but that he found the level of Talmud instruction to be unacceptably low;[35] and when Simhah Zisl sent three of his students to study with Eliezer Gordon, so that—according to Friedman—'they could draw the yeshiva of Rabbi Eliezer into the web of the musarists', Friedman reports that they did not possess the skills to pass the rigorous, public Talmud examinations which were given each month.[36]

Friedman's recollections show some of the ridicule and contempt that Lithuanian rabbinic culture directed towards the *musar* movement, and his characterizations are probably exaggerated. However, the other published critic of the *talmud torah*, Israel Isidor Elyashev (Ba'al Makhshoves), offered a similar assessment of Simhah Zisl's limited interest in promoting talmudic learning. Elyashev, who eventually went on to become the founder of Yiddish literary criticism, spent several years studying at Simhah Zisl's *talmud torah* in Grobin until he was expelled for his heretical tendencies.[37] He developed what he describes as a strong hatred of the *talmud torah*, and his descriptions (like Friedman's) often seem exaggerated, but his memories are nonetheless instructive:

In Grobin, they did not give particular value to the study of Talmud. I do not remember a time when each child had his own personal text of the Talmud. In the course of the whole time, they learned no more than ten pages—and these were studied without the commentaries of the Tosafists and without dialectical examination. Neither the students nor their rabbis could recognize all matters of concern on the pages of Talmud that they learned . . . . We were not directed to familiarize ourselves with the study of Talmud on our own at

---

[34] As Friedman puts it, the yeshiva 'had one goal: to spread knowledge of Torah among the students through the spirit of logic and a healthy intellect. And the students had one goal: to acquire deep knowledge in the Talmud and codes by means of deep logic and straight reason' (*Sefer hazikhronot*, 106). Later, however, when Gordon's yeshiva moved to Telz, Gordon incorporated some *musar* study into the curriculum, as discussed below.   [35] Friedman, *Sefer hazikhronot*, 84–5.

[36] Ibid. 100–3. According to Friedman, the students sent to 'infiltrate' Eliezer Gordon's yeshiva were Simhah Zisl's son Nahum Ze'ev Ziv, Bentsiyon Ze'ev Rosenos, and Elijah Dov Ber Lazarovitz. Friedman notes that even Simhah Zisl's most advanced students 'were considered, in comparison to the students of R. Eliezer, like dwarves in comparison to giants'. Friedman elsewhere writes that Simhah Zisl's students 'did not have great success in their studies of the Talmud and commentaries. The best of them, of the greatest ability, left with R. Simhah Zisl's encouragement, and they entered the yeshiva of the great R. Eliezer Gordon—may he live long—who was then the head of the rabbinic court of Kelm (now in Telz), whose yeshiva was great and highly esteemed—without the adornment and without the embellishment, without the *musar* preaching and without the *mashgiḥim* and without the total discipline. Rather, students sat and immersed themselves in Torah through the application of reason' (Friedman, 'Toledot ba'alei hamusar', pt. 2, p. 6–7).

[37] See M. Moseley, 'Bal-Makhshoves', in G. D. Hundert (ed.), *YIVO Encyclopedia of Jews in Eastern Europe*, <http://www.yivoencyclopedia.org/article.aspx/Bal-Makhshoves> (accessed 16 Feb. 2016).

all, and aside from the three hours [of daily Talmud study], our eyes never saw a single book other than *musar* books like *Mesilat yesharim* and *Reshit ḥokhmah*.[38]

There are contrary testimonies which suggest that additional time was allotted for reviewing Talmud studies in the evenings, but on the whole Talmud study seems to have been downplayed.[39] While the Talmud was certainly viewed as the repository of God's law and a source of great moral wisdom, dedicating time to traditional patterns of Talmud study and especially to analysing complex legal dialectics does not seem to have been viewed as a likely source of moral improvement. The *talmud torah* seems to have encouraged students instead to focus on studying *musar* literature and reflecting on their moral situations.[40]

MUSAR STUDY AT THE *TALMUD TORAH*

In fact, the evening time that might have been used for further Talmud study was generally dedicated to *musar*. While Talmud and general studies were taught by others, *musar* study centred on a sermon delivered each evening by Simhah Zisl himself, as his health permitted. These sermons focused on questions of proper belief and behaviour, the effort and discipline required for attaining moral excellence, and the rewards and punishments associated with virtue and vice. Sermons were often sparked by the particular moral failings of the students at the *talmud torah*—as well as Simhah Zisl's own failings—and Simhah Zisl intended the sermons themselves to provide *musar*, helping to heal flawed souls and to direct his students towards moral goodness. The sermons were designed, as Simhah Zisl put it, 'to renew the spirit of the human being, and place a new heart and new spirit in him, that he might use reason, and do good, and love Torah and revere the words of the sages'.[41] Dov Katz describes Simhah Zisl as conveying great emotion and sometimes shaking as he spoke, while at the same time maintaining self-control and equanimity.[42]

At times, evening sermons seem to have lasted for more than an hour and were often followed by extended periods of *musar* study, meditation, chanting, or group discussion.[43] After the sermon, Ya'akov Mark reports, the students 'would remain silent, meditating on the words that they had heard until it was time for evening prayers.[44] Katz, however, describes the students spending this time engaged in the

[38] Elyashev, 'Gerobin', pt. 2, *He'avar*, 2/2 (1918), 110. Elyashev admits that his memories of his time at the *talmud torah*, about which he was writing thirty-five years later, may not always have been completely accurate (ibid. 107).   [39] See Katz, *Tenuat hamusar*, ii. 209; Mondshein, 'Warsaw', 42.

[40] On the importance of in-depth study, where each individual would focus on *musar* in accordance with his own situation, see Katz, *Tenuat hamusar*, ii. 173.

[41] See ibid. 175; on the attention to students' moral failings, see Elyashev, 'Gerobin', pt. 1, p. 114; id. 'Gerobin', pt. 2, pp. 103–4.   [42] Katz, *Tenuat hamusar*, ii. 174.

[43] Dov Katz reports that sermons sometimes lasted for two or three hours; the sources typically describe half an hour to an hour for *musar* study (see e.g. ibid. 173–4; Elyashev, 'Gerobin', pt. 2, pp. 89, 91).   [44] Mark, *Bemeḥitsatam shel gedolei hador*, 220.

emotionally charged study of *musar* literature—typically chanting verses or passages from that literature to evocative melodies, seeking to imprint their messages in their souls. Simhah Zisl is said to have urged his students to raise their voices against the evil inclination that lurked in their hearts, calling out just as they would call out if they were being robbed on the street. But even when the students were engaged in this sort of exercise, Katz depicts an atmosphere that was marked by deep self-control at the same time that it was emotionally charged. The students sang, he writes, with 'stormy enthusiasm and very emotional voices . . . but at the same time they guarded against external outbursts or excited bodily movements'.[45]

Elyashev depicts a more emotionally expressive atmosphere, as students and teachers sat in the *talmud torah*, reflected on their sins, and sought to move their hearts to repentance by chanting phrases from *musar* literature. In this portrait, contrary to Katz's description, there were many outbursts and excited movements:

Before the evening prayer, our study and prayer room appeared as a space that was half-dark and fantastical, with scenes of people—children and adolescents and grown-ups—running here and there, gesturing with all their limbs. And amidst all the disorder, quiet sobbing would erupt, wavering amidst the shadows. The air was saturated with sighs and wails, the sound of drumming with a middle finger, the sound of a fist beating the heart, voices and echoes wailing: 'Akavia ben Mehalalel taught . . . "Know whence you came, whither you go, and before whom you will give justification and accounting" [Mishnah *Avot* 3: 1]'; 'Turn to us and we will return' [cf. Lam. 5: 21]; 'My own spirit is foreign to me' [cf. Job 19: 17]; 'Do not forget me in my old age' [cf. Ps. 71: 9]; 'Let us search and examine our ways and turn back to the Lord' [Lam. 3: 40]; and so on and so on.[46]

As Elyashev goes on to explain, everyone at the *talmud torah* considered himself in need of repentance. The students reflected on the events of the day and on their sinfulness each evening and sought through emotional arousal to move closer to God.[47] Simhah Zisl may well have trained his students to maintain equanimity even amidst this disorder, but *musar* study at his *talmud torah* may not have always been marked by emotional restraint.

Simhah Zisl also taught his students to regard the statutory prayers that followed these *musar* sessions—and all communal prayer at the *talmud torah*—as part of their *musar* study. Dov Katz, summarizing what he learned from Simhah Zisl's students, notes that prayer was seen as providing many moral benefits:

In addition to the value of prayer as words of supplication before God, they found in it an opportunity for comprehensive spiritual development: for focusing thought, for arousing emotion, for meditating on the wonders of creation and the greatness of God, for increasing faith and trust in apprehending God's loving-kindness and developing gratitude, and even for recognizing character traits and improving them.[48]

Realizing these benefits required taking one's time with the words of the liturgy.

[45] Katz, *Tenuat hamusar*, ii. 173–4.   [46] Elyashev, 'Gerobin', pt. 2, p. 91.
[47] Ibid. 91–3.   [48] Katz, *Tenuat hamusar*, ii. 176.

To help his students focus their minds on those words, Simhah Zisl urged them to remain still during prayer and to pray with the utmost concentration: if their concentration wavered, they were instructed to refocus themselves and try again.[49] In order to help students focus on ideal character traits, he urged them to move very slowly through descriptions of God's moral goodness so that they could meditate on these ideals and consider their own personal potential for improvement.[50]

All of these efforts meant that prayer services were remarkably lengthy. Morning prayer services, for example, which might have lasted for half an hour in standard Lithuanian yeshivas, are said to have lasted an hour or even two hours or more.[51] To accommodate the slow pace of prayer, some customary sections of the liturgy were skipped or postponed. Some liturgical poems, for example, were skipped on holidays, and the concluding prayers of Yom Kippur were postponed until after the Yom Kippur fast had been broken. Often, the concluding prayers of the sabbath morning service were postponed until after lunch. These sorts of non-traditional practices, while acceptable according to the letter of Jewish law, angered some traditionalists, who saw Simhah Zisl as disregarding time-honoured traditions.[52] Traditionalists were also angered, of course, that the length of prayers at the *talmud torah*, along with all the time spent in *musar* study and meditation, left less time for Talmud study.[53] On occasion, it seems, focused *musar* study occurred not only in the evening but in the morning as well, further cutting into the three hours reserved for Talmud study. At times, Talmud study or general studies classes were cancelled altogether so that the students could gather for additional sessions focused on moral improvement.[54]

Alongside the sermons and meditation and prayer sessions, the *talmud torah* also held group meetings. Students would gather in '*musar* groups' for mutual criticism and support. Group meetings sometimes took place in the evening during the week, although weekly meetings at the conclusion of the sabbath eventually

[49] Ibid. 176–7, 207; Elyashev, 'Gerobin', pt. 1, p. 110. Elyashev notes that a lack of intention in prayer was considered a serious sin which required repentance ('Gerobin', pt. 2, p. 91).

[50] Katz, *Tenuat hamusar*, ii 176–7. Katz notes that Simhah Zisl emphasized (following Moses Alshikh) that God's 'thirteen attributes' were to be imitated, not merely recited (ibid. 177).

[51] Elyashev speaks of the morning prayers as lasting for an hour and a half ('Gerobin', pt. 1, p. 110). Katz records that the three statutory prayer services (morning, afternoon, and evening) combined took 'several hours' (*Tenuat hamusar*, ii. 176). Simhah Zisl mentions dedicating three hours to the central part of the prayer service, the silent Amidah (Simhah Zisl Ziv, *Sefer ḥokhmah umusar*, 2 vols. (Jerusalem, 1957–64), ii. 340).

[52] Katz, *Tenuat hamusar*, ii. 213; Friedman, 'Toledot ba'alei hamusar', pt. 2, p. 7. The postponed sections of the Yom Kippur services were the *ma'ariv* (evening) services for the conclusion of the holiday; those of the sabbath services were the *musaf* (additional) services.

[53] This sort of critique had also been levelled against the hasidic movement.

[54] On *musar* chanting activities in the morning that would have inevitably cut into Talmud study time, see Katz, *Tenuat hamusar*, ii. 178; on the cancelling of classes, see Elyashev, 'Gerobin', pt. 1, pp. 114–15. Elyashev also recounts one rather unsuccessful attempt to dedicate more time to *musar* activities without cutting into the three hours a day reserved for Talmud study or the three hours a day reserved for general studies ('Gerobin', pt. 2, p. 97–9; see also Claussen, 'Rabbi Simḥah Zissel Ziv', 49).

became a part of the formal schedule.[55] Some groups dedicated each week to focusing on a particular character trait and spent the week engaging in exercises designed to strengthen it: on Saturday nights, a student appointed to lead the group would begin the session by offering a sermon on the character trait in question, and students would then discuss their experiences with that trait.[56] Other *musar* groups dedicated themselves to particular issues: one focused on love for others, one focused on the observance of the sabbath, and one group adopted Simhah Zisl's own practice of setting aside every tenth day as a special day for contemplation.[57]

In addition to the peer counselling made possible by these groups, Simhah Zisl also offered private counselling and made personal recommendations to students on how they could further their moral development.[58] The *talmud torah* employed a group of supervisors (*mashgihim*), generally former students in their twenties, who seem to have offered individual counselling as well. Whereas *mashgihim* in other yeshivas were primarily concerned with overseeing students' behaviour— making sure that they were keeping clean, following yeshiva rules, attending sessions on time, and so on—the *mashgihim* at Kelm Talmud Torah also gave considerable attention to their students' inner lives and came to be called 'spiritual supervisors' (*mashgihim ruhani'im*).[59] As Simhah Zisl himself also directed his attention to these matters, he seems to have functioned as a kind of chief spiritual supervisor.

MISSIONARIES FOR *MUSAR*: SPREADING STUDY BEYOND KELM TALMUD TORAH

With these *musar* activities at the centre of its programme, the *talmud torah* focused resolutely on the repair of its students' souls, and yet the institution's leaders were also interested in exporting their model to other yeshivas and thereby, ultimately, 'repairing' Jewish society throughout eastern Europe.

They did not try to reach out directly to the general public. Simhah Zisl had perhaps even less success than Israel Salanter with public preaching, and he and his students seem to have realized that they would have more influence focusing on elite yeshivas than on more broad swaths of society. As discussed above, Friedman

---

[55] See Elyashev, 'Gerobin', pt. 2, p. 89; id., 'Gerobin', pt. 1, p. 115; see also Claussen, 'Rabbi Simhah Zissel Ziv', 46–7, 59–60.

[56] Katz, *Tenuat hamusar*, ii. 202–3; Elyashev, 'Gerobin', pt. 2, p. 89; see Simhah Zisl Ziv, *Sefer hazikaron*, 1510; see also *Kitvei hasaba mikelm: pinkas hakabalot* (Benei Berak,1984), 147–72.

[57] See *Kitvei hasaba mikelm*; Katz, *Tenuat hamusar*, ii. 181–2, 204.

[58] Katz, *Tenuat hamusar*, ii. 183, 205.

[59] See Elyashev, 'Gerobin', pt. 1, p. 111; id., 'Gerobin', pt. 2, p. 89; for criticism of the supervisory system, see Claussen, 'Rabbi Simhah Zissel Ziv', 47–8; on the role of the *mashgihim* at a non-*musar* yeshiva in Volozhin, see Stampfer, *Lithuanian Yeshivas*, 89–92, 133–5; on the role of the *mashgihim* in the *musar* movement, see B.-T. Klibansky, 'Hayeshivot halitayot bemizrah eiropah bein shetei milhamot ha'olam', Ph.D. thesis (Tel Aviv University, 2009), 28.

was concerned that students from the *talmud torah* hoped to infiltrate Eliezer Gordon's yeshiva in Kelm. This may well have been their goal. Simhah Zisl clearly hoped that Gordon would adopt the model of *musar* study pioneered at the Kelm Talmud Torah, as evidenced by a letter he wrote to him filled with praise for *musar* study.[60] Friedman recalls Simhah Zisl pressuring Gordon to accept his *musar* methods (and to allow his three top students to 'infiltrate' Gordon's yeshiva):

> R. Simhah Zisl and his gang exerted great pressure on the rabbi, surrounding him with distress. Once the rabbi called me to his private room and implored me to agree to accept three young men from R. Simhah Zisl's Talmud Torah. 'Surely you know', said the rabbi, 'the extent to which I am pained by R. Simhah Zisl's institution and its behaviour. But I have no choice. This time I am compelled to fulfil his wish. Do you understand? I am compelled and forced to do this. For if I do not comply in this matter the flame of a great controversy will be lit in the town by his devotees. And those people are hard, the power of their speech is great, and I am soft spoken and despise argument. Therefore please agree to my request and persuade your companions to agree to it, and I will be very grateful to them.'[61]

Friedman is probably exaggerating Gordon's negative attitude towards Simhah Zisl, and he surely exaggerates the power that Simhah Zisl and his students had in Kelm,[62] but Simhah Zisl and his students do seem to have pressured Gordon to adopt their vision, pressure which seems to have continued even after Gordon left Kelm and became the *rosh yeshivah* at Telz (Telšiai), succeeding Tzevi Ya'akov Oppenheim, who had previously taught at Simhah Zisl's *talmud torah*.[63] Gordon initially discouraged *musar* study at Telz, too, but eventually developed an optional *musar* study time—apparently at the urging of his son-in-law, Rabbi Joseph Leib Bloch, who spent a number of years in Kelm and was apparently somewhat inspired by Simhah Zisl's model of *musar* study.[64] Despite considerable reluctance, but perhaps viewing *musar* study as a potential bulwark against the Haskalah, Gordon eventually incorporated more *musar* study into the Telz yeshiva.[65] By 1894 a half hour of *musar* study each evening had become mandatory. In 1897 a former student of Simhah Zisl's, Rabbi Aryeh Leib Hasman, was appointed as a *mashgiaḥ* at Telz. From Eliezer Friedman's perspective, Gordon remained 'a great opponent of R. Simhah Zisl's group and of all the sects of musarists', but, especially with growing interest in *musar* in his yeshiva, he 'found a place for one of the musarists of Kelm to join the Telz yeshiva'.[66]

[60] Simhah Zisl Ziv, 'Torah veyirah', *Moriah*, 12/7–9 (1983), 111–14. I am grateful to Benjamin Brown for drawing my attention to this letter. Shaul Stampfer suggests that the letter is congratulating Gordon for already having added *musar* study to his curriculum, but it does seem intended to persuade as much as to congratulate.

[61] Friedman, *Sefer hazikhronot*, 101. I follow Stampfer's translation (*Lithuanian Yeshivas*, 327 n. 124).   [62] See Stampfer, *Lithuanian Yeshivas*, 292–3.

[63] Ibid. 288–9. As Stampfer notes, the new Telz yeshiva also gained strength from the efforts of Simhah Zisl's student Natan Tsevi Finkel.

[64] Bloch 'saw the Musar movement at close hand. He accepted its conceptual path but was not drawn to its leaders' (ibid. 335).   [65] See ibid. 334–5.   [66] Friedman, *Sefer hazikhronot*, 106.

Hasman embodied the model of the *mashgiaḥ ruḥani* that had been developed at Kelm. He showed a fierce concern for the inner lives of the students at Telz, urging them to focus not only on Talmud but also on prayer and *musar*. As Telz student Yeruham Wahrhaftig recalled, Hasman 'considered the value of *musar* to be as weighty as that of Torah study' and saw *musar* study as a strict requirement for students of all ages at Telz.[67] Hasman showed a good deal of missionary zeal, and, without Eliezer Gordon's permission, he also invited students to his house on the sabbath to join him in *musar* study, an act which established, as Friedman put it, 'the foundation of a *musar* sect within the yeshiva'.[68]

Hasman was successful in convincing some Telz students to dedicate themselves to *musar* and even to make pilgrimages to learn with Simhah Zisl at the *talmud torah* in Kelm, to which Simhah Zisl had returned following the closure of the *talmud torah* in Grobin in 1886.[69] These pilgrimages did not sit well with Gordon, who ended up imposing the rule that 'only those who had [previously] been students of R. Simhah Zisl' were permitted to visit the *talmud torah* in Kelm. Gordon also prohibited Hasman from inviting students to his home, and he announced that *musar* study would only be mandatory for older yeshiva students.[70] Even so, students continued to object to what Wahrhaftig described as Hasman's 'authoritarian' efforts to impose the *musar* approach on them, and they complained that Hasman 'had weakened Torah study at the yeshiva in comparison with *musar* study'.[71] Gordon seems to have sympathized with these complaints: Hasman was eventually dismissed from the yeshiva, and he returned to Kelm.[72]

Hasman's effort to export the approach of Simhah Zisl's *talmud torah* was ultimately unsuccessful, and yet it is worth noting that aspects of his method continued to be accepted in Telz. Even after Hasman's departure, the Telz yeshiva kept the *mashgiḥim ruḥani'im* and the fixed time for *musar* study in its schedule, despite ongoing tensions among the students regarding the place of *musar* in their studies.[73]

One of the other notable yeshivas to which Simhah Zisl's model of *musar* study was exported was at Slobodka (Vilijampolė, Slabotkė) just outside Kovno, which was founded by another student of Simhah Zisl's, Rabbi Natan Tzevi Finkel. Finkel served as a supervisor and administrator at the Kelm Talmud Torah in the 1870s. Soon after it moved to Grobin, Finkel moved to Slobodka, where he founded a new yeshiva.[74] The Slobodka yeshiva, like Kelm Talmud Torah, featured sessions

---

[67] Stampfer, *Lithuanian Yeshivas*, 313.   [68] Friedman, *Sefer hazikhronot*, 109.

[69] Ibid. 107; see also the discussion of a Telz student taking up an extended residence at the *talmud torah* in Kelm (*Kitvei hasaba vetalmidav mikelm*, i. 188).   [70] Friedman, *Sefer hazikhronot*, 109.

[71] Stampfer, *Lithuanian Yeshivas*, 313–14.   [72] Ibid. 314–15.

[73] See esp. ibid. 318, 320. Another yeshiva similarly influenced by Simhah Zisl's *talmud torah* was the one in Mir.

[74] Katz, *Tenuat hamusar*, ii. 19–20; S. Tikochinski, 'Yeshivot hamusar melita le'erets yisra'el: yeshivat slabodka veshitatah haḥinukhit, aliyatah vehitbasesutah be'erets yisra'el hamandatorit', Ph.D. thesis (Hebrew University of Jerusalem, 2009), 23.

devoted to *musar* along with sessions devoted to Talmud study. More time could be devoted to Talmud at the Slobodka yeshiva, because there were no general studies courses there and because Finkel, his faculty, and his students generally held Talmud in higher esteem than did their colleagues in Kelm and Grobin.[75] Nonetheless, in Slobodka, as in Kelm and Grobin, '*musar* study . . . was considered its central activity in terms of importance, though not in terms of the amount of time devoted to it'.[76]

As Shlomo Tikochinski has shown, Finkel criticized his teacher for giving insufficient time to the study of Talmud and especially for his general studies programme. In fact, Finkel's complaints may have contributed to concerns about the reputation of the *talmud torah* in Grobin and, ultimately, to its closure in 1886.[77] As the *talmud torah* in Grobin struggled, Finkel's new yeshiva in Slobodka grew and flourished. With its greater focus on Talmud, the Slobodka yeshiva was much more within the mainstream of Lithuanian rabbinic culture and could more easily attract students and donors than the *talmud torah* could.

The flourishing of the Slobodka yeshiva, however, ultimately allowed many elements of Simhah Zisl's vision of *musar* to spread throughout the yeshiva world. Finkel's student Rabbi Yehiel Ya'akov Weinberg argued that it was thanks to Finkel's efforts to make *musar* more acceptable to talmudists and to do away with general education requirements that, ultimately, 'the *musar* method was accepted in the whole talmudic world, and it was elevated to be a part of the education of every Torah scholar'.[78] Much of the *musar* method that came out of Slobodka was based on that of the Kelm Talmud Torah.

Finkel followed Simhah Zisl's model of hiring others to teach Talmud and focused his own efforts on teaching and promoting *musar*. Like Simhah Zisl, Finkel 'saw himself primarily as a *mashgiaḥ*', responsible for the moral development of his students.[79] Like Simhah Zisl, he delivered regular *musar* sermons and urged his students to spend time reflecting on his words and on their inner lives. As at the *talmud torah*, students also spent *musar* study sessions focusing on classical *musar* literature, and, as they did this, some 'used to repeat choice maxims over and over in the *beit midrash*, sometimes shouting them out and weeping as they did so'.[80] As at Kelm, the focus was more on repairing individual souls than on tackling particular social problems, but there was nonetheless a hope that the focus on individuals would lead to social transformation. The Slobodka yeshiva 'strove for the perfection of society through the ethical reform of the individual'.[81] Finkel also, like Leib Hasman in Telz, encouraged his students to make pilgrimages to Kelm.[82]

[75] Tikochinski, 'Yeshivot hamusar melita le'erets yisra'el', ch. 4.

[76] Stampfer, *Lithuanian Yeshivas*, 267.

[77] See Tikochinski, 'Yeshivot hamusar melita le'erets yisra'el', 144–52.

[78] Cited ibid. 150.   [79] Stampfer, *Lithuanian Yeshivas*, 274–5.

[80] Ibid. 267–8; see Katz, *Tenuat hamusar*, iii. 214.   [81] Stampfer, *Lithuanian Yeshivas*, 260.

[82] See Tikochinski, 'Yeshivot hamusar melita le'erets yisra'el', 152–5.

As at Telz, the focus on *musar* did not sit well with many of the students of the Slobodka yeshiva. In 1897 students protested against *musar*, and about three-quarters of them abandoned Finkel and opted to join a new yeshiva in Slobodka where *musar* was not taught. However, Finkel's yeshiva retained great strength, and it spawned other branches in towns throughout the region. Moreover, a variety of other yeshivas throughout Lithuania came to employ *mashgiḥim ruḥani'im* and to require time in the curriculum for some study of *musar*, strengthening Weinberg's conviction about the acceptance of the *musar* method in the talmudic world. No yeshiva adopted the precise programme that Simhah Zisl Ziv had pioneered, but the *talmud torah*'s influence was felt through the efforts of its students such as Finkel, Hasman, and others, who sought to spread a culture of *musar* study throughout the Lithuanian yeshivas and thereby to transform the world.[83]

Some of Simhah Zisl's most ambitious students sought to spread his vision of *musar* to the land of Israel. Barukh Markus and Samuel Shenker set out from Lithuania in 1891 and settled in Jerusalem, where they established a *beit musar*, a *musar* study hall. In 1896/7 they founded a full-time yeshiva for young men, Or Hadash (New Light).[84] As the yeshiva developed, Simhah Zisl wrote to his students: 'How happy is the one with the good lot to merit [this opportunity] for awakening—acquiring a place in Jerusalem from which to spread both Torah and reverence together, [providing] for the maintenance of the world!'[85] He urged his students to dedicate themselves to spreading the vision of the *talmud torah*, with its commitment not just to the study of Torah but also to the cultivation of reverence, and expressed displeasure with those students who did not seek to spread their teaching to others. When one student opted to become a recluse in Jaffa, withdrawing from society in the style of the Vilna Gaon, Simhah Zisl railed against his failure to realize that one cannot repair one's own soul without also focusing on helping others to repair their souls as well. 'All philosophers describe the human being as "political",' he wrote, 'meaning that the world cannot be maintained except by means of everybody [assisting one another] . . . for a person needs to be concerned for the healing of his fellow's soul just as his own.'[86] As he put it elsewhere, 'true disciples of the sages . . . share the burden of their fellows, providing for the maintenance of the world—and this is the crown of the virtues'.[87] In Simhah Zisl's view, it was not just individual souls that were being repaired by the work of his *talmud torah*. He envisioned teaching *musar* as profoundly 'political' (or, one might say, 'social') work that would play a role in helping to sustain the entire world.

---

[83] The only yeshiva system to emerge that was more radical than Simhah Zisl's *talmud torah* in its focus on *musar*, and which seems to have drawn inspiration from it, was the system of Novaredok yeshivas. D. E. Fishman describes the Novaredok yeshivas as 'built on the model of the Musar *yeshivot* in Grobina [Grobin] and Slobodka' ('The Musar Movement in Interwar Poland', in Y. Gutman et al. (eds.), *The Jews of Poland between Two World Wars* (Hanover, NH, 1989), 248).

[84] Katz, *Tenuat hamusar*, ii. 83–5.   [85] Ziv, *Sefer ḥokhmah umusar*, i. 197.

[86] Ibid. 12.   [87] Ibid. 9.

CHANGING THE WORLD FROM BEHIND HIGH WALLS

Simhah Zisl's writings reveal his desire to spread the study of *musar* beyond his own *talmud torah*. As he wrote in one letter, 'most of the world finds this wisdom to be strange. And I have learned only a little of it—but now I am like a guardian for *musar*, [seeking to] spread it.'[88] Dov Katz explained that 'Rabbi Simhah Zisl was not content with his educational work being confined within the walls of his institutions, and he devoted himself also to strengthening reverence and *musar* beyond their boundaries'.[89] However, his efforts to spread *musar* focused almost exclusively on influencing elites, and the *talmud torah*s in Kelm and Grobin interacted very little with non-elites. As noted above, Simhah Zisl's efforts to preach publicly were unsuccessful, and he seems to have preferred to train students in isolation from the wider society that was sceptical of his vision. While he condemned students who isolated themselves, he himself isolated his students in many respects.

As Stampfer has shown, Simhah Zisl took unprecedented steps to isolate his students, especially through establishing dormitories, an effort which no traditional yeshiva had previously undertaken. The one in Kelm Talmud Torah 'seems to have been the first dormitory in a Jewish school to retain and foster traditional behavioural patterns in the setting of a total institution'.[90] Simhah Zisl 'believed that it was possible to shape the character of young students through education and create an ethical personality that would remain loyal to what the founders [of the *talmud torah*] saw as the true Jewish tradition. However, this could only be done in the setting of a total institution that could block out external influences.'[91]

The sociologist Erving Goffman coined the term 'total institution' to describe a place where 'a large number of like-situated individuals, cut off from the wider society for an appreciable period of time together, lead an enclosed, formally administered round of life'.[92] Commonly, the 'encompassing or total character' of such institutions 'is symbolized by the barrier to social intercourse with the outside and to departure that is often built right into the physical plant, such as locked doors, high walls', and the like.[93] Among the many examples of total institutions that Goffman cites are boarding schools and 'those establishments designed as retreats from the world even while serving also as training stations for the religious; examples are abbeys, monasteries, convents, and other cloisters'.[94] Simhah Zisl's *talmud torah* fits Goffman's description to a significant degree in ways that earlier Jewish institutions in eastern Europe did not. For one thing, as Stampfer points out, it was a boarding school that provided sleeping quarters and meals, breaking with more traditional arrangements whereby students would rent rooms from and

---

[88] Ibid. 57.　　　　　　　　　　　　　　　　　　　　　[89] Katz, *Tenuat hamusar*, ii. 73.

[90] Stampfer, *Families, Rabbis, and Education*, 222.　　　　　　　　　　　　[91] Ibid. 223.

[92] E. Goffman, *Asylums: Essays on the Social Situation of Mental Patients and Other Inmates* (Garden City, NY, 1961), p. xiii.　　　　　　[93] Ibid. 4.　　　　　　[94] Ibid. 5.

share meals with community members.[95] Such an arrangement may well have been pioneered by Israel Salanter in the previous generation: one writer reports that meals and sleeping quarters were provided for students at the Nevyozer *kloyz*.[96] Even so, Simhah Zisl developed the model of a yeshiva as a total institution even further, especially in Grobin, where the *talmud torah* was surrounded by a tall fence and was described by Dov Katz as truly being 'a world unto itself'.[97]

Students were encouraged to stay at the *talmud torah* for at least five years, and they were discouraged from spending time outside its walls.[98] Behind the fence in Grobin, students would not be challenged by traditionalists who opposed Simhah Zisl's innovations, as they seem to have been in Kelm; moreover, they could be shielded from the challenges to Orthodoxy and traditional religious observance that were increasingly found in Lithuanian towns. If students were to board with local residents, Simhah Zisl could not assume that they would be shielded from the heresies, self-indulgence, and lax religious observance that his sermons warned against, nor would students find support for their focus on *musar*. At the *talmud torah*, Simhah Zisl could create a total institution which would protect his students from these sorts of influences and place them under the constant watch of the *mashgiḥim ruḥani'im* who monitored their behaviour and kept them focused on the work of *musar*.[99]

Israel Elyashev described the atmosphere at the *talmud torah* in Grobin as akin to that of a Christian monastery, where the inmates renounced contact with the rest of the world. Students were even discouraged from much contact with their families, instead often regarding Simhah Zisl as a father figure.[100] Elyashev's sense was that Simhah Zisl was interested in developing what he considered to be a spiritual elite, raised in a cloistered environment, who could effect change in the wider world only after they completed a substantial period of training. He saw the *musar* movement as thus taking the same strategy that he associated with the Lithuanian Haskalah movement and also with Ahad Ha'am's elite Benei Mosheh Zionist movement. As Elyashev wrote, reflecting on his experiences in Grobin:

The *musar* movement, like the Haskalah movement in Lithuania, was not a popular movement. Rather, it was a movement of 'householders' [*ba'alei batim*] in the broad sense of the

---

[95] See Stampfer, *Families, Rabbis, and Education*, 211–28.

[96] Y. Halevi Lipschitz, *Zikhron ya'akov: historyah yisra'elit meḥayei hayehudim berusyah vepolin mishenat 520–656*, 3 vols. (Kovno, 1924–30), ii. 8; see Katz, *Tenuat hamusar*, i. 171–2; id., *The Musar Movement: Its History, Leading Personalities, and Doctrines*, trans. L. Oschry, 2 vols. (Tel Aviv, 1975–7), i/1, 231; I. Etkes, *R. yisra'el salanter vereshitah shel tenuat hamusar* (Jerusalem, 1982), 171–2; id., *Rabbi Israel Salanter*, 214.

[97] Katz, *Tenuat hamusar*, ii. 200; cf. Mark, *Bemḥitzatam shel gedolei hador*, 220. The writings of Elyashev contain ample references to the dormitories at Grobin (see also Katz, *Tenuat hamusar*). There is less evidence to confirm that there were in fact dormitories at the *talmud torah* in Kelm (see Claussen, 'Rabbi Simḥah Zissel Ziv', 53 n. 135).

[98] See Katz, *Tenuat hamusar*, ii. 200; Elyashev, 'Gerobin', pt. 1, pp. 109, 112, 116; id., 'Gerobin', pt. 2, pp. 92, 94, 95   [99] See Stampfer, *Families, Rabbis, and Education*, 222–3.

[100] Elyashev, 'Gerobin', pt. 1, p. 116; see also Katz, *Tenuat hamusar*, ii. 200.

term. It concerned itself only with the individual, aspiring to improve his path and to raise his spirit but not aspiring to bring the masses along. The Benei Mosheh movement was like this too, drawing a line between the prophets and the people. It, too, spread its Torah among individuals, and it was passed from person to person, seeing the masses (without clear recognition) as a concern for the future, as the passive material that would be [transformed] by the hands of the chosen prophets.[101]

From Elyashev's perspective, though, Simhah Zisl and his students were deluded in thinking of themselves as prophets who would eventually transform the world. Elyashev saw Simhah Zisl as having 'hypnotized' his students so that they would follow him, just as he saw Simhah Zisl himself as having been 'hypnotized' by the spell of Israel Salanter.[102]

Under such a spell, those who lived within the walls of the *talmud torah* became convinced that they could transform the world through their *musar* activities, and, despite their claims to be focused on developing humility, they thus developed a sense that they were spiritually superior to those outside the *talmud torah*'s walls. Elyashev recalled:

The student at Grobin considered himself to be on a level above all the Jews who could be found walking the streets. Whether they were rabbis or geniuses or merchants or doctors or whatever else—in the eyes of the Grobin [students], they had no value. It was precisely like the case of *ḥeder* students who believe with total conviction that souls were only given to Jews and that the brain of the non-Jew contained not a soul but, rather, the smoke from a candle. I related in the same way to all those who were not musarists . . . Whatever had a connection to Grobin and to R. Simhah Zisl Ziv was located in the world of truth, and the remainder of people, who lived in the world of error and worldly vanities, were nothing but shadows wandering in circles who did not even attempt to find repair for their souls.[103]

Elyashev's description should be understood in light of his eagerness to paint the *talmud torah* (and the *musar* movement more generally) in a negative light, but it would not be surprising if students at the *talmud torah* developed the sense of superiority that is characteristically felt by students living in 'total institutions'. The *musar* movement was criticized by some of its opponents for encouraging precisely this sort of sectarian attitude, especially in claiming that it offered salvific practices that ordinary Jews and even acclaimed rabbis did not undertake. Simhah Zisl saw his teachings as playing some significant role in 'the maintenance of the world'. Even if he modestly admitted that he had 'learned only a little', as noted above, he nonetheless saw himself as having learned more *musar* than most people, such that he was a 'guardian of *musar*' tasked with transmitting his wisdom to his students and, perhaps through them, to the broader Jewish world.[104]

This vision persisted after the closure of the *talmud torah* in Grobin in 1886,

---

[101] Elyashev, 'Gerobin', pt. 1, p. 109.
[102] Ibid. 116.   [103] Elyashev, 'Gerobin', pt. 2, p. 94, cf. 92, 95; id., 'Gerobin', pt. 1, p. 112.
[104] On Simhah Zisl's discussions of leaders serving or not serving as superior prophetic voices, see Claussen, 'Rabbi Simḥah Zissel Ziv', 230–6.

when Simhah Zisl returned to Kelm to organize a new *talmud torah* there. As opposed to the highly regimented junior yeshivas which had previously existed in Kelm and Grobin, this was a post-secondary, senior yeshiva, with older students and a framework for largely independent study. It accepted a limited number of pupils, which kept expenses down, and it was generously financed by a small number of donors—foremost among whom was a German banker, Samuel Strauss, a supporter of German neo-Orthodoxy who developed a deep admiration for Simhah Zisl's work.[105] Simhah Zisl was eager to focus on an even smaller group of excellent students who could be trained to be truly elite leaders and who could reach out to the rest of Jewish society with pure and loving hearts. As he wrote: 'I am far from wanting to increase the quantity, but rather I want to increase the quality . . . and only to draw in men whom I can examine and find that they share the burden of their fellows, without taking pleasure for themselves at all, neither from wealth nor from prestige.' People with the disposition to 'share the burden of their fellows', as he went on to explain, were people who would be active in engaging with others, focusing on the needs of others, and responding to them with compassionate love and concern.[106]

The number of students who spent substantial time in Kelm remained small, but the *talmud torah* was no longer dedicated to isolating young students from the dangerous influences of the broader society. The reconstituted Kelm Talmud Torah was more open to visitors, such as the students from Telz and Slobodka that Leib Hasman and Natan Tsevi Finkel sent to visit their teacher. In particular, it opened its doors wide during Elul, the month dedicated to introspection and repentance before the holy days of Rosh Hashanah and Yom Kippur. Students with an interest in *musar* streamed into Kelm from all over Lithuania and beyond, seeking to engage in the work of *musar* under Simhah Zisl's direction.[107]

THE EFFECTS OF GENERAL STUDIES AT
THE *TALMUD TORAH*

There is considerable evidence that the *talmud torah* attempted to shape its students, and through them Jewish society more broadly, through *musar* study, exemplified in its evening sessions of sermons, prayer, meditation, group discussion, and study of *musar* literature. But, as noted above, the time devoted to *musar* was not the only major innovation. The Kelm Talmud Torah was also the first yeshiva in eastern Europe to teach general studies alongside Jewish studies. Just as it scheduled three hours in the morning for Talmud study, the school

---

[105] Katz, *Tenuat hamusar*, ii. 72. Strauss was a resident of Karlsruhe, which was also the home of Simhah Zisl's brother Abraham Joseph. Abraham Joseph and Simhah Zisl's close disciple Reuven Dov Dessler introduced Strauss to Simhah Zisl's work.

[106] Ziv, *Hokhmah umusar*, i. 20–1; Katz, *Tenuat hamusar*, ii. 69–71.

[107] Katz, *Tenuat hamusar*, ii. 69; Friedman, *Sefer hazikhronot*, 83, 107; 'Meshiv kehalakhah', *Hamelits*, 1 July 1897, p. 84; *Edenu: lezikhro shel rabenu shelomoh poliachek* (New York, 1929), 10.

generally scheduled three hours in the afternoon for general studies, or, as Israel Elyashev described it, 'Haskalah studies'.[108] The teachers were Christians who otherwise taught in Russian government schools. They taught mathematics and Russian, and the study of Russian exposed students to geography and to Russian and world history and literature. When the *talmud torah* moved to Grobin, the general studies curriculum expanded to include bookkeeping, physical education, science, and an additional language that was common in Courland, German.[109] All of these subjects challenged the norms of what should be taught in a traditional Jewish institution: German instruction may have been a source of particular concern for traditionalists who were aware that German provided easy access to the heretical views of German-speaking Jews.[110]

As noted, one of the central goals of the Russian Haskalah in the mid-nineteenth century was to introduce subjects like mathematics and Russian into Jewish schools, a goal which was opposed by a wide range of traditionalists. Most traditionalists saw a commitment to non-Jewish learning as implying that there was truth to be found outside the Jewish tradition, an idea which they feared would lead to the abandonment of that tradition, and they saw the Russian government's encouragement of studying Russian as a tool to encourage assimilation and apostasy.[111] Israel Salanter was among those Lithuanian traditionalists who opposed the teaching of general studies in yeshivas, and he was joined by nearly all other figures in the *musar* movement. What did Simhah Zisl seek to accomplish by developing a yeshiva that accommodated the Haskalah and defied the norms of the movement and the wider culture with which he was associated?

Though there are no clear answers to this question, Simhah Zisl may well have seen his curriculum as helping students to pursue careers that he valued. Interest in general studies increased among Jews in the 1860s and 1870s because of reforms introduced by Tsar Alexander II that opened up new economic opportunities for Jews, opportunities that were only possible with the knowledge of Russian and the other subjects taught at his *talmud torah*. Aided by their studies, many of Simhah Zisl's students involved themselves in business activities with their teacher's support; indeed, whereas other yeshiva directors praised only the life of scholarship, Simhah Zisl's writings often praised the world of commerce.[112] He may have also supported his students' pursuing careers as rabbis, who, with Russian language skills, could communicate effectively with Russian government officials in

[108] Elyashev, 'Gerobin', pt. 1, p. 111; Broida, 'Kelm'; Lifshitz, 'Gan hashem'. Friedman, however, recalls that only 'an hour' was dedicated to such studies (*Sefer hazikhronot*, 81).

[109] On the subjects taught at the *talmud torah* in different periods, see Broida, 'Kelm'; Lifshitz, 'Gan hashem'; Tzizling, 'Liboya'; Frumkin, 'Kovno'; Mark, *Bemeḥitzatam shel gedolei hador*, 221; Shapira, 'Grobin'; Mondshein, 'Warsaw', 42; Katz, *Tenuat hamusar*, ii. 208; Elyashev, 'Gerobin', pt. 1, p. 111.

[110] See I. Etkes, 'Haskalah', in Hundert (ed.), *YIVO Encyclopedia of Jews in Eastern Europe*, http://www.yivoencyclopedia.org/article.aspx/Haskalah (accessed 17 Feb. 2016).

[111] See B. Nathans, *Beyond the Pale: The Jewish Encounter with Late Imperial Russia* (Berkeley, Calif., 2002), 202, 206, 235.   [112] Claussen, 'Rabbi Simḥah Zissel Ziv', 387–9.

ways that few traditional rabbis could: an 1873 newspaper article by Simhah Zisl's cousin Rabbi Mordecai Gimpel Yaffe praises the *talmud torah* and its general studies curriculum precisely because of its promise in this respect.[113]

Simhah Zisl may have also thought of the general studies programme as enticing to parents who would otherwise be tempted to send their children to the newly available gymnasia and technical schools. With its limited general studies programme, the *talmud torah* was hardly an elite gymnasium, but it was acclaimed in the Jewish press for combining the best of the gymnasium with the best of traditional Jewish education: one 1873 newspaper report by Rabbi Zevulun Barit, who sent his children to the *talmud torah*, praised it for having a 'curriculum used in gymnasia' and so 'educating young Jews in both the laws of Torah and wisdom together'.[114] Similarly, Israel Elyashev reports that his father, the businessman Simhah Zalkind Elyashev, saw it as an institution that could 'unite Haskalah with the fear of heaven', promoting traditional piety and values while also providing the modern knowledge appropriate for members of the emerging Jewish bourgeois.[115] As Simhah Zalkind saw it, the *talmud torah* could train 'a Jew who was expert in languages, polite and well behaved, possessing fine character traits, knowledgeable about the business world and, above all, following in the paths of his fathers'.[116]

Simhah Zisl may have seen the general studies curriculum as having limited intrinsic value but as important for enticing such prospective parents and winning them over to the cause of the *musar* movement. Such an approach would follow Israel Salanter's counsel to his students that they should entice adherents by appealing to their desires and especially that they should focus on attracting prominent businessmen to join the *musar* movement.[117] Salanter himself generally opposed general education, even publicly condemning his son at one point for his pursuit of secular studies, and he was troubled by the efforts in Germany led by Rabbi Samson Raphael Hirsch to develop 'neo-Orthodox' institutions that taught general studies. But Salanter seems to have conceded that Hirsch's general studies curriculum was acceptable insofar as it might appeal to modernizing German Jews and thereby draw them into Orthodox institutions that they would otherwise avoid. Salanter allegedly supported Simhah Zisl's experiments with general studies in Kelm and Grobin, and he may have viewed them in the same way, as a concession that could be part of an effective outreach strategy.[118]

[113] M. G. Yaffe, 'Shalom ve'emet', pt. 2, *Halevanon*, 31 Dec. 1872, pp. 145–6; see also Etkes, *Rabbi Israel Salanter*, 141–5.   [114] Z. L. Barit, 'Kelm', *Halevanon*, 19 Feb. 1873, p. 207.

[115] Elyashev, 'Gerobin', pt. 1, pp. 108–9.   [116] Cited in Elyashev, 'Gerobin', pt. 2, p. 101.

[117] See Claussen, 'Rabbi Simḥah Zissel Ziv', 77–8. On Salanter's interest in attracting prominent householders, 'the assumption being that, if these people are drawn toward Mussar study, many others will follow in their footsteps', see Etkes, *Rabbi Israel Salanter*, 111.

[118] Claussen, 'Rabbi Simḥah Zissel Ziv', 85–9; Etkes, *Rabbi Israel Salanter*, 246–7, 278–9, 283–6, 314–15; on Hirsch's neo-Orthodoxy, see N. H. Rosenbloom, *Tradition in an Age of Reform: The Religious Philosophy of Samson Raphael Hirsch* (Philadelphia, 1976).

Simhah Zisl's *talmud torah* was perceived as importing the model that Hirsch had pioneered in Frankfurt. Ya'akov Mark recalled that 'the yeshiva was organized to follow the example of the Orthodox "Frankfurt" school',[119] and Israel Elyashev described Simhah Zisl as creating 'a new sort of school, like those of the Orthodox in Germany'.[120] Elyashev and Friedman saw the *talmud torah*'s adaptation of this model as more superficial than substantive: Elyashev recalled Simhah Zisl's German-style clothes (such that 'he looked like a Protestant minister', following a style also adopted by German neo-Orthodoxy) and Friedman recalled the school's Western-style 'gleam, sparkle and beauty', but both saw this as part of an outreach effort and doubted that Simhah Zisl sought to promote any serious engagement with modern European ideas, as Hirsch did in Germany.[121]

Simhah Zisl's writings, however, seem to suggest that he was not merely providing attractive bait for unsuspecting parents but that he saw some intrinsic moral value in the *talmud torah*'s Russian and German classes. When he outlined the mission of the *talmud torah* in the 1870s, for example, Simhah Zisl described the general studies programme in strikingly positive terms, as one of the three foundational pillars of the yeshiva alongside Talmud and *musar* study. He described general studies as entailing the study of

the laws of the way of moral decency [*derekh erets*] in accordance with the spirit of the age, that one may behave [well] with people in speech and behaviour, and understand the subtleties of language. But know, and let it be known, that *all these studies are grounded in the path of reverence, the fulfilment of the Torah*—and this is done very wisely and carefully.

The way of moral decency is not only what is all over scripture but that one should 'keep the way of the tree of life' (Gen. 3: 24)—as the Midrash teaches, the way is the way of moral decency which precedes Torah. It also includes the art of writing, studying the language of the state, studying mathematics, and knowing geography, as is taught in this school under our supervision. We have implanted in their hearts a fixed understanding that *students should grasp these things as part of the fulfilment of the Torah*, not just on account of their desire, so that they not turn their steps away from the way of God.[122]

Simhah Zisl referred to general studies as the study of *derekh erets*, a term used in the newspaper report cited above to refer to the study of *musar*. Here, the term, which literally means 'the way of the land', refers to general knowledge about the world in which one lives. Using *derekh erets* to speak of general studies was popularized a generation before Simhah Zisl in Germany by Hirsch. Simhah Zisl here appears to follow Hirsch in interpreting the traditional Jewish requirement to 'study *derekh erets*' as requiring Jews to study and appreciate their surrounding cultures and 'the spirit of the age', with the goal of developing moral uprightness. Like Hirsch, Simhah Zisl by no means endorsed all the prevailing social

[119] Mark, *Bemeḥitsatam shel gedolei hador*, 219; see also M. G. Yaffe, 'Shalom ve'emet', pt. 1, *Halevanon*, 25 Dec. 1872, p. 145; Elyashev, 'Gerobin', pt. 1, p. 109.
[120] Elyashev, 'Gerobin', pt. 1, p. 109.   [121] Ibid. 109, 114; Friedman, *Sefer hazikhronot*, 81–2.
[122] Katz, *Tenuat hamusar*, ii. 193–4 (emphasis added).

conventions and he advocated 'care' when considering them, but he nonetheless felt their study to be necessary for the service and reverence of God. He saw general education as not merely utilitarian but as contributing to the 'fulfilment of the Torah'.

In another passage, Simhah Zisl explicitly argued that the German neo-Orthodox Jews under Hirsch's influence were more prone to empathy than his fellow Russian Jews and that this could be directly attributed to their general education, which focused on the importance of building a 'civilized' society:

When one habituates oneself to considering the way of moral decency [*derekh erets*] and the civilizing of the world, the consideration of justice will emerge from this and this will be the fulfilment of the Torah, for the Torah aims at civilizing the world as well as going beyond reason. . . . Indeed, in our countries, they do not study and habituate themselves to considering the civilizing of the world, as we have said a number of times. . . . It is not the case in the other countries [Germany] where, as I have seen myself, they study the wisdom of bringing civilization to the world, and so it is easy for them to arrive at this sentiment. . . . And so we can see with our eyes that he who is wiser regarding the human work of *musar*, such *musar* being part of moral decency as is known among the [non-Jewish] philosophers, is closer to knowing the Torah. He who understands will understand the greatness of this meditation and will be astonished and aroused in realizing that applying one's reason well to the wisdom of moral decency is part of *musar*.[123]

General education can provide real wisdom of the sort known to non-Jewish philosophers, and this wisdom can help to fulfil the purposes of the Torah and bring *musar* to human souls and greater justice to the world. Passages like this suggest that Simhah Zisl viewed general studies as contributing to the formation of his students, 'civilizing' them, making them fit to be citizens of the communities in which they lived, perhaps helping to build the habits of concern for others that he saw as present in German Jewry but lacking among his brethren in Russia.

Simhah Zisl did not advocate general education and the values of the Haskalah with the passion that Hirsch did.[124] In addition, the students at his *talmud torah* did not, on the whole, seem to envy German Orthodoxy. As indicated by the story at the beginning of this chapter, they saw the *talmud torah* as superior to the German universities with which Hirsch was aligned. Nonetheless, Simhah Zisl seems to have endorsed Hirsch's vision of Jewish and general education working together in pursuit of moral excellence. He seems to have harboured hopes that Russian Jewry could become a bit more like German Jewry through focusing on 'the way of moral decency', and he seems to have viewed his *talmud torah* as a force for realizing these hopes.

[123] Simhah Zisl Ziv, *Or rasaz: al hamishah humshei torah*, ed. H. S. Levin, 5 vols. (Jerusalem, 1960–5), i. 51–2.

[124] Compare Hirsch's much more direct discussion of the benefits of general studies ('The Relevance of Secular Studies to Jewish Education', in id., *The Collected Writings of Rabbi Samson Raphael Hirsch*, ed. E. Bondi and D. Bechhofer, trans. G. Hirschler, corrected edn., 9 vols. (New York, 1997), vii. 88).

THE LIMITS OF THE *TALMUD TORAH*'S INFLUENCE

Needless to say, this vision of shaping Russian Jewry through a Hirschian synthesis of Torah and general studies did not spread beyond the *talmud torah*, and it is doubtful whether Simhah Zisl was all that dedicated to such a vision. Perhaps the rhetoric did not reflect a heartfelt commitment to general studies but was, rather, the rhetoric of fundraising directed at the neo-Orthodox donors who supported the *musar* movement (like Samuel Strauss)[125] or the businessmen who sought a broad education for their children (like Simhah Zalkind Elyashev). Nonetheless, the general studies programme may have had some effect in making commercial careers possible for some of Simhah Zisl's students, it may have helped some students in their dealings with government officials, and, moreover, it may well have shaped the moral sensibilities of some students. Rabbi Aryeh Carmell, for example, noted that Simhah Zisl's student Reuven Dov Dessler stayed 'true to the principles of his rebbe, R. Simhah Zisl' in teaching his own son Eliyahu Eliezer 'classics of world literature in Russian translation', including works such as *Uncle Tom's Cabin* that seem to have been intended to enlarge his son's moral sympathies.[126] Eliyahu Dessler grew up to become an extremely influential rabbi, and it is possible that he was, through his father, shaped by the methods of the Kelm Talmud Torah, and that these methods had an influence on his own influential discussions of loving-kindness.[127] But Eliyahu Dessler himself, later in life, publicly denounced yeshivas that taught general studies along the lines advocated by Hirsch and Simhah Zisl.[128] Moreover, general studies ceased to be a part of the curriculum after the reconstitution of the *talmud torah* in Kelm in 1886. Although Reuven Dov Dessler may have sought to teach world literature to his son privately, none of the students from the *talmud torah* advocated spending much time at all on such literature. More commonly, like Eliyahu Dessler, they condemned such study, especially as traditionalists' fears about the threats from the outside world increased at the end of the nineteenth century. At the Slobodka yeshiva, for example, Natan Tzevi Finkel directed his assistants to spy on students and ensure that they were not reading secular literature.[129] Nearly all of the *talmud torah* students who remained committed to traditional observance came to be identified with an 'ultra-Orthodox' traditionalism that rejected the value of general studies to the greatest extent possible.

[125] On neo-Orthodox support for *musar* yeshivas, see Stampfer, *Lithuanian Yeshivas*, 268.

[126] A. Carmell, 'Harav eliyahu eliezer dessler zt″l', *Yated ne'eman*, 7 Jan. 1994, p. 12; see J. J. Schacter, 'Facing the Truths of History', *Torah U-Madda Journal*, 8 (1998), 200–2.

[127] This seems to be Carmell's conclusion (see Schacter, 'Facing the Truths of History', 251 n. 3).

[128] E. E. Dessler, *Mikhtav me'eliyahu*, ed. A. Carmell and A. Halpern, 5 vols. (London, 1955–97), iii. 355–8; see S. Z. Leiman, 'R. Shimon Schwab: A Letter Regarding the 'Frankfurt' Approach', *Tradition*, 31/3 (1997), 71–7.

[129] For suspicion of Haskalah literature at Slobodka, see Stampfer, *Lithuanian Yeshivas*, 271, 273, 274; see also Tikochinski, 'Yeshivot hamusar melita le'erets yisra'el', 120–3, 161–2, 180–1.

As noted, the *talmud torah* was more successful with its efforts to export its vision of *musar* study to other yeshivas. Simhah Zisl's students did seem to think that their *talmud torah* was the only place in the world that gave sufficient focus to 'the repair of human character traits' through *musar* study, and they lobbied for other elite yeshivas to take up their programme of impassioned study, lengthy prayer, *musar* sermons and counselling, and spiritual supervision. Their efforts were limited in the face of fierce opposition from traditionalists. Nonetheless, some rabbis who seemed hostile to institutionalized *musar* study came to accommodate it, especially when they realized that *musar* study might be a bulwark against the Haskalah, as Eliezer Gordon at Telz seemed to think. Above all, Natan Tsevi Finkel, although he rejected Simhah Zisl's general studies programme, did much to spread his focus on *musar*, such that *musar* study was accepted in many Lithuanian yeshivas.

Perhaps, though, the *talmud torah* had the most influence not in the specific programme of *musar* study that it developed but in its vision of how to effect social change through the creation of a total institution. In seeking to develop an elite group who would defend tradition, Kelm broke with tradition and introduced a yeshiva that was isolated from general society in unprecedented ways, especially through dormitories that obviated the need for students to lodge or eat with community members and that allowed them to be under constant supervision. As Shaul Stampfer has observed, 'the model of the Kelm/Grobin Talmud Torah was not quickly imitated', whether 'for lack of individuals who could take such an initiative because of the expenses and legal complications, or for other reasons'. But as traditionalist concerns about the dangers of general society increased at the end of the nineteenth century and the start of the twentieth, dormitories became more common.[130] With 'the growing concern about what was seen as the pernicious influences of the surrounding society', more and more yeshivas began to adopt the model that had been pioneered by Simhah Zisl's *talmud torah*.[131] Its clearest legacy for east European society was its model for separating traditionalists from the rest of society.

Although Simhah Zisl's *talmud torah* might have aspired to bridge that gap through its general studies programme, on the one hand, and its vision of 'maintaining the world' by spreading *musar* to the masses, on the other, its clearest legacy is a legacy of isolationism. The *talmud torah*'s own isolation was what allowed its students, even as they sought to cultivate their humility, to trust in their own superiority and imagine that they were envied even by German university chancellors. The institutions that were most influenced by the *talmud torah* did not adopt its general studies programme and downplayed its focus on *musar* study, but

---

[130] Stampfer, *Families, Rabbis, and Education*, 223.

[131] Ibid. 227. Among the examples noted by Stampfer is that of the Łomża yeshiva, a yeshiva very much shaped by the *musar* movement (ibid. 225). The *mashgiaḥ ruḥani* at Łomża, Moshe Rosenstein, was trained at the *talmud torah* in Kelm.

increasingly adopted its isolationism and began to tell the same sorts of stories about how they had mastered what other more 'worldly' institutions struggled to master. A later rumour developed among the students of the Telz yeshiva, for example, that one of their *rashei yeshivah* had been told by a university professor that he already knew 'everything we have to teach' based on his yeshiva education.[132] Students who believed this story were encouraged to turn away from the enticements of universities and from engagement with secular society altogether, and this pattern played itself out at many other institutions. In the twentieth century growing numbers of Lithuanian yeshivas and the institutions that they inspired around the world came to adopt the isolationism of the *talmud torah*s of Kelm and Grobin, as they sought to cultivate new communities of yeshiva students, 'chosen prophets', whom they hoped would eventually transform and repair Jewish society.[133]

[132] W. B. Helmreich, *The World of the Yeshiva: An Intimate Portrait of Orthodox Jewry*, aug. edn. (Hoboken, NJ, 2000), 66.

[133] On emerging patterns of yeshiva education in the twentieth century, see Fishman, 'Musar Movement in Interwar Poland'; Klibansky, 'Hayeshivot halitayot'; Tikochinski, 'Yeshivot hamusar melita le'erets yisra'el'; I. Fuchs, 'The Yeshiva as a Political Institution', *Modern Judaism*, 33 (2013), 357–80; Y. Finkelman, 'Haredi Isolation in Changing Environments: A Case Study in Yeshiva Immigration', *Modern Judaism*, 22 (2002), 61–82.

Legislation for Education

Rabbi Tsevi Elimelekh of Dynów's Regulations for the Support of Torah in Munkács

LEVI COOPER

IN THE LATE 1820s a set of *takanot* (regulations) regarding traditional Jewish education for all boys in Munkács, in Carpathian Ruthenia, at the time part of the Habsburg monarchy, was enacted by the local rabbinic leadership. They were titled *Takanot tamkhin de'orayta* ('Regulations for the Support of Torah'), and over the next century they were copied and printed in different locations in eastern Europe. This chapter examines the *takanot*, their objectives, circulation, and effectiveness.

The chapter begins by sketching the context of their enactment, before turning to the details of the *takanot* themselves: while the *takanot* ostensibly organized educational matters, they had a distinct socializing objective, and a careful reading highlights the particular socio-religious issues that troubled those who drafted them. The legacy of the *takanot*, as indicated by their legislative and publication histories, is then considered. The second half of the chapter explores the effectiveness of the *takanot* as a tool for the preservation and conservation of traditional education in the face of the winds of change that were blowing across the continent. It will examine the role of the *takanot* in their Munkács birthplace, from the end of the nineteenth century until the eve of the Second World War: that is, under the Hungarian government of the dual monarchy (1867–1918) and in the Czechoslovak Republic (1918–38). During this period, two processes were concurrently in play. Within the Jewish community, modernity was encroaching on traditional life, giving Munkács' Jews greater opportunities to leave the enclave

The research for this chapter was supported in part by the I-CORE Program of the Planning and Budgeting Committee and the Israel Science Foundation (grant no. 1798/12). It was written while I had the privilege of being a post-doctoral fellow in Bar-Ilan University's Faculty of Law. I am grateful for the opportunity. It is my pleasure to thank Meir Yosef Frankel, Shia Frankel, Uriel Gelman, Zeev Gries, Jossi Rabinovich, Amihai Radzyner, Yehudah Ber Zirkind, and Zvi Zohar for their assistance at various stages of this research.

and enabling the rise of political movements like Zionism. At the same time, the government was actively regulating education. The rhetoric, writing, and activism of rabbis in Munkács during this period suggest that *Takanot tamkhin de'orayta* were largely ineffective in preserving traditional education and preventing reform.

CONTEXT

The emancipation of the Jews in Europe began in the late eighteenth century, at the time of the Haskalah, and triggered discussions about traditional Jewish learning. At the same time governments were enacting new legislative measures concerning education. The 1781 Edict of Toleration and subsequent laws promulgated by Emperor Joseph II altered the legal situation of non-Catholics in the Habsburg lands.[1] On 2 January 1782 a further edict was issued, the Toleranz-Patent für die niederösterreichischen Juden, expanding existing compulsory education rules to Jews of Lower Austria and obligating Jewish children to study basic secular studies. Inter alia, the edict stated:

Since it is our purpose to make the Jews more useful and serviceable to the state, principally through according their children better instruction and enlightenment and by employing them in the sciences, arts, and handicrafts, we permit and command the tolerated Jews, in places where they have no German schools of their own, to send their children to the Christian upper elementary schools, so that they shall learn at least reading, writing, and arithmetic, and although they have no synagogue of their own in our capital, we yet permit them to build for their children, at their own expense, a normally equipped school, with a teaching staff of their own religion, which shall be subject to the same control as all the German schools here, the composition of the moral books being left to them.[2]

Joseph II continued to enact edicts for other provinces, as well as laws and instructions that applied to the whole realm. The various edicts differed based on local conditions and existing legislation, yet the central tenets were in concert: linguistic assimilation and related educational directives, permission to engage in previously forbidden occupations, and religious toleration for private worship. In October 1789 an edict issued for Moravia was extended to Hungary and Transylvania, which included Carpathian Ruthenia. The new legislation, however, did not change life in Carpathian Ruthenia, a region geographically removed from the seats of government, power, and official oversight.[3]

[1] 'Order *In Spiritualibus* to All Imperial and Royal Governments', in *The Habsburg and Hohenzollern Dynasties in the Seventeenth and Eighteenth Centuries*, ed. C. A. Macartney (New York, 1970), 155–7; *Das Toleranz-patent Kaiser Joseph II*, ed. G. Frank (Vienna, 1882), 37–40.
[2] 'Edict of Toleration for the Jews of Lower Austria', in *The Habsburg and Hohenzollern Dynasties*, 166; Toleranz-Patent für die niederösterreichischen Juden, §§ 7–8, in *Kaiser Josef II: Ein Lebens- und Charakterbild zur hundertjährigen Gedenkfeier seiner Thronbesteigung*, ed. J. Wendrinsky (Vienna, 1880), 153.
[3] For an overview of the legislation, see A. Moskovits, *Jewish Education in Hungary (1848–1948)* (New York, 1964), 1–10; *Habsburg and Hohenzollern Dynasties*, 164–5; R. Patai, *The Jews of Hungary:*

While the new laws may not have succeeded in imposing changes in Munkács' schooling, traditional Jewish education was nonetheless being re-examined and reassessed. By the beginning of the nineteenth century, traditionalists perceived modernity as a threat that needed to be countered, and education became the central battleground for ideological competitors in the region.

It was against this backdrop that in 1827 or 1828 an attempt was made to regulate the local Jewish education system in Munkács by Rabbi Tsevi Elimelekh Shapira (1783–1841), who would become famous as the hasidic master of Dynów and the author of acclaimed hasidic tracts, most notably *Benei yisaskhar*, which was published posthumously in 1850. At the time,[4] Tsevi Elimelekh was serving for a brief stint as official town rabbi of Munkács.[5] The legislation established the Society for the Support of Torah (Haḥavura Tamkhin De'orayta), which, it was hoped, would guarantee traditional Jewish education and thwart any attempt to change traditional mores.

Takanot tamkhin de'orayta do not detail specific factors that led to their enactment. It could be linked to Tsevi Elimelekh's arrival in Munkács, although there is scant evidence to suggest that he enacted similar *takanot* in other communities where he served as rabbi. At the time changes were afoot in the region, as Hungary was entering the period of reform diets (1825–48). On 15 September 1825 a general diet was convened in Pressburg (Bratislava) to discuss various social and economic matters, including education. The results of this meeting were negligible, yet in its wake the Jews of Pressburg convened their own meeting on

---

History, Culture, Psychology (Detroit, 1996), 211–25; S. O. M. Yanovsky, 'Facing the Challenge of Jewish Education in the Metropolis: A Comparative Study of the Jewish Communal Organizations of Budapest and Vienna from 1867 until World War II', Ph.D. thesis (Hebrew University of Jerusalem, 2013), 13–26. For the impact of the legislation in Carpathian Ruthenia, see S. Reinhardt, *Kehilot yehudei rusyah hakarpatit* (Culver City, Calif., 1989), 69–70, 79. A commemorative medal struck in 1781 depicts a bust of Joseph II, while the reverse side reads: 'Qvid Potvit Tota Contingere Vita Laetivs | Libertas | Religionis | A Iosepho II | in Terris Svis | Protestantibvs | et Ivdaeis Data' (That all might enjoy life, Joseph II gave the Jews and the Protestants in his lands freedom of religion). The 1781 Edict of Toleration did not actually include Jews: they were included in the 1782 edict issued a few months later.

[4] The *takanot* give the year they were enacted as 'tov leyisra'el' (Ps. 73: 1), that is [5]588 = 1827/8 (see Tsevi Elimelekh of Dynów, *Takanot tamkhin de'orayta* (Munkács, 1895), 8*a*, 9*b*, 19*a*). Elsewhere in his writings, Tsevi Elimelekh connected Psalm 73: 1 to the notion of supporting Jewish education (see *Benei yisaskhar* (Żółkiew, 1850), 'Kislev–tevet', 2: 37). I have used the Munkács edition which claims to have been copied from the author's manuscript. As I will explain, there are differences between this edition and the other three published editions: *Halakhot vetakanot shel havurat talmud torah* (Czernowitz, 1864); *Moznayim latorah* (Lemberg, 1896), 1*a*–9*a*; *Kakh hi darka shel torah* (Cluj, 1926), 2*a*–13*b*.

[5] On Tsevi Elimelekh, see S. A. Horodezky, 'Tsevi elimelekh midinov, perek betoldot hahasidut hagalitsa'it', *Metsudah*, 5–6 (1948), 284–9; N. Y. Urtner, *Harebi reb tsevi elimelekh midinov* (Benei Berak, 1972); M. Wunder, *Me'orei galitsya*, 6 vols. (Jerusalem, 1978–2005), v. 532–52; *Igerot shapirin*, ed. B. Weinberger (Jerusalem, 1983), 21–4; B. Brown, 'Hahmara: hamisha tipusim min ha'et hahadasha', *Dine yisra'el*, 20–1 (2001), 178–92; on his juridical authority in Munkács, see S. Weingarten, 'Munkatch', in Y. L. Maimon (ed.), *Arim ve'imahot beyisra'el*, 7 vols. (Jerusalem, 1946–60), i. 349–50.

11 October 1825. Thirteen districts of Hungary sent representatives, and a committee of eight was chosen to formulate proposals that would be presented to the government. The committee could not come to an agreement, and in the end two sets of proposals were submitted—one written by progressives stressed the importance of secular studies, while the other written by conservatives emphasized Talmud study and adherence to Jewish law.[6] Despite the proximity in time of the Pressburg meeting and Tsevi Elimelekh's *takanot*, there is no evidence to suggest a direct connection. Moreover, the tension in Pressburg was local and embryonic: the schism suggested by the two proposals had yet to grip Hungarian Jewry in its entirety. Nonetheless, the palpable general spirit, in particular modernity and the policies associated with Joseph II's legacy of enlightened absolutism, may have precipitated *Takanot tamkhin de'orayta*.

TAKANOT FOR EDUCATION AND SOCIALIZATION

Takanot tamkhin de'orayta include a preamble and six sections that governed the society. The first three sections reveal that the society had a dual purpose: in addition to its stated goal of providing universal Jewish education for males in Munkács, it was intended as a socializing tool. The fourth section focused on funding, while the final two sections related to the functionaries of the society, their responsibilities, appointments, and tenures.

Preamble

Tsevi Elimelekh used the preamble to recall the history of communal responsibility for Jewish education. He began his overview with the talmudic passage that credits Joshua ben Gamla, a high priest towards the end of the Second Temple period, with establishing schools in every locale. Jumping across centuries, Tsevi Elimelekh noted that responsibility for education was later undertaken by the Council of the Four Lands. Once the council was abolished in 1764, there was no longer a central authority responsible for Jewish education. Perceiving a need for new regulations for education and considering the history of Jewish concern, Tsevi Elimelekh embraced the task.

The central aim of *Takanot tamkhin de'orayta* was to provide community-sponsored schooling, thus guaranteeing that the education of the needy would not be neglected. In this vein, the preamble had harsh words to say about the wealthy who employed private tutors for their children. Tsevi Elimelekh saw this as no less than the work of Satan, in that it undermined the communal educational enterprise. He also rejected the suggestion that some students might not be able to study: 'Let not a person say: "Behold my child is incapable of Torah [study] and

---

[6] Moskovits, *Jewish Education in Hungary*, 11–12; H. N. Lupovitch, *Jews at the Crossroads: Tradition and Accommodation during the Golden Age of the Hungarian Nobility, 1729–1878* (Budapest, 2007), 173–4.

will not succeed in Torah [study]." Let not a person say so, for our Creator has already assured us "And all your children will be taught of God and great shall be the peace of your children" [Isa. 54: 13].'[7]

A further concern was the need to curb the spread of secular studies. Again the wealthy were targeted, for their private tutors were free of communal oversight and thus able to design their own curriculum, a situation that often led to instruction in general subjects. Tsevi Elimelekh adopted the position that, in the Middle Ages, the study of philosophy and other subjects had weakened commitment to Judaism. This, in turn, had led Jews to choose conversion rather than martyrdom at times of persecution and expulsion from European countries. While only mentioned briefly in *Takanot tamkhin de'orayta*, this was a theme that Tsevi Elimelekh developed extensively elsewhere in his writings.[8]

The *takanot* also served as the initial by-laws of the Society for the Support of Torah. The society's mandate was to oversee the implementation of the *takanot*, and to this end the society undertook responsibility for all males who arrived in Munkács to study for any period of time. The name of the society was innovative: similar societies, including the defunct Munkács society, adopted names such as the Society for the Teaching of Torah (Havurat Talmud Torah). Tsevi Elimelekh explained that *tamkhin de'orayta* was a reference to a passage in the Zohar about Jacob's night-time wrestle with an unnamed assailant (Gen. 32: 24–30): when the assailant realized that he could not overcome Jacob, he weakened him by injuring his thigh and causing him to limp. In the Zohar, this is interpreted as an attack on those who support Torah, the *tamkhin de'orayta*. Without *tamkhin de'orayta*, Torah cannot stand. Thus Tsevi Elimelekh's *takanot* turned the focus from *talmud torah* to *tamkhin de'orayta*; that is, from Torah study to support for Torah study.[9]

Section One: Membership

The first section dealt with membership of the society. The members voluntarily undertook responsibility for the implementation of the *takanot*. The *takanot* were designed to create a coterie of paragons, and the benchmark for membership was high: members were to avoid frivolity, social gatherings, the theatre, playing cards, and similar pastimes.[10] Members who were caught engaging in any of these vices

[7] Tsevi Elimelekh of Dynów, *Takanot tamkhin de'orayta*, 6*b*.

[8] Ibid. 4*b*–5*a*, 5*b*, 6*b*, 7*a*; see Tsevi Elimelekh of Dynów, *Ma'ayan ganim*, in Y. Ya'avets, *Or hahayim* (Żółkiew, 1848); id., *Kli haro'im* (Lemberg, 1848), Obad. 1: 8; id., *Derekh eidotekha* (Przemyśl, 1883), Josh. 1: 8; see also M. Piekarz, *Hahanhaga hahasidit* (Jerusalem, 1999), 336–62.

[9] Tsevi Elimelekh of Dynów, *Takanot tamkhin de'orayta*, 6*a*; citing *Zohar* i. 171*a*; the text appears as 'samkhin de'orayta' not 'tamkhin de'orayta', although there is no substantial difference in meaning. Tsevi Elimelekh cited this passage elsewhere in his writings (*Benei yisaskhar*, 'Kislev–tevet', 2: 37, 3: 22). Other hasidic masters also cited the passage as 'tamkhin de'orayta' (see e.g. Kalonymus Kalman Epstein of Kraków, *Ma'or vashamesh* (Breslau, 1842), 'Vayishlah'). The terms *tamkhin orayta* and *tamkhin le'orayta* appear in *Zohar* i. 8*a*, iii. 53*b*.

[10] Cf. L. Cooper, 'A Leisurely Game of Cards', *Jewish Educational Leadership*, 6/2 (Winter 2008), 59–63.

were to be fined and, for a second offence, thrown out of the society. The appearance of members was also to be exemplary: Tsevi Elimelekh was aware that many Jewish men were no longer careful about growing their side-locks and leaving their beard uncut: such people were automatically disqualified from membership. Similarly, members were not to have long hair. Clothing was also important: members were to wear *tsitsit* for the entire day and were warned against wearing clothes suspected of containing *sha'atnez*, the forbidden combination of wool and linen.

Society members undertook not to talk during the prayer service and were obligated to dedicate one hour a day to Torah study. That is not to say that members needed to be rabbinic scholars. On the contrary, there was a proviso for those who were unable to study Torah: they were to read the Psalms or *ma'amadot*, prescribed daily selections from the Bible and rabbinic literature. A further indicator of the intended membership is the language of the *takanot*. Tsevi Elimelekh explicitly stated that he did not use elaborate language 'because my intent with these words is that each and every person will understand these words of ours that are said with sincerity and with honesty'.[11] The recruitment pool was thus lay leaders and businessmen, a fact confirmed by the list of founding members appended to the *takanot*.[12] This model was reminiscent of the *ḥevra kadisha*, the burial society. Yet money alone could not buy membership: the *takanot* included a specific stipulation that a potential member whose conduct was considered inappropriate should not be admitted to the society 'even in exchange for a great sum'.[13]

Section Two: Eligibility for Assistance

Eligibility for assistance from the society was based solely on conduct and appearance: there is no mention of need-based criteria. Thus, the *takanot* detail the instructions that the beadle of the society was to give a new student upon his arrival. 'Do not waste time.' 'Study with diligence.' 'Review the material when the teacher is not present.' 'Wear kosher *tsitsit*.' 'If you are of barmitzvah age wear *tefilin*'—indicating that the society dealt with students younger than the age of 13. There is no mention of beards, presumably because the average student would have been too young to grow facial hair. Hair, however, was not ignored: if the student had cut his side-locks in the past or had previously grown his hair, he was to desist from these practices. 'Pray with concentration and do not talk during the service.' 'Do not wear "foreign" clothing'—fashionable garments that were not worn by Jewish traditionalists. These directives reflect the socializing objective of the *takanot*.

---

[11] Tsevi Elimelekh of Dynów, *Takanot tamkhin de'orayta*, 7*b*.
[12] Ibid. 12*b*–20*b*; the list was only printed in the Munkács edition.
[13] Ibid. 11*b*; cf. *Halakhot vetakanot shel ḥavurat talmud torah*, 9*b*–10*a*.

Section Three: Teachers

While Section Two dealt with students' appearance and conduct, Section Three applied similar guidelines to teachers, with the goal of ensuring that they provided suitable role models. Teachers were expected to attend daily communal prayer services. Bible teachers were to be well versed in the classic medieval commentaries such as those of Rashi, Rashbam, and Radak,[14] but one who was familiar with 'foreign commentaries in foreign languages' was automatically disqualified, even if he had no intention of teaching those commentaries, even if he was willing to guarantee that he would cease from studying them. As Tsevi Elimelekh explained, this was 'because there is a presumption that all his deeds are rotten'.[15]

Teachers were required to accompany the students to the *mashgiḥim* (overseers) on a weekly basis so that the students could be tested. The *takanot* make no secret of the fact that the goals of such examinations were not only to see whether the students knew the material, but also to check on the teachers: the *mashgiḥim* were explicitly 'obligated to oversee the teachers and their students'.[16]

Section Four: Funding

The success of the enterprise would have been dependent on procuring funding, a significant task undertaken by the society. To this end, Section Four outlines a fund-raising programme. This section is longer and more detailed than the others, containing more than twenty subsections (as opposed to ten in Section One, six in Section Two, five in Section Three, twelve in Section Five, and nine in Section Six).[17] The paratext of the Munkács edition suggests that those who prepared the booklet for publication also considered this section to be the most significant, as it alone was presented with a bold, double-spaced heading.

Initial membership dues were set, smaller weekly donations were collected, and an elaborate system of taxation was instituted. Thus, a member who purchased a new garment for himself or for a family member was required to donate half of 1 per cent of the value of the new item to the society coffers. A special tax was also imposed on members who purchased new barrels of wine. A set amount was to be donated for a variety of life-cycle events. If a member had a baby, began to teach his son to read Hebrew or to study the Bible or Talmud, celebrated a son's

---

[14] Specific commentators are not listed in the earliest (Czernowitz) edition. The mention of Rashbam and Radak—commentators favoured by the maskilim—is surprising. Rashbam was first printed in the early eighteenth century and first seriously considered by Moses Mendelssohn: Tsevi Elimelekh was unreservedly critical of Mendelssohn (*Ma'ayan ganim*, § 3, ¶ 4; Piekarz, *Hahanhagah haḥasidit*, 345). He was also critical of Radak's approach to studying subjects other than Torah (see *Derekh eidotekha*, Josh. 1: 8).

[15] Tsevi Elimelekh of Dynów, *Takanot tamkhin de'orayta*, 9*b*; cf. id., *Agra depirka* (Lemberg, 1858), § 271.   [16] Tsevi Elimelekh of Dynów, *Takanot tamkhin de'orayta*, 12*a*.

[17] In the Czernowitz edition, Section Four has twenty-three subsections; in the Munkács edition, twenty-two; in the Lemberg and Cluj editions, twenty-four.

barmitzvah or a marriage: all were occasions meriting a set donation. At these festivities, those honoured with roles in the ceremony, such as the *mohel* (who performed circumcisions), were also taxed. Each event was assigned a tariff, reflecting its relative significance in nineteenth-century Munkács. Other occasions, such as appointment to a position of responsibility in the society, also called for donations. Various *mi sheberakh* pronouncements (the public dedication of a blessing in the synagogue in honour of particular people and in lieu of a donation) were also a source of income for the society.

With such a pervasive system of taxation, only the wealthier members of the community could gain membership of the society, but the funds so raised were what made the society's objectives achievable. Despite the exclusivity of the society, the general public was not overlooked as a source of revenue. Collection boxes were placed in public places: guest-houses for visiting businessmen, the rabbi's home, and the women's *mikveh*—to encourage voluntary donations. At certain points during the year a public appeal was made in the synagogue, and voluntary donations for festivals and life-cycle events were declared for the benefit of the society. It is not surprising that dates connected to the giving of the Torah at Mount Sinai were singled out for public appeals: the festival of Shavuot and the two weekly portions when the Ten Commandments were read.[18] Representatives of the society would also frequent market-places to collect donations from local and visiting businessmen.

One aspect of funding was 'in kind'. Students relied on householders' generosity for their meals. A system of *esn teg* (eating days) was common, whereby each student would have a designated home for dining at on each day of the week. Society members were expected to bear a significant portion of this burden.

Section Five: Appointment of Functionaries

Each year, around the festival of Shavuot, three *borerim* (selectors) were chosen by lot from the society members. The *borerim* would meet to decide on the executive branch of the society, choosing three *gaba'im* (beadles), four *mashgiḥim*, and one *ne'eman* (trustee). The tenure of appointments was one year. At the annual general meeting—actually, an annual general feast—rules of the society could be abrogated or changed, and new members could be admitted. This was also the time for dealing with members who had not lived up to the high standards of the society as detailed in Section One. The *takanot* stipulated two disciplinary measures: fines and expulsion. The annual general meeting was also when compulsory donations were collected.

---

[18] Similar arrangements existed for other local charities. For instance, donations on two designated weeks—Shabat shekalim and the 'Re'eh' weekly portion—were earmarked for Jews from Carpathian Ruthenia who were living in the Land of Israel (see *Heshbon . . . mikolel munkatch . . .* (Mukačevo, 1937), 16).

Section Six: Jurisdiction of Functionaries

The *gaba'im* were responsible for collecting the dues of society members and were expected to keep meticulous records of the society's expenditure. If three weeks passed and the *gaba'im* had not collected the dues, they were to be removed from office. The *gaba'im* were responsible for hiring teachers, and as part of this task they determined class sizes. The *ne'eman* served as auditor, and each quarter he was expected to review the books kept by the *gaba'im*. The *mashgiḥim* monitored the students' progress and the teachers' performance through weekly examinations.

SOCIO-RELIGIOUS FOCUS: NEGLECT OF *TSITSIT*

Many aspects of *Takanot tamkhin de'orayta* were standard for societies constituted in Jewish communities for the advancement of local education or other purposes. For instance, mechanisms for financing a society's activities and rules of appointment of officers were typical of the by-laws of local societies.

As the preamble acknowledged, the goal of providing educational opportunities was not an innovation: providing schooling had been a Jewish value since the earliest times. More immediately, Tsevi Elimelekh may have been drawing on the example set by one of his teachers in Galicia, Rabbi Menaham Mendel of Rymanów (1745–1815), who had enacted *takanot* for his city just before his death, one of the thirteen sections of which dealt with providing traditional Jewish education for the impoverished: it aimed 'to supervise the needy and poor who learn Torah and also to support the study of Torah for the children of the needy'.[19]

Nonetheless, Tsevi Elimelekh's *takanot* went further than Menaham Mendel's in dealing with the financial aspects of providing universal education and in their socializing goals. A comprehensive comparison of the *Takanot tamkhin de'orayta* and the by-laws of other societies is beyond the scope of this chapter. It is, however, noteworthy that the particular issues emphasized by Tsevi Elimelekh's *takanot* are not identical to those in other education-related *takanot*. Broadly speaking, *Takanot tamkhin de'orayta* have a decidedly socializing focus, while educational questions are given less emphasis.[20]

Takanot tamkhin de'orayta devote more space to sartorial matters than to pedagogy, there is no discussion of classroom management or discipline, and it is

[19] Menaham Mendel of Rymanów, 'Beit menaham', § 9, in Y. A. Kamelhar, *Eim labina* (Lemberg, 1909), 17*a*–*b*.

[20] Reinhardt, *Kehilot yehudei rusyah hakarpatit*, 32; S. Assaf, *Mekorot letoledot haḥinuch beyisra'el*, new edn., ed. S. Glick, 6 vols. (New York, 2002–9), i. 704. See, for instance, the regulations of the Kraków *ḥevra kadisha talmud torah*, from 1551 and 1639 (ibid. 636–42). On the socializing goal of the modern yeshiva, see Y. Finkelman, 'Virtual Volozhin: Socialization vs. Learning in Israel Yeshivah Programs', in J. Saks and S. Handelman (eds.), *Wisdom from All My Teachers* (Jerusalem, 2003), 360–81.

entirely unclear how the schools at the centre of the legislation were expected to function. Fixing class size was the jurisdiction of the *gaba'im*, but there are no criteria set down for such a determination, no ideal class size, and no minimum or maximum number of students. Apart from approving classical medieval biblical commentaries and blacklisting 'foreign commentaries in foreign languages', there is no discussion of curriculum. When should a student begin studying Talmud? What other subjects were to be studied? It would appear, therefore, that Tsevi Elimelekh was not attempting to revamp prevailing educational norms (which are not detailed in the *takanot*) but to socialize students and teachers.

The *takanot* reveal the socio-religious issues that were rife in early nineteenth-century Munkács. Taking Tsevi Elimelekh's other writings into consideration, we can see which ones particularly vexed him. One obligation that is mentioned numerous times is the requirement to wear *tsitsit*. This obligation is not treated as extensively in the by-laws of other societies; hence, the attention it is given here is striking.

The ubiquitous neglect of *tsitsit* is mentioned in the preamble to *Takanot tamkhin de'orayta*: membership of the society was conditional on wearing *tsitsit* throughout the day, and the beadle was to warn new students that they must wear kosher *tsitsit*. Moreover, the wearing of *tsitsit* is one of the few topics that also appears in another set of instructions Tsevi Elimelekh wrote during his time in Munkács, published in 1909 under the title *Azharot mahartsa* ('The Warnings of our Master Rabbi Tsevi Elimelekh') and dealing with lax religious observance in a number of areas. In this context, Tsevi Elimelekh decried those who wore *tsitsit* that did not cover their entire bodies and further condemned those who hid the fringes in their trousers. *Tsitsit*—opined Tsevi Elimelekh—should be oversized and proudly displayed.[21]

Other topics are highlighted in both of Tsevi Elimelekh's Munkács works: avoiding *sha'atnez*, wearing *tefilin*, not trimming the beard or cutting side-locks, and not growing long hair.[22] Tsevi Elimelekh's concern for the vice of changing

[21] Tsevi Elimelekh of Dynów, *Takanot tamkhin de'orayta*, 6a, 8a, 9a; id., *Azharot mahartsa*, §§ 5–6, in Y. T. Yolles, *Kohelet ya'akov* and Tsevi Elimelekh of Dynów, *Azharot mahartsa*, ed. H. Fenig (Przemyśl, 1909). Tuvya Shapira, one of Tsevi Elimelekh's descendants, inherited some of his manuscripts. In 1908 he sold a few of them to Hersch Fenig who had *Azharot mahartsa* published bound together with Y. T. Yolles' *Kohelet ya'akov* (Yolles, *Kohelet ya'akov* and Tsevi Elimelekh of Dynów, *Azharot mahartsa* [ii], 1a (second pagination)). Fenig noted that the instructions were written when Tsevi Elimelekh was in Hungary (ibid. [iv], 1a, 11a (second pagination)). From the preamble, it is apparent that Tsevi Elimelekh was not addressing people in Galicia. On Yolles (1778–1825), see Wunder, *Me'orei galitsyah*, iii. 216–23; see also Z. Gries, *Sifrut hahanhagot* (Jerusalem, 1989), 135–6. There are a number of parallels between *Azharot mahartsa* and Menahem Mendel's *takanot*, including chaperones for women, accurate weights and measures, sabbath observance with particular emphasis on operating taverns, and *tsitsit*.

[22] Tsevi Elimelekh of Dynów, *Azharot mahartsa*, §§ 5, 7, 9, 12, 13. A third piece of Munkács legislation has been attributed to Tsevi Elimelekh. According to Weingarten, he founded the society that oversaw the purchase and repair of books in the large *beit midrash* and wrote its by-laws ('Munkatch',

traditional clothing is also mentioned elsewhere in his writings.[23] None of these issues, however, appear to have bothered him to the same extent as neglect of *tsitsit*.

Tsevi Elimelekh's concern for *tsitsit* was not new. In 1808 Menaham Mendel of Rymanów wrote to Rabbi Yitshak Isaak Taub of Nagykálló (1751–1821), lambasting the prevalent neglect of *tsitsit* amongst Hungarian Jews.[24] A few years later, Menaham Mendel instructed: 'Warn the tailors that when they sew four corners [*tsitsit*], that the four corners should reach the knees.'[25] Despite the possible influence, Tsevi Elimelekh seemed to go further than his predecessor in dealing with *tsitsit*.

Perhaps the emphasis on wearing *tsitsit* was due to the mystical value of this particular precept, as Tsevi Elimelekh understood it. The Bible indicates the importance of *tsitsit* by saying that the fringes act as an aid to recalling and keeping God's commandments (Num. 15: 39). Tsevi Elimelekh advised people who were having difficulty overcoming anger to look at their *tsitsit*. In fact, he cast the act of looking at *tsitsit* as a panacea for all types of temptation.[26] Elsewhere in his writings, he mentioned *tsitsit* as an example of a commandment that people neglect and that people assume they can achieve the goal of without the action that is supposed to lead to the goal: in the case of *tsitsit*, remembering God's precepts without wearing the four-cornered garment. Tsevi Elimelekh explained that the goals of commandments were not limited to the words of the biblical text: fulfilment of a particular commandment had other, perhaps unstated, purposes.[27]

It is also possible that the emphasis on *tsitsit* was due to a particular neglect of this precept in Tsevi Elimelekh's milieu. He noted that it was no wonder that sinning was so rampant in Munkács and the vicinity: since the commandment of *tsitsit* was being neglected, how were people to recall the other commandments?[28] Tsevi Elimelekh might have felt a personal affinity for the commandment of *tsitsit*.

---

367). Tsevi Elimelekh may have established the society, but the by-laws that Weingarten would have been familiar with were adopted in 1920 in order to satisfy insurance requirements. Not only is there no evidence of earlier by-laws but the lack of by-laws complicated the society's insurance claim following a fire in 1903, a complication that led to the 1920 by-laws. See M. Y. Frankel and N. C. Brody (eds.), *Munkatch: dos kleyn yerushalayim* (Brooklyn, 2011), [56–9]. For a reproduction of the 1920 by-laws, see ibid. [391–413]; for Weingarten as an office holder of the society, see ibid. [412]. Weingarten noted that the society listed 3,000 volumes in its possession. In 1942 the society published a list of its books (ibid. [417–54]).

[23] Tsevi Elimelekh of Dynów, *Hosafot mahartsa*, in Tsevi Hirsh Eichenstein of Żydaczów, *Sur mera va'aseh tov* (Munkács, 1900), § 86, ¶ 4; id., *Agra dekalah* (Lemberg, 1868), 'Mishpatim', s.v. *le'am*; id., *Ma'ayan ganim*, § 3, ¶ 5.

[24] Menaham Mendel of Rymanów, letter to Yitshak Isaak Taub of Nagykálló, Sun. [*sic*] 20 Feb. 1808, in *Beit va'ad lahakhamim*, 7 (1928), 56.

[25] Menaham Mendel of Rymanów, 'Beit menahem', § 10.

[26] Tsevi Elimelekh of Dynów, *Hanhagat ha'adam* (Lemberg, 1848; repr. Brooklyn, 2002), §§ 3, 25; id., *Hosafot mahartsa*, § 37.   [27] Tsevi Elimelekh of Dynów, *Ma'ayan ganim*, § 2, ¶ 2.

[28] Tsevi Elimelekh of Dynów, *Azharot mahartsa*, § 5. On the state of religious observance, as Tsevi Elimelekh perceived it, see *Takanot tamkhin de'orayta*, 7b–8a.

The notion that a particular precept might capture the attention of a person more than any other appears in hasidic writings and was one that Tsevi Elimelekh acknowledged with regard to customs and other practices performed as an expression of piety.[29]

Perhaps it was a combination of Tsevi Elimelekh's personal conviction and the backdrop of widespread neglect. There may have also been an element of family tradition, as Rabbi Elimelekh of Leżajsk (1717–87), Tsevi Elimelekh's maternal great-uncle and a key hasidic author, had written:

> Each and every generation is connected at its root to fix a specific commandment more than any other commandment. For example, this generation is connected at its root to fix the commandment of *tsitsit* more than any other commandment. And similarly each generation is connected at its root to uphold a specific commandment more than any other commandment.[30]

LEGACY: LEGISLATIVE HISTORY AND PUBLICATION HISTORY

Takanot tamkhin de'orayta were enacted in Munkács in the late 1820s, and for one hundred years they reverberated beyond their place of origin. Sometime between 1827 and 1864, the community of Kołomyja established a society to oversee education. They wrote to the Munkács community, asking for a copy of Tsevi Elimelekh's *takanot*. We know about this correspondence, because when a similar society was established in Czernowitz they wrote to Kołomyja asking for a copy of the copy. It was the Czernowitz society that first published the *takanot* in 1864, in a slim twenty-four-page booklet. It is unclear whether *Takanot tamkhin de'orayta* were considered binding legislation in Kołomyja or Czernowitz. At the very least, the Czernowitz publication had three stated objectives. First, the Czernowitz society sought to promote conduct that it deemed appropriate: the *takanot*, however, may have been read as guidelines rather than as legislation. Second, the Czernowitz society saw the publication of the *takanot* as a recruitment opportunity: readers would see the altruistic ethos of the Czernowitz society and be inspired to join. Third, the publication was part of a fund-raising effort, as proceeds from the sale of the booklet were earmarked for the needy.[31]

---

[29] Tsevi Elimelekh of Dynów, *Regel yesharah* (Lemberg, 1858), 'Ma'arekhet mem', § 161.

[30] Elimelekh of Leżajsk, *No'am elimelekh* (Lemberg, 1787), 3*b*. One of his interpretations of *tsitsit* was published in his lifetime (see B. Wolf, 'Igeret vesefer', *Heikhal habesht*, 17 (2006), 153–4).

[31] *Halakhot vetakanot shel ḥavurat talmud torah*, 1*b*. The booklet was printed together with a summary of relevant points from Shneur Zalman of Lyady, *Hilkhot talmud torah* (Shklov, 1794), which was published anonymously and is missing from Yehoshua Mondshine, *Sifrei hahalakhah shel admor hazaken* (Kefar Chabad, 1984). The copy in the National Library of Israel ends mid-sentence with a catchword at the bottom of the page indicating that the text continues on the next page (ibid. 11*a–b*). The following page is unnumbered and printed in a different font, and contains an announcement from the publisher about his intentions to print books without errors, an ironic statement under the circumstances.

Almost twenty years later, in 1881, Tsevi Elimelekh's grandson, Rabbi Shelomoh Shapira (1831–93), crossed the Carpathian Mountains with his family to take up the very position held by his grandfather as rabbi of Munkács. Soon after his arrival Shelomoh appended his name to the founding document of the society, indicating that the mechanism set in place by Tsevi Elimelekh was still functioning in some way.[32]

Shelomoh was succeeded in 1893 in the Munkács rabbinate by his son, Rabbi Tsevi Hirsh Shapira (1850–1913). Two years later, in 1895, the *takanot* were published in their Munkács birthplace. That year was an important one for Hungarian Jewry. A passage of legislation that had begun in 1880 was finally ratified as Law XVII of 1895. The first paragraph of that law announced: 'The Israelite religion is declared by law to be equal to other religions.' The law granted equal rights to Jews, permitted Christians to convert to Judaism, and allowed Jewish representatives to serve in the Upper House of the National Assembly. The law also provided for government educational subsidies to be allotted proportionally, which was a boon for Jewish schools.[33] The Munkács edition of the *takanot* makes no mention of this momentous legislation, and it is unclear what impact the legislation from Budapest had in Munkács. Nonetheless, it is possible that reprinting *Takanot tamkhin de'orayta* was a response to the passage of Law XVII of 1895.

In the introduction to the Munkács edition, the heads of the society acknowledged the role that the *takanot* could play—and did play—in other towns:

Why should we bury this precious charm in our satchels; is it not incumbent upon us to benefit our people the house of Israel with kindness, and to publish these holy regulations . . . so that also in other holy communities they will see it and thus they will do?

The introduction was signed: 'the *gaba'im*, administrators of the Society for the Support of Torah, here in the holy community of Munkács, may God protect it'.[34] The publication stated that the text was copied from the original *takanot* written by Tsevi Elimelekh himself, though this claim cannot be verified since the manuscript is lost. The copyist, Sulem Kalus, was a descendant of Tsevi Elimelekh. Like the Czernowitz printing, this publication had a fund-raising element, as proceeds from the sale of the booklet were earmarked for the Munkács Society for the Support of Torah.[35]

Whereas the first edition had only recapitulated the *takanot*, the Munkács edition also transcribed the names of the founding members of the society. These

[32] Tsevi Elimelekh of Dynów, *Takanot tamkhin de'orayta*, 13*b*–14*a*. According to Weingarten, Shelomoh reaffirmed the legislation ('Munkatch', 355).

[33] Moskovits, *Jewish Education in Hungary*, 163–4.

[34] Tsevi Elimelekh of Dynów, *Takanot tamkhin de'orayta*, 2*a*.

[35] Two versions of the Munkács edition were printed. The title page of one of them noted the publishing house and gave the address of the publisher, Samuel Kahn of Munkács, for obtaining the booklet; the title page of the other credited Kalus with copying and proofreading the text and gave his address for purchasing the work and the price. For a further difference, see n. 37 below.

names would have had scant significance for the Jews of Kołomyja or Czernowitz, but for Munkács Jewry the list included ancestors of residents of Munkács.[36] The Munkács edition also included a letter written by Tsevi Elimelekh to the community of Munkács, as well as to those of nearby Beregszász and Alsóverecke, offering words of comfort in the wake of the influenza pandemic that swept through Europe in 1830 and 1831.[37]

In 1896, shortly after the 1895 Munkács printing, the *takanot* were published with slight changes in Lemberg. This edition was published by a Kołomyja resident and was available for purchase in Kołomyja, and it introduced another city to the story of Tsevi Elimelekh's *takanot*: Horodenka. Rabbi Moses Teomim (1825–87) was appointed rabbi of Horodenka around 1859 and served in that position for almost thirty years until his death. When Teomim arrived to fill his post, he discovered that the original Horodenka regulations regarding education had been lost. In its place, the *pinkas* (community register) contained a copy of Tsevi Elimelekh's *takanot*. No details of this copy are given. A fire in Horodenka later destroyed the *pinkas*, and in the wake of the devastation the local society responsible for education disbanded. As part of an effort to reconstitute the local Society for Teaching the Torah, Teomim was charged with drawing up new regulations. Tsevi Elimelekh's *Takanot tamkhin de'orayta* served as source material for Teomim's effort.[38]

However, the efforts of Tsevi Elimelekh and Teomim were vastly different. Teomim felt that the situation in Horodenka was not as dire as circumstances had been in Munkács in the 1820s; hence, he did not need to recapitulate Tsevi Elimelekh's

[36] Tsevi Elimelekh of Dynów, *Takanot tamkhin de'orayta*, 12b–20b; *Igerot shapirin*, 46–9.

[37] Tsevi Elimelekh of Dynów, *Takanot tamkhin de'orayta*, 21a–22b; *Igerot shapirin*, 41–4. The community of Munkács was instructed to copy the letter and send copies to the two communities. On the pandemic, see A. W. Crosby, 'Influenza', in K. F. Kiple (ed.), *The Cambridge World History of Human Disease* (Cambridge, 1993), 809; Lupovitch, *Jews at the Crossroads*, 105–14. The pandemic is mentioned by Moses Sofer (*Ḥatam sofer: derashot*, 3 vols. (Cluj, 1929–59), i. 62a–63b) and possibly by Tsevi Hirsh Eichenstein of Żydaczów (letter to the Munkács community (n.d.), in *Peri kodesh hilulim* (Jerusalem, [1996]), 88–90). The title pages of *Takanot tamkhin de'orayta* promised to include the letter from Tsevi Elimelekh. Copies with the Kahn title page include a note from the publisher: 'Even though it [says] on the title page that we will also print a letter from the holy rabbi, the author of blessed memory, alas because of the costs of printing, for they are many, I omitted it' (in Tsevi Elimelekh of Dynów, *Takanot tamkhin de'orayta*, 16b); copies with the Kalus title page include no such note; a copy in the Rambam Library at Beit Ariela, Tel Aviv, has the Kahn title page but not the publisher's note. All copies of the Munkács edition that I have seen include the letter, whether or not they have the note.

[38] *Moznayim latorah*, 1a–9a (Tsevi Elimelekh's *takanot*); 10a–13a (Teomim's *takanot*). The majority of the volume contains a miscellany of items (ibid. 13a–84b). The fire may be the one in 1885 that destroyed the main synagogue (see *Pinkas hakehilot: polin*, 8 vols. (Jerusalem, 1976–2005), ii. 177). Teomim dated his *takanot* Sunday 24 Adar in the year 'kitro yeshuah' (*Moznayim latorah*, 13a). *Kitro yeshuah* (כתרו ישועה = 1017) does not give a realistic Hebrew year. It is possible that not all of the letters should be used: כתרו י"ו"ה gives the Hebrew year [5]647 (1887) when 24 Adar did indeed fall on a Sunday. On the Horodenka society, see S. Meltzer (ed.), *Sefer horodenka* (Tel Aviv, 1963), 170, 191; on Moses Teomim, see ibid. 69; Wunder, *Me'orei galitsyah*, v. 685–90; on his son David, see ibid. v. 654–5.

warnings to teachers and students.[39] More significantly, Tsevi Elimelekh's *takanot* had been a valiant attempt at socialization; by contrast, Teomim had a different objective, focusing on employer–employee obligations and other aspects of labour law. Regarding the challenge of financing local education, Teomim largely delegated the matter:

Behold, I have arranged a few regulations and rules regarding the laws of educators. And regarding the matter of revenue for the treasury of the society—what to add or to subtract from the *takanot* of the righteous rabbi of Dynów [Tsevi Elimelekh], of blessed memory— it should all be as the members of the society will agree. When they gather together they will consult privately on the matter—how and what it is appropriate to do and to enact in order to strengthen the Society for the Teaching of Torah in this community.[40]

Teomim's abdication of responsibility for fiscal legislation is surprising in the light of the mandate entrusted to him. In his own words: 'They demanded of me to instruct them in the path in which they should walk, and to institute the matter as I see fit: what to add or subtract from [Tsevi Elimelekh's *takanot*].'[41]

Teomim, however, did add an important directive that had not appeared in Tsevi Elimelekh's *takanot*: 'I perceive that this is appropriate to enact as a law that should not be transgressed: that a teacher from another city, who comes to our city, is obligated to give 5 per cent of his tuition fees to the society.'[42] While this rule concerns the finances of the society, it is really an extension of Teomim's other directives regarding labour relations.

Teomim's work was published posthumously by his son, David (*c.*1860–*c.*1920), in fulfilment of his father's will, in 1896. In his introduction, David praised the Munkács community, where, he reported, the impact of Tsevi Elimelekh's *takanot* was still felt:

And to this day, the city of Munkács, that faithful town [*kiryah ne'emanah*], is distinguished by inhabitants who fear God. Because the lofty righteous person, our master T[sevi] E[limelekh], may the memory of the righteous be a blessing, lived there and he sounded a voice that kindles flames of fire [see Ps. 29: 7] regarding support of Torah [*tamkhin de'orayta*]. And in many cities they will heed and rejoice over his *takanot*.[43]

The *takanot* had been published in Munkács only a few months earlier, but it is far from obvious that Tsevi Elimelekh's 'voice that kindles flames of fire' was more than a faint echo at the end of the century, as I will demonstrate below.

---

[39] *Moznayim latorah*, 10*b*.   [40] Ibid. 12*b*.   [41] Ibid. 9*b*.   [42] Ibid. 12*b*.

[43] Ibid. 3*b*. *Kirya ne'emanah* is a reference to Tsevi Elimelekh's own description of Munkács (*Takanot tamkhin de'orayta*, 6*a*). The Munkács edition included a warning against reprinting it without the permission of the Munkács society (ibid., title page); *Moznayim latorah* appears to be such an infringement. A copy of *Moznayim latorah* in the National Library of Israel belonged to Rabbi David Hakohen Zaltzer (1842–1908), who served on the rabbinic court in Munkács. The Lemberg edition appears to have used both the Czernowitz and Munkács editions: § 1, ¶ 3 is identical in the Munkács and Lemberg editions, but different in the Czernowitz one; while various turns of phrase in the Lemberg edition appear in the Czernowitz edition, as in § 1, ¶ 2.

The next stop on the journey of the *takanot* was Cluj, where they were published in 1926, a century after they were first enacted in Munkács. This edition was printed by students who studied in the yeshiva in Rodna, and their objective was to raise money. The yeshiva, which had between fifty and sixty students, was headed by Rabbi Asher Rubin—rabbi of Rodna from 1924 until his death in Auschwitz in 1944.[44] In addition to the *takanot*, the thirty-two-page pamphlet included an appeal for support from Rubin, as well as four letters on educational matters by the hasidic master Rabbi Simha Issachar Ber Halberstam of Cieszanów (1870–1914).[45] The letters were published from copies held by Rubin, who was a relative of Halberstam. This publication was not a legislative act, nor did it seek to regulate educational conduct in Rodna. Rather, publication of Tsevi Elimelekh's *takanot* was simply part of a fund-raising effort for the yeshiva.

The editions are not identical. Besides cosmetic and orthographic variations, the taxation systems differ from one edition to the next. Thus, for instance, the Czernowitz and Munkács editions both mention collections on Purim, whereas the Lemberg and Cluj ones do not. The Lemberg and Cluj editions consider the anniversary of a relative's death as a tax event, while the other editions do not. The Czernowitz, Lemberg, and Cluj editions instruct a member of the society to go the cemetery from the beginning of the month of Elul until Yom Kippur to collect donations from those who visit the deceased; there is no parallel instruction in the Munkács edition.[46] These variations are entirely in concert with the spirit of the *takanot*, as the Munkács edition explicitly praised 'anyone who adds to the aforementioned regulations'.[47]

Thus Tsevi Elimelekh's *Takanot tamkhin de'orayta* served two important non-legislative roles in the hundred years after they were first enacted: first, they were a source of inspiration for similar societies. Second, reprinting and selling the *takanot* helped to raise funds. While it is not explicitly indicated, it is possible that the *takanot* were adopted as legislation in Kołomyja and Czernowitz. In Horodenka, Lemberg, Cluj, and Rodna there was no pretence of enacting the *takanot* in order to regulate Jewish education. There is in fact no record of the actual societal impact of *Takanot tamkhin de'orayta* in Kołomyja, Czernowitz, Horodenka, Lemberg, Cluj, or Rodna.

---

[44] *Pinkas hakehilot: romanyah*, 2 vols. (Jerusalem, 1969–80), ii. 261–2; Y. Y. Cohen, *Hakhmei hungaryah vehasifrut hatoranit bah* (Jerusalem, 1997), 563.   [45] *Kakh hi darkah shel torah*, 14a–16b.
[46] *Halakhot vetakanot shel ḥavurat talmud torah*, 9a; Tsevi Elimelekh of Dynów, *Takanot tamkhin de'orayta*, 10b; *Moznayim latorah*, 4b; *Kakh hi darkah shel torah*, 11b. Besides differences in spelling and typographical errors, the Cluj edition is identical to that of Lemberg. For a comparison between the Munkács and Lemberg editions, see *Kuntras tamkhin de'orayta*, ed. A. M. Meisels (Brooklyn, 2000), 9–39.   [47] Tsevi Elimelekh of Dynów, *Takanot tamkhin de'orayta*, 10b.

EFFECTIVENESS: THE IMPACT OF
TAKANOT TAMKHIN DE'ORAYTA IN MUNKÁCS

Tsevi Elimelekh served in the Munkács rabbinate for a brief four years, between 1824 and 1828, before returning to Galicia.[48] There can be no doubt that his intention was to regulate Munkács's education system, although it is not known if he was successful. Was his detailed fund-raising mechanism effectively implemented? Did members pay their dues? Was taxation remitted willingly and promptly? Regrettably, no evidence as to whether the *takanot* operated smoothly and successfully in the late 1820s (or, for that matter, at any time afterwards) has survived. The fact that Tsevi Elimelekh left the city under acrimonious circumstances soon after enacting *Takanot tamkhin de'orayta* would not have furthered their effectiveness.[49]

While it is unclear how the Society for the Support of Torah fared after Tsevi Elimelekh's departure, when his grandson Shelomoh arrived in Munkács in 1881 he added his name to the founding document, suggesting that the society still existed in some form. This is the next surviving mention of *Takanot tamkhin de'orayta*—more than fifty years after Tsevi Elimelekh left Hungary—and it appears in the 1895 Munkács edition. This edition, printed two years after Shelomoh's death, includes an introduction by the *gaba'im* of the Society for the Support of Torah, perhaps suggesting that the group was active during Shelomoh's tenure in Munkács.[50] Regrettably, Shelomoh's writings—which were published piecemeal —give no clue as to the operation of the society or the effectiveness of the regulations during his rabbinate.[51]

The Hungarian revolution of 1848 and the Austro-Hungarian compromise of 1867 had far-reaching implications for many areas of Jewish life. Beginning with Law XXXVIII of 1868 concerning public education, the Hungarian government pursued changes in Jewish education. At the 1868–9 Jewish Congress in Budapest, education was one of the issues debated most fiercely. Rabbinic leaders in Carpathian Ruthenia (and elsewhere) actively fought against any change to traditional education practice.[52]

---

[48] Yosef Salmon suggested that Tsevi Elimelekh's appointment to the rabbinate on the other side of the Carpathian Mountains was connected to tension between him and Rabbi Naftali Tsevi Horowitz of Ropczyce (1760–1827) ('R. naftali tsevi miropshits: kavim biyografim', in I. Bartal, R. Elior, and C. Shmeruk (eds.), *Tsadikim ve'anshei ma'aseh* (Jerusalem, 1994), 100 n. 61; cf. Y. Berger, *Eser kedushot* (Warsaw, 1906), § 2, ¶ 35).

[49] The exact circumstances are a matter of debate (see Weingarten, 'Munkatch', 351; Reinhardt, *Kehilot yehudei rusyah hakarpatit*, 23; *Di shtot munkatch* (New York, 2005), 11 n. 21).

[50] Tsevi Elimelekh of Dynów, *Takanot tamkhin de'orayta*, 1b–2a.

[51] In his will, Shelomoh Shapira instructed that his writings not be published. With the understanding that Shelomoh had prohibited publication in book form, his son and grandson sporadically copied from manuscripts they had inherited, inserting passages into their own works. Recently, the scattered passages were collated and published: Shelomoh Shapira, *Osef torat shem shelomoh*, 2 vols. (Jerusalem, 2011).

[52] On the Hungarian legislation and the debates it caused, see Moskovits, *Jewish Education in*

Tsevi Hirsh, who succeeded his father in 1893, spearheaded the protest against change in Munkács. Information about Tsevi Hirsh's positions and activity in this arena comes from secondary sources,[53] which make no mention of *Takanot tamkhin de'orayta*, and Tsevi Hirsh never mentioned them in his own writings. This silence suggests Tsevi Hirsh felt that his great-grandfather's *takanot* were ineffective in dealing with the challenges he faced.

During Tsevi Hirsh's tenure, the Hungarian authorities zealously promoted the Magyarization of minorities. Thus children from the age of 6 were required to attend a Hungarian school, and any person who could not read Hungarian was declared illiterate, even if they could read Hebrew, Yiddish, German, or Russian. The official community rabbi was also required to be fluent in Hungarian and to have completed the first four grades of high school. Tsevi Hirsh did not fulfil these criteria: his mother tongue was Yiddish; he grew up in Galicia, where he would have heard German or Polish; and he had received a traditional Jewish education. He was therefore forced to forgo his state appointment and salary.[54]

Elsewhere in Hungary, rabbis supported Jewish schools that taught in Hungarian but were staffed by Jewish teachers and closed on the sabbath. Tsevi Hirsh viewed these institutions as particularly dangerous, seeing their apparent Jewish character as a facade for undermining traditional Jewish education, and urged his followers not to send their children to school. At first this was successful, but, as truancy fines were imposed, they, too, began sending their children there. By the

Hungary, 294–7; Reinhardt, *Kehilot yehudei rusyah hakarpatit*, 70–3; Yanovsky, 'Facing the Challenge of Jewish Education in the Metropolis', 64–76; for details of educational decisions from the congress and afterwards, see Moskovits, *Jewish Education in Hungary*, 61–104; for rabbinic responsa from Carpathian Ruthenia, see, for example, the 1875 responsum of Rabbi Mosheh Schick (1807–1879) (*She'elot uteshuvot maharam shik* (Munkács and Lemberg, 1880–3), ii: *Yoreh de'ah*, § 335); see also Shelomoh Tsevi Schick, *Mimosheh ad mosheh* (Munkács, 1903), 43*b*–44*a*.

[53] See e.g. D. Kahana [Gelb], *Toledot rabenu* (Mukačevo, 1938), § 90. The writings of Shemuel Hacohen Weingarten (1899–1987) are also an important source. Weingarten was born in Munkács, and his father, Aaron Mordecai, had been one of the community leaders during Tsevi Hirsh's tenure. Shemuel Weingarten had a close relationship with Hayim Elazar, a relationship maintained despite Shemuel's ardent Zionism and Hayim Elazar's vehement opposition to it. See S. Weingarten, 'Ha'admor mimunkatch, rabi ḥayim elazar shapira, ba'al teḥusha bikortit', *Shanah beshanah* (1980), 446–9; id., *Peirurim mishulḥanam shel gedolei yisra'el*, ed. A. Hakohen (Jerusalem, 2004).

[54] On schools in Carpathian Ruthenia during Tsevi Hirsh's tenure, see Reinhardt, *Kehilot yehudei rusyah hakarpatit*, 69–73; on the centrality of the language issue, see ibid. 65–6; on fluency in Hungarian amongst Subcarpathian Jews generally and rabbis in particular, see ibid. 84–5. According to Weingarten, Tsevi Hirsh's son and successor, Hayim Elazar, spoke Hungarian, albeit not fluently ('Munkatch', 358; id., *Peirurim*, 29). In 1904 Hayim Elazar was appointed rabbi of nearby Szentmiklós, and, in this capacity, he was the official state rabbi of the area which included Munkács (*Igerot shapirin*, 214). In a 1936 newspaper report, he was described as speaking classical German, using Hungarian, quoting Latin phrases, and of course being fluent in Yiddish (see B. Oberlander, 'Tsiyon halo tishali', *Heikhal habesht*, 31 (2011), 204). Weingarten wrote that Hayim Elazar spoke Hebrew, and, in preparation for his 1930 visit to the Land of Israel, Weingarten and Hayim Elazar secretly practised speaking Hebrew with Sephardi pronunciation together (*Peirurim*, 19).

beginning of the twentieth century, Hungarian could be heard even in hasidic homes in Munkács.[55]

Despite Tsevi Hirsh's attempts to prevent changes to the traditional educational system in Munkács, there is no evidence that connects his activity to the Society for the Support of Torah or to his great-grandfather's *takanot*. A 1903 publication mentions that the society still existed, alongside other charitable societies that operated in Munkács.[56] While the term *tamkhin de'orayta* and the attendant notion of supporting Jewish education appear twice in Tsevi Hirsh's writings,[57] there is no reference to *Takanot tamkhin de'orayta*. Moreover, it is surprising that he is not mentioned in the 1895 Munkács edition of the legislation. Regulations for establishing a different type of learning society were printed in Munkács during Tsevi Hirsh's tenure, and this publication carried his approbation.[58] This all occurred despite the familial link between the author of the *takanot* and the incumbent rabbi, and despite the socializing aspect of the *takanot* that was designed to prevent change—a mechanism and goal that fitted Tsevi Hirsh's purpose. While the fight over the direction of Jewish education in Munkács raged, it appears that *Takanot tamkhin de'orayta* were an ineffective, or at least insufficient, mechanism for blocking educational reform.

Tsevi Hirsh was well aware of his halakhic responsibilities as a communal rabbi and hasidic master. He enacted legislation with regard to a number of matters related to Passover: in 1894, soon after he took office, he issued directives for the preparation of slivovitz—liquor made from plums that contains no *ḥamets* (leaven) and is therefore kosher for Passover when prepared using appropriate vessels. The directives were co-signed by members of the Munkács rabbinic court. Ten years later, in 1904, an addendum was added to the slivovitz directives by the same legislative body.[59] In the lead-up to Passover 1900 Tsevi Hirsh printed a sheet in Hebrew and Yiddish with instructions for the infrequent occurrence of the eve of Passover falling on the sabbath, which also included directions for checking for *ḥamets* on the eve of Passover.[60] Each year, he also issued guidelines for the matzah-baking process in Yiddish, which were posted in each matzah bakery.[61]

Tsevi Hirsh's legislative activity was not limited to Passover. In 1907 he established the Kolel Munkatch Va'asarah Gelilot (Collective for Munkács and the Ten Regions), a charity to support Jews from Carpathian Ruthenia who had migrated to the Land of Israel. A local society for this charitable endeavour was established,

---

[55] Weingarten, 'Munkatch', 355–8.

[56] *Megilat b[eit] hamid[rash]* (Munkács, 1903), [4], reproduced in M. Y. Frankel and N. C. Brody (eds.), *Munkatch: dos kleyn yerushalayim* (Brooklyn, 2011), [381–7].

[57] Tsevi Hirsh, *Be'er laḥai ro'i*, pt. 1 (Munkács, 1903), 10; id., *Hagadah shel pesaḥ tiferet banim* (Munkács, 1914), 22*b*.

[58] Meshulam Feivish Halevi Heller of Zbaraż, *Yosher divrei emet* (Munkács, 1905), 14; cf. Gries, *Sifrut hahanhagot*, 135 n. 128.

[59] Y. M. Gold, *Darkhei ḥayim veshalom* (Jerusalem, 1974), § 573 (copied from the *pinkas* of the Munkács rabbinic court).   [60] Ibid., pp. 400–3.   [61] Ibid., § 545.

and Tsevi Hirsh enacted (or presided over the enacting of) rules for that society. There were two sets of regulations, one for the beneficiaries in the Land of Israel and the other for the donors in Carpathian Ruthenia. Each donation entitled the donor to a benefit: for instance, for 100 koruna, the anniversary of the donor's death would be commemorated by two *kolel* members dedicating their study to the deceased.[62]

Tsevi Hirsh also responded to legal questions about the by-laws of other communities.[63] In a lengthy responsum, he discussed communal by-laws whose records had been destroyed by fire that set a formula for dividing *mi sheberakh* revenue between the communal treasury and three local societies. In that particular case, communal officials wanted to change the allocation in order to direct more funds to the communal coffers. Tsevi Hirsh ruled against this unilateral re-allocation.[64]

In another responsum, Tsevi Hirsh dealt with a case involving a society whose purpose was to facilitate public Torah study. Members were fighting with the *gaba'im* of the society, because the *gaba'im* had admitted new members whom they thought were unworthy. The original members—with the support of the local rabbi—wanted to dissolve the society and establish an identical one under a different name, without the existing *gaba'im* or the newcomers. However, the by-laws of the society required two-thirds of the members to approve dissolution, and with the new members this majority could not be achieved. Tsevi Hirsh approved the proposed dissolution. Regarding the required majority, he emphasized the role of the community rabbi in validating society by-laws. He did not state that the rabbi could dissolve the society without the majority, but assumed that the rabbi would have the power 'to force the opinion of society members such that two-thirds will agree with his opinion'.[65]

In the light of Tsevi Hirsh's legislative activity, involvement, and awareness, it seems significant that he chose not to combat educational reforms with the existing *takanot* nor by enacting alternative legislation. It appears that Tsevi Hirsh well understood the limited potential for enforcing local rabbinic legislation and by-laws of voluntary societies. He may, therefore, have been hesitant to employ legislative mechanisms for the highly contentious matter of Jewish education. The upshot was that Tsevi Hirsh ignored *Takanot tamkhin de'orayta*.

---

[62] The requirements for beneficiaries appear in M. Goldstein, *Masa'ot yerushalayim* (Mukačevo, 1931; new edn., Jerusalem, 2004), 97–101. This transcribes the original 1909 document entitled *Takanot hakolel*, with the names and titles of the sixteen signatories. This list was headed by Tsevi Hirsh and included Hayim Elazar. Details of benefits for donors appear in *Ḥeshbon . . . mikolel munkatch . . .* (Munkács, 1912), 3.

[63] *Kuntras ya'anu vekol* (Paks, 1903), § 11; repr. in Tsevi Hirsh Shapira, *She'elot uteshuvot tsevi tiferet* (Munkács, 1912), § 7.

[64] Ibid., § 1. Tsevi Hirsh's contemporary Rabbi Shalom Mordechai Shwadron (1835–1911) wrote a responsum on the same issue (*She'elot uteshuvot maharsham*, 8 vols. (Jerusalem, 1902–68), vii. § 60).

[65] Shapira, *She'elot uteshuvot tsevi tiferet*, § 84.

Tsevi Hirsh was succeeded by his only son, Hayim Elazar (1871–1937), who also sought to combat educational reform. Hayim Elazar repeatedly insisted that traditional education practices continue without changing in the slightest.[66] Yet like his father, he did not use *Takanot tamkhin de'orayta*. To promote fidelity to traditional schooling and prevent educational reform, Hayim Elazar used blistering rhetoric in fiery sermons, in his writings, and in public protests. In his final years Hayim Elazar's students transcribed and published some of his sermons from the Days of Awe, and these sermons sound even more virulent.[67] Thus, in contrast to Tsevi Hirsh's legacy, which is apparent only from secondary accounts and by inference from his writings, there are rich sources that demonstrate Hayim Elazar's position and indicate his decision not to use existing regulations nor to enact new legislation in the local and regional battle over Jewish education.

There is much overlap between Hayim Elazar's sermons and the socializing themes of *Takanot tamkhin de'orayta*. For instance, Hayim Elazar followed Tsevi Elimelekh in casting the study of philosophy, and secular studies generally, as the cause of weakened commitment to Jewish tradition.[68] Despite the overlap, Hayim

[66] Hayim Elazar Shapira, *Divrei torah*, 9 vols. (Mukačevo, 1922–36), ii. § 132; *Kuntras divrei kodesh . . . behay shata [5]695* (Berehovo, 1934/5?), 6; M. Goldstein, *Tikun olam* (Mukačevo, 1936), 20; Hayim Elazar Shapira, *Tsava'ah* (Mukačevo, 1937), § 5; Kahana, *Toledot rabenu*, § 98; Hayim Elazar Shapira, *Ḥayim veshalom* (Sighet, 1938–40), 'Nitsavim', 29: 27–8; Gold, *Darkhei ḥayim veshalom*, § 1,072. This was also one of Hayim Elazar's reasons for opposing the *daf hayomi* (page-a-day) programme of Talmud study that was introduced in 1923 (*Kuntras divrei kodesh [5]695*, 5–6). On Hayim Elazar, see Weingarten, 'Ha'admor mimunkatch', 440–9; A. Ravitzky, 'Munkács and Jerusalem: Ultra-Orthodox Opposition to Zionism and Agudaism', in S. Almog, J. Reinharz, and A. Shapira (eds.), *Zionism and Religion* (Hanover, NH, 1998), 67–89; A. L. Nadler, 'The War on Modernity of R. Hayyim Elazar Shapira of Munkacz', *Modern Judaism*, 14 (1994), 233–64; L. Cooper, 'Ha'admor mimunkatch harav ḥayim elazar shapira', Ph.D. thesis (Bar-Ilan University, 2011); M. Inbari, 'Aktivizm meshiḥi befo'alo uvehaguto shel harav ḥayim elazar shapira mimunkatch bein milḥamot olam', *Cathedra*, 149 (2013), 77–104; L. Cooper, 'Neged zirmei hamayim hazeidonim: ha'admor mimunkatch r. ḥayim elazar shapira', in B. Brown and N. Leon (eds.), *Hagedolim: ishim she'itsvu et penei hayahadut haḥaredit beyisra'el* (Jerusalem, 2017).

[67] Sermons from 1928 to 1936 were printed, with the exception of 1929 and 1931. It has been argued that in the 1930s Hayim Elazar's rhetoric reached a fever pitch of messianic agitation (Nadler, 'The War on Modernity of R. Hayyim Elazar Shapira of Munkacz', 233; Inbari, 'Aktivizm meshiḥi befo'alo uvehaguto shel harav ḥayim elazar shapira', 97–100). While I do not discount this possibility, it is important to consider the different types of source material that have reached us. Sermons from Hayim Elazar's final years are student transcripts that were not vetted or edited by Hayim Elazar before publication (although Hayim Elazar instructed in his will that they be included in his posthumously printed works). It is possible that sermons from earlier years were just as fiery in their original medium, but Hayim Elazar edited them in preparation for publication. The fact that Hayim Elazar never appeared reticent about vociferously arguing his position suggests that strident words were not an innovation of his final years. An alternative possibility is that there is a correlation between the pitch of the rhetoric and the success of the Mukačevo gymnasium. On the growth of the gymnasium student body, see the figures in A. Sola, 'Bein shetei milḥamot olam', in Y. Erez (ed.), *Encyclopedia of the Jewish Diaspora: Karpatorus* (Jerusalem, 1959), 196, 198.

[68] M. Goldstein, *Divrei kodesh . . . [5]693* (Jerusalem, 1933), 7–9; *Kuntras divrei kodesh: rishmei*

Elazar did not refer to *Takanot tamkhin de'orayta*; instead, he used searing, evocative, and creative rhetoric to make his point. Hayim Elazar's sermons on the
importance of the beard and side-locks demonstrate this choice:

Behold in the image of God, he made man, with side-locks and a beard. . . . And this is the
straight and choicest path—not to shave his beard or side-locks at all, certainly not with a
razor which is a grave prohibition according to Torah law, but even [with] scissors or depilatories, there are great jurists who rule stringently that this is forbidden.[69]

While Hayim Elazar mentioned the legal angle, the thrust of his words was in a
different direction: being in the image of God meant that a Jew should have side-
locks and a beard. In a sermon from October 1933, some eight months after Hitler
rose to power, Hayim Elazar responded to the dire situation of German Jews.
He acknowledged that German Jews were being physically beaten and persecuted,
'even though most of them transgress the religion, and they are sabbath dese-
crators and have shaved their beards—not with depilatories, rather by means of
the severely prohibited scissors and a razor. And they have already left the Jewish people entirely.'[70] If German Jews were no longer considered part of the
Jewish collective, why were they being persecuted? Hayim Elazar explained that
they were still referred to as Jews, even though 'they lack the image of God and
form of Israel'. Undoubtedly, those who heard these sermons or read the transcripts were in no doubt that, at least in Hayim Elazar's eyes, a person who chose to
cut his side-locks or remove his facial hair was essentially removing any semblance
of God's image. Hayim Elazar made no mention of the regulations regarding
beard and side-locks in *Takanot tamkhin de'orayta*. It is apparent that in Hayim
Elazar's milieu, depicting the image of God as bearded and wearing side-locks
was a more effective socializing tool than the threat of expulsion from a voluntary
society.

Hayim Elazar's sermons were regularly laced with hope for an imminent messianic redemption, and his urgings regarding traditional schooling also reflected
this:

Teaching Torah to Jewish children should only be in the *ḥeder*, and we should teach as per
the custom of our forebears. In this way alone, we will merit the redemption speedily in our
days. Amen.[71]

hitorerut . . . behay shata [5]697 (Mukačevo, 1936/7?), 5–6. Hayim Elazar Shapira, *Sha'ar yisaskhar*
(Mukačevo, 1938–1940), 39, 117, 391.

[69] *Kuntras divrei kodesh* [5]695, 7; see also Goldstein, *Divrei kodesh* [5]693, 9.

[70] *Kuntras divrei kodesh . . . shenat* [5]694 (Mukačevo, 1933/4?), 5.

[71] Shapira, *Ḥayim veshalom*, 'Tsav', 6: 1; see also *Kuntras divrei kodesh* [5]697, 5–6. Regarding Jewish education for girls, and specifically the Bais Yaakov schools which Hayim Elazar denounced as *beit
esav* (the house of Esau), see *Divrei ha'igeret* (Jerusalem, 1932), 6; Goldstein, *Tikun olam*, 34, 148, 165;
Shapira, *Ḥayim veshalom*, 'Ha'azinu', 29: 27–8. Weingarten, however, recorded a trade school for girls
from poor families ('Munkatch', 368).

Hayim Elazar told his readers that this passage was taken from a sermon that he had delivered on Shabat Hagadol—the sabbath before Passover when a lengthy sermon was traditional—indicating the very public nature of his pronouncement. On another public occasion, Hayim Elazar harshly criticized any attempt to teach general studies, although he was aware that the authorities required students to study the vernacular language and that his father had unsuccessfully tried to rally his followers to ignore those rules. Hayim Elazar responded by demanding that, at the very least, general studies should not be taught in the same building where Torah was studied. In his understanding, using the same physical location was just like accepting other combinations that were forbidden according to Jewish law: kosher food with non-kosher food, wool and linen, and cross-breeding of seeds or animals.[72]

During Hayim Elazar's tenure, educational possibilities in the region expanded, although the rabbinic leadership continued to oppose changes.[73] In 1918 the local Zionists opened a primary school in Munkács (now Mukačevo) in newly formed Czechoslovakia. Hayim Elazar and his rabbinic court officially prohibited attendance at the school, but to no avail. In 1924 the cornerstone was laid for the Hebrew Reform Real Gymnasium (Hebrejské Reformní Reálné Gymnázium) in Mukačevo—the first institution of its kind in Carpathian Ruthenia. Hayim Elazar and his court declared that day a fast day and a day of public mourning. In the synagogue, the ancient rite of excommunication was pronounced, condemning all those involved in the venture.[74] Hayim Elazar would have realized that such bans issued by a Jewish court would not be effective, but he did not back down: from the pulpit, whenever he had the opportunity, he castigated anyone who dared send their children to the school.

The primary language of instruction in the gymnasium was modern Hebrew: Hebrew grammar was studied for five hours a week, and Bible classes were conducted in modern Hebrew. Czech was the second language, followed by English, and then German. In 1927 the school opened a course to train teachers. Textbooks were printed by Nekudah, the Mukačevo printing press affiliated with local Zionist leaders. The first graduating class was celebrated in 1932.[75] Later that year, on the

---

[72] Shapira, *Ḥayim veshalom*, 'Bereshit', 1: 4. The particular passage targeted Agudat Yisra'el. See also ibid., 'Vayishlaḥ', 32: 12; *Ketsat rishumei devarim imrot tehorot . . . shenat [5]691* (Jerusalem, 1931), 3 n; *Divrei ha'igeret*, 3; Goldstein, *Tikun olam*, 13.

[73] Reinhardt, *Kehilot yehudei rusya hakarpatit*, 73.

[74] S. L. Moškovič, *A dor vos geyt unter* (Mukačevo, 1937), 51; Weingarten, 'Munkatch', 363; Sola, 'Bein shetei milhamot olam', 189–90, cf. 186; 'Morim ve'ishei tsibur', in Erez (ed.), *Encyclopedia of the Jewish Diaspora*, 545. Other bans issued by Hayim Elazar were more effective: for a 1920 ban against Yiddish theatre in Mukačevo, see S. J. Harendorf, *Teater karavannen* (London, 1955), 168–70; id., 'The Yiddish Theater in Czechoslovakia', in *The Jews of Czechoslovakia*, 3 vols. (Philadelphia, 1968–84), ii. 553–4.

[75] Weingarten, 'Munkatch', 364; Sola, 'Bein shetei milhamot olam', 185–201; Z. Scharfstein, *Toledot haḥinukh beyisra'el bedorot ha'aḥaronim*, 2nd edn., 2 vols. (Jerusalem, 1960–6), ii. 298; A. Sola,

anniversary of his father's death as he stood by the graveside, Hayim Elazar publicly cried out:

Will not our strength fail and our heart dissolve in water, when we see how the heresy is gaining strength from every side, and the heretics made here [in Mukačevo] in the Hebrew school, the contaminated gymnasium of the Zionists, that from there will go forth forced conversion and heresy—may the Merciful One save us. . . . *And we have already warned and cried out regarding this, and we have announced that anyone who sends his son or his daughter to the aforementioned schools must rend [his garments] and mourn for them, just as is done for the deceased. And someone who causes them to sin in this way has even more so killed them—may it not be our fate, may God save us.*[76]

Thus Hayim Elazar evoked the troubling image of a parent mourning a child in his attempt to counter the gymnasium. He also made a point of expressing his indignation at the audacity of calling the institute Hagimnaziyum Ha'ivrit, the Hebrew Gymnasium, presumably because *ivri* is a term used to describe biblical heroes such as Abraham (Gen. 14: 13), Joseph (Gen. 39: 14; 41: 12), the courageous midwives in Egypt (Exod. 1: 15–16, 19), and Jonah (Jon. 1: 9).[77]

In subsequent years, Hayim Elazar's fiery rhetoric did not abate. On Yom Kippur 1934, before the solemn 'Kol nidrei' prayer, he declared:

And I say to you, and also to the 'complacent women' [see Isa. 32: 9]. You should know that whoever sends his children, even a grandchild or a great-grandchild, to the schools and the contaminated gymnasium of the Zionists—and all the more so the boy or the girl who goes there—then Yom Kippur does not atone for him![78]

It is not difficult to imagine the impact of this harsh prognosis as the opening volley of the Day of Atonement.

In 1935 Hayim Elazar decried what he considered to be the problematic religious approaches inherent in the gymnasium's curriculum:

Behold the *accursed Zionists* established schools and the contaminated gymnasium of theirs with a curriculum that actually denies the First Cause [God]—as if it were possible!—[that is, they deny] the novelty of the Creation of the world by the one and only Creator, may His

---

'Subcarpathian Ruthenia: 1918–1938', in *The Jews of Czechoslovakia*, i. 144–6. For vignettes of the gymnasium from a student's memoir, see P. Litman, *Hana'ar mimunkatch* (Haifa, 1996), 20–2. The Nekuda publishing house also printed traditional Jewish works. On printing in Mukačevo, see P. Y. Hacohen, 'Hadefus ha'ivri behungaryah', *Kiryat sefer*, 25 (1948–9), 206–28; 26 (1949–50), 111–12; N. Ben-Menahem, 'Hadefus ha'ivri bemunkatch', *Kiryat sefer*, 26 (1949–50), 201–15; H. Liberman, *Ohel rahel*, 3 vols. (New York, 1980–4), i. 221–67; Reinhardt, *Kehilot yehudei rusyah hakarpatit*, 73–8; Y. Spiegel, *Toledot hayehudim berusyah hakarpatit*, ed. Y. Alfasi (Tel Aviv, 1997), 157.

[76] Goldstein, *Divrei kodesh* [5]693, 12 (emphasis original); see also *Kuntras divrei kodesh* [5]695, 3, 5.

[77] *Kuntras divrei kodesh* [5]695, 5; *Kuntras divrei kodesh* [5]697, 5; see also Moškovič, *A dor vos geyt unter*, 17. Hayim Elazar also objected to the Agudah-affiliated Mesivta in Warsaw, condemning the sign in Polish that announced that the building housed the seminary of Polish rabbis (Goldstein, *Tikun olam*, 13).   [78] *Kuntras divrei kodesh* [5]695, 10.

name be blessed. And they ensnare the children of Israel in their net [taking them] to the depths of the netherworld—may the Merciful One save us.[79]

A few weeks later, Hayim Elazar sent a letter to Rabbi Jacob Hai Zerihan (1869–1953) in Tiberius, reiterating the charges against the curriculum.[80] An undated proclamation of protest issued no earlier than late 1934 condemned the Zionist gymnasium in Mukačevo and the similar institution in nearby Užhorod as being 'very dangerous for the souls of young Jewish boys and young Jewish girls' on account of the curriculum that promoted heretical beliefs and transgression of Jewish law. The document was signed first by Hayim Elazar, followed by the four members of the Mukačevo rabbinic court and eight other rabbis from the region. The proclamation singled out the sin of mixed dancing and declared that 'whoever sends his children to Hebrew schools, it is as if he is poisoning them with a death potion and erasing them from the book of life of Judaism!'[81] In 1936, Hayim Elazar's final year, he vociferously expressed similar sentiments:

In this era, they have damaged the holy study, and the Zionists have established their *house of impurity* . . . and there they learn and teach the young to deny the singularity of the God of the world, may His name be blessed; and [they teach the young] to deny the Torah of Moses, the written law and the oral law. And when the students of these houses of heresy grow up they are truly total heretics, ridiculing God and his anointed one, and they totally despise the honour of Heaven and his Torah and belief in him—may God save us. *Woe to us! There is a holy obligation incumbent upon us, and upon each and every person of the Children of Israel, to fight against this idol worship with real self-sacrifice.*[82]

Hayim Elazar's harsh words were not reserved for the High Holy Days, and they echoed beyond the confines of his hasidic following. He readily issued proclamations and penned public letters denouncing the gymnasium, and at times the tension led to blows in the streets of Mukačevo.[83] In 1935 *Selbstwehr*, the German-language Zionist newspaper published in Prague, reported on a sermon delivered by Hayim Elazar:

---

[79] *Kuntras divrei kodesh . . . behay shata* [5]696 (Mukačevo, 1935/6?), 4 (emphasis original).

[80] *Igerot shapirin*, 302.

[81] N. E. Roth, *Meir ḥayim*, 5 vols. (Benei Berak, 1990–2001), i. 442–3. The gymnasium in Užhorod opened on 1 September 1934. It is entirely possible that Hayim Elazar was the author or instigator of the proclamation, given its tone and language and the fact that he is the first signatory. A 1933 film of Mukačevo captures young men and women dancing in concentric circles with arms locked, somewhat incongruously singing words from the liturgy that evoke Jewish mystical tradition: 'May abundant bounty thereby be bestowed upon all the worlds' (Yad Vashem, 'Archival Footage: Jews Dancing the Hora in Munkács', *Youtube* (14 July 2010), <https://www.youtube.com/watch?v=LtqdqTlvXUQ> (accessed 25 Feb. 2017)).

[82] *Kuntras divrei kodesh* [5]697, 5 (emphasis original); see also Goldstein, *Tikun olam*, 158–9 n.

[83] Goldstein, *Tikun olam*, 158–60; Sola, 'Bein shetei milhamot olam', 199–200; id., 'Subcarpathian Ruthenia', 148–9; id., 'Modern Hebrew Education in Subcarpathian Ruthenia', in *The Jews of Czechoslovakia*, ii. 425–9.

Whosoever sends his children to the accursed Hebrew school shall be wiped out and shall not be permitted to live to raise his children. The children will not live to see the next year. A Zionist must not be called to the Holy Ark, and no one may partake of his wine. For the past ten years I have spat whenever I passed the godless Hebrew high school.[84]

The newspaper reported that the sermon had been delivered on 21 June 1934. According to Hayim Elazar's biographer, that day had been declared a half-day fast in Mukačevo to spiritually counter a raging typhus epidemic. Following traditional Jewish custom, Hayim Elazar delivered a sermon with the aim of inspiring those present to repent so that God would end the epidemic. The biographer offered a different version of the fiery sermon that squarely pinned the blame for the epidemic on the Zionist gymnasium.[85] Hayim Elazar was subsequently sued by the gymnasium in the district court of Užhorod. The court dismissed the case, but on appeal Hayim Elazar was found guilty of committing a misdemeanour and sentenced to a fine of 1,000 koruna or twenty days in prison. From other reports, it appears that court proceedings between the warring factions were conducted more than once.[86]

Hayim Elazar's rhetoric was not his only strategy for combating educational reform in Mukačevo. He also established competing institutions. In 1922 he departed from the custom of his predecessors and opened a yeshiva which he named, after his father's magnum opus on Jewish ritual law, Darkhei Teshuvah. Hayim Elazar took an active role in the institution: he delivered lectures twice a week and personally tested the students. Darkhei Teshuvah was popular and successful: reports suggest that in the 1920s it had up to 200 students.[87] This initiative, however, was unable to halt the decline of traditional Jewish education in Mukačevo.

Like his father, Hayim Elazar was familiar with the legislative mechanisms that were part of any community rabbi's arsenal. In 1927 he reissued his father's directives for the eve of Passover falling on a sabbath.[88] Then, during a pilgrimage to the Land of Israel in 1930, Hayim Elazar visited Kolel Munkatch Va'asarah Gelilot and enacted regulations for the conduct of *kolel* members. This legislation is particularly noteworthy in the present context, in that it mirrored rules that were

[84] 'Der Munkačer Rabbi verurteilt', *Selbstwehr*, 6 Sept. 1935, p. 3; A. M. L. Rabinowicz, 'The Jewish Party', in *The Jews of Czechoslovakia*, ii. 297–8.

[85] Moškovič, *A dor vos geyt unter*, 51; Kahana, *Toledot rabenu*, § 184.

[86] Kahana, *Toledot rabenu*, §§ 184–6; Sola, 'Bein shetei milhamot olam', 200–1; id., 'Modern Hebrew Education in Subcarpathian Ruthenia', 428; G. Fleischmann, 'The Religious Congregation, 1918–1938', in *The Jews of Czechoslovakia*, i. 308.

[87] Goldstein, *Masa'ot yerushalayim*, 17; Y. Adler, 'Introduction', in *Seder shana ha'aharona* (Mukačevo, 1937–40?); Kahana, *Toledot rabenu*, § 150; S. Weingarten, *Hayeshivot behungaryah: divrei yemeihen uva'ayoteihen* (Jerusalem, 1977), 89; Hayim Elazar Shapira, *Hagahot hayerushalmi* (New York, 1981), [9], [16].

[88] Hayim Elazar Shapira, *She'elot uteshuvot minhat elazar*, 4 vols (Munkács, 1902–30), iii. 26; Gold, *Darkhei hayim veshalom*, pp. 400–1.

included in *Takanot tamkhin de'orayta*. For instance, those who wished to pray in the *kolel*'s *beit midrash* were required to be 'distinguished in their clothing', to dress in traditional clothing rather than modern attire. Similarly, they were not to trim their beards nor grow their hair, and their conduct was to follow Jewish tradition in every way. When Hayim Elazar visited the *kolel*, he warned all those present against the trap of Zionist schools '"for many are those she has struck dead" [Prov. 7: 26]—may the Merciful One save us'. The writer who recorded these words pointed out that it was unnecessary to issue such a warning to 'our' *kolel* members, though he added: 'But who knows what the next day will bring, as the various impure parties gain strength. May God have mercy.' Hayim Elazar had issued this dire appraisal on his first Friday night after arriving in Jerusalem, and he repeated his ominous assessment a week later when visiting Safed. The *kolel* regulations formalized this warning: 'To distance from holy matters, as much as possible, those who send their sons or their daughters to schools that are not according to the ancient education [system] that has been practised since our forebears, [according to] the purity of holiness.'[89] Clearly Hayim Elazar felt that legislation was an effective socializing tool for the *kolel* in Jerusalem.[90] This is hardly surprising, given the economic dependence of *kolel* members and their families on their benefactors from Carpathian Ruthenia and considering Hayim Elazar's role as the head of the charity. But, for socializing Mukačevo's young Jews, it would appear that Hayim Elazar deemed legislation an ineffective mechanism.

It should be noted that the Society for the Support of Torah still existed in some form during Hayim Elazar's tenure. One of his students reported that during the afternoon prayer on fast days, funds were collected for it. Hayim Elazar himself, on occasion, would put coins in the collection box after morning prayers.[91] In interwar Mukačevo, the Society for the Support of Torah was one of a number of charitable societies originally set up for educational purposes. Another, Upholders of Torah (Mahazikei Torah) was also affiliated with Hayim Elazar. This society assisted the needy and more generally oversaw traditional Jewish education in Mukačevo.[92] There was also a society called Talmud Torah that had been estab-

[89] Goldstein, *Masa'ot yerushalayim*, 85–6, 99, 100, 150–1. It is unclear to what extent these regulations differed from the 1909 original. Goldstein mentioned that some *kolel* members lived in the old city of Jerusalem, and others lived in the new city where the *kolel*'s building was located. Consequently, *kolel* members were not necessarily studying together. Some of the regulations addressed this issue by delineating minimum attendance requirements in the *kolel*'s *beit midrash*. At the very least, these regulations were Hayim Elazar's addition.

[90] This is not to say that Hayim Elazar did not employ rhetoric as well. For instance, he lambasted the Hebrew University of Jerusalem (see *Rishumei divrei torah miseder hoshanot . . . bish[nat]* [5]689 (Jerusalem, 1931), 1–2, 3; *Ketsat rishumei devarim imrot tehorot* [5]691, 2).

[91] Gold, *Darkhei ḥayim veshalom*, §§ 128, 653.

[92] For a 1937 description of Upholders of Torah, see Moškovič, *A dor vos geyt unter*, 20–2. Gold referred to this society as being 'taḥat yadeinu', 'under our auspices' (*Darkhei ḥayim veshalom*, § 128). This is the only society mentioned in Hayim Elazar's will (see Shapira, *Tsava'ah*, § 5). According to Weingarten, Upholders of Torah was housed in a building constructed using funds from the estate of

lished by Rabbi Hayim Sofer (1821–86) during his tenure as rabbi of Munkács between 1867 and 1879. This society focused on providing traditional Jewish education for the poor who were not affiliated with the hasidim.[93] Thus in interwar Mukačevo, the Society for the Support of Torah was a legitimate charity for providing the needy, principally from the hasidic sector, with a Jewish education. Notwithstanding its collection box and Hayim Elazar's participation, the society and its pervasive system of taxation appear to have been unable to deal with the economic burden of educating Mukačevo's young Jews.

The late 1920s saw the Great Depression challenge the financial viability of Hayim Elazar's Darkhei Teshuvah yeshiva. Yet in grappling with this reality, there is no evidence that the funds of the Society for the Support of Torah were tapped or that the fund-raising mechanisms of its *takanot* were employed. Instead, Hayim Elazar granted permission to publish a travelogue of his 1930 pilgrimage to the Land of Israel written by one of his disciples. Proceeds from the sale of the book were earmarked for the yeshiva, and writers of approbations and introductions to the volume emphasized the importance and necessity of this financial support.[94]

In the final decade of his life, Hayim Elazar repeatedly mentioned the difficulties that parents had in paying tuition fees for traditional Jewish education. In his eyes, this difficulty precipitated a host of other problems: foremost among them being migration to America, which, he opined, almost guaranteed a lack of sabbath observance.[95]

There are places in Hayim Elazar's writings where a reference to Tsevi Elimelekh's *takanot* or to the notion of supporting traditional Jewish education might be expected, yet he is silent. For instance, when discussing Jacob's tussle with the angel, Hayim Elazar related the passage to the importance of educating young Jews but not in terms of *tamkhin de'orayta*.[96] However, Hayim Elazar was not unfamiliar with *Takanot tamkhin de'orayta*. In his commentary on the *Shulḥan arukh*, he referred to a particular legal issue that is discussed in the preamble of the *takanot*: Tsevi Elimelekh opined that once there is a rabbinic definition on how to fulfil a commandment, that commandment can only be fulfilled in the defined manner and there is no longer a concept of fulfilling the biblical commandment alone.[97] Clearly Hayim Elazar was familiar with the legislation, though he deliber-

Rabbi Moses Fuchs ('Munkatch', 357, 366–7). Fuchs died in 1921, and his widow financed the publication of Hayim Elazar's third volume of responsa (*She'elot uteshuvot minḥat elazar*, iii (Bratislava, 1922), title page verso). For a list of communal institutions in Mukačevo in 1930, see H. Dicker, *Piety and Perseverance: Jews from the Carpathian Mountains* (New York, 1981), 54–5; for a partial list of charities in Mukačevo in 1937, see *Ḥeshbon . . . mikolel munkatch . . .* (Mukačevo, 1937), 8. The list includes Upholders of Torah and a charity associated with Fuchs.

93 Weingarten, 'Munkatch', 367.

94 Goldstein, *Masa'ot yerushalayim*, 15–16, 18.

95 *Rishumei divrei torah* [5]689, 1; *Ketsat rishumei devarim imrot tehorot* [5]691, 1; *Kuntras divrei kodesh* [5]696, 3.   96 Shapira, *Ḥayim veshalom*, 'Vayishlaḥ', 32: 30.

97 Tsevi Elimelekh of Dynów, *Takanot tamkhin de'orayta*, 3a–4a; Hayim Elazar Shapira, *Nimukei oraḥ ḥayim* (Turnov, 1930), 267: 2.

ately chose not to cite it on educational matters. Despite his wide-ranging literary oeuvre and frequent citations of his predecessors' works and despite his ardent attempts to guide his disciples and mould their conduct and to prevent educational reform, he did not cite *Takanot tamkhin de'orayta*.

It is apparent that despite the existence of the Society for the Support of Torah and similar institutions and despite the legislative mechanisms at his disposal, Hayim Elazar fought reforms in Mukačevo's educational system from the pulpit and the printing press. It would seem that the strong socializing elements of *Takanot tamkhin de'orayta* were insufficient in twentieth-century Mukačevo. For this battle, Hayim Elazar's fiery tongue and quick pen were his weapons of choice.

CONCLUSION: LEGISLATIVE DECLINE

In the late 1820s Rabbi Tsevi Elimelekh of Dynów enacted a set of *takanot* that were designed to provide, oversee, and regulate traditional Jewish education for all males in Munkács. While the *takanot*'s stated purpose was to provide educational opportunities, they had undeniable socializing objectives. Thus financial support was not need-based, but dependent on conduct and appearance. Educational issues were given scant attention, while matters of appearance and sartorial guidelines were emphasized. The thrust of the socializing element was to stem educational reforms and to prevent modernity from making inroads into traditional Munkács society.

In the century that followed, Tsevi Elimelekh's *takanot* were lauded. It is unclear whether they were adopted as binding at the communal level outside their Munkács birthplace. It is apparent, however, that *Takanot tamkhin de'orayta* served as inspiration for the by-laws of similar societies in other towns. Their publication in Czernowitz, Munkács, Lemberg, and Cluj were not necessarily legislative acts. Rather, bringing Tsevi Elimelekh's *takanot* to the printing press was a public relations strategy: printing them demonstrated the ethos and altruism of local charitable societies, provided a backdrop for the enactment of their own by-laws, and promised a source of revenue from the sale of the booklet.

At the beginning of the twentieth century, education reforms that were making inroads in Jewish Munkács were countered by means other than legislation. What may have been an effective mechanism for defining the contours of local Jewish education at the beginning of the nineteenth century was not effective by the end of that century. Thus Tsevi Elimelekh's successors opted for persuasive and fiery rhetoric, rather than legislation.

Considering a broader perspective, *Takanot tamkhin de'orayta* tell two different tales, two tales that may evoke conflicting emotions. First, this is a case study of the erosion of rabbinic authority by the winds of change. Rabbinic legislation that was once central to the organization and regulation of the Jewish community was no longer effectual. In its stead, the rabbinic leadership sought alternative means to address their charges. In interwar Mukačevo, the substitute was primarily fierce and creative sermonizing. Inevitably, however, the rhetoric could only be of limited use: twentieth-century Mukačevo Jews did not feel bound to heed the admonitions and damning prognoses of the rabbi. Second, this is a case of the virtual disappearance of legislation as an institution for creating Jewish law. Legal systems require mechanisms for dealing with the vicissitudes of life, and legislation is a key source of law in most legal systems. While the ineffectiveness of the Munkács legislation reflects a victory over rabbinic hegemony, it also signals the decline of an important legal tool for responding to contemporary realities. The story of *Takanot tamkhin de'orayta* is therefore a chapter in the ongoing saga of an ancient legal system whose relics are floundering in exile.

The Narrative of Acculturation

Hungarian Jewish Children's Books during the Dual Monarchy, 1867–1918

DANIEL VIRAGH

SINCE the French Revolution, the modern state has had a definite stake in creating citizens who participate in civic life with vigour and 'patriotically' support the state's policies in military, political, and economic contexts. Feelings of patriotism are best developed in elementary and secondary school through the incorporation of teaching materials that expand the pupil's natural sense of attachment to the birth environment into an abstract feeling of love for the 'imagined community'[1] of the nation. As a number of historians have shown, in nineteenth-century European contexts the study of national geography and history were the prime tools that educators chose to effect this expansion of their charges' loyalties.

In *Peasants into Frenchmen*, for example, Eugen Weber devoted an entire chapter to the development of modern schooling in rural France at the end of the nineteenth century. As he noted, the function of the modern school was to teach a 'new patriotism'[2] which created a 'whole new language' providing 'common points of reference that straddled regional boundaries'.[3] The objective of modern schooling was in part to impress upon children 'what the state did for them and why it exacted taxes and military service'.[4] Weber showed that the 'vast program of indoctrination' created through compulsory elementary education relied heavily on French geography and history in order to 'persuade people that the fatherland extended beyond its evident limits to something vast and intangible called France'.[5] Thus the national map and the primary-school reading book were important tools for facilitating this inculcation of the idea of 'nation' into young minds.

So, too, in the German context, the idea of *Heimat* was introduced early in a child's education in order to expand the child's loyalty from the areas surrounding

---

[1] See B. Anderson, *Imagined Communities: Reflections on the Origin and Spread of Nationalism* (London, 2006).

[2] E. Weber, *Peasants into Frenchmen: The Modernization of Rural France, 1870–1914* (Stanford, Calif., 1976), 332.   [3] Ibid. 337.   [4] Ibid. 332.   [5] Ibid. 334.

his or her immediate physical context to places ever farther away that eventually merged with the unseen boundaries of the German state. The American historian Stephen Harp noted:

The closest English equivalent [to *Heimat*] may very well be the 'home' in 'homesickness', which implies some of the same *idealized nostalgia* and which can change according to context to mean everything from one's family to the nation-state.[6]

According to Harp, 'the meaning of *Heimat* changed according to context, embracing everything from one's village, to the surrounding area, to local vegetation, to customs and history, to the region, and, by suggestion, to the German nation-state'.[7]

Harp's study of elementary schooling in the French–German border district of Alsace-Lorraine in the period between 1850 and 1940 reveals that for both French and German state administrators the indoctrination of the population was especially important in a geographical area which had changed political ownership on three different occasions within living memory, and where the local population still remembered schooling under previous political regimes. But being in a border region only emphasized tendencies that were present in all other parts of Germany and France. As the British historian Jeff Bowersox has shown, by the beginning of the twentieth century the study of *Heimat* in geography lessons throughout the Wilhelmine school system was eventually expanded to include Germany's colonial holdings.[8]

For school administrators, a primary objective was to make the national narrative as appealing to children as possible. The Canadian historian Stephen Heathorn studied the construction of gender, class, and Englishness in British elementary schools by conducting a thorough investigation of reading material published for primarily working-class elementary schoolchildren in Britain between 1880 and 1914. Heathorn points to a central paradox with respect to the place that the study of history was accorded in the textbooks: after the promulgation of a revised Educational Code in 1862, history declined as an actual subject in school textbooks, while emphasis was squarely placed on reading, writing, and arithmetic.[9] However, by the 1880s schools had begun using historical reading books in order to teach basic reading skills; hence, the presence of a narrative that was partially based in history and partially mythologized in service to the nation actually increased. Heathorn points out that by reading romanticized versions of national history children 'could pass into the realm of semi-historical fantasy, into the imaginative enactment of possibilities beyond the restraints of their direct experience'.[10] Such

---

[6] S. L. Harp, *Learning to be Loyal: Primary Schooling as Nation Building in Alsace and Lorraine, 1850–1940* (DeKalb, Ill., 1998), 114 (emphasis added). [7] Ibid. 104.

[8] J. Bowersox, *Raising Germans in the Age of Empire: Youth and Colonial Culture, 1871–1914* (Oxford, 2013), 63.

[9] S. Heathorn, *For Home, Country, and Race: Constructing Gender, Class, and Englishness in the Elementary School, 1880–1914* (Toronto, 2000), 38. [10] Ibid. 46.

a result was actively encouraged by the Board of Education, which pointed out in a 1905 memorandum that

English history should be an inheritance of childhood; its characters and incidents should have the charm of a story which is not only interesting and true, but is also personal to the child, and should thus grow into his thoughts. History thus treated would not be a task, for the child would always be anxious to know more about it.[11]

History textbooks for children can thus sometimes be read in order to reveal the narrative construction of the nation that the authors meant to communicate to young readers at a time when the children's minds were plastic enough to have imprinted upon them a loyalty to the 'imagined community' of the nation. When used judiciously by historians, such materials can reveal the mythological ingredients that authors included in the hopes of inspiring children to love their nations. These ingredients are more often than not fragments of stories that are meant to evoke dedication to the state through showing some set of mythologized heroes.

The prime objective of this chapter is to analyse the message of belonging that was communicated to Hungarian Jewish schoolchildren in the second half of the long nineteenth century through six primary-school reading books that were written to introduce students in various degrees to Hungarian language and literature as well as to Jewishness. The purpose of these books—all written by Jewish educators—was to inspire in their readers a sense of loyalty to the abstract notion of the 'Hungarian nation' while also developing a sense of attachment to the similarly abstract concept of the 'Jewish people'. Given the context, the educators were faced with the difficult task of constructing a narrative that they felt was both 'Hungarian' and 'Jewish' enough to suit the needs of the time. The authors adapted the Hungarian cultural content of their reading books from similar books on the market, from which they excised Christian religious references. The Jewish cultural content usually consisted of biblical and talmudic stories, which the authors themselves translated into easy Hungarian.

The six reading books were chosen based first on their availability at the Hungarian Széchényi National Library and the Library of the Budapest Rabbinical Seminary. Both of these institutions hold some of the best resources for the study of education in Hungary. However, availability was not the only factor: the fifty-three years between the publication of the first and the last book (1861–1914) corresponds almost exactly to the lifespan of the Austro-Hungarian dual monarchy (1867–1918), a time during which the Kingdom of Hungary benefited from exclusive control over its internal affairs and experienced a vast industrial and commercial expansion. During this time, the kingdom forcibly encouraged the development of a modern national narrative in order to unify its population along the west European model. For reasons discussed below, this initiative met with

---

[11] Ibid. 47.

many difficulties. The period between 1861 and 1914 was also the time during which the Jewish population of Hungary grew to become the second largest in Europe, after that of the tsarist empire, and when Jews in Hungary achieved emancipation (1867) and religious equality with the other religious denominations of the kingdom (1895). In response to both of these developments, the leaders of Hungary's religiously progressive (Neolog) Jewish communities sought to develop a narrative of belonging that carved out for Jews living in Hungary at the time an identity as 'Hungarians of the Israelite religion'. These reading books show how, rather than rejecting the Hungarian government's cultural enterprise, as some members of Hungary's other nationalities did, Jewish cultural leaders embraced the enterprise and sought to make it their own.

The reading books studied here detail an organic and internal process of narrative creation. They reveal explicatory mechanisms and justifications for the sense of attachment to the kingdom and to the Hungarian nation that the authors suggest the children develop. These books track the development of a specifically Hungarian Jewish theory of acculturation that sought to negate all claims to Jewish peoplehood, replacing it with membership of 'Hungarians of the Israelite religion'. In these respects, the books provide invaluable clues to a local but diffuse process of identity creation, which, however, was not unique to Hungarian Jews. In a recent dissertation, Deborah Anna Brown explored the numerous ways in which German Jews in the late nineteenth century dealt with similar questions of belonging.[12] As Hillel Kieval has demonstrated, the Jews of Prague also had several different avenues for defining themselves vis-à-vis the modern state.[13]

The process of identity creation was facilitated by two institutions that also date from the dual monarchy: the National Israelite Teacher-Training Institute (Országos Izraelita Tanítóképző Intézet) and the National Association of Israelite Teachers (Országos Izraelita Tanítóegyesület), founded in 1857 and 1867 respectively. Both of these institutions provided teachers in Jewish schools and text-book writers throughout the kingdom with a sense of community and allowed for the exchange of ideas about identity formation. I will turn to them at the end of the chapter.

The Hungarian political context under the dual monarchy was vastly different from the French, Prussian, or English contexts, even though the ideas of nationhood as formulated by Hungarian statesmen clearly followed the west European model. These differences had to do, first, with area and population density and, second, with the sense of unity prevalent in the population as shown by linguistic abilities and religious affiliations. At the end of the nineteenth century, Hungary was much less densely populated than England, France, or Prussia but was

[12] D. A. Brown, 'The Order of Things and their Numerical Value: The Science and Politics of Category Creation and their Relationship to German and Jewish Identity in Germany, 1875–1933', Ph.D. thesis (University of California, 2012).

[13] H. J. Kieval, *The Making of Czech Jewry: National Conflict and Jewish Society in Bohemia, 1870–1918* (New York, 1988).

considerably more diverse in the linguistic and religious spheres. This geopolitical reality led Hungarian statesmen to pursue a policy of national integration and forced Hungarian cultural assimilation of other nationalities. The policy met with significant resistance from non-Hungarian speakers in the land.

The area of the Kingdom of Hungary totalled 125,426 square miles in 1900, and included Croatia-Slavonia.[14] At the turn of the century, this corresponded to 93 per cent of the territory of Prussia (134,617 square miles in 1903),[15] was more than double the area of England and Wales (58,324 square miles in 1901),[16] and 60 per cent of the territory of France (207,130 square miles in 1896).[17] The population of the Kingdom of Hungary was 19,122,340 in 1900.[18] All three of the other countries had larger populations. The British population was 1.7 times larger (32,327,843 in 1901);[19] Prussia's population of 34,472,509 in 1900 was 1.8 times that of Hungary's;[20] and France's population of 38,517,975 in 1896 was more than double.[21] These numbers show that the three other countries were also much more densely inhabited. In Hungary, 152 people lived on a square mile of land. Though roughly the same size as Hungary, Prussia's population density was 256 people per square mile; France's territory was double Hungary's and yet its population density was 186 people per square mile; and England and Wales were half of Hungary's size but 3.6 times more densely populated (554 people per square mile).

The census of England and Wales of 1901 did not report numbers for religious affiliation, nor did the French census of 1896, although according to Eugen Weber, 'in the mid-1870s 35,387,703 of the 36,000,000 people in France were listed in the official census as Catholics. The rest declared themselves Protestants (something under 600,000), Jews (50,000) or freethinkers (80,000).'[22] Sixty-three per cent of Prussia's population of 34,472,509 were of an Evangelical confession (Lutheran, Calvinist, or Unitarian). Together these 21,817,577 individuals formed an overwhelming religious majority in a country where most of the remainder of the population was Catholic (12,113,670 individuals, forming 35 per cent of the population). The Jewish population of Prussia (392,322) formed approximately 1 per cent of the total population.[23]

[14] Königliches Ungarisches Statistisches Zentralamt, *Ungarisches Statistisches Jahrbuch 1901*, NS, 9 (Budapest, 1902), 12.

[15] Königliches Statistisches Bureau, *Statistisches Jahrbuch für den Preussischen Staat: Erster Jahrgang 1903* (Berlin, 1904), 1.

[16] *Census of England and Wales, 1901 (63 Vict. C. 4.). Summary Tables: Area, Houses and Population; Also Population Classified by Ages, Condition as to Marriage, Occupations, Birthplaces, and Infirmities* (London, 1903), 44.   [17] *Annuaire Statistique* (Paris, 1901), xx. 3.

[18] Königliches Ungarisches Statistisches Zentralamt, *Ungarisches Statistisches Jahrbuch 1901*, 12.

[19] *Census of England and Wales, 1901*, 1.

[20] Königliches Statistisches Bureau, *Statistisches Jahrbuch für den Preussischen Staat: Erster Jahrgang 1903*, 3.   [21] *Annuaire Statistique*, xx. 3.   [22] Weber, *Peasants into Frenchmen*, 339.

[23] Königliches Statistisches Bureau, *Statistisches Jahrbuch für den Preussischen Staat: Erster Jahrgang 1903*, 14.

In 1900 Hungary was much more diverse religiously than either Prussia or France. A little more than half of its total population of 19,122,340 practised Roman Catholicism (9,846,533). The Evangelical population of the country only numbered 3,771,893 and formed 20.0 per cent of the population. Unlike Prussia or France, Hungary was home to sizable minorities of Eastern Catholics (1,843,634) and Eastern Orthodox (2,799,846), forming 9.6 per cent and 14.6 per cent of the population, respectively. The Jewish population was double the size of Prussia's (846,254) and represented 4.0 per cent of the total population of the country.[24]

Neither the English nor the French censuses reported statistics on linguistic use for the entire country. Eighty-nine per cent of Prussia's population reported speaking either German or German and one other language as their mother tongue. The only significant linguistic minority were the roughly 3 million Polish speakers who formed 8.8 per cent of the population.[25] Hungary was much more diverse linguistically than Prussia: of Hungary's total population, only 45.0 per cent reported speaking Hungarian as their mother tongue. Amongst linguistic minorities, Romanian was the commonest language reported (14.5 per cent of the population with 2,785,265 speakers). The German and Slovak speakers also formed important minority communities with 2,114,423 individuals and 2,008,744 individuals (11.0 per cent and 10.5 per cent respectively). The Croatian and Serbian communities formed smaller minorities of 1,667,377 and 1,045,550 (9.0 per cent and 5.0 per cent respectively). A small number of Ukrainian speakers (427,825) and speakers of other languages (394,142) each formed 2.0 per cent of the population.[26]

What these numbers show is that in 1900 there lived in Hungary—on a territory half the size of France and double the size of England and Wales—a population that was half as dense as either England's, France's, or Prussia's but that was concurrently much more diverse religiously and linguistically. Though the central government adopted the English, French, and Prussian models of state building, local realities prevented the full application of their project. Scholars have linked the aggressive Magyarization of the non-Hungarian-speaking areas of the kingdom with the rise of political forces that led to the dismantling of the kingdom following the First World War.[27] However, an interesting facet of the textbooks is that their authors accepted the policy of Magyarization and sought to inscribe Jewish identity within its boundaries.

The first two reading books discussed were published in 1861 and 1864. They

---

[24] Königliches Ungarisches Statistisches Zentralamt, *Ungarisches Statistisches Jahrbuch 1901*, 19.

[25] Königliches Statistisches Bureau, *Statistisches Jahrbuch für den Preussischen Staat: Erster Jahrgang 1903*, 19.

[26] Königliches Ungarisches Statistisches Zentralamt, *Ungarisches Statistisches Jahrbuch 1901*, 22–5.

[27] P. F. Sugar, 'External and Domestic Roots of Eastern European Nationalism', in id., *Nationalism in Eastern Europe* (Seattle, 1994); id., 'Government and Minorities in Austria-Hungary', in id., *East European Nationalism, Politics and Religion* (Aldershot, 1999); R. W. Seton-Watson, *Racial Problems in Hungary* (London, 1908); O. Jászi, *The Dissolution of the Habsburg Monarchy* (Chicago, 1929).

were intended for children of German-speaking, urban Jewish families who faced the task of learning both Hungarian and Hebrew in a cultural setting where the primary everyday language was German. The authors of both of these works were faced with the challenge of combining Hungarian, Jewish, and German cultural contexts into a usable, workable whole. Conversely, the last three reading books— published in 1889, 1909, and 1913—were meant to convey Jewish cultural and religious content within a Hungarian national and linguistic setting. Between the two sets of books, the emphasis shifted from purveying a trilingual cultural reality to a single national reality into which Jewish belonging was reframed and re-inscribed. Thus whilst the first two works emphasize an attachment to the Hungarian land, this attachment is expressed trilingually in German and in Hungarian, with the Hebrew linguistic content on an equal footing; in the later three books, the Hebrew linguistic content is either completely absent or conveyed only for the purpose of ensuring a minimal level of compliance and understanding of religious tradition, and Jewish history and tradition have been reimagined as coexisting within a Hungarian linguistic setting.

SÁMUEL KOHÁNYI'S *FIRST SOUND-MAKING READING BOOK FOR THE USE OF HUNGARIAN ISRAELITE PUBLIC SCHOOLS* AND SALAMON NEUMANN'S *READING BOOK FOR HIGHER ISRAELITE SCHOOLS*[28]

The *Hungarian Jewish Lexicon* of 1929 lists Sámuel Kohányi (born in Csábóc (Cabov, Slovakia), 15 April 1824, died in Budapest, 5 July 1905) as a composer of music.[29] Kohányi moved to Budapest at the age of 13 as an orphan, knowing neither Hungarian nor German. He supported himself by giving Hebrew lessons. In 1844 he obtained a Latin diploma from the Pest Lutheran gymnasium, as well a diploma from the National Music Academy. Kohányi held numerous positions during his career: he worked as a preceptor for children in Pest between 1846 and 1849 and operated a private school for boys between 1850 and 1862; from 1862 to 1872 he directed the congregational nursery at the Pest Israelite Community; and between 1872 and his retirement in 1895 he worked in the Jewish congregational boys' school behind the Dohány Street synagogue.[30] Kohányi liked using songs to teach children, and he wrote a number of books. His first, *Kinder-Lieder für Familienkreise, Elementarschulen und Kinder-Bewahr-Anstalten*, appeared in Pest in 1852. It was followed over the next forty years by at least ten other books in German and Hungarian, which used songs to introduce children to German and Hungarian language skills.[31]

---

[28] S. Kohányi, *Első hangoztatőó és olvasókönyv a magyarországi izráelita népiskolák számára* (Pest, 1861); S. Neumann, *Olvasókönyv felsőbb izraelita iskolák számára* (Pest, 1864).

[29] K. Kristóf, 'Kohányi Sámuel', in P. Újvári (ed.), *Magyar zsidó lexikon* (Budapest, 1929), 492.

[30] J. Szinnyei, 'Kohányi Sámuel', in *Magyar írók élete és munkái* (Budapest, 1914), available at <http://mek.oszk.hu/03600/03630/html/k/k11624.htm> (accessed 22 Feb. 2016).   [31] Ibid.

Kohányi's *First Sound-Making Reading Book for the Use of Hungarian Israelite Public Schools* (1861) is fascinating because it opens with a trilingual picture dictionary (Hebrew–German–Hungarian). The picture dictionary is geared towards German-speaking children whose parents expect them to learn the rudiments of Hebrew as well as everyday Hungarian. Kohányi did not provide Hebrew equivalents of some German words such as 'soup bowl', 'writing utensil', and 'coffee-grinder'.[32] Of course, the book was also meant to instil in Jewish children a love of the fatherland. It is interesting to observe the balance which Kohányi strikes between belonging to the people of Israel and being a member of the Hungarian nation: he avoids defining outright what it means to be a Hungarian of the Israelite religion. Instead, he presents the two types of information separately. At the beginning of the longer readings, the child could read:

My parents belong to the glorified people of Israel, who love the only God. They are therefore Israelites. My grandparents and ancestors have all been Israelites. I am also therefore an Israelite child. Our people have been a people for many millennia. Therefore, they are an *ancient* people. That which keeps itself up for a long time, is generally respected and illustrious; I am therefore the member of an ancient and illustrious people, which in many times could boast of pious and excellent men, and even now boasts of them. I also want to be good and pious.[33]

Several pages later, Kohányi tells children what it means to be patriotic:

The place, where we are born, is the land of our birth. This is where [our parents] rocked us in our cribs. This is where our dear parents take care of us, this is where we started going to school. This is where we played with our other children friends. Even if one day we were to move away from it we would always want to move back to [this] land. . . . The country where the land of our birth is located is part of our sweet home. This is where our friends from childhood live; where our community leaders are, who govern and protect us.[34]

Comparing Kohányi's two descriptions reveals that his description of the attachment to Hungary is formulated as an attachment to the *land* of the kingdom. This attachment is cemented in localities which children frequently explore while growing up: from the crib, to the school, to the friendships formed as a child. Primarily, Kohányi documents a personal connection based on intimate first-hand memories, which are equated to long-term attachment and thus happiness. Comparatively, Kohányi's description of the child's attachment to the Israelites (with whom the child presumably has daily contact) is anchored in an attachment to a *people*. It is a tribal description based on family origins, which is itself justified by and anchored in religious belief. The description specifically co-opts the child as a member of the Israelite people: 'our people', the child reads, 'have been a people for many millennia'. Here, the fact that the closest members of one's family are (supposedly) members of the Israelite people is used to convince the child that he or she is a member of the Israelite people.

---

[32] Possibly he did not know the Hebrew equivalents.

[33] Kohányi, *Első hangoztató és olvasókönyv*, 21.   [34] Ibid. 46.

Both parts of the definition are anchored in terms of the two types of information a child is likely to be most familiar with, in order to ensure loyalty to both Israelite and Hungarian ideals: spatial information regarding where the child has spent time and family-related information regarding his or her personal background. Most notable from the first definition is the absence of the words 'Jew' or 'Jewish'. Kohányi's editors probably felt it safer if the children reading the textbooks were not confused in this regard. Kohányi included two songs emphasizing nationality and how to behave with respect to foreigners. The other parts of Kohányi's book include short snippets about Abraham's youth, Moses as a shepherd, and Judah Maccabee. The collection is rounded out by short texts describing the beauty of Hungary's natural geography.[35]

Salamon Neumann's *Reading Book for Higher Israelite Schools* (1864) also seems to have been a transitional publication intended for children who spoke German fluently but were struggling to learn Hungarian, which was fast becoming the administrative language of the realm. Neumann's book contains three sections: the first with German and Hungarian on facing pages conveying simple and complex sentences; the second with more difficult readings on, for example, plants, animals, the Mediterranean Sea, London, St Petersburg, and Moscow; and finally, a third with longer, two-or-three-page, historical tales drawn from Jewish and Hungarian traditions. Sections 2 and 3 only contain Hungarian text, so it is evident that the first section was meant to raise the children's reading level to the degree that they could follow a Hungarian text. In his introduction, Neumann explained his reasons for writing the book:

During my many years of activity, I often found it difficult [to teach] without a helpful book which, aside from easing the learning of the Hungarian language additionally gave a good selection from the [required] school materials . . . *while also resonating with the Jewish spirit from its every line.* . . . In the end I decide to write and edit such a book by myself. Those who have like me felt so keenly the lack of a Hungarian reading book written in the Jewish spirit should judge whether I have succeeded in the execution of my main goal. . . . [While writing,] I had in my mind's eye especially those Israelite schools, where the teaching of the Hungarian language is meeting with some difficulty.[36]

For Neumann the reality of Hungarian-speaking Jewish children was still something of a dream to be achieved through the guidance of teachers such as himself. He argued for combining Hungarian and Jewish narratives into a usable whole, which a Jewish child with native Hungarian language skills could read in order to feel at home as a patriotic Hungarian of Jewish faith.

The second section of Neumann's book presents a variety of geographical readings; the third uses biblical tales and narratives of Hungarian heroes in order to hone advanced reading skills. But the real significance of Neumann's work for historians who are interested in questions of identity appears in the first section,

[35] Ibid. 29–31.
[36] Neumann, *Olvasókönyv felsőbb izraelita iskolák számára*, pp. iii–iv (emphasis added).

which he wrote in order to teach simple and complex sentences and moods. This section reveals the complexity of the world-view which Neumann purported to create for his young readers, in which he meticulously combined—sentence by sentence, paragraph by paragraph, on face-to-face German and Hungarian pages —strands from the Hungarian national canon, popularized references to Jewish stories, and a cultural context which can be seen as 'general European culture' or moral and ethical training. Take, for example, the following paragraph, from the section on phrases of intent:

God created the world. Joshua conquered Canaan. Cain killed Abel. Joseph was sold by his brothers. Árpád founded this national home. Stephen I defeated Kupa Somogyi.[37]

Or, on attributive sentences, from the same section:

The good God shows mercy. Solomon the Wise was once the king of the Jews. The valiant János Hunyadi is immortal. Let our beautiful homeland blossom! The pious Hillel was peace loving. The earnest shepherd stands guard.[38]

Or, on determinants of space:

The people of Israel wandered for forty years in the Arabian desert. The best iron products are made in England. Cotton is imported from America. Andrew II went to the Holy Land. At the top of the Carpathian Mountains, there are lakes.[39]

Or, on indeterminate sentences:

The righteous are not afraid of death. Do good and do not be afraid of anything! . . . What did Joseph dream of? The motherland does not forget about us. God provides for us. Judah guaranteed Benjamin's security. . . . God conveyed his will through Moses. The Germans offered Louis the Great the imperial crown. . . . I don't drink wine. . . . The funeral march is approaching the cemetery. The girl cuddles up to her mother. . . . We chose many of the books. . . . How do the Tatars make a living?[40]

Neumann provided model sentences for the various sections he had to fill. His objective was to convey a number of different types of sentences, in order for the child to learn to read. In this part of the book, it was not necessary for the sentences to match in theme; rather, the objective was to give examples of what might be said with the types of sentences. But Neumann was searching for sentences which

---

[37] Neumann, *Olvasókönyv felsőbb izraelita iskolák számára*, 14. Árpád (c. 845–907) was the leader of the confederation of Hungarian tribes which occupied the Carpathian basin. He is considered by many Hungarians (including Neumann) to be the founder of Hungary. Stephen I (970 or 980–1038) was the first king of Hungary. Kupa Somogyi, or Koppány, was a tenth-century Hungarian nobleman who challenged Stephen's claim to the throne.

[38] Ibid. 8. John Hunyadi (1407–56) was a Hungarian military commander of Transylvanian origin who defeated the Turks at the Battle of Belgrade in 1456.

[39] Ibid. 22. Andrew II was king of Hungary from 1205 to 1235.

[40] Ibid. 17–18. Louis I (1326–82) was king of Hungary and Croatia from 1342 and king of Poland from 1370.

focused on aspects of the Hungarian national historical canon (Árpád, Stephen I, János Hunyadi, Andrew II, Louis the Great) and the cultural heritage of the Jewish Bible and commentaries (Joshua, Cain, Joseph, Solomon, Hillel). There is also a hint of the idealizing adjectives usually reserved for describing the Holy Land. Agricultural professions are idealized. Finally, two overarching themes seem to be the fact that God cares for human beings and the nature of the nation of which the student is part. As a result, what comes across for the reader is a carefully constructed ideological frame of reference in which cultural signifiers exist on a level playing field, modulated by the all-encompassing belief in both the will of the divine and the children's partaking in the nation's destiny.

NÁTHÁN HALÁSZ'S *TREASURE CHEST*, IGNÁCZ KONDOR'S *HEBREW READING BOOK WITH PICTURES*, AND JÓNÁS BARNA'S *HUNGARIAN READING BOOK FOR THE FOURTH GRADE OF THE ISRAELITE PUBLIC ELEMENTARY SCHOOLS*[41]

When compared with the books produced by Neumann and Kohányi in 1861 and 1864, the reading books published by Náthán Halász, Ignácz Kondor, and Jónás Barna in 1889, 1909, and 1913 respectively show a shift in emphasis from helping German-speaking Jewish children acquire the rudiments of Hungarian idiom and national spirit to introducing Hungarian-speaking Jewish children to certain aspects of a very circumscribed version of Jewishness.

Halász (1834–1910) was the oldest of the three writers and was only ten years younger than Kohányi.[42] He was born into a family of industrial workers who could not afford to send him to school. As a result he seems to have been mostly home-schooled: he passed his exams for matriculation and teacher certification after lengthy periods of home study. Halász received his teacher certification from the Catholic Teachers' Training Institute in Pest in the mid-1850s. Thereafter, he was a schoolteacher in Kajászó-Szent-Péter, Lovasberény, and Sátoraljaújhely before moving to Buda in 1867, where he taught first in the public Israelite school. Sometime in the 1870s he became the principal of the Israelite girls' school in Pest.[43]

Barna and Kondor were approximately thirty years younger than Neumann and Kohányi, having been born in 1851 and 1852, in Kecskemét and Kaposvár respectively. Both graduated from the National Israelite Teacher-Training Institute

---

[41] N. Halász (ed.), *Kincses szekrényke: oktató, nevelő, mulattató elbeszélések és költemények a zsidó bölcsek irataiból a mindkét nembeli zsidó ifjúság részére* (Budapest, 1889); I. Kondor, *Képes héber olvasókönyv az elemi iskolák I. osztálya számára*, 4th edn. (Budapest, 1909); J. Barna, *Magyar olvasókönyv az izraelita elemi népiskolák IV. osztálya számára*, 6th edn. (Budapest, 1913).

[42] Z. Tieder, 'Halász Náthán', in Újvári (ed.), *Magyar zsidó lexikon*, 840.

[43] J. Szinnyei, 'Halász (Fischer) Nátán', in *Magyar írók élete és munkái*.

in Pest, Barna in 1870 and Kondor in 1872. Barna obtained teaching credentials in 1873 and continued his studies at university level, probably in Budapest. In 1876, according to two biographical entries in different encyclopedias, he delivered a strongly worded speech at the national congress of Israelite teachers, in which he argued for granting tenure to teachers in Jewish schools. Based on this speech, the Minister of Cults and Religions passed a decree forcing Jewish communities to grant tenure to their teachers. This created difficulties for Barna and he seems to have been forced to resign his position as director of a Jewish school. Thereafter, he worked as a primary-school teacher in several state elementary schools in Budapest.[44] Kondor's path was slightly different. His father died when he was 16, and he had to interrupt his studies at the local gymnasium in Kaposvár in order to pursue a career which required less formal training. He obtained his teaching degree after teaching at the Jewish school in Osztopán. After graduation he held various jobs, and taught from 1875 onwards at Jewish schools in Makó, Siófok, Sátoraljaújhely, and, from 1884, Pest.[45]

The five teachers wrote an average of seven schoolbooks each during their careers as educators. Kohányi was the most prolific, writing nine songbooks for children, a pedagogical work for the teaching of music to children, and three reading books in German and Hungarian for Jewish and general audiences. Only the first two of Kohányi's books were in German: after 1868 he only published in Hungarian. By contrast, all of Neumann's books were bilingual German–Hungarian, although as a sign of the changing linguistic conditions the titles of his works were given solely in Hungarian after 1859. Neumann wrote five Hungarian-language learning texts for a German-speaking audience and one 'short biblical history' in both Hungarian and German. After 1859 he completed a short history of Hungary in both languages, as well as a geography primer and the reading book for Jewish children discussed above.[46]

Halász, Barna, and Kondor generally wrote in Hungarian, although the titles of their works suggest that they were also proficient in German. Of the three, Barna wrote the greatest number of books (seven) of which only two were German textbooks. Apart from the reading book discussed here, it is unclear if Barna wrote any works for a specifically Jewish audience. He wrote a total of four Hungarian language-learning textbooks, a geography textbook, and a history textbook. By contrast, Halász wrote five books, of which four were on Jewish topics and were meant to convey Jewish beliefs to his readers: his first book was a Hungarian primer. It seems that Kondor only wrote three books, all on Jewish religion and beliefs.

Halász's *Treasure Chest: Educational and Entertaining Stories and Poetry from the Writings of the Jewish Sages for Young Jews of Both Sexes* (1889) was meant to be presented as a gift on special occasions or as a prize for the successful completion of

<hr/>

[44] 'Barna Jónás', in Újvári (ed.), *Magyar zsidó lexikon*; J. Szinnyei, 'Barna J(ónás)', in *Magyar írók élete és munkái*.   [45] J. Szinnyei, 'Kondor Ignácz', in *Magyar írók élete és munkái*.
[46] J. Szinnyei, 'Neumann Salamon A.', in *Magyar írók élete és munkái*.

examinations. In other words, it was a book given to children to reinforce their integration in and acceptance of a master narrative which had been communicated to them by means of the school system. The book itself is elegantly decorated with elaborate 'Oriental' prints of King Solomon and various places in the Land of Israel and elsewhere, such as Jerusalem and the tombs of Esther and Mordecai. At first glance there are many similarities between Neumann and Kohányi's books and Halász's. The *Treasure Chest* is essentially a story book with similar subject material to the works of Neumann and Kohányi. Neumann's work included adaptations of Psalm 1, the book of Jeremiah, and the story of the Maccabees.[47] Kohányi's work also included an adaptation of the life of Judah Maccabee, as well as stories about Abraham's youth and Moses as a young shepherd.[48] But Halász's work displays a consistency in style and tone which are lacking from the first two.

Halász's work was meant for children whose native tongue was Hungarian and who also felt Jewish. His work was not meant to be a linguistic primer; rather, it was a tool to introduce students to the stories of the Jewish tradition, which they might not have been exposed to in school. The book presupposes some familiarity with Jewish customs and texts but is clearly not intended for students with a yeshiva background. More importantly, while Kohányi's and Neumann's texts were also meant to introduce children to aspects of general Hungarian culture through geographical descriptions and selections from Hungarian literature, Halász's text was clearly written to reintroduce aspects of Jewishness into the lives of children who were becoming secularized. Halász's subject material is either biblical or talmudic, ethical or geographical (for example, it describes places in the Land of Israel). A retelling of 'Jews in Babylonian captivity'[49] follows 'King Solomon's wise judgement (with image)';[50] selections on 'Hillel's patience'[51] and David and Goliath[52] are interspersed with teachings about modesty and ostentatiousness[53] and descriptions of Rachel's tomb.[54] Though there is no price marked on the book itself, the decorated cover, high-quality paper, and elaborate images probably meant a higher price than the rather cheaply bound, unillustrated books by Kohányi and Neumann.

The fourth edition (1909) of Kondor's *Hebrew Reading Book with Pictures* reflects a different style of publication altogether. First and foremost, as its title indicates, the book is a Hebrew-language reading text meant to convey the essentials of the language of the prayer book to children who were by then at least one generation removed from a religious lifestyle. As mentioned in its subtitle, the book aims to convey 'knowledge of the Hebrew letters with reading exercises . . . elementary rudiments of religion, biblical history until Abraham [and] selections from the Hebrew prayers'. It was intended to be read by students in the first grade

---

[47] Neumann, *Olvasókönyv izraelita iskolák számára*, 228–30.
[48] Kohányi, *Első hangoztató és olvasókönyv*, 28–30.
[49] Halász, *Kincses szekrényke*, 108.   [50] Ibid. 97.   [51] Ibid. 159.
[52] Ibid. 145.   [53] Ibid. 157.   [54] Ibid. 117.

of elementary school and was published by the Pest Israelite Community, the largest and wealthiest of Hungary's Neolog congregations. The book is organized into three sections. The first introduces religious concepts, such as the belief in one God. The second contains adaptations of biblical stories from the first part of the book of Genesis (Creation, the first sin, Noah, the tower of Babel, and Abraham). The third part introduces the Hebrew alphabet and elementary prayers in that language. Although it is not a Hungarian reading book per se, I nevertheless choose to examine Kondor's work because on various occasions he seeks to define the relationship of Jews to their homeland of Hungary. He stumbles in arguing for the relevance of Jewishness for the Hungarian-speaking Jewish children for whom he is writing, and this makes his work interesting:

We are Hungarians, Hungary is our sweet home, Hungarian is our mother tongue; this prayer too is in Hungarian. . . . Our religion is Israelite (Jewish). We are Hungarians of the Israelite (Jewish) religion. . . . Human beings do not all love the good God in the same way. One is of a certain religion depending on how one loves the good God. Hungarians are also of varying religions. Our religion is the Israelite religion or in other words, the Jewish religion. As a result, we are of Israelite, that is, of Jewish, religion.[55]

The most intriguing part of this text is how Kondor falters repeatedly over the meanings of the words 'Israelite' and 'Jewish'. Since the book is written for 6-year-olds who presumably lack the sophistication to understand that by 'Israelite' one would be speaking of a member of the Jewish people, Kondor has to explain that the term 'Israelite' is applied to express the fact that one is Jewish. He also fumbles in showing why one ought to be Jewish (or Israelite) when one already considers oneself Hungarian. His awkwardness on this issue also underscores the fact that it is not necessarily self-evident either for him or for the children that Jewishness ought to be important at all within the context of Hungarianness and that some explanation has to be provided for why the cultural material of the reading book ought to be learned at all.

Kondor was writing for children whose native tongue was Hungarian. As a result, he had the arduous task of explaining why Jewish children still ought to learn to pray in Hebrew. He wrote:

Our fathers prayed in the Hebrew language. We, too, would like to pray according to the forms of our forefathers. Not all of those who are of the Israelite religion are Hungarians. There are Israelites with other mother tongues. But all Israelites love the good God in the same way and the language of their prayers is the same, which was also the language of their fathers. Our forefathers were Hebrews who were later called Israelites, or Jews. They prayed in Hebrew, and in Hebrew they wrote their holy books as well. As a result we would prefer, according to the ways of our fathers, to pray in Hebrew.[56]

Kondor thus had to stress that despite the ease with which Hungarian Jewish children could pray in their native tongue, there was still relevance to learning

---

[55] Kondor, *Képes héber olvasókönyv*, 7–8.   [56] Ibid. 8.

what (at that point) was a foreign language in order to connect with the past. This argument is all the more difficult for him to make because he had explained so clearly and arduously that the readers of his textbook were to think of themselves as Hungarians. However, an especially curious and quick-witted child could have asked Kondor the obvious question: who came first, the Hungarians or the Jews, and which group ought the child to think himself part of? Ultimately there was no correct answer; hence, Kondor's message was weakened by his attempt to define an organic fusion which had no simple definition.

By the 1913 edition, the sixth, of Barna's *Hungarian Reading Book for the Fourth Grade of the Israelite Public Elementary Schools* there is a completely organic version of Hungarian Jewishness, firmly integrated and combining strands of ethical teaching, Hungarian folktales and history, and Jewish traditions. Barna's book contains twelve sections. A first part on legends, teachings, and narratives is followed by one on stories from the Bible. Subsequent sections cover 'our holidays', 'sketches from our national home's history', and 'sketches from the history of Hungarian Jews'. These are followed by sections on 'geographical sketches' (physical descriptions of the land) and a generous selection of Hungarian literature and sayings, especially the poetry of Kálmán Tóth, Mihály Vörösmarty, Sándor Petőfi, and János Arany.

The section on Hungarian Jewish history is notable for demonstrating the narratological effects of five decades of cultural give and take. Barna wrote the entire section, presenting Jewish history to his young readers solely within the context of Hungarian history, and providing quasi-biblical legitimization for presenting Jewish history as such. The first line states: 'Great was the sin of our fathers . . . They turned away from God and thus God too turned away from them.'[57] He then states that even in punishment one can discern God's goodness, for though other great nations have disappeared, the Jewish nation has survived, notwithstanding persecution. Providence guarded the Jews and repaid to them a thousandfold for the loyalty of Abraham, Isaac, and Jacob. From the flames of persecution, Jews called out to God, and God pitied them: in time the situation of the Jews improved. He follows up with a part that is worth quoting in full:

Though the Jews have been scattered around the face of the Earth, no Jews have ever found as much protection as the Hungarian Jew has in our sweet homeland, Hungary. Love, my precious children, the Hungarian homeland! For as a result of the generosity of the Hungarian nation, we rejoice in having all of the same rights as any of the other sons of our homeland; and what is more, the crowned king and the nation have enacted into law the equality of our religion with that of the other faiths.[58]

Barna's aim was to reinscribe Jewish history squarely within the boundaries of the Hungarian historical narrative. Here, too, he presents a romanticized historical portrait. What is most interesting about the account is the lack of reference to any

---

[57] Barna, *Magyar olvasókönvy*, 117.   [58] Ibid. 117–18.

aspect of Jewish historical experience outside Hungary, aside from a few allusions
to the three patriarchs and the Khazar myth. There is no reference to the talmudic
academies of Babylonia or to Rashi; no reference to the Spanish expulsion; nothing
on Shabetai Tsevi; no discussion of other Jewish communities of Ashkenaz; no
allusion to hasidism, nor to the German Reform movements. Instead, there is a
lachrymose and superficial account of Jewish 'wanderings' before Jews reached the
Hungarian national homeland; a tenuous link—through the Khazar myth—
between the historical origins of the Hungarian and Jewish people; and accounts
of the condition of Hungarian Jews in Hungary at various crucial junctures of
history.

In the main, Barna focuses on those moments of Hungarian Jewish history in
which the distinction between Hungarian and Jewish cultural ascriptions can be
blurred through grandiose portraiture and rhetorical or explanatory flourishes.
These moments allow him to show his readers a subtle way to be proud of being
Hungarian nationals of the Jewish faith. Barna carefully chooses moments of great
importance in the Hungarian national story, for which the argument can be made
that Jews took part with great gusto. Two topics that he stresses in particular are
the medieval Hungarian king Matthias's entry into Buda in 1477 and the Hungarian revolution of 1848.

It is indicative that in explaining the long history of the Jews, Barna felt constrained to refer to them as a 'nation'. For all of his attempts to mask the existence
of Jewish ethnic affiliation, he could not avoid referring to Jewish nationhood in
biblical and pre-Hungarian times, and he also could not avoid contrasting the fate
of Hungarian Jews with that of other Jews 'scattered around the face of the Earth'.
One might call these two instances simple slips, as it can be difficult to distinguish
between the increasingly fine distinctions scholars assign to the words 'nation' and
'people'. I would argue, however, that it is better to think of these examples as the
first of two aspects of Barna's subsuming of the Hungarian narrative into an
extended and all-encompassing version of the traditional and premodern Jewish
narrative, present (with certain modifications) since biblical times.

Barna's ability to write a narrative in 1913 that inscribed Jewish history within
that of Hungary in a textbook with selections from Hungarian poets reflects the
consolidation of a Jewish narrative of belonging to the Hungarian nation that
Kohányi and Neumann could only faintly have imagined in the 1860s. The narrative presented in the reading books for Jewish children published across Hungary
benefited greatly from the establishment of the National Israelite Teacher-
Training Institute and the National Association of Israelite Teachers. Kondor and
Barna were graduates of the institute.

The establishment of Jewish schools in Hungary has been chronicled in English by the American historian Aron Moskovits[59] and in Hungarian by Viktória

---

[59] A. Moskovits, *Jewish Education in Hungary (1848–1948)* (New York, 1964).

Bányai.[60] Moskovits describes the foundation in 1857 of the National Israelite Teacher-Training Institute, the first institution of its kind in Hungary. Its financing came from a Jewish school fund which had originated from the fine imposed by the Austrian government on the Hungarian Jewish communities of Arad, Cegléd, Kecskemét, Irsa, Nagykőrös, and Pest for their participation in the failed revolution of 1848. That fine of 2.3 million florins had eventually been commuted to a school fund of 1.2 million florins payable by all the Jewish communities in the country.[61]

Throughout the dual monarchy, the National Israelite Teacher-Training Institute was the only institute that trained teachers to teach Jewish subjects in the country's Jewish public schools. A total of 793 students graduated from the institution between 1861 (the year diplomas were first awarded) and 1897, the year of the Hungarian millennial celebrations which prompted the publication of a Festschrift to celebrate the institution's achievements.[62] On average, 21 students matriculated from the institute a year. Three-quarters attended the institution full time and a quarter studied at home and passed exams after a period of preparation.[63] Most were 20 years old at the time of their graduation.[64] Until 1861 instruction was offered in German only, between 1861 and 1869 it was offered in both Hungarian and German, and after 1869 it was offered only in Hungarian.[65] As the institution matured, so too did the number of years of schooling which it offered: until at least 1872 the course of study was two years,[66] between 1872 and 1881 it was three years, and after 1881 an additional fourth year of study was added.[67] Extending the number of years of instruction provided the means to expand the number of hours devoted to Jewish religious subjects, Hungarian, and German.

As the educator József Bánóczi makes clear in his detailed history of the institution, its specific goal was to produce Jewish teachers who were fully Hungarian and devoted to national ideals:

[In 1861] the movement of Magyarization broke into the walls of the school. Let us add . . . this breaking in was not the result of a struggle, but was rather the victorious entry on lowered bridges and across open gates. And within, [there was found] not an adversary who leaned towards peace but a comrade-in-arms who was prepared to join [the fight].[68]

According to Bánóczi, by the 1880s the mother tongue of most students was Hungarian. He also provided data about the geographical provenance of the students. These data seem to correlate with an argument the French-Hungarian sociologist

[60] V. Bányai, *Zsidó oktatásügy Magyarországon 1780–1850* (Budapest, 2005).
[61] Moskovits, *Jewish Education in Hungary*, 17.
[62] J. Bánóczi, *Az Országos Izraelita Tanító-Intézet története 1857–1897* (Budapest, 1897), 69–79.
[63] Ibid. 66.   [64] Ibid. 67.
[65] 'Izraelita Tanítóképző, Intézet', in Újvári (ed.), *Magyar zsidó lexikon*, 403.
[66] Bánóczi, *Az Országos Izraelita Tanító-Intézet története*, 39.
[67] 'Izraelita Tanítóképző Intézet', 403.
[68] Bánóczi, *Az Országos Izraelita Tanító-Intézet története*, 35.

Viktor Karády made in 1997, to the effect that the popularity of specifically Jewish public elementary education ranked highest amongst the communities of the northern and western areas of the kingdom.[69] According to the admissions data which Bánóczi collated, more than 40 per cent of the students were originally from the western and northernmost counties, Nyitra, Veszprém, Pest, Trencsén, Fejér, Komárom, and Pozsony.[70]

Barna and Kondor were not the only graduates of the institute to write reading books. Twenty other graduates were included in the most complete Hungarian bibliographical encyclopaedia of the dual monarchy: the fourteen-volume *Lives and Works of Hungarian Writers* by bibliographer József Szinnyei (1830–1913), published posthumously in 1914. As Table 1 shows, these authors were committed to writing books on many aspects of the elementary school curriculum, and books on the Hungarian language form the largest single category.

The other institution that helped develop a sense of belonging amongst Jewish school teachers in Hungary was the National Association of Israelite Teachers. It too promoted a narrative of belonging presented in children's textbooks. It was established in 1867, and most of its founding members belonged to the modern Jewish school operated by the Pest Israelite Community and the Association of Teachers in Buda and Óbuda. The mission of the association was threefold: to 'raise the intellectual level of Jewish teachers', to care for the 'Hungarian national spirit', and to provide material care for widowed and sick teachers and orphans.[71] The association experienced a more than fivefold growth in membership between 1877 (the earliest year for which statistics are available) and 1905. In 1877 there were more than 171 members from around the kingdom,[72] and in 1905 the membership structure was expanded to four tiers. There were 96 honorary members, such as the world-famous orientalist Ignác Goldziher, who paid no fees; 145 founding members, who paid a one-time membership fee; 46 supporting members, who paid slightly less; and 570 ordinary members. Jewish communities, Jewish women's and burial societies, and Jewish schools from around the kingdom contributed funds at both the founding and supporting levels. The association had also established a vacation facility for teachers next to Lake Balaton, which had 6 founding, 9 supporting, and 67 ordinary members.[73]

The journal of the association has preserved some of the early debates regarding linguistic use in textbooks, which influenced the development of these learning materials. Vilmos Radó (1847–1919), a teacher, was one of the earliest redactors of

[69] V. Karády, *Iskolarendszer És Felekezeti Egyenlotlenségek Magyarországon, 1867–1945: Történeti Szociológiai Tanulmányok* (Budapest, 1997), 30.

[70] Bánóczi, *Az Országos Izraelita Tanító-Intézet története*, 68.

[71] 'Országos Izraelita Tanító Egyesület', in Újvári (ed.), *Magyar zsidó lexikon*, 667.

[72] 'Névsorozata azon tagoknak, kik a lefolyt év alatt a tagsági díjt egészen vagy részben lefizették', *Magyar Izr. Országos Tanító-Egylet értesítője*, 2/1 (Jan. 1877), 8–11.

[73] 'Az Országos Izraelita Tanítóegyesület tagjainak névsora az 1905. év végén', *Izraelita tanügyi értesítő* 31 (Jan. 1906), pp. i–x.

Table 1. Books by graduates of the National Israelite Teacher-Training Institute (1862–1906)

Subject	Number of books	Percentage
Hungarian	15	21.7
Hungarian translations of the Bible and prayer book	9	13.0
Jewish religious instruction	7	10.1
Mathematics	7	10.1
General Jewish history	6	8.7
Hebrew	6	8.7
German	5	7.2
Natural sciences	3	4.3
History of Jewish institutions in Hungary	3	4.3
Miscellaneous	8	11.6
Total	69	100.0

Source: J. Szinnyei, *Magyar írók élete és munkái.*

Hungarian reading books for Jewish schools. His books for students in the third and fourth grades of the Jewish public schools, published in the late 1870s and throughout the 1880s, provoked many arguments at meetings of the National Association of Israelite Teachers. Radó's biography in the *Hungarian Jewish Lexicon* also states that he was a writer of children's books, a teacher at the Hungarian National Teacher-Training Institute, and a devotee of Herbart's educational philosophy.[74] Throughout the early 1880s Radó argued in the association's journal in favour of the older, almost archaic literary form of Hungarian for the biblical translations which appeared in his reading books. His argument supporting the use of such language was that every literary genre commanded a specific style corresponding to the period in which the literary text to be translated had been produced.[75] One could not, for example, use the language of the modern novel for biblical passages, he stated. Radó acknowledged that the literary form he applied to the biblical passages was not everyday language, but he argued that the Hungarian literary language itself had been created by earlier translators of the Bible. Along these lines, he reminded his colleagues of the revolutionary effects of Luther's translation in the sixteenth century. Chief Rabbi Jakab Steinhardt (1818–85) of Arad was one of Radó's more vocal opponents on this issue. According to Steinhardt, if the purpose of the reading books was to impart to children a workable knowledge of the Hungarian tongue, why hand them a text which was simply 'incorrect' compared with everyday usage?[76] Steinhardt seems to have won this round of the debate.

[74] 'Radó Vilmos', in Újvári (ed.), *Magyar zsidó lexikon*, 780.
[75] V. Radó, 'Az olvasókönyvek ügyében', *Izraelita tanügyi értesítő*, 8 (1883), 25–8.
[76] [Series of exchanges about Radó's reading books], *Izraelita tanügyi értesítő*, 8 (1883), 41–5.

At the general meeting of 1883, the textbook committee enacted a resolution stating that, in future texts, the 'religious and patriotic element' would be in 'all ways subordinated to pedagogical and didactic requirements'.[77]

The fact that such debates occurred did not deter participants from uniting against attempts by Orthodox writers to produce Hungarian-language textbooks for young readers. (Such intra-communal polemics were occasioned by the religious schism that evolved from the late 1860s between the Neologs and the Orthodox, a process chronicled by Jacob Katz.[78]) In 1891 two authors from the Orthodox community, Gábel and Spitzer, published Hungarian reading books similar in tenor and scope to Radó's. Two reviewers of the books in the journal of the National Association of Israelite Teachers took issue with a number of minutiae: that the authors had designated Orthodox Jews as 'true to [the] religion'; that the readings had (apparently) been chosen at random from biblical sources and other, previously published reading books; and that (Magyarized) Hebrew-sounding names for biblical heroes had been used, instead of Hungarian translations of such names, as used in Radó's books. The second reviewer even concluded that the book could not 'move real religious sensibilities and true, pious Jewish thinking', for the moral examples presented in the work were unsuitable—why teach Lot's drunkenness to 7-year-olds?—and pedagogically the book was not in accord with the latest (scientific) advances.[79] This debate shows the extent to which the Orthodox–Neolog polemic had infiltrated even the most tangential aspects of Jewish communal life in Hungary by the end of the dual monarchy. It also shows, though, how similar both factions were in terms of their cultural strivings: both Neologs and Orthodox were struggling with similar issues of cultural transmission.

Finally, the early 1880s saw teachers debating methodological questions. On various occasions it was suggested that readings from the biblical and national Hungarian canons of similar ethical scope be taught together. Thus, Budapest teacher Ábrahám Lederer suggested in 1882, with respect to Radó's books, that the reading on David and Goliath be twinned with 'Prince Béla's Duel with the Pomeranian Lord'.[80] Radó himself commented—upon the publication of a new edition of his reading book in 1884—that the material had been culled and collated with the specific didactical purpose of combining Hungarian folktales, legends, and sagas with relevant stories from the Midrash and aggadah.[81] This willingness to combine both traditions minutely is thus the origin of the sense of balance evident

[77] 'A közgy lés', *Izraelita tanügyi értesítő*, 8 (1883), 151–62; 'Indítvány', *Izraelita tanügyi értesítő*, 8 (1883), 156–7.

[78] J. Katz, *A House Divided: Orthodoxy and Schism in Nineteenth-Century Central European Jewry* (Hanover, NH, 1998).

[79] P. Weisz, 'Új olvasókönyvek', *Izraelita tanügyi értesítő*, 16 (1891), 156–8; 'Megjegyzések a Gábel és Spitzer-féle olvasókönyvekhez', *Izraelita tanügyi értesítő*, 16 (1891), 202–4.

[80] A. Lederer, 'A Radó-féle izr. olvasó-könyvek olvasmányainak módszerü tárgyalásához', *Izraelita tanügyi értesítő*, 7 (1882), 33–7.

[81] 'Az egyesületi olvasókönyvek új kiadása', *Izraelita tanügyi értesítő*, 9 (1884), 59–60.

in Barna's book. Barna understood that in order to ensure the successful reception of his book he had to treat the Hungarian and the Jewish parts of his narrative as equals.

By the time of the general meeting of the association in 1883, the membership had produced an impressive series of resources. These included a Hebrew *aleph-bet* book; a Hebrew grammar; a dictionary of the Bible; a history of Israel as related in the Bible, including translations of biblical songs and parables; and a compendium of biblical Jewish history, with an appendix connecting Jewish religious ritual with its textual sources and ethical meaning.[82] The most striking aspect of this list is its length. It shows that religious teachers and authors in the National Association of Israelite Teachers were comfortable in the Hungarian cultural environment, viewing it as a suitable milieu for perpetuating their Jewishness. Perhaps the most striking aspect of the textbooks produced by these Hungarian Jewish teachers is that they were produced willingly, with the teachers' own resources and out of genuine love and interest in the country that had only recently given them the gift of legal emancipation. Theirs was a dedication to their new language and nation that knew very few boundaries.

[82] A. Lederer and Mór Kóhn, 'A vallástan tanításának módszere az izr. népiskolákban', *Izraelita tanügyi értesítő*, 8 (1883), 92–5.

The Reaction of the Polish Press to Baron Maurice de Hirsch's Foundation for Jewish Education in Galicia

AGNIESZKA FRIEDRICH

BARON MAURICE DE HIRSCH (1831–96) was one of the most important Jewish philanthropists of the late nineteenth century. One of the regions where he systematically engaged in charity was Galicia, whose Jewish population lived in particularly dire conditions. From the early 1880s he donated considerable sums to cover the needs of the people of Galicia (including, though not exclusively, its Jewish inhabitants),[1] and at the end of 1888 (the year after his son died, and Hirsch devoted himself almost entirely to charity work) he established a foundation whose aim was to develop a Jewish school system in Galicia.[2] Hirsch stressed that the schools he planned, although intended predominantly for Jewish students, were to be secular and he insisted that his foundation would not support 'exclusionary or purely religious tendencies'.[3] At the same time, he appealed to the Polish inhabitants of Galicia: 'Remove all the barriers, allow your Jewish brothers to enjoy all the rights and privileges of social life that you are enjoying, for only then you can achieve the unification that you openly state you would like to achieve. Proofs of that can be found in France and England.'[4] Despite Hirsch's statements, his generous donation, amounting to 12 million francs, provoked significant opposition. For entirely different reasons both Polish conservative circles and Orthodox Jewish groups protested against the establishment of the foundation. Operating in the difficult conditions of statelessness, Poles were afraid that the foundation, with the enormous amounts of money at its disposal, would engage in a large-scale process of buying land belonging to Poles which, in their view, constituted a guarantee of Polish national existence. Orthodox Jews, for their part, were wary

---

[1] See K. Rędziński, *Żydowskie szkolnictwo świeckie w Galicji w latach 1813–1918* (Częstochowa, 2000), 142–3.

[2] The foundation was officially registered by the authorities in Vienna on 2 January 1891 (see ibid. 144–89; S. Spitzer, *Maurycy baron Hirsch i jego działalność filantropijna* (Kraków, 1891), 33–52).

[3] Cited in Rędziński, *Żydowskie szkolnictwo świeckie w Galicji*, 144.   [4] Cited ibid.

of the advancement of secular Jewish education, which they saw as endangering traditional religious teaching.[5]

Hirsch tried to appease both groups, publishing a statement in early 1889 in which he explained that the goal of the foundation was to 'diminish the [Jews'] social exclusion, so that they can enjoy equality in matters of education, use the language of their fellow citizens, devote themselves to useful and productive endeavours, work in crafts and on the land, feel and think like citizens'.[6] Despite these assurances, Hirsch's foundation sparked a heated debate in the Polish press, both in Galicia itself and in the Kingdom of Poland. Particularly interesting was the reaction of Bolesław Prus, the leading commentator on social life in Warsaw. To understand Prus's critical reception of Hirsch's initiative requires an analysis of his attitude to the issue of vocational education for Jews in the years preceding the establishment of Hirsch's foundation.

Small-scale artisan activity was a common, low-income occupation among Jews. The work of tailors, umbrella-makers, and clockmakers was somewhat seasonal and such individuals frequently supplemented their income with other activities, often as hawkers. Few Jews had their own workshops. One of the most important reasons for this was the unwritten regulation that Jews could not be accepted into the guilds. Prus was aware of this state of affairs and saw it as discriminatory; however, he did not call for a radical solution to the problem, but merely advised Jews to be patient about a matter that he believed would be resolved satisfactorily sooner or later, writing in his article, 'Jews and the Question of the Guilds': 'It seems, then, that the question of accepting Jewish craftsmen into the guilds is merely a matter of time and it will happen sooner rather than later . . . After all, today, the biggest obstacle is not some kind of religious aversion, but the apathy of the guilds themselves.'[7] At the same time, Prus noted, with obvious satisfaction, all the positive changes in this area, including the organization of Jewish education in artisan trades.[8] Following the views of the English social theorist, Herbert Spencer,[9] whom he much admired, he saw it as very important to educate future craftsmen in special schools, where they would receive a more modern, all-round education than that acquired through the apprentice system. He set out his views as early as 1876, when he discussed the work of the High School for Trade, established a year earlier by Leopold Kronenberg.[10] He suggested that, along with

[5] Rędziński, *Żydowskie szkolnictwo świeckie w Galicji*, 144–5; cf. Spitzer, *Maurycy baron Hirsch*, 39–40.   [6] Cited in Rędziński, *Żydowskie szkolnictwo świeckie w Galicji*, 144.

[7] B. Prus, 'Żydzi wobec cechów', *Nowiny*, 1883, no. 72; see also id., 'Kronika tygodniowa', *Kurjer Warszawski*, 10 June 1883, in id., *Kroniki*, 20 vols. (Warsaw, 1953–70), vi. 137; id., 'Kronika tygodniowa', *Kurjer Warszawski*, 21 Mar. 1887, in id., *Kroniki*, x. 78.

[8] B. Prus, 'Kronika tygodniowa', *Kurjer Warszawski*, 2 Nov. 1884, in id., *Kroniki*, vii. 232.

[9] Cf. B. Prus, 'Kronika tygodniowa', *Kurjer Codzienny*, 6 Nov. 1887, in id., *Kroniki*, x. 224. Prus referred to one of the categories of Spencer's educational theory: teaching children how to earn their living by means of crafts and professional skills.

[10] B. Prus, in *Ateneum*, 7 July 1876, in id., *Kroniki*, ii. 520–3.

institutions of this type, it was necessary to create numerous schools at a lower level without which, in his view, it would be impossible to create a class of educated and efficient workers and craftsmen. His conviction of the need for such schools, which he insisted should be established in every district,[11] led him to express himself in drastic terms: 'Each year we fail to open such schools, we steal from the future and dig its grave.'[12]

It is therefore hardly surprising that he viewed critically the almost complete absence of such initiatives on the part of Poles, who, at the same time, observed with open resentment the creation of craft schools for young Jews. Prus's first observation on this topic was made on the occasion of what he described as the 'noble' initiative by Ludwik Natanson in establishing an elementary school for crafts that would educate children in such fields as shoemaking, tailoring, carpentry, locksmithing, and blacksmithing. This school, which admitted children regardless of their religious affiliation[13] and which was established by an assimilated Jew (which Prus failed to mention), was, however, exceptional. Meanwhile, as he argued, Jews 'had approached this problem right from the very beginning' and had funded several schools of this sort for young Jews seeking training in a craft. In addition, they had even founded an evening school to train adults in artisan trades.[14] The situation did not change in the following years, which in 1887 provoked Prus again to attack his compatriots: 'In our circles, even giving instruction on how to weave straw will meet with criminal charges; Jews, on the other hand, teach crafts in their schools with no accusations or arguments.'[15] In the same feuilleton, he announced the opening of a new Jewish craft school, this time providing training in textile production. In 1887 he also informed his readers about the opening of a craft school for Jewish boys in Mir in Navahrudak county[16] and in the following year about other schools opened by Natanson (for younger Jewish children).[17] Prus had a favourable view of Natanson, not only because he saw him as a man of action[18] but also because his ideas on Jewish integration were very close to his own. According to Natanson, 'the main task of the new [craft] schools is to move the masses of Israelites away from unproductive and usually harmful intermediate occupations and direct them towards the field of production.'[19]

Prus's reports on Jewish craft schools usually came with his own commentary.

[11] B. Prus, 'Kronika tygodniowa', *Kurjer Warszawski*, 8 Nov. 1879, in id., *Kroniki*, iv. 174.

[12] B. Prus, in *Ateneum*, 7 July 1876, in id., *Kroniki*, ii. 523.

[13] See B. Prus, 'Kronika tygodniowa', *Kurjer Warszawski*, 8 Nov. 1879, in id., *Kroniki*, ed. Szweykowski, iv. 173–5.

[14] B. Prus, 'Kronika tygodniowa', *Kurjer Warszawski*, 10 June 1883, in id., *Kroniki*, vi. 137.

[15] B. Prus, 'Kronika tygodniowa', *Kurjer Warszawski*, 1 Feb. 1887, in id., *Kroniki*, x. 28.

[16] B. Prus, 'Kronika tygodniowa', *Kurjer Warszawski*, 6 Nov. 1887, in id., *Kroniki*, x. 224.

[17] B. Prus, 'Kronika tygodniowa', *Kurjer Warszawski*, 19 Feb. 1888, in id., *Kroniki*, xi. 49–50.

[18] B. Prus, 'Kronika tygodniowa', *Kurjer Codzienny*, 21 Dec. 1890, in id., *Kroniki*, xii. 326–9.

[19] Statement at the inauguration of the Jewish crafts schools (*Kurjer Warszawski*, 5 Nov. 1879; cited in Z. Szweykowski, 'Przypisy', in Prus, *Kroniki*, iv. 537).

Since they reveal a lot about his approach to the question of craft schools as well as his general opinions about the Jewish question, they need to be examined in greater detail. In 1883 he wrote about the antisemitic weekly *Rola*:

What a great periodical! They condemn the wickedness of the Jews, but the Christian faults that undermine our future are politely overlooked. [They do not dare to] write to their own people: 'Look, you slouches, at the Jewish craft schools and start collecting funds for similar institutions for yourself . . . or otherwise in a few years we shall cry over Jewish domination in crafts as today we cry over Jewish domination in trade.'[20]

An article written in November 1887 employs the same kind of rhetoric. Describing additional craft schools funded by Jews, he addressed *Rola*, this time in the person of its editor-in-chief, Jan Jeleński:

Where are you, Mr Jeleński, that you fail to write anything about the new Semitic attack on Christians? Everywhere you look, Jews are educating masses of craftsmen and you fail to warn us about it. Is it because you would like some future antisemite to be able to lament about the incredible domination not only of Jewish 'capital' but also of Jewish 'work'?[21]

Two years later, taking Natanson's education in crafts as a model, he reminded his readers that there 'exists a legal solution developed by the state for similar schools', but then he added with irony and bitterness: 'Alas! We aesthetically educated Poles don't take advantage of it.'[22] Perhaps the best expression of Prus's opinion can be found in his statement from 1888, where he gave an account of new Jewish initiatives and suggested a vision of the immediate future:

Thanks to their intelligence and sacrifice, in a few years, the Jewish proletariat can produce, and certainly will produce, skilled craftsmen of various specializations, while we . . . we perhaps will be making efforts to find a place for our children in their *ḥeder*s. . . . This is because our capitalists are not concerned either with the teaching of crafts or with the fate of the working class.[23]

These quotations certainly illustrate the highly emotional nature of Prus's response to artisan education. Undoubtedly, he discerned the growing dispro-portion in interest in the matter from the two sides and, together with this, the danger of Poles in the future being gradually pushed out of yet another branch of the economy—after trade—or perhaps even more broadly, out of social life. He expressed this fear directly in a feuilleton of June 1883:

Jews—who are not accepted by guilds and are said to be very eager to learn crafts—imme-diately approached the matter correctly and are seriously considering opening craft schools—naturally, for their own kind. For this purpose, Mrs Petronela Bauman donated a house, several craft schools for young Jews have been opened, one evening school for adults,

[20] B. Prus, 'Kronika tygodniowa', *Kurjer Warszawski*, 10 June 1883, in id., *Kroniki*, vi. 138.
[21] B. Prus, 'Kronika tygodniowa', *Kurjer Codzienny*, 6 Nov. 1887, in id., *Kroniki*, x. 225.
[22] B. Prus, 'Kronika tygodniowa', *Kurjer Codzienny*, 21 Dec. 1890, in id., *Kroniki*, xii. 327.
[23] B. Prus, 'Kronika tygodniowa', *Kurjer Warszawski*, 1 Feb. 1887, in id., *Kroniki*, x. 28.

and, who knows, considering their well-known propensity for charity, they will probably open a university-level school.[24]

Worried by this state of affairs, he asked:

Has anyone considered what will happen when various skilled Jewish masters suddenly appear in the field of crafts, displaying thorough knowledge of their trade and technique? There is no doubt that with their skills in trade, they will soon become producers, while our craftsmen, educated in guilds, will be working for them.[25]

He then observed ironically: '*Rola* would have plenty of topics to address in their series of sermons, "What is to be done?"'[26]

In dealing with this issue, Prus's approach, typical of his journalism, used a tone and arguments very different from those employed in antisemitic rhetoric—indeed he often formulated his views as a polemic against the antisemites, as is clear in his exchanges with *Rola*. He avoided talk of Jewish conspiracies, accepted the right of Jews to open Jewish craft schools, approved of Jewish 'intelligence and sacrifice', and considered Jewish entrepreneurship a model for his fellow Polish citizens to follow. If Jews push us out of this field, he seemed to be saying, they will do it in an honest way, and only we will be to blame.

Prus's perspective changed significantly after the establishment of Hirsch's initiative in late 1888. This might seem surprising, for it would appear that Prus should have admired the project. Its goals were similar to his own: the spread of education, the encouragement of assimilation (since Polish was to be the official language of education), and the directing of at least some part of the Jewish population towards farming (a part of Hirsch's plan was to set up schools of agriculture). Nevertheless, Hirsch's plans provoked a harsh, though not immediate, rejection from Prus.

Prus first commented on Hirsch's initiative in *Kurjer Codzienny* on 2 December 1888.[27] The tone of this article was quite balanced and no different from what he had written before on the topic of Jewish craft schools. He saw the project as a 'highly reasonable and noble action' although he wondered whether it would not lead to the local population (that is, Poles and Ruthenians) being pushed out of the field of artisan trades. Again, he harshly criticized Poles, writing ironically that Hirsch's foundation was intending to use only the money squandered by Galician landowners abroad. Their wastefulness and recklessness had resulted in the fact that Hirsch's gigantic foundation found its Polish counterpart only in the far smaller foundation of Feliksa Maria Czarkowska, which, among its other goals, supported the provision of loans for Christians to open new workshops. Surprisingly, ignoring information available in the press[28] and his own knowledge of the

[24] B. Prus, 'Kronika tygodniowa', *Kurjer Warszawski*, 10 June 1883, in id., *Kroniki*, vi. 137.
[25] Ibid.   [26] Ibid.
[27] B. Prus, 'Kronika tygodniowa', *Kurjer Codzienny*, 2 Dec. 1888, in id., *Kroniki*, xi. 253–4.
[28] Cf. Szweykowski, 'Przypisy', in Prus, *Kroniki*, xi. 408.

matter,[29] Prus dealt only with that aspect of the work of Hirsch's foundation that concerned craft schools, completely omitting any mention of trade schools and agricultural schools. He adopted this same approach in his subsequent articles. This one-sided understanding of Hirsch's foundation determined his view of its proposals.

Before the new year, Prus addressed the topic again, again praising both Hirsch and the Alliance Israélite Universelle (AIU) that supported him and again criticizing the Poles, expressing the hope that 'among our "barons" there will emerge some as generous as Hirsch so that we can create at least as many professional schools as the Galician Jews will have!'[30]

A significant change came in a long article published in seven parts in *Kurjer Codzienny* in November 1889, with the very revealing title of 'Because of 12,000,000 Guldens'. The amount of Hirsch's donation provoked Prus into extended reflections on the Jewish question, and this is, in fact, his most important text on the topic.[31] Here, I will only examine those themes that concern directly economic matters, especially crafts and farming. However, before I do so, I would like to discuss the major change in Prus's opinions that emerged in the course of less than a year: between his first reaction to Hirsch's foundation and the articles of November 1889. Although initially Prus welcomed the donation as favourably as he had previously the foundation of Jewish craft schools in Poland, suddenly the entire process began to inspire serious reservations.

Firstly, he expressed doubt about the honesty of the intentions of the founder and argued:

We do not know . . . whose donation this actually is: whether it comes from the philanthropist Hirsch, who in memory of his deceased son supports his brothers in religion, or whether it comes from Baron Hirsch, the member of Alliance Israélite Universelle, who, together with Rothschild, is buying colonies for Jews in Canada. All this is not a clear matter, but some kind of dubious trickery.[32]

These doubts could have resulted from a discussion initiated earlier by the newspaper *Słowo* on an alleged appeal by the AIU to Galician Jews[33] in which the Jewish population was encouraged to take over the land, as well as professional positions in Galicia, and promised financial support for this task. Although this

[29] 'Baron Hirsch . . . donated *twelve million* francs for Jewish education, in particular, on teaching them crafts and opening workshops' (B. Prus, 'Kronika tygodniowa', *Kurjer Codzienny*, 24 Dec. 1888, in id., *Kroniki*, xi. 268 (emphasis original; Prus used 'francs' and 'gulden' interchangeably)).

[30] Ibid. 270.

[31] B. Prus, 'Z powodu 12,000,000 guldenów', *Kurjer Codzienny*, 6, 8, 14, 18, 20, 27, 30 Nov. 1889. That Prus saw this as a very important publication finds confirmation in that in his 'auto-bibliography', written in 1899 for Stefan Demby's *Album pisarzy polskich współczesnych* (Warsaw, 1901), he listed only three major pieces of journalism: *Szkic programu...*, the still unpublished *Najogólniejsze ideały Życiowe*, and 'Z powodu 12,000,000 guldenów' (cf. K. Tokarzówna, S. Fita, and Z. Szweykowski (eds.), *Bolesław Prus, 1847–1912: Kalendarz Życia i twórczości* (Warsaw, 1969), 543).

was an obvious forgery in which Prus did not believe,[34] it served him as a pretext to voice several sarcastic remarks about Jewish–Galician relations:

As far as the Jewish domination of Galicia is concerned, the manifesto of the Alliance Israélite Universelle provides no new guidelines and is a very clumsy interpretation of what is actually happening. After all, no Alliance Israélite Universelle existed when Jews attempted to take control of the Galician trade and of the flow of money by multiplying it through imposing very high interest rates, buying not only vast land properties but even small peasant farms and so on.[35]

Regardless of the anti-Jewish atmosphere provoked by the bogus AIU appeal, Prus's suspicions could also have been influenced by his generally unfavourable attitude towards emancipated, often wealthy, west European Jews. He gave this full expression in 'Because of 12,000,000 Guldens'. He seems to have been afraid of what he regarded as the excessive influence of the new Jewish elites on the public life of west European states. As he put it, 'what we are dealing with now is neither a "religion", nor a "nation", but a "state", which in the form of the Alliance Israélite Universelle is in the possession of both an energetic ministry of foreign affairs, as well as a wealthy treasury'.[36] In his view, the previous attempts to popularize education in crafts among the Jews were undertaken by emancipated local Jews. Prus was thus inclined to see them as a sign of an honest, though somewhat disquieting Jewish–Polish or Jewish–Christian competition, which Christians were losing because of their own faults and Jews were winning because of their virtues. Hirsch's initiative seemed rather to Prus a large-scale external intervention which would be bound to upset the already shaky balance. He described it in terms of a game of chess between 'Arya' and 'Semita'. What was at stake in the game was the position of the bourgeoisie who would be either 'Aryan' or 'Semitic'. The game was long and tiring, and both sides were left with only a few pieces, when suddenly Semita was given 'a castle worth 12 million guldens'. The angry Arya addressed Hirsch: 'What you are doing is disloyal and if you wish to continue like this, I will stop playing with your brother.'[37] This statement should be treated as an expression of emotions shared by Prus with wider circles of Polish public opinion.

Somewhat independently from these fears and stemming at least partly from strong emotions, Prus verbalized his fundamental reservations as to the practical impact of the foundation. Whereas previously he had been worried that Jews, by pushing Christians out of crafts, would make it more difficult for Poles and

---

[32] Prus, 'Z powodu 12,000,000 guldenów', pt. 7, *Kurjer Codzienny*, 30 Nov. 1889.

[33] Cf. Szweykowski, 'Przypisy', in Prus, *Kroniki*, xii. 371–2; see also P. [P. H. Peltyn], 'Humor antysemicki', *Izraelita*, 25 Oct. 1889, pp. 339–40.

[34] B. Prus, 'Kronika tygodniowa', *Kurjer Codzienny*, 21 Oct. 1889, in id., *Kroniki*, xii. 73–4.

[35] Ibid. 75. Prus's statement met with outrage at *Izraelita*, where he was called an antisemite. The editor of *Izraelita* added in a conciliatory manner: 'We would like to believe that this nastiness was merely an accidental remark coming from an otherwise rational writer and clear-headed observer' (P., 'Humor antysemicki').

[36] Prus, 'Z powodu 12,000,000 guldenów', pt. 2, *Kurjer Codzienny*, 8 Nov. 1889.   [37] Ibid. 7.

Ruthenians to earn a living, he was now concerned about the threat that Jewish expansion would pose to the Jews themselves. He stated that Hirsch's donation—which he understood as support for the Jewish orientation towards crafts—would further strengthen the belief that Jews could only be part of the middle class. In Prus's opinion, this belief was 'not only a source of failure for Christians but also . . . the source of misery, sickness and blight for Jews'[38] and would lead to 'a completely faulty Jewish social structure'.[39] In his eyes, it was the basis for the tensions and conflicts between Christians and Jews, rather than—as the anti-semites suggested—their race or religion.[40]

Prus spoke openly in favour of a social structure where particular fields of work would be distributed evenly. Jews should conform to this general rule, or else, in his opinion, the Jewish question would never be solved.[41] Instead, he claimed, Jews were too eager to work in particular trades and neglected others. They tended to choose 'easier, more profitable, and more privileged professions', avoiding those that were 'the hardest and those offering the smallest possibility of occupying a privileged position'.[42] The former he defined as middle-class professions, includ-ing crafts, while the latter was predominantly farming the land. This, in his view, was the central issue. In his words, 'Poles, who constitute 75 per cent of the country's population, should constitute 75 per cent in trade and among the educated, for this is their natural right, as it is your [the Jews'] natural right to be a nation and to have your own farmers.'[43] As a consequence, Prus argued that Jews should be encouraged by all possible means to work the land. He emphasized that he did not mean the occupations that Jews had traditionally undertaken in the countryside, such as leasing or trading farm products and definitely not running taverns, dealing in usury, or stealing horses, but actual 'work on the land', such as 'ploughing, harrowing, sowing, threshing, and breeding cattle . . . for only such tasks are actual farming'.[44] Accordingly, he argued that Hirsch would have done better if he had directed his generosity not towards Jewish craft schools, which would only increase conflict and deepen the faulty character of the social struc-ture—in his view they would 'put a Semitic head on the Slavic body'[45]—but to-wards agricultural schools. These, he claimed, would in the course of forty years educate around 90,000 farmers and farmhands, enough to create a farmer class among Galician Jews.

Prus estimated that this would ensure a good life in the countryside for around

[38] Prus, 'Z powodu 12,000,000 guldenów', pt. 2, *Kurjer Codzienny*, 8 Nov. 1889, 5.
[39] Ibid. 6.   [40] See Elkan, 'Z Życia', *Izraelita*, 1 Nov. 1889, p. 354.
[41] Prus's propensity for 'arithmetic sociology', according to which the proportions of population should be directly reflected in the proportions of employment in particular professions, was met with scathing criticism (see A. Świętochowski, 'Liberum veto', *Prawda*, 1889, no. 44, in id., *Liberum veto*, 2 vols. (Warsaw, 1976), ii. 45–6).
[42] Prus, 'Z powodu 12,000,000 guldenów', pt. 6, *Kurjer Codzienny*, 27 Nov. 1889.
[43] Ibid.   [44] Ibid.   [45] Ibid. 7.

420,000 Jews,[46] who would not have to live in crowded cities. Honest work in the country would additionally turn Jews away from tasks they traditionally performed in villages which were socially harmful, such as running taverns, engaging in usury, and handling stolen goods. At the same time, the space vacated by the Jews in the towns would be taken by hundreds of thousands of landless peasants, who thus would not have to emigrate in search of a better life overseas. These favourable results would follow the use of Hirsch's funds to create farm schools. Prus did not reject the possibility of the simultaneous opening of craft and trade schools; however, he thought that they should educate Christians, while Jews should be admitted only in numbers representing their proportion in society, that is, according to his estimation, about 14 per cent.

This was Prus's great social project formulated in response to Hirsch's foundation and meant to heal social divisions first in Galicia and then probably also in other Polish lands. It is clearly unrealistic, not to say hostile to the Jews. In his calculations, Prus not only based his analysis on false premises but clearly ignored reality. The ideas he presented in *Kurjer Codzienny* can only be seen as an example of wishful thinking. The quixotic idealism they contain is quite surprising, considering that Prus consistently tried to present himself as an advocate of reason and ridiculed what he described as Polish 'naive idealism'. Prus's project is clearly predicated on the typically positivist belief in education as a comprehensive solution to all social problems as well as on a reversion to the Enlightenment view that the Jews could be 'improved' by settling them on the land.

Prus's contemporaries viewed his project as inconsistent and unrealistic. Wincenty Kosiakiewicz, a columnist for *Gazeta Polska*, argued that it was difficult to imagine that thousands of Jews, shaped for generations in urban conditions and used to earning their living through trade, would suddenly become farmers. Moreover, he was realistic enough to notice that even if this happened, those who did so would never be able to establish themselves on individual farms but would merely join the landless rural proletariat.[47]

Similar arguments were raised by Aleksander Świętochowski, a liberal journalist and celebrated writer. In an article published in *Prawda* in November 1889, he argued that it was impossible to force Jews to abandon their right to choose what profession they wished to pursue, just as it was impossible to force Polish farmers to abandon agriculture and take up crafts. Prus's concepts were seen by Świętochowski as the product of a mechanical, strictly arithmetic understanding of society: 'How can one suggest that, since Jews constitute 10 per cent of the entire

[46] Admittedly, Prus did not simply translate the number of educated Jewish farmers into the number of Jews living from farming, yet in a different place in the same essay he did use the number of 420,000 people (ibid. 7). He did not explain his basis for such estimation, but he probably made use of a standard rate of four or five people per family.

[47] I recreated Kosiakiewicz's opinion on the basis of 'Kronika', *Gazeta Polska*, 1889, no. 272, in Szweykowski, 'Przypisy', in Prus, *Kroniki*, xii. 379–80.

population, they should constitute 10 per cent of doctors or craftsmen? . . . Is society a mixture prepared from a recipe or a chemical compound made according to some formula? Is it reasonable to rely on the ratio of its elements to determine arithmetically the ratio of their appropriate development?'[48] In his view, the actual establishment of these proportions could only be implemented through the introduction of exceptional legislation that would undermine the existing legal system. He noted that according to the laws of the Habsburg empire all individuals were allowed to donate funds to education and anyone willing to limit Jewish rights in this respect would have to question their equality before the law established by the Austrian constitution of 1868. Świętochowski did not formulate a clear stance about the most important problem, namely, whether the actions of Hirsch's foundation would be beneficial or detrimental. He even accepted the possibility that its activity could be deleterious to the Christian population of Galicia. This is suggested both in his articles of November 1889 and in a piece published a year earlier, in which he agreed that Prus was right to suspect that Hirsch's donation could have had a negative impact on the situation of the Polish and Ruthenian population of Galicia.[49] Regardless, however, of these reservations, Świętochowski was, above all, hostile to discrimination and a proponent of the rule of law, as is clear from his observations on the legality of Prus's proposals.

Although Prus and Świętochowski differed on this issue, both were in agreement at least on one thing: the Polish nobility, or more broadly the Polish privileged classes, were hardly willing to counter Hirsch's generous gift with an at-least-comparable donation of their own. Świętochowski allowed himself to criticize them for this lack of initiative: 'all our Hirsches of every kind, including the aristocrats, somehow fail to be affected by similar fits of generosity'.[50] Some time before, in his first article on Hirsch's foundation, Świętochowski had made an even more derisive comment on the difference between the generous Jew and the tight-fisted Polish nobleman: 'The generous donation of this selfish Jew casts a terrible shadow on our "kinglets", who argue about some dozen or some tens of roubles of tax imposed on them for a folk school. The disgrace of this comparison should immediately be dispelled with a comparable donation.'[51] The demand for an adequate response from privileged groups in Poland was also voiced by *Rola*. This was the only issue on which this journal agreed with Prus and Świętochowski, whom it considered 'philo-semites' and 'courtiers of the Jews'. At the beginning of 1889 Jeleński wrote: 'The Jewish magnate throws millions at the Jews; he throws them with utter cold-bloodedness, knowing that they will be used for the more effective crushing, flaying of Christians.' He then put the following words in Hirsch's mouth: 'Are you so well off? . . . Will you be worse off with my foundation? Well, then, defend yourselves! You have your own riches to protect you!' Jeleński's

---

[48] Świętochowski, 'Liberum veto', *Prawda*, 1889, no. 44.

[49] A. Świętochowski, 'Ofiara Hirscha i uwagi Prusa', *Prawda*, 1888, no. 49.

[50] Ibid.   [51] Świętochowski, 'Liberum veto', *Prawda*, 1888, no 28, in *Liberum veto*, i. 692.

response was pessimistic: 'Yes, we do, but what do they say? What do they, the Christian magnates, say to this philanthropy of Jewish wealthy stock brokers?'[52]

Apart from this critique of the wealthy Polish classes, there is hardly any resemblance between the positions of *Rola* and those of Prus and Świętochowski. Unlike Świętochowski, Jeleński was not concerned with the discrimination inherent in Prus's postulates. Basing his remarks on antisemitic stereotypes, he found Prus's main postulate—directing Jews towards farming—unrealistic, arguing that Jews were incapable of working the land and were also known for fraud in running their farms, citing examples from the Kingdom of Poland.[53] His pessimism in this matter is the more striking in that some ten years before he had also proposed projects to settle Jews on the land.[54]

A hostile approach to Prus's articles was also taken by the anonymous author of an article in *Przegląd Tygodniowy*,[55] who rejected the possibility of turning Jews into farmers by arguing that the implementation of such a project would be difficult to achieve because, while transforming lower elements of society into higher ones was not uncommon (for example peasants into bourgeois), transformations in the reverse direction were almost impossible.[56] He also criticized Prus's line of argument, accusing him of gaps in his knowledge of sociology, ethnology, and anthropology, as well as questioning the very relevance of the statistical data he used. Similarly, Michał Kolasiński accused Prus of a weak command of sociology, although he did not analyse Prus's project directly.[57] In contrast to Prus, he saw Hirsch's gift to Galicia in a positive light.[58] In response to both articles, Prus maintained his position and argued that only directing Jews towards farming would offer them a chance to organize themselves into a '"normal society" [which] would secure their existence, free them from their living in terrible lower class conditions and perhaps even undermine the common aversion to them'.[59] Prus's reply did not convince the journalist of *Przegląd Tygodniowy*, who responded ironically: 'It is well known that Prus was a writer of humorous texts for a long time before he decided to set sail onto the dangerous sea of sociology. For this reason, his marriage with science has produced merely humorous children.'[60] This discussion was also joined by the Jewish integrationist weekly, *Ojczyzna*, based in

[52] J. Jeleński, 'Magnaci i — magnaci', *Rola*, 1889, no. 1, p. 2.

[53] Kamienny [J. Jeleński], 'Na posterunku', *Rola*, 1889, no. 49, pp. 738–9.

[54] J. Jeleński, *O skierowaniu Żydów...* (Warsaw, 1873).

[55] 'Uczciwy antisemita', *Przegląd Tygodniowy*, 14 Dec. 1889, pp. 625–6, 21 Dec. 1889, pp. 637–9.

[56] Three years later Prus attempted to fight against this opinion (see 'Kronika tygodniowa', *Kurjer Codzienny*, 8 May 1892, in id., *Kroniki*, xiii. 203).

[57] Człowiek Szczery [Michał Kolasiński], *Polityczne samobójstwo*, i: *Antysemityzm zgubą* (Kraków 1889), 40; see Tokarzówna, Fita, and Szweykowski (eds.), *Bolesław Prus, 1847–1912*, 397.

[58] Człowiek Szczery, *Polityczne samobójstwo*, i. 32, 45.

[59] B. Prus, 'Kronika tygodniowa', *Kurjer Codzienny*, 29 Dec. 1889, in id., *Kroniki*, ed. Szweykowski, xii. 117.   [60] 'Jeszcze uczciwy antisemita!', *Przegląd Tygodniowy*, 11 Jan. 1890, pp. 19–21.

Lviv.[61] It took a favourable view of Prus's call for Jewish agricultural settlement, but noted that its implementation would require broad financial support, as well as a long-term effort dedicated to the gradual adjustment of the Jewish population to the new situation.[62]

Prus returned to the issue of Hirsch's foundation in 1896, on the occasion of his death. This time, he was eager to praise Hirsch. He recalled with special favour Hirsch's project to settle the Jews in Argentina and also revised his stance on the much-criticized Galician foundation. Recalling the circumstances of the never-executed donation for Galicia, Prus mentioned his past reservations, but claimed that this foundation would not have posed such a threat if it had found a reasonable counterbalance in the generosity of the Galician magnates.[63] He observed: 'This is a sad situation that when Jews are offered millions, Poles find it unacceptable. Yet Hirsch did not cause this kind of state of affairs, so this rather dangerous donation he made deserves respect.'[64] Prus's opinion of Hirsch called into question his general liberal principles. Clearly, he viewed the work of the Jewish millionaire from two perspectives at once: he criticized those actions that could have strengthened what he regarded as the faulty Jewish social structure, yet he praised those that could have led to an improvement of this structure, which is why he considered it crucial to direct Jews towards agriculture. For this reason the project of settling Jews on the land in Argentina met with his full acceptance, while the establishment of craft schools raised his doubts.

Prus's deliberations on Hirsch's foundation and its potential effects on the situation of the Jewish population in Galicia, as well as Polish–Jewish relations in general, raise many questions about his view of the Jewish situation in Poland. Not surprisingly, many contemporary statements on the foundation were formulated in reaction to Prus's articles. This does not mean that it was Prus who set the tone for the entire debate, as is clear from the articles on this topic published in *Rola*. Prus often set himself up as an adversary of *Rola*, on some occasions taking up real, on others imagined, polemics. He was right to perceive the stance of this weekly as being fundamentally different from his own. *Rola* was an openly antisemitic publication. It is hardly surprising, then, that Hirsch's foundation was considered by it as yet another manifestation of a co-ordinated Jewish offensive directed

---

[61] Cf. W. Feldman, *Asymilatorzy, syjoniści, Polacy: Z powodu przełomu w stosunkach Żydowskich w Galicji* (Kraków, 1893), 9, 12–16.

[62] [P.R.], 'Z powodu artykułów Bolesława Prusa', *Ojczyzna*, 1890, nos. 2–4; cited in Tokarzówna, Fita, and Szweykowski (eds.), *Bolesław Prus, 1847–1912*, 399.

[63] In 1891 Prus voiced a similar opinion: 'there is no money . . . that could counterbalance the 12 million francs that Hirsch donated for the Jewish crafts schools. A French or English Jew, who makes his money in Turkey, has more love for Galician Jews than the Galician noblemen, who make their money in Galicia, have for Polish and Ruthenian peasants!' ('Kronika tygodniowa', *Kurjer Codzienny*, 1 Feb. 1891, in id., *Kroniki*, xiii. 19).

[64] B. Prus, 'Kronika tygodniowa', *Kurjer Codzienny*, 3 May 1896, in id., *Kroniki*, xiv. 242.

against the Christian identity of Poland and Europe. It was characterized as a 'Trojan horse' and 'poisoned apple'.[65]

The most extensive reflections on Hirsch's donation were published in *Rola* by an anonymous author, Dr S.P. In a long, three-part article entitled '"Baron" Hirsch's Foundation', he described the issue at some length from an antisemitic perspective.[66] The very title, with Hirsch's aristocratic title in inverted commas, set the tone, intended as it was to discredit Hirsch by suggesting that he had no claim to this noble title. The author then claimed that for many years Galician Jews had been the beneficiaries of a specific socio-economic situation in Galicia. The population of Galicia was not very numerous, there was more money in circulation (due to the compensation paid to landowners for the abolition of compulsory labour service in 1848), there was a better market for grain, Jews could buy forests (according to the author, for 'next to nothing'), there were no legal regulations regarding usury, while Christians were largely 'passive' and 'apathetic',[67] limiting their professional activity to traditional farming and avoiding any engagement in trade or industry. In the author's view, this favourable situation for the Jews began to change gradually in the late 1870s, when new regulations regarding usury were introduced and when the centuries-old laws on the sale of liquor were abolished, causing many Jews to lose their source of income. Prices of agricultural products dropped, and this forced the Christian rural population to start taking other jobs and to compete with Galician Jews who had previously held a dominant position, particularly in the field of trade. These circumstances led to the situation in which the previously favourable situation of Galician Jews had deteriorated significantly, which was also aggravated by the increase in the number of Jews, resulting from natural growth as well as from the influx of Jews from other regions, such as Romania. All this resulted in Galician Jews suddenly being 'close to starvation'. This, claimed Dr S.P., motivated Baron Hirsch to take action.

This largely rational analysis was combined, however, with the antisemitic view that improving the economic status of Jews in Galicia would necessarily entail 'taking over the positions of Christians in crafts and ownership of land'.[68] In the view of the author, Hirsch created his foundation 'for purely aggressive, combative purposes, to provide the Jews in Galicia . . . with means for a more successful action against its local population'.[69] Dr S.P. was also sceptical about Polish hopes that Hirsch's schools would contribute to the assimilation of Galician Jews into Polish society. He argued that Hirsch's foundation was a purely Jewish initiative,

---

[65] Dr P., 'Sprawa Żydowska w Galicji', pt. 4, *Rola*, 1890, no. 40, p. 665. Most probably this is the same author as Dr S.P.

[66] Dr S.P., 'Fundacya "barona" Hirscha', pt. 3, *Rola*, 1891, no. 9, p. 130.   [67] Ibid.   [68] Ibid.

[69] Ibid. Several months before, the same thought was expressed in *Rola* in a more detailed manner. 'After having appropriated all the trade and industry, after having ruined large landowners and buying out hundreds of land properties, Jews now turned their greedy eye towards our crafts, up to now practised only by petit bourgeoisie' (Dr P., 'Sprawa Żydowska w Galicji', pt. 4, p. 665).

which was not significantly modified by the existence of a few non-Jewish trustees within it or assurances about providing access to these schools to Christian students. Moreover, even if the liberal Poles' hopes for assimilation were to be realized, this would have posed an even bigger threat. 'A dirty, uneducated Jew is repellent and dangerous only to the weakest of social organisms, that is, peasants; on the other hand, a "civilized" Jew, smooth and proficient in the Polish language, becomes a true threat to society, for he can sneak in anywhere, take it all, poison everything with his materialist-cynical venom.'[70] The author followed in the footsteps of Jeleński, who at the beginning of 1889, that is, shortly after Hirsch's foundation had officially been announced, wrote:

Whatever our independents [liberal journalists] . . . eager to kneel before the power and the gold argue, for all those who see clearly and think straight, the actual, real goal, and object of the foundation will be more than absolutely obvious: the final destruction and subjugation of the Galician 'goys', turning them into a bunch of hired servants, dogsbodies for the Jews. This is the plan of the 'noble benefactor' who offers Galicia his 'generous donation' . . . The country at large will not gain anything, but the Jewish population will gain new strengths to persecute Christian citizens.[71]

Even the birth of Hirsch's plans for a foundation provoked a heated, even violent discussion in the Polish press. What was revealed in its course was both the support for this initiative (largely in the Polish-language Jewish press which has not been discussed here), as well its powerful rejection. An apt summary of the reactions of the Polish press, as well as a record of the intense emotions aroused by the debate, can be found in the observation of Aleksander Świętochowski:

Because of the 12-million [gulden] donation by Baron Hirsch for Jewish schools in Galicia, there erupted a sudden polemic between newspapers, which soon enough gave vent to pro-semitic and antisemitic sentiments. As long as both sides are hardly reluctant to make use of disgusting insults, muddy accusations, suggestions neither serious nor reasonable, that is, as long as blind and wild emotions are having a dog fight here, I shall not enter this dispute either as an arbiter or as a backer.[72]

[70] Dr S.P., 'Fundacya "barona" Hirscha', pt. 2, *Rola*, 1891, no. 8, p. 116. The vision presented here follows completely the anti-assimilation line promoted by *Rola*. In 1883, the first year of the magazine's existence, Teodor Jeske-Choiński, the main representative of Polish antisemitism and one of the major collaborators of *Rola*, wrote: 'If you are a Jew, be a Jew. We prefer a dark Orthodox Jew than a civiliza-tional zero, for one believes in something, is something, while the other gives no guarantee' (cited in Z. Borzymińska, *Dzieje Żydów w Polsce: Wybór tekstów źródłowych. XIX wiek* (Warsaw 1994), 95).

[71] Jeleński, 'Magnaci i — magnaci', 2.

[72] Świętochowski, 'Liberum veto', *Prawda*, 1889, no 44, in *Liberum veto*, ii. 44–5.

A Story within a Story

The First Russian-Language Jewish History Textbooks, 1880–1900

VASSILI SCHEDRIN

> We should want a young Jewish man to know, although in brief form, the *entire* history of his people: to understand it and reflect on it. Then much would be revealed to him in the surrounding reality, in the spiritual and social life of his own nation.
>
> SIMON DUBNOW, Uchebnik evreiskoi istorii dlya evreiskogo yunoshestva

DESCRIBING his father's bookcase in their St Petersburg home, Osip Mandelstam wrote: 'I always remember the lower shelf as chaotic: the books were not standing upright side by side but lay like ruins. . . . This was the Judaic chaos thrown into the dust.'[1] The reddish volumes of the Pentateuch were shelved there along with 'a Russian history of the Jews written in the clumsy, shy language of a Russian-speaking Talmudist'.[2] Scholars of Mandelstam—Russian poet and 'autobiographical Jew'—identify this history book as either a study by Ilya Orshansky[3] or the Russian translation of the best-selling *History of the Jews* by Heinrich Graetz.[4] In fact, by 1900, the approximate year of Mandelstam's recollection, there were at least five publications that could have been described as a history of the Jews in the language of 'a Russian-speaking Talmudist' and could have been on the lower shelf of the poet's father's bookcase: the first volume of Graetz's *History of the Jews*, books by Mark Nemzer and Solomon Minor, and two books by Simon Dubnow.[5] Whichever book it actually was, the 'Russian history of the Jews'

---

[1] O. Mandelstam, *The Noise of Time: Selected Prose*, trans. C. Brown (Chicago, 1993), 78.   [2] Ibid.

[3] I. G. Orshansky, *Russkoe zakonodatel'stvo o evreyakh: Ocherki i issledovaniya* (St Petersburg, 1877).

[4] H. Graetz, *Istoriya evreev ot drevneishikh vremen do nastoyashchego*, trans. and ed. M. Ya. Khashkes, 5 vols. (Moscow, 1880–4) (incomplete); trans. O. Inber, 12 vols. (Odessa, 1904–8); Germ. orig.: *Geschichte der Juden von den ältesten Zeiten bis auf die Gegenwart*, 11 vols. (Leipzig, 1853–75); see M. Stanislawski, *Autobiographical Jews: Essays in Jewish Self-Fashioning* (Seattle, 2004), 93–4.

[5] H. Graetz, *Istoriya evreev*, i: *Istoriya evreev ot zaklyucheniya Talmuda do protsvetaniya evreisko-ispanskoi kul'tury* (Moscow, 1880); M. Nemzer, *Istoriya evreiskogo naroda (ot pereseleniya Evreev v Vavilon do razrusheniya vtorogo khrama) dlya obuchayushchikhsya Zakonu evreiskoi very v gimnaziyakh i*

represented an integral story within a story 'of the spiritual efforts of the entire family'.[6] According to Osip, in the case of his father, Emil Mandelstam—an escapee from the traditional Jewish world, a maskil-autodidact, and successful Russian merchant—this history might have paradoxically played a role both in the father's acculturation ('inoculating . . . [him] with alien blood') and in building a new sense of belonging to his people, or, rather, to his 'nation' ('In a fit of national contrition they went as far as hiring a real Jewish teacher for me.'[7]) Osip himself was very confused by the version of Jewish history taught to him by the private Jewish tutor. He recalled that the tutor's 'literate Russian speech sounded false' to him and that, while the tutor displayed striking 'national Jewish pride' during the lessons, he cautiously 'hid his pride when he went out in the street'. For these reasons Osip 'did not believe' his history teacher.[8]

However, the books by Nemzer, Minor, and Dubnow—as textbooks, tools of self-education, and popular histories—profoundly influenced the souls and minds of Mandelstam's contemporaries—the whole generation of Russian Jews who themselves made Jewish history in twentieth-century Russia and beyond. The stories recounted in these histories shaped the national consciousness of this generation and thus also shaped Jewish life in the modern world. In 1938 Lazar Kaganovich, a Bolshevik leader of the USSR, sternly told the Moscow State Yiddish Theatre (Gosudarstvennyi evreiskii teatr; GOSET) to present plays about the 'historical' Jewish courage and the rebellious spirit of the heroic national past. 'Where are the Maccabees? Where is Bar Kokhba?' he asked emphatically.[9] In the 1930s and 1940s Solomon Mikhoels, GOSET's principal star and unofficial leader of the Soviet Jews, planned a production of a 'historical' play about the sixteenth-century 'Jewish prince' David Reubeni. Mikhoels dreamed of playing Reubeni as an early Jewish nationalist, a 'political figure . . . a wild beast in international politics'.[10]

This chapter will focus on these four influential Russian-language textbooks on Jewish history. It will analyse their authors, goals, structures, sources, methodologies, narratives, and impacts on readers, but first and foremost, it will call attention to the key stories conveyed by these accounts.[11]

---

evreiskikh kazennykh uchilishchakh (Vilna, 1880); S. Minor (trans. and ed.), *Rukovodstvo k prepodavaniyu istorii evreiskogo naroda ot samykh drevnikh do noveishikh vremeni s kratkim ocherkom geografii Palestiny dlya evreiskikh uchilishch. Kratkii istoricheskii ocherk o evreyakh v Pol'she, Litve i Rossii* (Moscow, 1880); 2nd edn (Moscow, 1881); S. M. Dubnow (trans. and ed.), *Evreiskaya istoriya ot kontsa bibleiskogo perioda do nastoyashchego vremeni*, 2 vols. (Odessa, 1896–7); id., *Uchebnik evreiskoi istorii dlya evreiskogo yunoshestva*, 3 vols. (Odessa, 1898–9).

[6] Mandelstam, *The Noise of Time*, 78.
[7] Ibid.   [8] Ibid.   [9] Y. Sheyn, *Arum moskver yidishn teater* (Paris, 1964), 148.
[10] K. L. Rudnitskii (ed.), *Mikhoels: Stat'i, besedy, rechi. Stat'i i vospominaniya o Mikhoelse* (Moscow, 1981), 291.
[11] A recent study examined ten textbooks used in Jewish religion classes in Russian high schools from the 1870s to the 1890s, focusing on the authors' approaches to teaching Judaism as religion (E. R.

JEWISH HISTORY IN THE CURRICULUM OF
THE MODERN JEWISH SCHOOL

In the second half of the nineteenth century the reform and modernization of traditional Jewish education was among the key priorities of Russian official policy towards the Jews, as well as one of the most controversial and divisive issues of internal Jewish communal politics. In the 1840s the Russian Ministry of National Enlightenment under Count Sergei Uvarov had launched an ambitious reform project that resulted in the establishment of a network of state-sponsored Jewish elementary schools (*kazennye evreiskie uchilishcha*) and two institutions that served as both secondary schools and rabbinic seminaries in Zhitomir and Vilna. Traditional Russian Jews in the Pale of Settlement regarded these schools with distrust and even hostility. Jewish parents were afraid to enrol their children in them, believing that the primary goal of the official reform of Jewish education was the wholesale Christianization and Russification of the younger generation of Russian Jews. As a result, by the mid-1870s many of these schools, including the rabbinic seminaries, were officially deemed unsuccessful and closed down. However, Uvarov's reform of Jewish education had an impact on a small, yet important segment of Russian Jewry. The secular Russian-language curriculum studied in the *kazennye evreiskie uchilishcha* allowed for the students' acculturation and social integration into the Russian intelligentsia and bourgeoisie.

Forty years later the reform of Jewish education was revisited by the Russian government, along with other important issues of official Jewish policy. In 1887 it was the focus of the inter-ministerial Most High Commission on Re-examination of the Laws on the Jews (1883–8), dubbed the Palen Commission after its chair, Count Konstantin Palen. The government made a new attempt to reform and modernize traditional Jewish education. The new policy was no longer to be implemented through state-sponsored schools, alien and untrustworthy to most traditional Jews. Instead, the emphasis was to be placed on modernizing the academic curriculum of traditional Jewish educational institutions, *heder*s and yeshivas, which would now be officially recognized. This new curriculum was the focus of lengthy deliberations of the official Jewish experts invited by the Palen Commission.

These experts were drawn from the elite strata of Russian Jewish society. They included Baron Goratsii Gintsburg, Samuil Polyakov, and Abram Varshavsky, leading entrepreneurs and the wealthiest of Russia's Jews; Dr Avram Drabkin,

Adler, 'Reinventing Religion: Jewish Religion Textbooks in Russian Gymnasia', *Journal of Jewish Education*, 77/2 (2011), 141–56). A comparison of Russian and Hebrew Jewish history textbooks would yield an additional perspective on the teaching of Jewish history in contemporary Jewish schools. However, it is beyond the scope of this chapter. For an analysis of Hebrew Jewish history textbooks developed in the same time period, see D. A. Porat, 'The Nation Revised: Teaching the Jewish Past in the Zionist Present (1890–1913)', *Jewish Social Studies*, N.S. 13/1 (2006), 59–86.

government rabbi (*kazennyi ravvin*) of St Petersburg; and Dr Nikolai Bakst and Dr Adam Girshgorn, both medical doctors. In their opinion, the officially approved 'minimal essential curriculum of special Jewish disciplines for elementary Jewish school [*ḥeder*]' should include Jewish history, including 'biblical history' and 'major phenomena of Jewish history'.[12] The experts expressed the common belief that Jewish history should be one of the main subjects of study, along with Hebrew reading and writing, liturgy, Bible, and everyday and holiday rituals. The foundational subjects and key texts of traditional Jewish education, the Mishnah and Talmud, were not to be included in the 'minimal essential curriculum', but, in the experts' opinion, they could be studied as elective subjects.[13] The experts' emphasis on the study of Jewish history as a replacement for rabbinic literature in the core curriculum of traditional Jewish education prompted an emotional response from traditional Russian Jews, who were well aware of the experts' deliberations and did not hesitate to petition the Palen Commission. One such petition, signed by representatives of Jews from Vilna, called the decision of the government a 'grave mistake', which would 'completely eliminate [the study of Talmud] and replace [it] with plain instruction in the biblical history of Jewish people'.[14] The petitioners argued that the study of the Talmud was fundamental to the maintenance and transmission of traditional Jewish values, including religious piety, respect for the law, and loyalty to the government. And, they concluded, 'if there were no Talmud, Jews would long ago have become the worst kind of rationalists . . . harmful socialists and political agitators'.[15]

Apparently, the commission seriously considered the opinions of both the experts and the petitioners. While the question of the balance between Jewish history and Talmud in the core curriculum of elementary Jewish schools remained unresolved, the academic programme of the planned rabbinic institute, adopted by the Palen Commission, included both 'the Talmud (Babylonian and Jerusalem)' and 'history of the Jews in relation to the history of Jewish literature and [to the development of] Jewish religious outlook'.[16]

The official Jewish experts of the Palen Commission also paid much attention to the language of instruction and to special textbooks for students of Jewish subjects. Gintsburg pointed out that the traditional Jewish educational system could hardly be regulated. In his words, 'Jewish faith had never been dogmatized. [The Jews] have neither catechism, nor school textbooks. The laws of the Jewish faith are studied using original sources. This type of instruction cannot be circumscribed by an [academic] programme or limited by a certain amount of lectures and [study] hours.'[17] Gintsburg believed that this problem could be solved through the publication of 'the original sources, Jewish religious books' with a Russian translation

---

[12] Rossiiskii gosudarstvennyi istoricheskii arkhiv, St Petersburg, f. 821, op. 8, d. 246: Highest Commission for the Re-examination of the Laws on the Jews, materials regarding the reformation of elementary, secondary, and higher education of the Jews, 21 May 1887 – 12 Jan. 1890, fos. 68ᵛ, 86ᵛ, 94ᵛ.

[13] Ibid., fos. 68ʳ–68ᵛ.   [14] Ibid. fo. 164ʳ.   [15] Ibid.   [16] Ibid., fo. 216ᵛ.   [17] Ibid., fo. 46ʳ.

prepared by a 'competent assembly' of academic experts.[18] He also recommended the gradual replacement of 'Jewish jargon' (Yiddish) with Russian as the principal language of instruction in the study of religion and other Jewish subjects.[19]

The first Russian-language works on Jewish history appeared in the 1860s and 1870s. These pioneering studies dealt with many facets—anthropological, linguistic, and legal—of Jewish history in Russia from the eleventh to the nineteenth centuries. Their authors, the official Jewish expert Moisei Berlin, the collection curator of the Imperial Public Library Avraham Harkavy, and the independent lawyer Ilya Orshansky, sought to introduce Jewish history and the current status of Russian Jews to the Russian-reading public.[20]

In the 1880s the pressing need to modernize Jewish education, articulated both by Jews and Russian officialdom, demanded a new type of historical work: a universal Jewish history (whether academic or popular, original or translated) in Russian. Several histories meant to satisfy this demand, such as the synthetic works by Nemzer, Minor, and Dubnow examined in this chapter, were conceived of and prepared with the needs of modern Jewish schools in mind—as school textbooks, teaching aids, and material for self-education.

The works on Jewish history produced by scholars of Wissenschaft des Judentums, the nineteenth-century German attempt to investigate in a scholarly way all aspects of Jewish life, obviously helped the authors of Russian textbooks on Jewish history, providing them with inspiration, standards of scholarship, and an intellectual framework. The ideological foundations of Wissenschaft des Judentums, including the academic ethos, the critical approach to sources, and the social mission of scholarship, together with exemplary German textbooks and general accounts of Jewish history—by Moïse Elkan, Samuel Bäck, Marcus Brann, and Heinrich Graetz's monumental history—profoundly influenced Russian authors, shaping their conceptual thinking, research interests, and methods.[21]

---

[18] Ibid., fos. 48ᵛ–49ʳ.

[19] Ibid., fo. 49ʳ. According to Eliyana R. Adler, as early as the 1870s visions, such as Gintsburg's, were realized in the creation of a 'new genre'—Russian-language textbooks about Judaism—that sought 'to reformulate Judaism in a delimited, structured, and comprehensible idiom for students'. Adler also notes that due to a negative perception of the Talmud by the Russian government, writers of textbooks tended to avoid including talmudic texts with other study materials. See Adler, 'Reinventing Religion', 142, 152.

[20] Examples of such works include Orshansky, *Russkoe zakonodatel'stvo o evreyakh*; M. Berlin, *Ocherk etnografii evreiskogo narodonaseleniya v Rossii* (St Petersburg, 1861); A. Harkavy, *Ob yazyke evreev zhivshikh v drevnee vremya na Rusi i o slavyanskikh slovakh vstrechaemykh u evreiskikh pisatelei (Iz issledovanii ob istorii evreev v Rossii)* (St Petersburg, 1865). On the authors, see V. Schedrin, 'Neizvestnaya "Istoriya khasidizma": Raboty M. I. Berlina v kontekste russko-evreiskoi istoriografii XIX v', *Arkhiv evreiskoi istorii*, 1 (2004), 169–92.

[21] For an analysis of the relationship between German Wissenschaft des Judentums and Russian Jewish studies, see V. Schedrin, 'Wissenschaft des Judentums and the Emergence of Russian Jewish Historiography', in C. Wiese and M. Thulin (eds.), *Wissenschaft des Judentums in Europe: Comparative and Transnational Perspectives* (forthcoming).

Dialogue, either direct or indirect, between the Russian authors and their German teachers framed the conceptions and narratives of the textbooks on Jewish history analysed in this chapter. Even when translating German works, the creators of these textbooks acted as virtual co-authors, extensively commenting, emending, and editing the originals. Each of these textbooks emphasizes a very different short yet important story within the larger story of the Jewish people. Each of these stories focuses on very different heroes: pietists or freethinkers, conservatives or reformers. Finally, the main hero of all these stories, the entire Jewish people, is presented by textbooks' authors differently, as either a race, an ethnicity, a nation, or a religious community.

One remarkable feature that these textbooks have in common is the close attention they pay to Russian Jews, who were largely ignored by German authors as a backward community, an anachronistic culture, and even a historical anomaly. Russian authors consistently emphasized the inseparability of the historical experiences of west and east European Jewries. Thus, Russian translations of universal Jewish histories by German authors often contained amendments with original histories of the Jews in Poland and Russia by the translators. For one of them, Simon Dubnow, writing a textbook on the universal history of the Jews, which he compiled by translating the best German specimens, was an essential 'introduction', a preparatory stage on the path towards his principal objective—writing a history of Jews in Russia.[22]

PATRIOTIC HISTORY

The first textbook in this survey, *History of the Jewish People (from the Jews' Migration to Babylon to the Destruction of the Second Temple) for those Studying the Law of Jewish Faith in Gymnasia and Government-Sponsored Jewish Schools* (1880),[23] was compiled by Mark Osipovich Nemzer (1833–1912), a graduate of and former instructor at the Vilna rabbinic seminary, a former government rabbi of Vilna, and a teacher at the women's gymnasium in Vilna. This modest book, 152 pages printed in a large student-friendly typeface, was limited in chronological and thematic scope and lacked an overt conceptualization of Jewish history.

The unpretentiousness of *History of the Jewish People* is especially apparent when it is compared to the first volume of the Russian translation of Heinrich Graetz's *History of the Jews from the Earliest Times to the Present Day*, which appeared that same year.[24] Graetz's massive volume (398 pages) covered a comparable time period (just over 500 years); however, in contrast to Nemzer's account, it provided a rich picture of Jewish life—from its socioeconomic aspects to the development of Jewish literature and scholarship—against the wider background

---

[22] S. M. Dubnow, *Kniga zhizni: Vospominaniya i razmyshleniya. Materialy dlya istorii moego vremeni* (St Petersburg, 1998), 165.

[23] Nemzer, *Istoriya evreiskogo naroda*.   [24] Graetz, *Istoriya evreev*, vol. i.

of major events and developments of early medieval non-Jewish history. Graetz's work also featured its author's revolutionary conceptualization of the Jewish people and Jewish history. According to him, the unity of 'soul' (Jewish religion and tradition) and 'body' (the Jewish people) cemented the Jewish nation and shaped Jewish history. For centuries, the complex interplay of soul and body had been a major driving force of Jewish history, which had always been conspicuously 'national in character'.[25] Thus the Jews, living on different continents among different peoples in different periods of time, had never left their 'spiritual fatherland'.[26] The history of this fatherland was Graetz's principal focus. Jews and their non-Jewish hosts and neighbours might share historical space and time in the Diaspora, yet the core developments of Jewish society and culture always had a considerable degree of autonomy from non-Jewish societies and cultures. Thus, from the ninth to the twelfth centuries, during the European Dark Ages, the Jews in Spain experienced their golden age, marked by an unprecedented outburst of Jewish creativity.[27]

Graetz's idea of a fatherland of the Jews was one of the few conceptual problems discussed at considerable length in Nemzer's textbook. If Graetz's concept of spiritual fatherland was essentially cosmopolitan because it did not bind Jews to any specific polity, Nemzer's alternative could best be defined as patriotic. Unlike Graetz, Nemzer did not bother to summarize his views. However, he integrated them into his narrative by emphasizing certain stories while downplaying and even concealing others. Nemzer framed his narrative with two catastrophic events, the Babylonian captivity in the sixth century BCE and the destruction of the Second Temple in the first century CE, that set the theological, political, social, and institutional limits of the Jewish Diaspora for centuries to come. Nemzer linked these events with a narrative, a story of the consolidation of the Jewish people by way of preparation for their historical ordeal, *galut*, an indefinite exile from their homeland and life among other peoples. Stories of core Jewish spiritual and political institutes, such as the Temple,[28] the Torah,[29] and the Sanhedrin,[30] play a central role in Nemzer's account of the 'preparatory' stage of Jewish history. Nemzer's mostly negative portrayal of the kings of Israel and Judaea and his overly positive interpretation of the 'learned men' of the Sanhedrin are also telling. They condemn the disastrous historical role of the Jewish monarchy bent on the preservation of its political sovereignty at any price and contrast it with the constructive, historical role of Jewish institutions and values, such as spirituality, justice, and civic consciousness, which cemented the people's unity and ensured their national future. The actions of Jewish kings and their generals, who, like Flavius Josephus, put their personal ambitions before a 'commitment to the people's cause and earnest love of their fatherland',[31] led to the loss of the Jews' political independence along with 'the loss of their national and religious centre. Since then [Jews]

---

[25] Ibid., pp. i–ii.   [26] Ibid., p. iv.   [27] Ibid.
[28] Nemzer, *Istoriya evreiskogo naroda*, 18–20, 95–101.
[29] Ibid. 44–6, 106–14.   [30] Ibid. 34–6, 89–95.   [31] Ibid. 136.

considered their fatherland any country where they lived, [where they] were born and raised.'[32] Thus, the Jews were (and still are) divided by the borders of the many fatherlands, to which they were obliged to be loyal and patriotic.

Nemzer appended to his history a biographical index of a dozen of the most prominent Jewish historical figures featured in his narrative. Kings and military leaders are conspicuously absent from this appendix, 'Learned Men who Lived during the Times of Syrian Rule and the Maccabees', but included are the rabbis Shammai and Hillel, Rabban Gamliel, and other pillars of rabbinic Judaism.[33]

One contemporary reviewer sharply criticized *History of the Jewish People*, pointing out its lack of originality and the poor quality of its scholarship.[34] Nemzer promptly responded, painstakingly dismissing most of the criticism as irrelevant.[35] In fact, his history is a very well thought-out, structured, and written textbook drawing on the author's solid Jewish learning[36] and his knowledge of contemporary scholarship in Jewish studies, including works by Russian Jewish historians.[37]

DIDACTIC HISTORY

The next textbook, *Handbook for Teaching the History of the Jewish People from the Most Ancient to Modern Times including a Brief Survey of Palestinian Geography for Jewish Schools [together with] A Brief Historical Study of the Jews in Poland, Lithuania, and Russia*,[38] was published in 1880, the same year as Nemzer's *History of the Jewish People*. Like Nemzer, its creator, Solomon (Zalkind) Minor (1826–1900), was a graduate of and former instructor at the Vilna rabbinic seminary. However, unlike Nemzer, Minor, a rabbi and public figure, was a prominent leader of the Russian Jews. He was a government rabbi of Moscow, one of the largest Jewish communities in the late Russian empire, from 1869 to 1892. He was also the first Russian rabbi to deliver his regular sermons in Russian.[39] Minor also penned influential pamphlets and articles on pressing issues of Jewish life in Russia, such as antisemitism and the adaptation of Jewish tradition to modern realities.[40]

---

[32] Nemzer, *Istoriya evreiskogo naroda*, 147.

[33] Ibid. 147–52.   [34] A. Vol, 'Plagiator', *Vilenskii vestnik*, 206 (1 Oct.), 210 (7 Oct. 1880).

[35] M. Nemzer, 'Otvet na klevety', *Vilenskii vestnik*, 230 (31 Oct.), 233 (4 Oct.), 238 (10 Oct.), 239 (11 Nov.), 245 (19 Nov. 1880).

[36] For examples of using the Talmud as a historical source, see Nemzer, *Istoriya evreiskogo naroda*, 92–3, 98.

[37] For examples of using contemporary scholarship by Shemuel Yosef Fuenn and Daniel Chwolson, see ibid. 42, 69, 78.

[38] Minor (trans. and ed.), *Rukovodstvo k prepodavaniyu istorii evreiskogo naroda*.

[39] 'Minor, Solomon', in L. Katsenelson and D. G. Gintsburg (eds.), *Evreiskaya entsiklopediya: Svod znanii o evreistve i ego kul'ture v proshlom i nastoyashchem*, 16 vols. (St Petersburg, 1908–13), xi. 77.

[40] See e.g. S. Minor, *Posle pogromov* (Moscow, 1882); id., *Rabbi Ippolit Lyutostanskii i ego 'Talmud i evrei'* (Moscow, 1889); id., *Bibliya ob upotreblenii vina* (Vilna, 1899).

Handbook for Teaching the History of the Jewish People consisted of two parts. The first was Minor's translation of a German textbook on Jewish history by Moïse Elkan which had been first published in 1839.[41] The second was Minor's own study of Jewish history in eastern Europe, aimed at improving the German original by broadening its scope. Compared to Nemzer's work, Minor's textbook provided a wider and far more sophisticated perspective on Jewish history. His narrative spans more than 4,000 years, from biblical times to the mid-nineteenth century. It provided a remarkable panorama of Jewish life worldwide, including historical accounts of overlooked Jewish communities in China and India[42] and the marginalized community of Karaite Jews.[43] It also benefited from the overall quality and proven popularity of its authoritative German source. He used the sixth edition (1870) of Elkan's textbook, widely adopted 'in all Jewish schools of Germany and . . . recently translated into Hungarian'.[44] According to Minor, the first edition of his Russian translation was a comparable success in Russia, where it was 'selling quickly' and was officially approved by authorities in the Vilna educational district as 'the textbook to be used for teaching the history of the Jewish people to Jewish students in the higher grades of gymnasia and *Realschulen*'.[45] Thus, Minor undertook the second edition of *Handbook for Teaching the History of the Jewish People* based on the success of the first, and also in order to fix 'serious errors' found in both the original and the translation by his academic consultant, 'our prominent scholar' Avraham Harkavy.[46] In fact, Minor's own supplementary outline of Jewish history in Poland, Lithuania, and Russia, humbly aimed at emending the authoritative German textbook, was a major breakthrough in Jewish history textbooks. By telling a new story, Minor added an entirely new chapter to the established instructional narratives of Jewish history, such as Elkan's, where the Jews of eastern Europe were allotted only few lines.[47] Technically, *Handbook for Teaching the History of the Jewish People* was a huge step forwards compared to Nemzer's work. Its narrative is complete with chapter summaries; lists of key phenomena, developments, and concepts; and useful study aids, such as the 'Geographical Survey of Palestine',[48] listing natural and historical places, and a timeline extending from the creation of the world in the year 3988 BCE to the civic emancipation of the Jews of Austria-Hungary in 1868.[49]

Unlike Nemzer, Minor explicitly articulated his conception of Jewish history as well as his ideas about the social mission of historiography. His narrative could be

---

[41] M. Elkan, *Leitfaden beim Unterricht in der Geschichte der Israeliten, von den frühesten Zeiten bis auf unsere Tage: nebst einem kurzen Abriss der Geographie Palästina's, für israelitische Schulen* (Minden, 1839).

[42] Minor (trans. and ed.), *Rukovodstvo k prepodavaniyu istorii evreiskogo naroda*, 83, 88.

[43] Ibid. 86.

[44] S. Minor, 'Predislovie perevodchika ko vtoromu izdaniyu', in id. (trans. and ed.), *Rukovodstvo k prepodavaniyu istorii evreiskogo naroda*, 2nd edn. (Moscow, 1881), n.p.　　[45] Ibid.　　[46] Ibid.

[47] For example, see Minor (trans. and ed.), *Rukovodstvo k prepodavaniyu istorii evreiskogo naroda*, 114.　　[48] Ibid. 130–58.　　[49] Ibid. 159–61.

best described as a rationalist 'didactic' history aimed at enlightening Russian Jews, who, due to their long isolation, lacked 'culture' and 'aesthetics' in the contemporary Western understanding of these terms. Thus, Jewish life in Russia was not yet up to contemporary standards in having a true national history, but Minor recognized the attempts of Russian Jews, in secular education and in the introduction of a modern lifestyle, to live up to that standard. According to Minor, Russian Jews had first to 'refresh their spirit with the stream of the past [the history of western Jews]', and only then could they 'consciously start [their true] national, social, and spiritual life'.[50] *Handbook for Teaching the History of the Jewish People* established a close connection between the history of the Jews in eastern Europe and the Jews in the rest of the world. Minor's narrative, in both the translated and the original parts of the book, linked east and west European Jews by establishing common features of Jewish life in the Diaspora, such as the 'anti-aesthetical' and 'anti-social' role of the Talmud,[51] and by showing common historical developments, such as the inevitable civic emancipation of the Jews.[52] At the same time, Minor emphasized the close historical connection between the fate of Russian Jews and the 'fate of the whole of Russia, the fate of its other citizens'.[53] He believed that Jews should put all their efforts into self-improvement and work for the benefit of Russia in order to earn civic freedom and thus fully reunite with their progressive brethren in the west. He concluded with an appeal to Russian Jews 'to work and work honestly, work physically and work intellectually. Then there is no reason to be afraid of the future: it will bring certain freedom.'[54]

Like Nemzer, Minor singled out the principal heroes of his narrative and appended lists of them, including biographies, major works, and achievements, to most chapters. Minor's heroes were mainly the pioneers and active proponents of culture and aesthetics among the Jews, from the *paytanim* in medieval Spain[55] to the maskilim in Germany.[56]

A contemporary reviewer praised *Handbook for Teaching the History of the Jewish People*, observing that its principal source is 'the best textbook on Jewish history', as it 'links the political and religious history of the Jews'. However, the reviewer failed to recognize Minor's own achievement, a survey of the history of east European Jews, noting that it was 'an exposition of the article on Jews by Polish author [Tadeusz] Czacki'.[57] In response, Minor pointed out that he had

[50] Minor, 'Predislovie perevodchika ko vtoromu izdaniyu', n.p.

[51] S. Minor, 'Kratkii istoricheskii ocherk o evreyakh v Pol'she, Litve i Rossii', 22, in id. (trans. and ed.), *Rukovodstvo k prepodavaniyu istorii evreiskogo naroda*.

[52] Minor (trans. and ed.), *Rukovodstvo k prepodavaniyu istorii evreiskogo naroda*, 125–6.

[53] Minor, 'Kratkii istoricheskii ocherk o evreyakh v Pol'she, Litve i Rossii', 65.   [54] Ibid. 67.

[55] Minor (trans. and ed.), *Rukovodstvo k prepodavaniyu istorii evreiskogo naroda*, 102–3.

[56] Ibid. 120.

[57] Mevakker [Judah Leib Gordon], 'M. Elkan, Rukovodstvo k prepodavaniyu istorii evreiskogo naroda ot samykh drevnikh do noveishikh vremen s kratkim ocherkom geografii Palestiny dlya evreiskikh uchilishch. Kratkii istoricheskii ocherk o evreyakh v Pol'she, Litve i Rossii. Per. s nem. i dop. Z. Minor. Moskva, 1881', *Voskhod*, 5 (1881), 60–8 (second pagination).

'significantly improved Czacki'.[58] Actually, Minor's account of east European Jewish history had been seriously researched using his own previous publications,[59] a study by Alexander Kraushar,[60] numerous publications of primary sources,[61] and other materials in addition to Czacki's work.[62]

PRAGMATIC HISTORY

While condemning the Talmud in principle, Minor paradoxically singled out Elisha ben Abuyah (also known as Aher), the archetypal apostate condemned by the Talmud, as a major villain in his textbook, comparable to the greedy kings and corrupt generals, the principal villains of Nemzer's narrative. However, the same historical figure was idealized as an exemplary Jew by Dubnow, author of the two last textbooks in this survey, who intellectually and emotionally identified with Aher.[63] In April 1881, at the beginning of his literary and scholarly career, Dubnow 'proclaimed to the Russian Jews . . . a gospel of freethinking' in a debut article entitled 'A Few Moments in the History of the Development of Jewish Thought'.[64] In Dubnow's opinion, 'if all Jews knew their history well, they would see the difference between the core of Judaism and its later developments, and they would get rid of the latter, from the Talmud to the *Shulḥan arukh*'. Thus, a knowledge of history would allow for the spiritual regeneration of the Jewish people, whose freedom had for centuries been constrained by strict religious law and rigid tradition. 'What might the historical mission of the Jewish people have been, Dubnow asked, if Elishas (and not Akivas . . .) had constituted its predominant element? If that mission could have been more universal and its results, from a point of view common to all mankind, much broader?'[65]

Ten years later, Dubnow, now a mature and accomplished author with a strong interest in east European Jewish history and a consciousness of his mission as a historian, enthusiastically moved from words to deeds. At the end of 1891 he developed a plan for a general textbook on Jewish history in Russian, which, he believed, had not yet appeared.[66] In fact, he was carrying on Minor's work. Like Minor, Dubnow envisioned his textbook as a translation of some authoritative

---

[58] S. Minor, 'Otvet g. Mevakkeru', *Voskhod*, 6 (1881), 21–5 (second pagination).

[59] M.R., 'O zapadno–russkikh evreyakh', *Prilozhenie k Gakarmelyu*, 11 (1866). M.R. was Minor's pen name, signifying 'Minsk rabbi' (see Minor, 'Kratkii istoricheskii ocherk o evreyakh v Pol'she, Litve i Rossii', 4).

[60] A. Kraushar, *Historya Żydów w Polsce* (Warsaw, 1865); see Minor, 'Kratkii istoricheskii ocherk o evreyakh v Pol'she, Litve i Rossii', 16.

[61] e.g. *Akty, otnosyashchiesya k istorii Yuzhnoi i Zapadnoi Rossii* (St Petersburg, 1846); see Minor, 'Kratkii istoricheskii ocherk o evreyakh v Pol'she, Litve i Rossii', 8.

[62] T. Czacki, *Rozprawa o Żydach* (Vilna, 1807).   [63] Dubnow, *Kniga zhizni*, 75.

[64] Dubnow, 'Neskol'ko momentov iz istorii razvitiya evreiskoi mysli', *Russkii evrei*, 16, 17, 18, 24, 27, 28, 32, 35, 36 (1881); see also id., *Kniga zhizni*, 85.

[65] Dubnow, *Kniga zhizni*, 85–6.   [66] Ibid. 165.

German work, such as an abridged version of Graetz's *History of the Jews*, appended by his own account of Jewish history in eastern Europe. Like Minor, Dubnow considered basic knowledge of general Jewish history an essential prerequisite for Russian Jews, helping them to overcome their social isolation and spiritual stagnation and thus prepare for their debut in the historical arena. 'It seemed abnormal to me', wrote Dubnow, 'to prepare a broad [account of the] history of the Jews in Poland and Russia for readers who have not yet learned the general history of the Jews.'[67] In 1894 a new, revised edition of a popular one-volume textbook on Jewish history by Samuel Bäck was published in Germany.[68] Dubnow, who had then just secured funds for his project, considered Bäck's work 'at first sight, appropriate' for his plan and decided to translate it into Russian and publish it with his own 'supplement on the history of eastern Jews'.[69]

In contrast to the works of Nemzer and Minor, Dubnow's *Jewish History*, published in 1896/7, was more than an ordinary school textbook. It was an advanced tool for self-education and self-improvement, or, according to Dubnow, 'a source of knowledge and an instrument [for the acquisition] of self-knowledge'. This deliberately 'pragmatic' and 'accessible' history aimed to satisfy 'the most obvious urgent need . . . of the average Russian Jew . . . to learn about the past of his people'. Because that need was so urgent, Dubnow abandoned his ambitious plan to write a brand new account of Jewish history based mainly on primary sources and decided to translate an authoritative German work instead.[70] He found Bäck's textbook suitable for this purpose, since it featured a 'vivid and consistent' narrative and conceptually followed Graetz, whom Dubnow admired. However, in Dubnow's opinion, Bäck's work was also full of 'omissions and serious flaws' due to the author's inadequate knowledge of primary sources. In order to improve on Bäck, Dubnow used another German source, a textbook by Marcus Brann.[71] Brann's narrative, dry and didactic, substantiated Bäck's vivid account with solidly researched material that 'stood closer to the primary sources'.[72] When neither Bäck nor Brann fitted Dubnow's scheme, he turned to other influential scholars, such as Isaac Hirsch Weiss and Heinrich Graetz, or looked directly at primary sources.[73] As a result, *Jewish History* told at least three stories of the Jewish people: Bäck's, Brann's, and Dubnow's own. Yet Dubnow's ideas, overall plan and structure, narrative and distinctive authorial voice cemented this two-volume history into a coherent whole. Dubnow acknowledged that while working on the textbook he 'had to deviate [from the German original], increasing the original element of the book at the expense of [its] translated [element]'.[74]

---

[67] Dubnow, *Kniga zhizni*, 85–6.

[68] S. Bäck, *Die Geschichte des jüdischen Volkes und seiner Litteratur vom babylonischen Exile bis auf die Gegenwart* (Frankfurt, 1894).   [69] Dubnow, *Kniga zhizni*, 180.

[70] S. M. Dubnow, 'Predislovie', in id. (trans. and ed.), *Evreiskaya istoriya*, vol. i, p. v.

[71] M. Brann, *Geschichte der Juden und ihrer Litteratur: Für Schule und Haus* (Breslau, 1893–5).

[72] Dubnow, 'Predislovie', p. vi.

[73] Ibid., p. vii.   [74] Ibid., p. vi; Dubnow, *Kniga zhizni*, 182–3.

Dubnow was the first author of a Russian-language textbook on Jewish history to approach his subject with a sophisticated pedagogical methodology of his own, meticulously developed, well articulated, and carefully implemented. In his words, 'strict objectivity and pragmatism' were the main features of his method. Dubnow exposed the facts 'logically and philosophically', linking them into one coherent narrative 'without wasting words and emotions . . . in order to give the reader's mind and feelings enough freedom for independent work'.[75] Using this approach, Dubnow sought to engage his readers in the active learning of history. In his opinion, most authors of textbooks on Jewish history mentioned rather than described facts for the sake of brevity and thus turned history into 'dead' didactic material. Dubnow believed that 'in order to create a clear image of a historical event in the reader's mind, it was necessary *to recount*, if possible, all the important details of this event. The more details, the more concrete the fact and the stronger its impression [on the reader].'[76] Thus, Dubnow's principal pedagogical objective was to 'stir up the reader's thoughts and feelings'.[77]

Dubnow's textbook was a significant contribution to the development of Jewish historiography and Jewish studies in general. His revolutionary theory about the shifting centres of Jewish cultural hegemony in the Diaspora made its first appearance in the pages of this work. His theory provided the conceptual framework for a narrative that spanned 'eastern' (antiquity and the early Middle Ages, 'from the Babylonian captivity to the end of the Gaonic period', totalling 323 pages) and 'western' (high and late Middle Ages, and modern times, 'from the emergence of Judaeo-Spanish culture to our day', totalling 474 pages) periods of Jewish history. This context shifted the conventional perspective on the history of the Jews in Poland and Russia, seen as a marginal chapter in universal Jewish history, but considered in Dubnow's textbook as the culmination of the 'western' period, similar to the golden age of Jewish civilization in medieval Muslim Spain during the 'eastern' period. Dubnow believed that to exclude the history of Polish Jews in the 'Ashkenazi [western] period was as unthinkable as to write about the Sephardi [eastern] period without including the history of Spanish Jews'.[78] Thus, contrary to Minor's *Handbook for Teaching the History of the Jewish People*, the story of east European Jewish history in *Jewish History* was not separated from the main narrative, but 'in the interest of pragmatism it was integrated into the relevant chapters of national history, an organic part of which it represents'.[79]

The socioeconomic history of the Jewish people is the primary focus of *Jewish History*. It was Dubnow's first substantial historiographical work, and, building

[75] Dubnow, 'Predislovie', pp. ix–x.

[76] Ibid., p. vii (emphasis original). Dubnow gave an example of one such textbook based on 'dead' facts, D. Cassel's *Lehrbuch der jüdischen Geschichte und Literatur* (Leipzig, 1879), which 'despite all its academic quality . . . could only kill the reader's . . . desire to learn about Jewish history' (see Dubnow, 'Predislovie', p. x).   [77] Dubnow, 'Predislovie', p. x.

[78] S. M. Dubnow, 'Predislovie ko vtoromu tomu', in id. (trans. and ed.), *Evreiskaya istoriya*, vol. ii, p. vi.   [79] Ibid.

upon an extensive source base, he approached the Jewish people as a political nation, both before and after the actual loss of Jewish political sovereignty in the first century CE. He thus proposed a serious alternative to 'the erroneous method of most authors [including Bäck and Brann], who were turning the history of the western period into the history of Jewish literature'. In contrast to such authors and their histories, Dubnow's narrative provided a detailed account of 'the outward developments of a dispersed nation during the Middle Ages and modern times, and [of] its spiritual life in different countries'. At the same time he only 'briefly referred' to 'developments of a purely literary nature'[80] and arranged the material in 'main divisions', corresponding to the major outward developments of national history, such as the periods of Ashkenazi and Sephardi hegemony, and 'minor divisions', corresponding to the stages of 'intellectual development' of the people, such as 'rabbinic-philosophical', 'enlightening', and other epochs.[81]

While working on his textbook, Dubnow made use of a vast pool of historical sources and contemporary scholarship, both Jewish ('major works of old Jewish literature') and non-Jewish ('raw materials published in various Polish and Jewish collections'). In addition to translating, editing, and considerably emending Bäck and Brann, he was not afraid to challenge the authorities of the older generation of Jewish historians, from Leopold Zunz and Heinrich Graetz to Tadeusz Czacki and Sergei Bershadsky, whose works figured prominently among his sources.[82]

Dubnow's work resulted in a history that 'in addition to its theoretical significance also had a twofold social import . . . as a source of self-knowledge for the Jews . . . and a source of a humane and positive attitude [towards the Jews] for non-Jews'.[83] The attitude of the official Russian censors was a peculiar test of its actual effect on non-Jews. Anticipating problems, Dubnow submitted his manuscript for preliminary censorship in Odessa. He was counting on the lenient attitude of the preliminary censorship procedure to authorize publication, with a few blackouts at worst, in contrast to post-publication censorship that could prohibit the book from circulating altogether and could confiscate its entire run after publication.[84] In addition, Dubnow relied upon his connections in the Odessa censorship committee and the overall reputation of his publisher, Isakovich, who also published the official *Vedomosti Odesskogo gradonachal'stva* ('Journal of the Odessa Authorities'). Even more cautiously, Dubnow omitted the 'sacred history' (i.e. most of the biblical period) and opened his narrative with the story of the Babylonian exile in order to avoid dealing with the harsh clerical censorship of the Holy Synod of the Russian Orthodox church.[85] Despite this precaution, Dubnow's censor

---

[80] S. M. Dubnow, 'Predislovie ko vtoromu tomu', in id. (trans. and ed.), *Evreiskaya istoriya*, vol. ii, p. v.   [81] Ibid.   [82] Ibid.   [83] Dubnow, 'Predislovie', p. x.

[84] Dubnow well remembered such a disaster with the publication of the Russian translation of the first volume of Graetz's *History of the Jews* in the early 1880s (see *Kniga zhizni*, 183).

[85] Later, Dubnow 'decided to add an introductory chapter with a brief survey of the biblical period, so that the reader would have some impression about the epoch that preceded the Babylonian captivity. Cautiously . . . [he] reworked for this purpose an introductory chapter—mainly consisting of biblical

ordered a few corrections and deletions. Dubnow fiercely disputed the censorship, fighting for every word and every paragraph, which, if deleted from the textbook he believed would also be deleted from the historical consciousness of the people that he sought to cultivate. He managed to save a 'little paragraph' recounting the 'beautiful legend' of the Khazars' conversion to Judaism, which the censor considered 'propaganda dangerous for the church'.[86] The censor allowed this story to remain in the book, but Dubnow had to omit several details and, in his words, he felt that he had 'deprived [the story] of colour' and ultimately made it a 'dead fact'.[87] The censor also found 'impermissible an aphorism of [Judah] Halevi, that Israel among nations performs the same function as the heart in the human organism'. This time, Dubnow's arguments were not effective, and Halevi's words were purged from the manuscript.[88]

In general, Dubnow's *Jewish History* firmly linked the past and present of the Jewish people and built a solid foundation for Jewish national consciousness. It brought a new historical perspective about the major developments of Jewish life, including many contemporary issues. In early 1897, concluding the second volume on the 'western' period of Jewish history, Dubnow observed that 'in view of contemporary publicity about Herzl's *Judenstaat* . . . Palestinians [champions of Palestine, i.e. Zionists] wanted to turn the wheel of [Jewish] history back from the western to the ancient eastern period'. He called this vision 'one-sided', while acknowledging its 'instrumentality in awakening national consciousness'.[89]

REVOLUTIONARY HISTORY

After finishing *Jewish History*, Dubnow did not consider his mission as a historian accomplished. He devoted special attention to the problems of modern Jewish education and its key issue, the study of Jewish history, in *Letters on Old and New Judaism*, a comprehensive exposition of his philosophy and politics, written and first published in 1897. In Letter 5, 'On National Education', Dubnow argued that the Jewish people was experiencing a major cultural crisis and therefore had to think seriously about strengthening the very foundations of its national life. The sweeping reform of Jewish schooling was an immediate priority in this context. Dubnow saw the main dilemma to be the widening gap between race and culture. For a modern Jew, 'educated outside his people's culture, by race and by blood his

quotes—from Brann's book and supplemented it with excerpts from [his own] article "What is Jewish History?"' (Dubnow, *Kniga zhizni*, 183).

[86] Ibid. 184–5. In his letter to the censorship committee, Dubnow argued that 'this choice [by the Khazar king] does not speak to the detriment of Christianity and Islam, nor to the advantage of Judaism. It is nothing more than an indifferent fact. . . . I do not comment on this story by taking sides. . . . I am committed to complete objectivity.' He also noted that the story of the Khazars' conversion to Judaism had long ago been accepted by Russian historians (cited in V. Kelner, *Missioner istorii: Zhizn' i trudy Semena Markovicha Dubnova* (St Petersburg, 2008), 236).

[87] Dubnow, *Kniga zhizni*, 184.   [88] Ibid. 187.   [89] Ibid. 188.

nation is one [thing] and by culture quite another. The latter overshadows the former.'[90] Dubnow believed that the re-evaluation and nationalization of Jewish cultural values, historical heritage, and education would solve that dilemma in the future. He proposed to

teach Jewish boys and girls so that the Jewish people could become a nation by culture and not only by blood; they should be given the opportunity, like children of other nations, to imbibe the national through the universal; Jewishness should become for them the closest source for meeting their cultural interests, the focus of their vital social and spiritual ideals. Education has de-Judaized young Jews [in the past], and it should now Judaize them.[91]

Dubnow considered the universal academic discipline of history, applied to the singular phenomenon of the chosen people, the best means of nationalizing modern Jewish identity. For this reason, he devoted most of 'On National Education' to the current status of teaching Jewish history and to the development of textbooks on Jewish history in Russian, a 'universal' means of communication for Jews in the vast Russian empire.

Dubnow deemed the contemporary status of the teaching of Jewish history unsatisfactory. He observed that Jewish parents rarely took the opportunity to have their children instructed in Jewish history in non-Jewish secondary schools (such as gymnasia, *Realschulen*, or commercial and municipal schools), where, according to the law, this subject could be a legitimate part of the curriculum nominally taught as 'the law of the Jewish faith'.[92] And in schools of the north-western educational districts, where, according to Dubnow, this subject was taught, 'abridged textbooks more suitable for elementary school' and lacking a serious scholarly approach were in use. Dubnow considered such instruction 'dead', as it was 'unable to instil students with love for Jewish studies or to awaken in them national or religious or ethical feelings'.[93] In Dubnow's opinion, Jewish schools desperately needed a decent textbook on Jewish history 'in which, beside an all-encompassing general knowledge [of history], not tailored to suit any particular narrow agenda [i.e. Russification and assimilation], there must be all-encompassing special Jewish knowledge (. . . Jewish history, literature, etc.), pursuing one lofty goal: self-knowledge'.[94]

This 'lofty goal', along with the commercial success of *Jewish History*,[95] led Dubnow to embark on the project of preparing a new, original work, *Textbook of Jewish History for Jewish Youth*, which he completed and published in 1898. Despite his obvious interest and passionate involvement in the current issues of

[90] S. M. Dubnow, *Pis'ma o starom i novom evreistve (1897–1907)* (St Petersburg, 1907), 125.

[91] Ibid.   [92] Ibid. 142.   [93] Ibid. 139.

[94] Ibid. 146. On Dubnow's plan to prepare such a sweeping account of Jewish history, see Kelner, *Missioner istorii*, 242–3.

[95] According to Dubnow, all 3,600 copies were sold instantly and he continued to receive orders from impatient readers, 'whose orders testified to the eagerness with which this first Jewish history in Russian was awaited' (*Kniga zhizni*, 188).

Jewish cultural politics in general and of Jewish education in particular, he considered them a distraction that prevented him from focusing on his principal mission, the creation of a comprehensive history of the Jews in Poland and Russia. However, in his words, 'the old trouble—material insecurity—impeded serene scholarly work'.[96] Then he remembered 'a friend's advice' once given by his senior colleague, Odessa neighbour, and classic Yiddish writer Sholem Yankev Abramovitsh (Mendele Moykher Sforim): 'Write a school textbook on Jewish history and you . . . will [have enough money to] live and continue your studies.'[97] The proven demand for a Jewish history textbook also helped Dubnow calm his conscience that was 'torturing [him] for deviation from [pure] scholarship'. He followed Abramovitsh's advice and spent the entire year of 1898 working on it 'with great diligence but without much enthusiasm'.[98]

It is true that the final product featured a more systematic approach and less emotional involvement than his adaptation of Bäck and Brann. *Jewish History* had been Dubnow's first attempt at a dialogue, sometimes very emotional, with his readers and also with other authors (namely, his senior German colleagues), aiming to promote a new understanding of Jewish historical experience as a national rather than just an intellectual and literary history. *Textbook of Jewish History* was intended in the first place to be a study aid, and Dubnow envisioned his task as a 'reconciliation of the demands of scholarship, pedagogy, and censorship that often contradict each other'.[99] According to Dubnow, scholarship demanded that an analysis of 'sacred history' should conform to the standards and findings of contemporary research; pedagogy demanded that the integrity and poetics of biblical legends be preserved in order to keep their literary and educational import; censorship, in its turn, simply 'threatened punishment for [taking] any liberties'.[100]

In an introductory chapter that covered the origins of biblical Judaism, Dubnow managed to reconcile and even link the 'unscientific' material of the Bible, such as the story of Creation and its traditional Jewish interpretation, with recent scientific discoveries and methods, such as archaeology and comparative linguistics.[101] These two intertwined perspectives, which he called 'biblical religious pragmatism' and 'heretical secular pragmatism', allowed for a coherent narrative, linking events with their deeper causes and revealing their greater implications, fusing many

---

[96] Ibid. 202.

[97] This was practical and helpful advice indeed. Abramovitsh might have been referring to contemporary Russian Jewish authors who published very successful textbooks providing study aids to the growing number of young Jews seeking Russian-language education as means of social integration and advancement. One such author, a graduate and instructor of the Vilna rabbinic seminary Mikhail Vol'per (1851–1912?), invested thirteen years in the creation of a textbook for students of the Russian language. The investment paid back enormously as this textbook, *Russian Speech: Study Aid in the Russian Language Adapted to the Needs of the Alien Population [of the Russian Empire]*, had over 60 editions in three decades from the late 1880s to the late 1900s and served as a source of steady income for its author. See 'Vol'per, Mikhail Ioakimovich', in Katsenelson and Gintsburg (eds.), *Evreiskaya entsiklopediya*, v. 752.   [98] Dubnow, *Kniga zhizni*, 203.   [99] Ibid. 202.

[100] Ibid. 203.   [101] Dubnow, *Uchebnik evreiskoi istorii*, i. 5, 6, 16.

voices and stories into one all-encompassing history of the people.[102] Thus, biblical history, in Dubnow's view, 'was not only a religious but also a national history of the Jews'.[103]

However, the author's emotions also entered into the narrative. *Textbook of Jewish History* was an extended message, as indicated in its full title, to young Jews, with historical knowledge as its main substance and 'the pathos of history', the main feature of Dubnow's historiography in general, as its energizing spirit.[104] It was this spirit that inspired the endeavours of the young Dubnow as an aspiring Jewish writer who in 1881 dreamed of writing a history of Jewish rebels, ideological missionaries who might expand the special mission of their people into a truly universal one.[105] It was this spirit that in 1892 helped Dubnow to set his life's goal, 'the dissemination of historical knowledge about Judaism with special focus on the history of the Russian Jews', and thus turned the young historian himself into an ideological missionary—'a missionary for history', in his own words.[106] Essential to this mission was his scholarship, the search for and reflection on the national Jewish component within universal human civilization. This mission provided the spiritual framework for his studies and was their virtual 'soul'. Thus, for example, Dubnow's polemic with Graetz was not strictly academic. Dubnow admitted that he 'took under his protection, against Graetz, freethinkers of all epochs, from Aher to Uriel Dacosta, [Leon] Modena, to Spinoza, all heroes of the "romance" of his youth . . . [he] even found extenuating circumstances for female heroines of the Berlin salons, explaining their abandonment of Judaism as a consequence of "the spring flood" of the revolutionary epoch'.[107]

Like Nemzer and Minor before him, Dubnow drew up his own 'honour roll', singling out those who, in his opinion, were the true heroes, mainly his favourite 'freethinkers of all epochs' who had been overlooked or marginalized by other authors. The continuity of their stories underlies the narrative of *Textbook of Jewish History*. In antiquity, Jewish freethinkers championed the national independence of the Jewish people. The sacred goal of their struggle, the restoration of Jewish political sovereignty and religious freedom, justified their means, even if they clashed with the basic tenets of Judaism. Thus, Dubnow called the Maccabees, who did not hesitate to fight on the sabbath, pious 'patriot-Hasideans . . . engaged in a sacred struggle with enemies of their faith and homeland'.[108] During the Judaean war in the first century CE, 'Akiva, a spiritual leader of the Jews, recognized Bar Kokhba . . . [who] was not sufficiently pious . . . who was too brutal and authoritarian . . . as a military leader [of the Jews], and co-operated with him.'[109] When, after Bar Kokhba's revolt was crushed by the Romans, 'the last episode of the

[102] Dubnow, *Uchebnik evreiskoi istorii*, i. 2; Kelner, *Missioner istorii*, 244–5; Dubnow, *Kniga zhizni*, 203.   [103] Dubnow, *Kniga zhizni*, 203.
[104] 'Pathos of history' is a phrase coined by Dubnow and used in the title of a chapter dealing with his philosophy of history in his memoirs (ibid. 165).   [105] Ibid. 85–6.   [106] Ibid. 165.
[107] Ibid. 166.   [108] Dubnow, *Uchebnik evreiskoi istorii*, i. 80.   [109] Ibid. 107–8.

Jewish people's struggle for independence ended lamentably',[110] and a period of exile began, Jewish rebels and freethinkers directed their efforts at overcoming the self-imposed spiritual and intellectual isolation of the Jewish community. *Textbook of Jewish History* exposed a multitude of such tough yet tragic figures: from Aher, 'a great yet unfortunate freethinker . . . belonging to the circle of the finest [rabbinic] scholars';[111] to 'prince' David Reubeni, 'about whom it is hard to say if he was an impostor or a dreamer';[112] to Baruch Spinoza, 'the greatest philosopher to come from the Jewish milieu . . . for whom reason became the only source of wisdom, ranking high above religious tradition'.[113] In Dubnow's narrative, these were the heroes of a transitional epoch, the link between a glorious past and a hopeful present. They 'stood on the crossroads', like one of them, Moses Hayim Luzzatto, who, 'as a kabbalist . . . belonged to the past and as a poet . . . was a pioneer of a new creative process that culminated in the nineteenth century'.[114] Dubnow considered the late eighteenth century as the major watershed of Jewish history, when not only the freethinking elite but also the wider masses of Jewish people were blazing new paths out of the ghetto of 'rabbinism' and aiming to overcome stagnation in Jewish spiritual and national life. Thus, Moses Mendelssohn, 'a poor young Jew from Dessau, who . . . illuminated his people and all of Germany . . . argued that Judaism did not demand faith from its adherents, it demanded only rational knowledge [that makes one] adhere to historical and ethical laws'.[115] Mendelssohn's contemporary, Israel Ba'al Shem Tov, 'a humble Jew from Podolia', created a 'teaching of piety', hasidism, that 'best fit the needs of the Jewish populace . . . [He] emphasized genuine faith and prayer that were accessible to the people as a replacement for inaccessible bookish learning.'[116] Finally, the nineteenth-century Russian Hebrew thinkers and poets, synthesizing national and universal elements in their works, ushered in a new era of Jewish national rebirth. According to Dubnow:

> Between two opposite strata—the backward orthodox masses and a part of [Jewish] society torn away from their people—there were truly enlightened people, who considered it their duty to raise the level of Jewish social and spiritual life. This work was done by the enlightened, 'maskilim', who reanimated Hebrew literature. Abraham Mapu . . . [Judah] Leib Gordon . . . Peretz Smolenskin [among them].[117]

Dubnow's fresh look at Jewish history was revolutionary both for Russian Jews and the Russian government. The goals set forth in *Textbook of Jewish History* hardly conformed to the limits established by the official doctrine of modern Jewish education, which, in contrast to Dubnow's approach, still aimed at 'de-Judaizing' Jewish students. As a result, while authorizing classroom use of the first and second volumes of *Textbook of Jewish History*, spanning antiquity and the early Middle Ages, the Expert Committee of the Imperial Ministry of National Enlightenment

---

[110] Dubnow, *Uchebnik evreiskoi istorii*, i. 108. [111] Ibid. 109. [112] Ibid. 167. [113] Ibid. 171.
[114] Ibid. 170. [115] Ibid. 182, 184. [116] Ibid. 186–7. [117] Ibid. 194.

was reluctant to recommend these volumes officially to Jewish schools. Moreover, the committee considered the third volume, dealing with the rest of the Middle Ages and the modern era, 'inappropriate for school use in its current version',[118] citing the author's 'bias' and general lack of objectivity, the difficulty of the material, and many factual errors. In the committee's opinion, Dubnow provided a one-sided account of events of European history in which Jews figured prominently. For example, in describing the persecution of the Jews in medieval Spain and Germany, according to the committee, the author failed 'to explain these as a consequence of Jewish vices and faults, but [explained them as a result of] Christians' envy of the "skills" and "business talents" of the Jews'. Also, according to the committee, describing Jewish life in contemporary Russia, where, in Dubnow's words, 'an order of things analogous [to medieval persecution] prevailed', the author 'did not say a single word about the corruptive influence of the Jews on the economic well-being of the Christian population in the Vistula provinces [Russian Poland]'.[119] The committee also pointed out that the overabundance of 'various facts, personal and geographical names' in *Textbook of Jewish History* would cause 'great difficulty for students'. In addition, many issues, such as 'religious philosophy . . . a comparison of the philosophical views of [Ibn] Gabirol and those of Plato and Philo of Alexandria . . . works by Maimonides . . . kabbalah and the Zohar . . . and the [philosophy of] Spinoza', would be beyond the comprehension of secondary-school students. Finally, the committee mentioned the many 'historical errors', such as the author's 'identification of the western Roman empire with Italy' and his discussion of the Jewish origins of Islam, as unacceptable in a school textbook.[120]

This detailed criticism reveals the overall nationalist focus and approach of *Textbook of Jewish History*. The revolutionary bias of Dubnow's narrative, rather than particular historical facts and details, provoked an enthusiastic reception of the work by Jewish readers. In addition to its instant success, it was in steady demand for the next two decades, running through eighteen editions by 1917. It thus provided for the financial security of its author[121] and filled the minds and everyday lives of his readers with fresh spirit and new substance. In 1945 Aron Perel'man, former St Petersburg publisher and public figure, emphasized in his memoirs 'the special role Dubnow played in Russian Jewish historiography':

In Russian Jewish life, Dubnow's [*Textbook of Jewish*] *History* played a role similar to that of [Nikolai] Karamzin's *History* [*of the Russian State*] in the life of nineteenth-century Russian society. Dubnow's *History* has many defects; Karamzin's *History* is full of them. However, both Karamzin and Dubnow played an unforgettable role in their peoples' histories. Dubnow was the first major historiographer of Russian Jewry to draw the attention of his contemporaries to the glorious past of the Jews, like Karamzin who drew the attention of his educated Russian contemporaries to their national past. Dubnow believed that the his-

---

[118] Kelner, *Missioner istorii*, 246–7.   [119] Ibid.   [120] Ibid. 250.   [121] Ibid.

torian, in addition to being a scholar, should be an architect able to use material collected by other scholars to build an edifice of history according to his own plan.[122]

CONCLUSION

In the 1880s and 1890s creators of Russian Jewish history textbooks set out to resolve a host of immediate as well as imminent problems of modern Russian Jews.[123] First and foremost, they sought to introduce Jewish history into the curriculum of modern Jewish schools as a core subject. In the long term, they envisaged the study of Jewish history as a major tool of Jewish national revival.

The stories and heroes of Nemzer's, Minor's, and Dubnow's textbooks achieved most of these objectives. In addition to making the subject of Jewish history integral to modern Jewish education, they made the Jewish historical past integral to the national consciousness of many generations of Russian Jews. These textbooks were widely circulated in the classroom and beyond, profoundly influencing many readers. Prominent Zionist Shmarya Levin purposely avoided 'dry catechism, dates, rules' and chose 'the histories of Simon Dubnow' as his principal study material while teaching Judaism to his enthusiastic Jewish female students at the Ekaterinoslav gymnasium in the early 1900s.[124] Historian Mark Vishnitser recalled that in 1900 he 'immersed himself in [Dubnow's] textbook'. 'We, the young', he wrote, 'considered Dubnow our teacher in the field of history and regarded him with great respect.'[125] The Russian Jewish revolutionary and author Lev Teplitsky confided in a letter to Dubnow that he first read one of his textbooks in the 1900s. 'The book virtually captured my imagination', he wrote. '[It] provoked a storm in my mind so strong that since that moment I have never ceased to read with ever growing enthusiasm all of the best historiographical works on the Jews, and also dreamed of serving our people in some way.'[126] The 'historical' proof-texts, such as the stories of the Maccabees and David Reubeni, which figured so prominently in the minds of Lazar Kaganovich and Solomon Mikhoels, also suggest that the Russian-language textbooks from the 1880s and 1890s on Jewish history helped raise a whole generation in which 'Elishas . . . constituted a predominant element',[127] making Dubnow's dream a reality.

Methodologically and ideologically, in just two decades, the creators of these textbooks came a long way, from Nemzer's conformist 'patriotic' history to Minor's *kulturträger* 'didactic' history, to Dubnow's lucid 'pragmatic' and nationalist

---

[122] A. Perel'man, *Vospominaniya* (St Petersburg, 2009), 51.

[123] The textbooks by Nemzer, Minor, and Dubnow far exceeded the modest goals of authors of contemporary Russian textbooks on Judaism of providing basic knowledge about the Jewish religion. See Adler, 'Reinventing Religion', 154.

[124] S. Levin, *Forward from Exile* (Philadelphia, 1967), 367–8; see also Adler, 'Reinventing Religion', 150.   [125] Kelner, *Missioner istorii*, 238.

[126] Ibid. 239.   [127] Dubnow, *Kniga zhizni*, 85–6.

'revolutionary' histories. This progression was crucial for modern Jewish education, in which the study of Jewish history played a key role.

The development of Russian-language textbooks of Jewish history was linked
to the overall development of Russian Jewish historiography in the late nineteenth
century. The main contributions of Russian Jewish scholarship to academic Jewish
studies first appeared in these textbooks, including the history of the Jews in
eastern Europe as a whole new field of study and the influential concept of shifting
centres of Jewish cultural hegemony in the Diaspora as a driving force of Jewish
history.

The creators appropriated universal Jewish history by translating and
expanding German sources. They made this previously inaccessible Jewish history
into an important part of the Russian Jewish heritage and legitimized the history
and heritage of Russian Jews, who had been previously neglected, as an integral
part of universal Jewish history. The textbooks also helped a nascent Jewish
national consciousness bridge the gap between 'blood' and 'culture', solving what
Dubnow called the main dilemma of the modern Jew. Thus, the history textbook,
an advanced tool for self-education and self-improvement developed at the end of
the nineteenth century, effectively transformed the backward, anachronistic, and
essentially marginal community of Russian Jews into a self-confident vanguard of
modern Jewish nation-building at the beginning of the twentieth century.

In the end, the Russian-language Jewish history textbooks of the 1880s and
1890s virtually 'refresh[ed] . . . the [Jewish] spirit with a stream of the past',[128]
linking that past to the present and shaping the generations of the future.

[128] Minor, 'Predislovie perevodchika ko vtoromu izdaniyu', n.p.

Clothes Make the Man

A Photo Essay on Russian Jewish School Uniforms

ELIYANA R. ADLER

IN ONE of his beloved short stories, 'On Account of a Hat', Sholem Rabinovitz, better known by his pen name, Sholem Aleichem, describes the tragi-comic mishaps of a ne'er-do-well would-be businessman on his way home for the Passover holidays.[1] Because of the train schedule, Sholem Shachnah has to sleep at the station. Before lying down on a bench already occupied by a Russian official, he issues strict instructions to the porter to wake him for his train. At the appointed time, in his haste to catch the train, instead of grabbing his own hat, however, Sholem Shachnah inadvertently grabs the hat belonging to the still slumbering tsarist official. He boards the train only to walk past a mirror, where he sees, to his horror, the official:

Twenty times I tell him to wake me and I even give him a tip, and what does he do, that dumb ox, may he catch cholera in his face, but wake the official instead! And me he leaves asleep on the bench! Tough luck, Sholem Shachnah old boy, but this year you'll spend Passover in Zlodievke, not at home.[2]

The story is, obviously, a farce, yet another misadventure for the antihero Sholem Shachnah Rattlebrain. Such comedy was Sholem Aleichem's bread and butter. This ability to laugh at all of the indignities of Jewish life in Russia gained him tremendous popularity. But there are serious themes embedded even in these light stories. In fact, it is not only Sholem Shachnah who is fooled by the hat with the red band. Even the ticket seller and conductor treat him with unusual courtesy for those few minutes. The mere addition of a hat transforms a poor Jew into a respected representative of the government.

The story is a popular one, and has been analysed from a variety of perspectives

I am grateful to Sean Martin and Victoria Khiterer for providing thoughtful comments on this chapter.

[1] Sholem Aleichem, 'On Account of a Hat', trans. I. Rosenfeld, in *A Treasury of Yiddish Stories*, ed. I. Howe and E. Greenberg (New York, 1954), 111–18.

[2] Sholem Aleichem, 'On Account of a Hat', 117.

by literary scholars. It is a story about Jewish identity, about Jewish psychology, a Jewish response to Gogol's 'The Overcoat'.[3] David Roskies has demonstrated that the story ultimately originates in an old Jewish joke.[4] At the same time, at the most basic level, it is a social commentary. Sholem Aleichem was playing with costumes partly because they were meaningful in the world in which he lived.

In his autobiography Sholem Aleichem includes a telling scene. The son of a local man not known for his piety has returned to town from the Russian high school where he is studying. That Saturday the young man and his father come to the synagogue. The congregation is overwhelmed by the experience:

Next to him stood his son, Sholom, or Solomon, wearing his uniform with silver buttons from top to bottom and a strange cap—a cap with a badge. He held a little Siddur and prayed, just like a normal person. Neither the adults nor the children took their eyes off this gymnasium student with the silver buttons. He seemed to be like everyone else—an average boy—yet he was different. He was a gymnasium student.[5]

But why should a group of Jews who go to synagogue regularly and know the prayers backwards and forwards find themselves unable to concentrate simply because of the arrival of a visitor? Surely visitors came through their town with some frequency. It is not the fact of a relative stranger, but the juxtaposition of this stranger's uniform with his setting. The worlds of the traditional Jewish house of worship and the imperial gymnasium were as yet strangers. Just as Sholem Shachnah could not assimilate his own face in the hat of a tsarist official, the congregation was unprepared to process a young man who felt at home both in a synagogue and a gymnasium.

Throughout the later decades of the nineteenth century, as young Jews increasingly entered Russian schools, communities and individuals would learn to assimilate these two worlds. As they did so, the school uniform remained a potent symbol, both in writing and in visual culture. This chapter seeks to probe the meanings assigned to the school uniform through an analysis of memoirs and photographs. The discussion of uniforms, in autobiographies and then in images, will follow a brief historical introduction to the entry of Jews into Russian schools.

FRAMING THE PICTURE

The 1804 Statute on the Jews in the Russian Empire, the first major attempt to respond to the integration of the Polish lands and their large Jewish population, included an open invitation for Jews to attend all of the schools in the empire.[6]

---

[3] For an overview of literary criticism of 'On Account of a Hat', see D. Roskies, 'Inside Sholem Shachnah's Hat', *Prooftexts*, 21 (2001), 40.

[4] D. Roskies, 'Yiddish Storytelling and the Politics of Rescue', in E. R. Adler and S. L. Jelen (eds.), *Jewish Literature and History: An Interdisciplinary Conversation* (Lanham, Md., 2007), 22.

[5] Sholem Aleichem, *From the Fair*, trans. and ed. C. Leviant (New York, 1985), 156.

[6] *Polnoe sobranie zakonov Rossiiskoi imperii, 1649–1825*, 45 vols. (St Petersburg, 1830), xxviii. 731–7 (9 Dec. 1804).

In point of fact, at that time there were not yet many schools in the empire, and most Jews lacked the prerequisites for attending them. Nonetheless the law signalled an early desire to acculturate the Jews into Russian society, and a few Jews did take the government up on its generous offer.

In 1827, when the city of Vilna wanted to define the area of Jewish residence, certain individuals were asked to move. One Jew, by the name of Pines, refused to relocate to the Jewish area. In his ultimately successful petition to the city, he brought as evidence of his special status the educational achievements of his children. Two of Pines's daughters worked as midwives and a third was taking examinations to serve as a teacher. His son was in the fifth class of the gymnasium. Interestingly, Pines also saw fit to mention that he himself did not wear Jewish garb.[7] In the early decades of the nineteenth century a family that sent its children to Russian schools and dressed in the Russian style was, quite literally as it turns out, outside of the bounds of the Jewish community; however, over the course of the century this would change with surprising rapidity.

As of 1853, in all of the *gimnazii* and *progimnazii* of the empire there were 159 Jewish students, or 1.2 per cent of the total number of students. Ten years later in 1863 there were 552 Jewish students, or 3.2 per cent. In 1873 Jewish enrolments surpassed 5.0 per cent.[8] These same years saw major expansion in secondary educational institutions across the empire. Whereas in 1871 there were 145 *gimnazii* and *progimnazii* in Russia, by 1879 there were 201.[9] Thus the fact that by 1881 Jews constituted 12.0 per cent of the students in all Russian educational institutions demonstrates the burgeoning Jewish interest in Russian schooling.[10]

It is also worth noting that these young pioneers of Russification included girls as well as boys. In 1886 Jewish girls made up 8.6 per cent of the total population in women's *gimnazii* and *progimnazii*. In Odessa, they were over 26.0 per cent. In 1887 the government began to introduce quotas to limit Jewish numbers in universities and secondary schools across the empire. However, the new laws only explicitly addressed Jewish males. In practice Jewish women sometimes also faced obstacles, but their numbers remained legally unconstrained throughout the tsarist period. By 1911 Jewish boys were 9.1 per cent of the pupils in men's *gimnazii*,

---

[7] P. Kon, 'Yidishe froien in der akusherie-shul baym vilner universitet (1811–1824)', *Historishe shrift*, 1 (1929), 767.

[8] S. V. Pozner, *Evrei v obshchei shkole: K istorii zakonodatel'stva i pravetel'stvennoi politiki v oblasti evreiskogo voprosa* (St Petersburg, 1914), 38. Russian *gimnazii* were academic secondary schools of seven years. *Progimnazii* were parallel schools typically of four years and roughly equivalent to middle schools. Both were elite institutions that often had entrance examinations. *Real'nye shkoly* were more modern secondary schools modelled on German *Realschulen*. However, it is important to note that not only did these schools change over time but they were often different depending on the auspices and sponsorship of the school and the gender of the students. Thus the curriculum and rigour of a private *gimnaziya* for girls might bear little resemblance to that of a military-sponsored *gimnaziya* for boys.

[9] D. K. Howard, 'Elite Secondary Education in Late Imperial Russia, 1881–1905', Ph.D. thesis (Indiana University, 2006), 55.   [10] Pozner, *Evrei v obshchei shkole*, 39.

progimnazii, and *real'nye shkoly*, whereas Jewish girls were 13.5 per cent of those in the women's schools.[11]

EXPERIENCE OF UNIFORMITY

In pursuing the effects of this educational sea change on the Jewish community, I have relied on enrolment figures, faculty lists, newspaper articles, textbooks, almanacs, legislation, and memoirs. A number of factors jump out from a perusal of memoirs of Jewish students who attended Russian schools. The former students speak about the joy of engaging in study, the first stirrings of political activism, the frustrations of official and social antisemitism, distance from family, and many other aspects that one might expect. Less predictable was their sartorial consciousness. Students in Russian secondary schools typically wore uniforms, and this proved very significant for Jews. School uniforms—for boys paramilitary in style, for girls less flashy, often a particular tie or pinafore over a plain coloured dress—were a mark of the Russian upper classes. Thus attending Russian secondary schools meant leaving not only one's home and neighbourhood but also even one's sense of self. It meant wearing what must have felt at first like a costume.

In the early years of Jewish attendance at Russian schools, this was a source of embarrassment. In his treatment of Jewish education in Russia, Petr Marek quotes a Jewish gymnasium student from the 1840s living a dual life. Once he arrived at school the student would take off his Jewish garb, tuck his *peyes* behind his ears, and put on his school uniform. Before leaving, he would switch back into his other persona.[12] Whereas this young man had to perform a Superman-like identity switch in order to attend the gymnasium, and could wear neither his Jewish self in school nor his school self in the streets, over time other Jewish students felt more pride in their uniforms.

B. Kruglyak describes looking forward to returning to his native town in his university uniform:

You start to dream about how pleasant it will be when you appear in the provinces as a student, in your peaked cap with the blue band around it. Won't that be great! With reverence and envy the provincials will say: 'Ah, the former *melamed*—what a fellow, he's preparing for his doctorate!'[13]

[11] G. Voltke, 'Prosveshchenie', in L. Katsenelson and D. G. Gintsburg (eds.), *Evreiskaya entsiklopediya: Svod znanii o evreistve i ego kul'ture v proshlom i nastoyashchem*, 16 vols. (St Petersburg, 1908–13), xiii. 58. For more on the education of Jewish girls, see E. R. Adler, *In Her Hands: The Education of Jewish Girls in Tsarist Russia* (Detroit, 2011).

[12] P. Marek, *Ocherki po istorii prosveshcheniya evreev v Rossii: Dva vospitaniya* (Moscow: 1909), 167; cited in B. Nathans, *Beyond the Pale: The Jewish Encounter with Late Imperial Russia* (Berkeley, Calif., 2000), 207.

[13] B. Kruglyak, 'Vospominaniya o zhizni eksternov v Odesse (1896 g.)', *Evreiskaya starina*, 1916, no. 9, p. 282; cited in Nathans, *Beyond the Pale*, 239.

In reality his family was horrified by his transformation. Likewise Leon Trotsky describes the deflation of his enormous pride on the first day of school when a young shop-apprentice spat on the shoulder of his new uniform.[14] These young men wore their school uniforms with a great sense of purpose but found that other members of their community, as well as those outside it, understood the uniforms differently.

The uniforms were in fact multivalent signifiers. Kruglyak's family saw his distance from his roots. Trotsky, of course, interpreted his encounter as class based. In both cases, all of the parties involved shared an understanding that the uniform was meaningful. The student uniforms were immediately recognizable. However, interpretations of the meaning differed. Kruglyak's inherent valuation of a *melamed*, or teacher of children in a traditional Jewish elementary school, compared with a doctoral student was not in fact shared by his family. Trotsky's assailant may have been offering a commentary on Trotsky's class status or may have been more concerned about his ethnic background. In either case he perceived the young student as an unwelcome interloper.

This is not to suggest that only the wearers of uniforms could appreciate their value. For two Jewish sisters in Suwałki (Suvalkskaya guberniya), the gymnasia students returning from classes on the sabbath were the unattainable other: 'Tsivia and I were envious of the strolling pupils for their starched uniforms. Their dresses were brown with a white collar all around. A black pinafore fluttered when they walked.'[15] The two sisters knew that their father would never allow them to attend a school that met on Saturdays. Although the author, Hanah Kotzer, had been an eager and successful student at her Russian grammar school for two years, she describes her longing for more education not in terms of the books and lessons, but by way of the smart, neat uniform that would never be hers.

Rivka Guber, who would later become the first girl in her agricultural settlement to go to the city to attend a gymnasium, described the reaction of her community to an earlier student visiting his family: 'When he would come to visit from great distances, once every two years, and would cross the road, straight and proper in his blue jacket and student hat, the elderly would bless him with affection and reverence—the young girls ceased breathing as he passed before them.'[16] In Guber's retelling the entire community participated in welcoming the student and all that he stood for. Yet the other Jews were also distinguished from their visitor. He stood out among his own people because of his uniform.

Uniforms were a meaningful focus because they clearly signalled 'the Other'. This designation was most important for the first-generation students, reaching cautiously beyond the confines of their homes. For those Jews already significantly

[14] L. Trotsky, *My Life: An Attempt at Autobiography* (New York, 1970), 47.

[15] H. Kotzer [Bat Shalom], *Netivei ḥayim* (Tel Aviv, 1977), 24.

[16] R. Guber, *Morashah lehanḥil* (Jerusalem, 1981), 12.

Russified, the Other was at times the world of tradition. Anna Vygodskaya, born in 1868 to a rapidly acculturating family, mentions her own school uniform only in an incident she relates about getting into trouble for forgetting to wear her bow.[17] Rather it is specifically Jewish accoutrements that surprise her. In her section on her student years she points out with obvious humour the oddness of her stepbrother being expected to pray daily in *tefilin* by his grandparents. To Vygodskaya the image of a Russian schoolboy wearing phylacteries was far more anomalous that that of a Jewish boy wearing a school uniform.[18]

However, for those Jews just emerging from the traditional Jewish milieu, by far the majority, the school uniform was a concrete representation of their transformation, a rite of passage not just of adolescence but also of the gradual merging of the Jewish community with the Russian educated classes. Indeed many of these excerpts expose the reactions of both the student and the Jewish community, because of course the thousands of Jewish students who attended Russian educational institutions did so not in isolation, but as members of families and communities.

It is also worth highlighting that almost from the beginning of the annexation of the Polish and Lithuanian lands, the tsarist government had issued a number of rulings aimed at getting the Jews to abandon their distinctive garb. Programmes that were initially voluntary were gradually replaced by mandatory laws with hefty fines attached.[19] Yet not only was it necessary to continually reissue and refine such laws, but clearly, as these memoirs reveal, they had not been all that successful. Indeed some have suggested that the laws had the opposite effect, causing some Jews to sacralize their traditional clothing.[20] It was only later, and through involvement with Russian education, that Jews truly began to change their garb and to experience the transformation inherent in that act.

For any child, donning a uniform for the first time is an important act. For the Jewish authors of these memoirs the uniform meant not only becoming a student but also joining the Other, becoming part of the Russian environment. Part of the task of the social historian is to trace the paths of change. Rather than just noting that many Jews were attracted to what Russia had to offer in the later imperial period, we seek to discover how and why. Although there is obviously much more to be mined in these autobiographical texts—and undoubtedly many more to read—they demonstrate a fascination with the school uniform and help to explain the preponderance of photographs of Jewish students in uniforms from the late tsarist period.

[17] A. P. Vygodskaya, *Istoriya odnoi zhizni: Vospominaniya* (Riga, 1938), 86; Eng. trans.: *The Story of a Life: Memoirs of a Young Jewish Woman in the Russian Empire*, trans. and ed. E. M. Avrutin and R. H. Greene (DeKalb, Ill., 2012). [18] Vygodskaya, *Istoriya odnoi zhizni*, 81.

[19] On these efforts, see E. M. Avrutin, 'The Politics of Jewish Legibility: Documentation Practices and Reform During the Reign of Nicholas I', *Jewish Social Studies*, 11/2 (2005), esp. 149–55; Yu. Gessen, 'Odezhda', in Katsenelson and Gintsburg (eds.), *Evreiskaya entsiklopediya*, xii. 46–50.

[20] E. Silverman, *A Cultural History of Jewish Dress* (London, 2013), 75.

PORTRAITS OF ASPIRATION

Photography developed in Russia much as it did elsewhere in Europe and the United States of America.[21] The equipment was originally unwieldy and expensive and initially provided an alternative method of having portraits made only for the wealthy. However, as methods, techniques, and equipment improved, it became possible to produce smaller portraits for considerably less cost. The advent of the *carte de visite* in the mid-1850s—multiple small portraits produced simultaneously and mounted on cards for display and disbursement—led to an international fad and a true democratization of the medium.[22] This trend, along with changes in the international postal system, would in turn usher in the postcard craze towards the end of the century.[23]

Members of the rising and aspiring middle classes were especially keen on photography, as it not only made family and individual portraits available to a larger swathe of the public but also allowed them to participate in the construction of their public images. By the late nineteenth century the Jewish community of eastern Europe was, as the educational trends discussed above suggest, deeply engaged in the modernization project. East European Jews were also on the move, migrating in unprecedented and disproportionate numbers. In the words of David Shneer, 'for Jews, photography was a means of maintaining memory across long distances'. Shneer adds that the late emergence of the field, its relatively low status, and its entrepreneurial demands meant that Jews were overrepresented among photographers.[24] For all of these reasons, the development of a means of sending idealized images to friends and family far and wide was particularly attractive and accessible to Jews.[25]

[21] D. Elliot, 'The Photograph in Russia: Icon of a New Age', in id. (ed.), *Photography in Russia, 1840–1940* (London, 1992), 11.

[22] T. Saburova, 'Early Masters of Russian Photography', in Elliot (ed.), *Photography in Russia*, 31–5; W. C. Darrah, *Cartes de Visite in Nineteenth Century Photography* (Gettysburg, Pa., 1981), ch. 2; E. A. McCauley, *A. A. E. Disderi and the Carte de Visite Portrait Photograph* (New Haven, Conn., 1985), 1.

[23] For more on the development of the postcard, see e.g. C. M. Geary and V.-L. Webb (eds.), *Delivering Views: Distant Cultures in Early Postcards* (Washington DC, 1998). Frank Staff discussed the causal link between the earlier and later cards. 'With a stretch of the imagination it could be said that these pictorial visiting cards are the direct ancestors of the picture postcards, especially when it is remembered that messages were sometimes written on them' (*The Picture Postcard and its Origins* (New York, 1966), 10).

[24] D. Shneer, *Through Soviet Jewish Eyes: Photography, War, and the Holocaust* (New Brunswick, NJ, 2011), 15.

[25] Perhaps one of the most famous of the Jewish photographers from the early twentieth century was Alte Katz, the grandmother of Yaffa Eliach, whose photographs were featured in the 'Tower of Life' exhibition at the United States Holocaust Memorial Museum (see Y. Eliach, *There Once was a World: A 900-Year Chronicle of the Shtetl of Eishyshok* (Boston, 1998), 323–4). For two excellent articles on the importance of postcards in the Jewish context, albeit slightly outside the geographical and chronological bounds of this chapter, see E. Smith, 'Greetings from Faith: Early-Twentieth-Century

All of the photographs included in this chapter come from the archives of the YIVO Institute for Jewish Research. YIVO was founded in Vilna in 1925 as a central location to collect and analyse material related to the history and culture of east European Jews.[26] In 1940 the institution and some of its documents moved to New York. Those documents and the scholars fortunate enough to survive the war followed afterwards, and YIVO has continued to serve its original purpose up to the present. Although some of the photographs in the collection pertain to a particular individual or come from a single photographer, most are the bequests of American offspring or relatives of the subjects and have been donated individually. A significant portion of YIVO's photograph archive can be accessed on-line.[27]

Families had the opportunity to work together with the photographer to craft the image they wanted to send out. All photography is both art and artifice, but this latter aspect is perhaps most transparent in staged studio portraits. Most photographers had an array of backdrops, furniture, and props available.[28] But even before setting foot in the studio, families signalled their actual or desired level of wealth and culture in dressing for the session. Of course most would wear their finest garments to impress the recipients of the cards. It is thus noteworthy that many such portraits include a son in a school uniform.

The uniform, which had to be specially tailored according to each school's specifications, was in many cases the most expensive suit of clothes that the young man owned. In some cases, it may well have been his only presentable outfit. Nonetheless, including the uniform in the photo was a symbolic choice. The uniform, even more than other symbols such as books, let the viewer know that this family was committed to modern education. Even as it made the child stand out from his family, it simultaneously showed the aspirations of the entire group. By embracing a child in uniform, they were symbolically embracing what modern Russia had to offer.

To some degree this aspiration can be demonstrated with reference to its opposite. Indeed, while there are many extant family photographs showcasing a son in uniform, there are also a few that show a son in the garb of a traditional yeshiva student. Discussing the reasons east European Jews sought to have themselves photographed, Jeffrey Shandler notes: 'Their motives for this engagement were anything but uniform; they included the thorough embrace of modernity as well as efforts to resist or counteract it.'[29]

American Jewish New Year Postcards', in D. Morgan and S. M. Promey (eds.), *The Visual Cultures of American Religions* (Berkeley, Calif., 2001); S. Sabar, 'Between Poland and Germany: Jewish Religious Practices in Illustrated Postcards of the Early Twentieth Century', *Polin*, 16 (2003), 137–66.

[26] For more on the origins of YIVO, see C. E. Kuznitz, *YIVO and the Making of Modern Jewish Culture: Scholarship for the Yiddish Nation* (Cambridge, 2014).

[27] <http://www.yivoarchives.org/?p=pages/photo_archives> (accessed 18 Feb. 2017).

[28] Darrah, *Cartes de Visite*, ch. 4.

[29] J. Shandler, 'What Does it Mean to be Photographed as a Jew?', *Jewish Quarterly Review*, 94 (2004), 10.

In these images, it is the son standing in for the entire family by virtue of his clothing style. The fathers in Figures 1–3 do not look dramatically different. All are dressed in relatively modern clothing. While only one wears a hat (Figure 1), he does not have a beard. Another of the fathers has a trim beard, but no hat (Figure 2) while the third is bearded and holds his hat in his hand (Figure 3). These are ambivalent signals. The women are even more challenging to read for clues. In the two images where they appear, both are dressed modestly, as was the style of the time, and neither appears to have her hair covered, but it is difficult to discern details. It is only by viewing the school-age sons that the public stances of these families, with regard to modernity and tradition, become clear.

These three photographs stand in contrast to Figure 4, in which the majority of the family members clearly broadcast their modern and Russian commitments. Not only are the two older boys dressed in school uniforms but the father is as well. He was, according to the documentation accompanying the photograph, a teacher in a Russian school. Instead of wearing or holding a traditional hat that could be worn for prayer services, he rests his hand on the cap of a tsarist official. Even the younger sons, not yet attending school, are dressed in sailor suits, as if highlighting the martial quality of the men in the family. While the mother wears a fairly traditional, if expensive, dress, the two daughters, strikingly, are outfitted in the matching white starched pinafores of a Russian school uniform.

In addition to family portraits, individual portraits on *cartes de visite* became increasingly popular in the latter half of the nineteenth century. As well as being sent to family abroad, these photographs could be given to teachers, close friends, sweethearts, and family members as signs of friendship and respect. Whereas the family photo was often elaborately staged, with backgrounds and props, the individual portrait could be more simple. Popular trends included head and bust shots and vignetted photos, with only the subject visible. There were also a variety of full-body poses sometimes designed to highlight the character, profession, or figure of the subject.[30]

The head and bust shots in the YIVO collection tend to show boys older than those in the family portraits. These are young men in secondary school, thinking already of their futures, who might well have had a need or desire to share their photograph with others. The earliest in the collection comes from 1878 and was taken in Minsk: it shows a man who would later become a doctor (Figure 5). At the time the photo was taken there were 114 Jewish students attending gymnasia in Minsk, representing 26 per cent of the school population.[31] Figure 6 shows the young P. Marik, who in 1884 presented his *carte de visite* to a certain M. Gurvitsh. By the time Michal Szabad posed for his portrait in Vilna in 1908 (Figure 7), Jews in school uniform were already a regular sight in the city. Although their numbers had dropped from the 20 per cent before the introduction of the *numerus clausus*, in 1911 they were still over 15 per cent in the Vilna educational district.[32] Beyond the

[30] Ibid. 26–30.   [31] Pozner, *Evrei v obshchei shkole*, 67.   [32] Voltke, 'Prosveshchenie', 57–8.

Figure 1. Studio portrait of man and three boys, Radomsko, *c.*1900: studio of Emilia
YIVO Archives, New York, RG 120 'Territorial Photographic Collection, 1860s–1970s', Poland before
World War II, Radomsko, 3262

Figure 2. Studio portrait of the Rachlen family, Mariupol (Ekaterinoslavskaya guberniya), 1906. The eldest son wears a proper school uniform; his brothers are dressed in a similar style but are too young to be in secondary school.

YIVO Archives, RG 120, Russia II, Bilson, 15059

Figure 3. Studio portrait of the Nikolayev family (Khersonskaya guberniya), *c.*1900: studio of V. Z. Ronesa. It shows a family: two parents, four daughters, and one son. It is not possible to tell if any of the girls is in school uniform, but the boy certainly is, as, in addition to his distinctive shirt, the telltale cap is beside him.

YIVO Archives, RG 120, Russia I, Nikolayev, 108

Figure 4. Studio portrait of the Tolpin family, Ostrog (Volynskaya guberniya), 1906.
YIVO Archives, RG 120, Poland, before World War II, Ostrog, 2766

Figure 5. An oval-framed studio portrait of a young man in school uniform, Minsk, 1878. Inscribed on the back in Russian: 'Dr M. Lurie in his youth, 1878'. A later hand, possibly belonging to a YIVO archivist, has translated the inscription into Yiddish.

YIVO Archives, RG 120, Russia, Minsk, 4

Figure 6. *Carte de visite* of P. Marik, Shavli (Kovenskaya guberniya), 1884. Inscribed on the back in Russian: 'As a memento to M. Gurvitsh . . . 13 February 1884'.

YIVO Archives, RG 2 'Lithuanian Jewish Communities, 1844–1940', 76975

Figure 7. Studio portrait of Michal Szabad in school uniform, Vilna, 1908. The folder containing this photo also contains an image of Szabad as a child. He would appear to be a relative, perhaps a nephew, of Dr Tsemah Szabad (1864–1935), a prominent physician and educational and political activist in Vilna. On the basis of photographic evidence, it seems that he was also one of the two stepbrothers of Anna Vygodskaya, whose memoir is mentioned above.

YIVO Archives, RG 120, Poland before World War II, Vilna, 5996.1

age of the subject, these small photographs provide little information about the context of their production.

Slightly more information is available from the full-body images. At times the boys were posed to highlight their status. Despite the somewhat garish backdrop, Yu. Ofnaem's being seated with a table and a book clearly conveys his status as a student (Figure 8). Leaning slightly on his arm and with his feet crossed, he looks at ease in his role. Meir Gordon's photographer tried for a less obvious, and arguably less successful, pose. Gordon is standing and holding what appears to be a stick (Figure 9). Yet the military-style look is undercut by the boy's youth and poor posture. Figure 10 presents a compromise between the two poses. The unidentified student stands proud and straight in his uniform, leaning lightly on what appears to be a writing desk.

All of these highly staged poses highlight the conventions of the time. Given the relatively low price of the *cartes de visite*, it was necessary for the photographers to produce as many as they could. Darrah claims that sixty to a hundred sittings per day was not unusual during the height of their popularity.[33] It was thus not always

---

[33] Darrah, *Cartes de Visite*, 24.

Figure 8. Studio portrait of Yu. Ofnaem, Siedlce, 1914. The title of the book he is holding is simply *Album*, suggesting that it is a prop rather than his actual schoolbook. Inscribed on the back in Russian: 'From Yu. Ofnaem, 7 April 1914'.

YIVO Archives, RG 120, Poland before World War II, Siedlce, 3436

Figure 9. Studio portrait of Rabbi Elijah Gordon's son, Meir, Vilna.
Although it is not dated, there is reason to believe that this photo may actually be from after the
First World War. A second photo, showing Meir Gordon with his family (YIVO Archives,
RG 120, Poland before World War II, Snipzki, 3564.01) is captioned only 'Before 1930'.
Gordon's uniform is actually from a Jewish rather than a Russian school. Such schools existed
in the early twentieth century, but they became much more popular later.
YIVO Archives, RG 120, Poland before World War II, Vilna, 6002

Eliyana R. Adler

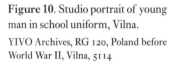

Figure 10. Studio portrait of young man in school uniform, Vilna.

YIVO Archives, RG 120, Poland before World War II, Vilna, 5114

possible for a photographer to know his or her subject or to be responsive to their particular character. It was far easier to revisit a formulaic tableau or pose considered generally appropriate. Even more than schoolboys, soldiers were the most frequently photographed men in uniform. Given the risks of their profession, as well as the cachet of their uniforms, it was common for them to give loved ones mementos. *Cartes de visite* depicting handsomely uniformed soldiers may well have influenced the popularity of other uniformed photographs, such as those of students, and photographers might well have become over-reliant on this sort of pose.

Despite the larger number of soldiers, as with the family photographs, the prevalence of individual *cartes de visite* of young Jewish men in school uniforms is noteworthy. It is certainly possible that there was an overlap between the kind of person who would attend a modern Russian school and one who would choose to spend money on a personal portrait. Both were part of the modernizing package. And yet, as we have seen, a diversity of families invested in portraits. An added factor would appear to be pride. Especially after the introduction of quotas, acceptance into a Russian school was a difficult feat for a Jewish boy. The cost of the uniform and tuition were also substantial. An individual or family might well want to publicize their successes as well as their cultural leanings.

What is missing from this collection is individual portraits with Jewish girls obviously in school uniforms. A number of factors go into explaining this. First of all the girls' school uniform was less dramatic and recognizable. This means that both the contemporary and the historian would be less likely to notice it. As a result, some of the girls in similar portraits may in fact be wearing their school uniforms, but, even if they were, the impact on the viewer is less without the jaunty cap and shiny buttons of the boys' uniforms. Unlike with boys, an individual or family could not rely upon making a statement by showing a girl in her school uniform. Figure 11 shows a girls' gymnasium in Romny. All of the girls are wearing dark-coloured garment of some sort over dark-coloured dresses. En masse, it is easy to see that they are wearing their uniforms. In a black-and-white photograph it is impossible to see either the colours or any other distinguishing characteristics. It is possible that these girls would have been recognized on the street for their academic achievements, but a photograph does not do their uniforms justice. The girls at the mixed school in Keidan from 1904 (Figure 12) wear white aprons that contrast sharply with their dark dresses and make a stronger impression.

Yet the fact that boys' school uniforms stood out more was not accidental. Secondary schools in Russia originally existed to train the sons of noble families to fill positions in the state bureaucracy. This was to be a sort of state service, complete with a table of ranks and regular promotions, much like the military. Some of these boys were in fact in training to enter the officer corps, and it is understandable that their school uniforms should have a military style. Schools for girls came later and with less of a clear professional progression. The first were more like finishing schools for the daughters of the wealthy and required no

Figure 11. Studio portrait of teachers and students at a girls' gymnasium, Romny (Poltavskaya guberniya), c.1905.

YIVO Archives, RG 120, Russia I, Romny, 1

Figure 12. Outdoor portrait of students and two teachers from a school in Keidan (Kovenskaya guberniya), 1904

YIVO Institute for Jewish Research, RG 120 Lithuania 1

uniforms. Eventually more academic schools for girls appeared, and some introduced uniforms, but not all did and never in a martial design. As Jennifer Craik has noted in a more general context, while male uniforms typically demonstrate societal notions of masculinity, female uniforms are less easily defined.[34]

Additionally, Jewish and other families may have felt more ambivalent about their daughters' educational careers than about those of their sons. As discussed above, the image of a son in a school uniform in a family picture conveyed a move towards modernity, Russification, and bourgeois respectability. A Jewish man with a high-school education could aspire to become a teacher in a modern school, a state rabbi, or even to higher education and a career in medicine or law. All of these brought financial reward and respect, at least in progressive circles. A daughter in a school uniform in a photograph would have been a more radical statement. A limited number of professions were also open to women, but families aspiring to a higher socio-economic status largely did not expect their wives and daughters to work.

Anna Vygodskaya, mentioned above for her family's progressive attitudes and commitment to secular education, was sent to gymnasium as a matter of course. However, when she expressed a desire for higher education, her parents begged her to desist, claiming that sending a single daughter to a distant city for schooling would bring shame on the family.[35] She finally managed to secure the permission required from her father to attend the Higher Women's Courses in St Petersburg only by threatening to enter the even less respectable midwifery courses that did not require his permission.[36] When Rivka Guber's father sent her to a gymnasium, her grandfather expressed concern that all of her dowry money would be spent on education and she would thus be unable to marry.[37]

CONCLUSION

'Uniforms shape who we are and how we perform our identities. As well as becoming a leitmotif of our clothed self, uniforms have equally shaped our ways of seeing and become central to the visual language and spatial conventions of photography.'[38] This brief examination of references to school uniforms in memoirs by nineteenth-century Russian Jews and photographs of Jewish students in school uniforms held in the YIVO collections raises a number of issues connected with education, modernization, and the social history of images. The autobiographies and photos, while they must be read differently, both ultimately point to the significance of the school uniform in Russian Jewish culture.[39] In words and in

[34] J. Craik, *Uniforms Exposed: From Conformity to Transgression* (Oxford, 2005), 12.
[35] Vygodskaya, *Istoriya odnoi zhizni*, 63.   [36] Ibid. 76.
[37] Guber, *Morashah lehanhil*, 12.   [38] Craik, *Uniforms Exposed*, 4.
[39] The YIVO archives also contain numerous photographs of Jewish boys from the Austrian empire in their school uniforms. Although there was certainly overlap in the cultural meanings of education

images, they give a sense of the laden quality of first encounters. Just as a Jewish student arriving in a town in the late nineteenth century, especially if he or she was among the first to do so in uniform, attracted attention both positive and negative, so too the impact of the photographs, especially those showing a child in uniform in the midst of a family grouping, is startling.

In all cultures and settings, dress is meaningful. In nineteenth-century Russia the short hair, glasses, and simple black dresses of nihilist women, like the long hair and peasant shirts of populist men, had a cultural valence. So too did the sharp, neat, embellished styling of the boys' gymnasium uniform. In the 1850s this was still very much a sign of the Russian nobility and elite. Over time, however, both circumstances and symbols evolve. In the ensuing decades, as more and more secondary schools opened, the ethnic, social, and gender make-up of Russian educational institutions began to change. This was reflected in debates over the curriculum, discussions of what girls and the lower classes ought to be taught, the introduction of multiple religion classes, and expanded meanings and venues for the uniform.[40]

The memoirs and photographs in this chapter capture the Jewish community in the midst of transition. In these images, the uniform carries weight and meaning, but that meaning is unstable and multivalent. The uniform is disruptive, capturing attention, but it is also a source of pride, a marker of aspiration. As is clear from the memoirs, the evolution of the meaning of the uniform was gradual and highly varied. In some towns, communities, or families the school uniform remained a shock right up until the end of the century. In others it was accepted and even expected by then. Jacob Shatzky quotes the poet and activist J. L. Gordon in 1864, with perhaps a bit of wishful thinking, stating that in Lithuanian Jewish communities, Jewish children no longer had to hide their uniforms.[41] Thus although the photographs and memoirs span a period of several decades, with the written records beginning earlier and the visual ones lasting longer, they capture an ongoing and evolving sense of wonder about the school uniform.

By the end of the century, it was more common to see children in Jewish schools also sporting uniforms. In the early decades of the twentieth century youth groups

among Jews in the neighbouring regions, the conditions were also different in significant ways. This chapter thus only includes photos and memoirs from the Russian empire.

[40] On these changes, see e.g. G. J. Makowski, 'The Russian Classical Gymnasium, 1864–1890', Ph.D. thesis (Indiana University, 1993); S. T. Duke, 'Educating Non-Russians in Late Imperial Russia: An Historical Study of Educational Development in a Multiethnic Setting', Ph.D. thesis (Indiana University, 1999); A. Sinel, *The Classroom and the Chancellery: State Educational Reform in Russia under Count Dmitry Tolstoi* (Cambridge, Mass., 1973); E. R. Adler 'Reinventing Religion: Jewish Religion Textbooks in Russian Gymnasia', *Journal of Jewish Education*, 77/2 (2011), 141–56; V. Schedrin, 'A Story within a Story: The First Russian-Language Jewish History Textbooks, 1880–1900' (this volume, pp. 109–30).

[41] Y. L. Gordon, cited in J. Shatzky, *Kultur-geshikhte fun der haskole in lite: fun di eltste tsaytn biz hibas tsien* (Buenos Aires, 1950), 127.

Eliyana R. Adler

of all sorts, including those within the Jewish community, used uniforms to distinguish themselves and their ideologies. Photographs of the distinctive scarves and emblems of the various Zionist and socialist Jewish youth groups could easily fill a second chapter. By the interwar period the sight of a Jew in uniform was ubiquitous. In the course of a few decades, the meaning of uniforms in the Jewish community had changed entirely and Sholem Shachnah would no longer have needed to miss Passover at home on account of his hat.

How Jews Gained Their Education in Kiev, 1860–1917

VICTORIA KHITERER

RUSSIAN governmental policies on Jewish education changed several times during the nineteenth and early twentieth centuries. As Michael Stanislawski has shown, the Russian government actively intervened in affairs related to the traditional Jewish educational system. The law of 1844 led to the establishment of Jewish state schools in many cities and towns in the Pale of Settlement, subordinating traditional religious Jewish schools, *ḥeder*s, to the Ministry of National Enlightenment (Ministerstvo narodnogo prosveshcheniya). The Russian government planned to transform Jewish society through this new educational system and achieve rapprochement between Jews and the general population.[1] Hence, the Russian language was part of the curriculum in Jewish state schools. From 1864 the government required that all private Jewish teachers, *melamedim*, pass an examination to show proficiency in Russian.[2] Jewish state schools thus served as a tool for the Russification of the Jewish population.

The imperial authorities allowed Jews to establish state and private Jewish schools in the Pale of Settlement and, starting in the 1860s, outside it. Jewish schools were opened in many cities outside the Pale, even in the Russian capitals of St Petersburg and Moscow.[3] A private school for impoverished Jewish boys and girls was established in St Petersburg by Lazar and Anna Berman in 1867. In 1873 their daughter Sara 'received permission to open a private school for Jewish girls', also in St Petersburg.[4] In Moscow, a *talmud torah* was established in 1872

---

[1] M. Stanislawski, *Tsar Nicholas I and the Jews: The Transformation of Jewish Society in Russia, 1825–1855* (Philadelphia, 1983), 44.

[2] P. Marek, 'Borl'ba dvukh vospitanii', in A. Lokshin (ed.), *Evrei v Rossiiskoi Imperii XVIII–XIX vekov: Sbornik trudov evreiskikh istorikov* (Moscow, 1995), 573.

[3] S. Vermel, 'Iz nedavnego proshlogo (K istorii Aleksandrovskogo remeslennogo uchilishcha v Moskve)', in Yu. Snopov and A. Klempert (eds.), *Evrei v Moskve: Sbornik materialov* (Moscow, 2003), 264–5.

[4] E. R. Adler. *In her Hands: The Education of Jewish Girls in Tsarist Russia* (Detroit, 2011), 54; Yu. Gessen, 'Sankt-Peterburg', in L. Katsenelson and D. G. Gintsburg (eds.), *Evreiskaya entsiklopediya: Svod znanii o evreistve i ego kul`ture v proshlom i nastoyashchem*, 16 vols. (St Petersburg, 1908–13), xiii. 945.

and the Aleksandrovskoe Jewish artisan school was founded in 1880. This school was named after Alexander II and opened to commemorate the twenty-fifth anniversary of his reign.[5]

However, rights that were granted to Jews in St Petersburg and Moscow were often not extended to Kiev. Kiev was always an exception to the rule: its first official Jewish schools were permitted by the authorities only in the early twentieth century. In this chapter, I analyse why the official Jewish schools in this city were opened significantly later than in other cities and towns within and beyond the Pale of Settlement. I will also discuss the education of Jews in general, pointing out situations faced by schools and universities in Kiev.

Before the 1880s Russian authorities encouraged Jews to send their children to state schools and universities. In the 1860s and 1870s the ideas of the Haskalah spread among Russian Jews, and the number of Jewish students in general schools grew significantly. Ironically, just as Jews were developing an increased interest in general education, the tsarist government restricted their access to Russian state schools. In 1887 the *numerus clausus* for Jewish students was established in gymnasiums and universities. This limitation was part of the policy of state anti-semitism that was implemented by the Russian government from 1881 until the collapse of the monarchy in February 1917.

The situation with regard to Jewish education in Kiev can be understood only in the context of the overall history of Jews in Kiev. In Sholem Aleichem's words, 'the large, beautiful gentle city of Yehupets [Kiev] . . . is certainly not the kind of city that would seek to have even a token Jewish population. Quite the contrary, it is well known that, from time immemorial Jews have been as welcome to the people of the city as a migraine.'[6] The persecution of Jews in Kiev was always harsher than in other places in the Russian empire, and the religious intolerance of the non-Jewish population was stronger, due to the special significance of Kiev for Orthodox Christians as a holy city, 'the Jerusalem of the Russian Land'.[7]

Jews were expelled from Kiev several times by various rulers. The last expulsion of the city's entire Jewish population occurred in 1835 by order of Nicholas I, because the city was excluded by law from the Pale of Settlement. Kiev remained beyond the Pale until the February 1917 revolution. However, between 1859 and 1861 new laws allowed Jewish merchants of the first guild, craftsmen, Jews who were university graduates, students of gymnasiums and universities, retired soldiers, and some other categories of Jews to reside in Kiev.[8]

Jews were always attracted to Kiev despite the hostility of the authorities and

---

[5] Vermel, 'Iz nedavnego proshlogo', 264–5.

[6] Cited in Gennady Estraikh, 'From Yehupets Jargonists to Kiev Modernists: The Rise of a Yiddish Literary Centre, 1880s–1914', *East European Jewish Affairs*, 30/1 (2000), 21.

[7] A. Anisimov, *Skorbnoe beschuvstvie: Na dobruyu pamyat' o Kieve, ili Grustnye progulki po gorodu, kotorogo net* (Kiev, 1992), 36.

[8] V. Khiterer, 'Jewish Life in Kyiv at the Turn of the Twentieth Century', *Ukraina Moderna*, 10 (2006), 75.

many of the Christian residents. Kiev was a commercial hub, an educational and cultural centre, and the only large city in the south-western region of the empire. It was reputed to be an easy place to make money.[9] Thus none of the official restrictions and prohibitions could completely 'protect' Kiev from Jews, many of whom dwelt there illegally. The authorities repeatedly expelled Jews from Kiev, but they always came back, and, despite the restrictive measures, the Jewish population of Kiev grew steadily from 1861 to 1917. The Jewish population found better conditions in Kiev than in overcrowded shtetls, and Jews made major contributions to the city's overall economic development. While Judaeophobes complained that Kiev had become a Jewish city, Jews still ranked the city as one of the most hostile towards them in the Russian empire. Sholem Aleichem's name for it—Yehupets— means Egypt, a place of despair.

The government's negative attitude towards the growth of the Jewish population resulted in ongoing prohibitions against the opening of any Jewish institutions: synagogues, schools, or cultural or philanthropic organizations. The authorities were afraid that such institutions and organizations would attract even more Jews to Kiev.

JEWISH SCHOOLS IN KIEV

For many years, the government forbade the establishment of Jewish schools in Kiev, and *melamedim* were not allowed to teach. With the establishment of quotas in gymnasiums and universities in 1887, even more obstacles blocked the path of education for the Jews of Kiev. The majority of Jewish children were denied schooling altogether. The authorities appreciated this situation, accurately judging that if Jews had fewer options to educate their children, then the community would decline. Because the authorities tried to keep the number of Jews as low as possible, they continuously rejected requests to establish Jewish schools, and they closed underground schools as soon as they were detected.

The struggle for Jewish education in Kiev continued from the creation of a new Jewish community in the 1860s until the beginning of the twentieth century. However, despite the prohibitions, Jewish schools and *melamedim* worked clandestinely. The vast majority of Kiev's Jews in the 1860s and 1870s were traditional and more than reluctant to send their children to general schools, as Russian state education was based on Orthodox Christian ideals. Jewish parents were concerned that such education would encourage their children to abandon their faith.[10] The language barrier was also a serious obstacle, especially for children of poor Jews, who typically knew little Russian. Furthermore, the number of Russian state schools in Kiev was too low to accommodate the city's population. Thus, even before the introduction of the *numerus clausus*, it was difficult for any child to obtain

[9] Ibid. 74–5.   [10] Stanislawski, *Tsar Nicholas I and the Jews*, 69–96.

a place in Kiev's Russian schools, and the *numerus clausus* greatly exacerbated this problem.[11]

Jews felt an obligation to educate their children, or at least the boys. Literacy was a requirement of Judaism, without which religious Jews could not fulfil the commandments to read the religious books and pray in Hebrew. They thus ignored the ban. Well-to-do parents hired *melamedim* to teach their children. Some Jewish communities appealed to the government to change the situation. For example, Izrail Beniaminovich Grinshtein sent a petition from the Jewish community to the chancellery of the governor-general of Kiev, Podolia, and Volhynia, on 15 March 1879, in which he complained that the Kiev police often arrested *melamedim* in the city and detained them until the parents of their pupils bribed the authorities to release them.[12] Grinshtein asked that the work of *melamedim* in Kiev be legalized. His request was rejected.

Poor Jewish families could not afford to pay *melamedim*, so the Jewish community of Kiev opened and financed a *talmud torah* for poor children and orphans. But if private lessons could usually be hidden from the authorities, the existence of a *talmud torah* with sixty-eight students was hard to keep secret. The director of administration of the Kiev educational district wrote a confidential report to the governor-general, Count Aleksandr Mikhailovich Dondukov-Korsakov, stating that the inspector of national schools of the first district of the Kiev province, Chechet, reported to him on 29 April 1874 that he had discovered an illegal Jewish school in 'Bazilevskaya's house' in the Plossky district of Kiev:

Entering this school, he found sixty-eight Jewish boys and three teachers of Jewish subjects. The students, located in three separate rooms, were engaged in reading the Bible and other Jewish books. Considering the similar uniforms of the students and the quite comfortable furniture of the school, Chechet assumes that this school has good financial backing.

When asked by whom, when, and with whose permission the school had been opened, the teachers answered that it had been opened by the Jewish trusteeship, financed by the Jewish community, and had operated since January 1873. However, they knew nothing about permission to operate the school.

The inspector instructed one of the teachers to provide information from the trustees about the opening of the school. The next day, inspector Chechet received the by-laws of the Kiev Jewish Orphanage, which had not been approved by any authority. Afterwards, Kiev [State] Rabbi Tsukkerman came to Chechet and explained that the Jewish community did not yet have sufficient funds to establish a shelter for Jewish orphans, children of soldiers who had died in the cholera epidemic, and had not had the opportunity to petition for a formal opening of the orphanage. However, the Jewish community did not want to leave

[11] Tsentrall'nyi derzhavnyi istorychnyi arkhiv Ukrayiny, Kiev (hereafter TsDIAK), f. 442, op. 535, d. 280, fos. 1–3: Rabbi Nikolaev and Mark Osipovich Kogan, teacher of Jewish religious law, petition to governor-general of Kiev, Podolia, and Volhynia, 25 Sept. 1882.

[12] TsDIAK, f. 442, op. 829, d. 51, fos. 1–4: I. B. Grinshtein, petition to the chancellery of the governor-general of Kiev, Podolia, and Volhynia, 15 Mar. 1879.

orphans wandering on the streets without care and thus opened the institution before receiving official permission for the orphanage, temporarily settling and teaching them, as they did not speak or understand Russian.[13]

Governor-General Dondukov-Korsakov demanded that Nikolay Pavlovich Gesse, the governor of Kiev, explain why he had for several months delayed the closure of the illegal school. Gesse's response demonstrates his lenient attitude towards the Jewish 'orphanage'. He explained that he gave an order to the Kiev police to investigate this case:

During further interrogation Tsukkerman, Fainberg, Markovich, and Lander, and also the clerk's wife Bazilevskaya, claimed that no school existed in Bazilevskaya's house, but from the beginning of the spring the Jewish community, which was afraid of a flood, gathered the orphans left after the deaths of soldiers and artisans. The orphans lived on the allowance of different Jews, mostly in Obolon [district] and were settled temporarily in the house of the clerk's wife Bazilevskaya who was living there with the Jew Lander, who was already caring for eight orphans. More than sixty orphans were placed there; and so that they would make good use of their time, the community entrusted Lander to take care of them, and he gave them the Bible to read.[14]

The governor of Kiev also suggested approving the request of Assistant Rabbi Wolf Bronshtein to open a boarding or private school for Jewish children. The governor, as well as the city's chief of police, wrote that if 'Jews, according to article 284 of volume XIV of the statute about passports, have the right to live in Kiev with restrictions . . . so it is necessary to give them the opportunity to teach their children'.[15]

Jewish merchants and artisans also asked, in a petition to the governor-general on 16 April 1877, for permission to establish a private Jewish school, which would be subsidized by the community: 'We, artisans, very much need such a school, in which our children aged 6 to 10 can study the Holy Scripture and the Russian language. Because of the absence of such a school our children remain without any moral and religious education, which makes us concerned about their future behaviour as adults.'[16] Despite the petitions of the Jewish community of Kiev and support for their request from Governor Gesse, a Jewish school did not open in Kiev until many years later. Governor-General Dondukov-Korsakov rejected all requests by the Jewish community and wrote in a letter to the chief of police on 19 April 1877: 'Kiev has schools of the Ministry of National Enlightenment, where

---

[13] TsDIAK, f. 442, op. 53, d. 356, fos. 1–2: director of administration, Kiev educational district, confidential report to Governor-General Dondukov-Korsakov, 29 Apr. 1874.

[14] TsDIAK, f. 442, op. 53, d. 356, fos. 6–8: governor of Kiev, report to governor-general of Kiev, Podolia, and Volhynia, 19 Oct. 1874.   [15] Ibid.

[16] TsDIAK, f. 442, op. 53, d. 356, fo. 12: Jewish merchants and artisans of Kiev, petition to governor-general, 16 Apr. 1877.

Jewish children can study, so I ask you to tell the above-mentioned Jews that their request cannot be satisfied.'[17]

On 20 October 1881 the former rabbi of the city of Nikolaev, Mark Osipovich Kogan, who had moved to Kiev in 1880 to have his five children educated at Kiev's St Vladimir University and secondary schools, petitioned the director of administration of the Kiev educational district to allow him to open a private school for Jewish boys. The director passed this request on to the board of trustees of the Kiev educational district. The trustees, according to Kogan, postponed their decision, claiming that 'opening such a school in Kiev is contrary to the views and desires of the high authorities'.[18] On 25 September 1882 Kogan sent a petition directly to the governor-general, Aleksandr Romanovich Drenteln, explaining why the opening of a private Jewish school was absolutely necessary:

Kiev has a very significant Jewish population. . . . Meanwhile, the children of local Jews (more than one thousand Jewish boys live there) are deprived of any education, as is necessary for any Russian subject, general courses as well as those providing basic knowledge of the Jewish Holy Scripture and even the ability to read and translate everyday Jewish prayers. The cause of such an aberrant and unusual situation among Jews in this particular city is quite clearly the result of the following circumstances: on the one hand, it is impossible even to increase slightly the number of Jewish students in the few general elementary and middle schools due to the large number of local Christians. On the other hand, this is a direct result of the absence in Kiev of at least one legal Jewish elementary school, especially now, when according to the order of the Kiev municipal police, the few *melamedim* who lived in Kiev and previously taught Jewish children without impediment, had to leave the city. Thus, almost all of the large number of Jewish children in Kiev, whose numbers increase each year, grow up without any knowledge about religion and faith and without any knowledge of the most necessary general subjects such as the Russian language, arithmetic, and the history of their country, the Russian empire. . . . Private Jewish schools have long been open with the permission of authorities even in the Russian capitals, St Petersburg and Moscow.[19]

Kogan's explanation did not convince the local authorities, and his request to open a private Jewish school was rejected, like those of all previous petitioners.

The authorities responded in a similar way to a petition by the Jewish women of Kiev to allow the opening of a boarding school for Jewish girls who were either left without supervision while their parents worked or were orphans. The wives of the wealthiest Kiev Jews, whose husbands held leading positions in the Jewish community, Berta and Eva Brodskaya, Sofia Mandelstamm, Elka and Maria Rozenberg, and others, signed the petition and submitted it to the governor of Kiev in December 1885. In his letter of 31 December 1885, the governor advised the

[17] TsDIAK, f. 442, op. 53, d. 356, fo. 13: Governor-General Dondukov-Korsakov, letter to chief of police, 19 Apr. 1877.
[18] TsDIAK, f. 442, op. 535, d. 280, fos. 1–3: M. O. Kogan, petition to Governor-General Drenteln, 25 Sept. 1882.   [19] Ibid.

governor-general to decline the request, as he doubted that the petitioners had the means to finance the boarding school. He feared that as a consequence, this 'would provide them subsequently with a reason to ask that this school be financed from the means of the basket tax. In addition, its by-laws allowed the school to accept the children of Jewish non-residents of Kiev, which would give their parents the legal right to live in Kiev.'[20] Governor-General Drenteln concurred with the governor of Kiev, refusing the request on the grounds that such a school 'would promote the further isolation of Jews'.[21] Before 1881 it was the Russian government's official policy to work against such isolation and in favour of their merging with the general population. Subsequently, the government changed its official course to one of isolation and further persecution. However, the authorities still continued, for a while, to employ the old rationale in denying the opening of a boarding school for Jewish girls in Kiev, as well as other Jewish schools. The negative attitude of local authorities towards the establishment of Jewish schools was in accord with the government's policy towards Jewish education in the 1880s. A circular from the Ministry of National Enlightenment of 30 March 1888 affirmed that 'the establishment of Jewish schools outside the Pale of Settlement cannot be permitted, especially when there is a sufficient number of general elementary schools'.[22]

A few years later, on 11 May 1890, the Kiev rabbi Evsey Tsukkerman and two men responsible for the care of the city's Jewish orphans, the merchant Leon Ashkenazi and the hereditary honourable citizen of Kiev Saul Levin, again appealed to the governor-general to permit the opening of two Jewish elementary schools in the Lybedskoy and Plossky districts to 'teach Holy Scripture and Russian grammar to Jewish children'.[23] Their petition stated:

Because Jewish home teachers [*melamedim*] do not have the right to teach and live in Kiev and also because Your Highness has ordered that an end be put to all teaching which is not completely legal, the Jewish children of Kiev are in a desperate situation with regards to the possibility of studying Jewish religious law . . . and also because private education at home is inaccessible for the majority of the population. Thus almost all Kiev's Jewish children are deprived of the chance to receive at least an elementary religious and moral education. The sum of 3,000 roubles annually allocated from the basket tax is used only for teaching poor Jewish orphans artisan skills: the religious and moral side of their education is entirely neglected, so these children like all the others remain illiterate and without any religious education.[24]

[20] TsDIAK, f. 442, op. 539, d. 11, fos. 1–2: governor of Kiev, letter to governor-general of Kiev, Podolia, and Volhynia, 31 Dec. 1885.
[21] TsDIAK, f. 442, op. 539, d. 11, fo. 3: governor-general of Kiev, Podolia, and Volhynia, letter to governor of Kiev, 20 Jan. 1886.
[22] TsDIAK, f. 707, op. 175, d. 39, fo. 41: Ministry of National Enlightenment, circular no. 5035, 30 Mar. 1888.
[23] TsDIAK, f. 442, op. 53, d. 356, fo. 19: Rabbi E. Tsukkerman, L. Ashkenazi, and S. Levin, petition to governor-general of Kiev, Podolia, and Volhynia, 11 May 1890.   [24] Ibid.

Kiev's governor, Lev Pavlovich Tomara, responded to the governor-general on 24 May 1890:

This petition should not be acceded to, because, first of all, there does not exist a law that allows Jewish schools to be opened outside the Pale of Settlement, and, second, because the opening of such schools will be a cause for Jews from other towns to settle in Kiev to educate their children in these schools, and it could become the cause of an influx of Jews into Kiev, which already has a significant Jewish population. Then, little by little, still more new Jewish schools will be opened, because the existing ones will be too crowded. Modern Kiev will be no different from the places where Jews are allowed to live.[25]

Aleksey Pavlovich Ignatyev, governor-general of Kiev, Podolia, and Volhynia, supported the governor and rejected the request.[26]

Education in Russian schools became less available to Jews after the introduction of a quota for Jewish children in gymnasiums and universities in 1887. The attitude of the authorities towards establishing Jewish schools in Kiev deprived the majority of Jewish children of any chance of receiving a formal education. Even the director of the Kiev educational district pointed out the absurdity of this situation. He wrote to the governor-general on 31 March 1894 that Jews, on the one hand, were not allowed to open *heder*s and have *melamedim* in Kiev; on the other hand, in the city

there lives permanently a significant Jewish population for whose children the secondary schools are largely inaccessible due to the quota; the elementary schools also restrict as much as possible an excessive influx of the Jewish element due to its harmful influence on the schools. Thus, in the current year, Jewish students number not more than sixty in all thirty-eight parish schools in the town, while only three Jewish students are enrolled in the Kiev City School.[27]

He therefore asked the governor-general to accede to the repeated requests of the 'honoured Jewish citizens' for permission to open an elementary school in Kiev financed by the Jewish community. However, the request was rejected, because

only Jewish merchants of the first guild and individuals with higher education have the right of permanent residence in Kiev: all other Jews who live there (artisans, retired soldiers, and others) for whom the opening of the school is important have only the right of temporary residence. The establishment of this school could confirm the settlement of these Jews in Kiev and even provoke the further undesirable influx of others.[28]

---

[25] TsDIAK, f. 442, op. 53, d. 356, fo. 17: governor of Kiev, report to governor-general of Kiev, Podolia, and Volhynia, 24 May 1890.

[26] TsDIAK, f. 442, op. 53, d. 356, fos. 20–1: Count Ignatiev, governor-general of Kiev, Podolia, and Volhynia, letter to director of Kiev Educational District, 6 June 1890.

[27] TsDIAK, f. 442, op. 624, d. 249, fos. 1–2: director of Kiev educational district, letter to governor-general of Kiev, Podolia, and Volhynia, 31 Mar. 1894.

[28] TsDIAK, f. 442, op. 624, d. 249, fo. 3: governor-general of Kiev, Podolia, and Volhynia letter to director of Kiev Educational District, 30 July 1894.

Figure 1. St Vladimir University, Kiev, *c.*1900. Postcard.

The governor-general's concerns about the potential increase in the Jewish population of Kiev were well founded, since parents of Jewish students had the right of temporary residence while their children were being educated. This temporary residence could extend for many years, as was the case with Yudka Yanovsky, who in 1899, when the police checked his 'temporary' residence, had lived there for fifteen years. As the governor reported to the governor-general on 8 October 1899: 'The Jew Yanovsky . . . has lived in Kiev since 1884 because of the educational needs of his eleven children, who range from 26 to 5 years old. . . . At present 139 Jewish families live in Kiev, in accordance with the right to educate their children.'[29] Because of the size of Jewish families, it is likely that in 1899 more than one thousand Jews 'temporarily' lived legally in Kiev in accordance with 'the right to educate their children'. This temporary residence could last for decades depending upon the number of children, as is shown by the Yanovsky case.

Jewish families who received the right to education sent their children to study in Russian gymnasiums, commercial and artisan schools, St Vladimir University (Figure 1), the Kiev Polytechnic Institute (Figure 2), and the School of Music.[30] However, after the introduction of the *numerus clausus*, entrance of Jews into

[29] TsDIAK, f. 442, op. 629, d. 408, fo. 7: governor of Kiev, letter to governor-general of Kiev, Podolia, and Volhynia, 8 Oct. 1899.
[30] TsDIAK, f. 442, op. 629, d. 408, fos. 8–20: list of Jewish residents of Plosskii and Lybedskoi police districts who are living there according the right of the residence for education of their children in educational institutions, May 1900.

Figure 2. Kiev Polytechnic Institute, *c.*1900. Postcard

Russian schools was again severely restricted. Thus, local authorities could ensure that the number of Jewish students and their parents temporarily residing in Kiev would remain small.

In spite of all the bans, illegal Jewish schools again opened. On 18 November 1897 the governor-general was informed by two Jews from Kiev about an illegal Jewish school that contained 'six departments' at 23–24 Yaroslavskaya Street.[31] Consequently, that school was closed.

To obtain permission to open a school, the Jews of Kiev sometimes proposed that the school accept Christians as well. However, the possibility of establishing a general school would immediately raise the question of the language of teaching and the curriculum. By the early twentieth century, when Kiev Jewry was more or less Russified, such a combination of students did become possible. For example, the honorary hereditary citizen of Kiev Gerts Grigoryevich Balakhovsky petitioned the authorities in 1900 for permission to open a Jewish teaching farm. His request was denied, as were all other petitions related to the establishment of Jewish schools in Kiev. Then four years later Balakhovsky asked for permission to open a farm for the education of Jewish children whose parents had the right to reside in the city, as well as for orphans of other religions, 'especially the children of warriors fallen in the Far East [in the Russo-Japanese War]'.[32] On 29 October 1905, five years

---

[31] TsDIAK, f. 442, op. 847, d. 288, fos. 1–2: two Kiev Jews [the signatures are illegible], denunciation to the governor-general of Kiev, Podolia, and Volhynia, 18 Nov. 1897.

[32] TsDIAK, f. 442, op. 633, d. 40, fo. 6: Gerts Grigoryevich Balakhovsky, petition to governor-general of Kiev, Podolia, and Volhynia, n.d.

after Balakhovsky's original petition, the governor-general allowed the farm to open as a general educational institution for both Christian and Jewish children.[33]

For more than forty years after restricted categories of Jews were allowed to settle in Kiev, Jews were not legally permitted to open schools. This situation was finally changed by the leader of the Jewish community of Kiev, the wealthy sugar industrialist and philanthropist, Lazar Brodsky. When Brodsky petitioned the government to found a Jewish state elementary school in Kiev in 1901, he was granted permission. Why the local authorities changed their minds in this case is unclear. Possibly Brodsky's connections in St Petersburg played a role, or he may have bribed somebody, or perhaps his request was more significant for local authorities than that of other Jews, as Brodsky was one of the most prominent industrialists in the region and a generous philanthropist for many city organizations and institutions, both Jewish and non-Jewish. The administrator of the chancellery of the governor-general wrote to the governor-general on 17 November 1901:

Kiev is located beyond the Pale of Settlement; however, a large number of Jews live here and need to educate their children. The law does not require, but also does not forbid, the opening of Jewish state schools in Kiev. On the other hand, the law's intent does not allow the influx of Jews into Kiev.

Therefore, I assume it would be right to allow [the opening of a Jewish school in Kiev], but with the condition that this school will accept only the children of parents (or even orphans living with their relatives and guardians) who have the right of residence in Kiev.

These conditions will also serve as a response to the request of Mr Brodsky, who envisages the school as catering to the poorest sector of Kiev's Jewish population.[34]

The governor of Kiev supported this request, and Brodsky received permission to open a two-grade Jewish state school financed by the Jewish community. Then the question was raised about the right of residence in Kiev for the teachers at the school. The governor-general declared that they could reside in the city while employed there. However, it took three more years to construct the school. Even though it was a state institution, it was built and financed by Kiev's Jews. The brothers Lazar and Lev Brodsky donated 300,000 roubles for its construction; the Jewish community provided 6,000 roubles a year from the basket tax for the school budget; and other expenses were covered by the founders. The students paid 20 roubles a year for tuition. The school formally opened on 7 November 1904 and was named after Solomon, the late brother of Lazar and Lev Brodsky (Figure 3). The school, which reported to the Ministry of National Enlightenment, had a principal, eight teachers of general subjects, and several arts and crafts teachers.

---

[33] TsDIAK, f. 442, op. 633, d. 40, fo. 5: government clerk of Kiev province, letter to governor-general of Kiev, Podolia, and Volhynia, 28 Oct. 1904; governor-general of Kiev, Podolia, and Volhynia, resolution 29 Oct. 1905.

[34] TsDIAK, f. 442, op. 631, d. 410, fo. 1: administrator of the chancellery of the governor-general of Kiev, letter to the governor-general of Kiev, Podolia, and Volhynia, 17 Nov. 1901.

Figure 3. Solomon Brodsky Jewish State School, Kiev, *c.* 1900.
Courtesy of the Center for Studies of the History and Culture of East European Jewry

It thus provided not only elementary education but also vocational training.[35] Students studied the Russian and Hebrew languages, Russian and Jewish history, Judaism, arithmetic, geography, and natural sciences. Those who wished also to receive a vocational education studied at the Department of Arts and Crafts. The school was designed for 300 students, with 100 more accepted into the arts and crafts department.[36] Lev Brodsky, who managed the institution after the death of his brother Lazar, asked the authorities in 1905 to establish two inspectors and provided 1,000 roubles a year for this purpose. Although the status and size of the school did not entitle it to be granted these positions, the governor-general, Sukhomlinov, allowed their appointment. The inspectors received the right of residence in Kiev for the term of their work at school.[37]

Less than a year after its opening, the Solomon Brodsky Jewish State School was targeted by rioters during the October 1905 pogrom. Senator Evgeny Fedorovich Turau wrote in his report about the Kiev pogrom: 'On 19 and 20 October the well-

[35] TsDIAK, f. 442, op. 631, d. 410, fo. 7: director of Kiev Educational District, report to governor-general of Kiev, Podolia, and Volhynia, 13 Nov. 1901.

[36] M. Kalnitskii and B. Khandros, 'Gde uchilisl' kievskie evrei', *Evreiskii Obozrevatel'* 21/64 (Nov. 2003), <http://www.jewukr.org/observer/eo2003/page_show_ru.php?id=390> (accessed 16 Mar. 2009).

[37] TsDIAK, f. 442, op. 658, d. 209, fos. 1–2: Deputy Minister of National Enlightenment, letter to governor-general of Kiev, Podolia, and Volhynia, 10 Oct. 1905.

equipped Brodsky Jewish school, belonging to the Ministry of National Enlightenment, was completely looted.'[38] Kiev's chief of police, Tsikhotsky, had received several warnings about an attack on the school, but did nothing to protect it. Perhaps he was not concerned about the property of the Jewish state school, as he knew that the Jews were financially responsible for it. The Brodsky school was the only Jewish school in Kiev for three years and functioned until at least 1918 (the exact date of its closure is unknown).

Along with the opening of the first Jewish school in Kiev, the authorities allowed the Jews of Kiev to open a branch of the Society for the Promotion of Enlightenment among the Jews of Russia (Obshchestvo dlya rasprostraneniya prosveshcheniya mezhdu evreyami v Rossii; OPE) in 1903. Established late compared to other branches of this organization, the Kiev society soon became one of its largest branches. Its first meeting took place on 23 December 1903, and Lazar Brodsky was elected chairman, while Max Mandelstamm, the vice president of Kiev's Jewish community, was to serve as vice president.[39] Although its wealthy donors preferred most of their funds to be spent locally, its activities were spread throughout Kiev, Podolia, and Volhynia provinces.[40]

The opening of the first Jewish state school in Kiev created a precedent. It was now easier for Jews to receive permission to establish other private Jewish schools in the city. In 1907 the governor-general granted permission to the OPE to open four private Jewish schools in Kiev, two for boys and two for girls.[41] In addition, in 1908 the OPE financed Jewish schools in Kiev province and a Jewish kindergarten, a Jewish Saturday school, and a Jewish library.[42]

Thus, in the early 1900s, after Lazar Brodsky's initiative, the local government came to accept the existence in Kiev of a variety of Jewish schools and Jewish teachers. Subsequently, the authorities even allowed *ḥeder*s and *melamedim* to operate there. Several *ḥeder*s existed after 1910, one of them financed by the renowned jeweller Iosif Marshak. In 1911 the industrialist and philanthropist David Margolin built, financed, and opened a *talmud torah*, with room for 300 to 400 students, located on Konstantinovskaya Street in Podol, the district where the majority of poor Jews lived.[43]

---

[38] TsDIAK, f. 316, op. 1, d. 382–V, fos. 3–8: Senator Evgenii Fedorovich Turau, report on the Kiev pogrom, n.d.

[39] B. Horowitz, *Jewish Philanthropy and Enlightenment in Late-Tsarist Russia* (Seattle, 2009), 192, 196; I. Sergeeva and O. Gorshikhina, 'Deyatel'nost' Kievskogo otdeleniya Obshchestva dlya rasprostraneniya prosveshcheniya mezhdu evreyami v Rossii v kontse XIX–nachale XX vv.', in D. A. El'yashevich (ed.), *Istoriya evreev v Rossii: Problemy istochnikovedeniya i istoriografii: Sbornik nauchnykh trudov* (St Petersburg, 1993), 125–6.　　　　　　　　　　　　　　　　[40] Ibid.

[41] TsDIAK, f. 442, op. 660, d. 208, fos. 1, 3–4: Governor General Sukhomlinov, Kiev, Podolia, and Volhynia, correspondence with governor of Kiev and director of Kiev Educational District, 4–31 Oct. 1907.　　　　　　　　　[42] Sergeeva and Gorshikhina, 'Deyatel'nost'', 126.

[43] Kalnitskii and Khandros, 'Gde uchilis'' kievskie evrei'.

The number of Jewish schools and teachers grew so rapidly in Kiev that in 1911 the teachers established a professional organization, the Society for Aid to Jewish Teachers and Melamedim Residing in Kiev and the Pale of Settlement (Obshchestvo vspomoshchestvovaniya evreiskim uchitelyam i melamedam, zhivushchim v gorode Kieve i v cherte evreiskoi osedlosti). Its board was located in Kiev and provided financial support to 'Jewish teachers of state and private schools and *melamedim*' if they became unemployed or ill and to their families in the case of their death. According to its by-laws published in 1911, the society also intended to organize pedagogical courses for Jewish teachers in the summer, publish a journal, and arrange lectures and libraries for teachers, while supporting the establishment of Jewish schools, *ḥeders*, and kindergartens.[44]

At the beginning of the twentieth century, traditional Jewish religious schools attracted mainly indigent Jews. The upper and middle classes sought more modern schools, where their children could receive both Jewish and general education. In response to this demand, A. Kozarinsky and B. Shummer opened private Jewish gymnasiums in Kiev during the First World War.[45] Students were taught the same subjects as in Russian gymnasiums, as well as courses in Judaism, Jewish history, and Hebrew. The schools provided places for Jewish children rejected by Russian state schools because of the *numerus clausus*.

As a result, despite difficulties and obstacles, the Jewish community of Kiev ultimately won its struggle for Jewish education. By 1 January 1917 the Solomon Brodsky Jewish State School (with 421 students), eleven private elementary Jewish schools (for 1,206 boys and 522 girls), twenty-nine *ḥeders* (for 669 boys), the two Jewish private gymnasiums, and several Jewish libraries were functioning in Kiev.[46] The Jewish community of Kiev never before and never subsequently had so many schools. Although it was the golden age of Jewish education in Kiev, there was no guarantee of safety for Jewish schools, Jewish students, or their teachers in times of pogroms and violence. In addition, many students would probably have preferred to attend general schools had there not been a quota.

The achievements of the Jewish community of Kiev seem especially significant compared to the even more difficult situation of other national minorities in Kiev. Ukrainians, Poles, and Czechs were not allowed to establish their own national schools. Russian authorities showed a somewhat more lenient attitude towards Jewish schools at the beginning of the twentieth century, preferring them to allowing the education of Jewish children in the general Russian schools.

[44] TsDIAK, f. 442, op. 636, d. 647, part VII, fo. 642: *Ustav Obshchestva vspomoshchestvovaniya evreiskim uchitelyam i melamedam, zhivushchim v gorode Kieve i v cherte evreiskoi osedlosti* (Kiev, 1911).

[45] Kalnitskii and Khandros, 'Gde uchilisl' kievskie evrei'.

[46] *Istoriya Kieva*, ed. O. K. Kasimenko, 2 vols. (Kiev, 1963), i. 584–5.

JEWISH STUDENTS IN GENERAL SCHOOLS IN KIEV

From the late nineteenth century young Russian Jews strongly desired higher education, preferably in universities or at the least in professional schools. The increased interest in higher education is usually attributed to the processes of assimilation and acculturation. However, the roots go even deeper. In late imperial Russia, obtaining a university or professional school diploma was the principal means for Jews to escape the Pale of Settlement. The laws of the Russian empire allowed their settlement outside the Pale if they were graduates of universities or professional schools or were students at gymnasiums or universities. Thus, the efforts of young Jews to receive diplomas were motivated not only by their wish to acquire knowledge. However, the *numerus clausus* presented a major obstacle.

The Russian government's attitude to Jewish attendance at gymnasiums and universities changed radically during the nineteenth century. From the early 1800s to the beginning of the 1880s the government followed the policy of 'merging' the Jewish population with 'native' Russian people and of acculturating Jews into Russian culture. Higher education was thus encouraged by Russian officials. Often the Jewish students of these schools received state scholarships.

The first Jewish students were accepted into Kiev's St Vladimir University in the 1840s. There were three Jewish students enrolled there in 1842, and by 1848 their numbers had increased to twenty-seven.[47] In those years Jews were not allowed to live in Kiev or stay in the city for more than a few days for business, so the government made an exception for Jewish students, a factor that indicates the special significance the government assigned to the education of Jews as a means of assimilation.

In the late 1850s and the beginning of the 1860s, when some categories of Jews were allowed to settle in Kiev, the number of Jewish students at St Vladimir University increased continuously. However, the Jewish community was still small and could not provide financial aid to its students, who typically had great difficulties paying tuition fees. Nikolay Ivanovich Pirogov, director of the Kiev educational district from 1858 to 1861, well known for his Judaeophilia, attempted to come to their assistance. He maintained good connections with the Jewish community of Odessa, where he had served in a similar position from 1856 to 1858 and had promoted education for Jews. In 1861 Pirogov wrote to Abram Markovich Brodsky, a leader of the Jewish community of Odessa: 'Jewish students at St Vladimir University in Kiev live in great poverty, and some of them may be excluded from the university as they cannot pay their tuition fees. Kiev's Jews are not wealthy enough to provide support for their co-religionists.'[48] Pirogov hoped that

---

[47] A. E. Ivanov, *Evreiskoe studenchestvo v Rossiiskoi imperii nachala XX veka: Kakim ono bylo?* (Moscow, 2007), 30.

[48] A. de-Ribas [Deribas], *Staraya Odessa: Istoricheskie ocherki i vospominaniya* (Moscow, 2005), 210.

the Jewish community of Odessa would assist Jewish students in Kiev. Brodsky, an ardent adherent of the assimilation of Jews, perhaps surprised Pirogov in his response:

According to the demands of our time, well-to-do people should help the poor without distinction of faith. Therefore, it is preferable that the Jewish community make a donation for poor students in general, not only for Jewish students. This can be a first step towards the elimination of exclusiveness, which was and is a barrier against Russian Jews merging with Russian people.

The majority of Jews . . . wish to do good deeds for all their fellow citizens without the distinction of religion.[49]

In addition to this letter, Brodsky expressed to Pirogov his willingness to provide a scholarship for two poor students at St Vladimir University, one Christian and one Jewish, for five years, giving each of them 200 roubles a year.

Pirogov considered Brodsky's letter a *profession de foi*. On his initiative, it was published in newspapers in Kiev and Odessa, stimulating a public outpouring of support for students. Many donations arrived from different strata of the population of Odessa, from Jews, Russians, and foreigners, often with the note 'without the distinction of religion'.[50] However, the euphoria and the mood of brotherhood of the early 1860s did not last, and the ethnic and religious differences among students in Kiev did not disappear, neither then nor a decade later. This was emphasized in an article published in the newspaper *Kievlyanin* in 1876:

The Poles were slim and gracious, dandies with their cocked hats, thin, turned-up moustaches, and self-assured gait. The Jews, sharp-featured, moved quickly and stuck together. They spoke quietly, but with animated gestures. Some, from wealthy homes in Odessa, wore massive golden chains. Their distinctive Russian accent made you uncomfortable. The Little Russians [Ukrainians] were hefty, well-built and strongly featured, and spoke in a loud, animated dialect. They laughed loudly, were a bit rude, even cynical. There were only a few Russians, and they kept to the background. Poles predominated, then Little Russians, then Jews.[51]

When the government policy towards Jews changed from assimilation to isolation after the pogroms of 1881 and 1882, this attitude was reflected in the lower acceptance rate of Jewish students into Russian educational institutions. Between 1883 and 1885 several universities set limits to the numbers of Jewish students. On 5 December 1886 and 28 June 1887 the Council of Ministers issued circulars which established percentages for admitting Jews into universities and gymnasiums, under the supervision of the Ministry of National Enlightenment. The quota was set at 10 per cent in the Pale of Settlement, 5 per cent outside the

---

[49] de-Ribas, *Staraya Odessa*, 210.   [50] Ibid.
[51] Cited in M. F. Hamm, *Kiev: A Portrait, 1800–1917* (Princeton, NJ, 1993), 67.

Pale, and 3 per cent in St Petersburg and Moscow.[52] The figures in these circulars were ultimately adopted by law in 1908.[53]

The introduction of the quota was motivated by the need to maintain a 'right' proportion between Jewish and non-Jewish students. Russian officials also claimed

that the flood of Jews was depriving non-Jews of educational opportunities; that Jewish students were exercising a negative moral influence on their Christian counterparts; that Jewish students were supporting the revolutionary movement; and that the disproportionate Jewish presence in higher education threatened to shift the balance of power within the technical and professional elites into the hands of a non-Russian, non-Christian minority whose loyalty to the Tsarist state appeared at best doubtful.[54]

At the same time the Russian authorities only reluctantly allowed the creation of specifically Jewish schools, especially outside the Pale of Settlement. The Minister of National Enlightenment, A. N. Shvarts, wrote in 1908 that 'it is necessary to consistently refuse all requests of non-Russian people for any isolation and nationalization of schools. The united Russian school at all levels should be the main educational provision for all non-Russian people of the empire without exception.'[55] Thus Jews were simultaneously not allowed to open Jewish schools and were given very restricted rights to send their children to Russian state schools. The Russian administration, in effect, deprived the vast majority of Jews of any access to education. Kiev's young Jews, especially, felt the negative impact of these policies.

The quota was initially imposed by the publication of special circulars, not by laws, and had some exceptions and variations from place to place. For example, the percentages could change from year to year. In the 1904/5 academic year, the quota for Jews was increased from 10 to 15 per cent in the Pale, from 5 to 7 per cent outside the Pale, and from 3 to 5 per cent in the capitals 'as a special privilege due to the birth of the heir Cesarevitch'.[56]

St Vladimir University had a 10 per cent allowance for Jewish students.[57] However, the actual percentage enrolled was considerably higher. In the 1890/1 academic year some 2,000 students studied there, including 361 Jews (18 per cent). A note on the list of students states that in 1890 a total of 67 Jews were accepted to the university according to the percentage quota, but 43 Jewish students were admitted above that number following orders from the Minister of National Enlightenment and the director of the Kiev educational district. Among the 361

[52] B. Pinkus, *The Jews of the Soviet Union: The History of a National Minority* (Cambridge, 1988), 24.

[53] G. Voltke, 'Prosveshchenie', in Katsenelson and Gintsburg (eds.), *Evreiskaya entsiklopediya*, xiii. 55.

[54] B. Nathans, *Beyond the Pale: The Jewish Encounter with Late Imperial Russia* (Berkeley, Calif., 2002), 259–60.

[55] Cited in Ivanov, *Evreiskoe studenchestvo v Rossiiskoi imperii*, 76.   [56] Ibid. 65.

[57] Ivanov, *Evreiskoe studenchestvo v Rossiiskoi imperii*, 59; Nathans, *Beyond the Pale*, 296.

Jewish students, 289 studied in the Department of Medicine, 64 in the Department of Law, and 8 in the Department of Physics and Mathematics (2 specialized in natural sciences and 6 in mathematics). Jews did not enter the Department of History and Philology, because of the limited career opportunities this provided:[58] a Jew making a career as a university professor in imperial Russia would have been required to convert to Christianity, as Russian schools did not hire Jewish teachers. Accordingly, Jews sought more practical professions such as medicine and law. At that time, university education was almost exclusively reserved for men. St Vladimir University accepted its first female students (20 of about 4,000) in 1907, including 6 Jewish women. In addition, the courses offered to women by the Kiev Institute of Higher Education were popular among Jewish female students, who always constituted more than 16 per cent of all such students. The Kiev courses were opened in 1878 and at first offered a two-year programme which was expanded to four years in 1881. It contained two departments: History and Philology and Physics and Mathematics, in which 357 women studied in 1881 (compared with 1,270 male students at St Vladimir University). Jewish girls also attended higher-education courses for women, which were offered in Moscow, St Petersburg, and Kazan.[59] The majority of women who graduated from these courses worked as teachers, although some continued their education abroad. The Kiev courses were closed in 1889, however, owing to a drop in the number of students. Society was not ready yet to accept emancipated women, and the opponents of women's education scared young girls away from higher education by presenting a negative image of an educated woman—a bluestocking who took no interest in familial duties and motherhood. Another reason for the drop in numbers was that the Kiev courses were quite expensive and difficult, especially physics and mathematics.[60] They were reopened in 1906 and continued until 1920, when they were reorganized by the Soviet authorities as pedagogical courses for both men and women.[61] The number of students in these courses increased to 4,021 in 1915 and to 4,919 in 1917. There were then four departments: History and Philology, Physics and Mathematics, Law, and Economics and Commerce.[62] In 1909 the director of the courses petitioned to change their status and the name to the Women's University of St Olga. It was to be the first women's university in imperial Russia. However, the proposal was rejected by the authorities as it was not deemed appropriate for 'provincial' Kiev to have a women's university before Moscow and St Petersburg. The project also proposed giving female university graduates equal rights to males, particularly for obtaining scholarly and science degrees. This, too, was rejected by the authorities. A similar request by the Bestuzhev courses in St

    [58] TsDIAK, f. 442, op. 840, d. 211, fo. 7: list of students enrolled at St Vladimir University, Kiev, 1890/1.

    [59] Nathans, *Beyond the Pale*, 222–4; K. Kobchenko, 'Zhinochyi universytet Svyatoyi Ol' hy': Istoriya Kyivs'kykh vyshchykh zhinochykh kursiv (Kiev, 2007), 70.

    [60] Kobchenko, 'Zhinochyi universytet Svyatoyi Ol' hy', 63–6.   [61] Ibid. 241–2.   [62] Ibid. 135.

Petersburg, the largest women's higher education institution in Russia, was also denied.[63]

To avoid the quota, wealthy Russian Jews sent their children to study in foreign universities, but the majority of young Jews who desired a university education had to find a way to get one in Russia. Even graduation from the gymnasium with a gold medal did not guarantee acceptance into a university. If the university had already reached its quota of Jewish students, it could not accept any more, regardless of their educational excellence. Some young Jewish men committed suicide, despairing of breaking into the Russian state school system. Vladimir Jabotinsky wrote about the situation in 1912:

Every Jewish child [in Russia] grows up with the understanding that a diploma is the only path towards elementary human rights. . . . [Government regulations] compel tens of thousands to dream about attending a gymnasium, adapt their psyche to its demands, train themselves on its discipline even outside of the school—therefore [school] is the only way for deliverance from the terrible torture of the denial of their civil rights.[64]

Many young Jews chose the path of independent studies, taking tests as 'external students'. However, most external students repeatedly failed their equivalency examinations for diplomas for universities and gymnasiums. Without teachers and formal instruction, it was difficult to acquire the full range of knowledge required to pass the examinations. The vast majority of external students were from poor Jewish families that could not afford to pay for private schooling or tutors. Many Jewish external students also came to the large cities from shtetls.

To understand the plight of poor external students, it is important to note that to graduate from a Russian gymnasium was difficult even for a Russian student. Fewer than one-third of gymnasium students graduated, mainly because the very complicated curriculum devoted up to 40 per cent of class time to Latin and Greek. This classical education was made mandatory by the Ministry of National Enlightenment for all supervised gymnasiums.[65]

But for the brightest among the poorer young Jews, being an external student was the only possible way to receive a higher education. According to a survey of Jewish students at St Vladimir University in 1910, a total of 38 per cent 'reported having received their gymnasium diplomas as externs'.[66] Jews constituted a large percentage of the external students and the government continued to strive to prevent them from receiving gymnasium diplomas in any significant numbers, even establishing a quota for Jewish external students in 1909.[67]

Some professional and private schools were exempted from the *numerus clausus*, but many still required a gymnasium diploma for enrolment. All state gymnasiums had a quota for Jews, so only a very limited number could study there. Some young

[63] Ibid. 125–7.   [64] V. Jabotinsky, *Fel'etony* (Berlin, 1922), 74.
[65] N. V. Riasanovsky, *A History of Russia*, 7th edn. (New York, 2005), 437.
[66] Nathans, *Beyond the Pale*, 275.   [67] Voltke, 'Prosveshchenie', 56.

Jews found creative solutions for this situation. A scandal in 1906 revealed that more than 600 Jewish students in Kiev dentistry schools (about 80 per cent of the entire student body) had falsified gymnasium diplomas or held diplomas from private schools that did not have gymnasium credentials. Fifty-seven Jewish students had diplomas from non-existent gymnasiums. The Ministry of the Interior investigated the case and ordered the expulsion of the Jewish students with fake diplomas. Jewish dentistry students in their third, fourth, or fifth semesters with diplomas from private schools that did not have gymnasium credentials were allowed to finish their studies, but they also had to pass the exam for the sixth-grade state gymnasium within five years after their graduation from dentistry school.

According to *Kievlyanin*, most of the expelled Jewish students disappeared from Kiev after the scandal. Most left because they only had the right of residence in the city as students. Also, after their expulsion from the schools, they could be drafted into the Russian army.[68] Thus these young Jews were motivated by a desire not only to obtain a good profession but also to receive the right to live outside the Pale of Settlement and to avoid military service.

Commercial schools in Russia were under the supervision of the Ministry of Finance, and for a time did not restrict the number of Jewish students. The absence of a quota made such schools very popular among Jews. The Russian Jewish writer Isaac Babel and the prominent Jewish actor and director of the Moscow State Yiddish Theatre (Gosudarstvennyi evreiskii teatr) Solomon Mikhoels studied at the Kiev Commercial Institute. Often, wealthy Jewish merchants were among the trustees of these commercial schools, giving them generous donations. According to Nathans, 'Jewish donors contributed over four-fifths of the 280,000 rouble start-up funds for Kiev's two commercial schools.'[69] This allowed Jewish trustees to monitor and influence the attitude of the administration and the teachers towards Jews. In Nathans's view, the private and public educational institutions that were not subordinate to the Ministry of National Enlightenment were havens for Jews. However, the Russian government soon realized this and began to pressure such institutions to establish a quota for Jews, under the threat of depriving them of accreditation. By the end of the 1911/12 academic year, the Minister of National Enlightenment L. A. Kasso 'imposed a five percent quota on Kiev's two commercial schools', at a time when nearly 60 per cent of the students were Jewish.[70]

Among Kiev's non-Jews were many who felt compassion for the Jews and attempted to help them overcome the limitations imposed by Russian law. For example, the Russian writer Konstantin Paustovsky wrote in his autobiographical novel *Distant Years* that before the final examinations at the First Kiev Gymnasium (Figure 4), reputedly the best gymnasium in the city, students of his class came to a meeting:

---

[68] *Kievlyanin*, 282, 286, 300 (1906).   [69] Nathans, *Beyond the Pale*, 299.   [70] Ibid. 296–9.

№ 301.   Кіевъ — Kiev
Первая гимназія — Le gymnase I.

Figure 4. First Kiev Gymnasium, *c.*1900. Postcard.

To this meeting were invited all the students in my class, except the Jews. The Jews were to know nothing about this meeting.

We decided in the meeting that the best Russian and Polish students must intentionally receive a grade of '4' in at least one course in the examinations so that they did not receive gold medals. [The gold medal granted university acceptance without entrance examinations.] We decided to give all the gold medals to Jews. They were not accepted at the university without these medals.

We swore to keep this decision a secret. To the honour of our class, we did not reveal this secret either then, or later, when we had already become students at the university.[71]

A similar event occurred while Volodymyr Miyakovsky, a Pole and one of the founders of the Ukrainian Free Academy of Arts and Science in the United States, was studying at a Kiev gymnasium.[72] Miyakovsky was four years older than Paustovsky, and so probably wasn't in the same class. Thus, philosemitism at Kiev gymnasiums was a tradition that was transferred from the older to the younger students. While the Russian government attempted to enforce the quota for Jews at gymnasiums and universities strictly, many students and professors ensured that Jews, despite the quota, had access to education in these institutions.

Since gymnasium and university education gave young Jews the right to live outside the Pale of Settlement, the government opposed any attempt to abolish or

[71] K. Paustovsky, *Dalekie gody* (Moscow, 2005), 325.

[72] L. Zaleska-Onyshkevych, 'Volodymyr Miya'kovs'kyi (1888–1972)', in M. Antonovych (ed.), *125 rokiv Kyivs'koyi ukrayins'koyi akademichnoyi tradytsiyi 1861–1986: Zbirnyk* (New York, 1993), 518.

increase the quota. In 1905, under the influence of revolutionary changes, universities were granted autonomy and self-government. Between 1905 and 1907 academic boards accepted students solely on the basis of their grades. The result of this policy was a rapid increase in the number of Jewish students. In 1906 Jews constituted 28 per cent of students at St Vladimir University and 40 per cent in the Department of Mechanics at the Kiev Polytechnic Institute. In 1907 a total of 240 Christian and 159 Jewish students were accepted at the institute. In general, Jewish students constituted 23 per cent of all students there. According to rules approved by the institute's academic board, all students were accepted on the basis of equal competition: there was no national and religious discrimination.[73]

This situation angered Russian nationalists, who were convinced that the policy would inevitably be followed by Jewish domination of the professional and intellectual life of the country. Nationalists called for a restoration of the quota for Jews, for the sake of Russian 'national self-protection'.[74] In 1907, after the suppression of the first Russian revolution, the government re-established the quota. In the same year, Prime Minister Petr Stolypin gave an order to the director of the Kiev Polytechnic Institute to expel 100 Jewish students and replace them with Russians. In response, the director, Timofeev, proposed instead to accept more Christian students without expelling the Jews. But Stolypin would not change his mind, leading to the resignation in protest of the director, three of four deans, and several professors. The governor-general of Kiev, Podolia, and Volhynia, Sukhomlinov, sent a telegram to Stolypin, noting that the resignation of the administration at the Kiev Polytechnic Institute was a protest against the government's policy.[75]

The position of the administration and professors at the Kiev Polytechnic Institute was not unique. A significant part of the Russian academy was quite liberal and had objections to the *numerus clausus*. According to the Minister of National Enlightenment, P. M. Kaufman, the councils of all institutions of higher education were 'unanimous and persistent' in their desire 'to open the doors of higher education to all who received a secondary education, regardless of their nationality'.[76] On 2 September 1905 the Academic Council of Moscow University sent a petition to the Minister of National Enlightenment, V. G. Glazov, requesting the abolition of the quota.

The Minister of National Enlightenment Count Ivan Ivanovich Tolstoy, who served briefly in this position (November 1905 to April 1906), was, in his own words, 'an opponent of the existent system of Russification through the school, and on the Jewish question a supporter of complete equality for this persecuted nation

---

[73] TsDIAK, f. 442, op. 857, d. 383, fo. 32: Governor-General Sukhomlinov, Kiev, Podolia, and Volhynia, telegram to Prime Minister Petr Stolypin, 14 Sept. 1907 [draft].

[74] *Kievlyanin*, 255 (1906).

[75] TsDIAK, f. 442, op. 857, d. 383 fo. 49: Governor General Sukhomlinov, Kiev, Podolia and Volhynia, telegram to Prime Minister Petr Stolypin, 29 Sept. 1907.

[76] Ivanov, *Evreiskoe studenchestvo v Rossiiskoi imperii*, 66.

to receive all rights with other citizens of Russia . . . and an advocate of the immediate abolition of the percentage quota for enrolment in educational institutions.'[77] On 20 January 1906, on Tolstoy's initiative, the Council of Ministers discussed the abolition of the quota for Jewish students. Ten of thirteen ministers, including Tolstoy and the chairman of the council, Sergey Witte, voted for its abolition, while three voted to retain it. However, Nicholas II supported the opponents of abolition. The Council of Ministers sent its resolution for consideration to the tsar, emphasizing that Jews saw in the *numerus clausus*, which was not established by law but by special circulars, 'administrative arbitrariness'. It said that the quota often provoked disturbances: 'Young Jews, embittered by such obvious inequality, joined and supported the revolutionary parties, and at the same time the institutions of the higher education, as shown by recent events, although restricted from the influx of Jews, were still not sealed off from revolutionary propaganda.'[78] In his response, Nicholas II wrote: 'the Jewish question should be thoroughly considered, when I find it necessary'.[79] Unfortunately, Tsar Nicholas II never found it necessary. The liberal ministers who supported the abolition of the quota, such as Witte and Tolstoy, were fired after the suppression of the first Russian revolution. They were replaced by more conservative ministers, who continued the policy of restricting Jewish access to university. The quota, which was spontaneously ignored in the revolutionary years by many universities, was again re-established. Furthermore, it was made into law in 1908 and was extended to schools that had been exempted— and therefore had not reported to the Ministry of National Enlightenment—and to Jewish external students. Consequently, the number of Jewish students at the universities decreased by half from 4,266 (13 per cent of all university students in Russia) in 1905 to 2,133 (6 per cent) in 1914. The total number of Jewish students in Russian state higher education institutions was 4,440 in the 1913/14 academic year, 8 per cent of the total number of students.[80]

  The struggle over the quota for Jewish students continued in the Russian empire until the February 1917 revolution and the abdication of the tsar. It was one of the most oppressive restrictions imposed on Russian Jews. Its abolition could have resulted in the opening of many prospects for young educated Jews. Conservative tsarist authorities always opposed the lifting of this restriction. The quota created divisions within the Russian government. In the years of the first Russian revolution, when several liberals were appointed to the government, the majority of them supported the abolition of this restriction, which they viewed first of all as harmful to state interests. The *numerus clausus* also radicalized young Jews, continuously creating new enemies for the tsarist regime. However, Nicholas II, in spite of the opinion of the majority of his government and public opinion, repeatedly refused until the collapse of the monarchy to abolish this most odious restriction.

---

[77] Cited ibid. 68.   [78] Cited ibid. 69.
[79] Cited in Ivanov, *Evreiskoe studenchestvo v Rossiiskoi imperii*, 69.   [80] Ibid. 73.

CONCLUSION

The Russian authorities did not allow the formation of Jewish schools, synagogues, and other Jewish institutions in Kiev for many years and tried to keep the Jewish community as small as possible in what they regarded as an Orthodox Christian holy city. However, despite all the restrictions, the Jewish population grew rapidly. In 1862 a total of 1,411 Jews lived in Kiev; in 1863 there were 3,013; in 1910 more than 50,000; and in 1913 the official count was 81,256. In 1917 officials estimated that 87,240 Jews lived there (about 15 per cent of the total population).[81] Hence, the plan of the authorities to keep the Jewish community of Kiev small by prohibiting all Jewish institutions failed dismally. But the situation of Kiev's Jews was unique. Perhaps it was the only Jewish community in the Russian empire which in spite of its size was deprived of the right to a Jewish education. This contradicted Russian laws, which allowed Jews to have Jewish schools within and beyond the Pale.

The ban on Jewish schools in Kiev, which the authorities maintained for forty years, created a peculiar situation in which all Jewish education was forced underground. There were illegal *talmud torah*s, *heder*s, and *melamedim* throughout the city. Deprived of official Jewish schools, the Jewish elite sent their children to Russian schools. However, when the Russification desired by tsarist authorities succeeded among wealthy Jewish circles, the Russian government reversed its policy. The quota raised a high barrier, preventing an influx of Jews into secondary schools and universities. Therefore, in the late nineteenth century Kiev's Jews were deprived of the right to either Jewish or general education.

The authorities eventually recognized the flaws in the situation, and the Jewish community of Kiev finally received permission to open Jewish schools, synagogues, and other institutions at the beginning of the twentieth century. Perhaps Lazar Brodsky's connections with the higher authorities helped to break the ice and establish the first Jewish school in Kiev in 1901, or perhaps the authorities, who recognized the need to provide Jews at least some access to education, decided that it was better to allow Jewish schools than to have an influx of Jews into Russian schools.

The editor of the pro-government newspaper *Novoe Vremya*, Aleksey Suvorin, in an 1880 article 'The Yid is Coming', warned that Russian education was opening the way for Jewish domination of Russian intellectual life.[82] The state-sponsored newspaper *Kievlyanin* stated that Russian education made Jews only superficially Russian and cleared the path for the rule of aliens over the Russian intelligentsia.[83] It noted on 5 November 1880: 'We must take care that in the future there will always be a compact majority of the native race in the educated ranks of

---

[81] Khiterer, 'Jewish Life in Kyiv', 75.
[82] See J. D. Klier, *Imperial Russia's Jewish Question 1855–1881* (Cambridge, 1995), 403–4.
[83] See ibid. 405.

Russian society, and not aliens, be they the Jerusalem nobility, Baltic barons, or Georgian princes.'[84]

Despite the opening of various Jewish schools in Kiev in the early twentieth century, many young Jews wished to earn either university or Russian vocational school diplomas, as these would give them the right to live outside the Pale of Settlement. Jews in Kiev, as well as throughout the tsarist empire, used all possible means to circumvent the obstacles that the authorities placed in their way to obtaining an education and to break through the quota for admission to Russian schools and universities. Heated debates about the quota divided Russian society. Conservatives supported it, justifying it as a necessary protection for the Russian people from Jewish domination and competition. Liberals struggled together with Jews for its abolition, considering this restriction harmful not only to Jews but to the entirety of Russian society.

[84] Cited ibid.

The Return of the *Ḥeder* among Russian Jewish Education Experts, 1840–1917

BRIAN HOROWITZ

T HE ROLE of the *ḥeder* in the modernization of Jewish education in the tsarist empire is a fascinating, albeit little-known, story. Most laymen and even scholars view the *ḥeder* monochromatically. They repeat the criticisms of the maskilim of the 1840s and later decades: the *ḥeder* was the obstacle to the successful integration of the Jews of Russia; nothing was learned there; the *melamed* beat the children, destroying them physically and spiritually; it was one of the vilest of religious institutions. However, there was a change in attitude towards the *ḥeder* at the beginning of the twentieth century among some of the most important specialists in the field of Jewish education in Russia. Some of these experts discovered in the *ḥeder* previously unnoticed dimensions that could be salvaged in future schools, while others saw parallels between the values of the *ḥeder* and the new nationalist-leaning Jewish institutions. Still others were impressed by the *ḥeder*'s longevity, its success with the public, and its low costs. Individuals associated with the School Commission of the Society for the Promotion of Enlightenment among the Jews of Russia (Obshchestvo dlya rasprostraneniya prosveshcheniya mezhdu evreyami v Rossii; OPE) along with certain Zionists, Bundists, and other independent intellectuals were involved with these questions.

Research into the *ḥeder* and modern schools in the tsarist empire is largely divided between those who studied the question during tsarist times and those who approached these issues starting in the 1960s in Israeli and American universities. The kinds of questions each group posed were different, because each group had its own political and cultural agenda.

During tsarist times the *ḥeder* was the object of study by 'activists', individuals, mainly men, who sought either to eliminate the *ḥeder* or to transform it. Attitudes changed, growing more positive around 1900 and reflecting new views on politics and the Jewish cultural ferment of the time. The experts gradually and

Parts of this chapter appear in B. Horowitz, *Jewish Philanthropy and Enlightenment in Late-Tsarist Russia* (Seattle, 2009): used with permission.

begrudgingly discovered much to like in the *ḥeder*. The majority of these individuals, non-Zionists such as Menashe Morgulis, Pinkhus (Petr) Marek, Leon Bramson, Jacob Katsenelson, Hayim Fialkov, and Shaul Ginzburg, were trained as lawyers but worked as journalists, teachers, or activists. Zionists, such as Avram Idelson and Chaim Zuta, admired the institution, although they demanded its modernization.[1] Incidentally, some of the statistical information and much of the anecdotal material come from studies produced in tsarist times.

The other group is composed of university professors in Israel and the United States of America. Individuals such as Zevi Scharfstein, Shaul Stampfer, Steven Zipperstein, Michael Stanislawski, Jacob Shatzky, Yossi Goldstein, Eliyana Adler, and Brian Horowitz intended to produce objective scholarship independent of political motives, although they relied on earlier statistics and to a degree on previous analyses. Despite their professed objectivity, these university-trained professors were sometimes influenced by revisionist thinking about Jewish history in Russia that was typical of the late years of the Cold War. Such thinking was characterized by the rediscovery of a good deal of positive aspects of Jewish life ('it was not all gloom and doom'). The 're-imagination' of Jewish life in Russia was undoubtedly connected with disappointment regarding Jewish life in the West, which was seen as decaying in spite of or because of the free atmosphere for Jewish religious observance. Russian Jews, it turned out, had much to offer in the construction of Jewish community.[2] Although this chapter does not deal directly with the differences between these two groups and their agendas, it implicitly shows the premises that underlie sympathies towards the traditional *ḥeder*.

The history of the *ḥeder* in the Russian empire is connected largely with struggles between the religiously orthodox and the maskilim (supporters of the Haskalah). The maskilim emphasized learning Russian, basic secular knowledge, and the acquisition of useful skills, such as mathematics. Despite a good deal of support from the government, including subsidies and even free tuition, for most of the nineteenth century few parents would permit their male children to attend secular schools. Besides the religious obligation to teach their children Torah, study at a *ḥeder* conveyed prestige. Parents showed they could afford a place in a *ḥeder* and implied at the same time their assent to the established order in the community. In addition, a *ḥeder* education gave their boys a chance at upward mobility: success at the *ḥeder* might lead to study in a yeshiva and in some cases to a coveted rabbinic position.[3] With success in Torah and talmudic learning came other potential tangible benefits such as marriage to the daughter of wealthy parents and status in the community. For these and other considerations, parents

[1] Y. Goldstein, '"Haḥeder hametukan" berusiyah kebasis lemerekhet hahinukh hatsiyonit', *Inyanim beḥinuch*, 45 (1986), 147–57.

[2] S. Zipperstein, *Imagining Russian Jewry: Memory, History, Identity* (Seattle, 1999), 3–4.

[3] S. Stampfer, 'Heder Study, Knowledge of Torah and the Maintenance of Social Stratification in Traditional Eastern European Jewish Society', *Studies in Jewish Education*, 3 (1988), 271–89.

continued to send their boys to the *heder* even when schools were available. Regarding the education of girls there were more options.

Alternatives to the *heder* began to appear in the 1840s when the Russian government established special Jewish schools. The government's goals appear contradictory to us now, but at least some of the intentions were positive: to educate young Jews in order to facilitate their integration into Russian society.[4] The government opened over a hundred schools as well as two teacher-training and rabbinic seminaries in Vilna and Zhitomir. After the schools were up and running, the government still had trouble convincing parents to send their children there, because the government's intentions did not appear unambiguous to the Jewish communities: perhaps the schools were the first step towards conversion to Christianity; why educate Jewish children for jobs that were closed to them?[5]

When the OPE was established in St Petersburg in 1863, its members devoted their energies to reforming government schools to make them more attractive to parents.[6] The unanimous opinion of the early leaders was that the *heder* was retrograde and unredeemable. From the mid-1860s until the 1890s the society spent the bulk of its resources on sending small numbers of students to universities. The idea was to produce university graduates who could serve as role models.[7] What little the organization devoted to primary and secondary education was earmarked for private schools. Such schools appeared to satisfy the society's goals of providing a secular education to Jews with the aim of integrating them into Russian society and giving them vocational skills.

Private schools for Jews promised instruction in reading, writing, mathematics, geography, and literature. The teachers of these schools purposely avoided religion and usually allowed students a choice of a half day of instruction in order to give boys the opportunity to attend *heder* in the morning. Private schools catered primarily for girls who, as Eliyana Adler has shown, had more choices than boys.[8] They could do without any education, acquire training in crafts, engage in home schooling, attend a state school, a private Russian school, or even a modern Jewish school. Girls were permitted to study secular subjects more readily than were boys, since parents condoned non-religious education if it helped a woman acquire

---

[4] M. Stanislawski, *Tsar Nicolas I and the Jews: The Transformation of Jewish Society in Russia, 1825–1855* (Philadelphia, 1983), 172.　　　　　　　　　　　　　　　　　[5] Ibid. 72–6.

[6] Benjamin Nathans gives the St Petersburg elite enormous credit for its services to the Jewish people of Russia; Brian Horowitz similarly lauds the elite, while underscoring their limitations (B. Nathans, *Beyond the Pale: The Jewish Encounter with Late Imperial Russia* (Berkeley, Calif., 2002), 55–6; Horowitz, *Jewish Philanthropy and Enlightenment in Late-Tsarist Russia*, 178–84).

[7] Scholars of the OPE such as Ilya Cherikover and Horowitz share the view that in its early period the society was top-heavy with wealthy members who sought to create a small elite among university-educated Jews (I. Cherikover, *Istoriya Obshchestva dlya rasprostraneniya prosveshcheniya mezhdu evreyami v Rossii, 1863–1913* (St Petersburg, 1913), 23–4; Horowitz, *Jewish Philanthropy and Enlightenment in Late-Tsarist Russia*, 17–20).

[8] See E. R. Adler, 'Private Schools for Jewish Girls in Tsarist Russia', Ph.D. thesis (Brandeis University, 2003), 55–90.

gainful employment so that her husband could devote his time to Torah study—
the Jewish tradition asserted that the religious responsibilities for a woman were
less onerous, and therefore girls did not need to study Hebrew or the Talmud.
It was enough to read the Pentateuch with simple commentaries in Yiddish translation (*Tsene rene*). Adler notes that, in opposition to what many people think, in
the nineteenth century 'many [Jewish] girls were educated, and secondly, their
educational paths differed significantly from that of their brothers'.[9]

Just as private schools found a way to supplement the local *ḥeder*, *shraybers*,
itinerant private teachers of Russian and secular subjects, complemented the *ḥeder*
by providing instruction in subjects that were not included in the *ḥeder* curriculum. The *shraybers*, mostly young unmarried men, gave lessons in private homes
and were widely employed.[10] *Shraybers* underscored how a single institution could
not fulfil the function of educating Russia's Jews: at least two, the *ḥeder* and something else, were needed.

The need for multiple educational institutions irked modern educators. In the
1890s experts—secular Jews who had studied the question of Jewish education—
were still bewildered by the enormous popularity of the *ḥeder*. Although educators
thought that private schools lost the competition because they were too costly, in
fact studies of the *ḥeder* found that massive sums were spent on its upkeep. What
was especially disconcerting was the fact that the masses had the money to fund
modern schools if they really wanted them. Jacob Katsenelson, a journalist who
wrote on Jewish education, calculated that in Russia 700,000 families paid a
minimum of 30 roubles a year for a *ḥeder*, *talmud torah*, or yeshiva, and therefore at
least 21 million roubles were spent annually on Jewish education.[11] That sum was
more than the total budget for elementary education in Austria and one and a half
times the amount spent in Italy, a country of thirty million people. Clearly, the
ḥeder could not be displaced, because it was popular; and it was popular, because it
met the needs of the population. This at least was the conclusion of Katsenelson
and Menashe Morgulis, a lawyer, civic leader and editor of the Jewish newspaper
Den' from 1870 to 1871.

What were the needs of the Jewish community? According to Morgulis, who
wrote a great deal about Jewish education, the existing schools did not meet the
community's basic needs, for example, for cheap childcare.[12] Children arrived at
the *ḥeder* early and stayed until late in the evening, thereby allowing mothers to

---

[9] Adler, 'Private Schools for Jewish Girls', 84.

[10] *Shraybers* (lit. 'writers') are depicted in the fiction of Shimon An-sky (Rapoport) and Sholem
Aleichem (Rabinovich). Sholem Aleichem was himself a *shrayber* in his youth.

[11] J. Katsenelson, 'Shkol'noe delo', *Ezhenedel'naya Khronika Voskhoda*, 9 (1894), 12. On the
korobochnyi sbor (meat and candle tax), see Yu. Gessen, 'Korobochnyi sbor', in L. Katsenelson and
D. G. Gintsburg (eds.), *Evreiskaya entsiklopediya: Svod znanii o evreistve i ego kul'ture v proshlom
i nastoyashchem*, 16 vols. (St Petersburg, 1908–13), ix, 758–71; see also id., 'K istorii korobochnogo
sbora v Rossii', *Evreiskaya starina*, 1911, no. 3, pp. 305, 484.

[12] M. Morgulis, *Voprosy evreiskoi zhizni: Sbornik statei*, 2nd edn. (St Petersburg, 1903).

spend longer days in the shop or market stall. By contrast, the schools let their pupils out in the early afternoon. Additionally, the school had higher expenses (rent for a building, the teacher's salary) and sometimes the instruction offended parents' religious principles.[13] It was hard to argue with Morgulis, although a number of critics objected to his proposition that schools needed to provide longer hours.[14]

Among other reasons for the *ḥeder*'s survival was its reliability. Parents considered that it had served Jewish children well over the centuries. Nonetheless, Jews, especially in the south-western region, began to favour Russian schools during the 1870s and 1880s until restrictions on Jewish enrolment were enacted in 1887. Significantly these quotas had the twin result of enhancing the value of Russian schools and reviving interest in the *ḥeder*, since Jews were now forced to attend exclusively Jewish educational institutions.[15]

The attitude of the modernizers towards the *ḥeder* did not drastically change in the 1890s. For example, in 1893, when the OPE set out to design its ideal elementary school, its members divided the existing types of schools into four categories, according to the time spent on Jewish and general subjects. *Ḥeder*s had only Jewish subjects; *talmud torah*s concentrated on Jewish subjects but included secular subjects as well; government Jewish schools had a mixture of religious and secular with an emphasis on the secular; and private schools gave preference to secular knowledge. In part because of the law of March 1893 which prohibited secular subjects from being taught in *ḥeder*s and perhaps because of a personal animus of the members of the commission, the members gave the *ḥeder* short shrift. They were convinced that the *ḥeder* could 'not be transformed into a modern school'.[16]

The organization and curriculum of the OPE's modern Jewish school were conceived both in opposition to and in conformity with the *ḥeder*. The way the schools were organized—with proper ventilation, furniture, and a concern for the hygiene and health of the students, including breaks between classes and for lunch, as well as proper bathing—showed a desire to break with the *ḥeder*. The request that the schools have their own buildings and that the classrooms not be used as the teacher's home was also directed against the *ḥeder*, since in the *ḥeder* the *melamed*

---

[13] Ibid. 200.

[14] L. I. Mandelshtam, 'Iz zapisok pervogo evreya-studenta v Rossii', ed. S. Ginzburg, *Perezhitoe*, 1 (1908), 4–5.

[15] Many scholars see the rise of Jewish nationalism as a response to the pogroms of 1881–2. Horowitz regards the government's educational quotas in 1887 as a large factor in producing activities that furthered national interests (*Jewish Philanthropy and Enlightenment*, 80–96).

[16] Rossiiskii gosudarstvennyi istoricheskii arkhiv, St Petersburg (hereafter RGIA), f. 1532, op. 1, d. 49: 'Otchet o deyatel'nosti obshchestva za 1894', 15. Nevertheless, the members had noted that they had recently received indications that several *melamedim* in the south-western region had petitioned the Ministry of Education for the right to offer instruction in Russian. Therefore, it was important to wait and see how the law was applied.

lived in the same room in which he taught. In the *ḥeder* there was often inadequate lighting, few windows, and filth on the walls because of the smoke from the oven. Little thought was given to ventilation. In addition, there were no breaks between classes or concern about back-breaking benches.[17]

During the 1890s the administrators of the OPE's education programmes, such as Leon Bramson, slowly began to realize the *ḥeder*'s strengths. In his 1896 essay 'On the History of the Elementary Education of Jews in Russia', Bramson set himself the goal of explaining why Jews had remained isolated from Russian society, why government-sponsored Jewish schools had been necessary, and why Jews themselves now had to take control of their own education.[18] In addition, at the end of the essay Bramson sketched his ideal school. In contrast to those who wanted a completely secular school and those who preferred the *ḥeder*, Bramson sought a compromise:

In a modern school there should be enough of those subjects that attract Jewish children to the *ḥeder*—that is, the Jewish religion—and one should give the school a vocational character as much as possible. In addition, instruction should be at the highest pedagogical level. Only in these conditions, so the advocates of this view contend, can the school be ready to replace our unique age-old institution.[19]

Although Bramson preferred vocational schools—he became the head of the Society for Trades and Agricultural Labour (Obshchestvo remeslennogo i zemledel'cheskogo truda)—others continued to see positive aspects of the *ḥeder*, especially as national feeling began to grow among the Jewish intelligentsia. The revival of Hebrew in particular had a strong influence on reconsiderations of the *ḥeder*, as did the emergence of political Zionism.[20]

There were many signs of Hebrew's revival in the Russian empire, but the school debates in the Odessa branch of the OPE in 1902 best embody the relationship between schools, Hebrew, and the nationalist-leaning Jewish intelligentsia. Challenging the ideology of integration, nationalists, predominantly Zionists, launched an attack on the number of hours of Jewish and secular subjects in schools subsidized by the society. Their goal was to get more hours of Hebrew and fewer of Russian. They gave their opponents the mocking epithet 'assimilators'.

The nationalists were represented by Ahad Ha'am, Ben-Ami (Mark (Mordecai) Rabinovich), Meir Dizengoff, Yehoshua Ravnitsky, and Simon Dubnow. Dubnow was the only non-Zionist. They pressed the point that Jewish schools had to instil national values; anything less would amount to yielding to assimilation. The school must be occupied not with preparing a vocation or advancing integration but with

---

[17] Some modern historians view the *ḥeder* more positively as a place where students learned religious values, Hebrew, and the essential texts of the Jewish religion (Goldstein, '"Haḥeder hametukan" berusiyah', 147–8).

[18] L. Bramson, 'K istorii nachal'nogo obrazovaniya evreev v Rossii', in *Sbornik v pol'zu nachal'nykh evreiskikh shkol* (St Petersburg, 1896), 280–333.

[19] Ibid. 353.   [20] Goldstein, '"Haḥeder hametukan" berusiyah', 148.

a series of courses in Hebrew, the Bible, and Jewish history to instil nationalist feelings. Moreover, at least twelve of the thirty school-hours in the week had to be given over to Jewish subjects and Hebrew should serve as the primary focus of the curriculum in order to spur an interest in the 'customs, way of life, and literary creativity of the Jewish people'.[21] The study of the Bible, they wrote, also had the goal of 'acquainting students with Judaism's main religious and ethical precepts'.[22]

Although both the assimilators and the nationalists were in favour of schools, the 1902 debates reflect a major change in attitude. Most significant is the focus on Hebrew (rather than Yiddish) as the means to attaining a proper Jewish identity and purpose. With a cluster of hours devoted to Hebrew and the Bible, the nationalists' school curriculum had elements in common with the traditional ḥeder.

Similar positive attitudes towards the ḥeder appeared elsewhere. At the meeting of provincial representatives with the OPE board in 1902, the question of the ḥeder was widely debated and the seeds of a new, positive evaluation could be detected. Lev Katsenelson, the long-standing leader of the OPE and well-known Hebrew writer, explained that 'educated' Jews had long been convinced that even in the instruction of Hebrew the ḥeder was a worn-out institution that had to yield to the superiority of the modern school. However, results proved otherwise: 'Experts in Hebrew, which the ḥeder produced, did not emerge from the modern school.'[23]

At the beginning of the twentieth century the dominant viewpoint among nationalists was that the ḥeder provided Jewish children with an important part of a total educational package. However, the ḥeder needed to be supplemented by secular studies. Both the ḥeder and the school were needed, but ideally they would not be separate but joined in a single institution.

Serious discussions on how to restructure the relationship between the school and the ḥeder took front-and-centre place in the first journal devoted to Jewish education in Russia, *Evreiskaya shkola*. The journal, which appeared monthly for almost two years from 1904 to 1905, expressed the nationalist viewpoint that assimilation was the primary danger to the Jewish people and much more dangerous than antisemitism. Among the contributors were some of the major Jewish intellectuals: V. O. Harkavy, Dubnow, Avram Idelson, J. Katsenelson, Mikhail Krol, Mikhail Kreinin, Marek, A. Ravesman, A. Konshtam, and Ya. Galpern.

Arguing in favour of the ḥeder, individuals such as Marek, Kreinin, and Idelson insisted that it be included in any comprehensive Jewish educational programme. Marek wrote:

Over the course of two centuries, fifty years after their appearance in Russia, our modern schools for boys (state, private, and community schools) have barely reached 400 in the Pale of Settlement (outside Poland). In the Pale of Settlement, several tens of thousands of ḥeders can be counted. The simple comparison of these figures shows how little the opponents of ḥeders have accomplished in half a century. And if, instead of a politics of neglect for the ḥeder, on the contrary, we had paid it serious attention, and if, instead of an

---

[21] Bramson, 'K istorii nachal′nogo obrazovaniya evreev v Rossii', 353.   [22] Ibid.   [23] Ibid.

unrealizable dream about uniting it with the school, we had studied the conditions for the joint, equal, and peaceful coexistence of both schools and tried to help them cooperate, then our schools would function better than they do now.[24]

Marek added that it was an illusion to think that the school would 'swallow' the *ḥeder*. More likely, the *ḥeder* would swallow the school.[25] Because of the loyalty of Jewish parents to the *ḥeder* and the difficulty and expense of organizing two schools at once, the School Commission came to realize that no progress could be made without some idea of how the school interacted with the *ḥeder*. As one member put it, 'naturally, the two contradictory systems of education cannot be justified by logical and practical considerations. A pedagogue must do everything in his power to diminish the abyss between the school and the *ḥeder* in order to bring them as much as possible closer together.'[26]

Despite much hard work to promote the modern school, it became clear that a stalemate had occurred: the *ḥeder* could not replace the school, nor the school the *ḥeder*. Simultaneously, it was equally impossible to unite them in a single institution, as much as the educators wanted to. The problem was the uncompromising difference in programmes and goals and the difference in the kind of teachers that each school required. For one thing, legally, secular courses could not be introduced into the *ḥeder*. Moreover, the institutions catered to different audiences: attendance in the *ḥeder* was the natural decision for parents in areas where traditional Jewish life was still strong, such as the north-western territories, while secular schools were popular in the south. For example, there were eighteen *ḥadarim metukanim* (improved *ḥeders*) in the south-west in 1903, which had been established by medical doctors.[27]

The idea of gaining information about *ḥeders* had actually been realized to an extent by the beginning of the twentieth century. In fact, as early as 1895 the OPE, in collaboration with the Russian Imperial Free Economic Society (Imperatorskoe vol'noe ekonomicheskoe obshchestvo), set out to learn more about 'Jewish home schools', their name for the *ḥeder*. Sending a questionnaire to several hundred state rabbis and civic leaders, the OPE hoped to 'gain a full portrait of folk education in [the] country'.[28] The questions focused on the age and experience of the *melamed*, the number of students in the school, and whether the students attended other schools besides the *ḥeder*. In addition, members of the OPE School Commission wanted to know if Russian was taught and whether Yiddish was used in teaching Torah.

[24] P. Marek, 'Natsionalizatsiya vospitaniya i evreiskie uchebnye zavedeniya', *Evreiskaya shkola*, 3 (1904), 9.   [25] Ibid. 10.

[26] P. Marek, 'Nablyudeniya i vyvody po shkol'nomu voprosu', *Nedel'naya Khronika Voskhoda*, 20 (1902), 6.

[27] M. Kreinin, 'Nablyudeniya po shkol'nomu delu', *Nedel'naya Khronika Voskhoda*, 5 (1903), 15.

[28] J. Katsenelson, 'Sovremennyi kheder, kak ob"ekt' issledovaniya', *Nedel'naya Khronika Voskhoda*, 12 (1895), 308.

From this and another survey conducted in 1898–9, members of the OPE School Commission were able to get reliable statistics about *ḥeder*s.[29] According to the Jewish Colonization Association (JCA), there were approximately 24,540 *ḥeder*s in a population of 4,874,636 Jews. According to these statistics, there were 13 students per *ḥeder* in the Pale, which meant that there were 343,000 children in *ḥeder*s, plus another 20,000 in organized schools. Combined, these figures give a total of 363,000 Jewish elementary school students in the Pale.[30]

According to this survey, of the students in *ḥeder*s, 95 per cent were boys and only 5 per cent were girls.[31] This fact was surprising because it differed radically from other groups in the empire. For example, although Muslims also refused to part with folk schools, 17 per cent of the students in Muslim schools were girls. Educational experts also asserted that among students, the largest group in the *ḥeder* were under school age, 7 years old (23 per cent). In addition, the majority of students came from the middle class (55 per cent), as opposed to the poor (28 per cent) or wealthy (17 per cent). The concept of middle class may be misleading, however, since it meant a family with a single room to themselves.

The study also found that for the most part the *ḥeder* teacher was either a representative of the synagogue, the *gabai*, for example, or someone who had failed at another profession: a former contractor, storeowner, confectioner, or craftsman.[32] Often such *melamedim* were older men. Among the *melamedim* in the Kiev district, for example, 66 per cent were between the ages of 40 and 60. The majority had received some training in a yeshiva, although about 25 per cent had left the yeshiva by the age of 16. The statistics supported prejudices regarding the average *melamed*'s lack of skill.

According to statistics from the OPE, each student paid on average 25 roubles annually in cities and 18 roubles in rural regions. Adding up the number of *ḥeder*s with these prices, the investigators calculated that Jews spent between 6.5 and 7.5 million roubles on *ḥeder*s every year. Furthermore, the *ḥeder* composed 31 per cent of the total of 'unorganized' schools in the empire, which showed that Jews were particularly attached to their traditional 'folk' education.

In the years following the revolution of 1905, some educators had come around to the view that the best school was the *ḥeder metukan*. Zionists in particular were enamoured of the *ḥeder metukan*, because it permitted a mixed curriculum and was designed to teach and use Hebrew in the classroom.[33] At the same time, under the

[29] *Spravochnaya kniga po voprosam obrazovaniya evreev: posobie dlya uchitelei i uchitel' nits evreiskikh shkol i deyatelei po narodnomu obrazovaniyu* (St Petersburg, 1901), 287. In the second investigation, educational experts from the Imperial Free Economic Society conducted interviews in various locations and their findings were compared with responses from the OPE questionnaire. On the Free Economic Society, see J. Pratt, 'The Russian Free Economic Society, 1765–1915', Ph.D. thesis (University of Missouri, 1983). [30] 'Sovremennyi kheder, kak ob"'ekt' issledovaniya', 293.

[31] Adler, 'Private Schools for Jewish Girls in Tsarist Russia', 74–7.

[32] S. Avirom et al., *Sovremennyi kheder po obsledovaniyu OPE* (St Petersburg, 1912), 14.

[33] Z. Scharfstein, *Toledot hahinukh beyisra'el bedorot ha'aharonim*, 5 vols. (Jerusalem, 1960–5), ii. 42–7.

influence of what appeared to be life-changing events, OPE professionals lost interest in the *ḥeder* as optimism grew in the society's ability to expand its school programme throughout the country. Unfortunately, events unfolded in ways that were inimical to these plans.

In the last years before the First World War many intellectuals came out strongly in favour of the *ḥeder*, reversing their former views. In a meeting of the OPE with its provincial members in 1912, speaker after speaker defended the *ḥeder*, attributing to it the virtue of keeping the Jewish people united and strong.[34] The thrust of the discussion pivoted around the indifference of Jews to Judaism, the threat of assimilation, and the potential dissolution of the Jewish people. Hayim Nahman Bialik, the renowned Hebrew poet, fulminated against the intelligentsia's traditional attitude towards the *ḥeder*:

For the past fifty years 'smart thinking' excluded a concern with Jewish subjects, the Bible was something religious, rather than educational. Pushkin, yes, he's a poet, but Jewish poets —why should one know them? . . . Your child, the generation you brought up lies dead. The living child, the future Jewish generation, is ours. And we will not give him up![35]

Bialik's hostility was perhaps too simple, since he characterized the Zionists as defenders of everything Jewish and everyone else as defectors from a just cause. Nevertheless, his passionate speech in favour of the *ḥeder* was influential. Even Hayim Fialkov, the leading educator of the OPE, changed his mind about reform-ing *ḥeders*. 'Vilna's improved *ḥeders* show how one can initiate huge projects if one wants to meet the needs of the broad masses of Jews. . . . I want to acknowledge respect for those who labour on behalf of these schools, whose activities do not entirely coincide with our educational ideals.'[36]

Action went with the words. In 1911 the St Petersburg OPE established a *ḥeder* commission,[37] whose goal was to incorporate the *ḥeder* into the society's school programme. As a consequence, St Petersburg sent four educational experts to dif-ferent areas: the south, Volhynia, Lithuania, and Poland. The research was pub-lished in 1912 in a volume entitled *The Contemporary Ḥeder According to an OPE Study*.[38] Acknowledging the importance of the *ḥeder* for Jewish life, the editors nonetheless expressed overwhelmingly negative opinions. That conclusion did not interfere with expressions of nostalgia, however:

Despite our consciousness of the extremely anti-pedagogical, distorted, and often distort-ing aspects of the *ḥeder*, we nevertheless feel that this special ancient school of traditional

---

[34] The proceedings were published as *Otchet o soveshchanii komiteta OPE s predstavitelyami otdelenii, 25–27 dekabrya 1912* (St Petersburg, 1913).

[35] Ibid. 19; see also Zipperstein, *Imagining Russian Jewry*, 48–57.

[36] *Otchet o soveshchanii komiteta OPE s predstavitelyami otdelenii*, 34.

[37] It was the second in the society: Odessa had opened a *ḥeder* commission in 1904.

[38] Avirom et al., *Sovremennyi kheder po obsledovaniyu OPE*. It was also published in *Vestnik Obshch-estva rasprostraneniya prosveshcheniya mezhdu evreyami v Rossii*, 17 (1912). S. Avirom was responsible for the south, I. Shulkovsky for Volhynia, F. Shapiro for Lithuania, and B. Alperin for Poland.

Judaism has left an intimate mark on our soul. The *ḥeder* with its unique Jewish atmosphere, in spite of all its dark aspects, has a warm spot in our distant memories, and together with the synagogue gives strength to our connection with Judaism.[39]

The scholars concluded that, while it had much to offer the modern Jewish school, the *ḥeder* itself had to be transformed. On the eve of war the educational experts among the Jewish intellectuals embraced the notion that they had to be involved in the running of *ḥeder*s, in curricular development, teacher training, and reform of the institution's format—from the design of the chairs to the location of instruction. It is hard to say what would have happened had war not broken out, but the war changed the situation drastically.

Jewish educators reacted slowly to the war. The chaos that interfered with Jewish civil life can only be imagined: men were drafted, women found themselves without work, and families were exposed in the war zones. It was only in August 1915 that Jewish organizations in Russia, members of the Jewish Committee for Aid to the Victims of the War (Evreiskii komitet pomoshchi zhertvam voiny; EKOPO), the Society for the Preservation of the Health of the Jewish Population (Obshchestvo okhraneniya zdorovya evreiskogo naseleniya), the OPE, and the JCA organized a meeting to co-ordinate efforts and assign responsibilities. The job of organizing schools for refugees was turned over to the OPE. By the end of 1915 the OPE had opened or subsidized ninety-three schools, eighteen for boys, sixteen for girls, and fifty-nine mixed.[40] The Petrograd board was responsible for forty-seven, the Moscow branch ran twenty-six, and the Kiev branch, twenty. In 1916 the number of schools and *ḥeder*s supported by the OPE reached 222, serving 29,688 students.

Although the St Petersburg OPE was working with a limited budget, OPE leaders immediately understood the need to expand their reach. They turned to Russian Jewry with a plea for money:

We believe that if Jewry's vital forces work together, the destructive whirlwind of war will pass over our heads without rupturing our internal life, which would occur if we were not organized. The ark of our cultural life, the Jewish school, must survive the present deluge. Twenty centuries ago the Jewish school saved our nation when it stood on Jerusalem's ruins. The school will save our present generation after the collapse of the Polish–Lithuanian cultural centre.[41]

The appeal was signed by leading educators, Hayim Fialkov, A. Strashun, E. Kantor, and S. Groisman.

OPE experts set out to design a curriculum for schools for refugees that would be familiar and contain a large selection of Jewish subjects. However, they made the fateful decision to use Yiddish as the language of instruction. This decision was based on solid pedagogical grounds: Yiddish was the refugees' native language.

---

[39] Avirom et al., *Sovremennyi kheder po obsledovaniyu OPE*, 3.
[40] RGIA, f. 1532, op. 1, d. 1308: 'Otchet o deyatel'nosti komiteta Obshchestva za 1914–1917', p. 16.
[41] Ibid. 11–12.

'The board is convinced that the Jewish school must replace that national environment which the children of refugees lost when they left their homes and faced the alienating, de-nationalizing influence of the new environment.'[42] The decision also meant that the school resembled the traditional *ḥeder*.[43] Educators in the OPE explained:

Concerning the language of instruction, besides Russian and Hebrew as subjects in their own right, all the other subjects in the school for refugees will be taught in most cases in Yiddish. In addition to general considerations about the significance of using one's native language in teaching, one should also keep in mind that even at home these shtetl children did not attend normal schools. They studied in *ḥeders* where they acquired knowledge of Hebrew, but they are total beginners when it comes to secular subjects. They have not been prepared for school. They do not even know how to study. We have to teach them how to pay attention and teach them discipline. The *ḥeder*, in which they studied independently, did not teach them these things. Children of various ages are coming to the school for refugees, therefore one has to use Yiddish.[44]

Although strong condescension towards traditional Jews is apparent from the St Petersburg elite, especially in the claim that the refugees had to be taught to concentrate and that Yiddish had to be used because students of various ages studied together, the educators intended to promote real learning. 'Simultaneous with the establishment of the old type of *ḥeder*, which undoubtedly will appear in these new communities, we will try to make several improvements.'[45]

Permitting children as young as 6 into the school, OPE leaders decided that the schools should have twenty-six or twenty-seven hours per week of instruction for the younger classes and up to thirty-six hours for the older ones. It was necessary to increase the school day, wrote one educator, in order to find time for secular subjects in addition to Hebrew, the Bible, Yiddish, and Jewish history.[46] The length of the programme was five years for boys and four for girls.

[42] RGIA, f. 1532, op. 1, d. 1308: 'Otchet o deyatel'nosti komiteta Obshchestva za 1914–1917', 11. In his memoir Ben-Zion Dinur credits himself with the use of the student's native language, since it made no sense to teach Baltic Jews whose native language was Russian or those students who were proficient in Hebrew in Yiddish. Actually, Dinur tried first to advance Hebrew as the language of the future Jewish state. He describes how the Yiddishists perceived him as a Hebraist and the Hebraists condemned him as a Yiddishist (*Biyeme milhamah umahpekhah: zikhronot ureshumot miderekh hayim* (Jerusalem, 1960), 76).

[43] See *OPE na voine* (Petrograd, 1917), 13. In December 1914 the OPE presented the government with a new charter for the Grodno Teachers Academy that requested instruction in Yiddish and of Jewish history in Hebrew. Although there was already some Yiddish in the school and a 1914 law permitted Yiddish (or any native language) to be used in elementary schools, the changes in the charter were requested to prepare teachers to offer a more intensely Jewish school experience. The government, however, rejected the new charter, making it more difficult for the OPE to prepare teachers for schools that were closing the gap with the *ḥeder*.

[44] *Obshchestvo dlya rasprostraneniya prosveshcheniya mezhdu evreyami v Rossii na voine* (St Petersburg, 1918), 12–13.   [45] *OPE na voine*, 8.

[46] RGIA, f. 1532, op. 1, d. 1446: 'Otchet o deyatel'nosti komiteta Obshchestva za mart-avgust 1916', p. 2.

It is impossible to deny both that the study of Yiddish as an academic subject was a novelty and the decision to teach in Yiddish had ideological underpinnings. OPE leaders were strongly influenced by Simon Dubnow's ideas of cultural nationalism, especially his view that east European Jews formed a 'centre' with their own native culture. Although Dubnow favoured trilinguism, the idea of the east European centre presumed Yiddish as a legitimate language, while, at the same time, Bundists and other Jewish socialists expropriated Yiddish as the language of the folk and the Jewish proletariat.[47] Yiddishists, such as Kreinin, Shaul Ginzburg, and Israel Zinberg, viewed Yiddish as the national language of the Jewish people, powerfully influencing school policy.[48] Hebrew, previously the darling of the nationalists, was still advanced by Zionists and older intellectuals who remembered the services Hebrew had rendered in the struggle for enlightenment. Nonetheless, a Yiddish-speaking school with Jewish subjects had a strong resemblance to the *ḥeder*, and the *ḥeder* was the model on which the educational experts built their wartime schools.

The picture of Jewish education in the 1920s is part of the larger context of the communist government's treatment of Russia's Jews generally. As complicated as that story is, a few general observations can be made. Immediately after the revolution the Zionists, the Bund, and the communists established their own independent school programmes.[49] Nevertheless, with the outbreak of the Russian civil war, Jews gravitated towards supporting the Bolsheviks, viewing them as defenders against the pogrom-making of the Whites. In time the Bolsheviks consolidated their power and the new regime made it more and more difficult for independent educational organizations to survive. In 1924 the communist government uniformly closed all the *ḥeder*s, eliminating in a single day an institution many centuries old and denying religious Jews and Zionists an institutional foothold. The attack on the *ḥeder* occurred simultaneously with attacks on Jewish religious institutions, synagogues, study-houses, and rabbis.

[47] S. M. Dubnow, 'O sovremennom sostoyanni evreiskoi istoriografii', *Evreiskaya starina*, 1909, no. 1, pp. 149–58.

[48] S. M. Dubnow, *Kniga zhizni: Vospominaniia i razmyshleniia. Materialy dlia istorii moego vremeni* (Moscow, 2004), 360–1.

[49] On Zionists, see J. Gilboa, *A Language Silenced: The Suppression of Hebrew Literature and Culture in the Soviet Union* (Rutherford, NJ, 1982), 25–5; on the Bund, see Z. Gitelman, *Jewish Nationality and Soviet Politics: the Jewish Sections of the CPSU, 1917–1930* (Princeton, NJ, 1972), 178.

From Theory to Practice

The Fight for Jewish Education in Vilna during the First World War

ANDREW N. KOSS

IN 1916—while the eyes of the world were fixed on the bloody battle between France and Germany at Verdun—Moyshe Shalit, a Yiddish-language journalist in Vilna, proudly described a recently created elementary school as 'the first experiment with a model elementary school [*folks-shul*] in Yiddish'.[1] A few decades later, another Yiddishist writer, K. S. Kazdan, would claim that 'in the whirlwind of the First World War the Jewish [*yidishe*] secular school was born'.[2] These statements raise several important questions, most importantly: why did the First World War bring about such a long-awaited development? At first sight, it would seem that a time of intense social, political, and economic crisis (which would in fact lead to the collapse of the tsarist empire), when Russia's Jews suffered from pauperization, antisemitic violence, and physical dislocation and when most of the Pale of Settlement was turned into a war zone, would be an unlikely moment for major changes in education. Furthermore, there were Jewish schools in tsarist Russia that offered secular education and used Yiddish as a language of instruction: in what way, then, were these new schools different? Finally, what were the long- and short-term consequences of these new schools?

The statements by Shalit and Kazdan were, if anything, understatements. The First World War led to major changes in Jewish education that were by no means limited to advances in Yiddish-language secular education. Jewish Vilna experienced a particularly dramatic wartime transformation of its educational

I would like to thank Aron Rodrigue, Steven Zipperstein, and Brian Horowitz, who read this chapter at various stages and provided invaluable feedback, as well as the staff of the JDC and YIVO archives, especially Fruma Mohrer and Ettie Goldwasser. The research was made possible by the Jewish Studies Program at Colgate University and the Andrew W. Mellon Foundation.

[1] M. Shalit, 'Vilner shuln', in *Vilner zamlbukh*, ed. T. Szabad, 2 vols. (Vilna, 1916–18), ii. 137. Technically speaking, two similar schools in Russia, of which Shalit would have been unaware, might have preceded the Folks-Shul far Yingelekh (see K. S. Kazdan, *Fun kheyder un 'shkoles' biz 'tsysho': dos ruslendishe yidntum in gerangl far shul, shprakh, kultur* (Mexico City, 1956)).

[2] Kazdan, *Fun kheyder un 'shkoles' biz 'tsysho'*, 216.

institutions, as documented by a substantial body of archival and contemporary published sources. Here the war gave a group of Jewish activists and intellectuals an opportunity to carry out one of their longstanding goals: the creation of a network of modern Jewish elementary and secondary schools that would give children both a secular education and a strong sense of Jewish identity. The war saw the founding of Vilna's first Jewish kindergartens, its first Yiddish-language primary schools, and its first Hebrew and Yiddish gymnasia. These institutions came into being despite the burdens of wartime poverty and constant lack of communal funds. They succeeded, in part, because wartime population movement and economic devastation uprooted existing educational systems, leaving some children without access to schooling, while simultaneously creating room for new kinds of institutions. New schools also succeeded because of the educational policies of the German military occupation (1915–18), which were liberal in comparison with those of the tsarist regime.

The wartime flourishing of modern schools, however, dashed any hopes of a unified system of Jewish education. Ideological differences eventually undermined co-operation between the various proponents of school reform. By the end of the war, multiple organizations, representing different political and cultural ideologies, ran competing Jewish school networks. While debates over schools often pitted socialists and diaspora nationalists against Zionists, the conflict was not simply the pedagogical manifestation of pre-existing ideological and political divisions. The very process of creating new schools shaped ideological stances and in fact led to political realignments. In other words, education became the tail wagging the dog of politics.

JEWISH SCHOOLING DURING THE FIRST YEAR OF WAR, JULY 1914–AUGUST 1915

When war broke out in 1914 most children in Vilna continued to attend school as usual. The war's effects were, at first, only gradually felt. A few teachers were called up for military service or auxiliary civilian activities. Growing economic problems may have affected enrolment patterns, but they would only have significant effect later on. The first major strain on wartime education came from the influx of refugees from nearby provinces. Between the outbreak of war in July 1914 and Vilna's occupation by the German army in September 1915, over 22,000 Jews fled to Vilna, many of whom were victims of the Russian army's violent expulsions of Jews from the areas near the frontlines. Jewish organizations in Vilna, in addition to having to provide food, clothing, and shelter for these refugees, faced the daunting task of educating their children. The response of these organizations to the refugee crisis prefigured changes in Jewish education that would occur under the German occupation.[3]

---

[3] See J. Wygodzki, *In shturm: zikhroynes fun di okupatsye-tsaytn* (Vilna, 1926), 20–66; id., 'Vilne in

Communal leaders used the task of ameliorating the humanitarian crisis as an opportunity to create new kinds of educational institutions. First, in October 1914, a group of activists and philanthropists established a Jewish *kinderheym*, or children's home, the first of its kind in Vilna.[4] This institution, something between a kindergarten, a day-care centre, an orphanage, and an elementary school, served the primary purpose of giving roughly a hundred displaced boys and girls a place to spend their days under adult supervision. The all-female staff consisted entirely of volunteers. Children received at least one meal per day, as well as clothes and shoes. Teachers ensured that children bathed once a week—a crucial activity when hygienic standards were low and the refugee crisis presented a growing hazard to public health. The curriculum, although circumscribed by limited resources, included Yiddish, Russian, arithmetic, reading, crafts, singing, drawing, and outdoor exercise. The school received support from the Petrograd-based Jewish Committee for Aid to the Victims of the War (Evreiskii komitet pomoshchi zhertvam voiny; EKOPO) and from individual local benefactors.[5] During the subsequent years of the war, several children's homes would be founded in Vilna that would take in native children as well as refugees.[6]

The *kinderheym* differed starkly from the dingy, pedagogically conservative, and boys-only *ḥeder*, which was the only form of education most of these children had previously experienced. Furthermore, even those Jews who sent their children to modern schools did not send them to kindergarten, since none existed. (There were only a handful of kindergartens in all of Russia at the time.) The school's avoidance of rote learning and emphasis on hands-on activities such as crafts and drawing reflected the most modern trends in pedagogy. The use of Yiddish as a language of formal secular instruction alongside Russian, while not unheard of, was rare and conformed to the programme of a particular segment of the Jewish intelligentsia. (I will discuss the significance of Yiddish at length below.) As a result, poor children —rather than children of the acculturating Jewish bourgeoisie—gained exposure to the most innovative educational approaches.

In the summer of 1915 the local branch of the Society for the Promotion of Enlightenment among the Jews of Russia (Obshchestvo dlya rasprostraneniya prosveshcheniya mezhdu evreyami v Rossii; OPE) resolved to organize proper elementary schools for refugee children to supplement the *kinderheym*. Since the 1880s the St Petersburg OPE had been the major institutional force behind

veltkrig', in *Pinkes far der geshikhte fun vilne in di yorn fun milkhome un okupatsye*, ed. Z. Reyzen (Vilna, 1922), 45, 64; 'Vegn opfohren fun di heymloze', *Letste nayes*, 4 Apr. 1916, p. 4.

[4] Y. Frankfurt, 'Di kinder-heymen', in *Vilner zamlbukh*, i. 11–12; Szabad, 'Forverts', in *Vilner zamlbukh*, i. 4–6; Reyzen, 'Hakdome', in *Pinkes far der geshikhte*, 3–4. Unfortunately, I have found little information about who founded the children's home or explicit documentation of their motives.

[5] Frankfurt, 'Di kinder-heymen', 12–13; G. Pats, 'In kinder heym (ayndrukn)', in *Vilner zamlbukh*, i. 7–11; Y. Rubin, 'Der yidisher tsentraler bildungs-komitet in vilne (ts.b.k.)', in *Pinkes far der geshikhte*, 716.   [6] T. Szabad, 'Iberzikht', in *Vilner zamlbukh*, ii. 14; Shalit, 'Vilner shuln', 154.

reforming Jewish education in Russia. It had established its first *ḥeder metukan* (reformed *ḥeder*) in Vilna, which served as a model for similar institutions opened subsequently. However, the OPE's efforts to further the cause of modern Jewish education were checked by suspicious local and provincial authorities on the one hand and the rabbinic establishment on the other. Its major successes in Vilna in the decade before the First World War were in the founding of schools for girls, which provoked less opposition from the traditionalists than modern schools for boys. Thus, on the eve of war, Vilna had an OPE-run modern elementary school for girls where pupils studied the Hebrew language along with secular subjects, and an equivalent private gymnasium for girls directed by OPE activist Sofia Gurevitsh.[7]

By stepping in to provide for the refugees, the OPE saw the possibility of circumventing the Orthodox establishment by using funding from its parent organization in Petrograd to provide modern elementary schools for children who were not attending school. It would thus avoid competing with either traditional educational institutions or with state-run schools. Zionists on the OPE committee, generally more sympathetic to religious education, proposed the moderate course of creating a *shul-kheyder*, intermediate between a *ḥeder metukan* and a modern school. Yiddishist members wished to take the more radical step of creating a *folks-shul*—a modern secular school that taught such subjects as Jewish history and literature in Yiddish. (Russian law continued to dictate that general subjects be taught in Russian.) The rapid pace of the war, however, prevented this debate from reaching a conclusion.[8]

After losing its hold on Poland and Galicia and faced with the threat of complete military collapse, the tsar's army opted for a scorched-earth retreat east of Vilna in the late summer of 1915. The evacuation gave Jewish education—along with every other aspect of life—a much greater shock than the refugee crisis. The army ordered not only Vilna's military garrison to depart but also the city's civilian administration, including the staff of state-run schools. In addition, many of Vilna's residents fled voluntarily, including most of the teachers and administrators from those private schools where Russian was the language of instruction.[9] (The

---

[7] I. Klausner, *Vilna: yerushalayim delita, dorot aharonim*, 2 vols. (Tel Aviv, 1983), ii. 574–6. For the history of the OPE, see B. Horowitz, *Jewish Philanthropy and Enlightenment in Late-Tsarist Russia* (Seattle, 2009); for the education of girls, see E. R. Adler, *In her Hands: The Education of Jewish Girls in Tsarist Russia* (Detroit, 2011); for the early history of schools for girls in Vilna, see esp. ibid. 28–46; for Russian policy, see A. Sinel, 'Educating the Russian Peasantry: The Elementary School Reforms of Count Dmitrii Tolstoi', *Slavic Review*, 27/1 (1968), 49–70.

[8] R. Valt, 'Der kamf in der khevre "mefitsey haskole" in vilne 1915–1917', *Yivo-bleter*, 2/1–3 (1937), 420–1; H. Abramowicz, *Farshvundene geshtaltn: zikhroynes un siluetn* (Buenos Aires, 1958), 119–23.

[9] Rubin, 'Der yidisher tsentraler bildungs-komitet in vilne', 716; Wygodzki, *In shturm*, 38; G. Pludermakher, 'Tsu der geshikhte fun dem yidish-veltlekhe shul-vezn in vilne', in *Shul-pinkes: finf yor arbet fun tsentraln bildungs-komitet, 1919–1924* (Vilna, 1924), 22–3; F. Frech, 'Russische und deutsche Schule', in *Das Land Ober Ost: Deutsche Arbeit in den Verwaltungsgebieten Kurland, Litauen und*

departure of these teachers was part of a larger pattern of ethnic Russians fleeing the city.) Thus, for instance, M. Prizurov's Gymnasium for Girls, a private non-denominational school where Jews made up a significant portion of the student body,[10] had to close its doors during the Russian retreat.

Those Jews who fled mostly belonged to elite groups; among them were many teachers and students at secular Jewish schools. In the wake of the Russian evacuation, Sofia Gurevitsh, for instance, managed to transfer her entire gymnasium to Poltava, where it remained until after the war's end.[11] (Like the planned *folksshul*, this school—the flagship of secular Yiddishism in Vilna—used Russian as its primary language of instruction, but taught some classes in Yiddish.) Similarly, when Hayim Ozer Grodzenski, Vilna's de facto chief rabbi, fled, the students at his advanced institute for talmudic study followed him. By the time German soldiers marched into Vilna, the Jerusalem of Lithuania had already lost some of its most prominent educational institutions.

GERMAN EDUCATIONAL POLICY IN VILNA, SEPTEMBER–DECEMBER 1915

After a rapid series of victories in 1915, the German army found itself in possession of a large swathe of formerly Russian territory. While Berlin placed an area corresponding roughly to Congress Poland under civilian rule, it kept areas further to the east, including Vilna, under direct military control. Governance of these territories fell under the purview of Paul von Hindenburg and his second-in-command, Erich Ludendorff. The region became known as Ober Ost (an abbreviation of Hindenburg's title, Oberbefehlshaber Ost, Supreme Commander of the Eastern Front) and, in the apt words of one historian, constituted a 'quasi-state'.[12] Ober Ost developed its own economic, ethnic, and educational policies as it sought to exploit the area's human and natural resources and take advantage of local ethnic rivalries.[13]

In the weeks following the arrival of the Germans, normal life began to re-emerge out of the chaos. The *ḥeder* required only the most rudimentary resources —a room with tables and chairs, a single teacher, and books—and thus could

Bialystok-Grodno (Stuttgart, 1917), 375; V. G. Liulevicius, *War Land on the Eastern Front: Culture, National Identity and German Occupation in World War I* (New York, 2005), 32, 123. Wygodzki asserts that after the evacuation only 'a certain portion of the Jewish intelligentsia' continued to speak Russian; otherwise the language ceased to be heard among Jews and non-Jews alike (*In shturm*, 38).

[10] Klausner, *Vilna*, ii. 574.

[11] YIVO Archives, New York, RG 51 'Sofia M. Gurevitch Gymnasium, Vilna (1905–1922, 1930's)'; Sofia M. Gurevitsh, 'Gimnazye fun s. m. gurevitsh', in *Shul-pinkes*, 287–8.

[12] W. Sukiennicki, 'Ober Ost Land: Ludendorff's "Another Kingdom" (1915–1918). A Chapter from the History of the Territories between Germany and Russia during the First World War', *Antemurale*, 22 (1978), 194.

[13] Ibid. 179–220; Liulevicius, *War Land on the Eastern Front*, 54–81, 113–44.

resume functioning easily. Poor *melamedim* were certainly not among those likely to have left during the evacuation. The *talmud torah*s, charged with educating the poorest children, also managed to keep their doors open: some 1,000 boys attended such schools in 1916. However, the combination of a ballooning number of refugees, economic crisis, and the disappearance of income from both local donors and organizations based in the Russian interior completely overwhelmed the ability of these schools to expand and keep pace with the rising number of poor children.[14]

The remnants of the Jewish intelligentsia initially responded to the educational crisis in an ad hoc and clandestine manner. Teachers gathered together with small groups of students who had previously attended modern schools and conducted improvised classes in private homes. These classes remained secret because the German occupation authorities had not yet clarified their position on educational activities. They had occasionally closed local schools and looked askance at any social or political activity on the part of the occupied population.[15]

When the new German rulers of Vilna became aware of the secret schools, their primary concern was with their use of Russian as the language of instruction.[16] At this point, Ober Ost was in the midst of developing a policy best described as de-Russification. That is, it wished to encourage the local population to use either German or non-Russian local languages, specifically Lithuanian, Polish, and perhaps Belarusian. It hoped that by doing so it could sever its subjects' already shaky loyalty to the tsar and instead foster a perception that Germans had liberated them from Russian rule. Thus local administrators moved to forbid the use of Russian in schools.

However, during the first weeks of occupation, Ludendorff and his subordinates were still in the process of learning about the unfamiliar realm they now governed and did not yet have a sense of its complex ethnic makeup.[17] Consequently, when Captain von Beckerath, chief administrator of the Vilna district, summoned Jakub Wygodzki, who had stepped into the position of chief representative of the Jewish community, to express his concern about reports of secret Jewish schools conducting classes in Russian, the former did not have a sense of what language should be used in Jewish schools instead.[18]

[14] Shalit, 'Vilner shulen', 156–65; Frech, 'Russische und deutsche Schule', 375; Szabad, 'Iberzikht', 12; on the *talmud torah* in general, see Horowitz, *Jewish Philanthropy and Enlightenment in Late-Tsarist Russia*, 125–8.

[15] Wygodzki, *In shturm*, 38–9; H. Abramowicz, 'Der baginen fun praktishn yidishizm in vilne', in *Almanakh fun yidishn literatn- un zhurnalistn-farayn in vilne, ershter zamlbukh*, ed. M. Shalit (Vilna, 1938), 156–7; Szabad, 'Iberzikht', 12; Liulevicius, *War Land on the Eastern Front*, 124.

[16] Wygodzki, *In shturm*, 38.

[17] Liulevicius, *War Land on the Eastern Front*, 30–44; see also the various reports concerning internal Russian politics and ethnic relations in the borderlands from 1 January 1915 to 27 October 1916 (Hoover Institution Archives, Stanford University, XX301, 'Germany: Oberste Heeresleitung records, 1914–18', Box 2).

[18] Wygodzki, *In shturm*, 39; cf. V. Klemperer, *Curriculum vitae: Erinnerungen 1881–1918*, 2 vols. (Berlin, 1996), ii. 464–6; on Beckerath, see Sukiennicki, 'Ober Ost Land', 214–17.

According to Wygodzki's recollection of the conversation, he proposed to Beckerath that schools be allowed to function openly and use Yiddish as the language of instruction. Beckerath responded by asking what exactly Yiddish was. Wygodzki replied that it was the local Jewish dialect and succeeded in convincing Beckerath that Yiddish, as the mother tongue of the majority of Vilna's Jewish denizens and a close linguistic relative of German, ought to be the approved language of instruction in Jewish schools.[19] With the support of Tsemah Szabad, director of the Vilna OPE, and the sympathy of Rabbi Isaac Rubinstein, who served as chief rabbi in Grodzenski's absence, Wygodzki got support from official Jewish organizations to turn the secret schools and the remnants of other local institutions into government-approved Yiddish-language schools.[20] Thus, after years of conflict within the Jewish community and between Jewish institutions and the Russian government, modern Yiddish schools suddenly attained official recognition.

Wygodzki's coup for Yiddish did not bring a decisive end to the intra-Jewish controversies concerning schooling (religious versus secular; Hebrew versus Yiddish) that would smoulder on throughout the war and flare up immediately afterwards. It nonetheless constituted an important victory for proponents of Yiddish, especially by gaining official legitimacy for a language many still referred to simply as 'jargon'. Such a development could happen with relative ease because of the removal of the Russifying forces of the tsarist regime, the weakening of the positions of both the Russophone Jewish elite and the old religious elite, the de facto recognition of Jewish nationality by the German regime, and the sheer chaos and disruption of 1915.

As stability gradually returned to Vilna, Jewish schools continued to reopen and community organizations tried to recover from the severing of financial support from Petrograd. On 22 December 1915 Ober Ost clarified its educational policy by publishing a series of orders regulating schooling. These orders ratified as law what was already becoming fact in Vilna. The primary language of instruction in all schools was to be the students' 'mother tongue', but schools were also required to teach German. A classified corollary to these regulations explicitly forbade attempts at Germanization.[21] The end of Russian rule and demographic changes resulting from evacuation served to bolster the mother-tongue policy by removing much of the impetus for Russian-language education.

Beyond linguistic requirements, the orders contained detailed prescriptions concerning pedagogy and curriculum, but, apart from affirming the principle of

[19] Wygodzki, *In shturm*, 39–41.
[20] The title of chief rabbi was a wholly unofficial one. Since the late eighteenth century, Vilna had had no chief rabbi at all. The community gave salaries to several prominent rabbis who shared halakhic judicial authority. In the 1880s the position was offered to Grodzenski. Although he turned it down, he was nonetheless recognized by the community at large and by other rabbis as the city's foremost rabbinic figure. Rubinstein was elected government rabbi (*kazennyi ravvin*) in 1910, with Grodzenski's enthusiastic support. [21] Liulevicius, *War Land on the Eastern Front*, 125–7.

universal education in basic secular subjects, these measures had little effect on actual practice. Germany's resources were spread too thinly to invest much money or manpower in creating and administering schools in its occupied territories.[22]

The new Ober Ost educational policies aimed first and foremost to instil a sense of orderliness and obedience in local young people through primary education. Second, schooling played a role in Ober Ost's broader programme of bringing *Kultur* to the supposedly backward people of the east, which involved the cultivation not merely of individual but also of national consciousness. Furthermore, the policy of fostering education in the students' mother tongue not only advanced de-Russification but also undermined the aspiration of the Poles—the most powerful ethnic group in the area—to use the new situation to Polonize Belarusians, Lithuanians, and perhaps even Jews. At the same time, such a policy could mollify Poles by giving them greater cultural and linguistic freedom than they had enjoyed under the Russians. The Central Powers, deeply concerned that mishandling the Polish question could cause them grave strategic problems, viewed care in this delicate situation as crucial.[23]

Given the variety of concerns that went into shaping Ober Ost's educational policies, the Jewish question was hardly of primary importance. Despite the military regime's penchant for micro-managing everyday life and despite the specificity of Hindenburg's orders on schooling, Vilna Jewry experienced a degree of laissez-faire when it came to educational policy, especially in comparison with the constant, and sometimes hostile, interference of the tsarist regime. A flourishing of new educational institutions ensued, along with the continued existence of old ones.

THE VILNA OPE: THE JEWISH MINISTRY OF EDUCATION

At the forefront of these changes was the Vilna OPE, which itself underwent a fundamental transformation. From 1874 the OPE throughout the Russian empire had began to pay increased attention to primary education. With the establishment of its School Commission in 1894, supporting modern Jewish primary schools became the focal point of its activities. By this time, the OPE's leadership had become concerned not only with providing Jews with secular education (its original goal) but also with providing good Jewish education, however construed. It wished to combat both ignorance of secular subjects and assimilation. A lively debate thus began over what Jewish education ought to entail. What place ought to be given to Hebrew and Yiddish vis-à-vis one another and Russian? How should

---

[22] Liulevicius, *War Land on the Eastern Front*, 125-7; YIVO Archives, RG 29 'Vilna Collection (1822–1940)', folder 188. For manpower and occupation, see I. Hull, *Absolute Destruction: Military Culture and the Practices of War in Imperial Germany* (Ithaca, NY, 2005), 243–8.

[23] Liulevicius, *War Land on the Eastern Front*, 113–50, esp. 125–8; J. Kauffman, 'Sovereignty and the Search for Order in German-Occupied Poland, 1915–1918', Ph.D. thesis (Stanford University, 2008), 155–97; Klausner, *Vilna*, ii. 608; Sukiennicki, 'Ober Ost Land', 195–202.

religion be taught, and how much? Did modern Jewish literature deserve a place in the curriculum? Did Jewish history? These debates intensified in the wake of Russia's failed 1905 revolution, when Zionists and Bundists turned to cultural work and became increasingly interested in establishing schools in keeping with their respective ideologies. In 1908 the OPE reorganized to expand its membership and to make it easier for local branches to form, a move that intensified squabbling as different factions vied for control of local boards. Diaspora nationalists too joined the fray, with their own ideas about Jewish schooling.[24]

Yet prior to the First World War these debates were largely theoretical. They affected the *heder metukan* to some extent, but largely revolved around ambitious plans for radical departures from traditional schooling that were made difficult by restrictive state policies and, to a lesser extent, by opposition from religious conservatives. The OPE served more as a forum for these debates than as an institution that could make far-reaching changes to Jewish education. But in Vilna the war allowed it to become exactly that.

Just before the evacuation, the Vilna OPE had received 10,000 roubles from the main branch in Petrograd and hence began the occupation on a relatively firm financial footing, although it did not take long to deplete these funds. The moment Hindenburg issued his orders on education, the Vilna OPE seized the opportunity to create new forms of Jewish education in Vilna. It did so by creating a *folks-shul* for boys like the one proposed by the Yiddishist faction a few months earlier. It also took control of the elementary school for girls that had been founded in 1912 by OPE activists Hayim Fialkov and Dvoyre Kupershteyn and transformed it into a sister school for girls.[25]

The Vilna OPE also gained a great deal of power and authority through its connection with the Jewish Central Committee, an organ that served as the quasi-official Jewish government during the German occupation. Founded at the beginning of 1916 at the instigation of a German Jewish army chaplain, the Central Committee's original purpose was to serve as a central address in Vilna to which the American Jewish Joint Distribution Committee could send relief funds. Thus its membership consisted of representatives of Vilna's major philanthropic organizations, who distributed these funds through their own institutions or funnelled them to smaller charities. The Central Committee used its role as a conduit for aid to become much more: it served as the representative of the Jewish community to the German regime and to Vilna's other ethnic groups, and to all intents and purposes functioned, like the *kehilah* of old, as an autonomous Jewish government.

[24] Horowitz, *Jewish Philanthropy and Enlightenment in Late-Tsarist Russia*, 97–143, 161–89; S. G. Rappaport, 'Jewish Education and Jewish Culture in the Russian Empire, 1880–1914', Ph.D. thesis (Stanford University, 2000), 73–80, 105–21; E. [Frumkin], *Tsu der frage vegn der yidisher folkshul* (Vilna, 1910); J. D. Zimmerman, *Poles, Jews, and the Politics of Nationality: The Bund and the Polish Socialist Party in Late Tsarist Russia, 1892–1914* (Madison, Wis., 2004), 254.

[25] Pludermakher, 'Tsu der geshikhte fun dem yidish-veltlekhe shul-vezn in vilne', 23; Klausner, *Vilna*, ii. 530–9, 584–5.

The Central Committee and the Vilna OPE were closely connected and not only because the one funded the other. Their boards were intertwined: Szabad and Wygodzki (among others) played leading roles in both organizations. It was Szabad who in 1916 convinced the Central Committee to spend 10 per cent of its income on cultural and educational activities: the decision that made most of the educational changes discussed here possible. In keeping with its policy of nonpartisanship, the committee channelled funds to all of Vilna's Jewish schools, but the Vilna OPE maintained a privileged position, running an entire network of schools. Soon the Vilna OPE began to function as a sort of ministry of education for the Central Committee.

THE JEWISH *FOLKS-SHUL*

The *folks-shul* created by the Vilna OPE shortly after the beginning of the German occupation reflected the long-held aspiration of Jewish educational activists. Members of the different ideological streams within the pre-war OPE had largely concurred in their desire to create such an institution, and it is necessary to understand precisely what it entailed. *Folks-shul* itself was the term favoured by Yiddishists; Hebraists preferred *beit sefer amami*. Both terms were literal translations of the Russian *narodnoe uchilishche*, generally used to denote the state-sponsored public elementary schools first established in the 1860s. (The Russian phrase is itself a translation of the German *Volksschule*, originally coined by the Prussian government to refer to government-run schools.) Although the word *folk* (like *narodnoe*) could also connote ethnic or national peculiarity, here it meant 'of the people'. Thus, like the American 'public school', a *folks-shul* was intended for the common people, as opposed to private schools intended for a narrow elite.[26]

Pre-war discourse on the Jewish *folks-shul* was full of proposals for national-cultural, extra-territorial autonomy for Jews from Jewish nationalists of various stripes. Theorists of the *folks-shul* had envisioned a special Jewish ministry tasked with overseeing government-funded Jewish public schools, which would exist alongside public schools for other ethnic groups.[27]

Then, as now, public schools were generally understood to be free and state sponsored. The boys' *folks-shul* was neither, as students paid a tuition fee of 1½ roubles per month. (Its equivalent for girls charged 3 roubles a year for textbooks and supplies, in lieu of tuition fees.[28]) Supporters of these schools nevertheless

[26] See B. Eklof, *Russian Peasant Schools: Officialdom, Village Culture, and Popular Pedagogy, 1861–1914* (Berkeley, Calif., 1986). The Hebrew equivalent of *folks-shul* is *beit sefer amami* (people's school) rather than *beit sefer le'umi* (national school). For the distinction between *folks-shul* and a *natsyonale shul*, see [Frumkin], *Tsu der frage vegen der yidisher folkshul*, 3–5.

[27] See Horowitz, *Jewish Philanthropy and Enlightenment in Late-Tsarist Russia*, 111–26, 169–73; see also J. J. Weinberg, 'Schulfragen im Ostjudentum', *Jeschurun*, 3/9 (1916), 490, 493–4. It seems to me that Horowitz does not give sufficient weight either to the importance of the *folks-shul* per se or to the importance to the OPE of providing universal free education to the Jewish population.

[28] Shalit, 'Vilner shulen', 145, 148.

insisted on seeing them as a kind of Jewish public school system. In part, they viewed them thus out of the hope that they would one day become publicly funded institutions connected to official Jewish cultural autonomy. But in many ways, the *folks-shuln* had the hallmarks of public institutions. More than half of the students at the boys' school had their tuition fees partially or completely waived.[29] Furthermore, although the impoverishment of Vilna's Jews was well under way by the time the school opened its doors, even full tuition was but a small sum. These schools were not free, but they were close to it.

A more fundamental distinction, however, made these schools public in the minds of contemporaries, namely that they were run by the OPE, a public institution, membership of which was in theory open to all. This fact set them apart from schools run by closed groups of philanthropists or private individuals.[30] And as the Vilna OPE began to act as if it were the ministry of education for Vilna's Jewish community, the *folks-shuln* came to be seen as public institutions in a way other schools were not.

Unlike any school that had previously existed in Vilna, the *folks-shuln* used Yiddish as the primary language of instruction for both general and Jewish subjects and also taught reading and writing in Yiddish, which would have been illegal under Russian rule. Of course, Yiddish had been the language of instruction in the *ḥeder* for centuries; furthermore, some *ḥadarim metukanim* and *talmud torah*s had used Yiddish for general subjects, depending on uneven enforcement. However, two features distinguished the new *folks-shul* from anything that had existed before: first, all subjects, both Jewish and general (with the exception, perhaps, of other languages), were taught in Yiddish; and, second, Yiddish reading, writing, and grammar were taught formally, just as Russian was taught in Russian schools and German in German schools. (As noted above, this pro-Yiddish policy did not preclude children from studying Hebrew as well.) In addition, the *folks-shul* did what few Jewish schools before it had done: teach a full complement of secular Jewish subjects, most importantly, Jewish history.

The two *folks-shuln* quickly became models for other institutions. The Vilna OPE added a third, co-educational *folks-shul* in the suburb of Antokol. Kinder-farzorgung (Care for Children), an organization that gradually came to function as a subsidiary of the Vilna OPE during the war, transformed its own girls' elementary school into a *folks-shul* similar to the others. Prior to 1914 the OPE school for girls, as well as the Kinder-farzorgung school, had mainly attracted students from the poor and the lower middle class; wealthier parents sent their daughters to private or state-run schools. During the war, these schools began to attract girls from the upper middle class who had previously attended Russian public schools,

---

[29] Ibid. 145.

[30] Even before the war, important distinctions were made among 'societal' (*gezelshaftlikh* or *obshchestvennye*) schools (such as those run by the OPE and Kinder-farzorgung), private schools (such as the Prizurov school), and state-run schools.

since such schools had ceased to exist.[31] This was but one example of how the German occupation turned Jews away from a cosmopolitan imperial culture towards a distinctively Jewish culture.

The *folks-shuln* simultaneously drew other children away from traditional education. The boys' *folks-shul*, for instance, recruited a student body that represented nearly the entire spectrum of Jewish children in Vilna. When it first opened, it accepted students from 8 to 12 years old. (This was a consequence of the Vilna OPE's limited resources; in mid-1916, the school added additional classes and began accepting 6- and 7-year-olds.) Since children normally began elementary school at age 6, and *heder* even earlier, all the original students had attended some sort of school previously. Students came from state-run schools, private elementary schools, and *heder*s. This variety of prior experience caused numerous problems: there were children who had studied Talmud but could not compose a sentence in Yiddish, let alone in a non-Jewish language; at the other extreme were children who could read, write, and speak Russian but did not know the Hebrew alphabet. Students also applied for admission to the school with no prior schooling whatsoever and had to be turned away.[32]

While the need to integrate such a diverse student body posed a major challenge for educators, it also marked the school's ability to recruit students who would have otherwise attended *heder*. Parents of such children were attracted to the *folks-shul*, because it provided a thoroughly Jewish environment and taught boys Hebrew and the Bible, while also giving children such skills as knowledge of mathematics and non-Jewish languages that could provide them with greater economic opportunities. Information about dropouts also sheds some light on parental concerns. According to a report compiled by Moyshe Shalit in 1916, many of the younger children whose parents took them out of the boys' *folks-shul* did so because they had second thoughts about deviation from traditional schooling. On the other hand, most of these parents intended to return their children to *heder* for two or three years to ensure a minimum of religious instruction and then send them back to the *folks-shul* in order to get the best of both worlds.[33]

More mundane considerations also played a role in educational decisions. As before the war, poorer parents tended to prefer traditional education, while wealthier parents were more likely to consider the modern kind. Yet *heder*s were private institutions, and their *melamedim* lived off fees they collected from students, and the wartime economic crisis made even the meagre *heder* fee a burden. The *talmud torah*s could only take in so many children. The schools operated by the Vilna OPE and Kinder-farzorgung, however, charged minimal fees and offered scholarships.

[31] See YIVO Archives, RG 22 'Hevra Mefitsei Haskalah Society (1909–1938)', folders 48, 51; Rappaport, 'Jewish Education'; Shalit, 'Vilner shuln', 147; Gurevitsh, 'Gimnazye', 287.

[32] Shalit, 'Vilner shuln', 137–40.

[33] Ibid. 141. For the phenomenon of 'dual attendance' in general, see Rappaport, 'Jewish Education', 244–5.

Modern schools also had the advantage of providing more than education. The OPE schools took responsibility for pupils' medical needs and provided students at the girls' school with shirts and smocks.[34] The Kinder-farzorgung school gave pupils tea with sugar every morning and provided breakfast for the poorest among them. Torat Emet, a progressive *talmud torah*, gave students breakfast, as well as clothes and shoes. The Vilna OPE soon realized that it could recruit more students by offering food as well. In June 1916 it opened a joint cafeteria for the boys' and girls' schools. Officially children paid for each meal, but 45 per cent received meals for free, and an additional 25 per cent at half price.[35] The provision of food and social services during a period of desperate poverty thus facilitated a major victory for modern national education. The general scarcity, devastating pauperization, and sporadic epidemics that reigned during the German occupation meant that even the offer of a few extra items of clothing could have significant appeal.

EDUCATION IN HEBREW

While the Vilna OPE focused primarily on Yiddish schools, other educational activists sought to create new opportunities for education in Hebrew. The greatest achievement came from Dr Yosef Epshteyn (1874–1916), himself a member of the Vilna OPE's governing committee. Epshteyn decided that Hindenburg's orders concerning education provided an opportunity to do what had long been an aspiration of Vilna Zionists: establish in Vilna a modern, Hebrew-language gymnasium. In December 1915 he gathered fifteen students in his house and began teaching them Hebrew, the Bible, and Jewish history along with mathematics, geography, science, and world history.

This Hebräische Normalschule expanded its student body to seventy-five boys and girls divided into four grades over the course of the next two months, forcing it to move into its own space. As it continued to grow, it added Latin and other subjects to its curriculum and changed its name to the Hebräische Gymnasium. All classes were conducted in Hebrew, in keeping with the cultural-Zionist linguistic orthodoxy of the day. By the summer of 1916 it had 250 students and multiple classes for each grade and once again had to move to larger premises.[36] It was the first school of its kind in Europe, and would become the flagship school of the Tarbut school system in interwar Poland.[37]

---

[34] Shalit, 'Vilner shuln', 140, 149.

[35] Ibid. 141, 145, 154, 157; Szabad, 'Iberzikht', 14; YIVO Archives, RG 22, folders 38, 40.

[36] T. Szabad, 'D"r Yosef b"r Shabsay Epshteyn', in *Vilner zamelbukh*, i. 252–3; M. Y. Nadel, 'Di gimnazye ivrit', in *Pinkes far der geshikhte*, 757–60; 'Tsum yor fun d"r Epshteyns gimnazye', *Letste nayes*, 29 Dec. 1916, p. 4; I. Klausner (ed.), *Sefer yovel ha'esrim shel hagimnasyah ha'ivrit a.y. 'tarbut'* (Vilna, 1936).

[37] Epshteyn modelled the school on the Herzliyah Gymnasium in Jaffa, which had until then been one of a kind (see B. Halpern and J. Reinharz, *Zionism and the Creation of a New Society* (New York, 1998), 115–17).

The decrees of 22 December 1915 had not specified how the mother tongue of the students was to be determined. For the majority of Vilna Jews, it was Yiddish, and Wygodzki had already obtained the language's official recognition. The remaining Jews were native Russian speakers, but education in Russian was forbidden. There were no Jews who were native speakers of Hebrew, making the Hebräische Gymnasium technically illegal.[38] Nonetheless, it did not remain a secret that Hebrew played a key role in the school's curriculum. Ober Ost's inclination to grant educational freedom outweighed its inclination to regulate new forms of Jewish education.

The Hebräische Gymnasium did not affiliate with the Vilna OPE, nor did it compete with it, since the Vilna OPE did not administer any secondary schools during the first years of German occupation. Epshteyn continued to be a leading voice for Hebraism within the Vilna OPE, where he worked to compromise with the Yiddishists. Other Vilna Zionists, however, sought to establish purely Hebraist elementary schools, outside of the Vilna OPE framework. The newly formed Tse'irei Tsiyon (Young People of Zion) league took action and on 8 February 1916 opened a *folks-shul* for girls, Beit Sefer Amami Levanot.[39]

The school had four grades, for students aged 6 to 13, and its curriculum centred on instruction in Hebrew. Only third graders studied traditional religious texts; fourth graders received lessons in Judaism not based on textual study. German was not introduced until the third grade, thus fulfilling the minimal legal requirement.[40] This curriculum made Beit Sefer Amami Levanot the most secular Jewish elementary school in all of Vilna during the German occupation. The latitude towards girls' education in traditional circles, along with the decidedly Yiddishist bent of the Vilna OPE school for girls, made a girls' school a logical goal and may explain why Tse'irei Tsiyon never attempted to create an equivalent boys' school.

Funding for these schools came from the dues of Tse'irei Tsiyon members, tuition fees, and some supplemental money provided by the Central Committee, which strove to remain neutral and support all ideological tendencies, especially at a time when many children were not attending school at all. In May, Tse'irei

---

[38] Nadel, 'Di gimnazye ivrit', 757. Nadel reports that, when government inspectors visited the school, Hebrew education ceased for the day. (Presumably, classes were conducted in German or Yiddish.) Once an inspector walked into a class unannounced, catching students and teacher in the act of studying in Hebrew, but was so fascinated at the prospect of the ancient language being used as a living idiom that he decided to turn a blind eye to the infraction. The German government's negative attitude towards Hebrew may have also stemmed from its hope that Yiddish could serve as a stepping-stone to Germanization. Some official correspondence from German officials refers to the schools as 'Die hebräische Gymnasium' (YIVO Archives, RG 29, folder 199: Stadthauptmann, letter to to Regensburg, 4 Dec. 1918,), but it is possible that only the general liberalization of 1918, especially after the collapse of Germany in November, made this school's linguistic orientation acceptable.

[39] Shalit, 'Vilner shuln', 159–60.

[40] Ibid.; YIVO Archives, RG 29, folder 197: Devorah Berkovits' report card, 1917.

Tsiyon launched another girls' school in the Šnipiškės district. Both schools remained open for the duration of the war. These schools, like the others, provided students with food.[41] Thus, Tse'irei Tsiyon set itself up in competition with the Vilna OPE, advancing its own programme of modernized, but thoroughly national, Jewish education, and making use of Hebrew to the fullest extent permitted by German regulations—far beyond what the Russian regime would ever have tolerated. For the first time, Vilna Jews faced a choice among very different Jewish, secular educational institutions to which they could send their daughters.

THE LANGUAGE WAR REIGNITES

In late summer of 1916 the leaders of Tse'irei Tsiyon wrote a letter to the American rabbi Judah Magnes, after learning of his interest in visiting Vilna. Tse'irei Tsiyon saw Magnes as an important potential source of financial assistance, especially since he shared Tse'irei Tsiyon's commitment to Zionism and its loosely Ahad Ha'amist Hebraism and was an influential member of both the Joint Distribution Committee and the American Zionist movement.[42] In the midst of the usual complaints about the dire situation of Vilna's Jews, the letter noted the particularly grim situation of the Hebrew cause and the consequent importance of its efforts to establish a Hebrew-language elementary school: 'Above all, we are saving our small children from the powerful force of the movement that has grown strong of late, namely the movement of opposition to our Hebrew language and to all our entire historical and national achievements.'[43] The unnamed movement was undoubtedly Yiddishism.[44] The Zionists saw Yiddish as the great, and growing, threat to their cause.

The success of Yiddish in becoming the standard language of secular education explains part of the sense of looming defeat felt by Tse'irei Tsiyon. However, Yiddishists also saw their own cause as having suffered serious blows at the hands of Zionists over the school question during the war. In June 1916 the newly created Arbeter Kultur Farayn (Workers' Culture Union) issued a resolution condemning the Vilna OPE in response to what it saw as a Zionist coup, and began advocating the secession of left-wing Yiddishists from the organization.[45] The Arbeter Kultur

[41] Shalit, 'Vilner shuln', 160–1; YIVO Archives, RG 29, folder 197: Tse'irei Tsiyon budget, Aug. 1917.

[42] Z. Szajkowski, 'Concord and Discord in Jewish Overseas Relief', *YIVO Annual*, 14 (1969), 101, 103, 132, 141–4.

[43] YIVO Archives, RG 29, folder 197: Tse'irei Tsiyon, letter to Magnes, 4 Sept. 1916.

[44] Yiddishism had made great strides in Vilna since the autumn of 1915, while Russian culture's appeal to Jews had declined drastically. Orthodoxy, especially the anti-Zionist kind, was decidedly on the defensive. The adoption of Polish culture among Vilna's Jews did not begin in any significant way until the 1920s. Despite German hopes, adoption of German culture made only minimal headway. Thus no other cultural tendency besides Yiddishism can be active here.

[45] Valt, 'Der kamf in der khevre "mefitsey haskole" in vilne 1915–1917', 424; 'Di algemeyne farzamlung funem yidishn arbeter-kultur-farayn', *Letste nayes*, 10 June 1916, p. 3.

Farayn began working to set up a counter-organization to the Vilna OPE that would conduct its own activities, despite the fact that the pro-Yiddish Szabad remained chairman of the Vilna OPE and the organization ran schools with Yiddish as the primary language of instruction. Why did both sides simultaneously feel that they were losing?

The conflicts that arose within the Vilna OPE during the German occupation stemmed from a debate that came to the fore during the 1911 and 1913 OPE congresses. Although Yiddish versus Hebrew became the central point of contention at these congresses, the underlying question concerned the relative importance of three languages: Hebrew, Yiddish, and Russian. Virtually everyone affiliated with the OPE agreed that Jewish schools ought to teach children the language of the land in which they lived: only the Orthodox opponents of the OPE believed that Russian had no place in Jewish schooling. Furthermore, education exclusively in Hebrew or Yiddish was impossible. The law mandated that Russian be the primary language of instruction for all schools, with the exception of traditional *heder*s.[46]

In understanding both pre-war and wartime debates, it is important to note that there were no direct correspondences between Zionism and Hebraism, on the one hand, and Bundism and Yiddishism, on the other. It is true that these positions had begun to take shape and that both the Bund and the mainstream Zionist leadership had officially endorsed Yiddishism and Hebraism, respectively. But it would be wrong to project the more rigid alignments of the 1920s and 1930s on to this earlier period. Yiddish still had a great deal of support from within the Zionist movement. (Wygodzki himself was a committed Zionist, as well as a member of Hovevei Sefat Ever, Vilna's Hebraist circle.) Much of the general Zionist leadership in Russia, although committed to Hebrew culture, believed in Yiddish as an important tool for political propaganda—founding, for instance, Yiddish newspapers—as well as a means of maintaining Jewish identity. Thus, during the negotiations surrounding the Minorities Treaty in the aftermath of the First World War, Zionist leaders would campaign for official recognition of Yiddish in their struggle for Jewish national rights. Furthermore, many left-wing Zionists favoured Yiddish over Hebrew.

Similarly, support for Hebrew did not necessarily imply Zionism. It was the belief of most of the founding members of the OPE—an organization that predated both Bundism and Zionism—that Jewish schools ought to teach both Hebrew and Russian. They did not think that Hebrew would one day be revived as a spoken language but simply that it was the language of the Jewish cultural and religious heritage and, unlike Yiddish, was capable of becoming a *Kultursprakh* (a language of high-level cultural activity). Although this sort of attitude towards language was a holdover from the pre-1880 Haskalah, it was alive and well in 1914, despite the presence of a new generation with new ideologies.[47]

[46] See Horowitz, *Jewish Philanthropy and Enlightenment in Late-Tsarist Russia*, 42–51, 97–205.

[47] On this persistence in general, see M. Stanislawski, *For Whom do I Toil? Judah Leib Gordon and*

The language debate in wartime Vilna, as in pre-war Russia, involved a spectrum of positions. At one end, there were radical Zionist-Hebraists who believed in the ultimate goal of eventually doing away with Yiddish completely, teaching all subjects in Hebrew, and only teaching the language of the land as a second language. At the other end, there were a few radical Yiddishists who wanted to do away with Hebrew completely. However, the positions of most of Vilna's OPE members were somewhere in between.

The Russian evacuation brought about a realignment within the Vilna OPE. As mentioned, Russian disappeared from the linguistic picture; legal restrictions on Jewish education changed drastically; teachers fled the city; and schools closed down or relocated. At the same time, the makeup of the Vilna chapter shifted dramatically. Eight of the original twenty-four members of the governing committee departed during the evacuation, including the writer and socialist activist Shmuel Niger, who had led the Yiddishist faction within the Vilna OPE. An element of randomness permeated these departures, but they had major consequences.

While the Vilna OPE's decision in December 1915 to create a model Jewish *folks-shul* for boys was unanimous, the same questions that had previously divided the OPE arose once more concerning language of instruction, religious education, and whether the organization should support schools in a variety of languages, among which parents could choose according to their preferences. Some Hebraists seized the opportunity provided by the disappearance of the Russian Ministry of Education to make the radical demand of Hebrew as the sole language of instruction, adding a new stance to the mix.

In a series of meetings over the space of a few weeks, the Vilna OPE came to decisions on these questions. Its members overwhelmingly supported uniformity when it came to education, believing that Jews had to demonstrate to their new rulers that they constituted a separate nation and ought to be treated as such. Setting up schools in various languages might imply that Jews ought to be considered a confessional group of indeterminate ethno-national identity. This final point acquired particular significance because those involved believed that precedent set during the occupation would become the status quo of a post-war order which was likely to be very different from what had existed beforehand.[48]

The decision to create uniform schools only served to heighten the intensity of the Hebrew versus Yiddish debate. Szabad, who at this point could best be

the Crisis of Russian Jewry (New York, 1988); B. Nathans, *Beyond the Pale: The Jewish Encounter with Late Imperial Russia* (Berkeley, Calif., 2002); on its implications for Jewish education, see Abramowicz, *Farshvundene geshtaltn*, 122. Horowitz also addresses these fluidities throughout his work (see esp. *Jewish Philanthropy and Enlightenment in Late-Tsarist Russia*, 1–10, 161–77).

[48] Z. R—n [Reyzen], 'Tsu di valn in komitet fun khevre m"h', *Letste nayes*, 12 Mar. 1916, p. 3; Valt, 'Der kamf in der khevre "mefitsey haskole" in vilne 1915–1917', 420–2. The argument that linguistic unity could hinder the case for recognition of Jewish nationhood on the part of non-Jews was not

described as a Yiddishist fellow traveller, prioritized consensus and brokered a compromise between Yosef Epshteyn, leader of the Hebraists, and Gershon Pludermakher, the committee's leading Yiddishist. Eventually, deliberations ended with a reversion to the 1913 compromise, whereby Hebrew would be taught in addition to Yiddish, which would remain the primary language of instruction. Furthermore, the curriculum of the *folks-shuln* would include classical religious studies, so as not to alienate the traditionalist masses.[49] The possibility of developing separate Hebrew schools at a later point was left open. For the time being, the unifying goal of seizing the opportunity to modernize Jewish schools and implement an educational programme premised on the hope of Jewish national-cultural autonomy trumped party-specific concerns and linguistic preferences.

Over the course of the following months, as the OPE's educational project went into effect, conflicts over language began to re-emerge. These conflicts stemmed in part from procedural issues. In order to replace the committee members who had fled, those remaining had selected four new temporary delegates, who would hold their offices until the next annual meeting of all members of the Vilna OPE, which would then properly elect a new committee. When the meeting did eventually take place, an overwhelming majority of Zionists was elected to the committee. The new committee began incrementally introducing more instruction in Hebrew and the Hebrew Bible into the *folks-shuln*. The teachers at these schools, who were mostly Yiddishists, objected to these measures. It was the growing conflict between the committee and the teachers' union that reignited the language war.[50]

Responding to the complaints of the teachers' union, the Yiddishist opposition began to raise objections concerning the elections and qualifications for membership. Yosef Izbitski,[51] at the time the leader of the Bund in Vilna, called upon socialist members to forsake the OPE. He questioned its legitimacy, pointing out that it was an elitist (and thus non-proletarian) organization where only dues-paying members could vote in elections. The new circumstances, in his view, called for a truly democratic institution to co-ordinate Jewish educational activity in keeping with the wishes of Jewish workers. Leftist members began to resign from

---

without merits: in 1919 one Polish parliamentarian cited the fact that Jews could not even agree on a national language as evidence that they were merely a confessional group (see I. Lewin, 'The Political History of Polish Jewry, 1918–1919', in I. Lewin and N. M. Gelber, *A History of Polish Jewry during the Revival of Poland* (New York, 1990), 109).

[49] Valt, 'Der kamf in der khevre "mefitsey haskole" in vilne 1915–1917'; Szabad, 'Iberzikht', 13–14.

[50] Valt, 'Der kamf in der khevre "mefitsey haskole" in vilne 1915–1917'; B. Zilberbakh, 'Di yudishe lerer-gezelshaft', in *Vilner zamlbukh*, ii. 241–3.

[51] Izbitski, better known by his pseudonym, Beynish Mikhalevitsh, had been among the founding members of the Bund in Vilna in 1897. The Bund leadership sent him to Vilna from Petrograd in August 1915, anticipating the German occupation and hoping he could lead socialist agitation under German rule. See S. Kleyt, 'Di arbeter bavegung in vilne in der tsayt fun der daytsher okupatsye', in *Vilne: a zamlbukh gevidmet der shtot vilne*, ed. E. Jeshurin (New York, 1935), 224–8; M. V. Bernshteyn, 'Mikhalevitsh, b.', in *Leksikon fun der nayer yidisher literature*, 8 vols. (New York, 1956–81), v. 608–12.

the OPE, and turned to Izbitski's newly created Arbeter Kultur Farayn.[52] By this time Tse'irei Tsiyon had already begun running its own independent elementary schools.

With radical Hebraists creating their own educational institutions, on the one hand, and the Arbeter Kultur Farayn threatening to become a Yiddishist alternative to the Vilna OPE, on the other, the organization seemed to be in danger of losing its relevance. However, it regrouped and successfully, if temporarily, preserved its status as a powerful and unifying force in Jewish education, although it never gained the sort of absolute authority it ultimately desired.

The Vilna OPE avoided a complete split because of the power (and money) it enjoyed through its closeness to the Jewish Central Committee, and also because of two powerful personalities: Tsemah Szabad and Zalmen Reyzen. Reyzen's radical Yiddishism led him to oppose Izbitski's secessionist moves. Although he appreciated the Jewish socialists' efforts to promote Yiddish, he fiercely criticized them for limiting their efforts to Jewish workers. Reyzen believed Yiddish ought to be the language of all social classes of east European Jewry. He thus objected vociferously to the proletarian-centred educational endeavours of the Arbeter Kultur Farayn. Instead, he wanted the Vilna OPE to be the sole official authority in Jewish education, promoting Yiddish as the exclusive Jewish national language. Consequently, Vilna's most intense devotee of Yiddish remained in favour of compromise.[53]

Szabad shared many of Reyzen's convictions, although in more moderate form. He remained a liberal nationalist unwilling to throw in his lot with the socialists. Like Reyzen, he believed that the Jews of Vilna ought to present a unified front to other nationalities and to the German rulers, but, unlike Reyzen, he thought this need surpassed any particular cultural or political preference.[54] Furthermore, Szabad was a gifted politician who could put his considerable personal authority to good use. After much negotiation, he brokered a deal: the Yiddishists remained in or rejoined the Vilna OPE; the Hebraists scaled back their demands; a new executive committee was formed giving roughly equal representation to Yiddishists and Hebraists; and a compromise was reached on issues of membership and electoral procedure. The Arbeter Kultur Farayn refrained from setting up its own schools, although it sponsored classes for adults and other cultural activities.[55]

Both Hebraists and Yiddishists complained of setbacks, because both sides hoped not merely to build new institutions but to dominate Jewish education. The project of the *folks-shul* was wedded to the idea of a uniform, official system of

[52] Valt, 'Der kamf in der khevre "mefitsey haskole" in vilne 1915–1917', 420–33; Pludermakher, 'Tsu der geshikhte fun dem yidish-veltlekhe shul-vezn in vilne'.

[53] S. Kassow, 'Zalmen reyzen un zayn gezelshaftlekh-politishe arbet 1915–1922', *Yivo bleter: naye serye*, 2 (1994), 67–98; Abramowicz, *Farshvundene geshtaltn*, 171–6.   [54] Szabad, 'Iberzikht', 13.

[55] YIVO Archives, RG 29, folder 33; American Jewish Joint Distribution Committee Archives, New York, Records of the New York Office of the American Jewish Joint Distribution Committee, 1914–1918, folder 140.16: 'Appendix 40'.

Jewish elementary education, not to an educational marketplace where different kinds of schools competed with one another. The Vilna OPE continued to exist as a unified organization as long as this goal seemed possible.

THE POST-WAR LEGACY

The compromises that kept the Vilna OPE intact as a unified organization began to unravel at the very end of the war, when competing Jewish school networks began to emerge and the Vilna OPE lost its claim to be Vilna's ministry of Jewish education. The first sign of this new development came in 1917: Nahman Rachmilewitz, a member of the Central Committee with ties to the German Orthodox Agudat Israel party, decided greater effort and co-ordination were required to maintain Vilna Jewry's traditional religious educational institutions, which were increasingly losing potential students to modern schools. He began soliciting Orthodox communities in Germany for funds specifically for this purpose, hoping to create a centralized platform for supporting Orthodox primary education equivalent to the Vilna OPE. In 1918 he set up an ad hoc commission to this end.

In the spring of 1918 the situation in Vilna began to change rapidly. After the signing of the Treaty of Brest-Litovsk in March 1918, movement between Russia and Ober Ost became possible. Trade revived, somewhat, easing the economic situation. At the same time, prominent Jewish figures across the political and cultural spectrum were coming to the conclusion that Soviet Russia was not a particularly hospitable place for them and began arriving in Vilna. These included many who had fled at the beginning of the war, such as Shmuel Niger, Sofia Gurevitsh, and Hayim Ozer Grodzenski. The returnees brought new energies and abilities, as well as the new perspectives they had gained from their experiences in revolutionary Russia.

The course of the war was also changing. After the Allied offensive at Amiens on 8 August 1918, it began to become clear that the Central Powers were losing, and local German officials started to display increasing laxity. In September Lithuanian leaders began to organize their own government and promised Jewish leaders the autonomy they desired. In November armistice was declared, and Germany agreed that it would remove all its troops from the occupied areas by 31 December 1918. These various internal and external factors encouraged a new spurt of educational activities that would lead to the breakdown of communal co-operation in the post-war period. A new system would emerge whereby each major ideological group would develop its own network of schools.

As 1918 drew to a close Grodzenski returned to Vilna. He had spent his years in exile trying to create a framework for co-ordinating Orthodox efforts to establish and maintain *heder*s and other religious institutions. He had also become convinced that the quality of religious education had to be improved and that *heder*s had to offer some degree of secular education in order to keep parents from sending their children to secular Jewish schools.[56] The combined efforts of Grodzenski, Rubinstein, and Rachmilewitz led to the creation in 1919 of Va'ad Hame'uhad (The Unified Council) for overseeing all religious schools in Vilna.[57] Such an organized network was new not only to Vilna but to Russian Jewry in general. Traditionally, *melamedim* ran their *ḥeders* privately and independently, while the organized Jewish community and individual donors ran a few public *talmud torah*s for poor students. Now Vilna had an Orthodox counterpart to the Vilna OPE.

Yiddishist education underwent a parallel development. In the autumn of 1918 Zalmen Reyzen convinced the recently returned Gurevitsh to aid him in establishing a Yiddish-language *Realshule* (mathematics- and science-focused high school) under the auspices of the Vilna OPE.[58] This was the first secondary school (except yeshivas) anywhere with Yiddish as its primary language of instruction. At about the same time, a new organization called Kultur Lige (Culture League) opened a branch in Vilna that began to take over some of the Vilna OPE's activities, although schools remained firmly in the latter's purview. Kultur Lige had been founded in Kiev in early 1918 and placed Yiddishism at the centre of its ideology. Its arrival in Vilna was the first step in the unravelling of the Yiddishist–Hebraist compromise achieved in 1916.[59]

In the final days of 1918 the Jews of Vilna elected their first democratic *kehilah*. It was assumed that it would co-ordinate all educational activity, ushering in a new era of Jewish autonomy; however, the arrival of the Red Army ten days later put a halt to any significant activity. The Soviets encouraged the use of Russian and Yiddish, while repressing Hebrew and religious education. Although their policies encouraged Yiddishists, never before had freedom of cultural activity been so restricted. In April Polish forces seized Vilna, and Yiddish lost state sponsorship. After a period of chaos and anti-Jewish violence, the *kehilah* resumed its activities, and the conflict between Yiddish and Hebrew flared up once more. This time, however, compromise failed.[60]

Szabad concluded that he could no longer mediate between the two sides. The demands of Hebraists—and their power within the *kehilah*—had become too great, while Yiddishists had themselves become less willing to compromise. In May 1919 the Yiddishist faction, together with Kinder-farzorgung, decided to merge into the Central Education Committee (Tsentral Bildungs Komitet; TsBK), which would oversee all secular Yiddish schools in Vilna—and in fact continued to do so until

[56] See A. N. Koss, 'War Within, War Without: Russian Refugee Rabbis during World War I', *AJS Review*, 34/2 (2010), 231–63.

[57] 'Havad hameukhad', *Unzer osid*, 17 (16 Oct. 1918), 30; Klausner, *Vilna*, ii. 605–6.

[58] YIVO Archives, RG 10 'Vilna Jewish Community Council (1800–1940)', folder 250.

[59] Reyzen, 'Hakdome', in *Pinkes far der geshikhte*, p. iv; K. B. Moss, *Jewish Renaissance in the Russian Revolution* (Cambridge, Mass., 2009), 30–8, 52–9.

[60] Szabad, 'Iberzikht', in *Pinkes far der geshikhte*, 12–15; Pludermakher, 'Tsu der geshikhte fun dem yidish-veltlekhe shul-vezn in vilne'; Klausner, *Vilna*, ii. 609; S. D. Kassow, 'Jewish Communal Politics in Transition: The Vilna Kehile, 1919–1920', *YIVO Annual*, 20 (1991), 61–91.

the Second World War. In 1921 the TsBK affiliated itself with the newly created Central Yiddish School Organization (Tsentrale Yidishe Shul Organizatsye; TSYSHO)—directed by none other than Izbitski—which co-ordinated secular Yiddish education throughout Poland.

With the Vilna OPE now dissolved (along with the Russia-wide OPE, which did not survive the revolution) and Yiddishists having created their own, self-contained school administration, Hebraists decided to circumvent the *kehilah* entirely and create a parallel organization. In June 1918 Hovevei Sefat Ever reconstituted itself as the local chapter of the newly created Tarbut organization. Like the Kultur Lige, Tarbut had been formed in revolutionary Russia, and the opening of the borders after the Treaty of Brest-Litovsk had exposed Vilna Hebraists to the organization. In the words of Kenneth Moss, Tarbut's leaders 'aspired not only to support and institutionalize Jewish cultural creation in all of the arts, but also to provide intensive Hebraist education to children and adults—and to serve both of these very different goals through Hebrew theaters, art exhibitions and clubs'.[61] The Vilna Tarbut made its first order of business the takeover of the Hebrew Gymnasium and the Tse'irei Tsiyon girls' schools and then began planning the establishment of further Hebrew-language schools.

A similar splintering took place within the newly formed Hava'ad Hame'uhad. While wartime changes in religious education in Vilna are a topic unto themselves, it is worthwhile to compare briefly the organizational parallels to secular schooling. Not long after the war, Hava'ad Hame'uhad became exclusively associated with the religious Zionist Mizrachi movement, while the non-Zionist and more religiously conservative Agudat Israel created its own school network. Both local Orthodox school organizations—like their Zionist and Yiddishist counterparts—affiliated with larger networks that operated throughout Poland and beyond. Neither defenders of Orthodoxy nor proponents of modernization could present a united front. The idea of Jewish education as something that could transcend ideology perished along with the OPE. Schools now became parts of networks whose ideologies determined curricula.

School reformers were thus successful when it came to opening schools based on the principle that Jews constituted a separate nationality that ought to have its own educational institutions. However, they failed in their goal of creating a unified Jewish public school system. When the democratic *kehilah* re-emerged from the post-war chaos in 1922, it was unable to co-ordinate (or fund) educational activities: a task that had been essential in the eyes of those who had dreamed of such an institution in the previous decades.

Before the First World War Jewish parents in Vilna could choose from a range of schools extending from wholly traditional *heder*s to state-run Russophone schools; yet, across the board, education remained relatively independent of ideology. Fierce ideological debates surrounded education, individual educators might have

---

[61] Moss, *Jewish Renaissance in the Russian Revolution*, 50.

been ideologically motivated, and ideology could influence decisions of parents when it came to school selection, but schools themselves remained ideologically unaffiliated. Organizations that ran schools uniformly claimed to be without party affiliations: whether the official pre-war Jewish community (responsible for the municipal *talmud torah*), Kinder-farzorgung, the Vilna OPE, or the association of benefactors that ran the Torat Emet Talmud Torah. This situation changed during German occupation, when the overtly Zionist Tse'irei Tsiyon established Zionist schools and ideological conflicts threatened to tear the Vilna OPE apart just as its power reached its zenith. In the year after the war, education in Vilna became the province of unified organizations with distinct party affiliations: Hava'ad Hame' uhad for Orthodox Zionists, Tarbut for other Zionists, and TsBK for socialists and folkists. Education had become an ideological matter.

VILNA'S JEWISH SCHOOLS IN A COMPARATIVE PERSPECTIVE

To understand fully the causes, consequences, and significance of wartime developments in Jewish education, some comparison with areas outside Vilna is in order. Throughout other areas of Ober Ost, Jews—as well as Poles, Lithuanians, Belarusians, and Latvians—opened new schools, emboldened by the freedoms the new regime granted.[62] Extremely little is known about such schools, and primary source material is quite sparse.

More can be said of the area to the west that came under the control of the German General Government in Poland (roughly corresponding to the pre-war Congress Kingdom) and the areas to the east that remained under Russian control. Jewish communities in these regions, despite important differences in governance, followed a trajectory similar to Vilna's. The first year of war brought about a refugee crisis: first, Jews from areas closest to the fighting fled to Warsaw; later, Jews from Poland and the Pale fled or were expelled to the Russian interior. The OPE, the EKOPO, and other philanthropic organizations tried to help refugee children, their first step being the establishment of children's homes. These organizations also worked to set up modern schools for them. The creation of modern Jewish schools led to fierce debates over questions of language and a proliferation of schools with both Hebrew and Yiddish as the language of instruction. The tsarist regime allowed for greater latitude when it came to these schools than it had before the war. After the February revolution, the freedom allowed Jewish educators briefly became even greater.[63] The Soviet regime reversed this trend, but it was not until a

---

[62] Liulevicius, *War Land on the Eastern Front*, 124–6.

[63] Kazdan, *Fun kheyder un 'shkoles' biz 'tsysho'*, 208–16; S. J. Zipperstein, 'The Politics of Relief: The Transformation of Russian Jewish Communal Life during the First World War', in J. Frankel (ed.), *Studies in Contemporary Jewry*, iv: *Jews in the European Crisis, 1914–1921* (New York, 1988), 22–40; Horowitz, *Jewish Philanthropy and Enlightenment in Late-Tsarist Russia*, 206–27.

few years after the war that Hebrew schools were stamped out and Yiddish schools came completely under the control of the Evsektsii (Jewish sections of the Communist Party).[64]

The General Government in Poland, which, unlike Ober Ost, was under civilian rule, had ambitious plans for educational reform and initially sought to transform all *heders* into modern schools and replace Yiddish with German. The latter task was soon abandoned completely, and little headway was made with the former.[65] In Warsaw and other major cities, however, Jewish school activists founded many modern schools, especially Yiddish-language ones.[66]

However, despite these general similarities, certain factors distinguished Jewish communities in Ober Ost in general and Vilna in particular. Throughout Ober Ost, the assimilationist option was completely marginalized when it came to education.[67] Even before the war the lack of any one predominant culture in the area had weakened the appeal of assimilation: with the disappearance of Russian as the language of the state and its suppression by the German occupiers, very little opposition existed to the principle of Jewish schools for Jewish children. In the General Government, however, there were groups of Polonized Jews in major cities (Warsaw and Łódź), and segments of the Polish national movement sought to encourage further Polonization. To the east, Russia saw the arrival of tens of thousands of largely Yiddish-speaking Jewish refugees from the shtetls of the ethnically mixed borderlands in cities and towns outside of the Pale of Settlement where Russians were the dominant ethnic group and local Jews were acculturated to a greater degree. The children of these refugees for the most part attended schools run by the OPE and the EKOPO where the Russian language played an important role.[68]

Few cities in any region matched Vilna in terms of the sheer zeal with which educational activity was undertaken during the war. Even after the evacuation, Vilna had a number of outstanding activists and intellectuals ready to devote themselves to founding schools and courses. Vilna's residents' sense of themselves as living in the Jerusalem of Lithuania—the intellectual capital of the Jewish world—perpetuated a desire to support educational activity.

Jewish Vilna had led the way before the war in matters of education and continued to do so afterwards. The founding of TsBK, devoted solely to activity

---

[64] Z. Y. Gitelman, *Jewish Nationality and Soviet Policy: The Jewish Sections of the CPSU, 1917–1930* (Princeton, NJ, 1972), 299–301, 335–50.

[65] Kauffman, 'Sovereignty and the Search for Order in German-Occupied Poland', 128–38; K. Zieliński, 'Świeckie życie kulturalno-oświatowe Żydów Królestwa polskiego w czasie pierwszej wojny światowej', *Studia Judaica*, 1999, no. 1, pp. 41–60.

[66] Kazdan, *Fun kheyder un 'shkoles' biz 'tsysho'*, 213–15.

[67] A possible exception to this trend was Courland, where the presence of an influential ethnic-German minority had led acculturating Jews to adopt German prior to the war and where Germanization efforts during the occupation were more pronounced.

[68] Zipperstein, 'Politics of Relief'; Koss, 'War Within, War Without'.

within Vilna, took place five years before the establishment of TSYSHO, its all-Polish equivalent. Vilna's Tarbut chapter was the first to preside successfully over a Hebrew gymnasium. Hava'ad Hame'uhad too was the first council of its type, created before Mizrachi and Agudat Israel formed international networks of schools. In these ways, Vilna became a trendsetter for interwar Poland.

With these comparisons in mind, it is possible to isolate some determining factors behind the explosion of educational activity in wartime Vilna. First, every development discussed here stemmed in one way or another from crisis and disruption, with the arrival of refugees and the closing of schools during the evacuation serving as the initial impetus. Most of the creative activity began with efforts to solve the ensuing problems: the resulting educational experiments then became arenas for testing new ideas that had crystallized during the previous decade. Furthermore, the lack of normal sources of funding for schools spurred greater organizational sophistication. Vilna shared these destructive experiences, in varying forms, with Jewish communities throughout the Russian empire.

In addition to disruption there was a second factor: relative freedom for Jewish education. Although Ober Ost encouraged education in Yiddish, this decision was largely the result of urging from Jewish leaders. Thus, the rapid growth of modern Jewish education did not require active state intervention of the kind considered by the Evsektsii in the early Soviet period, nor state support of the kind envisioned by the post-war Minorities Treaty, but simply enough latitude to allow the modern Jewish educational project to be carried out. This combination of freedom and crisis brought about the multifaceted changes during the First World War.

Building new educational institutions and changing the nature of Jewish schooling were major preoccupations of Jewish intellectuals and community leaders (including many rabbis) at the turn of the century. They saw education as the crucial arena in which the battle over the future of the Jewish people would take place. The First World War brought these plans from theory into practice and created schools that would last until 1939/40 and provide models for similar institutions. In Vilna, and perhaps elsewhere, the process of creating these schools brought to the surface deepening fissures within Jewish society, forcing individuals to take sides and ultimately contributing to the fractured politics of the interwar period.

Creating a New Jewish Nation

The Vilna Education Society and Secular Yiddish Education in Interwar Vilna

JORDANA DE BLOEME

IN 1935 Max Weinreich, the Yiddish historian and a founder of YIVO, set out his views about the needs of young Jews in Poland. In summarizing the subject of his work, *The Way to our Young People*, Weinreich wrote: 'He who holds the young, holds the future.'[1] His study was intended as the beginning of a larger project of socio-psychological research into young Jews, undertaken with the hope of providing a better future for Polish Jewry and ensuring a future for Yiddish in eastern Europe. Seen in a broader context, his statement embodies the goals of Jewish leaders in Poland between the First and Second World Wars. Education, the young, and a preoccupation with the future of Polish Jewry were intensely intertwined with issues involving the political and cultural rights of the Jewish minority in the Second Polish Republic.

Jewish pedagogues and intellectual and political leaders considered language as the basis for identity formation, an all-the-more complex issue in the city of Vilna, with its multi-ethnic population. During the interwar period, Polish Jewry had a wide choice of schools, spanning the political spectrum from right to left, religious and secular, and operating in Polish, Yiddish, Hebrew, and sometimes a combination of all three. While most were represented by a cognate political party, the secular Yiddish school system in Vilna, formally organized by the Central Education Committee (Tsentraler bildungs komitet; TsBK) from 1919 and later the Vilna Education Society (Vilner bildungs gezelshaft; Vilbig), founded in 1924, shunned overt political alliances and looked to Yiddish language and culture as the basis of its curricula, while also attempting to act as a voice for all of Vilna Jewry, supplying what it felt was best for its immediate and future needs. Its proponents championed Yiddish language and culture as the foundation of a new secular Jewish identity intended to lead east European Jewry into the modern world.

---

[1] M. Weinreich, *Der veg tsu unzer yugnt: yesoydes, metodn, problemen fun yidisher yugnt-forshung* (Vilna, 1935), 12.

Jewish educational institutions were prevalent throughout interwar Poland, yet Vilna was the only region to have an all-encompassing organization that sought to speak for all of Vilna Jewry, permeating all areas of their lives at all ages. As Andrew Koss has demonstrated, Jewish pedagogues and leaders in Vilna were able to establish educational institutions, which had not been possible under the tsarist regime, as a result of the German occupation during the First World War, the influx of Jewish refugees into the city, and the flight of those sympathetic to the Russian regime.[2] Similarly in Warsaw, the German occupation provided a laboratory in which Jewish leaders and pedagogues established schools based on a variety of ideologies, in an attempt to ensure some form of Jewish identity. As in Vilna, those in Warsaw were unable to find common ground to establish a single Jewish school system. In addition, significant differences developed between secular Yiddish educational programmes in Vilna and elsewhere in Poland. The unique character of Vilna and its educational institutions continued throughout the interwar period.

When Poland was re-established at the end of the First World War, its leaders were compelled to sign the Minorities Treaty formulated at the Paris Peace Conference of 1919, guaranteeing, among other stipulations, students' rights to education in their mother tongue and government funding for Poland's Jewish minority, the second largest in the state. Although these rights were never fully implemented and the Polish government disavowed the treaty in 1934,[3] Jewish leaders throughout the country used the Minorities Treaty to lobby for government funding for Jewish-language schools. Jewish national and ideological movements with their origins in the late nineteenth century were able to flourish during this twenty-year period, establishing schools or school systems that adhered to their ideologies, and spanning the whole political and religious spectrum. The main issue at stake in the conflict between the different school systems, as it had been from the early twentieth century, was the question of choosing a Jewish national language as the language of instruction.[4]

Vilna was uniquely positioned during this period. It had a key role in the world of the Jews of Poland–Lithuania and was claimed by Lithuanians, Poles, and Belarusians. During the First World War, while the city was under German occupation, the Russian-speaking Jewish intelligentsia fled to the Russian interior. Those who remained established new organizations and societies for a destitute population, offering schools that provided education in the student's mother tongue for the city's large influx of Jewish orphans.[5] In 1918 the first communal

---

[2] A. N. Koss, 'From Theory to Practice: The Fight for Jewish Education in Vilna during the First World War' (this volume, pp. 195–220).

[3] S. Horak, *Poland and her National Minorities, 1919–1939* (New York, 1961), 78.

[4] See Y. Iram, 'The Persistence of Jewish Ethnic Identity: The Educational Experience in Interwar Poland and Lithuania 1919–1939', *History of Education*, 14/4 (1985), 273–82; K. S. Kazdan, *Fun kheyder un 'shkoles' biz 'tsisho': dos ruslendishe yidntum in gerangl far shul, shprakh, kultur* (Mexico City, 1956); K. Weiser, *Jewish People, Yiddish Nation: Noah Prylucki and the Folkists in Poland* (Toronto, 2011), ch. 4.   [5] 'Fun der yidisher folks-shul in vilne', *Letste nayes*, 6 Feb. 1916, p. 3.

elections were held and a showdown between Yiddishists and Hebraists ensued for control over much-needed funds for Jewish schooling and thus over the cultural future and identity of Vilna Jewry.

SECULAR YIDDISH EDUCATION IN VILNA

No other region in interwar Poland had an institution as all encompassing as Vilbig. The multi-ethnic make-up of the city and the precarious political situation during the immediate post-war period meant that Jewish leaders were less likely to advocate acculturation and instead championed Jewish national autonomous aspirations.

Although Yiddish secular schooling in Vilna owed much to the German occupation during the First World War, it was after this period that its proponents were able to organize and experiment by appealing to a larger audience rather than solely to the parents of children attending their schools. After the Germans retreated, a short-lived democratic Lithuanian state was established. Not long after that, the Red Army marched in and took control of the region. A major turning point in the history of Yiddish schooling in Vilna occurred under Soviet occupation: secular Yiddish schools in Vilna first received state financial and organizational support from the TsBK. All institutions were taken over by the state, while religious institutions, including schools, were liquidated, education for all children aged 8 to 17 in state-run schools was made mandatory.[6] Although all other Jewish institutions were closed, the Yiddish schools, because of their apparently non-religious nature, were allowed to remain open under the jurisdiction of the TsBK, which also organized a publishing house, evening courses for workers, and pedagogical courses for teachers. Three journals were published: *Di naye velt*, devoted to Yiddish literature, art, and scholarship; *Folksbildung*, answering questions and providing information on Yiddish secular education and schooling; and a youth journal, *Grininke beymelekh*, a revival of a pre-war publication edited by Shloyme Bastomski and his wife M. Khaymson. Plans were also made to publish Yiddish-language textbooks for children and a journal on Yiddish linguistics.[7] These publications enabled Yiddishist pedagogical leaders in the city to create a unified formal and informal education system that reached all sectors of Vilna Jewry, not solely those who attended Yiddish secular schools. Despite its brief three-month existence, in its attempt to implement a cultural programme embodying all aspects of Yiddish culture and intended for a mass Yiddish-speaking audience, the TsBK can be seen as a precursor to Vilbig.

During this period, three pedagogues—Gershon Pludermakher, Zalmen Reyzen, and Shlomo Bastomski—were key members of the TsBK. Before the Lithuanian–Belarusian Soviet Republic (Litbel), all three had been highly influen-

---

[6] 'Vegn di reorganizirn fun di shuln', *Folksbildung*, Apr. 1919, p. 32.
[7] 'Di yidishe farlag-opteylung bam bildungs komisaryat', *Folksbildung*, Mar. 1919, pp. 30–1.

tial in Yiddish secular schools and would continue to be influential as members of the TsBK and later Vilbig. This factor solidified hopes among secular Yiddishists in the city for state-funded education as well for promoting the notion that Yiddish was the language of the Jewish working class. Under the Soviets, all recognized educational institutions received state funding but were forbidden to teach religion. Nonetheless, even in 1919 each 'national' school was expected to cultivate its own national ideology in a Soviet incarnation. A debate ensued on the pages of *Folksbildung* regarding the use of the Hebrew Bible in the Soviet-funded Yiddish secular schools in Litbel. Although all non-communist political organizations were dissolved during this brief period, *Folksbildung* acted as the voice of Yiddish-speaking Jewry. It was in its pages that questions on the nature of the Yiddish secular schools in Vilna were debated for the first time with a mass audience.[8]

THE CENTRAL EDUCATION COMMITTEE (TSBK)

From January 1919, during the rule of the Lithuanian–Belarusian Soviet Republic, secular Yiddish schools in Vilna enjoyed state support.[9] In May 1919, shortly after Poland took control of Vilna, the TsBK was established to unite these schools and to establish curricula. However, it soon became evident that without financial support, either from the state or through a single governing body able to funnel philanthropic donations, the schools were unsustainable, and the TsBK found itself mostly dealing with financial issues and had little control over individual schools until 1922 when Vilna was formally annexed by Poland.[10]

During the eighteen months from October 1920 to April 1922 when Vilna was part of Central Lithuania (Litwa Środkowa), which was nominally independent but in fact under Polish control, Yiddish secular schools under the TsBK's tutelage addressed educational issues and curricula content both from a practical standpoint and as a means of declaring political allegiances. In anticipation of international recognition of Polish rule in the region, the merits and problems of teaching Polish language and history were discussed. Yet at the same time, the Yiddishist intelligentsia affiliated with the TsBK used the *Vilner tog* to promote its ideology. In its pages, Reyzen and Pludermakher, among others, stressed the need for Yiddish secular schooling and modern Yiddish culture while openly declaring their allegiance to Lithuania.[11] These pedagogues and communal leaders saw themselves as distinct from the Polish Jews of the former Congress Kingdom, with whom they would soon be united. There was a sense of elitism, along with the practical hope

---

[8] By 'first time', I mean that there were no formal secular Yiddish-language journals dedicated to secular Yiddish schooling in Vilna prior to this publication.

[9] On Yiddish secular schools under Litbel, see *Folksbildung*, Mar., Apr. 1919.

[10] 'A tsentraler yidisher bildungs-komitet', *Vilner tog*, 19 May 1919, p. 3; Pludermakher, 'Tsu der geshikhte fun dem yidish-veltlekhn shul-vezn in vilne', *Shul-pinkes: finf yor arbet fun tsentraln bildungs-komitet, 1919–1924* (Vilna, 1924), 22–9.

[11] G. Pludermakher, 'Vilne muz ir koved bashteyn!', *Vilner tog*, 4 Jul. 1921, p. 2.

that incorporation into independent Lithuania would provide resources for Yiddish education, since the Lithuanian government had granted cultural autonomy to its country's Jewish minority, including state funding for secular Yiddish education, in 1919.

At the same time, the TsBK as an organized entity was on the brink of collapse. In 1921 Pludermakher complained about the lack of 'systematic organization' in the school system, which the TsBK was intended to remedy. He noted that much had been achieved: evening schools, youth clubs, cultural centres, and people's universities had been established. Above all, though, he emphasized the importance of Yiddish educational endeavours for adolescents, stressing that cognitive development and formation of opinions took place then rather than in earlier childhood. The fact that Yiddish education was mostly confined to elementary schools meant that this other segment of the population was ignored at a critical moment. He therefore suggested the creation of a *yugnt-shul* for those who had attended elementary school but were unable to go on to secondary education. This was not to be a professional school but would focus on the humanities and Yiddish language and literature, while cultivating artistic abilities, including providing curricular time for drawing, singing, and drama. It would also foster 'free and friendly' relationships between male and female students.[12]

These far-reaching plans could not be implemented, because in February 1921 the TsBK faced financial catastrophe which even impeded the unification of the various institutions that were already established. By then the TsBK had forty-six institutions under its control, providing Saturday lectures for children and teachers, a choir, lectures for parents, student co-operatives, and artistic centres, all in addition to formal schooling.[13] As a result, in 1922, immediately after Poland's annexation of Vilna, the Yiddishist intelligentsia's focus turned to obtaining government funding for education in the students' mother tongue in elementary schools, as it was seen as the only way to ensure the continuation of Jewish national culture in the region. Some, like pedagogue Avrom Golomb, who championed government funding of the Yiddish secular schools, dismissed the argument that graduates of such elementary schools would be unable to attend Polish-language secondary schools and universities.[14]

LANGUAGE POLITICS

After Poland annexed Vilna, the TsBK was absorbed by the Warsaw-based Central Yiddish School Organization (Tsentrale Yidishe Shul Organizatsye; TSYSHO), although it still retained some autonomy. The two school systems were significantly different, mostly due to the dissimilar political climates of the two cities.

[12] G. Pludermakher, 'Bildungs far yugnt un dervaksene', *Di naye shul*, Feb. 1921, p. 29.

[13] 'Der tsentraler yidisher bildungs-komitet (tsbk) in vilne un zayn tetikeyt', *Di naye shul*, Feb. 1921, pp. 9–11. [14] A. Golomb, 'Numerus klozus in folkshuln', *Vilner tog*, 26 Mar. 1923, p. 2.

Jewish pedagogical leaders in Warsaw were heavily involved in politics, a factor less significant in Vilna. Although TSYSHO was not openly affiliated with the socialist Jewish Labour Bund, in Warsaw parents of pupils in its schools were more likely to have links to the Bund. The Bund unofficially championed these schools, and many pedagogues were also ardent Bundists. In Vilna, by contrast, TsBK leaders spanned the gamut of left-wing Jewish political parties, including the Bund, the Territorialists, and the socialist-Zionist Po'alei Tsiyon Left. Here it was held, according to Max Weinreich, that the Yiddish secular schools and the education of the Yiddish-speaking Jewish child should be 'above' politics, and that the Yiddish secular schools should not be connected to any single political party.[15] As early as 1920 there was anxiety about subordinating Yiddish schools in Vilna to a secular Yiddish school organization located in Warsaw. At a meeting in April 1920, Pludermakher noted that one would need to travel a long way (from Vilna) 'to knock on the doors of political parties and when these doors don't open, teachers will need to act as politicians rather than be teachers'.[16]

Aside from political issues, the greatest difference between the schools in central Poland and those in the Vilna region seems to have involved the curriculum, specifically the question of language and especially the teaching of Hebrew. After the first meeting of the two school organizations in 1923, it was decided not to make the teaching of Hebrew obligatory in all schools. In addition, it was decided that the only permissible form of Hebrew was biblical, not modern. This apparent consensus masked significant differences.[17] In Vilna, it was feared that the absence of Hebrew from the curriculum would alienate more traditionalist parents. According to Pludermakher, the omission would make the schools too 'radical' and disconnected from Jewish tradition, inducing parents to send their children elsewhere.

THE VILNA EDUCATION SOCIETY (VILBIG)

Reservations now began to be expressed within the Yiddishist intelligentsia about the impact of the TsBK on Vilna Jewry as a whole. In 1922 people affiliated with secular Yiddish education in Vilna also expressed concern over the state of Yiddish education and young Jews in the city. Parents of students attending the Yiddish secular schools run by the TsBK were worried that the partnership with the Bundist-oriented TSYSHO would ultimately corrupt young Jews. While both school systems had been established to unite schools in Poland, promoting a modern, secular Yiddish education and the championing of the Yiddish language,

---

[15] YIVO Archives, New York, RG 11 'VILBIG (Vilner Yidishe Bildungs Gezelshaft) (1923–1940)', folder 1: Vilbig statute 1924.

[16] 'Barikht fun unzer tsveyter shul-baratung', *Di naye shul*, Apr. 1920, p. 89. At this meeting, TSYSHO was formally established as the central school organization for all Yiddish secular schools in Poland, Lithuania, and Belarus. There were to be school committees in Warsaw and Białystok in addition to TsBK in Vilna.   [17] 'Di yidishe lerer konferents', *Vilner tog*, 28 Dec. 1923, p. 3.

TSYSHO had a much more political character. In addition, in 1922 the parents' association of the TsBK called for an institution of higher learning for graduates of its schools. This was intended to promote modern, secular Jewish identity and champion the Yiddish language by providing scholarly courses on Jewish history, Yiddish literature, and the Yiddish language itself, as well as general subjects taught in Yiddish at university level in order to further a national Jewish consciousness and promote scholarship on and in the language. The parents' association approached the TsBK with this proposal, but to no avail.[18] One year later, various members of the community met to discuss the TsBK's role in bridging what was perceived as a cultural gap between the intelligentsia and the Yiddish-speaking masses. Although the committee was supposedly in charge of the schools, it lacked ultimate authority; similarly, the Kultur Lige, which was in charge of cultural endeavours, failed to assume this role and closed soon afterwards. Although the TsBK's leaders had begun working towards creating Hebrew and Yiddish curricula, financial difficulties resulted in the closure of schools, teachers not being paid, and the postponement of the publication of textbooks and curricula. It was argued that, as an organization, the committee did little to build up the schools. Although an evening school and a children's library existed, these facilities could not accommodate everyone who had been unable to attend the elementary schools. The debate ended with two recommendations: that a committee be established to lobby the Polish government for funding for the schools and that something be done about what was perceived as a 'cultural crisis' of Vilna Jewry, which the TsBK had failed to address. It was decided that another governing body should be established, which would have authority over extra-curricular activities and the proposed people's university.[19]

A year later, in 1924, Pludermakher argued in the *Vilner tog* that the TsBK and the Kultur Lige were failing to accomplish their mission of disseminating modern, secular Yiddish culture to the majority of Yiddish-speaking Vilna Jews. Pludermakher, along with other members of the TsBK, called a meeting to discuss what was perceived as the low cultural level of Vilna Jewry and the Vilna Yiddishist intelligentsia's lack of commitment to modern, secular Yiddish culture. He was particularly disturbed that the anniversary of the Yiddish writer Y. L. Peretz's death had not been commemorated by the Jewish community of Vilna. Pludermakher, along with others at the meeting, decided to create a new educational society to unite the Yiddishist intelligentsia in one organization, while simultaneously raising the cultural level of the Yiddish-speaking masses in Vilna by disseminating modern, secular Yiddish culture. They hoped that this society would bridge the cultural and intellectual gap between the Yiddishist intelligentsia and everyday Yiddish speakers.[20]

[18] M. Bernshteyn, 'Vilner yidisher bildungs gezelshaft (vilbig)', in *Vilner almanakh*, ed. A. Y. Grazenski (Vilna, 1939), 223.   [19] 'Di yidishe shuln in vilne', *Vilner tog*, 16 Nov. 1923, p. 4.
[20] G. Pludermakher, 'Der vilner yidishe bildungs gezelshaft', *Vilner tog*, 26 Sept. 1924, p. 3.

Thus, Vilbig was established in 1924. According to its founding statute, its mission was to raise the cultural level of the Jewish people and its ultimate goal was to promote cultural autonomy and the prestige of Yiddish language and culture in the Jewish Diaspora and specifically in Vilna and the surrounding region.[21] Vilbig sought to achieve this primarily through education, hoping to transcend the highly politicized contemporary Polish Jewish environment. The society believed that only through education could a Jewish national consciousness be disseminated within the majority of Yiddish-speakers, thereby raising the cultural level of the people and providing prestige for the national language and culture. Although it often petitioned the Polish government for funding for Jewish schools and for payment of Yiddish, and at times Hebrew, teachers, its main focus was on education and the very real needs of Vilna Jewry. Executive committee members included Max Weinreich, the staunch advocate of keeping Yiddish schooling separate from politics.[22] Instead, he and others sought to create a world in which Yiddish-speaking children and adolescents could be reared in a non-political environment away from the adult world.

What was unique was Vilbig's combination of a formal Yiddish education with extracurricular activities, including scouting and activities to provide productive occupations for young Jews, with the goal of creating a new and moral younger generation. Vilbig sought to raise the cultural level of Vilna Jewry by disseminating a modern, secular Yiddish culture beyond the formal school system. Among the means to achieve this was the establishment of the children's group Kinderland, which provided after-school activities and weekend assemblies for children attending Yiddish secular schools and later for Jewish students at Polish public schools. The society also created evening schools and provided lectures for adolescents, which were to become part of a Yiddish-language university for graduates of the Yiddish secular schools. By the late 1930s these aims culminated in a project for the 'educated worker'.

Vilbig sought consistently to remain non-political in its struggle for Yiddish language rights. As a proponent of Yiddishism and diaspora nationalism, it expressed loyalty to Poland as the host country and, in particular, to Vilna and its region: this loyalty was evident throughout the organization's seventeen-year history.[23] The executive also had to take into consideration the expectations of its members. Until 1937 Vilbig was self-funded and member-driven,[24] and the executive often vacillated between its desire to create a cadre of Yiddish-speaking scholars and satisfying its members' demands for more practical educational endeavours.[25]

[21] Vilbig statute, 1924.   [22] YIVO Archives, RG 11, folder 67: Vilbig, minutes, 24 Mar. 1925.
[23] On Yiddishism in Vilna, see G. Estraikh, 'The Vilna Yiddishist Quest for Modernity', in *Jüdische Kultur(en) im Neuen Europa Wilna 1918–1939* (Wiesbaden, 2004), 100–16.
[24] In 1937 Vilbig appealed to the American Jewish Joint Distribution Committee for funding in order to continue its programmes. YIVO Archives, RG 11, folder 23: Vilbig, letter to director of the JDC in Europe, 25 May 1937.
[25] As late as 1937 Vilbig executive member Meir Bernshteyn refused to support any endeavour

The language politics of Vilna Jewry were the subject of heated debates at Vilbig's executive meetings. In 1925 the executive established a commission to support its 'struggle for Yiddish' as part of the language rights of Vilna Jewry. Weinreich stressed the significance of education and the dissemination of Yiddish language and culture among young Jews as integral to this struggle. Rather than petitioning the Polish government for specific Yiddish-language rights and recognition, he and others within Vilbig felt that their energies should be channelled into attracting young Yiddish-speaking Jews to Yiddish culture as part of a specifically national endeavour, separate from the practicalities of the language question in the schools.[26]

Simultaneously, the Vilbig executive and parents of students expressed intense fear of Polish linguistic acculturation among Vilna Jewry. Chone Shmeruk noted in his seminal article on the trilingual Jewish culture of interwar Poland that the linguistic lines among Polish Jewry were often blurred and that Polish linguistic acculturation did not necessary result in assimilation.[27] Nonetheless, Yiddishists throughout Poland continued to berate those who sent their children to Polish public schools, despite the obvious socio-economic incentives, or who chose Polish-language newspapers, journals, or other forms of Polish Jewish culture over Yiddish. At the heart of this debate was an intense fear of the loss of culture and language. Without Yiddish, Yiddishist diaspora nationalists believed that the Jewish nation, as a non-religious and non-territorial entity, would be unable to sustain itself in a modern, secular world. However, without discussing the problematic nature of the 1931 Polish census, it would seem as though Yiddish remained the mother tongue of the great majority of Polish Jews, since 79.9 per cent declared it to be so.[28] Nonetheless, as early as 1926 the chair of the TSYSHO executive, Khayim Shloyme Kazdan, publicly expressed concern about Polish linguistic acculturation among the children of Jewish workers.[29] There was also a sense among parents in Vilna that speaking Polish was only for non-Jews. In his autobiography submitted to YIVO in 1939, F. explained that when his uncle suggested that he attend a *szabasówka* school, one of the Polish state-run schools intended for Jewish

that did not have the potential to lead Vilbig into establishing a Yiddish-language university (YIVO Archives, RG 11, folder 23: M. Bernshteyn, letter to all TsBK elementary schools, 28 Jun. 1937).

[26] YIVO Archives, RG 11, folder 14: Vilbig, minutes, 1 Nov. 1927.

[27] C. Shmeruk, 'Hebrew–Yiddish–Polish: A Trilingual Jewish Culture', in Y. Gutman et al. (eds.), *The Jews of Poland between Two World Wars* (Hanover, NH, 1989), 285–311.

[28] E. Mendelsohn, *The Jews of East Central Europe between the Wars* (Bloomington, Ind., 1983), 31. However, as Mendelsohn notes, the 1931 Polish census did not ask for national affiliation. Therefore, various political movements in Jewish communities throughout Poland launched campaigns urging those filling out the census to declare Yiddish or Hebrew, depending on political affiliation, as their mother tongue in lieu of national affiliation. While the data on Yiddish as a mother tongue is more reliable than the data on Hebrew, it still must be interpreted carefully. Furthermore, it cannot be compared to the 1921 Polish census, since that did not include the territory of Vilna and the surrounding region, which was only annexed by Poland in 1922 and where a larger number of Yiddish speakers resided.

[29] K. S. Kazdan, *A shul af yidish oder af poylish* (Warsaw, 1926).

children with lessons conducted in Polish, his mother responded that she did not want her son to be a 'goy'.[30]

At Vilbig's first annual meeting in 1925, Weinreich affirmed his belief that secular Yiddish education must be non-political. Politics, and especially socialism, had no place in children's and adolescents' education.[31] A major problem encountered by Vilbig was the dissonance between its articulated goal of championing Yiddishism as a form of linguistic Jewish nationalism and its refusal to take a political stance. In 1927 Vilbig organized a commission to champion the 'struggle' for Yiddish-language rights in Poland. The commission concluded that the Yiddish language should be spread through the publishing of books and journals alongside the provision of education. Vilbig's leaders looked to professional unions to champion Yiddish publishing and specifically argued that, whether intentionally or not, the Bund had failed to champion Yiddish-language rights.[32] Above all, Weinreich stressed the significance in this struggle of education and the dissemination of Yiddish language and culture among young Jews. Rather than petitioning the Polish government for language rights and recognition, he and others in Vilbig felt that energy should be channelled into attracting young Yiddish-speaking Jews to Yiddish culture through both formal and informal education. Vilbig's first such informal endeavour geared directly at children was Kinderland.

KINDERLAND

In 1925 representatives of Vilbig began discussing the need for an educational programme to deal with the divide between Yiddish secular schools and the home. Since it was believed that many of the parents of children in TsBK schools were not themselves acquainted with the basic concepts of secular Yiddishism, it was feared that the children reared in these schools would not grow up to become 'proper' Yiddish cultural consumers and producers. This dictated the need for activities aimed at such pupils outside school hours. While TsBK schools were praised as modern, light, and airy, the Yiddishist intelligentsia affiliated with the TsBK and Vilbig expressed concern that the school experience was not enough. A similarly light and airy place was needed in the evenings and at weekends to provide a refuge for TsBK students whose own homes, it was feared, were not as progressive as the schools. Some went so far as to express concern that any education imparted in school might be undone at home, if such a location were not created. Therefore, Kinderland was created to develop Yiddish-speaking children mentally and physically. It sought to offer extracurricular educational activities, including commemorations of important events, discussion groups, and clubs, in an atmosphere intended to develop bodies and minds not only through educational

[30] YIVO Archives, RG 4, 'Autobiographies of Jewish Youth in Poland (1932–1939)': Autobiography 3627, 2.   [31] YIVO Archives, RG 11, folder 67: Vilbig, minutes, 24 Mar. 1925.
[32] YIVO Archives, RG 11, folder 14: Struggle for Yiddish Committee, minutes, 1 Nov. 1927.

courses and lectures but also through scouting and sport.[33] Originally run jointly by Vilbig and the TsBK, Kinderland held a number of assemblies for young children on Saturday mornings. As early as 1925 Vilbig organized assemblies for children in conjunction with YIVO, on folklore and legends, intended for those in the sixth grade onwards.[34] Although Kinderland as an organization soon ceased to operate, it represented Vilbig's first attempt to cultivate a historical and traditionalist consciousness among Yiddish-speaking children outside a formal educational setting.

DI BIN

Vilbig's goal of promoting the productivization of Vilna Jewry, alongside its championing of Yiddishism as a linguistic-based diaspora nationalism, highlights the problematic nature of diaspora nationalism but also the extent to which even those reared within a Yiddishist milieu were still affected by connections with Poland. In an attempt to further Vilbig's mandate of regeneration and productivization through a new Jewish national-cultural identity, Vilbig turned to scouting and to the inculcation of its young people with moral values. In 1927 Di Bin (the Bee) was founded as a non-political scouting organization under Vilbig's jurisdiction and was one of the organization's most significant programmes.

Di Bin was modelled on the German youth movement Wandervogel. It established circles known as 'beehives', divided by age, with groups located in Vilna and the surrounding region. Each beehive had a leader, with Max Weinreich serving as head of the entire organization. Initially, Vilbig principally promoted the merits of scouting and camping, providing each Di Bin member with a manual containing minute details of Vilna and the surrounding territory.[35] Vilbig believed that members needed to be socialized away from the urban setting of Vilna and not to be morally corrupted by adult and urban vices and to establish a connection to the land and its people, the Yiddish-speaking 'folk' of Vilna and the surrounding region.[36]

In order to create a Jewish diaspora nationalist consciousness, Di Bin sought to expand beyond Vilna: the only organization under Vilbig that did so. Weinreich wrote in 1932 that 'Di Bin will bring to young Jews the idea that work in general and especially agricultural work is holy, not only in remote places but also where we live and where we will live. This is our home that we have built and our land.'[37] This remark echoes the notion of *doykeyt* (hereness) championed by the Bund and other Jewish diaspora nationalist groups. While it promoted an international concept of Yiddish-speaking Jewry, it also assumed loyalty to the host country. In the 1932 volume *Binishe lider* ('Songs of the Hive'), intended to inspire new

[33] M. Weinreich, 'Di vilbig: a naye kulturele pozitsye in vilne', *Vilner tog*, 19 Dec. 1924, p. 3.
[34] YIVO Archives, RG 11, folder 12: M. Bernshteyn, letter to pedagogical council of the Yidishn tekhnikum, 2 Dec. 1925.   [35] Bin komisye, Vilbig, *Instruktsyes far vanderung* (Vilna, 1927).
[36] M. Weinreich, 'Ver zaynen mir: vos viln mir', *Binishe lider* (Vilna, 1932), 11–17.   [37] Ibid. 15.

beehives outside Vilna, Weinreich also claimed that Vilna would always remain the centre of the movement.[38]

The actual role of Vilbig in Di Bin was rather ambiguous. Tensions between the group's original members, especially Leyzer Ran, a native of Vilna who succeeded in removing Di Bin from Vilbig's jurisdiction in 1934, and Weinreich, were evident from its inception. It was argued that as a scouting organization, Di Bin should seek to move in new directions, which it eventually did through creating agricultural communes: in 1932 Vilbig dedicated itself to providing a plot of land in order to fulfil its mandate of scouting and productivization.[39] However, Vilbig's executive was unhappy with the group's direction. The focus on child-rearing away from overt adult intervention resulted in a backlash by some Di Bin members against the very ideologies upon which Vilbig had been founded, principally its commitment to high culture and scholarship and its apolitical mandate.

Through scouting, Di Bin members were expected to develop a connection with the Polish landscape. For Ran and other early members this aspect was more important than the group's Yiddishist ideology. Di Bin members were encouraged to sing songs during their expeditions in order to create a joyful atmosphere of camaraderie. Members were encouraged to write their own songs, rather than sing those they had learned in school. Nature and the Vilna landscape featured prominently. These were published in the group's newsletter that was distributed to all members. It was also suggested that Di Bin members make contact with those in other cities and countries by sending pictures of Vilna, so that others could see the group's environment.[40] The fact that this occurred before Di Bin groups were established outside Vilna suggests that not only was Poland, and specifically Vilna, the centre of Di Bin but it was also the centre of Yiddishism and modern Yiddish culture. Therefore, despite the rhetoric of diaspora nationalism and its simultaneous focus on internationalism and *doykeyt*, it seems that young Jews in Vilna acquired a romantic sense of belonging to Poland in addition to some degree of linguistic acculturation.

THE POLISH LANGUAGE AND THE EDUCATED WORKER

Part of what made Vilbig unique as an educational organization were the activities it supported outside the classroom. While it sought to create a particular future in which Jews had a secular but unique role and identity within eastern Europe, it also acknowledged the complex situation of young Jews in Vilna, including the increase in Polish linguistic acculturation and the fact that not all Yiddish-speaking children in Vilna could attend a Yiddish secular school. Although Vilbig sought to establish a Yiddish-language university and aimed to create an educational system

[38] Weinreich, 'Ver zaynen mir', 19.

[39] YIVO Archives, RG 11, folder 2: Protocols of the Ninth Annual General Meeting of Vilbig, 18 July 1932. [40] 'Noent un vayt', *Bin bletlekh*, 27 Apr. 1928, p. 2.

from kindergarten through high school to post-secondary education, it felt compelled to recognize what it saw as the real needs of Vilna Jewry. The 'educated worker' project is an example of this endeavour.

In the mid-1930s the leaders of Vilbig reviewed its intended audience and overall mandate. Since its foundation in 1924 Vilbig had sought to balance its ideology of non-political Jewish nationalism with the real needs of Vilna Jewry. However, Vilbig's continued financial problems limited what it could achieve. It relied mostly on revenue from membership dues and entrance fees, as well as on precarious funding from the Vilna *kehilah*. From 1925 to 1940 it ran a continuous deficit. Tuition fees for its classes were heavily subsidized, as most students lacked the financial means to pay them. In 1934 Vilbig's executive members complained that it was very difficult to find teachers for evening courses, since funds were not available to pay their wages. In the same year Vilbig reported that a record number of students were turned away from classes because of the inability to provide adequate subsidies, and the organization lost the use of some classrooms as it could not afford the rent.[41]

From its inception Vilbig saw itself as a school of higher learning into which graduates of Yiddish secular schools, both elementary and high, could progress. This was part of the goal of building up the prestige of Yiddish and its culture through education, scholarship, and cultural activities. However, there were intense debates about exactly who these students were supposed to be. By the mid-1930s Vilbig switched its attention from students of Yiddish secular schools to Yiddish-speaking students of state-run Polish public schools.[42] The majority of Jewish students in interwar Poland attended Polish public schools intended for Jewish children, primarily to avoid the cost of Jewish private schools and the slim socio-economic prospects for those lacking Polish-language skills.

The place of Polish in Jewish circles also began to change during this period. Although a significant number of the autobiographies submitted as part of YIVO's contests in the 1930s refer to antisemitic and brutal teachers in Polish state schools, whose hostile atmosphere is often contrasted with the feeling of comfort and belonging which marked the private Jewish schools, individual autobiographies and even the activities of Vilbig tell a less clear-cut story. They demonstrate that Yiddish, Polish, and Hebrew were used for different purposes and were part of an evolving non-religious Jewish ethnic identity.

Those who took part in secular Yiddish organizations, including the Bund's organizations for young Jews, Tsukunft and the Socialist Children's Union (Sotsyalistisher Kinder Farband; SKIF), and even those who attended TsBK schools, did not necessarily speak Yiddish with ease and often felt more comfortable

[41] YIVO Archives, RG 11, folder 2: Protocols of the Tenth Annual General Meeting of Vilbig, 23 Feb. 1935.
[42] YIVO Archives, RG 11, folder 19: Vilbig, letter to the head of the Vilna *kehilah*, regarding subsidies for evening schools, 1933; YIVO Archives, RG 11, folder 23: Vilbig, letter to the head of the Yiddish Teachers' Union, 21 Jun. 1937.

in a Polish-language setting. In one autobiography from 1939, a young woman, T., states that she spoke Yiddish when she was at Tsukunft or SKIF events and Hebrew when she attended Hashomer Hatsa'ir meetings, yet she felt most comfortable using her mother tongue, Polish.[43] In 1938 a student from a TsBK school in Vilna described his visit to YIVO in the Yiddishist youth journal *Grininke beymelekh*. What struck him most was that YIVO, as an academic institution, conducted itself entirely in Yiddish.[44]

As the interwar period progressed, Vilbig reluctantly acknowledged the linguistic situation of Vilna Jewry. It became the only Yiddishist institution in Vilna that specifically provided educational programmes for those attending Polish public schools. By the mid-1930s Vilbig had begun to shift its focus away from those reared solely in a Yiddishist milieu and to direct its interest towards students in Polish public schools who could attend evening courses.[45] Yet Vilbig still remained split regarding its target audience. After a series of debates about where the society should funnel its perpetually limited financial resources, the chair of the Vilbig executive, Meir Bernshteyn, insisted that the society not abandon its original goal of becoming an institution of higher education operating in Yiddish. He maintained that if the education sponsored by Vilbig did not raise the cultural level of students, then it could not be considered a worthwhile endeavour. A compromise was reached: two streams of evening classes were established, one for graduates of Yiddish secular schools, which was intended eventually to develop into a Yiddish-language university, and one for those unable to complete their education in Yiddish secular schools. This ultimately became an entirely separate project to which Vilbig gave the name the 'educated worker', and was intended to raise the cultural level of working-class Jews.[46]

However, in their attempt to target what they described as 'the Yiddish-speaking masses', Vilbig's executive members realized as late as 1937 that it was not entirely clear who made up this oft-discussed group. In 1934, in the Yiddish-language journal *Literarishe bleter*, Nakhman Mayzel asked where the graduates of Yiddish secular schools had gone. A network that was intended to create future cultural producers who would raise the literary, linguistic, and scholarly status of Polish Jewry was, according to him, nowhere to be found.[47]

The campaign for the educated worker began in 1937, when Vilbig launched a search for students who had left Yiddish secular schools before graduation as well as for those who attended *szabasówki* schools.[48] In an attempt to attract workers to

[43] YIVO Archives, RG 4: Autobiography 3749.

[44] 'Oshmener yidishe shul in vilne', *Grininke beymelekh*, 213 (Feb. 1938), 97.

[45] YIVO Archives, RG 11, folder 2: Protocols of the Tenth Annual General Meeting of Vilbig.

[46] YIVO Archives, RG 11, folder 12: M. Bernshteyn, letter to all TsBK elementary schools, 28 Jun. 1937; YIVO Archives, RG 11, folder 2: minutes of the Fourteenth Annual General Meeting of Vilbig, 5 Feb. 1939.   [47] N. Mayzel, *Literarishe bleter*, 23 Mar. 1934, p. 185.

[48] YIVO Archives, RG 11, folder 12: M. Bernshteyn, letter to all TsBK elementary schools, 28 Jun. 1937.

Vilbig, the executive sent circulars to unions, asking them to suggest beginners' courses for their workers and advertised the courses in the Polish-language Jewish press. Despite an initially poor response, by 1938 a total of 3,842 students were attending Vilbig's evening and weekend lectures.[49] According to the organization, the most popular courses were about Jewish history and Yiddish literature; however, according to questionnaires distributed by Vilbig in 1937 and 1939, more than half of its members requested Polish- and Lithuanian-language courses, while some even openly stated that they no longer wished to see Vilbig running Yiddish language and literature classes.[50]

CONCLUSION

Vilbig, whether consciously or not, successfully aided Vilna Jewry in adapting to its new political and social environment as part of the Second Polish Republic through its educational and cultural programmes, while continuing to pursue its ideological goal of championing a modern, secular Yiddish culture and diaspora nationalism. Yiddish pedagogue and folklorist Shlomo Bastomski wrote in 1939 that Vilna, traditionally known as the 'Jerusalem of Lithuania', should be renamed the 'Jerusalem of Yiddish'.[51] Despite a rise in Polish linguistic acculturation during this period, secular Yiddish education in the city managed to extend beyond formal schooling, into after-school and weekend children's clubs, youth groups, and scouting organizations.

In October 1939 the city of Vilna was handed over to the Lithuanian government after a brief Soviet occupation, as part of the Molotov–Ribbentrop Pact. Vilbig had high hopes for Lithuanian rule and appealed to the Lithuanian government for state support of Yiddish-language education, as had been provided in 1920 when the city had been briefly under Lithuanian control. However, in February 1940 the government refused to provide such funding and Vilbig came under intense police scrutiny and was subsequently liquidated.[52] By then, Vilbig had shifted its programmes completely from propagating Yiddish culture towards the more practical linguistic and immediate needs of Vilna Jewry.

[49] YIVO Archives, RG 11, folder 2: minutes of the Thirteenth Annual General Meeting, 1937–8, Apr. 1938. Lectures were divided into humanities and natural science and mirrored the curriculum of the Yiddish secular high schools in Vilna. The humanities courses included Jewish history, Yiddish literature, and contemporary Poland. Yiddish and Polish language classes were also offered. According to Vilbig's own statistics, humanities and natural science courses were evenly attended, as were Yiddish and Polish courses. The majority of students were about 17 years of age and did not have a high school education but had achieved an elementary-level Yiddish secular education.

[50] Lietuvos centrinis valstybės archyvas, f. 625, ap. 1, b. 7: members comment cards, 1937, 1939; YIVO Archive, RG 11, folder 2: minutes of Fourteenth General Meeting of Vilbig, 5 Feb. 1939.

[51] S. Bastomski, 'Der yidish-veltlekher shulvezn in vilne', in *Vilner almanakh*, 197.

[52] YIVO Archive, RG 11, folder 26: Republic of Lithuania, memorandum announcing the closure of Vilbig, 13 Feb. 1940.

Although it might seem that Vilbig's leaders strayed from the society's original mandate to bring high Yiddish culture to all of Vilna Jewry, in reality their overall goal was to bring about an improved future for them. Through education and culture, Vilbig provided the next generation with a leadership that could steer them towards national cultural autonomy and a collective Jewish consciousness after the First World War. In acting in this way and, more importantly, in targeting all of Vilna Jewry and not solely those in Yiddish secular schools or affiliated with a particular political ideology, Vilbig fulfilled its role as a communal organization championing the very real and urgent needs of the population during this tumultuous period.

Between a Love of Poland, Symbolic Violence, and Antisemitism

The Idiosyncratic Effects of the State Education System on Young Jews in Interwar Poland

KAMIL KIJEK

INTRODUCTION

THE ESTABLISHMENT of new states after the First World War constituted a revolution for the people affected and had a major impact on every aspect of their lives. The Second Polish Republic was the largest of these new states and also contained the most sizeable Jewish community, numbering some three million. Throughout its existence this state was enmeshed in the contradictions of a nation state aspiring to be a democratic republic in a situation in which one-third of its citizens did not consider themselves or were not recognized as Polish. The term that perhaps most accurately describes the new state's character and, more specifically, its internal policy towards the Polish majority and its ethnic minorities was that coined by Rogers Brubaker: 'a nation-oriented state'. The Second Polish Republic was formed in the name of and for an ethnically defined Polish nation, whose interests it was first of all to guarantee.[1] Although it was meant to be democratic and all its citizens were to enjoy equal rights, the failure to put this into practice fully led to serious tensions between the ethnic minorities and the government, which defined the new polity in exclusivist terms as the state of the Polish nation.

The aim of this chapter is to examine how this contradiction manifested itself in the state education system and how this affected young Jews in interwar Poland. In order to do this, I will firstly describe how Jewish children, who until 1918 had been educated mostly in traditional institutions, entered the Polish public school system. I will then investigate the relationship between Jewish pupils enrolled in

---

[1] R. Brubaker, *Nacjonalizm inaczej: Struktura narodowa i kwestie narodowe w nowej Europie* (Warsaw, 1998), 107–8; Eng. orig.: *Nationalism Reframed: Nationhood and the National Question in the New Europe* (Cambridge, 1996).

state institutions and in the private Jewish school systems. Finally, I will evaluate the experience of Jewish children studying in government schools. Did the education system attempt to integrate its youngest Jewish citizens? If so, how did it attempt to connect them to the state? What attitudes did it try to promote, and was it successful? What emerges is the paradox of a state successfully acculturating young Jews, inculcating in them an attachment to Polish national symbols and to the national historical narrative, while at the same time reinforcing their alienation and, instead of reducing, increasing their political radicalism and opposition to the political system.

From the emergence of Polish nationalism in its modern form at the end of the nineteenth century, the 'Jewish question' had been a subject of internal debate. At the time, discussions over whether and how to assimilate Jews frequently evolved into arguments about whether the assimilation of the Jews was, in fact, possible and whether their absorption by the Polish nation was not actually harmful to it.[2] This position was closely linked to the birth of modern antisemitism in the Polish lands, to the increased popularity of racial ideology, and finally to integral nationalism, which a priori also excluded from the ranks of the Polish nation even those Jews whose consciousness, identity, and daily culture were Polish.[3] At the same time, the nascent Jewish national movement, in its various Zionist and diaspora autonomist forms, began to acquire increasing support. At the beginning of the twentieth century, its supporters started to make increasingly specific demands, not only for equal civil rights but also for collective rights which would guarantee Jews cultural and political autonomy, including their own national school system.[4]

These phenomena and processes became more significant after 1918. Most Jews now supported nationalist or Orthodox groups, which declared their attachment to the Polish state, while simultaneously being in favour of retaining their own religious and national identities. Various forms of antisemitism, ascribing an array of negative attributes to Jews, took centre stage in the Polish public arena and differed from the xenophobia directed against other ethnic groups: Germans, Ukrainians, Belarusians, and Lithuanians. According to those who held these views, Jews

[2] See M. Wodziński, '"Civil Christians": Debates on the Reform of the Jews in Poland, 1789–1830', in G. Safran (ed.), *Culture Front: Representing Jews in Eastern Europe* (Philadelphia, 2008), 46–76; T. R. Weeks, *From Assimilation to Anti-Semitism: The 'Jewish Question' in Poland, 1850–1914* (DeKalb, Ill., 2006); A. Cała, *Asymilacja Żydów w Królestwie Polskim (1864–1897)* (Warsaw, 1989), 173–314.

[3] R. Blobaum, 'Criminalizing the "Other": Crime, Ethnicity, and Antisemitism in Early Twentieth-Century Poland', in id. (ed.), *Antisemitism and its Opponents in Modern Poland* (Ithaca, NY, 2005), 81–102; B. Porter, *When Nationalism Began to Hate: Imagining Modern Politics in Nineteenth-Century Poland* (Oxford, 2000), 157–238; G. Krzywiec, *Szowinizm po polsku: Przypadek Romana Dmowskiego (1886–1905)* (Warsaw, 2009), 79–120, 232–69, 374–90, 410–17.

[4] S. Ury, *Barricades and Banners: The Revolution of 1905 and the Transformation of Warsaw Jewry* (Stanford, Calif., 2012); M. Silber, 'The Development of a Joint Political Program for the Jews of Poland during World War I: Success and Failure', *Jewish History*, 19/2 (2005), 211–26; id., 'Ambivalent Citizenship: The Construction of Jewish Belonging in Emergent Poland, 1915–1918', *Jahrbuch des Simon-Dubnow-Instituts*, 10 (2011), 161–83.

were a hostile element, harmful to Polish interests, no matter what their vision of the world, degree of assimilation, or social and cultural attributes.[5] Such phenomena have led Rogers Brubaker to characterize the Second Polish Republic and its institutions as aiming to exclude or to 'dis-assimilate' Jews.[6] By the 1930s Polish antisemitism manifested itself in a wave of anti-Jewish violence and calls for anti-Jewish legislation; Jews themselves, regardless of their status and convictions, felt themselves to be discriminated against and rejected in Poland. A clear majority felt that they belonged to a separate nation, so dis-assimilationist in character was national policy.

Analysis of one of the most important institutions in the 'nation-oriented state', state schooling and the ways in which it affected the first (and only) generation of Polish Jews to experience it, reveals a far more complex and interesting picture. The goal of state schooling throughout the interwar period was to integrate young Jews and to build ties to the Polish state. This chapter attempts to explain why these efforts had very different results from those intended.

JEWISH CHILDREN IN THE EDUCATION SYSTEM OF THE SECOND POLISH REPUBLIC

The creation of the Second Polish Republic caused a revolution in children's education, especially for former subjects of tsarist Russia and Austrian Galicia (where more than 90 per cent of the new state's Jewish citizens lived). The Decree on Compulsory Schooling, issued on 7 February 1919, made schooling obligatory up to the age of 14 and established a state-mandated curriculum, which for the first time was applied to all the territories that had previously been under the partitioning powers.[7] Despite the appalling economic situation and the poor state of development of the rural and eastern areas of the country, the state succeeded relatively quickly in establishing a network of schools and bringing nearly all of its youngest citizens into the system.[8] At the same time, however, universal access to primary education went hand in hand with huge disparities in opportunity and

---

[5] On different forms of antisemitism in Poland between the wars, see e.g. J. Michlic, *Poland's Threatening Other: The Image of the Jew from 1880 to the Present* (Lincoln, Neb., 2006), 69–130; S. Rudnicki, 'Anti-Jewish Legislation in Interwar Poland', in Blobaum (ed.), *Antisemitism and its Opponents*, 148–70; Y. Gutman, 'Polish Antisemitism between the Wars: An Overview', in Y. Gutman et al. (eds.), *The Jews of Poland between Two World Wars* (Hanover, NH, 1989), 97–109; A. Cała, *Żyd—wróg odwieczny? Antysemityzm w Polsce i jego źródła* (Warsaw, 2012), 325–418; R. Modras, *The Catholic Church and Antisemitism in Poland, 1933–1939* (Jerusalem, 1994).

[6] Brubaker, *Nacjonalizm inaczej*, 118.

[7] K. Trzebiatowski, *Szkolnictwo powszechne w Polsce w latach 1918–1932* (Wrocław, 1970), 68.

[8] See S. Mauersberg, 'Reformy szkolne w Drugiej Rzeczypospolitej (1918–1939)', *Kwartalnik Pedagogiczny*, 1995, no. 4, p. 26; K. Sanojca, *Obraz sąsiadów w szkolnictwie powszechnym Drugiej Rzeczypospolitej* (Wrocław, 2003), 22–4; B. Szyja, *Ludność żydowska w okresie międzywojennym: Studium statystyczne* (Wrocław, 1963), 178–81.

access to secondary and tertiary education.[9] Both the eight-form secondary school, which operated until 1932, and the four-form secondary school and two-year grammar school, introduced as a result of the so-called Jędrzejewicz reform of that year, charged fees. The average fees in 1934 in a state secondary school were between 200 and 300 zlotys (poorer pupils paid only half). Private secondary schools, including Jewish schools, were two to three times more expensive, with tuition costs ranging from 700 to 1,300 zlotys.[10] For most citizens, these sums were astronomical.[11] Furthermore, most parents needed their children to help on the farm or in the shop or depended on the income they brought in from other jobs. Although the Sanacja government did attempt through the Jędrzejewicz reform to democratize public education in some ways, secondary and grammar schools continued to be elite institutions.[12] This had enormous significance for the specific models of socialization and for developing the socio-political consciousness of the young, including young Jews, especially those from the lower merchant or artisanal classes.[13]

Primary-school education presented a different situation. While the objective consequences of many of the policies of the Second Polish Republic can be described as dis-assimilation, efforts were made, regardless of who was in power at the Ministry of Education, to ensure that as many Jewish children as possible attended state schools. The Provisional Instructions on Primary Schools in the Kingdom of Poland, issued on 29 October 1917, made provision for state schools to observe the sabbath or offer separate classes which would take into account that day's prohibitions and dictates (the school week in Poland was six days long). Beginning in 1923, in an effort to increase the number of children from traditional Jewish homes entering state schools, such students were not required to write on Saturdays.[14] At the same time, throughout most of the interwar period, the Polish state refused to give financial support to private Jewish schools, which taught in Hebrew or Yiddish, even though it had obligated itself to do so by signing the Minorities Treaty, ratified by the Sejm on 31 July 1919. In order to attract the greatest number of Jewish children to state schools, the republic set up special state schools for Jews, which respected religious tradition by not holding classes

[9] M. Falski, *Środowisko społeczne młodzieży a jej wykształcenie* (Warsaw, 1937), 11–13, 15, 23; Mauersberg, 'Reformy szkolne w Drugiej Rzeczypospolitej', 30; id., *Komu służyła szkoła w Drugiej Rzeczypospolitej? Społeczne uwarunkowania dostępu do oświaty* (Wrocław, 1988), 38–9.

[10] Mauersberg, *Komu służyła szkoła w Drugiej Rzeczypospolitej?*, 49; B. Garncarska-Kadary, *Żydowska ludność pracująca w Polsce 1918–1939* (Warsaw, 2001), 136.

[11] C. Brzoza and A. L. Sowa, *Historia Polski, 1918–1945* (Kraków, 2006), 379.

[12] For the dramatic class differences between the populations in primary and secondary schools, see Falski, *Środowisko społeczne*, 31; Mauersberg, *Komu służyła szkoła w Drugiej Rzeczypospolitej?*, 40.

[13] Peasant children, both Polish and those from the national minorities of the Kresy, were in an even worse situation.

[14] A. Landau-Czajka, *Syn będzie Lech… Asymilacja Żydów w Polsce międzywojennej* (Warsaw, 2006), 347–8.

on Saturdays. These schools were commonly known as *szabasówki*, and their curriculum allowed lay and assimilated teachers to teach Jewish religion for two hours a week, but in all other ways they followed the curriculum of the other state schools.[15] The goal of national policy was not primarily to incorporate the greatest possible number of Jewish children within the ranks of the Polish nation and to achieve complete Polonization. Rather it sought to promote patriotism, loyalty, and respect for the achievements of the Polish nation. To achieve this, Jewish private schools were also gradually compelled to introduce more subjects taught in Polish.[16] Educational policy with regard to the Jewish minority was focused not so much on inclusion as on subordinating it to the interests of the Polish state.

Despite its unprecedented expansion after 1914, secular, national, and Orthodox modern Jewish schooling in the Second Polish Republic lost out to the state education system, which a majority of Jewish pupils attended.[17] This phenomenon indicated a significant revolution. For the first time in the history of the Polish lands, the majority of Jewish children were attending secular, modern state schools. Data from the Nationalities Institute show that during the 1928/9 school year 60 per cent of Jewish school-age children attended public primary schools and this percentage grew steadily over the next few years. According to Arie Tartakower—a leading Jewish sociologist of the interwar period who was favourably disposed to the Zionist movement and the Tarbut network of Hebrew schools—during the 1934/5 school year, some 343,700 Jewish children attended state schools, representing 84 per cent of Jewish children of that age.[18] Regionally the

---

[15] In 1931 only 1,900 teachers out of 5,000 in the *szabasówki* programmes were Jewish. These schools were limited in scope. In the 1920s, of more than 200,000 Jewish pupils in state schools, 34,200 (17 per cent) went to *szabasówki* schools. After the Jędrzejewicz reform, the *szabasówki* began gradually to be phased out, and Jewish children were meant to go to 'ordinary' state schools. In 1938 there were only sixty *szabasówki* in the whole country. In Jewish schools, both religious and state, there was general agreement on the disastrous, secularizing influence of *szabasówki* schools on the children: it was felt that the students were being turned into Poles. The Jewish teachers working in them were lay and strongly acculturated, and yet even there they represented a clear minority in relation to the Christian teachers. See S. Mauersberg, *Szkolnictwo powszechne dla mniejszości narodowych w Polsce w latach 1918–1939* (Wrocław, 1968), 160–3; C. S. Heller, *On the Edge of Destruction: Jews of Poland between the Two World Wars* (New York, 1977), 221; S. Frost, *Schooling as a Socio-Political Expression: Jewish Education in Interwar Poland* (Jerusalem, 1998), 32.

[16] Frost, *Schooling as a Socio-Political Expression*, 29–30, 76–9, 126, 136–9; M. Eisenstein, *Jewish Schools in Poland, 1919–39: Their Philosophy and Development* (New York, 1950), 31–3; S. Levin, 'Observations on the State as a Factor in the History of Private Jewish Elementary Schooling in the Second Polish Republic', *Gal-ed*, 18 (2002), 65–6; K. S. Kazdan, *Di geshikhte fun yidishen shulvezen in umophengikn poyln* (Mexico City, 1947), 217; Trzebiatowski, *Szkolnictwo powszechne w Polsce*, 147.

[17] On Jewish education in the Second Polish Republic, see Frost, *Schooling as a Socio-Political Expression*; Kazdan, *Di geshikhte fun yidishen shulvezen*; Eisenstein, *Jewish Schools in Poland*; G. Bacon, *Politics of Tradition: Agudat Yisrael in Poland, 1916–1939* (Jerusalem, 1996), 147–62; id., 'National Revival, Ongoing Acculturation: Jewish Education in Interwar Poland', *Jahrbuch des Simon-Dubnow-Instituts*, 1 (2002), 71–92.

[18] Mauersberg, *Szkolnictwo powszechne dla mniejszości*, 163–4. According to other estimates, in 1935 81 per cent of Jews of school age attended Polish schools (see S. Chmielewski, 'Stan szkolnictwa wśród

percentage varied greatly: in the former Galicia it exceeded 90 per cent; in the east, on the territory of the former Russian Pale of Settlement, it did not exceed 60 per cent.[19]

Unlike in the primary sector, most Jewish secondary school pupils attended private schools. The growing trend in the 1930s to send Jewish pupils to non-state schools, accompanied by a simultaneous decrease in the percentage of such pupils in secondary schools, was caused by the application of the *numerus clausus* in state secondary and grammar schools.[20] However, even in the private sector, many institutions chose to teach exclusively or mainly in Polish, sticking closely to the national curriculum.[21]

STATE SCHOOLS: OPPORTUNITY OR COERCION?

According to Tartakower, economic factors compelled Jewish parents to send their children to state primary schools.[22] A number of modern historians have shared this view.[23] Unquestionably, economic factors were important, but another factor had some weight as well: in the smallest towns and villages the only available educational opportunity for 'country Jews', given the lack of *heder*s, was the state school.[24] In addition, various sources show that parents' motivations in sending their offspring to Polish schools were more complex. *Hinuhenu*, a paper focusing on Hebrew instruction, observed that local Tarbut schools were losing the battle with Polish schools even among parents who could afford to pay for primary education

Żydów w Polsce', *Sprawy Narodowościowe*, 9/1–2 (1937), 13; S. Rozenak, 'Al ma'arehet hahinukh hayehudi bepolin bein shetei milḥamot ha'olam', in I. Halpern (ed.), *Beit yisra'el bepolin*, 2 vols. (Jerusalem, 1948–53), ii. 153). Approximately 20 per cent of Jewish schoolchildren attended a state school in the morning and a Jewish secular school or *heder* in the afternoon.

[19] S. Chmielewski, *Stan szkolnictwa wśród Żydów w Polsce* (Warsaw, 1937), 15; S. D. Kassow, 'Communal and Social Change in the Polish Shtetl, 1900–1939', in R. Dotterer, D. Dash Moore, and S. M. Cohen, *Jewish Settlement and Community in the Modern Western World* (Selinsgrove, Pa., 1991), 87. The fact that a relatively large number of Jewish private schools operated in the poor north-eastern areas, where the numbers of their pupils were slightly higher than those of Jewish students in state schools, can be attributed to the exceptionally strong secular and modernized Jewish religious instruction in those areas, dating back to the times of tsarist Russia. The region also saw the lowest levels of Polonization.

[20] Whereas in 1921/2 there were 48,849 Jewish pupils in secondary schools (24 per cent of pupils in secondary schools), by 1936/7 there were only 33,320 (16 per cent). That same year as many as 73 per cent of all Jewish secondary and grammar-school pupils attended private schools (Heller, *On the Edge of Destruction*, 229).

[21] Frost, *Schooling as a Socio-Political Expression*, 49–50; C. Schmeruk, 'Hebrew–Yiddish–Polish: A Trilingual Jewish Culture', in Gutman et al. (eds), *The Jews of Poland*, 294–5; Mauersberg, *Szkolnictwo powszechne dla mniejszości*, 164–5.

[22] See J. Zineman (ed.), *Almanach Szkolnictwa Żydowskiego w Polsce*, Trzeci Zeszyt Okazowy (Warsaw, 1936), 7–8.   [23] See e.g. Kassow, *Communal and Social Change in the Polish Shtetl*, 88 n. 23.

[24] See e.g. M. Adamczyk-Garbowska, A. Kopciowski, and A. Trzciński (eds.), *Tam był kiedyś mój dom… Księgi pamięci gmin żydowskich* (Lublin, 2009), 141.

and who had access to such schools. This was attributed to the 'snob value' associated with their children having a good knowledge of the Polish language and culture which outweighed their fear of their children's 'assimilation'.[25] Teachers at the Tarbut secondary school in Kołomyja shared this view.[26] Zalmen Reyzen, a leading Yiddish linguist and activist for the Vilna Central Education Committee (Tsentraler bildungs komitet; TsBK) affiliated with the Central Yiddish School Organization (Tsentrale Yidishe Shul Organizatsye; TSYSHO), regarded the state schools' popularity with Jewish parents as the greatest long-term threat to 'the future of the Jewish nation in Poland'.[27] This view was also shared by Zionists. Natan Bystrycki, who visited Poland at the end of the 1920s as a representative of the Jewish National Fund, described growing Polonization and feared the resulting inevitable 'intensifying assimilation' of the Jews in Poland.[28]

There were clearly a number of reasons for the growth of support for state schools, as well as for private schools (Jewish and non-Jewish) whose language of instruction was Polish. They included demography (above all, the post-war rise in the birth rate), economics (in particular, the impoverishment of most Jewish social classes as a result of the Great Depression, which made it harder to send children to relatively expensive private schools), and state policy that clearly aimed to weaken the Jewish private education sector. All private Jewish schools charged tuition fees, and most parents could not afford to send their children to these institutions. In addition, these schools suffered chronic financial problems and were unable to operate in many small towns. The private Jewish schools that did exist fiercely competed with one another, often accusing their rivals of betraying Jewish interests and values. The Tarbut and TSYSHO school networks were secular in character and many religious leaders believed that their impact was even more negative than the acculturation attempts of non-Jewish teachers in the state system. For all these reasons, to the horror of national politicians and educators, a great many traditionalist parents preferred to send their children to state establishments.[29] The Jewish *Kulturkampf*, the internal cultural rivalry of various Jewish socio-political streams, made the task of Polish schools seeking to attract Jewish children easier, but this is not the whole explanation. Pragmatic considerations were also often an important factor in parents choosing to send their children to Polish schools. A good knowledge of the national language was considered crucial for employment and made it possible to be active in public life. What was needed was not merely a limited technical fluency in the language but the ability to use it reasonably

[25] *Hinuhenu*, special edition (Jan. 1932), 3.

[26] Tarbut, *Wychowanie dziecka żydowskiego dawniej a dziś / Di Ercijung fonim jidiszen Kind amal un hajnt* (Kołomyja, n.d.), 10.

[27] Z. Reyzen, 'Der kamf far der yidisher shul iz der kamf far undzere recht', in S. Bastomski (ed.), *Far undzer shul* (Vilna, 1933), 14.

[28] N. Bystrycki, *Erets yisra'el behinukh hayehudi bepolin* (Jerusalem, 1929), 4–6.

[29] Heller, *On the Edge of Destruction*, 222–3, Adamczyk-Garbowska, Kopciowski, and Trzciński (eds.), *Tam był kiedyś mój dom*, 145; Frost, *Schooling as a Socio-Political Expression*, 42.

correctly on a daily basis. A growing number of Jewish parents, not only those from the acculturated, big-city elite, recognized that a child's chances of success in life were improved not only by a secular education but also by having deeply inter-nalized the Polish cultural code. This was even more important for those families who wished to send their children to secondary schools. For the most part, only those schools in which the language of instruction was Polish and which followed the national curriculum received full state accreditation, and their school-leaving certificates were recognized for admission to Polish universities. National Jewish schools were usually denied the right to issue these state certificates, and their graduates, with few exceptions, had to pass additional qualifying examinations if they were to continue their education in Poland. As a result, Jewish parents, regardless of their political and cultural views, usually chose Polish teaching estab-lishments for their children's secondary education.[30]

The best sources for examining why children from very different Jewish back-grounds attended state schools are the autobiographies of the generation that was socialized in the Second Polish Republic, collected in the three competitions run by the Vilna YIVO in 1932, 1934, and 1939.[31] These autobiographies were written by young people born between 1910 and 1922 and who attended school in the 1920s and 1930s.[32] Representative of the majority of Jewish primary-school pupils, most of the YIVO entrants came from traditionalist, neither strongly Orthodox nor secular, homes. As they were growing up, a decided majority of them joined or sup-ported one of the secular Jewish political parties and, less frequently, the Orthodox Agudah or Mizrachi. In line with the ideologies of their movements and that of YIVO, most wrote their autobiographies in Yiddish. Even the minority who wrote in Polish had a hostile attitude to assimilation and acculturation (despite the fact that they themselves were subject to certain processes of acculturation). The parti-cipants in the YIVO competition, like the organization sponsoring the competition,

---

[30] Heller, *On the Edge of Destruction*, 231.

[31] YIVO Archives, New York, RG 4: 'Autobiographies of Jewish Youth in Poland (1932–1939)'; see also *Awakening Lives: Autobiographies of Jewish Youth in Poland before the Holocaust*, ed. J. Shandler (New Haven, Conn., 2002); *Ostatnie pokolenie: Autobiografie polskiej młodzieży żydowskiej okresu międzywojennego*, ed. A. Cała (Warsaw, 2003); *Alilot ne'urim: otobiyografyot shel benei no'ar yehudim mipolin bein shetei milḥamot olam*, ed. I. Bassok (Jerusalem, 2011).

[32] For the YIVO competitions and young Jews' autobiographies, see, inter alia, I. Bassok, 'Lishe'elat erkhan hahistori shel otobiografiyot benei no'ar me'osaf yivo', *Madei yahadut*, 44 (2007), 137–64; id., 'Ma'amadot utefisah ma'amadit etsel yeladim uvenei no'ar yehudi bepolin bein hamilḥamot', *Gal-ed*, 18 (2002), 225–44; id., 'Ne'urim ve'erkhei ne'urim bitenu'ot hano'ar bepolin shebein shetei milḥamot', in I. Bartal and Y. Gutman (eds), *Kiyum veshever*, ii: *Yehudei polin ledoroteihem* (Jerusalem, 2001), 573–604; K. Kijek, 'Max Weinreich, Assimilation and the Social Politics of Jewish Nation-Building', *East European Jewish Affairs*, 41/1–2 (2011), 25–55; M. Kligsberg, 'Di yidishe yugent bavegung in poyln tsvishn bayde velt milchomes', in J. Fishman (ed.), *Studies on Polish Jewry, 1919–1939: The Interplay of Social, Economic and Political Factors in the Struggle of a Minority for its Existence* (New York, 1974), 137–228; B. Kirshenblatt-Gimblett, 'Coming of Age in the Thirties: Max Weinreich, Edward Sapir, and Jewish Social Science', *YIVO Annual of Jewish Social Science*, 23 (1996), 1–103.

were not well disposed to the state primary schools and showed a preference for national or Orthodox (but not traditional) educational institutions. Despite this, the majority of participants in the competitions had attended such schools, and their autobiographies, whatever their authors' intentions, reveal the schools' enormous influence on their socialization and consciousness.

The growing popularity of the Polish language as a key element in educational choice is apparent in the YIVO autobiographies even in those circles least inclined to send their children to non-Jewish schools. Beniamin R. had received an elite traditional education and, despite his political views (he was a left-wing Zionist), supported himself from his salary as a private teacher of Jewish religion. He was appointed over older teachers because of his command of spoken and written Polish. Although he was a graduate of a Hebrew secondary school, he had also been sent for a short time by his religious father to a state school. Traditionalist parents valued such qualifications in teachers of religion for their children.[33] However, Beniamin R. grew up in the Lithuanian Jewish community, which was the least influenced by Polish culture. Many religious Jews placed stress on their children achieving competence in Polish, even though the older generation probably had no personal command of the language. An extreme example comes from the auto-biography of Yecheskiel Twerski, who grew up in Bełz, one of the most conservative hasidic communities that closed itself off from non-Jewish influences. He revolted against his mother's prohibition on learning Polish, claiming that her stubbornness meant that no rabbi would marry their daughter to his elder brother, despite the family's very high *yikhes* (traditional status), because his elder brother lacked knowledge of Polish. Yecheskiel Twerski taught himself Polish, without his mother knowing. He stressed in his autobiography that such knowledge was widespread in Orthodox circles and even among some Bełz hasidim.[34]

Beniamin R. and Yecheskiel Twerski came from the religious and financial elite who could afford to have their children taught Polish at home by private tutors.[35] The equally devout parents of Jafet, raised among hasidim in central Poland, whose financial situation was similar to that of the majority of Jewish families in the Polish Second Republic, did not have this option. Following tradition, the boy studied in a *ḥeder* from the age of 3. As he approached the age of 7 his parents were faced with a serious dilemma:

Now that it was time for me to enter primary school, a quarrel broke out between my mother and father. My father claimed that primary school was the path to abandoning the

[33] YIVO Archives, RG 4: Autobiography 3542, 2.
[34] YIVO Archives, RG 4: Autobiography 3668, 20–1, 46–50.
[35] On the education of Orthodox and wealthier families, which differed markedly from that of poor, traditionalist families, see K. Kijek, 'Światopogląd i aspiracje życiowe ortodoksyjnej młodzieży żydowskiej w Polsce międzywojennej', in T. Stegner (ed.), *Religia a społeczeństwo II Rzeczypospolitej*, Metamorfozy społeczne, 5 (Warsaw, 2013), 291–331; YIVO Archives, RG 4: Autobiography 3548, 11–12, 16; Autobiography 3713, in *Awakening Lives*, 306–7.

Jewish faith. In a dramatic voice he asked my mother: 'This child could become a rabbi, and you want him to convert?' My mother replied that even if he wanted to become a rabbi, he still needed to know Polish . . . If she had the money, she would hire a private tutor, but since that was out of the question, the boy ought to go to school.[36]

Jafet's autobiography illustrates a problem faced by most Jewish families in the Second Polish Republic. Even his father, a *shames* (assistant) in a synagogue of the Ger hasidim, was not opposed to his son learning a non-Jewish language, as it would allow him to operate in the wider world and was even essential for a rabbinic career. What he feared was not so much the acquisition of Polish as the fatal influence of a non-Jewish school. He worried that after spending time among non-Jews (including sitting in a classroom with girls) and being taught by people for whom the traditional Jewish world was quite alien, his son would feel increasingly estranged from Jewish society. In Jafet's case (as subsequent events in his life showed), and for many other writers of YIVO autobiographies, such fears were not groundless.

What distinguished the majority of Jewish children from Jafet is the fact that most parents could not dream of rabbinic careers for their sons. Children of traditional craftsmen, minor merchants, or *luftmenschen* (those with no definite occupation) were destined to learn a trade, assist in the family business, or master a craft. The basics of a secular education were key to these plans.[37] Primary school education could provide useful intellectual, cultural, and social tools for children from poor families. Boys were usually sent there after a few years of study at a *ḥeder*. For girls from this background, primary schools were the only educational institutions (excluding later informal instruction in political organizations and their youth branches) which they would ever attend. Apart from mathematics, the most important elements of secular education for future craftsmen, workmen, merchants, and service-sector workers were Polish and a basic knowledge of the country's cultural code, which prepared them to function in the reality of the Second Polish Republic. Only a minority of poor, traditionalist parents who were not planning a talmudic career for their children opposed their children attending a state primary school. As the autobiographies show, even they were frequently forced to send their children to such schools.[38] One paradox of the situation was that far less

---

[36] YIVO Archives, RG 4: Autobiography 3782, in *Ostatnie pokolenie*, 188.

[37] Parents in poor, traditionalist homes feared, of course, that school might secularize their children, leading them to break the laws of halakhah. This problem was less acute in primary school than in secondary school. The latter had no obligation to excuse Jewish children from writing on Saturdays, and teenage peer groups plus students' natural tendency to rebel led much more frequently to non-religious behaviour. Religious parents were more afraid of these schools and were more likely to express their opposition to sending their children there. See e.g. YIVO Archives, RG 4: Autobiography 3732, 10; Autobiography 3770, 13; Autobiography 3764, in *Ostatnie pokolenie*, 400; Autobiography 3801, in *Ostatnie pokolenie*, 152; Autobiography 3819, 2, 13; Autobiography 3816, in *Ostatnie pokolenie*, 382.

[38] See e.g. YIVO Archives, RG 4: Autobiography 3504, 2; Autobiography 3510, 8; Autobiography 3514, in *Awakening Lives*, 392; Autobiography 3645, 19; Autobiography 3701, 4–5; Autobiography 3861, 16–21.

religious or even non-religious parents who spoke Polish on a daily basis, had Zionist convictions, and came from wealthier circles, often had the means to send their children to Tarbut schools. In the same way, workers or craftsmen with socialist or left-wing views or supporters of the Bund and the Po'alei Zion Left or Right were sometimes able to send their sons and daughters to TSYSHO schools or the Shul-Kult schools sponsored by Po'alei Zion Right. Among the Orthodox, only the wealthy could afford a religious education from the age of 3 in a *ḥeder* and finishing in an adult yeshiva. Poor, traditionalist parents, especially in small towns, had no choice but to send their children to a state school, a place that represented a quite foreign world of values and educational content.

THE GATES OF MODERNITY

A majority of youngsters who wrote autobiographies for the YIVO competition belonged to Jewish youth groups opposed to assimilation and one of its strongest elements, the instruction of Jewish children in state schools. However, the strongest connection between young Jews (apart from the Orthodox) and their political leaders was forged by attacks on Jewish tradition, on 'outmoded' customs in the shtetl or the Jewish districts of great cities, or on the traditional norms of social and economic life and the values which upheld them. In the autobiographies, the most important symbol of the world that young people rejected was the traditional *ḥeder*.[39] As Michael Steinlauf noted, 'school, whether Jewish or Polish, was loved. Anything but the heder.'[40] For those young people who were unable to attend Jewish schools, the positive antithesis of the much-maligned *ḥeder* was a state school. For most it was the first place that brought them into contact with the 'modern', non-Jewish world, granting them the childhood of which poverty and tradition had deprived them. School was meant to give them an opportunity to gain greatly desired secular knowledge and to earn cultural and intellectual capital which would make social advancement and a different life possible. School was the first institution of the 'great outside' world that young Jews wanted to enter.

The uniqueness of school in the life of a Jewish child was symbolized by its actual physical reality. An inhabitant of Włodzimierz Wołyński, G.W., an activist in the Bund's youth movement, Tsukunft, who wrote his autobiography in Yiddish, recalled his delight at seeing the state elementary school's building, so very different from the one that had housed his *ḥeder*.[41] Another writer, also a supporter of the Bund, had her first experience of the 'outside world' in a state pre-school:

---

[39] See K. Kijek, 'Świadomość i socjalizacja polityczna ostatniego pokolenia Żydów Polskich w II Rzeczypospolitej', Ph.D. thesis (Institute of History, Polish Academy of Sciences, 2014), 112–20.

[40] M. C. Steinlauf, 'Jewish Politics and Youth Culture in Interwar Poland', in Z. Y. Gitelman (ed.), *The Emergence of Modern Jewish Politics: Bundism and Zionism in Eastern Europe* (Pittsburgh, Pa., 2003), 98.   [41] YIVO Archives, RG 4: Autobiography 3713, in *Awakening Lives*, 309.

The building was magnificent . . . it had red shining floors. . . . Every day we had a great number of extracurricular activities . . . we sang, we jumped, we played all kinds of games we made up. In the pre-school there were also great big beautiful dolls, puppets, boxes of building bricks. . . . We spoke Polish.[42]

The material reality of the school and pre-school seemed to be a function of their modernity. Compared to the small rooms of the *ḥeders*, the spacious sun-lit classrooms, clean corridors, large brick buildings, school gyms, and desks all made a huge impression on young people. Mendel Man,[43] who wrote a great deal about the 'satanic' antisemitism of the state schools, still described their enormous value in terms of the opportunity to gain a secular education. Learning there was something diametrically different from the monotonous 'repeating after the rabbi words read from a tattered *sidur*'.[44] Em Tepa, a Bund sympathizer, wrote in a similar vein about school, contrasting it with the 'dirty' and 'unfair' *ḥeder*:

Even the way I was prepared for my first day of state school was different and had nothing in common with *ḥeder*. . . . When I saw how clean the state school was, I became disgusted with the filthy, smoky room of the *ḥeder*. The state school teacher's dignified appearance . . . made me despise the other 'teacher' in his dirty, long, black coat, who always had a cap on his head and particles of food in his unruly, black beard . . . Only after I found myself in a classroom where, for the first time, I sat on a nice, smooth bench, did I experience a wave of revulsion and contempt for the *ḥeder*, with its long tables and grimy benches.[45]

Em Tepa's comments touch on key themes that appear in most of the traditionalist autobiography writers, who, between the ages of 6 and 8, had started attending primary school. His words highlight the powerful and, significantly, first truly institutional factor in the secularization of his generation, in the weakening of traditional social control, and in the process of estranging children from their parents' values. The state school provided this generation with new norms and values, new categories and points of reference in perceiving the world, and contested the educational content dispensed in their own homes. The tragedy for most traditionalist parents lay in the fact that they were paying an enormous price for handing over their children to the schools in order to increase their chances in life.

Of course, what Jewish children were looking for in non-Jewish schools was not assimilation, understood as abandoning their own Jewishness. In rejecting 'tradition', young people were simply looking for 'modernity': knowledge and education, which at that stage in their lives generally could be provided only by the state schools. In offering knowledge of Polish language and culture, the schools were now reaching just about every Jewish community. A writer using the pseudonym

[42] YIVO Archives, RG 4: Autobiography 3720, 1.

[43] Mendel Man was one of a few participants in the YIVO competition who survived the Second World War. In 1948 he emigrated from Łódź to Palestine, where he dabbled in painting and writing, was an important advocate on behalf of the development of Yiddish culture in Israel, and contributed to the well-known Yiddish publication *Di goldene kayt*. In 1961 he emigrated to Paris and died in France in 1975.   [44] YIVO Archives, RG 4: Autobiography 3802, 18–19.

[45] YIVO Archives, RG 4: Autobiography 3792, in *Awakening Lives*, 276–7.

Pionier furnished an example of this process. He had been brought up in a traditional religious home, had joined the Haluts organization, and was a committed Zionist who dreamed of emigrating to Palestine. He came from a small town near Łuck in Volhynia, from a community which did not, on the whole, speak Polish. In the 1930s, even there, however, the longed-for door to modernity was a state school, followed by a trade school.[46] Pionier had to interrupt his schooling early on to go to work, since his father became seriously ill. Despite having completed only three classes of primary school, he knew Polish. Thanks to this, he hoped to obtain a state qualification as a locksmith and be able to leave for Palestine. He enrolled in a state 'professional trade school'. For him, along with the Haluts organization, this institution provided a semblance of a different, better life.[47] Another writer, A. W. Sztoimeszan, came from a poor, traditionalist family and wrote that thanks to primary school (which he had to leave after a few years to work) he was 'not illiterate, like [his] parents'. In his view, illiteracy meant having no spoken or written command of Polish, understood as the language of 'normal' secular life, the country, and the modern world.[48] Mendel Man's mother, who used Yiddish on a daily basis, shared this attitude and sent her son, who had already attended a *ḥeder*, to a state school, saying that she 'would not have him be an illiterate; he must learn Polish'.[49] Gitman G., the son of a poor, traditionalist family from Bełżyce near Lublin, reacted to the news that he was going to be transferred from a *ḥeder*, which he had been attending since the age of 4, to a state school in the following manner: 'School, I said to myself, is the fount of knowledge. . . . I shall become a pupil and will then start to learn everything which I have been asking about and receive answers to those questions which until now no one has been able to give.'[50]

There was a characteristic way in which writers from very different social circles created their narratives on school (and on *ḥeder*s and the world of tradition). Despite the fact that their views were defined by adherence to conflicting political ideologies, almost all shared radical, modernist views. Without a doubt, these young people derived their general social philosophy from the ideologies of the political organizations to which they belonged, which promoted the need for a battle for a 'new world', whether 'here' in Poland and Europe, or 'there' in Palestine.[51] The germs of this 'new world' they found in the political movements and

[46] YIVO Archives, RG 4: Autobiography 3501, 7–8.

[47] Ibid. 19–22.   [48] YIVO Archives, RG 4: Autobiography 3663, 9–11.

[49] YIVO Archives, RG 4: Autobiography 3802, 17.

[50] YIVO Archives, RG 4: Autobiography 3519, 9.

[51] That the writers rarely had internally coherent ideas is unimportant, given their youth, lack of political knowledge, and low educational level. For the 'radical modernism' which marked the socio-political consciousness of young Jews and the eclectic manner in which they drew on competing political ideologies, see K. Kijek, 'Haradikalizm hapoliti shel hano'ar hayehudi beshtetl polani bein milḥamot ha'olam', *Yalkut moreshet*, 92–3 (Apr. 2013), 20–59; Pol. orig.: 'Radykalizm polityczny sztetlowej młodzieży okresu międzywojennego', in A. Sitarek, M. Trębacz, and E. Wiatr (eds.), *Zagłada Żydów na polskiej prowincji* (Łódź, 2012), 55–98).

youth organizations which they joined in their teens. Most of them, especially those from traditionalist homes, were linked by a Manichean vision of a 'dark and dirty' world, which they were trying to escape and which defined their present situation (at home and in their hard jobs after school) and which they contrasted with the 'bright and clean' world they were trying to create.[52] The first institution in these young people's lives to represent this second world was school, more often than not a state school. In accordance with young people's modernistic imaginations, the school represented the 'modern' and 'clean' world which was to supplant the world of tradition.

As the autobiographies show, state schools, secular Jewish political parties and organizations, and the educational institutions connected with them intensified generational conflict in traditional Jewish families, estranging children from their parents' world. But there was another very important connection between state schools and the state's Jewish policy. One of the Second Polish Republic's educational goals for ethnic minorities was to defuse political radicalism and anti-state attitudes among the young. In the case of young Jews, the goal was to reduce the influence of the Jewish nationalist parties, whose activities both domestically and abroad were interpreted as inimical to Polish interests. No less important was the obsession with *żydokomuna*, the Jews' supposed predilection for revolutionary activities directed against everything that was truly Polish and Christian, which had taken firm root in general discourse and among many members of the Second Polish Republic's elite.[53] In promoting Polish patriotism among young Jews, the schools sought to defuse their radicalism. However, while estranging young people from their parents' world and placing them in a position of being both unable and unwilling to return to it, school and the Second Polish Republic's socio-political environment offered them no alternative. Young people from poor, traditionalist homes were unable to continue their education. Even if, with enormous effort, they somehow managed to obtain further schooling, they encountered constant discrimination and lack of opportunity in the employment market. The resultant disillusionment and anger fed political radicalism. The seeds of such revolt were found not just in the reality beyond school but also in the state school itself.

LOVING POLAND WHILE NOT BEING A POLE

It might appear that the state education system had enormous success in its dealings with the Jewish community. Upon leaving state or private schools, Jewish children not only knew the Polish language and culture but were also distinguished

[52] See A. Selzer, '"Vos vayter?" Graduating from Elementary School in Interwar Poland: From Personal Crisis to Cultural Turning Point' (this volume).

[53] See M. Zaremba, *Wielka Trwoga: Polska 1944–1947. Ludowa reakcja na kryzys* (Kraków, 2012), ch. 1; J. Michlic, '*Żydokomuna*: Anti-Jewish Images and Political Tropes in Modern Poland', *Jahrbuch des Simon-Dubnow-Instituts*, 4 (2005), 304–9.

by a respect and often a love for its symbols.[54] A committed Zionist writer from Ostróg wrote that her favourite subject in primary school had been history. Above all, she recalled national holidays, to which the teachers had attached enormous importance. When she had been asked to deliver a speech in honour of Marshal Józef Piłsudski on one of them,[55] she had been filled with enormous pride.[56] The testimony of another girl, writing from Bereza Kartuska, noted that Jewish pupils in Polish, as well as at TSYSHO, schools had grown up with the same adulation of Piłsudski.[57] The autobiography of Esther, a teacher at the Bais Yaakov Orthodox school for girls, further confirms the strength of the Polish schools' attempts to transmit patriotism. Though her school promoted Yiddish and opposed assimilation, Esther still described patriotic feelings about the years she had spent as a pupil in a state *szabasówka*:

I kept a diary in Polish. I was becoming more and more immersed in the Polish language. I especially loved Polish literature. I idolized the Polish Romantic poets Mickiewicz and Słowacki. Polish history was also a subject I loved and learned easily. I was enthralled by everything connected to Polish history. I was consumed by the martyrdom of Polish heroes in their struggle for Poland's independence. I venerated Marshal Józef Piłsudski.[58]

Another writer, who at the time of the competition was a supporter of the Bund, wrote about his attendance for a few years at a Zionist Tarbut school: 'I was reading more and more, simply "devouring" books and I was living with my story-tale heroes. I felt closest to the heroes of Sienkiewicz's *Trilogy*.'[59]

Young Jews from various backgrounds showed attachment to the state, pride in some of its achievements, and reverence for a specific interpretation of the history of the Polish nation, which after years of foreign rule had finally regained its own country. It might appear, then, that the Second Polish Republic's educational policy had achieved enormous success in integrating the youngest Jewish generation and turning them into loyal and faithful citizens. However, that was not what had happened. The young people quoted above, like the decided majority of participants in the YIVO competitions, despite their knowledge of Polish culture, their attachment to Polish national symbols, and the dominant historical narrative which was the basis of the ideology of the new state, did not feel at ease in Poland.

[54] The YIVO autobiographies prove that Polish language and culture, as well as the most important symbols and interpretations of Polish national history, were also transmitted and internalized by young people in Jewish schools (see e.g. YIVO Archives, RG 4: Autobiography 3516, 26–7; Autobiography 3542, 25, 46–7; Autobiography 3568, 30, 44–8; Autobiography 3598, in *Ostatnie pokolenie*, 88, 98; Autobiography 3707, in *Awakening Lives*, 233).

[55] On the cult of Józef Piłsudski in Polish schools in the 1930s, see A. Landau-Czajka, *Co Alicja odkrywa po własnej stronie lustra: Życie codzienne, społeczeństwo, władza w podręcznikach dla dzieci najmłodszych 1785–2000* (Warsaw, 2002), 366–73.

[56] YIVO Archives, RG 4: Autobiography 3516, 16–17.

[57] YIVO Archives, RG 4: Autobiography 3823, 4.

[58] YIVO Archives, RG 4: Autobiography 3559, in *Awakening Lives*, 326.

[59] YIVO Archives, RG 4: Autobiography 3504, 5.

There was an ambivalence in their patriotism, which was accompanied by feelings of anger, bitterness, and disappointment with the state and the position it allotted Jews. The last generation of young Jews in Poland before the Holocaust, instead of rejecting political radicalism, supplied it with the largest percentage of its representatives. Paradoxically, one of the most significant reasons for this was the nature of the curricular content, the specific structure of the historical narrative and of Polish patriotism which Polish schools were transmitting to their Jewish pupils.

A NATION OF CITIZENS OR AN ETHNIC NATION?
POLISH SCHOOLS' SYMBOLIC VIOLENCE AND
AMBIGUOUS EDUCATIONAL MESSAGES

In the interwar years, the goal of Polish schools was to produce patriotic members of the newly independent country.[60] The state school, throughout the period, promoted Polish as the sole national culture, considering it to be superior to the languages, literatures, customs, and traditions of minorities. As Włodzimierz Mędrzecki notes, the state was 'widely defined as a nation state, whose sole sovereign power and host was the Polish nation'.[61] An important element of educational policy was to instil in pupils from minorities the conviction of the superiority of Polish culture. The schools reinforced the Second Polish Republic's social and ethnic hierarchy, stressing the inferiority of the other nationalities in the state to the dominant Polish nation. The acculturation of young Jews in the sphere of language and imagination and their undoubted patriotism was not accompanied by their integration or their full identification with the state. Jewish students were not given the opportunity to acknowledge the state as fully 'their own'.

The concept of the Polish nation which dominated the public domain of the Second Polish Republic and which was transmitted in the state schools was to blame for this state of affairs. Throughout the interwar period, the notion of detaching state patriotism from an ethnically and religiously defined concept of the Polish nation was considered undesirable and impossible to achieve. This was the situation during the period of parliamentary governments (1918–26), during the relatively mild authoritarianism until the death of Piłsudski (1926–35), and even during the final four years of the Second Polish Republic, when the political system was drifting towards authoritarianism.[62] The subtext of state solidarity promoted by

---

[60] J. Żarnowski, 'Społeczeństwo polskie wobec szkoły w XX wieku', *Kwartalnik Pedagogiczny*, 1995, no. 4, p. 7; Landau-Czajka, *Co Alicja odkrywa po własnej stronie lustra*, 247–8; Mauersberg, *Komu służyła szkoła w Drugiej Rzeczypospolitej?*, 6–7.

[61] W. Mędrzecki, 'Polskie uniwersum symboliczne w Drugiej Rzeczypospolitej', in W. Mędrzecki and A. Zawiszewska (eds.), *Kultura i społeczeństwo w II Rzeczypospolitej*, Metamorfozy Społeczne, 4 (Warsaw, 2012), 30.

[62] Some scholars take a different view, pointing out that in the years 1926 to 1935, during the first phase of the Sanacja government, attempts were made to support a policy of 'state patriotism', which

the Sanacja, which stated officially that the Second Polish Republic was the homeland of all its citizens, was national solidarity. As a result, educational policy did not promote a national unity that transcended ethnic boundaries—a concept which would have meant that Jews, Ukrainians, Belarusians, and Germans could feel themselves equal to Catholic Poles as members of the state. Patriotism for minorities was to be created using the symbolic resources of Polish ethnic nationalism, an impossible task. Representatives of the ethnic minorities were almost never mentioned in school textbooks. If they did appear, and if their appearance had a positive character (as in the case of Berek Joselewicz), they were extolled only in the context of their subordination to the Polish ethnic group, participating alongside it in its battles and its history.[63] In practice, 'state education' (the inculcation of the ideology of the state) was based exclusively on Polish culture. Even during the period of the Sanacja's educational reforms, the schools had to conduct their integrationist activities by focusing on Polish national symbols. In Sanacja educational practice, the Polish nation continued to be a unified community of ethnic Poles: it was hierarchical, controlled by elites and reflected the 'national interest' as defined by them.[64] The ethnocentric and religious character of national symbols made it impossible for young Jews to envisage themselves as part of this Polish community. Many Jewish pupils in primary school had educational experiences similar to that of Leopold Infeld:

At the time I identified with the Polish nobility so strongly that I imagined that my forebears, clad in heavy armour, had fought the Teutonic Knights. The class's smiles reminded me that my ancestors had probably been studying the Talmud or had been lending the same

---

also included and integrated ethnic minorities. Sanacja educational reforms were meant to increase and build attachment to the most important institutions of state, to reduce the education system's Polonocentrism, and to strengthen ethnically non-Polish citizens' identification with the state (see, inter alia, D. Wojtas, 'Learning to Become Polish: Education, National Identity and Citizenship in Interwar Poland, 1918–1939', Ph.D. thesis (Brandeis University, 2003), 43; J. Sadowska, 'Stosunek Zrębu do reformy oświaty w latach 1931–1932', *Kwartalnik Pedagogiczny*, 1995, no. 4, pp. 216–17; Mauersberg, 'Reformy szkolne w Drugiej Rzeczypospolitej', 31–3; Trzebiatowski, *Szkolnictwo powszechne w Polsce*, 287). However, assessments of this kind tend to rely on politicians' aims and statements rather than on analysis of the effects of Sanacja's education policy and its real influence on minorities. In the case of young Jews, their experience of school between 1918 and 1926 differed little from those coming later.

[63] A. Landau-Czajka, 'Obraz mniejszości narodowych w podręcznikach szkolnych okresu międzywojennego', *Biuletyn Żydowskiego Instytutu Historycznego*, 183–4 (1997), 3–7; J. Sadowska, 'Ustawodawstwo jędrzejewiczowskie wobec szkolnictwa mniejszości narodowych w II Rzeczypospolitej', in A. Bilewicz, R. Gładkiewicz, and S. Walasek (eds.), *Edukacja – państwo – naród w Europie Środkowo-Wschodniej XIX i XX w.* (Wrocław, 2002), 301. In the *Szkolna Gazetka Ścienna*, published by the Ministry of Religious Denominations and Public Enlightenment, for the 1933/4 school year, which all state schools were obliged to hang on their walls, ethnic minorities were all but invisible. If they did appear, it was when their representatives were paying homage to the most important institutions of state, usually the army or Piłsudski (see e.g. *Szkolna Gazetka Ścienna*, 15 Jan. 1933).

[64] Trzebiatowski, *Szkolnictwo powszechne w Polsce*, 287–91.

nobles money. . . . That smile was a lesson for me, making it clear to me that I had no right to identify my family with the family of a Polish nobleman.[65]

The overwhelming majority of Jewish pupils in state primary schools came from communities with deep roots in Jewish tradition, language, and culture. It was much harder for them to imagine themselves as descendants of the knights at the Battle of Grunwald than it had been for Infeld, who came from an assimilated family. A splendid example of educational content, which was bound to seem foreign to young Jews, is a fragment of the poem 'My Golden-Haired Little Boy' by Maria Ilnicka, which was placed at the beginning of the first volume of *Legends, Tales, and Stories from History* by the popular writer of school reading books, Cecylia Niewiadomska:

> My golden-haired little boy
> I know you really love the songs
> I sometimes hum to you
> .   .   .   .   .   .
>
> But there are other songs too,
> At whose sound an innocent heart
> Feels an unknown emotion:
> About times gone by and men of yore,
> Kings, hetmans, famous knights,
> Who 'neath tombstones slumber.
> They are your grandfathers and your fathers!
> They have taken their winged armour to their graves.
> .   .   .   .   .   .
>
> So listen, little son, to what I sing
> When I cuddle you to my breast
> Under the picture of Our Lady;
> She is the Queen of those who lie sleeping in their tombs.
> She will bless you and me,
> When we sigh to her together.[66]

This kind of message had a clearly exclusionary character. It did not allow young Jews to feel part of the Polish 'imagined community'.[67] The tradition was addi-

---

[65] L. Infeld, *Kordian, fizyka i ja. Wspomnienia* (Warsaw, 1968), 153, cited in Landau-Czajka, *Syn będzie Lech*, 144.

[66] M. Ilnicka, 'Mój złotowłosy synku maleńki', in C. Niewiadomska, *Legendy, podania i obrazki historyczne*, i: *Czasy przedchrześcijańskie* (Warsaw, 1918), 4. This textbook was first published in 1918 and saw many reprints. See also an interesting extract from a later volume: C. Niewiadomska, *Legendy, podania i obrazki historyczne*, xix: *Resurrecturis* (Warsaw, n.d.), 6. Especially before 1932 the textbooks were characterized by a great range of views. They differed, amongst other things, in terms of Catholic symbolism and their treatment of the problems of social divisions and issues of gender. However, none promoted the concept of a national community of citizens beyond or outside the ethnic community of the Polish nation.

[67] See B. Anderson, *Imagined Communities: Reflections on the Origin and Spread of Nationalism* (London, 1983).

tionally reinforced by the specific treatment of 'Jewish subjects' in the curriculum. In religious instruction textbooks for the higher classes in primary schools, Jews were unambiguously presented negatively, often as 'Christ killers'.[68] In geography or social studies, Jews were portrayed as 'separate, hated, and parasitical creatures', 'cut off [from the Polish nation] by virtue of their religion, their fanatical superstitions'.[69] This message was in line with views about the negative economic role of Jews that were widespread in the Second Polish Republic. Sanacja textbooks, which were milder on this subject, would at times call for the emigration from Poland of at least some Jews.[70] One seeks in vain in the textbooks for images of Jews as schoolmates or holding important civic positions as engineers, doctors, or politicians. Things were different in Polish lessons, where the romantic and positivist literary tradition sometimes presented the Jew as a patriot. These texts, nonetheless, stressed the need to 'enlighten' the benighted Jewish people. Enlightenment was usually seen as synonymous with assimilation and with the conviction that Jews as a group were inferior in civilizational terms. The only way for Jews to change their situation and status was for them to abandon their traditional ethnic and religious identity in favour of Polish identity.[71] Educational material based on the principle of an ethnically Polish and religiously Catholic national community did not reduce the strong traditional distance between Jews and Poles: Jews still appeared as 'foreign'. At best this could mean that Jews were seen as operating at the margins, as people whose existence in the country was not fully legitimate. Young Jews entered school with a strong sense of their own ethnic identity and with a deeply internalized mistrust and often clear dislike of non-Jews.[72] All these factors explain why Jewish pupils, conscious of their separate ethnicity and often defining themselves according to the criteria of modern Jewish nationalism, had little chance of feeling part of the Polish community.

Young Jews with positive feelings for Poland and the Polish national mythology experienced something akin to unrequited love, full of pain, bitterness, and resentment, resulting from a sense of rejection. Pierre Bourdieu's definition of 'symbolic violence' explains convincingly the simultaneous love and resentment felt by young Jews and the role of the Polish state's educational institutions in creating such feelings. 'Symbolic violence is exerted whenever any Power imposes meanings and imposes them as legitimate by concealing the power relations which

---

[68] On the specific role played by teachers of religion in spreading antisemitism in schools, see Adamczyk-Garbowska, Kopciowski, and Trzciński (eds.), *Tam był kiedyś mój dom*, 312–13.

[69] Landau-Czajka, 'Obraz mniejszości narodowych w podręcznikach szkolnych', 3–4.

[70] Ibid. 7.   [71] Ibid. 8–9.

[72] See e.g. YIVO Archives, RG 4: Autobiography 3505, 41–3; Autobiography 3598, in *Awakening Lives*, 352; Autobiography 3673, 23; Autobiography 3702, 8; Autobiography 3740, 50; Autobiography 3802, 11; Autobiography 3812, 19–20; Autobiography 3837, in *Ostatnie pokolenie*, 466. On the subject of inter-ethnic and social distances stemming from the hierarchy and prejudices between acculturated participants in the YIVO competition writing in Polish and their Christian contemporaries, see A. Cała, 'The Social Consciousness of Young Jews in Interwar Poland', *Polin*, 8 (1994), 44–50.

are the basis of its ability to impose those meanings.'[73] What was concealed was the Polish attitude of domination over Jews and other minorities. This domination was imposed by the symbols of Polish patriotism, examples of heroism on the part of the Polish nation, as well as by the hidden, but implicitly expressed, message that Jews did not participate in these acts. This domination was reinforced by the cultural arbitrariness of the school's message.[74] Jewish identity and culture (in the form of language, customs, and beliefs), both traditional and modern, were unambiguously not desirable in Polish schools. Thus, the content of lessons on Polish language, history, or general knowledge fulfilled all the criteria of 'language as an instrument of power'.[75] Schools reinforced the domination of the controlling Polish nation. Meanings that required respect for the myths of Polish heroism and the nation's united struggle for independence were imposed on young Jews. As a subjugated group, they felt the need to demonstrate these types of convictions in order to legitimize their right to live in the country. They also internalized, more or less consciously, the conviction of the primacy of Polish culture, its dominant position in every area of life in the Second Polish Republic, and how essential it was for obtaining a school-leaving certificate, entering higher education, or getting factory work or a trade qualification.[76] The strength of this kind of oppression was reinforced by the fact that this generation was the first to attend Polish state schools, which, for a great many of those from traditionalist homes, were the sole institutions representing the 'modern world'. The influence of Polish schools on young Jews can also be interpreted in terms of 'symbolic violence', because the transmitted contents 'did not belong' to young Jews, but came from an elite which was not their elite and which did not recognize them as members of the Polish nation. Thus was the symbolic domination of a nationalistically inclined state over its ethnic minorities achieved. One of the crucial characteristics of 'symbolic vio-

---

[73] M. S. Mander, 'Bourdieu, the Sociology of Culture and Cultural Studies: A Critique', *European Journal of Communication*, 2 (1987), 432; see P. Bourdieu and J.-C. Passeron, *Reprodukcja: Elementy teorii systemu nauczania*, translated from the French by E. Neyman (Warsaw, 2006), 71; published in English as *Reproduction in Education, Society and Culture* (Thousand Oaks, Calif., 1990); P. Bourdieu and L. J. D. Wacquant, *Zaproszenie do socjologii refleksyjnej*, translated from the French by Anna Sawisz (Warsaw, 2001), 131; published in English as *An Invitation to Reflexive Sociology* (Chicago, 1992).

[74] 'Every pedagogical action objectively represents symbolic violence as an imposition of cultural arbitrariness by an arbitrary authority' (Bourdieu and Passeron, *Reprodukcja*, 75, see also 78–84).

[75] P. Bourdieu and T. Eagleton, 'Doxa and Common Life: An Interview', in S. Žižek (ed.), *Mapping Ideology* (London, 1994), 265.

[76] 'Language relationships are always relationships of symbolic power, and through them . . . relations of power between speakers and—appropriately—between the groups to which they belong flourish. . . . Even the most straightforward linguistic exchange sets in motion a complex and extensive network of relationships of historically defined forces' (Bourdieu and Wacquant, *Zaproszenie do socjologii refleksyjnej*, 133, see also 134–5, 139). Hence the attachment, mentioned above, of young Jews from traditionalist homes where Yiddish was spoken to Polish national mythology, the works of Sienkiewicz, and the Polish language as a 'tool of modernity' was not just a neutral exchange, but was an expression of the master–subordinate relationship between the Polish state and the Jews.

lence' is that it is one of the 'soft' tools of political power. Not every Jewish pupil had the ability of Leopold Infeld to fully understand the arbitrary character of the educational message of the Polish school. Others were unable to perceive this, and, as the autobiographies suggest, most sincerely loved Poland and its national symbols without reservation. But these symbols had a hidden, exclusionary content. The negative implications of this content were made clear by other elements of the generational experience of young Jews growing up in interwar Poland.

As a result of this symbolic violence, Polish culture played an ambiguous role in the lives of young Jews: it was very close and at the same time very alien. Many participants in the YIVO competitions illustrate this ambivalent attitude towards things Polish, as well as the resentment caused by feelings of inferiority and exclusion. Mars, a committed Zionist, wrote:

Only then did the baleful image of the Jews' eternal misery appear before me! One day, when going through the reading room, I heard a 'Strzelcy' choir.[77] I longed for such a song, but who would sing it? The 'Strzelcy' had their own country and sang of their love for it, while I had nothing. I burst into tears.[78]

Abraham Rotfarb, another competitor, had fled from the 'bad' world of tradition, sought a 'new home' in the Young Communists' Association, and finally found it in the Zionist movement and dreams of Palestine. Earlier, however, he had sought and not found it in 'Polishness':

I am a Jew and am far from calling myself a Pole. . . . I read and write in Polish, I know Poland's history, and so on. I see myself precisely as a real twentieth-century Jew of the diaspora. So forgive me for writing in Polish and not Yiddish, because it's not my fault. Poland is all around me, and I've fallen under its influence. But I want to get close to Jewishness, so that Polishness becomes only something I am acquainted with and not a part of my psyche.[79]

Abraham Rotfarb, as he himself admitted, spoke, wrote, and 'felt' Polish. At the same time, although he of course did not say so, he appeared to accept his 'symbolic subordination', declaring his unbreakable tie to Polishness while simultaneously feeling that it was not his forever and that he needed to 'break free' from it.

ANTISEMITISM

The Polish schools' symbolic violence played an enormous part in creating an antisemitic atmosphere; however, it was not the sole factor. Also important was the

---

[77] Związek Strzelecki 'Strzelec' (Riflemen's Association 'Rifleman') was a para-military organization founded in 1910. Between the wars it was closely linked to Józef Piłsudski. The organization engaged teenagers through sport and military training, and propagated a specific militarist form of Polish patriotism through a cult of the army.

[78] YIVO Archives, RG 4: Autobiography 3832, in *Ostatnie pokolenie*, 329–30.

[79] YIVO Archives, RG 4: Autobiography 3598, in *Ostatnie pokolenie*, 88; *Awakening Lives*, 344–5.

antisemitism manifested by the teachers and classmates of Jewish pupils. This did not have a planned character. In contrast to symbolic violence and the idea of Polish superiority over minorities, it cannot be attributed to the school curriculum or to the state's educational policies. These, although 'nationalistically inclined', did aim at integrating young Jews. The state failed to achieve this not so much because it applied an antisemitic exclusionary policy in schools, but because it did not counteract the prevailing antisemitism. It often failed to react to teachers' hostility towards Jews, and some teachers, if not antisemites themselves, often did not want or were unable to oppose the prejudices of their Christian pupils.[80] The attacks in the 1930s on Jews at universities must also have had an enormous effect on the participants in the YIVO competition. The incidents were widely reported in the Jewish press, became the topic of parliamentary questions by Jewish members of the Sejm, and were extensively discussed.[81] The motif of harassment and violence by right-wing teachers and pupils, as well as the authorities' failure to react, appears frequently in these autobiographies. Antisemitism was the most commonly recalled experience from a state school education.

This is most powerfully evident in the autobiographies written in Polish by writers from highly acculturated Jewish families. The small number of contestants in the YIVO competition who had been admitted to university belonged to both the Jewish and the Polish elite. Just about all of them had graduated from Polish schools and used Polish at home. Hence they were most forcefully affected by antisemitism. It is not surprising that their memoirs contain the greatest layers of pain and disappointment, as well as powerful resentment towards people who rejected Jews' claims to Polishness and their attachment to the country. The more the writer related culturally to ethnic Poles, the stronger the resentment. Antisemitism undermined the basis of the identity of children of acculturated families, the way in which they were brought up, and the values passed on to them by their parents.[82] It was an 'internally felt antisemitism', reflecting their identification with those who displayed the hostile attitude, not, as was the case with Jews from more tradi-

---

[80] Of the 100 autobiographies that I examined, only two testify to changes in teaching staff after the 1932 education reform and to improvements in teachers' attitudes towards Jewish pupils. M. Stein, having earlier experienced harassment by teachers friendly to the cause of National Democracy, wrote: 'In the next form of my grammar school, the seventh, as the result of a change of direction by the government, "our" trio of ND types retired and were replaced by BBWR [Bezpartyjny Blok Współpracy z Rządem; Nonpartisan Bloc for Co-operation with the Government], that is neutral, teachers. The situation of Jews in those three subjects changed impressively' (YIVO Archives, RG 4: Autobiography 3732, 19; see also Autobiography 3669, 32–3).

[81] On anti-Jewish incidents at universities in the 1930s, see E. Melzer, *No Way Out: The Politics of Polish Jewry, 1935–1939* (Cincinnati, 1997), 71–80; M. Natkowska, *Numerus clausus, getto ławkowe, numerus nullus, 'paragraf aryjski': antysemityzm na Uniwersytecie Warszawskim 1931–1939* (Warsaw, 1939); Cała, *Żyd—wróg odwieczny*, 380–1.

[82] This also explains why acculturated parents often decided to send their children to Jewish private schools, including those with Hebrew and Zionist flavours (see Landau-Czajka, *Syn będzie Lech*, 362–3).

tionalist backgrounds, something which was professed by alien, abstract 'goyim'. This bitterness is reflected in the experience of Ludwik Stoeckel, the son of an estate administrator in eastern Galicia. He devoted a great deal of his auto-biography to antisemitism and the bad relations between Jews and Christians in his secondary school.[83] However, for him the greatest impact, influential in his later life and identity, came from anti-Jewish incidents that occurred while he was a stu-dent at the University of Lviv. He describes in detail how right-wing action groups beat up Jewish students and passers-by, while policemen standing nearby failed to react.[84] Two problems occupy a central place in his autobiography. One was the almost entirely Polish nature of the cultural reality around him. The second was antisemitism, whose sting was sharpened by his deep acculturation, his education, his high social status, his aspirations, and finally his associated high self-esteem, especially in relation to his antisemitic persecutors. In his autobiography, Stoeckel describes himself as 'a Jew' and only as 'a Jew'. As he was not religious and had joined the Zionist left, he adopted the national definition of Jewishness. At the end of his first year, he abandoned his studies to seek a better life in a kibbutz in Palestine.[85]

The autobiography of Bronka exemplifies how acculturation increased the sense of antisemitic rejection in young people. She came from a Warsaw *haute bourgeois* family which had a rather loose relationship with Jewishness: 'A year at school taught me quite a few things beyond addition and subtraction. It sowed in me a mistrust of people, it awakened a feeling of loneliness and, quite by accident, national consciousness. . . . I learnt of the centuries of wandering, the eternal rest-lessness and the boundless, centuries-old martyrology.' Until then, while knowing that she was Jewish, she did not attach much importance to that fact.[86] As in the case of a great many other acculturated writers, her Jewish self-awareness rein-forced her antisemitic rejection. The same was true of G.S.:

I myself don't know how it happened that, despite my upbringing, such a powerful feeling of Jewishness awoke in me, but the strongest influence was the antisemitism that flourished then in schools. My sister and brother also became ardent Zionists at this time, which had an influence on our parents. To the extent that they began to contribute to Jewish causes,

[83] YIVO Archives, RG 4: Autobiography 3675, in *Ostatnie pokolenie*, 366–7; *Awakening Lives*, 141–96.

[84] Ibid., in *Ostatnie pokolenie*, 369–71. Events that took place in the universities also had an enor-mous influence on Gerszon Pipe, who belonged to the small group of writers who, despite having grown up in poor, traditional Jewish communities, managed to obtain a school-leaving certificate. He wrote that when he was in the final form in secondary school he knew that, despite his marks, he had no chance of completing his studies due to antisemitism. By this he meant the difficulty of getting into university and harassment there by other students and lecturers (YIVO Archives, RG 4: Autobiogra-phy 3770, 41).

[85] YIVO Archives, RG 4: Autobiography 3675, in *Ostatnie pokolenie*, 376.

[86] Bronka, 'Autobiography', in *Ostatnie pokolenie*, 58–9 (this autobiography is not in the YIVO archives).

shop in Jewish stores, and socialize in Jewish circles. Today, a portrait of Herzl and a map of Palestine hang over my father's desk.[87]

University students and grammar school pupils were the best educated of the participants in the YIVO competition. They knew more about the legal system and demanded greater state protection of their civil rights than did the other participants. The experience of antisemitism made them not only hostile towards supporters of the National Radical Camp (ONR), the National Democrats, and the other antisemitic elements in Polish society, but also alienated them from Polish state institutions that broke their promises of full civic equality. Antisemitism radicalized and 'nationalized' these young people, forcing them to redefine their own identities.

The success and widespread acceptance of state education by the Jewish community created yet another paradox. The greater the number of young Jews in state schools, the more effectively these institutions promoted 'symbolic acculturation', love for the 'Polish nation's heroic history', and Polish cultural identity. Ironically, these factors strongly reinforced the experience of antisemitism among young traditional Jews. For the majority of their parents and grandparents, who had grown up before 1914, traditional anti-Judaism as well as modern antisemitism were culturally foreign and socially remote. Their children and grandchildren in interwar Poland experienced antisemitism at the hands of their schoolfellows; from authority, in the shape of their teachers; from representatives of the nation which they were learning to love; and in the state institutions which they had been taught to regard as their own. This 'internalized experience of antisemitism', touching the very heart of young Jews' identity, for the first time in history affected most young Jews in the Second Polish Republic. Polonization and state education brought with them a universalization of the experience of modern antisemitism. The autobiographies are filled with testimonies to this effect. They were written by people from traditional Jewish families, who almost always had first come into contact with new forms of dislike and even antagonism in a state school. Ajzyk R. wrote of pupils and teachers insulting or hitting Jews in primary schools and trade schools.[88] The majority of these young writers mentioned not only their schoolmates' antisemitism. The discrimination, dislike, or even contempt on the part of teachers affected them even more painfully. Gitman G. entered a primary school from a *szabasówka*, attending school with Christian children for the first time: 'The Jewish children were divided between four forms and they had a hard time of it with their new schoolfellows. They were all antisemites. . . . There were those of us who "complained" about the Christian children to both the men and the women teachers, who did nothing whatsoever about it.'[89]

A young hasid, who signed his autobiography 'Stormer', and attended primary

---

[87] YIVO Archives, RG 4: Autobiography 3739, in *Awakening Lives*, 267.

[88] YIVO Archives, RG 4: Autobiography 3669, 8–9, 11–12, 29.

[89] YIVO Archives, RG 4: Autobiography 3543, 21.

school as well as a small yeshiva, wrote:

From my school years I also recall a whole gallery of teachers of various types. One teacher, Mr Fachalczyk, sticks in my memory. He caused me a great deal of trouble and used to make fun of my *peyes* and my long coat. He taught history and Polish. Today he is the leader of the Endek Party in our area and is known to be very antisemitic. I was very fond of the director of the school, Mr Kowalski, who in his time had gained a reputation as a great humanist. I had wonderful conversations with him (in the seventh grade) about the Bible and Talmud, which pleased him quite a bit. On the whole, I remember him as a very refined person with great pedagogical abilities. However, he, too, has now moved over to the antisemitic camp, although he still holds the same post.[90]

M. Szeinberg began his secular, non-Jewish education in a small rural school in the countryside near Kielce, where he was the only Jewish student. Although he liked school, emphasizing that in the end he became used to this 'community of rogues' and learned a great deal from them, he was persecuted by an antisemitic schoolmistress. In the third grade he was moved to another school where the Jewish pupils were beaten up by their Christian schoolfellows, inspired by what they had heard in religious instruction lessons or from nationalist teachers.[91] Another author, M. Stein, wrote of his time in primary school:

Some antisemitic teachers arrived and for them making the life of Jewish pupils a misery was their greatest pleasure. . . . At break all I did was to find a safe nook where I could hide away from Catholic clobbering. Finally, at the end of the day, a few solid 'rogues' were usually waiting for us by the gate to feed us their fists usually armed with wooden knuckledusters. . . . I would then go home beaten up, covered in bruises, with no will to live or to go to school. . . . All our complaints to the school authorities went unanswered and, what's more, they even seemed pleased.[92]

Mendel Man began to attend primary school after a few years in a *ḥeder*. Hitherto, his only contacts with Christian children had been on the streets of his native Sochocin, where fights often ensued. He began his description of his experiences as follows:

I went there for two years during which a great deal happened. The school was gripped by antisemitism. We suffered on account of the teacher's malice and the Christian pupils' hatred. The teacher would put Jews on a special bench, which of course was not based on any school rule. We were beaten up and he pretended not to notice. In any case, he himself with his nasty comments turned everyone against the Jews. He built a wall of hatred between Christian and Jewish pupils.[93]

Another young woman, using the *nom de plume* Jesz, wrote that a schoolmistress's open antisemitism in primary school provoked deep hatred in the Jewish girls.[94]

[90] YIVO Archives, RG 4: Autobiography 3707, in *Awakening Lives*, 236.
[91] YIVO Archives, RG 4: Autobiography 3702, 3–4.
[92] Ibid. 8–9.   [93] YIVO Archives, RG 4: Autobiography 3802, 17–18.
[94] YIVO Archives, RG 4: Autobiography 3735, 8–9.

And in 1939 Esther, whose idols were the 'Polish national heroes' Mickiewicz, Sienkiewicz, and Piłsudski, wrote:

Relations between Jews and Poles had deteriorated significantly. This, too, had a powerful impact on me. The loyal Polish patriot in me suffered. Now I, whose soul was so bound to Poland, had to give up my cherished dream of Poles and Jews living together in harmony. . . . And now all of this had vanished. . . . My faith in Poland's 'heart' was tarnished. I no longer saw a nation with brotherly feelings for all of its citizens, as Poland had been in her pre-war dreams.[95]

Coming from a completely different background, Abraham Rotfarb wrote:

I love Poland. Her language, her culture, but most of all her hard-won freedom and the heroism of her struggles for independence all speak to my heart, my feelings, and enthusiasm. But I do not love that Poland which hates me for no reason! Which tears my heart and soul, which pushes me into apathy, into melancholy, and into dark aimlessness. I hate that Poland which not only does not want me as a Pole and sees me as nothing but a Jew but which then wants to drive me out of Poland, the country where I was born and which has brought me up. I hate that Poland; I hate antisemitism. I blame you, the antisemites, for my inferiority complex and for the fact that I don't know what I am, a Jew or a Pole! Poland has broken my heart, has turned me into a dog who abjectly asks not to be abandoned alone in a cultural desert and to be taken along the path of Polish cultural life. Poland has brought me up to be a Pole, and now shouts that I am a Jew who must be chased out![96]

CONCLUSION

Shulamit Volkov, in an essay on the reception of what has been described as modern antisemitism before 1914, points out the basic difference between east and west European Jews. The former, more deeply rooted in their ethnic culture and for the most part not identifying with the nations around them, were inclined to treat modern antisemitism as external and threatening but not as attacking the roots of their own identity. The situation was very different for most German Jews, who deeply identified with their own Germanness and for whom antisemitic attacks not only undermined their legally obtained emancipation but also struck at the intellectual and spiritual basis of their way of life. East European Jews, who had relatively quickly and painlessly adopted a modern national posture, appeared to understand better how widespread and inevitable antisemitism was. They were able to come to terms with it and to move on and finally to make antisemitism just another piece in the political puzzle on the road to achieving their goal of collective, national self-emancipation.[97] The situation of Jews and the evolution of Jewish attitudes in the Second Polish Republic—the shift by a majority of traditional

---

[95] YIVO Archives, RG 4: Autobiography 3559, in *Awakening Lives*, 329.

[96] YIVO Archives, RG 4: Autobiography 3598, in *Ostatnie pokolenie*, 119; *Awakening Lives*, 375–6.

[97] S. Volkov, 'Views from East and West', in ead., *Germans, Jews and Antisemites: Trials in Emancipation* (New York, 2006), 20–32.

Jewish society to either an Orthodox or a nationalist posture—suggest that Polish Jewish society confirms Volkov's description of the east European Jews' reaction to modern antisemitism. However, the autobiographies of young Jews examined here provide a more complicated and much more interesting picture. This was the first and only generation that was in its entirety subject to the influence of the Polish state's educational institutions. While young people identified en masse with modern Jewish national policies and acknowledged themselves as part of the Jewish nation, because of the simultaneous intensity of the acculturation processes they saw antisemitism very similarly to the 'un-national' German Jews. In addition, in their case, antisemitic rejection undermined the very basis of individual identity. In fact, it was never described calmly as an inherent element of life in the Diaspora with which one had to live and come to terms. Young Zionists and Bundists saw anti-Jewish attitudes in moral terms as a hateful, undeserved, unjust injury inflicted on them personally.

Thus Polish state education aimed at young Jews had an effect opposite to that intended. This generation was the first in which almost all its members not only spoke Polish but also moved easily within the surrounding non-Jewish culture and were characterized by their attachment to its most important symbols. It is one of the greatest paradoxes of the Second Polish Republic that its modern institution, the school, which was meant to integrate ethnic and national minorities, functioned in a manner which contradicted its official aims. Instead of bringing young Jews closer to the state to counteract political radicalism, it ended up making them even more antagonistic towards it. The state school was the first and often the only institution of the Polish state with which young people came into contact in their childhood and adolescence. It was there that the 'democratic promise' of the Second Polish Republic was offered to young Jews, while at the same time, they were made aware that this promise would in no way be fulfilled. There were two basic reasons for this failure. The first was the dominance of the ethno-religious concept of the Polish nation and the lack of a similarly strong narrative of the communal bond linking all the state's citizens. The other was widespread antisemitism. Because of the strength of these two factors, school in some ways provided a foretaste of what young people would encounter in adult life, in the job market, in politics and in social life.

Once again, following Bourdieu, the influence of the Polish school on young Jews can be seen as 'unconscious submission, which may indicate a lot of internalized tension, a lot of physical suffering'.[98] The conflict between love for an abstract Poland and the hostility experienced everywhere at the hands of its real-life representatives led to tension and suffering. The response to this tension, to the 'symbolic violence' of the state, and to the antisemitism which it fostered was widespread political radicalism. The majority of writers of the YIVO autobiographies, after leaving school, taking on hard, poorly paid work and seeing no better

98 Bourdieu and Eagleton, 'Doxa and Common Life', 276.

prospects, would join one of the Jewish political movements contesting the surrounding reality. They sought future salvation 'here' through revolution in Poland, or 'there' by building a new society in Palestine. Undoubtedly there were a great many reasons why young Jews joined movements of this type. One of them, was, paradoxically, the Polish school.

Between Church and State

Jewish Religious Instruction in Public Schools in the Second Polish Republic

SEAN MARTIN

JANUSZ KORCZAK, physician, writer, pedagogue, and Jewish community leader, described a public school classroom in which religion was being taught in 1932:

I see a classroom: a class of forty or fifty students. Young and old, in the third or fourth lesson of the day, in the days before or after a holiday, during spring or fall. I see a teacher: sometimes feeling good, sometimes not. A teacher repeating the same material for the fourth or fifth year. I see a bored class and a bored teacher, who has to teach the lesson because of the mandatory curriculum. The hour, which lasts sixty minutes, passes slowly. And in these hours, on a topic that is supposed to enthral children, to give them eternal truth, the task is not easy. In each kind of work there are hours that are tiring and torturous and hours that are noble and beautiful.[1]

Korczak's depiction of the bored teacher and students may not necessarily describe every classroom in which the Jewish religion was taught to Jewish students, but he thought this scene typical enough to introduce his short remarks on the topic of religion and the child, which he published in *Dziecko*, a journal of the Central Organization of Care for Jewish Children in Poland. The Jewish religious instruction in Poland's public schools described by Korczak may have been intended to impart the values of a living tradition, but it is difficult to see how this could have been done successfully in such an environment.

After the First World War, when Poland regained her independence from the partitioning powers of Prussia, Russia, and Austria, the new Polish government needed to integrate the school systems left behind by the fallen empires. Students in independent Poland's public schools received two hours of religious instruction a week. This chapter explores the role of Jewish religious instruction in these schools and how the new government's requirements affected Jewish children and the Jewish community. Efforts to ensure that Jewish children grew up within the Jewish tradition were certainly not limited to the public schools, but it was in

---

[1] J. Korczak, 'Dziecko a religja (odczyt Janusza Korczaka)', *Dziecko*, 1/3 (1932), 5–6.

the public schools that the conflict between the religious faith of a national minority and public institutions that were meant to support that faith but, in the eyes of many Jewish observers, often failed in their task can be most clearly seen.

A survey of the role of religion in public schools and the related legislation reveals the value placed on religious education by most citizens in the Second Polish Republic. Many Poles and Jews expected religious instruction to be part of the curriculum, but for many within the Jewish community the subject was never accorded the treatment or consideration it deserved. Nonetheless, the effort to provide Jewish religious instruction in public schools is a further example of the complex relations between Jews and Poles. While private Jewish educational networks developed and flourished, the remaking of public schools in Poland and the inclusion of Jewish religious education compelled Jews to define and defend their religious practices in public and to confront their relationship to both their religion and the Polish state. At the same time, the Polish government, on both a national and local level, was forced to consider the needs of a religious and national minority. Examination of religious instruction in the public schools of the Second Polish Republic offers insights into the role of religion in multi-ethnic democracies.[2]

The problems associated with religious instruction in the Second Polish Republic included both the practical logistics of scheduling and the challenge of accommodating minority religious views and practices within the modern educational system of the majority. Even as the problems themselves illustrate increasing interaction, and sometimes conflict, between different national communities living under the same government, the Jewish response to these problems reveals the often innovative nature of minority communities. While the majority of Jewish students in independent Poland attended public schools, there has been little research on their experiences or on how the authorities developed and implemented the system of religious instruction.[3]

RELIGIOUS INSTRUCTION BEFORE 1918

Religious instruction among Jews in Polish lands is most often associated with the *ḥeder*, which Jewish children, usually boys, but sometimes girls, attended as young

---

[2] The challenge of accommodating religion within the public sphere was certainly not unique to Poland. The situation of students in government-supported schools in England presents an interesting comparative case, since in England assimilation, which was resisted by Polish Jews, was seen as significantly more acceptable. See S. K. Greenberg, 'Anglicization and the Education of Jewish Immigrant Children in the East End of London', in A. Rapoport-Albert and S. J. Zipperstein (eds.), *Jewish History: Essays in Honour of Chimen Abramsky* (London, 1988), 111–26.

[3] Most overviews of Jewish education in Poland include only a brief mention of religious instruction in public schools (see C. S. Heller, *On the Edge of Destruction: Jews of Poland between the Two World Wars*, 2nd edn. (Detroit, 1994), 221, 236–7; J. Tomaszewski, *Najnowsze dzieje Żydów w Polsce* (Warsaw, 1993), 242–4).

as 3.[4] For centuries it was the basic educational institution for Jewish children, a central institution of the shtetl, and often romanticized in Yiddish folk songs such as 'Afn pripetshik'. Through it, Jewish communities passed on the Hebrew language and Jewish values, focusing on the study of the Bible and Talmud, prayers, and elementary reading and writing and avoiding secular education of any kind. The *ḥeder* served as both a school and a day-care facility, enabling parents to work and to provide for the education of their children. Intended to educate Jewish boys, the traditional *ḥeder* excluded girls and so buttressed the community's social values as well.[5]

The *ḥeder* epitomized Jewish education and insistence on the importance of learning. As Shaul Stampfer has pointed out, it identified students who were talented enough for advanced study and so was a fundamental part of the maintenance of the Jewish religious elite.[6] The *ḥeder* provided basic literacy to many, and, together with the yeshiva, it helped to create a respected cadre of religious scholars. The traditional system of education was concerned with perpetuating the elite within Jewish society: it was not meant to prepare students for future careers.

The *ḥeder* had long been a target of reform for the maskilim of the Russian empire.[7] The various groups of the Jewish elite, religious and secular, wanted education to reflect and replicate the values of the community. The *ḥeder metukan*, or 'improved *ḥeder*', which was introduced after the pogroms of the 1880s, aimed to introduce young Jews to Jewish nationalism and to teach Hebrew as a spoken language. Writing decades after their experiences, some Jewish leaders recalled the miserable conditions and disorderliness of the classroom (often in a private home) and the poor attitude of the teachers. Chaim Weizmann claimed that the word *melamed* (teacher) was synonymous with *schlemiel* (fool).[8] Indeed, the *melamedim* have been described as 'embittered, poverty-stricken, weak and sometimes sadistic men'.[9] Stampfer has shown how cultural and social circumstances led to poor teaching: women were proscribed from learning Hebrew and more talented men had better economic options, so the quality of men who sought posts as *melamedim* was low. The *ḥeder*, however, should not be seen as simply a backward institution. It was a fundamental tool in the maintenance of tradition.

[4] See E. Gamoran, *Changing Conceptions in Jewish Education* (New York, 1924); B.-Z. Gold, 'Religious Education in Poland: A Personal Perspective', in Y. Gutman et al. (eds.), *The Jews of Poland between Two World Wars* (Hanover, NH, 1989), 272–4; id., *The Life of Jews in Poland before the Holocaust* (Lincoln, Neb., 2007), 43–54; I. Etkes and D. Assaf (eds), *Haḥeder: meḥkarim, te'udot, pirkei sifrut vezikhronot* (Tel Aviv, 2010).

[5] See A. Greenbaum, 'The Girls' Heder and Girls in the Boys' Heder in Eastern Europe before World War I', *East/West Education*, 18/1 (1997), 55–62.

[6] S. Stampfer, '*Heder* Study, Knowledge of Torah, and the Maintenance of Social Stratification', in id., *Families, Rabbis and Education: Traditional Jewish Society in Nineteenth-Century Eastern Europe* (Oxford, 2010), 271–89.

[7] See S. J. Zipperstein, 'Transforming the Heder: Maskilic Politics in Imperial Russia', in Rapoport-Albert and Zipperstein (eds.), *Jewish History*, 87–110.

[8] C. Weizmann, *Trial and Error: The Autobiography of Chaim Weizmann* (New York, 1949), 4–5.

Jewish religious instruction had existed in non-Jewish schools before 1918. The system was most developed in Galicia, where organizations and at least one journal aimed to provide support to instructors. Naftali Schipper was the editor and publisher of the monthly *Wychowanie i Oświata*, the journal of the Association of Teachers of the Mosaic Religion in Primary and Divisional Schools in Galicia, which first appeared in Lwów in 1905.[10] It represented the assimilationist movement, and the course of religious instruction it promoted also included lessons in Polish nationalism. It featured information about regulations governing teachers and schools, articles about Polish authors writing on Jewish topics, and explications in Polish of passages from the Torah. Schipper continued his work promoting Jewish religious instruction after 1918, publishing a textbook used in Jewish religion courses throughout Poland.[11]

New secular elites eventually put in place institutions that replaced the traditional *ḥeder*. As Jewish leaders adopted new social and political goals, such as promoting Yiddish as a national language and developing Palestine as a Jewish national home, they began to establish different types of private Jewish schools. In response to the government's educational initiatives and because of their own cultural priorities, private Jewish educational networks grew throughout Poland, reflecting the community's significant diversity and offering alternatives that could be seen as distinctively Jewish.[12]

The new private and public schools represented a revolution in education which led to significant changes within the Jewish community. In her study of Jewish religious textbooks in Russian schools in the late nineteenth century, Eliyana Adler argues that the authors of these textbooks 'reinvented religion' for the Jewish community.[13] The adoption of non-Jewish languages and participation in non-Jewish institutions meant at the very least a reconsideration of the boundaries of Jewish identities and a rethinking of the definition of Judaism. Contact with non-Jewish students and non-Jewish traditions slowly broke down barriers between Jews and Poles in the 1920s and 1930s. The two religious and national communities were increasingly less isolated from each other. The public schools helped to make this possible.

[9] J. Sarna, 'American Jewish Education in Historical Perspective', *Journal of Jewish Education*, 64/1–2 (1998), 8–21.

[10] A. Karbowiak, 'Polskie czasopisma pedagogiczne', *Wychowanie w domu i szkole*, 3/1 (1912), 82–85.

[11] N. Schipper, *Historja Żydów oraz przegląd ich kultury*, i: *Od upadku państwa żydowskiego (r. 70) do końca wieków średnich (1492)*; ii: *Od końca wieków średnich (1492) do doby najnowszej (1928)* (Lwów, 1929–30).

[12] See M. Eisenstein, *Jewish Schools in Poland, 1919–1939* (New York, 1950); S. Frost, *Schooling as a Socio-Political Expression: Jewish Education in Interwar Poland* (Jerusalem, 1998).

[13] E. R. Adler, 'Reinventing Religion: Jewish Religion Textbooks in Russian Gymnasia', *Journal of Jewish Education*, 77/2 (2011), 141–56.

THE SYSTEM OF RELIGIOUS INSTRUCTION

Poland between the wars was a society 'where everyone was expected to have a religious designation'.[14] For better or worse, separate religious instruction in public schools was a reminder of the divisions within society, revealing how Poles and Jews lived both separately and together and the innovative ways in which citizens of east European states attempted to maintain their religious and cultural traditions even as they were undergoing fundamental political, social, and cultural changes. Teaching religion in public schools was one way for both government and society to maintain the religious values of the country's varied populations. Compulsory religious instruction was written into the new Polish constitution. Thus, meeting the educational needs of the country's different religious groups became in part the responsibility of the state. Almost 65 per cent of Poland's 30 million residents during this period were Roman Catholic. Greek Catholics (Uniates), Eastern Orthodox, and Jews made up about 10 per cent each of the remaining population; Lutherans, Calvinists, and smaller Protestant and Christian groups amounted to about 5 per cent.[15] The task of integrating these diverse groups into the school system was just one of many the state faced after 1918, and, given the significance of social stability, it was certainly one of the most important.

Illiteracy was high throughout the lands that came together to make up the new state, more than 50 per cent in some eastern provinces and 33 per cent for the country as a whole.[16] Public schools were needed to train the masses and develop the state. The Polish educational system was most developed in the Habsburg empire, where autonomy and decentralization had led to the adoption of Polish in the classrooms from 1867. The Prussians were the most successful pedagogically, but they insisted that the language of instruction be German, including religious lessons, and eliminated Polish cultural influences from schools. Elementary education was least developed in the Russian empire. There restrictions on the teaching of Polish language and literature were part of various campaigns to minimize the effect of Polish culture. However, underground educational efforts helped to impart both basic skills and Polish national and cultural values.[17] The Polish government had to unify three completely different systems and set nationwide standards for development and growth of both children and of the educational system. On 7 February 1919 elementary education was made obligatory for all children aged 7 to 14.[18] This was part of the modernization of Poland as the nation

[14] Heller, *On the Edge of Destruction*, 189.

[15] J. Rothschild, *East Central Europe between the Two World Wars* (Seattle, 1974), 36.   [16] Ibid. 44.

[17] For a review of pre-1918 educational policies, see D. Wojtas, 'Learning to become Polish: Education, National Identity, and Citizenship in Interwar Poland, 1918–1939', Ph.D. thesis (Brandeis University, 2003); W. Garbowska, *Szkolnictwo powszechne w Polsce w latach 1932–1939* (Wrocław, 1976), 11–46.

[18] S. Mauersberg, *Szkolnictwo powszechne dla mniejszości narodowych w Polsce w latach 1918–1939* (Wrocław, 1968), 162.

transformed itself and developed institutions in line with those of other, more advanced countries.

The Minorities Treaty of June 1919 specifically allowed 'for the existence of Jewish schools, controlled by Jewish authorities and funded by the state'.[19] In addition, the treaty guaranteed that Jews could not be forced to violate the sabbath, a provision that was especially important in the educational context. The new system did not force all children to attend public schools. Minority populations were able to establish and develop their own private educational systems, and Polish officials also made accommodation for children from minority groups in the public schools.[20] Polish schools were open from Monday to Saturday, and instruction on the sabbath was always problematic. Most public schools attended by Jewish children were ethnically mixed, but the government did establish some exclusively for Jews. In these schools, children did not have to attend on Saturday but could attend on Sunday, with the approval of local Catholic Church officials, and they were also free to stay away on Jewish holidays in addition to state holidays (nearly all of which were Christian holidays). Jewish children in some schools did have to attend on Saturday, but they could refrain from writing, drawing, or performing any other activity forbidden on the sabbath. Private schools could conduct lessons in any language, but all public schools used Polish, including for religious instruction. Jewish delegates to the Sejm tried throughout the life of the Second Polish Republic to gain approval for the use of Hebrew in public schools but to no avail.

The public school was still a relatively new experience for the Jews of eastern Europe. According to Stampfer, 'traditional east European Jewish society' had already broken down by the end of the nineteenth century,[21] and some Jewish children were studying in private non-Jewish elementary and secondary schools, but mandatory education in a public setting only became the norm in the Second Polish Republic. Generally speaking, the Jewish community saw public education as a threat to the Jewish way of life. The public school was a manifestation of a government policy explicitly intended to unify the new country's disparate regions and, to some extent, its diverse populations. Public education meant that boys and girls would be taught together, which alone was reason enough for some traditional Jews to object to it. Distinctive markers of language, dress, political status, custom, and religious practice had marked Jews as different from Poles for centuries. *Ḥeder* study did not challenge Jewish identity; public school clearly threatened how Jewish children would dress, how they would speak, and what they would think about themselves and their neighbours.[22]

The Polish government set the conditions for religious instruction and for the continued interaction between Jewish community leaders and Polish officials

---

[19] E. Mendelsohn, *The Jews of East Central Europe between the World Wars* (Bloomington, Ind., 1987), 35.   [20] See Mauersberg, *Szkolnictwo powszechne dla mniejszości narodowych*, 162–6.

[21] Stampfer, '*Ḥeder* Study, Knowledge of Torah, and the Maintenance of Social Stratification', 164.

[22] On the failure of the *ḥeder* to maintain Jewish identity, see ibid. 163.

regarding that instruction.[23] Article 114 of the Constitution stated: 'The Roman Catholic creed, being the creed of the majority of the people, shall have a preponderating authority in the state among other religions which shall enjoy equal treatment.'[24] However, Catholicism's 'preponderating authority' meant that allowing equal treatment for other religions would not be an easy task. Article 120 of the Constitution established religion as a compulsory subject for students under the age of 18 in the Polish public school system:

In all educational establishments, supported or subsidized by the state, whose curriculum embraces the education of youth under 18 years of age, the teaching of religion shall be compulsory for all pupils. The conduct and control of such teaching shall rest with the respective religious association, with the reservation of a supreme right of control by the educational authorities of the state.[25]

While the necessity of religious instruction in public schools was taken as a given by the government, some voices in Polish society argued vehemently against it. Poland was not without those opposed to the church and its influence. Such prominent Polish figures as the writer Tadeusz Boy-Żeleński, the philologist Jan Badouin de Courtenay, and the philosopher Tadeusz Kotarbiński suggested that the teaching of religion actually prevented the development of a sincere religious identity in addition to violating fundamental principles of democracy.[26] Boy-Żeleński wrote: 'In the higher classes we have an obtuse boor as a religious instruction teacher, someone without education, without intelligence, without substance, on whom students look with disdain. . . . Religious instruction in the school not only does not teach religion, it ruins it.'[27]

The influence of the church on schools was consolidated when the Sejm ratified the Polish Concordat with the Holy See in 1925.[28] In addition to compulsory religious instruction, the concordat made it clear that church authorities would oversee the moral education of children and could also hold teachers accountable for their behaviour. The Catholic Church hoped its representatives would also influence events in schools, including parties and commemorative ceremonies.[29] Thus,

---

[23] See H. Seidman, *Dos yidishe religyeze shul-vezn in di ramen fun der poylisher gezetsgebung* (Warsaw, 1936/7). This is the best summary of laws affecting Jewish religious instruction in independent Poland.

[24] Konstytucja Rzeczypospolitej Polskiej z dnia 17 marca 1921, art. 114, cited in F. J. Drobka, *Education in Poland: Past and Present* (Washington DC, 1927), 61.

[25] Ibid., art. 120; cited in Drobka, *Education in Poland*, 62.

[26] See T. Boy-Żeleński, 'Rozmyślania przed Popielcem', *Kurjer Poranny*, 23 Feb. 1930, in *400 lat walki o szkołę świecką w Polsce*, ed. M. Szulkin (Warsaw, 1960), 140–1; J. Baudouin de Courtenay, 'Pogadanki szkolne o "Bogu" i o innych sprawach pokrewnych a drażliwych', *Wolnomyśliciel Polski*, 1929, nos. 11–12, in *400 lat walki o szkołę świecką w Polsce*, 138–9; T. Kotarbiński: 'Trzechsetlecie procesu Galileusza', *Racjonalista*, 1933, no. 1, pp. 1–5, in *400 lat walki o szkołę świecką w Polsce*, 160–6.

[27] Boy-Żeleński, 'Rozmyślania przed Popielcem', 141.

[28] See N. Pease, *Rome's Most Faithful Daughter: The Catholic Church and Independent Poland, 1914–1939* (Athens, Ohio, 2009), ch. 3.

[29] K. Trzebiatowski, *Szkolnictwo powszechne w Polsce w latach 1918–1932* (Wrocław, 1970), 228–32.

the Polish state demonstrated that it would guarantee the role of Catholicism in public education. Speaking in the Sejm, Stanisław Grabski, the Minister of Religious Confessions and Public Education, remarked: 'The Holy See is confident that the Polish State will allow no undermining of religion in its schools. . . . If the Vatican expresses such confidence why should we not take the same attitude?'[30]

In individual schools, Roman Catholic priests or representatives of other religious groups taught religion for two hours a week. In cities where there were enough children of one faith, they were to attend the same school in order to make the teaching of religion easier. When fewer than twelve students of one faith attended a public school, they would be taken to a nearby school, so that there would be at least twelve students in the class. Instruction for Jewish children was provided in schools with twelve or more Jewish students.[31] The difficulties of this system are obvious. Simply counting the students and determining how and when instruction could be provided were significant bureaucratic tasks. That some children remained outside the system is very likely, and that others were not always provided for adequately is a certainty. Still, the attempt to provide instruction was made, an attempt that attests both to the sincerity of Polish efforts to create a society where religion was sanctioned by the state and to the commitment of religious leaders to educating their children.

The percentage of Jewish students in the public school system varied from city to city, but a majority of Jewish students in Poland attended public schools throughout the interwar period. Roughly 60 per cent of Jewish children in the mid 1930s went to non-Jewish schools (public or private); the remaining 40 per cent attended private Jewish schools of varying orientations (Yiddishist, Zionist, or religious).[32] Jewish private educational initiatives were quite successful, despite the relatively high costs of tuition, which illustrates the strong desire among Jews for private schools. In addition, many Jewish parents whose children went to public schools felt that they should also attend supplementary schools in the afternoon for religious instruction.[33] However, the need for public schools was real, and parents' desire to prepare their children to make a living in Poland in Polish ensured that, while public school might not be the preferred option, it was an option that many Jewish parents needed and at least some wanted. Even as the number of children in private Jewish schools grew throughout the 1930s, public schools remained a viable choice.[34]

[30] Cited in Drobka, *Education in Poland*, 109.
[31] Okólnik Ministra Wyznań Religijnych i Oświecenia Publicznego z dnia 5 stycznia 1927 r. Nr 1, 148/27; repr. in Seidman, *Dos yidishe religyeze shul-vezn in di ramen fun der poylisher gezetsgebung*, 47–50.
[32] A. Landau-Czajka, *Syn będzie Lech...: Asymilacja Żydów w Polsce międzywojennej* (Warsaw, 2006), 349; M. Fuks et al., *Żydzi polscy: Dzieje i kultura* (Warsaw, 1982), 90.
[33] For an example, see Gold, *The Life of Jews in Poland before the Holocaust*, 55–6. More research on how many Jewish parents sought additional religious education for their children outside the public school is needed.   [34] Landau-Czajka, *Syn będzie Lech...*, 350.

Statistics from the American Jewish Joint Distribution Committee (JDC) suggest the alarming speed of educational change. In 1927 a JDC report noted that the number of Jewish children attending government schools was increasing while the number attending Tarbut or Yiddishist schools was decreasing. The local childcare committees financed by the JDC were 'forced to take advantage of free education, for financial reasons', meaning that orphans were sent to public schools, not private ones.[35] The JDC also noted that the number of children attending *ḥeder*s or *talmud torah*s was steadily decreasing, 'chiefly because parents desire to have their children receive general education'.[36] Such a rapid change can only have been alarming to both traditional and progressive Jews who wanted to influence the direction of their people.

While the number of Jewish students in public schools was quite high, there was much local variation. For example, the private Jewish school system in Vilna and Kresy was particularly well developed, and Jewish parents in these areas had the option of sending their children to several different types of private Jewish school, supported by the *kehilah* and by private Jewish organizations. During the school year 1929/30 only 913 of a total 4,065 Jewish students in Vilna attended public schools; 3,152 were in private schools: that is, just over 22 per cent of Jewish students in Vilna attended public schools, whereas nearly 78 per cent were in private schools.[37] In Kraków, a Jewish community of similar size, the numbers were nearly the reverse. There, according to a 1929 report of *Sprawy Narodowościowe*, almost 90 per cent of the city's Jewish students were in public schools and just over 10 per cent were in private schools.[38] These local variations suggest the continuing effects of the pre-partition regimes. In the Russian empire, where elementary education was least developed, Jews developed stronger private educational options, which perhaps accounts for the later successes of Jewish leaders there. In contrast, Habsburg rule allowed for educational options in Polish, perhaps accustoming Kraków's Jews to the greater role of the state in education.

A 1922 JDC report on the schools in the small town of Nowogródek offers a more detailed look at the various options parents had for their children's education. Nowogródek was a town of about 10,000 residents, of whom 60 to 65 per cent were Jewish. A total of 155 boys and girls attended the one public school in the town. There was also a Hebrew school with 135 students, mostly boys; a yeshiva and a *talmud torah* where 60 boys studied; and five private *ḥeder*s, with

---

[35] American Jewish Joint Distribution Committee Archives, New York, 1921–32, 'Poland: Subject Matter', folder 341: Irma May, letter to John Hyman: 'Cultural life in Poland, according to data gathered in Warsaw, Poland, from Mr. Leon Neustadt, in charge of the Childcare work in Poland, in July 1927'.   [36] Ibid. The report also noted that 'there are no repressions on the part of government'.

[37] A. Hirschberg, 'Zarys historyczno-statystyczny szkolnictwa na ziemiach północno-wschodnich (1913–1929)', in *Wilno i ziemia wileńska*, 2 vols. (Vilna, 1930–7), ii. 65 tables 30, 25.

[38] 'Powszechne nauczanie wśród ludności żydowskiej w Polsce w świetle cyfr', *Sprawy Narodowościowe*, 2 (1929), 297.

a total enrolment of 90 children, again mostly boys.[39] More students were in private Jewish schools than public schools, but these numbers suggest that the public school had been accepted as an option by Jewish parents relatively early. The most pedagogically developed of the schools was the public school, to which Jewish orphans were sent because it was free. Next best was the Hebrew school, which included religious subjects in its curriculum. The JDC report describes conditions in the *ḥeder*s and *talmud torah*s as 'broken down' and 'out of date'. Writing was taught in these schools, but only as copying. 'Arithmetic' was also taught. Private educational alternatives remained strong, but public school was a competitive option.

TRAINING INSTRUCTORS OF RELIGION IN PUBLIC SCHOOLS

Some of the characteristics of Jewish religious instruction in the Second Polish Republic were apparent well before 1918. For all the importance of religion in both Christian and Jewish society, the subject was often seen as simply a supplement to an educational programme that focused on more practical skills. Jewish community leaders wanted religion to be as respected as any other topic in the schools, but it never was. Evidence shows that Jewish community leaders in Galicia contacted imperial authorities regularly with specific requests, such as increasing the hours of religious instruction or raising teachers' salaries.[40] This dynamic of petition and response was repeated in the Second Polish Republic. Nineteenth- and early twentieth-century community leaders also complained about the lack of full-time positions in secondary schools. Low salaries made it difficult to recruit teachers. Teachers of religion were not treated as well as teachers of other subjects: they were not given the resources to participate in conferences and felt that, although their subject was 'the entire basis of life outside of the classroom and of life as a citizen',[41] it was not respected and that the students knew this.

Providing high-quality religious instruction in non-Jewish schools might have been a way to assuage Jewish parents' fears about sending their children to public schools, but the proper instruction of teachers of religion had been a concern among some Jewish leaders since the late nineteenth century. Jewish religious instruction in non-Jewish schools in nineteenth- and early twentieth-century

---

[39] American Jewish Joint Distribution Committee Archives, New York, 1921–32, 'Poland: Localities: Niebylec to Szydlowiec', folder 410: 'The School System in the Novogrodek Section', 29 Aug. 1922.

[40] Żydowski Instytut Historyczny, Warsaw, 107, 'Gmina Wyznaniowa Żydowska w Krakowie', 740/1, Korespondencja z C.K. Radą Szkolną Okręgową m. Krakowa w sprawach nauczania religii mojżeszowej w szkołach; podanie w sprawie posad nauczycieli religii mojżeszowej w szkołach m. Krakowa: 'Do Rady Wyznaniowej Gminy Izraelickiej w Krakowie', 31 Aug. 1908.

[41] Żydowski Instytut Historyczny, Warsaw, 107, 740/1: 'Do Wysokiej c. k. Rady Szkolnej Krajowej we Lwowie', 9 Dec. 1908.

Galicia was hard to regulate.[42] While some teachers of religion in both public and private secondary schools held doctorates from European universities, others, especially those in elementary schools, were poorly trained. There was no institution of higher education to prepare them to teach, and pay for teachers of religion was lower than that of other teachers.[43] There was a concern that badly educated teachers would have a negative influence on their students. In addition, in the nineteenth century few Jewish children took religious instruction in non-Jewish schools. In the Russian part of pre-war Poland, Jewish religious instructors were meant to stem Polonization; thus, neither Jewish community leaders nor Polish educators respected their work. As in Galicia, the quality of training and low pay were ever-present issues.[44]

Community leaders were well aware of the need for better training and also of the changes happening in education, both in pedagogy and in the building of new public and private schools. The State Seminary for Teachers of the Mosaic Religion was founded in Warsaw in October 1918.[45] Samuel Poznański was the first director of the seminary, which was located at Pańska 32. The initial five-year programme included a two-year preparatory course and three years of more advanced study for Jews aged 14 to 18. Poznański secured a building for the seminary at Gęsia 9, and twelve students attended its first class in December 1918. After Poznański's death in 1921 and a temporary replacement, Majer Tauber became director. Tauber unified the five years of instruction and adopted the principles being used in seminaries for teachers for bilingual schools. The school's 338 graduates from 1918 to 1938 received a diploma allowing them to teach religion in the country's public elementary schools. The seminary's faculty consisted of ninety teachers over the twenty years of its existence, including such well-known figures as Majer Bałaban, Roman Brandstaetter, Janusz Korczak, and Michał Weichert. There was a director of physical education and physician on its staff as well.

In spite of the efforts of the state seminary, the poor reputation of religion teachers persisted. The sociologist and community leader Arie Tartakower shared the opinion of Boy-Żeleński: poorly trained 'teachers of religion did more harm

[42] M. Łapot, 'Nauczanie religii mojżeszowej we lwowskich szkołach publicznych w dobie autonomii galicyjskiej: Zarys problematyki', in K. Dormus and R. Ślęczka (eds.), *W kręgu dawnych i współczesnych teorii wychowania: Uczeń – Szkoła – Nauczyciel* (Kraków, 2012), 166–83.

[43] M. Stinia, 'Dorobek wielokulturowego środowiska gimnazjalnego Krakowa w okresie autonomii galicyjskiej: Nauczanie i nauczyciele religii mojżeszowej', in S. Walasek (ed.), *Wśród 'swoich' i 'obcych': Rola edukacji w społeczeństwach wielokulturowych Europy Środkowej (XVIII–XX wiek)* (Kraków, 2006), 203–12; B. Łuczyńska, 'Towarzystwo Nauczycieli Szkół Wyższych organizacją integrującą zróżnicowane narodowościowo środowisko nauczycieli Galicji', in Walasek (ed.), *Wśród 'swoich' i 'obcych'*, 161–75.

[44] E. Kula, 'Nauczyciele religii mojżeszowej w rządowych miejskich szkołach średnich Królestwa Polskiego w drugiej połowie XIX wieku', in Walasek (ed.), *Wśród 'swoich' i 'obcych'*, 213–30.

[45] Z. Hoffman, 'Państwowe Seminarium dla Nauczycieli Religii Mojżeszowej w Warszawie', *Biuletyn Żydowskiego Instytutu Historycznego*, 149 (1989), 101–5.

than good, since they degraded in the eyes of the children the meaning of the Jewish religion and Jewishness in general'.[46] Jewish religious instructors in the public schools of the Second Polish Republic held what were essentially part-time positions, working an average of twenty to thirty hours a week and often being assigned to three or four different schools with two or three different classes in each. Many of the religion teachers had taught in some capacity within the Jewish community before 1918; the younger ones were often students at the local university. Even in cities as large as Kraków and Lwów, the number of Jewish religious instructors was rather small, usually no more than twelve to fifteen.

In addition to the worries of underemployment, religious instruction teachers also had to take responsibility for a demanding curriculum. The two hours of weekly instruction were intended to cover the daily prayers, Torah, Psalms, liturgy, biblical history, rabbinic literature, and Jewish history from the earliest times to Poland's Constitution of 3 May 1791. Two hours could not replace the long, often ten-hour, day of the *ḥeder*. Naftali Schipper's *Historja Żydów oraz przegląd ich kultury* proved quite useful, as it offered instructors a concise interpretation of a complex history, albeit one sympathetic to Polish national aims. It covered nearly two thousand years in just two brief volumes, and two major sections of the second volume concerned the participation of Jews in the struggles for an independent Poland.

RELIGIOUS INSTRUCTION IN PRACTICE

The classroom Janusz Korczak described was far removed from the traditional *ḥeder*. Korczak devoted his life to improving the conditions of those around him. He was a modern figure, quite unlike the traditional embittered *melamed*. His involvement in Jewish education suggests just how much it had developed in a few short decades. Studying in the *ḥeder* and then in the *beit midrash* or *shtibl* and going on to study at the yeshiva was no longer the typical pattern of education for young Polish Jews. In a description of his educational experiences before the Second World War, the memoirist Ben-Zion Gold wrote: 'In Poland secular education generally meant a break with tradition.'[47] As Poland developed, educational patterns changed, both because of government decrees mandating education and because of Jewish parents' recognition that their children needed more practical skills than just those they learned in the *ḥeder*. Gold concluded: 'What only recently had been the accepted norm became in my time an exception.'[48]

The implementation of religious instruction in schools proved more complex than Polish officials had at first thought. The state set guidelines for religious instruction, but, naturally, local authorities made any necessary decisions about the implementation of them. For example, school authorities carefully monitored

---

[46] A. Tartakower, 'Yidishe kultur in poyln tsvishn tsvey velt milkhomes', *Gedank un Lebn*, 4 (Apr.–June 1946), 20; cited in Heller, *On the Edge of Destruction*, 237 n. 39.

[47] Gold, 'Religious Education in Poland', 275.   [48] Ibid. 278.

the teaching of Hebrew in Jewish religious classes. While Hebrew was accepted as necessary for Jewish religious instruction, school authorities stressed that only the minimal amount of Hebrew necessary for prayer be taught, explicitly forbidding the teaching of Hebrew reading, writing, and grammar.[49] They did not specifically mention a fear of Hebrew as an alternative national language, but the restrictions indicate the authorities' consideration of issues of Jewish nationalism within the context of the teaching of the Jewish religion. It also indicates one of the dangers of teaching religion in a public school system. Government officials simply did not understand that the teaching of Hebrew was not simply philology but an essential part of the religious identity Jewish leaders wished to impart to Jewish children. Local authorities did allow *kehilah* leaders to establish Hebrew as an elective course in three public schools where there were enough Jewish students to justify it.[50] Such an elective course did not, however, exempt them from religious instruction.

The system of religious instruction, however flawed, perpetuated the religious divisions within the population. It was designed to maintain them, for the benefit of all religious groups. Even in the best of times and under the best conditions, however, minorities would be likely to suffer unfair treatment. Both the *kehilot* and Agudat Israel, the modern Orthodox political party founded in 1916, criticized the system of religious instruction and continually petitioned school and state authorities for improvements to it. Lwów provides an important example of how the *kehilah* interacted with Polish governmental authorities. Unless their parents enrolled them in private schools, Jewish children in Lwów, as Polish citizens, received a public education. The teaching of the Jewish religion ensured that they would at least receive some instruction in their parents' religious tradition, but community leaders wanted to improve it as much as possible.

Public schools held classes on Saturday, which meant Jewish children at those schools were unable to attend synagogue services on the sabbath. As this was an integral part of Jewish religious instruction, in 1930 *kehilah* leaders planned a programme that would periodically allow Jewish secondary school students to be excused from classes early on Saturday.[51] This was a complicated task that involved the administration and teachers of religion from ten different schools and consideration of the sensitivities of religious Jews, who objected because the Jewish students might come to the synagogue dressed inappropriately and, carrying all their materials for school, might break the sabbath restrictions. Issues of timing and transportation were also a concern. Students could not attend in the late afternoon because winter afternoons were too short. In many cases, the children lived too far away from the synagogue, and they could not use transport on the

---

[49] Tsentral'nyi derzhavnyi istorychnyi arkhiv Ukrayiny, Lviv (hereafter TsDIAL), f. 701, op. 3, spr. 672: 'Protokoły, plany nauczania', letter to directors of all public and private secondary schools from Sobiński, Kuratorium Okręgu Szkolnego Lwowskiego (n.d.).

[50] TsDIAL, f. 701, op. 3, spr. 846: 'Spiski uchiteli'.

[51] TsDIAL, f. 701, op. 3, spr. 1121: 'Protokoły konferencji'.

sabbath. Eventually, a plan was devised for the Jewish students of the ten schools to attend synagogue services every third Saturday. While some Jewish leaders objected to the programme, calling it much too modest to meet the real needs of Jewish religious instruction, the *kehilah* presented the plan to the city's school authorities. While there was some protest because it would require some Jewish students to miss classes each Saturday, the authorities eventually approved. Jewish leaders even succeeded in gaining an important concession. While the teacher of Jewish religion accompanied the students, in schools where most students were Jewish a teacher of a secular subject, Jewish or non-Jewish, accompanied them as well. The *kehilah* leaders argued that releasing the teacher of a secular subject was necessary in order to impress upon the students the importance of attending the synagogue.

Other examples show how Polish authorities responded to Jewish requests about specific issues. A rabbi in Będzin led an effort to make it possible for Jewish children to pray in the mornings before school began. However, in winter, if school began at 8:00 a.m., prayers had to be at 7:00 a.m., when it was still too dark to pray according to Jewish religious law. The rabbi petitioned the Ministry of Education to allow the school day to begin at 8:30 from 1 October to 31 March, allowing prayers to begin at 7:30.[52] Similarly, the school authorities in Warsaw granted parents' request that their children study the Torah in Hebrew for two extra hours each week, as long as the costs of the instruction were covered by the parents.[53] Such requests involved significant effort by parents and Jewish community leaders, similar to *shtadlanut*, the official lobbying of the authorities on behalf of the Jewish community. The system of religious instruction was still not firmly established, and Jewish parents and community leaders often tried to change it to their children's advantage. The *kehilah* certainly did not have any real power over the public school system, but it could hire and fire religious instruction teachers, arrange special programmes for synagogue attendance, influence the school's opening hours, and establish elective courses in Hebrew. Jewish leaders were not satisfied with the system, but they worked within it to improve the education of their children. They recognized that public schools would be a permanent feature of the new state and that many Jewish children, perhaps a significant majority, would attend them. The back and forth of Jewish requests and Polish responses suggests a degree of flexibility on the part of Polish authorities and a strong desire on the part of Jewish parents to improve religious instruction.

According to Dorota Wojtas, 'the noticeable presence of the Church in schools constituted one of the peculiarities of the Polish state's attempts at nation-building',[54] and it meant that the Catholic Church was present in the daily lives of

[52] Seidman, *Dos yidishe religyeze shul-vezn in di ramen fun der poylisher gezetsgebung*, 47.

[53] C. Statkiewicz, Board of Trustees, Warsaw School District, answer to letter 273 of 26 Dec. 1933, 29 Jan. 1934, in Seidman, *Dos yidishe religyeze shul-vezn in di ramen fun der poylisher gezetsgebung*, 50.

[54] Wojtas, 'Learning to become Polish', 36–7.

Jewish students. Fourteen of the fifteen school holidays were specifically Christian; the other one was 3 May, Constitution Day.[55] Religious instruction in public schools was fundamentally about the importance of Catholicism in Poland: Catholics wanted religion in schools, and consequently there were daily prayers, holiday rituals, and religious instruction as well as accommodations for those of other faiths. Catholic rituals permeated the school, and Jewish children often sang hymns or Christmas carols and, in some cases, attended Catholic religious lessons. Judaism was not absent from public schools, but Polish customs intruded even in Jewish events. Thus, students danced the *mazur* and *krakowiak* at a Hanukah ball sponsored by one public school.[56] The culture of the majority could not be denied. In his 1927 study of education in Poland, Frank Drobka concluded: 'While the schools are not *de jure* strictly Catholic, they are so *de facto*. The schools now publicly acknowledge Christ and His teachings, and try to instil religious practices into the pupils.'[57] For Catholic leaders, this may have been a positive development; for the Jewish community, it was a reason to support private Jewish education.

The autobiographies of young Polish Jews submitted to the YIVO autobiography competitions in the 1930s and post-war memoir literature allow a glimpse into Jewish students' experiences in public schools. While these sources are not necessarily representative of all students' experiences, they do offer interesting details about how Jewish children experienced religious instruction and, more generally, their encounter with Catholicism and Polish culture. The story of Esther reveals just how a young person's life could change in the 1920s and 1930s.[58] Esther came from a hasidic family, attended a Bais Yaakov school, and was active in the school's youth organization, but she wanted to go to the public school and her father eventually granted his permission. Esther was truly caught between tradition and assimilation:

I didn't consider the public school to be 'ours', even though we were taught by Jewish men and women. Since they didn't observe the Sabbath and always spoke Polish, as far as I was concerned they were 'unfortunate people'. I also felt that the way that they taught religion was wrong. More than once I found myself in tears outside the classroom door as a consequence of challenging my teacher. I had no intention of making myself important; I only wanted to point out where the teacher had erred. I would explain that this or that in the school's teaching of history didn't conform with what we were taught in Beys Yaakov and therefore was wrong. For this I got paddled liberally. While I continued to protest at every opportunity, this didn't prevent me from getting straight 5's on my report card. Father was very pleased and stopped talking about my becoming a '*shikse*'. He was glad that I opposed the lessons in religion.[59]

[55] Drobka, *Education in Poland*, 72–3.
[56] See Landau-Czajka, *Syn będzie Lech...*, 367; for additional examples, see ibid. 374, 378.
[57] Drobka, *Education in Poland*, 113.
[58] YIVO Archives, New York, RG 4 'Autobiographies of Jewish Youth in Poland (1932–39)': Autobiography 3559, in *Awakening Lives: Autobiographies of Jewish Youth in Poland before the Holocaust*, ed. J. Shandler (New Haven, Conn., 2002), 321–43.   [59] Ibid. 322–3.

While Esther took her values from Bais Yaakov into the public school and opposed what she was taught in the state-sanctioned religion course, public school was not without its effects. She fell in love with Polish literature, she venerated Piłsudski, and she eventually made friends with girls from different backgrounds. Despite missing her chance to attend either a gymnasium or the Bais Yaakov teachers' seminary in Kraków, she nonetheless established a Bais Yaakov school in a small town. The public school had helped to shape her intellectual horizons, but it had not necessarily effaced her Jewish identity. Esther eventually read widely in secular Yiddish literature as well, and her first writing in Yiddish was her YIVO autobiography, submitted in 1939.

According to Celia Heller, the teaching of Jewish religion in public schools did little to stem secularization, since the teachers were subjected to ridicule and pranks and not respected. Heller quoted from one of the YIVO autobiographies: 'the greatest disorder was during the lesson of religion'.[60] Furthermore, as Heller explained, the bent back of the traditional Jew stood no chance against the image of the brave Pole: 'large numbers of young middle class Jews—those belonging to the intelligentsia or aspiring to it—had internalized the Polish ideals of manhood'.[61] According to Jakub Wygodzki, doctor, Zionist activist, and member of the Minorities Bloc in the Sejm, the schools were clearly 'a tool of forced assimilation'.[62] Some students were indeed attracted to the rituals of Catholicism. One recalled his experience in public school:

I went to the Jewish religion class every week. But every day, with everyone else, I sang the morning prayer 'Kiedy ranne wstają zorze'. . . . When Marshal Piłsudski died I took part in the school church service. I painted Easter eggs with Marysia for Easter and I glued together chains for the Christmas tree. In spite of all of Mr Segal's efforts, I never learned to read in Hebrew, but I knew all the Christmas carols by heart.[63]

Assimilation, or at least acculturation, could happen at lightning speed in the public schools.[64]

Anna Landau-Czajka challenges Heller's conclusion about the schools and assimilation. Writing specifically about assimilation, Landau-Czajka explains that Polonization did not necessarily mean a move away from Jewish identity, as Esther's story attests. She points out that the public schools were limited as agents of assimilation precisely because they were also full of antisemitism. Public schools were often places where Jewish children felt alienated from their peers. Landau-Czajka cites a Polish memoirist who describes Jewish children shamefacedly leaving

---

[60] YIVO Archives, RG 4: Autobiography 3577, cited in Heller, *On the Edge of Destruction*, 237, 354 n. 38.   [61] Heller, *On the Edge of Destruction*, 237.

[62] J. Wygodzki, 'Budżet Państwa Polskiego na 1929–30r. a Żydzi', in 'Mowy w Sejmie i Senacie w dyskusji budżetowej', *Biuletyn Klubu Posłów i Senatorów Żydowskiej Rady Narodowej*, 3 (1929), 66, cited in Heller, *On the Edge of Destruction*, 221.

[63] K. Winiecka [I. Wilder], *Od Stanisławowa do Australii* (Cieszyn, n.d.), 48–9, cited in Landau-Czajka, *Syn będzie Lech...*, 377–8.   [64] Landau-Czajka, *Syn będzie Lech...*, 383.

the classroom when it came time for religious instruction.[65] Throughout her discussion of the experiences of children from assimilated families, she suggests that simply feeling different from their classmates was more of an issue for students than their occasional participation in Catholic prayers or singing carols.

The presence of the church in schools was one of the most important reasons why Jewish leaders sought to establish private Jewish schools. Those promoting private Jewish education did not hesitate to associate public schools with assimilation and Polonization.[66] More religiously observant parents did not want to send their children to public school but often had no choice.[67] The influence of the Catholic Church in Poland led to religion in schools and, consequently, to difficult situations for those who did not practise Catholicism. Religious practice in school blurred the distinction between public and private behaviour: for Catholics in Poland, religious practice was public behaviour that merited the approval and protection of the state. The government made accommodations because the circumstances of minority faiths warranted those accommodations.

CONCLUSION

Part of the task of the education system of the newly created Polish republic was the integration of diverse populations and the public schools aimed to teach children what it meant to be a Polish citizen in a Polish nation. School rituals, such as the observance of Constitution Day and name days of Polish government officials, prayers, and singing, reinforced Polish national belonging. Religion complicated this educational effort. The Catholic Church was not officially involved in integrating the country's diverse populations: the national and religious minorities in Poland were simply too large for such an effort at forced assimilation to have worked, but the daily presence of Catholicism in schools and the 'preponderating authority' of the church in relation to other faiths reinforced the culture of the majority and sometimes damaged children of other faiths, who wondered how to fit in and why they were different. The Polish authorities' failure to provide adequately for minority students led many Jews to see the public schools as simply a tool to bring about the assimilation they were anxious to avoid.

Jews in Poland had no reason to trust a nascent government and every reason to fear establishments set up by non-Jewish rulers. Religious instruction for Jewish children—in Polish and in Polish schools—simply could not satisfy those who viewed this instruction as an imposition from outside the Jewish community.

[65] S. Berenda-Czajkowski, *Dni grozy i łez* (Warsaw, 2001), 28–9, cited in Landau-Czajka, *Syn będzie Lech…*, 373.

[66] Some of the leaflets in the collection of the National Library in Poland refer directly to the threat of assimilation in public schools (see B. Łętocha, A. Messer, and A. Cała, *Żydowskie druki ulotne w II Rzeczypospolitej w zbiorach Biblioteki Narodowej* (Warsaw, 2004), nos. 296, 320, 325).

[67] Landau-Czajka, *Syn będzie Lech…*, 348.

Writing in *Miesięcznik Żydowski*, Jeremiasz Frenkel noted that for the Orthodox the study of religion was something like '"artificial breathing": unnecessary for the religiously healthy organism and of not much help to the sick'.[68] The inclusion of Jewish religious instruction simply highlighted that the state privileged secular education and implicitly relegated Jews to the status of a religious, rather than a national, minority within the Polish state. Moreover, government regulations, in the form of mandatory education and oversight of religious instruction and private schools, ensured that the culture of the majority, including their Catholic faith, would somehow always be officially present in the lives of Jewish students.

Yet if the goal of the Polish authorities was to assimilate Jewish children, their policy on religious instruction could only undermine it. The presence of religion in the classroom introduced a distinction among schoolchildren. This distinction led to inequity, but it also preserved difference. This was a difference some Jewish children felt acutely, a difference that could only limit their assimilation. The policy on religious instruction in public schools was about religion, not assimilation. In retrospect, it was a remarkable attempt to bridge significant differences within state institutions. The effort to teach Judaism in public schools is an excellent example of how the interaction of a smaller group with the culture and institutions of a larger group is necessarily transformative. Public schools were one of the successes of the Second Polish Republic. Polish educational leaders developed and stabilized a network of elementary and secondary schools and, however inadequately, included Jews in their plans. Poland's model of religion in the public sphere accommodated groups outside the majority faith and suggests that accommodations such as those in the public schools helped to transform the relationship of Jews to the Polish state. Teachers of Jewish religion in Poland's public schools offered their students a way to implement and exercise a Jewish identity in a Polish environment. Public schools were helping to make Jewish children into Polish citizens and Poles, further increasing and testing internal Jewish diversity.

[68] J. Frenkel, 'Znaczenie nauczania religji i wychowania religijnego', *Miesięcznik Żydowski*, 2/7–12 (July–Dec. 1932), 240.

'Vos vayter?' Graduating from Elementary School in Interwar Poland

From Personal Crisis to Cultural Turning Point

ADVA SELZER

IN 1932 YIVO announced its first autobiography competition for young east European Jews with the goal of learning about the problems they faced. Two years later YIVO established a special department for youth research in order to develop and deepen knowledge of the lives of young Jews, which held two additional competitions in 1934 and 1939:

Through these autobiographies we want to learn about the lives of young Jews in these painful days. We want to understand what are the obstacles that stand in the way of young people who wish to establish their status in life, what kind of conflicts they have with their immediate and remote surroundings and amongst themselves.[1]

Around 370 autobiographies survived the Second World War, affording a rich and rewarding resource for this period, especially the experience of growing up as a Jew in Poland.[2]

The autobiographies have been the subject of several important studies, starting with that of Max Weinreich, one of YIVO's founders and head of its youth department. His book,[3] published before the third competition, stands out for its psycho-social approach that emphasized the cultural context in which the autobiographies were written. Sociological and statistical methods were also employed by Moshe Kligsberg, who focused on the cultural and political mentality of the young

---

[1] *Yediyes fun YIVO*, Nov.–Dec. 1939, p. 16.

[2] YIVO Archives, New York, RG 4: 'Autobiographies of Jewish Youth in Poland (1932–1939)'; see also *Awakening Lives: Autobiographies of Jewish Youth in Poland before the Holocaust*, ed. J. Shandler (New Haven, Conn., 2002); *Ostatnie pokolenie: Autobiografie polskiej młodzieży żydowskiej okresu międzywojennego*, ed. A. Cała (Warsaw, 2003); *Alilot ne'urim: otobiyografyot shel benei no'ar yehudim mipolin bein shetei milḥamot olam*, ed. I. Bassok (Jerusalem, 2011).

[3] M. Weinreich, *Der veg tsu unzer yugnt: yesoydes, metodn, problemen fun yidisher yugnt-forshung* (Vilna, 1935).

writers.[4] Gershon Bacon used the autobiographies alongside additional sources to examine gender issues.[5] Ido Bassok and Alina Cała both made use of the auto-biographies to map political and ideological consciousness.[6] Bassok's latest book sought to evaluate the 'truth' and 'falsehood' in these writings—a rather old-fashioned approach—and to assess their literary value—despite the fact that the official contest announcements by YIVO specifically stressed that the participants should not try to write 'literature'.[7] An interesting perspective is provided by Marcus Moseley, who describes the development of these youngsters from young enthusiastic readers through nascent authors to their emergence as autobiographers.[8]

This chapter analyses the experience of growing up as a Jew in interwar Poland.[9] I have tried to penetrate the inner, emotional lives of the autobiographers, concentrating on their emotional reactions to the events, circumstances, and institutions encountered during childhood and adolescence. This provides new understandings of the institutions and activities at the centre of their lives, as emotional spheres that channel feelings and actions in new directions. Thus, on a broader level, the chapter seeks to demonstrate how an emotional experience can have a transformative effect by focusing on one such moment in the world of interwar Polish Jews: graduation from elementary school.

The first section analyses how the novelty of access to education and its abrupt and painful discontinuation (for economic, familial, or other reasons) provoked a deep crisis for young Jews, who found their hopes for a future as participants in a modern Polish state cut short by the needs of their family and by political, social, and economic reality. The second section outlines their responses: from writing personal diaries to continuing the quest for education in political Jewish youth movements. The last section places these findings in the context of ideology and examines how their personal crises transformed their political orientation.

[4] M. Kligsberg, *Child and Adolescent Behavior under Stress: An Analytical Topical Guide to a Collection of Autobiographies of Jewish Young Men and Women in Poland (1932–1939) in the Possession of the YIVO Institute for Jewish Research* (New York, 1965); id., 'Di yidishe yugnt-bavegung in poyln tsvishn beyde velt-milkhomes', in J. A. Fishman (ed.), *Studies on Polish Jewry, 1919–1939* (New York, 1974), 137–228.

[5] G. Bacon, 'The Missing 52 Percent: Research on Jewish Women in Interwar Poland and its Implications for Holocaust Studies', in D. Ofer and L. J. Weitzman (eds.), *Women in the Holocaust* (New Haven, Conn., 1998), 55–67.

[6] A. Cała, 'The Social Consciousness of Young Jews in Interwar Poland', *Polin*, 8 (1994), 42–66; I. Bassok, 'Ne'urim ve'erkhei ne'urim bitenu'ot hano'ar bepolin shebein shetei milḥamot', in I. Bartal and Y. Gutman (eds), *Kiyum veshever*, ii: *Yehudei polin ledoroteihem* (Jerusalem, 2001), 573–604; id., 'Ma'amadot vetefisa ma'amadit etsel yeladim uvene no'ar yehudim bepolin ben hamilḥamot', *Gal-ed*, 18 (2002), 225–44.   [7] *Alilot ne'urim*, ed. A. Novershtern (Tel Aviv, 2011).

[8] M. Moseley, 'Life, Literature: Autobiographies of Jewish Youth in Interwar Poland', *Jewish Social Studies*, 7/3 (2001), 1–51.

[9] See also A. Selzer, '"Freedom still my soul demands": Growing Up in a Jewish Family in Inter-War Poland', Ph.D. thesis (Bar-Ilan University, 2009).

EXISTENTIAL CRISIS

In reading the autobiographies of young Jews in interwar Poland, one special occasion emerges almost immediately as one of existential crisis, the day they graduated from elementary school and left its desks, never to return:

Vos vayter? [What next?] The question burst out of my chest with the strength of thunder. I'm not the only one who shouts. A whole camp like me: Mendele, Moishale, Avremale, and more and more, everyone shouts in one voice: What next?[10]

The end of elementary school was also the end of formal education for the majority of these writers. Research has revealed that only 8 to 10 per cent of Jewish children continued their studies in either high schools or vocational schools, while the rest were forced to enter the job market at the ages of 13 to 15, primarily in order to contribute to the family budget and avoid the expenses which would be incurred had they continued their studies.[11]

The expressions of pain and sorrow caused by leaving school are puzzling, for this certainly was not the first generation that was forced to end its formal education at such a young age. The majority of the older generation and, in all likelihood, the preceding one as well, especially those who lived in the parts of Poland that had been in the tsarist empire, did not have the opportunity to continue their education. Boys may have gone to the *ḥeder*, but most girls did not, and only a small minority, mainly from the elite, received a formal Jewish and general education in public and private schools.[12] Yet, instead of a neutral description of this 'natural' stage in the course of their lives or at most a painful acceptance of it, the reactions are quite different:

Yet when the time came to go to the [Bais Yaakov teacher-training] seminary, I was the one who remained at home. The reason for this was simple, but tragic! 'Why? Why?' a voice within me cried. 'Why do I have to suffer like this, when I have such an urge to learn? Why must I suffer within the narrow confines of my limited duties, when everything in me longs to broaden my horizons?'[13]

Why was graduating from elementary school at the age of 13 or 15 portrayed in such desperate terms?

[10] YIVO Archives, RG 4: Autobiography 3802, 25.
[11] S. Lewin, 'Some Aspects of the History of Secondary Education for Jews in Congress Poland during the Late Tsarist Period and Between the World Wars', *Gal-ed*, 17 (2000), esp. 23–4; S. Frost, *Schooling as a Socio-political Expression* (Jerusalem, 1998), 48–50; J. Marcus, *Social and Political History of the Jews in Poland 1919–1939* (Berlin, 1983), 156–61.
[12] E. Adler, 'Rediscovering Schools for Jewish Girls in Tsarist Russia', *East European Jewish Affairs*, 34/2 (2004), 139–50; ead., *In her Hands: The Education of Jewish Girls in Tsarist Russia* (Detroit, 2011); S. Stampfer, 'Gender Differentiation and Education of the Jewish Woman in Nineteenth-Century Eastern Europe', *Polin*, 7 (1992), 63–87.
[13] YIVO Archives, RG 4: Autobiography 3559, in *Awakening Lives*, 329.

Emphasis on learning had always been central to Jewish culture, although only a limited circle enjoyed the privilege. These scholars—all men—usually came from the elite, although occasionally they also came from lower strata aided by financial support from the community. Being a *talmid ḥakham* (scholar in Jewish scriptures) promised them not only social prestige but also better prospects for a good marriage, which meant a better material situation. Learning Torah was a sacred obligation even for groups like artisans and merchants who were predominantly concerned with earning a living. Being well versed in Jewish scriptures thus afforded significant cultural and social capital.[14] When the Haskalah movement developed in eastern Europe during the nineteenth century, new types of education became available to the Jewish public, and women started being included in the process of learning.[15] Higher education became synonymous with modernity and the path towards better integration into non-Jewish circles. Gradually general subjects were added to the traditional curriculum or even sometimes replaced it, and educated men (doctors, lawyers, engineers) came to enjoy prestige among their fellow Jews.[16]

Thus, the thirst for education that characterized young Polish Jews between the wars was based on a mixture of tradition and more recent trends. Yet, as has been noted, this was not the first generation of Polish Jews compelled to leave school at such a young age. The inability to continue at school does not, therefore, in itself explain why their fate was experienced as particularly cruel.

One possible explanation is that appetite tends to increase by eating. When the First World War ended and the Second Polish Republic was established, compulsory education was introduced. All children, including those of the minorities, were obliged to attend either state-funded or private elementary schools. Compulsory education thus opened the doors of public schools to all Jewish children, boys and girls alike.[17] Around 80 per cent of them took this opportunity to study without

[14] C. S. Heller, *On the Edge of Destruction: Jews of Poland between the Two World Wars* (Detroit, 1994), 153; M. Zborowski, 'The Place of Book Learning in Traditional Jewish Culture', in M. Mead and M. Wolfenstein (eds.), *Childhood in Contemporary Cultures* (Chicago, 1955), 118–41.

[15] Stampfer, 'Gender Differentiation and Education of the Jewish Woman in Nineteenth-Century Eastern Europe'; Adler, 'Rediscovering Schools for Jewish Girls in Tsarist Russia'.

[16] On modernization and education in nineteenth-century eastern Europe, see M. Zalkin, *El heikhal hahaskalah: tahalikhei modernizatsyah baḥinukh hayehudi bemizraḥ eiropah bame'ah hateshaesreh* (Tel Aviv, 2008).

[17] In some areas of Poland, mainly those that were under Austro-Hungarian and German rule, these doors were opened even earlier, in the second half of the nineteenth century. In territories controlled by tsarist Russia, the situation was more complicated. During the nineteenth century the Russian government, in collaboration with the maskilim, tried to promote educational reform among the Jews, including a quota for Jews in Russian educational institutions and the establishment of government-run Jewish schools. These endeavours were to leave a permanent mark on Jewish society; however, they required the co-operation of the Jewish public, which was still very traditional and perceived the innovations as a threat, and the good will of the government, which fluctuated according to the political and ideological atmosphere. See B. Nathans, *Beyond the Pale: The Jewish Encounter with Late Imperial Russia* (Berkeley, Calif., 2002), 201–56; Adler, *In her Hands*.

having to pay tuition, while the remaining 20 per cent paid for private Jewish schools that were obliged to include general subjects in their curriculum (Polish history, literature, and language) if they wanted to obtain government approval.[18] The years spent in those institutions opened their eyes to new possibilities and reinforced their appetite for education. Even those who suffered from the discrimination and antisemitic attitudes of their classmates and teachers acknowledged the positive sides of school and the advantages it gave them:

These were the dark sides from which I suffered in school but on the other hand, I got familiar with new things that until now I had no idea about. Public school for me was the complete opposite of the old and mouldy *ḥeder* in which I spent a few months repeating the *melamed*'s words. . . . I breathed freely, the curiosity and exciting conversations and classes in school exceeded the antisemitic hate. Although the latter existed, I rarely missed days in school.[19]

For the first time modern education was widely available and not the prerogative of the elite. This new state of affairs, combined with the fact that in the Second Polish Republic minorities were guaranteed equal rights under the constitution, created a euphoric sense among Jews: for a certain period it seemed as if the sky was the limit. Although this feeling evaporated with the increasingly antisemitic atmosphere and discrimination,[20] the idea that education could secure a better future had by the 1930s become deeply rooted.

For young Jews, education seemed to be the only way to escape poverty and backwardness. As with the bulk of Poland's population, the majority of Jews suffered from impoverishment. In some shtetls almost 90 per cent of the Jewish inhabitants had to rely on welfare. Unemployment was widespread in the country as a result of the underdevelopment of the Polish economy and the impact of the Great Depression, while antisemitism did not make it easier for Jews to find jobs. In 1930 35 per cent of Jewish businesses were bankrupt, and in 1931 29 per cent of Jewish breadwinners were unemployed (compared to 21 per cent of non-Jews).[21] Education was the only 'capital' left for young Jews and they actively sought its advantages.[22] One girl described this very clearly:

Mother fought with Father even harder over how I and my eldest sister . . . were to be educated. Father wanted a melamed to teach us how to sign our names and nothing more. But Mother knew better; she understood that life was a struggle. To avoid failing as she had, we

[18] G. Bacon, 'National Revival, Ongoing Acculturation: Jewish Education in Interwar Poland', *Jahrbuch des Simon-Dubnow-Instituts*, 1 (2002), 73.

[19] YIVO Archives, RG 4: Autobiography 3802, 18–19.

[20] After the death of Józef Piłsudski in 1935 the situation changed for the worse. Nationalistic tendencies became widespread and antisemitism was employed for political ends (see E. Melzer, 'Antisemitism in the Last Years of the Second Polish Republic', in Y. Gutman et al. (eds.), *The Jews of Poland between Two World Wars* (Hanover, NH, 1989), 126).

[21] J. Schatz, *The Generation: The Rise and Fall of the Jewish Communists of Poland* (Berkeley, Calif., 1991), 25.

[22] Kligsberg, 'Di yidishe yugnt-bavegung in poyln tsvishn beyde velt-milkhomes', 154.

had to see everything with open eyes. To do this we had to be armed with knowledge. . . .
After a week of feuding, my parents enrolled me in a Jewish public school.[23]

There was also another reason, less rational and future-oriented, why public
school was attractive. School was experienced as a haven, a refuge from the chaos
and turmoil outside its walls. For some children, school was the only place they felt
happy and secure; while at home, their parents, absorbed in survival, could not
provide them with the needed emotional support and comfort:

In time I became very attached to my teachers. My greatest joy was to hear a kind word
from them; a caress on my cheek was the greatest pleasure. Little by little, I began to like
school more than home. The more I suffered at home, the more I valued school. I felt that
they understood me much better. My teacher paid much more attention to me than Father
did.[24]

The emotional and moral support derived from school thus meant that leaving
at a young age was not simply a matter of sacrificing one's chances for a better
future. For some it meant giving up the only sheltered place in their lives, and in
leaving it they felt that they were being exiled from an earthly paradise. When they
left school, they found themselves facing a suffocating reality with a quite gloomy
horizon. No wonder the day of graduation from elementary school found some
emotionally shattered: 'I feel impoverished—just as I am poor in daily life, I am
poor in knowledge. My mind is thirsty. . . . For me the struggle for existence is
tied to the great drive for knowledge.'[25] When a 'whole camp', the majority of a
generation, experiences such an existential crisis, it leaves its mark on the whole
society and its culture. Graduating from elementary school became a formative
and transformative event.

How did this great drive for knowledge affect their lives? In what ways did it
change Jewish culture and particularly its youth culture? What impact did this
personal crisis have on their conduct as a generation? How did an emotional
experience of this type become a driving force, an historical agent?

TRAGIC VISION

Not only were they miserable because they had to leave school, probably forever,
they were also afraid. Afraid to find themselves working long and tedious hours in
workshops or joining the small family business and standing with their parents
behind the counter of a shop. In 1931 37 per cent of Jews made their living in trade
and 42 per cent in industry, mainly in small workshops as artisans and appren-
tices.[26] For their fathers and grandfathers this had not been an issue, since, in more

[23] YIVO Archives, RG 4: Autobiography 3539, in *Awakening Lives*, 125.

[24] Ibid., in *Awakening Lives*, 126.

[25] YIVO Archives, RG 4: Autobiography 3713, in *Awakening Lives*, 311.

[26] R. Mahler, *Yehudei polin bein shetei milḥamot olam: historyah kalkalit-sotsialiyit le'or hastatistikah*
(Tel Aviv, 1968), 37.

traditional societies children generally followed their parents and inherited their occupations.[27] However, things had changed, and with the spirit of modernity came individualism—personal wishes and hopes began to be recognized as legitimate factors in life decisions. The fear of becoming like their parents (perhaps a universal phenomenon) resonated in small towns and big cities alike: 'My father didn't give me time to choose an occupation. Instead, I was ordered to come and work in our business. This commandment had a horrible influence on me, like Isaac when his father called him to be sacrificed.'[28]

Feeling helpless was also very common among the young autobiographers. They left school against their will, usually due to circumstances that were beyond their own or even their parents' control. In the face of economic reality it seemed that they were compelled to accept their fate: 'I finally realized that higher education wasn't for me, that my father's income didn't afford me the possibility of going to school. I had to make peace with reality and abandon my dream.'[29]

On top of these feelings of despair, fear, and helplessness came anger and frustration at what was perceived as an injustice. They blamed the social order, capitalism, and the lack of equality in the world. Combined, these emotions created what Lucien Goldman described as a 'tragic vision',[30] which became widespread among the young after the First World War. Those who were unable to obtain high positions, influence, resources, or authority and found themselves with no control over their fate were attracted to this tragic vision. In their view, while individuals cannot overcome the circumstances and limitations that surround them, they should compromise or accept their reality. The 'tragic man' longs for a better world. He experiences the ambivalent desire both to fight and to withdraw.[31] Not surprisingly, this attitude is widely found in the autobiographies: 'I came into contact with "true reality", with its minimum of possibilities and maximum of impossibilities.'[32]

ALTERNATIVE SOURCES OF EDUCATION

Youth Movements

In response to this crisis, many young Jews turned to youth movements, including those of the trade unions and political parties. At the peak of their activity, more than 100,000 of the 450,000 Jewish adolescents in interwar Poland were active in

[27] J. Katz, 'Ḥevrah masoratit veḥevrah modernit', in *Le'umiyut yehudit: masot umeḥkarim* (Jerusalem, 1983), 165.   [28] YIVO Archives, RG 4: Autobiography 3780, 4.

[29] YIVO Archives, RG 4: Autobiography 3713, 312.

[30] Lucien Goldman, a French Jew and Marxist intellectual, had been a member of the youth movement Hashomer Hatsa'ir (see M. Evans, *Lucien Goldmann: An Introduction* (Brighton, East Sussex, 1981), 60).

[31] O. Nordheimer Nur, 'Ha'estetikah ha'anarkhistit shel "hashomer hatsa'ir" bishenot ha'esrim utefisat ha'olam hateragit', in Y. Hotam (ed.), *'Tor hane'urim': no'ar yehudi-germani ba'idan hamoderni* (Jerusalem, 2008), 35–6.   [32] YIVO Archives, RG 4: Autobiography 3792, in *Awakening Lives*, 292.

such organizations.[33] Research has tended to emphasize the ideological and political aspects of these movements as they competed for support within the Jewish community.[34] While turning to ideology as a source of hope and an explanation of reality is not unusual, the ideological intensity of this particular generation seems to have been very strong.[35] The psychological and cultural aspects of the youth movements—the emotional support of a peer group, the search for authenticity through the formation of personal and generational identities, and the development of youth culture—have been investigated from various points of view.[36] The experience of togetherness provided in these youth movements' *lokale* (clubs) not only comforted their members but also gave them a feeling of strength and competence. By joining such groups, young Jews also made it clear that talking was not enough, action was necessary.

The autobiographies reveal another important aspect of the youth movements. In taking part in their activities, their members gained an informal education, which provided some solace in the emotional crisis caused by leaving school: 'This involved me more closely with the Union, which I considered to be a place that offered cultural and educational opportunities for those who had been dragged out of their homes while still very young and pushed into fetid workshops.'[37] In the *lokal* they continued to broaden their horizons by participating in lectures on a variety of subjects: general and Jewish history, geography, economics, literature and philosophy, and even sex education. They also arranged for themselves special evenings for study and reading circles and initiated local newspapers and cultural soirées. These opportunities to educate themselves made it worth spending their limited spare time in the youth movement branch: 'The pioneers roused me from my intellectual stagnation by appealing to my ambition to learn, which was one of the organization's many virtues.'[38]

The *lokal* became a substitute for school, and, as in school, its members found emotional support and understanding. They met with members from their peer group, who like them had been forced to leave school and were now either trying to find work or struggling to cope with a tedious job. The instructors at the *lokal*, who were mostly only a few years older and had been through similar hardships and

[33] I. Bassok, 'Tenuot hano'ar hayehudiyot bepolin bein shetei milḥamot olam', in A. Novershtern (ed.), *Alilot ne'urim*, 769–93.

[34] Bassok, 'Ne'urim ve'erkhei ne'urim bitenuot hano'ar'; Z. Lam, *Tenuot hano'ar hatsiyoniot bemabat le'aḥor* (Tel Aviv, 1991).

[35] E. Mendelsohn, 'Zionist Success and Zionist Failure: The Case of East Central Europe between the Wars', in R. Kozodoy, D. Sidorsky, and K. Sultanik (eds.), *Vision Confronts Reality: Historical Perspectives on the Contemporary Jewish Agenda* (Rutherford, NJ, 1989), 202–3.

[36] S. N. Eisenstadt, 'Archetypal Patterns of Youth', in E. H. Erikson (ed.), *The Challenge of Youth* (New York, 1965), 29–50; Kligsberg, 'Di yidishe yugnt-bavegung in poyln tsvishn beyde velt-milkhomes'; Bassok, 'Ma'amadot utefisah ma'amadit etsel yeladim'; Nordheimer Nur, 'Ha'estetikah ha'anarkhistit shel "hashomer hatsa'ir"'.

[37] YIVO Archives, RG 4: Autobiography 3690, in *Awakening Lives*, 83.

[38] YIVO Archives, RG 4: Autobiography 3598, in *Awakening Lives*, 365.

disappointments, inspired them and infused them with hope for a better personal future and a just and fair collective future: 'Here I discovered a new life, a life full of belief in the future.'[39]

Like school, youth movements offered a chance to develop and advance in rank. From being a simple participant, a member could progress to being an instructor or the chairman of a cultural or political committee in the local branch or even become the leader of the *lokal* itself. Members got recognition for their activities and received rewards for their contributions to the organization, in the same way that they had received grades and prizes not so long before in school: 'I was considered among the promising "girls" that developed spiritually. . . . They loved me and my heart was filled with love! There was something to do for yourself and for the Jewish public. I was very happy when the leader expressed his sympathy towards me and all the seniors always smiled at me. I became a group leader.'[40]

Many Jewish political parties addressed this desire for knowledge and organized evening schools.[41] The curriculum was planned according to the political agenda of each party, but it included diverse subjects. Young boys and girls hurried to these courses after long and tedious days at work and as soon as they finished their chores at home, and there they satisfied their craving for education:

An unfulfilled passion developed in me and followed me like a shadow. In each way I went I felt thirst for knowledge and education. After a while I started to visit the evening school of Po'alei Tsiyon Left. There I discovered a whole new world and environment. The attitude of the teachers towards the students was warm and friendly. They provided all sorts of courses, like Yiddish, Polish, mathematics, natural sciences and economics. I took it seriously and never missed a session.[42]

Reading

The members of this generation engaged in reading whenever they could. One autobiographer wrote: '[Books] replaced within me the role of school, gradually I forgot my former misery. With all my might I tackled reading.'[43] Libraries, no matter how small, became their favourite places. Jewish libraries constituted about a fifth of all libraries in Poland and held some 850,000 volumes, about 14 per cent of the country's library books.[44] Some of the autobiographers describe the library as a sacred temple were they could find refuge and solace from the chaos and turmoil outside, just as they had in school: 'My heart pounding with deep reverence and respect, I would slip quietly into the library, where everything was clean, neat,

---

[39] YIVO Archives, RG 4: Autobiography 3713, in *Awakening Lives*, 316.

[40] YIVO Archives, RG 4: Autobiography 3520, 13–14.

[41] Kligsberg, 'Di yidishe yugnt-bavegung in poyln tsvishn beyde velt-milkhomes', 198, 221; Bassok, 'Ne'urim ve'erkhei ne'urim bitenuot hano'ar', 578.

[42] YIVO Archives, RG 4: Autobiography 3586, 27.

[43] YIVO Archives, RG 4: Autobiography 3562, 41.

[44] N. Cohen, 'Sifriyot yehudiyot vekoreihen bepolin bein shetei milḥamot ha'olam', *Tsiyon*, 67 (2002), 163–88.

and pleasant. For me this was the holiest place there was, holier than a synagogue is for someone devoutly religious.'[45]

The library not only served as a refuge: inside its walls, self-education and collective learning were carried on in the same way as in the youth movements, through reading circles and study evenings. The librarians, who were often themselves young, advised on books that might enrich the readers' understanding and knowledge of certain subjects. Visiting the library was almost like going back to school.

Thus, between work, youth movement activities, and chores at home, the members of this generation sat down to read. Reading was so vital that they were willing to fight about it with their mothers, who were worried they might ruin their eyesight or, worse, waste expensive lamp oil. The writers emphasized that they also reduced sleeping hours, time with friends, and even abstained from love in favour of reading.

In their daily lives, they saw themselves as victims of circumstance. Since they had been forced to abjure key aspects of their lives such as continuing their education or choosing their career, there remained one thing that they categorically refused to abandon—books: 'With my whole body and soul I devote myself to literature. There isn't a day that goes by without me reading over one hundred pages. I sit for hours at home and occupy myself with reading.'[46]

Books conferred freedom, and literature, as Marcus Moseley has demonstrated, was perceived in terms of the liberation of the self.[47] The autobiographers could educate themselves independently through books, and they read everything: fiction and non-fiction, poetry and political literature. Many of them, especially those who lived in small shtetls, read all the books they could from their local library and ran out of reading material. To overcome this, they taught themselves new languages. Most of them were quite well versed in Polish, which they had learned at school, but in some places the library mainly held books in Yiddish and Hebrew: 'Then I started to read only Hebrew. I knew that by reading I will learn the language. . . . It also gave me an opportunity to get familiar with Hebrew literature— to know the past of my people . . . I hardly left home—and read . . . and read.'[48]

Books replaced also the guiding hand of teachers and the empathy of peers. Young Jews identified with the characters they encountered in them and found comfort and reassurance in the plots:

I love . . . poetry that serves the interest of the working class, which helps the proletariat in its heroic struggle to free itself, that reflects the needs and pain, the joy and suffering of the worker. I love books in which the author describes the wealth and prosperity of the bourgeoisie that result from exploiting the workers. When the present order is exposed in all its

---

[45] YIVO Archives, RG 4: Autobiography 3690, in *Awakening Lives*, 70.
[46] YIVO Archives, RG 4: Autobiography 3814, 15.
[47] Moseley, 'Life, Literature', 6.
[48] YIVO Archives, RG 4: Autobiography 3820, 10.

forms in a genuine and artistic way, it makes workingmen stronger and gives them the energy to fight against their class's enemy.[49]

In the past, sitting in school for a few hours a day had helped them to forget the hardships at home, the hunger and the cold, their wretchedness and their parents' helplessness. Now they could endure all of these while reading at night, delving into the stories and theories that the books offered them:

Winter. Our house is horribly cold. Nothing to heat the kitchen and the stove with. The windows are covered with frost, like beautiful leaves and flowers. I sit and read until late at night. The cold is breaking my bones, [tearing at] my organs. My face shrinks and freezes. When I sit down and read I feel nothing. I just see in front of me the open book and the dripping candle that burns for me with red fire.[50]

Writing

At some point reading was not enough and from passive reading, some of these young Jews turned to active writing, finding ways to express themselves and develop their talents. They started to imagine, even if only for themselves, a new better world. If daily life and leaving school made them feel helpless, the blank sheet of paper, awaiting them alone, filled them with faith, strength, and courage. Holding a pen, they gained control of their narrative. It was the perfect platform to dare and to actualize the potential hidden within them. In their school days their teachers used to listen and absorb their questions, thoughts, and contemplations; now the notebook fulfilled these functions: 'Nowadays I don't enjoy anything as much as I enjoy writing. Writing has become for me a source of pleasure. When I am exhausted from work and want to rest, I sit down to write.'[51]

At school their talents might have been recognized by their teachers and fellow students; outside school they sought recognition from new sources. Usually the first step was writing a diary, but many reached the next level and sought to publish their work. They submitted poems, prose, and political essays to the youth movements' newspapers, 'wall-newspapers' displayed in the local branches, and magazines.[52] They even read their compositions aloud at assemblies and cultural evenings. Public recognition meant that they were capable, productive, and talented. This allowed them to believe that maybe all was not lost:

Generally, I felt compelled to write during every spare moment I had, when hunger didn't torture me too strongly. I felt compelled to write, thinking that, by writing, I could rise above my friends . . . a 'solace' for the fact that I couldn't study in high school and had to become an artisan. Generally, writing became for me a daily phenomenon.[53]

[49] YIVO Archives, RG 4: Autobiography 3794, 46–7.
[50] YIVO Archives, RG 4: Autobiography 3814, 15.
[51] YIVO Archives, RG 4: Autobiography 3709, 65.
[52] Political parties, youth organizations, welfare institutions, and education networks all produced periodicals and newspapers for young Jews (see A. Bar'el, *Bein ha'etsim hayerukim: itonei yeladim beyidish uve'ivrit bepolin 1918–1939* (Jerusalem, 2006)).
[53] YIVO Archives, RG 4: Autobiography 3562, 68–9.

The significance of this textual realm was fully realized in the autobiography competitions. The hours they spent in the library and at home, reading, writing, and reflecting on their lives, allowed them to develop the ability to write a comprehensive autobiography at a young age.[54] Even YIVO's researchers were surprised by the responses to the competitions. In the first competition in 1932 only 34 autobiographies were submitted, the second competition of 1934 attracted 304 responses, and the third and last in 1939, 289. Since composing autobiography is quite a complicated task, why did so many youngsters take it on?

Composing their life narratives gave meaning to their lives. They interpreted their personal stories just as they interpreted their favourite works of fiction. Aided by the world-view they had adopted and developed for themselves, they examined their lives and considered their actions and choices in order to define their identities.[55] As Max Weinreich explained: 'What they submitted was for them not literature but life.'[56]

Examining their lives also provided coherence in otherwise chaotic situations, which could prove therapeutic: 'For the first time, I gave an accurate account of myself. Until now I have tried to repress every memory. Now, when I can think about everything quietly, it may be possible to be released from this appalling apathy.'[57] In a way, the act of writing an autobiography was an act of auto-emancipation. On paper, the autobiographers were free from all constraints and could cross every boundary.

The youth movements, the evening courses, the libraries, the books, and the notebooks that characterized Jewish youth culture in interwar Poland functioned in many ways as an alternative to school. They enabled youngsters to keep learning against all odds, whether independently or in groups, and provided them with hope, comfort, and refuge. No wonder that so many of them participated in these activities so enthusiastically.

Of course, many of the lucky ones who remained at school and studied in gymnasiums or vocational schools also participated in these activities. Some youth organizations like Mesada, Gordonia, and Hashomer Hatsa'ir were essentially organizations of high-school students.[58] The autobiographies of those who had to leave school early describe their difficulties in joining these organizations and feeling at home in them: 'All of us decided to leave "Hashomer Hatsa'ir".

---

[54] Moseley, 'Life, Literature', 26.

[55] J. A. Singer and S. Bluck, 'New Perspectives on Autobiographical Memory: The Integration of Narrative Processing and Autobiographical Reasoning', *Review of General Psychology*, 5/2 (2001), 91–3.

[56] Weinreich, *Der veg tsu unzer yugnt*, 140.   [57] YIVO Archives, RG 4: Autobiography 3708, 19.

[58] The 'more fortunate' joined and played active roles in youth organizations for diverse reasons that are beyond the scope of this chapter. Youth organizations were, broadly speaking, driven by ideology, identity conflicts, radicalism, and secularization (see Kligsberg, 'Di yidishe yugnt-bavegung in poyln tsvishn beyde velt-milkhomes', 192–226; Bassok, 'Ne'urim ve'erkhei ne'urim bitenuot hano'ar').

We supported the youth from poor homes and joined together. Everyone enjoyed equality.'[59]

Attending high school had social implications. It divided young Jews into privileged and underprivileged. Even when members of these different groups shared the same ideology, co-operation was difficult; usually they did not join forces and took separate paths.[60]

LEAVING SCHOOL AND FINDING AN IDEOLOGY

From a very young age, members of this generation were involved in politics and ideology, which explained their reality, provided a way to overcome their predicament, and reduced their feelings of helplessness by giving them a vision of a better world.[61] The inflation of ideologies that characterized the period was both a symptom and a remedy: a symptom of the crisis and distress among young Jews and a remedy that brought hope and assuaged the pain.[62]

Adolescence is a stage of life characterized by the quest for autonomy and self-expression, and attempts at crystallizing a personal identity both separate from and as part of a generational identity. Identity formation is a process of individualization which takes place in reaction to others, whether by rejection or acceptance.[63] In modern society, the family unit cannot on its own satisfy these fundamental psychological needs.[64] Ideological movements became one of the central reference points for this generation: participation in their activities aided the urgent task of identity formation.[65]

Many members of this generation, in their search for the 'true' ideology, turned to socialism or communism.[66] This inclination is easily understood, since most of them came from poor worker or artisan families who had to struggle to survive. Marxism in its various forms promised a solution to their hardships by changing the world order and building a new and just one, whether through revolution or social evolution. These young men and women felt that the only way to break through the suffocating and narrow walls of injustice was by uniting the exploited and the wretched and abolishing class oppression and taking away power from

[59] YIVO Archives, RG 4: Autobiography 3562, 29–30.

[60] Bassok, 'Ma'amadot utefisah ma'amadit etsel yeladim uvenei no'ar', 241.

[61] Lam, *Tenuot hano'ar hatsiyoniot*, 21.   [62] Ibid. 17.

[63] R. Josselson, 'Identity and Relatedness in the Life Cycle', in H. A. Bosma et al. (eds.), *Identity and Development: An Interdisciplinary Approach* (Thousand Oaks, Calif., 1994), 82–3.

[64] R. G. Braungart and M. M. Braungart, 'Life Course and Generational Politics', *Annual Review of Sociology*, 12 (1986), 210.

[65] R. Kahane, *The Origins of Postmodern Youth: Informal Youth Movements in a Comparative Perspective* (Berlin, 1997), 23.

[66] Kligsberg, 'Di yidishe yugnt-bavegung in poyln tsvishn beyde velt-milkhomes', 192–216; Bassok, 'Ne'urim ve'erkhei ne'urim bitenuot hano'ar', 575–8, 580–3; M. Mishkinsky, 'The Communist Party of Poland and the Jews', in Gutman et al. (eds.), *The Jews of Poland between Two World Wars*, 56–74.

those responsible for it. Radicalism exercised a seductive charm, providing an alternative to the old failed ways of life responsible for the hopeless situation in which they found themselves.[67]

The 'Jewish factor' also drove them towards Marxism. It promised a utopian, universalist, and humanist world with no national and ethnic barriers and consequently attracted those who felt rejected because of their Jewish origins.

Class and personal identity formation, reasons for and solutions to the wretchedness of the present, and the search for a better future explain the ideological choices of this generation. However, a close reading of the autobiographies also shows the importance of these political orientations for dealing with the crisis of having to leave school. Marxist ideologies not only promised a new economic and social order, they also offered a new set of values: only work skills and work ethics were to count in the future, in which at the top of the social scale would be the outstanding worker and conscious avant-garde and not the wealthy man or the intellectual. Education would lose its value, and work and professional expertise would be appreciated instead: no more 'tse ulemad!' (go and learn!), but 'ha'avodah hi hayenu!' (work is our life!).

Because of the internalization of these concepts, the experience of leaving school was tinted with brighter and more optimistic colours. It was no longer seen as a personal failure or a cruel fate; instead, it was perceived as the free choice of a lofty ideal. This helped the members of this generation to make peace with the biggest loss of their lives, to accept it, and to invest it with new meaning:

I came to the conclusion that I mustn't go on like this, I must have a plan for the future, now and immediately. I'm not young anymore. I'm a grown-up. The only way that was left for me was productivization, because I had been a parasite and as such, I must become productive, a worker. . . . I was educated in capitalist, religious, backward surroundings, spoiled society, and spiritually poor. . . . I went against all the things that smelled of exploitation and inequality. I disconnected myself from the bourgeoisie, and started to look for a path in life in which I could connect with the proletariat. And I've found one.[68]

Another writer recalled her instructor and leader of her group in the Bund's Kultur Lige: 'She gave us special attention. She comforted us and contributed a lot to our lives; she gave us moral lectures concerning our attitude towards work and explained to us that not everyone should study. . . . Conversation with her made an impact on us.'[69]

Leftist ideologies not only supplied an explanation of present injustices but also made them bearable. Manual work, workshops, and leaving school were all integrated into the process of becoming productivized, a process that was highly valued. With this new interpretation, their stories and their lives were perceived in

[67] Kligsberg, 'Di yidishe yugnt-bavegung in poyln tsvishn beyde velt-milkhomes', 185–6; Schatz, *The Generation*.   [68] YIVO Archives, RG 4: Autobiography 3794, 14–15.
[69] YIVO Archives, RG 4: Autobiography 3666, 44.

a totally different light and graduating from elementary school became a day of revelation.

FROM PERSONAL CRISES TO CULTURAL TURNING POINT

The day they left elementary school never to return was, for many of the auto-biographers, an emotionally shattering experience. In this pivotal moment they started to develop the 'tragic vision' that characterized them, a world-view that was shaped by feelings of helplessness, frustration, and despair, but that at the same time contained the willingness and readiness to oppose and rebel against their destiny. Of course there would be other turning points in their lives, but the day they left elementary school was their most defining moment.

The gap that was created between their passion for education and the dis-appointing reality of their lives forced them to look for ways to bridge it. With courage and creativity, they found alternative sources of education in youth movements, at libraries, in reading, and in writing. At the same time they adopted ideologies that supplied them with a different explanation of reality, with new meanings, and with a new scale of values. These ideologies enabled them to reassess their own lives and to redefine education and learning. Their emotional crisis, an existential crisis that almost each and every one of them experienced, became a major driving force that left its mark on Jewish society and culture in interwar Poland.

Jewish Youth Movements in Poland between the Wars as Heirs of the *Kehilah*

IDO BASSOK

THIS CHAPTER is a part of a research project focusing on 150 autobiographies out of the collection of about 350 by young Jews, which are in the possession of YIVO.[1] Of the 150, 93 were written in Yiddish, 46 in Polish, and 11 in Hebrew; 109 were composed by young men and 41 by young women. They were sent to YIVO, then in Vilna, as entries in three contests the institute organized in 1932, 1934, and 1939. The contests, as was made clear,[2] limited the age of the contestants to between 16 and 22 years, but some writers a few years younger or older managed to 'infiltrate' them using various stratagems.[3]

The chapter proposes a new understanding of the mental characteristics[4] of Jewish children and adolescents in Poland between the two world wars, especially their feelings regarding the future of the traditional Jewish world and their solidarity and identification with their 'ethnic' community. Though from a quantitative point of view the autobiographers cannot be regarded as 'representative' of their generation, they nevertheless express the views typical of broad sectors of young people at the time, rather than the more ideologically extreme ones, such as

---

This chapter is adapted from I. Bassok, 'Hebetim baḥinuch shel no'ar yehudi bepolin bein milḥamot ha'olam le'or otobiografiyot shel benei no'ar yehudiyim me'osef YIVO', Ph.D. thesis (Hebrew University of Jerusalem, 2009); an abridged version was published as *Teḥiyat hane'urim: mishpaḥah veḥinukh beyahadut polin bein milḥamot ha'olam* (Jerusalem, 2015).

[1] YIVO Archives, New York, RG 4: 'Autobiographies of Jewish Youth in Poland (1932–1939)'; see also *Awakening Lives: Autobiographies of Jewish Youth in Poland before the Holocaust*, ed. J. Shandler (New Haven, Conn., 2002); *Ostatnie pokolenie: Autobiografie polskiej młodzieży żydowskiej okresu międzywojennego*, ed. A. Cała (Warsaw, 2003); *Alilot ne'urim: otobiyografyot shel benei no'ar yehudim mipolin bein shetei milḥamot olam*, ed. I. Bassok (Jerusalem, 2011).

[2] See *Yediyes fun YIVO*, Sept. 1932, pp. 2–4; Apr.–May 1934, pp. 1–3.

[3] See B. Kirshenblatt-Gimblett, M. Moseley, and M. Stanislawski, 'Introduction', in *Awakening Lives*, xi–xlii; A. Cała, 'Przedmowa', in *Ostatnie pokolenie*, 9–28.

[4] See J. Le Goff, 'Les Mentalités: Une histoire ambiguë', in J. Le Goff and P. Narra (eds.), *Faire de l'histoire* (Paris, 1974), 76–94; C. Ginzburg, 'Introduction', in *The Cheese and the Worms: The Cosmos of a Sixteenth Century Miller*, trans. J. Tedeschi and A. Tedeschi (London, 1981).

those of the radical assimilationists or the radical hasidic courts. The justification for such an argument stems primarily from the heterogeneity and variety of the autobiographers' backgrounds: they represent the three cultural-historical zones of Poland (Kresy, the former Congress Kingdom, and Galicia), although not in exact proportion to the size of the Jewish populations in each; they lived in large cities and small towns; they belonged to all classes of Jewish society (with a tendency towards the lower socioeconomic levels, who were the majority); they attended all sorts of educational systems, both Polish and Jewish, secular and religious, traditional and modern; they were affiliated with all sorts of youth movements—communist, Zionist, and Bundist—or none. However, many of the autobiographies conveyed similar information and led to similar conclusions, and therefore I selected 150 that provided a balanced representation of these factors. Literary criteria, such as richness of detail, length, and the quality of the writing, also influenced my decisions for inclusion. My aim is to examine—through these autobiographies—two significant and complementary topics: the means developed by the various youth movements to position themselves as leaders in the new Jewish public sphere and their attempt to supersede the *kehilot* (traditional communal structures) still operating in the Polish Jewish communities at the time. The members of the youth movements were seeking answers to an array of issues relating to lifestyle choices: interpersonal communication (relationships with friends, the opposite sex, and their elders); work and employment (in terms of a new value system which saw work as transforming Jews economically, socially, and psychologically); and various aspects of society (political allegiances, participation in public life and religious ritual, however this was expressed).

In the second part of the chapter I attempt to show that the efforts of youth movements to achieve public leadership found different expression in each of the three 'cultural zones' of interwar Poland: the east (Kresy), the centre (the former Congress Kingdom), and the south (Galicia). Against the background of long-term historic developments, there evolved different concepts of the connections between the Jewish past, present, and future, between religiosity and secularization, and between tradition and modernization in each of these zones. The typical attitude of the Jewish population of Kresy involved a strong sense of dialectic continuity; the Galician attitude was marked by a belief in 'synthesis', which was possible but difficult to attain; and Congress Poland was characterized by the widespread belief in a deep split between the processes of secularization and Polonization, on the one hand, and the need to adhere to one's Jewish 'roots', on the other. In addition, differences can be observed between the attitudes of the youth movements in the various regions towards the values, customs, and leadership of the past and the best ways to renew, transform, or supersede them.

JEWISH YOUTH MOVEMENTS IN INTERWAR POLAND

Jewish youth movements in Poland can be divided into four major categories in accordance with their ideological stance: (1) Zionist, to which the majority of the adherents of youth movements belonged, from Yugnt of Po'alei Tsiyon Left to Betar; (2) cultural autonomist and its associated outlooks, such as sejmism and folkism: included in this category are Tsukunft, the youth movement of the socialist Bund, and Di Bin (the Bee), a youth movement active in Vilna and vicinity, established by Max Weinreich; (3) communist; and (4) assimilationist, whose leaders aspired to see Jews integrate into the Polish state as equals, without compromising their unique identity.

The first Polish Jewish youth movement, Hashomer Hatsa'ir, was established in Galicia. This was no accident: while seeking temporary shelter in Austria during the First World War, the young people who founded the movement were inspired by the pioneering 'free youth movement', the German Wandervogel. The Wandervogel sought to imbue in its followers a critical approach towards the bourgeois way of life of the older generation, encouraging them to 'discover themselves' in small peer groups. A second source of influence was Robert Baden-Powell, whose *Scouting for Boys* was tremendously popular immediately after its publication in 1908 (first Polish translation, 1911). Hashomer Hatsa'ir and other scouting movements borrowed from Baden-Powell the idea of educating children and adolescents in discipline and order through a semi-military way of life.[5]

The first cells of Tsukunft were organized towards the end of 1918. Tsukunft, in contrast to Hashomer Hatsa'ir, was a political rather than a scouting movement. Its principal mission was to inculcate the values of the Bund itself in its young followers with the goal of subsequently integrating them into the party. In the early 1920s other leftist Zionist youth movements were also established: Gordonia, similar to Hashomer Hatsa'ir, and Hehaluts Hatsa'ir, which resembled Tsukunft in its connection to an adult organization, the socialist Zionist Hehaluts. The late 1920s also saw the appearance and flourishing of right-wing youth movements: Betar and Hano'ar Hatsioni.

The Jewish educational networks which developed in interwar Poland had complicated relationships with the youth movements. In religious and *haredi* schools, being affiliated with a matching youth organization was considered a matter of course, and teachers frequently tried to persuade their students to join them: in the Bais Yaakov system of girls' schools, there was no real distinction between the network's schools and the girls' youth movements, Agudat Israel,

---

[5] J. Springhall, *Youth, Empire, and Society* (London, 1977). On the formative influence of scouting and the Wandervogel on Hashomer Hatsa'ir and, through it, on other Jewish youth movements, see T. Lam, *Shitat hahinukh shel hashomer hatsa'ir: sipur hithavutah* (Jerusalem, 1998); R. Peled, '*Ha'adam hehadash*' shel hamahapekhah hatsiyonit: hashomer hatsa'ir veshorashav ha'eiropiyim (Tel Aviv, 2002), 65–75.

Bnos, and Basie. The students of the Tarbut Hebrew Zionist schools and of the bilingual Hebrew and Polish elementary and high schools inclined towards Hashomer Hatsa'ir but also towards other diametrically opposed groups, Betar and the communist youth movement. *Talmud torah* pupils often opted to join Betar. The majority of children studying in Central Yiddish School Organization (Tsentrale Yidishe Shul Organizatsye; TSYSHO) schools naturally inclined towards the Socialist Children's Union and Tsukunft, often because of their close relationships with their socialist teachers.

THE CREATION OF A NEW TOTALITY

The informal Jewish educational frameworks of this period and those established by Jews which were not specifically identified as Jewish (such as some of the communist youth movements where Jews were in the majority) display a dimension of transformative continuity in relation to traditional Jewish society rather than an attempt to destroy it. Just as hasidism originally created new tools to revive Jewish communal solidarity,[6] so the Jewish youth movements created tools of various kinds—institutional (institutes of learning and judgement), ceremonial (festivals, days of commemoration and mourning), recreational (trips, camps), and even occupational (the *hakhsharot* of the Hehaluts movements which sought to train potential emigrants to the Land of Israel)—which replaced, or tried to replace, the *kehilot*, which were already in the process of losing their effectiveness, their ability to mobilize the whole community, and the almost absolute authority they had enjoyed in previous generations.[7] At the same time the institutions they established and the services they provided were aimed almost entirely at the young.

Jewish youth movements in Poland between the wars felt themselves capable of replacing the *kehilah* and the whole traditional framework that had previously dictated educational practices, social relationships, and economic behaviour.[8]

---

[6] By creating a new social cohesion and obedience to authority, hasidism enabled the renewal of collective commitment in a Jewish community which was fragmenting following the Shabatean crisis, precapitalist economic pressures, and other factors. On hasidism replacing the *kahal*, see C. Shmeruk, 'Haḥasidut ve'iskei hakhakhirot', *Zion*, 35 (1970), 182–92; J. Katz, *Masoret umashber* (Jerusalem, 1986), 264–70; E. Etkes, *Polin: perakim betoledot yehudei mizraḥ eiropah vetarbutam* (Tel Aviv, 1991), ch. 8.

[7] Some scholars maintain that hasidism itself began as a youth movement, intended to handle intergenerational tensions: see D. Assaf, 'Hebetim historiyim veḥevratiyim beḥeker haḥasidut', in id. (ed.), *Tsadik ve'edah* (Jerusalem, 2001), 14; G. D. Hundert, *Jews in Poland–Lithuania in the Eighteenth Century* (Berkleley, Calif., 2004), 179–81). On how Jewish autonomy functioned during this period in Poland, see G. Bacon, 'Hatslaḥah ḥelkit, hesegim gedolim: al ha'otonomyah hayehudit bein shetei milḥamot olam', in J. Kaplan (ed.), *Kehal yisrael*, 3 vols. (Jerusalem, 2001–4), iii. 351–71; on Jewish youth movements and their handling of the community crisis, see Z. Lam, *Tenuot hano'ar hatsiyoniyot bemabat le'aḥor* (Tel Aviv, 1991); I. Bassok, 'Ne'urim ve'erkhei ne'urim bitenu'ot hano'ar bepolin shebein shetei milḥamot', in I. Bartal and Y. Gutman (eds), *Kiyum veshever*, ii: *Yehudei polin ledoroteihem* (Jerusalem, 2001), 573–604.

[8] On the internal organization of the Jewish community, including associations for social welfare

Their confidence was based on the relative weakness of the old Jewish institutions and the sense of power typical of youth movements convinced they possess a greater understanding of new social realities. They also believed that they better embodied the Jewish 'ethnic' spirit and served its objectives more efficiently than the old institutions. Given that, for many of the previous generation, the Jewish religion was a marker of identity rather than an object of enthusiastic and devoted faith which was being replaced by new markers such as Jewish languages—Hebrew and Yiddish—and the secular cultures nurtured through them,[9] the attraction and strength of youth and similar movements is easily understood.

One of those who submitted an autobiography to the YIVO competitions, Ben Ami from Borszczów, discussing his experiences from a theoretical and ideological perspective, explained why the youth movements felt they were the true successors of the *kehilot*. Being a member of Betar had developed in him a sense of solidarity and social responsibility, 'a quality which we Jews have lost as well as [our] homeland'. In his opinion, only the younger generation was able to identify with the interests of the people, while traditional society throughout history had failed to recognize the young generation's importance and its unique values and was, as a consequence, 'sterile, inert, and backward'.[10]

All the youth movements—Zionist, Bundist, and also, as is implied by the autobiographies, communist (at least in part)—constantly referred, both in their ideological discussion and in their practical activity, to the essential and chronic failings of the *kehilot* in dealing with the community's needs and aspirations. Their members felt strong solidarity with the community and sought ways of solving the problems it faced, even when this solidarity was not compatible with the official ideology of the movement to which they belonged and with the message of its leadership.

Jewish youth movements in Poland saw themselves as working for the whole community in the manner of the *kehilot*. This was demonstrated both in the general commitment of their members and in the creation of a net of 'societies', which reproduced the social and cultural structure of traditional Jewish society. They all sought to create institutions and organizations which fulfilled the functions of *batei din* (religious courts with the power to impose *ḥerem*); *bikur ḥolim* (lit.: 'visiting the sick') societies, and *ḥevra kadisha* (funeral and burial) societies. In addition, they made use of a secularized version of the Jewish religious calendar to

and study and those of the workers' unions, see M. Bałaban, 'Ma'amadam haḥuki shel hayehudim ve'irgunam', in Y. Heilperin (ed.), *Beit yisra'el bepolin*, 2 vols. (Jerusalem, 1948), i. 44–65; Katz, *Masoret umashber*, ch. 10.

[9] These included new mores which were interpreted as embodying Jewish values, such as devotion to secular and academic studies and, probably, even proficiency in the languages of the people among which the Jews dwelt, especially by those tending to acculturation.

[10] YIVO Archives, RG 4: Autobiography 3712, 41. That the Jews had lost their sense of belonging as well as their homeland was a teaching of Ahad Ha'am (see *Lo zeh haderekh* [1899], in *Kol kitvei aḥad ha'am* (Tel Aviv, 1965), 11–16).

create a substitute national religion, based on values such as asceticism and benevolence, which was intended to reshape their members' lifestyle. This can be well demonstrated from the autobiographies.

ALTERNATIVES TO THE *KEHILAH*'S ROLES

Beis Din and Ḥerem

Ba'al Makhshoves from Będzin, born in 1919 and 20 years old when he submitted his autobiography to the YIVO competition, described how the youth movement of which he was a member banned someone for not following its approved life-style and values. *Ḥerem* had been used in traditional Jewish society against those deviating from accepted norms or disobeying the edicts of the *kahal*.[11] According to Ba'al Makhshoves, the local branch of Gordonia expelled an orphan boy who was known as a *badkhen* (lover of jokes), a card player, and an 'honour-seeker and popular with the girls'.[12] The initial reason for the ban was the boy's love for a girl who was considered to have deserted the movement, and he was denounced by his comrades as unproductive. He worked in a damp cellar and contracted a lung infection. As he lay on his deathbed in his parents' home his comrades were called upon to visit him and ask his forgiveness. The author and the head of the local branch went to see him. After his death they agreed they were not responsible for the tragedy, because they had done what they did to reform the boy's behaviour.[13]

Even when not resorting to *ḥerem*, youth movements attempted to control criminal tendencies among their members. Binyomin Rothberg from Bielsk Podlaski wrote about a friend, the son of a village pedlar, who was involved in theft as a child. At the time of when he wrote his autobiography, the boy had become an active member of Hashomer Hatsa'ir and 'had become somewhat humanized' and rejected his thieving past.[14]

Bikur Ḥolim Societies

Shing-Shing (Yudke) from Ostrowiec described activities for sick comrades as one of his main occupations in Tsukunft.[15] B.R.H.5 from Oździutycze related how members of the Hehaluts movement in his little town collected money to take a female member of the local branch to the city to receive medical treatment.[16]

Ḥevra Kadisha Societies

B.R.H.5 also gave a detailed description of a funeral in which traditional and socialist elements were mingled. His girlfriend, a member of Hehaluts, fell sick, died, and was given 'a funeral in the manner of the Hehaluts movement': her

---

[11] See Katz, *Masoret umashber*, 124–9. The *kahal* was declared illegal in the Russian empire in 1848, but local *kehilot* continued to function.   [12] YIVO Archives, RG 4: Autobiography 3554, 24.

[13] Ibid. 26.   [14] YIVO Archives, RG 4: Autobiography 3542, 23.

[15] YIVO Archives, RG 4: Autobiography 3514, 38.

[16] YIVO Archives, RG 4: Autobiography 3504, 26–7.

corpse was wrapped with a red flag 'tied with black'.[17] An unprecedented number of people in the small town attended the funeral, showing that the movement had succeeded in invoking in the community the solidarity that seemed to have been lost. The local Tarbut school students followed the Hehaluts members in the funeral procession, with black crêpe-paper flowers on their clothes.[18] The ceremony combined non-Jewish and Jewish customs, the non-Jewish or socialist ones being integrated into the traditional customs. The author writes that there was 'a holy silence' (as at the revelation at Mount Sinai) and that he succeeded in eulogizing the deceased 'with simple and passionate words'.[19] In the context of a 'collective' ceremony, fusing tradition and innovation, he found the strength to make a speech, strength he had not possessed on previous occasions when all that had been involved was himself.

Burial and mourning ceremonies interpreted in a secular manner also played a significant role in the Bund. The funeral of Beinish Michalevitch, the head of TSYSHO, took place in the presence of tens of thousands of people, including many Tsukunft members, and became a 'political demonstration'.[20]

'Miracles'

Youth movements also took on the functions of charismatic figures, such as the *tsadik* or rebbe.[21] According to some autobiographies, youth movements had the ability to cure handicaps or weaknesses in speech and expression. This capacity was linked to psychological processes which, in and of themselves, were reasonable and even expected, but their intensity made them seem miraculous.

Certainly, many young people felt comfortable in the movement's *lokal* (club), a feeling they did not get, or got only rarely, in school, particularly those in the public system. Even in their parents' home this sensation was quite rare.[22] The feelings of comfort and intimacy with people of their own age, including those of the opposite sex, and the existence of a space for activities important for their emotional, physiological, and intellectual needs—met sparingly by school and hardly at all in their parents' home—empowered the members of the movements. They felt capable of performing actions they could not otherwise have carried out. Frequently, the *lokal* provided them, for the first time in their lives, with the satisfaction of making a public presentation, declamation, or artistic performance.

[17] Ibid. 28.

[18] This was not a traditional Jewish custom but was common among Jews at the time: for example, at fund-raising events. [19] YIVO Archives, RG 4: Autobiography 3504, 28.

[20] G. Pickhan, *Gegen den Strom* (Stuttgart, 2001), 164–5. For a description of a communist funeral replacing the traditional one, see M. Friedman, 'Sochaczew tsvishn beyde velt-milkhomes', in A. S. Stein and G. Weissman (eds.), *Pinkes sochaczew* (Jerusalem, 1962), 115.

[21] On miraculous healing by *ba'alei shem* at the beginning of hasidism and before, see M. Rosman, *Founder of Hasidism: A Quest for the Historical Ba'al Shem Tov* (Berkeley, Calif., 1996), 21–40; I. Etkes, *Ba'al hashem. habesht: magia, mystika, hanhaga* (Jerusalem, 2000), 15–87.

[22] See Bassok, 'Hebetim baḥinuch shel no'ar yehudi bepolin bein milḥamot ha'olam'.

These activities had, to some extent, also been nurtured in school, but often students had the feeling that, even when given the opportunity to perform there, they failed because of the lack of encouragement or belief in their abilities.

The story of Ba'al Makhshoves is remarkable in this context: he was cured of his stammer as a result of membership of Hashomer Hatsa'ir.[23] The supportive ambience and the reinforcement provided by the society of his peers helped him to overcome traumatic fears, perhaps the result of his father's stern and domineering behaviour. The youth movement seems, therefore, to have power beyond its role as a communal institution: it was endowed with the magical or charismatic power of a *ba'al nes* (miracle maker).

As mentioned above, B.R.H.5's 'simple and passionate' words at his girlfriend and comrade's funeral were of almost miraculous character, since he had failed in the past at similar tasks. He succeeded then because he did it within a framework with significance for him and his comrades, and which they controlled.

The same kind of influence, rational in itself but on the margins of the magical in its capability to transform, may be attributed to what the authors relate about the connection between their youth movement activity and improvements in their ability in the language of instruction in their schools after years of mediocre performance. This emerges in two anecdotes by authors who struggled with the language of instruction, probably as a result of inner identity struggles which were only resolved by the movement. Gershon Pipe from Sanok, who studied in a Polish elementary school and later in a municipal Polish gymnasium, was strongly attached to his traditional Jewish identity. He describes himself as, in his childhood, more religious than his father and fond of Yiddish, but weak in Polish. When he joined Hashomer Hatsa'ir, just before or after he entered the gymnasium, he did not even understand the orders given in Polish by his scoutmasters. Because of his admiration for them, sons of assimilated families whose first language was Polish and who despised his and some of his comrades' Yiddishized Polish, his attitude towards the language changed fundamentally and he cut himself off from Yiddish and the kind of Judaism it had represented for him: 'I began aspiring to master the Polish language, because I saw in my future comrades at Hashomer more noble and intelligent youths.'[24]

Bjel from Włocławek also had an identity problem. He was a student at a local Polish and Hebrew gymnasium where his father taught Jewish subjects. As a result of his deep-rooted Polonization (and maybe also due to reservations about his father which he does not elucidate[25]), he encountered difficulties in studying Hebrew. He describes his change of attitude in the youth movement:

---

[23] YIVO Archives, RG 4: Autobiography 3554, 28.

[24] YIVO Archives, RG 4: Autobiography 3770, 21.

[25] See M. Korzen, 'Hagimnasyah hayehudit', in K. P. Tchursh and M. Korzen (eds.), *Wlotslavek vehasevivah* (Tel Aviv, 1967), 390.

By addressing my emotions and intelligence, Hashomer Hatsa'ir deepened my love for my people and Palestine. What the school did not succeed in doing over eight years with the son of the Jewish studies teacher, the movement did in only one year. I studied Hebrew because I wanted to, because I understood that only knowledge of my people's language would help further the first stages of my career in Hashomer.[26]

Because of his general tendency to self-criticism, he attributed his success in studying Hebrew to his career ambitions, but even his own words show that this success derived mainly from his emotional stake in the movement that caused him to understand the significance of Hebrew and comprehend his real need for it.

Youth movements restored to their members those words lost or silenced by traditionalist parents who often did not know how to deal with questions from children and adolescents. By endowing their members with the ability to express themselves, the youth movements granted them the power to create their own symbols.

Calendar and Festivals

Sheikewits from Międzyrzecz Korecki, a graduate of the Równe Hebrew gymnasium, described how, during his childhood, the members of Zionist youth movements appropriated for themselves the traditional festival which was so significant for *ḥeder* children, Lag Ba'omer. In an era when 'political parties flourished', the members of the movement would transform the valley near the town into 'a piece of the Land of Israel', in the same way as the *ḥeder* children used to go with their *melamed* on an excursion to a hill near the town which they considered to be 'Mount Sinai'.[27] According to the author, the Lag Ba'omer procession was converted into a demonstration in favour of Zionist settlement in the Land of Israel.[28] The children from the youth movements and the Jewish children from the Polish public school would march through the town and sing Zionist songs until reaching the valley. However, after several years the police banned the activity.[29]

The leftist Zionist youth movements added national and socialist festivals to their calendar and these were observed with the same reverence as traditional religious holidays. Ben Tikveh from Święciany, who had settled in Vilna with his parents as a child, depicts the 1 May celebration in the *hakhsharah* in Grochów, a

---

[26] YIVO Archives, RG 4: Autobiography 3647, 25.

[27] YIVO Archives, RG 4: Autobiography 3758, 33. Lag Ba'omer is mentioned in the collection of autobiographies as a real day of liberation from *ḥeder* norms, when children enjoyed equal status with the rebbe and he shared in their games, all carrying toy rifles. Some of these sources mention naming a hill outside the town 'Mount Sinai'. For partially comparable descriptions in fiction and memoirs, see Sholem Aleichem, 'A farspilter lagboymer', in id., *Yidishe kinder: alle werk sholem aleichem* (Warsaw, 1911), 61–8; Y. Kotik, *Mayne zikhroynes*, 2 vols. (Warsaw, 1912–14), ii. ch. 21.   [28] Ibid. 34.

[29] This prohibition was most probably connected with the intensification of government measures against any activity understood as 'political' in 1932 and even more drastically after 1935.

suburb of Warsaw,[30] by using images that evoke a sacred ceremony: on this day everything celebrated, 'from human beings to domestic animals, from grains of wheat to agricultural implements'.[31] He may have borrowed this expression from a speech he had heard or an article he had read, but there is no doubt that, as a pupil at a *ḥeder*, he was aware of the connotations of his words and had fully assimilated them. The communal meals were also depicted in his story as a type of rite: at the end of the meals the *ḥalutsim* (potential emigrants to the Land of Israel) sang: 'We have nobody [to rely on] and we need nobody', 'We are *ḥalutsim*, the army of work', and a woman sang a song by Abraham Reisin, 'Orems leben' ('Life of the Poor').[32] Ben Tikveh was very involved with Yiddish and seems to have had difficulties studying Hebrew: he explicitly states that rejection of Yiddish was not part of his own understanding of Zionism, which he had only embraced after inner conflicts. In this sense he was not really an ordinary *ḥaluts*. Yet in his description of *hakhsharah* life, incorporating the various components of *ḥaluts* culture, he not only expresses his personal approach but conveys a world of images common to him and the *ḥalutsim*.

Aizik Zeidenberg, who lived in Białystok from his early childhood, reveals how religious youth movements also introduced new anniversaries alongside traditional Jewish festivals. At the age of 12 or 13, while studying at the Beis Shmuel Yeshiva in Białystok, '[he and some of his friends in the yeshiva] would mark the memorial days of Zionist leaders'. The memorial day of Shmuel Mohilever,[33] after whom the yeshiva was named, was used by the author and his colleagues to preach Zionism in a remote *beit midrash*.[34]

The Bund and its Tsukunft youth movement celebrated 1 May with processions, which sometimes degenerated into violence. They also added the civil New Year to their festivals, to demonstrate their being 'citizens of the world' without religious distinction. In addition, the Tsukunft celebrated International Youth Day every year to indicate its dual identity as Jewish and Polish. From 1936 the event was celebrated over two days: Saturday and Sunday. Every 24 June the International Socialist Sport and Child Day was celebrated. There were also one-off dates, such as the thirty-sixth anniversary of the establishment of the Bund on 18 March 1933.[35] The list of communist festivals and dates was even longer and

[30] S. Zaromb, 'Beshadmot grochov', in M. Bassok (ed.), *Sefer heḥaluts* (Jerusalem, 1940), 453–5.

[31] YIVO Archives, RG 4: Autobiography 3623, 25–6. He is probably alluding to the description of the revelation on Mount Sinai in *Shemot rabah* (29: 9).   [32] Ibid. 27.

[33] Shmuel Mohilever (1824–98), considered one of the fathers of religious Zionism, was a leader of Hibat Tsiyon. Hamerkaz Haruhani (The Spiritual Centre), which he established, was the basis of the Hamizrahi movement. In his last years he served as a rabbi in Białystok. Regarding marking the memorial days for him and S. H. Landoy in Hashomer Hadati, the youth movement to which Aizik Zeidenberg belonged, see Y. Elihay, *Hamizraḥi utenuat torah ve'avodah bepolin 1928–1939* (Jerusalem, 2001), 153.   [34] YIVO Archives, RG 4: Autobiography 3552, 7.

[35] See Y. S. Hertz, *Di geshikhte fun a yugnt* (New York, 1946), 423–6. For the cultural concepts the Bund derived from its ideology, see Y. Gorni, *Ḥalufot nifgashot* (Jerusalem, 2005), chs. 3, 5.

included, among others, memorial days for Rosa Luxemburg, Karl Liebknecht, and Vladimir Lenin (16–21 January), International Working Woman's Day (8 March), 1 May, and Struggle against War Day (1 August).[36]

Since the great majority of youth movements were secular and several even anti-religious, they not only added festivals to the traditional calendar but also removed or profaned existing ones that they considered old-fashioned or opposed to their message. The *Folkstsaytung*, the Bund's daily newspaper, was published on Saturday and Yom Kippur.[37] Even eating on Yom Kippur was considered a commendable act.[38]

AN ENTIRE LIFESTYLE

Absolute Authority

The autobiographers saw youth movements as controlling all aspects of their members' lives, in the same way that Jews in traditional society felt themselves subject to the *kehilah* and also, at certain times, to autonomous national organizations such as the Council of the Four Lands.[39] This is especially evident in descriptions of how they joined youth movements, the activities in which they took part, and the circumstances in which they left them, very often using terms of relationship to the sacred.

The perception of youth movements' authority as all-embracing is seen in the autobiographers' declarations of absolute dedication to the movement, such as Szklarowski from Ostryna, who, as an adolescent of 16 or 17 devoted entirely to Hehaluts and having become, in his own words, 'a one hundred percent *ḥaluts*, an extremist', went to all the movement's public assemblies and lectures.[40] Ben Yisroel from Oszmiana worked as a delivery boy for a bank. He would come to work wearing his Hashomer Hatsa'ir uniform.[41] Belonging to the movement was understood to demand total identification, not only in major matters but in minor ones, including clothing.

Nana Kenerman, from the small town of Sterdyń, spoke of her membership in the youth movement using the religious terms of Jewishness and apostasy (*shmad*). She had studied in the local Polish school and joined the Freiheit movement at the age of 15. In her autobiography she frequently made analogies between her own life and a religious Jew's daily schedule, comparing the *lokal* to a *beit midrash* and

---

[36] J. Schatz, *The Generation: The Rise and Fall of the Jewish Communists of Poland* (Berkeley, Calif., 1991), 107.   [37] N. Cohen, *Sefer sofer ve'iton* (Jerusalem, 2001), 313–16.

[38] See e.g. Y. Bialovrode (Biale), 'A tsenter fun idealen un kultur', in D. Shtokfish (ed.), *Sefer falenits* (Tel Aviv, 1967), 87. Bialovrode belonged to leftist circles, but it is unclear whether he himself was Bundist or communist.

[39] See H. H. Ben-Sasson, *Retsef utemurah* (Tel Aviv, 1984), 156–6, 239–57.

[40] YIVO Archives, RG 4: Autobiography 3518, 29.

[41] YIVO Archives, RG 4: Autobiography 3521, 15.

the assembled company to the *minyan* required for prayer. On abandoning the local movement, she declared that although she refused to go to the *hakhsharah* (and therefore also failed to observe the commandment of *aliyah*), she would stay faithful to what were to her the two fundamental components of Judaism: religion and Zionism. For her, they are combined: 'I won't forsake my religion; I won't convert to another religion'; 'I was born a daughter of Jews and will die a daughter of Jews, even in the worst possible conditions. The same is true for my [Zionist] ideals . . . Erets Yisra'el is the land I have dreamt of for so long.'[42]

For several of the autobiographers, the youth movement defined their lifestyle and imbued them with a total commitment by controlling their cultural choices and even the criteria for selecting a partner. This was most obvious in the case of young members of leftist movements—communists, Bundists, and members of the Zionist pioneer movements—who saw themselves as revolutionaries seeking to overthrow the society they rejected.

Gershon Pipe dramatically described the transition from scrupulous religiosity to no less enthusiastic adherence to the youth movement. The rite of passage in his case occurred during his barmitzvah party. On that occasion he incorporated Hashomer Hatsa'ir injunctions into his religious practice. In the section headed 'When I was a Barmitzvah', he wrote:

When I reached 13 years old, I was already imbued with the essence of two conflicting worlds: the *ḥeder* and the movement that had been penetrating more and more into my heart.

I did not serve cigarettes at my barmitzvah celebration, as other boys since did. Hashomer strictly prohibits smoking, alcohol, and playing cards.[43] Cakes and spirits were served in the Yad Harutsim Synagogue and I served cakes separately in the *lokal*.

The day of my first *hanokhes tefillen* [putting on phylacteries] was very important for me. All night I could not sleep. At 3:30 in the morning, I got up and went to the *mikveh*; I washed myself thoroughly and went back home . . . . I was determined to be punctilious in fulfilling the *mitsves*.[44]

Proletarian Values

Members of non-Zionist leftist movements were no different from members of Zionist ones in their conviction of the need for a system of rules and, specifically, a comprehensive code of behaviour for themselves and their comrades. The 'proletarian' way of life was mandatory for them in all areas, including such personal matters as selecting reading material and choosing a partner. This is evident, for example, in the description of the movement's meetings by Tsukunftistike from Maków Mazowiecki. The leaders of the local cell tried to impart the party's philosophy through decrees and prohibitions of the sort the movement's members had

[42] YIVO Archives, RG 4: Autobiography 3780, 6.

[43] As explicitly mentioned in the 'tenth commandment' of Hashomer's 'Aseret ha'dibrot', written by 1916 (see Y. Gothelf (ed.), *Sefer hashomerim* (Warsaw, 1934), 16).

[44] YIVO Archives, RG 4: Autobiography 3770, 22.

met in their families' religious world.[45] The chairman of the cell imposed a ban on social connections with those opposed to the Bund's ideology, and on reading books condemned by the Bund, especially *shund* (trash) literature because of its lack of a social message or subliminal support for the status quo. Reading was among the positive commands imposed by the chairman, including reading *Der yugnt veker*, the Bund youth weekly.

When Ben Tikveh was about 14, he and his younger brother joined Di Bin.[46] The movement 'began to give us what we lacked . . . a life of togetherness, character development, and relationships between comrades'. He emphasizes at length the obedience to rules: he and his comrades learned the movement's 'ten commandments'; 'we would work and act according to Di Bin's orders'.[47] The movement brought about a change in his behaviour at school and his life outside the home in general.

The proletarian identity, which the leftist movements, including to some extent the leftist Zionists, aimed to inculcate in their followers, was characterized by living modestly in material matters, while strongly adhering to popular culture and showing a keen interest in topics that might promote the hoped-for social transformation. These cultural elements were intended to overcome petit-bourgeois tendencies and philistinism, understood as the pursuit of material pleasures combined with a conservative and passive outlook.

Shing-Shing described how, at 14, he was a member of a professional union which for him constituted a sort of youth movement.[48] Later, he became for a short time a member of Betar, which he came to detest, and then joined Tsukunft.[49] This restored to him the sense of identity he had lost on leaving his religious home. Joining Tsukunft enabled him to lead an entirely proletarian way of life. He earned six zlotys a week, five of which he gave to his family. He used the remaining zloty to pay his party dues, go to the cinema and eat a modest meal.[50] He took considerable pride in living as a 'real manual worker' on one zloty a week. He participated in activities to help sick colleagues and took part in arguments and presentations. Even after leaving the Tsukunft 'for a certain reason', he remained 'a pure, conscious Jewish worker'.[51] Similarly, Tsukunftistike combined such pleasures as going to the cinema (considered proletarian because it was cheap and non-elitist) with material sacrifices for the party, such as subscribing to the party journal.[52]

Jerzy Tomaszow from Łódź aspired to live a proletarian lifestyle, which extended to the qualities he looked for in friends and even girlfriends. He left the Communist Party after being imprisoned and tortured, but abandoning the movement only intensified his thirst for social contact with people with a proletarian

[45] YIVO Archives, RG 4: Autobiography 3749, 61–2.

[46] See I. Bassok, 'Bin', in G. D. Hundert (ed.), *The YIVO Encyclopedia of Jews in Eastern Europe*, <http://www.yivoencyclopedia.org/article.aspx/Bin> (accessed 17 Feb. 2017).

[47] YIVO Archives, RG 4: Autobiography 3623, 23.

[48] YIVO Archives, RG 4: Autobiography 3514, 28–9.   [49] Ibid. 32.   [50] Ibid. 35.

[51] Ibid. 28.   [52] YIVO Archives, RG 4: Autobiography 3749', 7–8.

spirit. He tried to make friends with a person he described as 'elegant and mis-
chievous, cheerful—the mark of a proletarian'.[53] He also joined a study circle of
people who, like him, had left the Communist Party, but still adhered to its ideas,
'proletarians: of pure metal!' When depicting the young girls he was interested in,
he described one who seemed to him the incarnation of a proletarian: she was energetic, inquisitive, and possessed strong bodily features: 'Healthily built. Among
the girls she looks like a hero and besides she is a fountain of energy.'[54]

THE HEIRS OF THE *KEHILAH*

As argued above, the youth movements considered themselves to be the successors
of the traditional *kehilot* and saw their activities as legitimately continuing functions which they had performed. Though this phenomenon also existed in non-
Zionist movements, it was much more evident in Zionist ones. These movements
tended to present themselves both as continuing in the traditional spirit and as
creators of a new set of rules, the old system having lost its ability to run the Jewish
community successfully. Significant differences can be perceived in the way the
Zionists sought to achieve these goals within the three Jewish cultural zones of
interwar Poland.

The basic attitudes to the Jewish heritage in the three zones, as reflected in the
autobiographies, can be described as 'dialectic' in Kresy, 'synthetic' in Galicia, and
'confrontational' in the former Congress Poland. The origins of these differences
lie in the specific history of the Jews of each of these regions, a somewhat complex
topic which I cannot examine here in detail.[55] I use the term 'dialectic' to describe
an interpretative and transformative approach which does not treat the culture of
the past as something to be rigidly followed but as open to interpretation and from
which different elements can be taken, provided the attempt is made to remain
faithful to its spirit and ideals. The synthetic approach seeks to combine the cultures of the past and present, on the assumption that they can coexist comfortably,
without conflicting with each other or becoming conflated. The confrontational
approach assumes that past and present cultures cannot be harmonized and that
any attempt to unite them would be more or less mechanical, rather than interpretative (as in the first approach) or integrative (as in the second).

These different attitudes are clearly reflected in the autobiographers' decisions
to join or leave a youth movement, for example. Some of the autobiographies from

---

[53] YIVO Archives, RG 4: Autobiography 3701, 32.   [54] Ibid. 37.

[55] See E. Mendelsohn, 'Zionist Success and Zionist Failure: The Case of East Central Europe
between the Wars', in R. Kozodoy, D. Sidorsky, and K. Sultanik (eds.), *Vision Confronts Reality: Historical Perspectives on the Contemporary Jewish Agenda* (Rutherford, NJ, 1989), 190–209; id., *On Modern
Jewish Politics* (New York, 1993), ch. 2. For a useful categorization, congruent in great measure with my
own, of the three cultures as intellectual, political, and 'inchoate behavioural' secularization, see T.
Endelman, 'Secularization and the Origins of Jewish Modernity: On the Impact of Urbanization and
Social Transformation', *Jahrbuch des Simon-Dubnow-Instituts*, 6 (2007), 158.

Volhynia which represent the spirit of deep faithfulness to Jewish culture and the feeling of 'renovating continuity' which characterized the Jews of Kresy will illustrate this. Speakers, representatives, and activists from political movements in the region saw the youth movements as self-evidently the heirs of Jewish identity and touching a deep messianic impulse. Deliberately using a literary style, B. Ziger from Beresteczko described events which had occurred when he was about 10 or 11 (in about 1924). He relates how a youth who was 'deep-eyed, wearing a *rubashka* [embroidered Russian blouse]' appeared in the town and addressed the youngsters on how 'the long and stable existence of healthy [Jewish] life' had been under-mined and how it was the responsibility of young people to make the changes that would bring about redemption. The writer implied that this orator did not present the Diaspora existence, in itself, as shameful but stressed the problematic character of Jewish life in recent times, threatened as it was by the danger of assimilation. He asserted that what was required of the new generation—to speak Hebrew and move to the Land of Israel—would, paradoxically, be the realization of their ances-tors' dream.[56] He established a branch of Hehaluts in the town and re-established the Hashomer Hatsa'ir one. For B. Ziger, long walks in the youth's company 'gave great satisfaction to [his] sensitive soul' and 'the wild *horah* around the fire would ignite his imagination'. He understood then that he had no place 'here' (in Poland). His duty to guard his grandfather's empty shop symbolized for him 'the sin of Goles [exile]'.[57]

D. Pochalnik, also from Beresteczko and aged 24 when he wrote his autobiog-raphy, described his emotional situation and ideological consciousness when he was about 18 or 19: 'The national sentiment in me grew stronger. I felt the great and difficult task of being a Jew resting on my shoulders. I longed for a Jewish land, a Jewish state, and a Jewish army.'[58] But the content of the Zionist movement did not satisfy him. When he was 20 he established a 'national sport movement' named Haganah which he later transformed into a branch of Betar.

For Leidener (Sufferer) 1001 from the agricultural colony of Osowa Wyszka there was no question of dialectical continuity but rather of directly taking over the values of traditional Judaism. The local organization was probably conceived by the youngsters, depicted here scornfully by the author, as a society of believers.

The organization in the town had a different [educational and ideological] programme from that of the general organization. Thus, for example, it was forbidden to come to the 'club' bare headed, and the illiterate members of the organization believed that Hashomer was a religious organization. For them it was inconceivable: how could a Jewish organization not

[56] YIVO Archives, RG 4: Autobiography 3545, 28–9.

[57] Ibid. 41. It should be noted that the author tended towards Yiddishism or cultural autonomism and perhaps even to communism and was, therefore, reluctant to use Zionist slogans about 'productiv-ity' and 'return to physical labour'. These would have seemed to him to be contrary to Jewish identity, which he believed should be characterized by intellectual pursuits, not physical endeavours.

[58] YIVO Archives, RG 4: Autobiography 3547, 13–14.

be religious? The only thing they knew was that one should move to the Land of Israel, precisely in order to build the Temple.[59]

Other autobiographies from this region demonstrate the 'dialectical' approach to innovative ideas and trends which was widespread among young people. They easily assimilated the new concepts into a strong and well-based Jewish identity but without religion as a central or essential factor (contrary to the crude primitivism of members of Hashomer Hatsa'ir in Osowa Wyszka). The sons and daughters of the community moved from the *beit midrash* to the Zionist or Bundist *lokal* or even the communist cell without their strong ethnic sense being shaken.

In Galicia, especially its eastern part, which had already experienced powerful trends of Polish acculturation in the nineteenth century, the Zionist youth movements were frequently seen as the last 'line of defence' against the assimilation that had already deeply infiltrated family life and the educational system. Some of the autobiographers even described themselves as having joined youth movements, usually Zionist, with the sole intention of not being considered assimilationists. In contrast to the strong sentiment and emotion which characterized the Zionists in Volhynia, in the autobiographies from Galicia the inner struggle over whether to join or remain in a movement was more rational and analytical.

Mez from Zaleszczyki was born in 1912 and joined Betar while studying at teacher training college at the age of 16 'so people would not say that I was an assimilationist'. He was even a *rosh kitah* (head of a group), but really 'without knowing what revisionism was about and what goals Betar sought'.[60] When Lud from Tłuste was in seventh grade (about 13), his friend Symek joined Hashomer Hatsa'ir and tried to convince him to follow in his footsteps to prevent him from 'totally assimilating'.[61] Youth movements were thus seen as a means of asserting Jewish identity when this identity had no other means of expression.[62] Through his friend's invitation he came, despite his hesitations, to see an exhibition of drawings in the movement's *lokal*, but was shocked by the noise and the behaviour of the *ḥalutsim*: perhaps, for him, it was too 'Jewish', although he does not put it this way. In any case, his encounter with the social reality of the movement made him more determined not to join it.

Later in his autobiography Lud writes that, as a young boy seeking an outlet for his energies, he probably should have joined a youth movement, but his parents' home had not nurtured the required spirit, whether Jewish or Zionist. A deep attachment to Judaism should have been expressed, in his opinion, in systematic Talmud study and learning Hebrew, which he had not done since entering the gymnasium.[63] Nonetheless, the problem of antisemitism, which began to be felt

---

[59] YIVO Archives, RG 4: Autobiography 3511, 10.

[60] YIVO Archives, RG 4: Autobiography 3652, 22. *Rosh kitah* is transliterated in Polish letters.

[61] YIVO Archives, RG 4: Autobiography 3675, in *Ostatnie pokolenie*, 346.

[62] Lud had had a Hebrew teacher in his childhood.

[63] YIVO Archives, RG 4: Autobiography 3675, in *Ostatnie pokolenie*, 347–8.

more acutely in Poland while he was in tenth grade (1930/1),[64] led him to the conclusion that assimilation was not a feasible solution, given the impossibility of Jews and Catholics living harmoniously together.

ES-WU from Brody, who was born in 1912, had a deep attachment to Zionism, though he described his joining Zionist youth movements—first Hashomer Hatsa'ir when he was in the sixth or seventh grade and later Hano'ar Hatsioni—as mainly motivated by the group instinct and a wish to avoid loneliness. When invited, while studying law, to join 'a movement of Jewish university students', he strove to be active in it and to give lectures, and was even a member of the anti-Nazi committee which organized a boycott of German goods.[65] His affinity with Zionism was similar to that of Mez and Lud and in a great measure to that prevalent in his social sphere. His Zionism had a paradoxical character: it was both natural to him but imposed no obligations. It satisfied his need to identify with Jewish national aspirations and thus to realize the cultural separateness of the Jews but lacked any political content or desire to emigrate to the Land of Israel. In his words: 'From my earliest youth I was a Zionist. In the beginning I had no idea of Zionism's objectives; I was not aware of the differences between the Zionist parties. I knew only one thing . . . the aim of this movement is to acquire a land for the Jews so that the Jewish people could develop its original culture there.'[66] Later he wrote about his desire to realize himself in the Land of Israel and Hebrew culture, but voices his apprehension about wasting his talents in this way.[67]

ES-WU, like the other autobiographers from Galicia discussed here, belonged to an educated and culturally assimilated Jewish elite, which in spite of all their difficulties in Poland, feared the consequences of emigration to Palestine, which would adversely affect their personal circumstances. Like a significant proportion of Galician Jews, he tried to harmonize his links to Polish culture with an appreciation of and identification with Jewish culture, yet the result of this attempted synthesis was often polite respect for Jewish culture, with little commitment to the Jewish national idea.

Zyg. Hor. from Zakopane identified even more fully with Polish culture. In his view, he had been 'transplanted' into the Polish national soil and could not make a true, 'internal' return to his Jewish identity. He came from a family which could be called traditionalist and had even attended *ḥeder*. When he was 19 or 20, after abandoning Hano'ar Hatsioni and subsequently being expelled from the local committee of Hahistadrut Hatsionit, he tried to reflect on the Jewish question 'coldly'. The key issue seemed to him to be antisemitism, while the social content of Zionism—the character of the society to be created in the Land of Israel—was

[64] Especially in his immediate surroundings, according to 'Czortkow', in D. Dąbrowska, A. Wein, and A. Weiss (eds.), *Pinkas hakehilot polin*, ii: *Galitsyah hamizraḥit* (Jerusalem, 1980), 445–7.

[65] See E. Melzer, *Ma'avak medini bemalkodet* (Tel Aviv, 1982); Eng.: *No Way Out: The Politics of Polish Jewry, 1935–1939* (Cincinnati, 1997); Y. Weiss, *Etniyut ve'ezraḥut* (Jerusalem, 2001), 207–25.

[66] YIVO Archives, RG 4: Autobiography 3658, 76.   [67] Ibid. 77.

unimportant. His lack of interest in the practical aspect of Zionism stemmed from his experience of growing up in a town where there were relatively few Jews and where he had had many friends among the Górale, the local mountain people. He identified with them, ascribing to them the 'call of [his] ancestors' and claiming their 'rite of the water of fire' had led to his addiction to alcohol. The seventeenth-century characters in Sienkiewicz's trilogy, *With Fire and Sword*, *The Deluge* and *Sir Michael*,[68] seemed to him vivid and alive, while Jewish history was 'something legendary'.[69] The study of Hebrew was, in his eyes, 'dilettantism' with no practical purpose.

Another writer from Galicia, Ben Ami, who was raised in a much more traditional Jewish environment than Zyg. Hor., initially discovered in himself, from the moment he abandoned the study of the 'holy writings', a deep sense of alienation from the Jewish society he encountered and the Jewish national idea. He claimed that his town 'had become assimilated' (in the negative sense) in the late 1920s which was proved by the lack of Jewish youth movements. Like some of the other autobiographers, particularly those from Galicia, he was convinced that membership of a youth movement was the only way for young Jews to express their Jewish identity. When he was about 17 or 18 (in 1929) and engrossed in the Yiddish literature which virtually led him to heresy, propagandists from a neighbouring town came and established youth organizations in Borszczów.[70] He joined Betar and was transformed 'both ideologically and practically', attending lectures on Herzl, Pinsker, and Trumpeldor. '[Trumpeldor's] life and death convinced me that Zionism is a sublime idea'.[71] In the spirit of Jabotinsky he asserted that it is impossible for an idea for which blood is shed to be 'frivolous and fantastic'; blood makes it possible to wipe away the 'dust and rags by which the Jewish flag is covered'.

His radical transformation can be traced mainly to the inner conflicts he felt in relation to his Jewish identity. From the moment he ceased to be religious and abandoned Talmud study, despite his specific family background, he experienced the same sense of shame at the nature of the local Jewish community articulated by some of the other autobiographers from Galicia. The dust and filth covering the Jewish flag could only be removed by violent and radical measures, in this case those advocated by Jabotinsky's revisionist movement.

In summary, the attitudes of the youngsters of Galicia towards the new definitions of Jewish identity were significantly different from those in Kresy. They were characterized by the attempt, sometimes more and sometimes less successful, to connect and integrate cultural assimilation to Polishness with support for a Zionist Jewish identity. These young Jews felt a strong sense of Jewish identity, but

[68] H. Sienkiewicz, *Ogniem i mieczem* (Warsaw, 1884); *Potop* (Warsaw, 1886); *Pan Wołodyjowski* (Warsaw, 1887–8).

[69] YIVO Archives, RG 4: Autobiography 3654, 497.

[70] Compare the totally different picture drawn in N. Blumenthal (ed.), *Sefer borscziw* (Tel Aviv, 1960), 138–40.   [71] YIVO Archives, RG 4: Autobiography 3712, 37.

it lacked the ardour and readiness to sacrifice and to transform life patterns which can be observed among their counterparts in Kresy.[72]

The autobiographies from the former Congress Kingdom reveal internal fractures and contradictions rather than either continuity or synthesis. Sh.R. from Radzyń, who was born in 1913, was the son of a religious but 'modern' father who was responsive to new social currents (he was employed in Lublin, perhaps as a clerk). The writer studied in both a *ḥeder* and a Polish elementary school. When he was 16 or 17 he joined Hashomer Hatsa'ir but was attracted to communism. He presented his ideological world as torn between intellect and emotion: in his opinion, speaking on the level of 'cold logic', the solution suggested by Zionism was impossible to implement, but he felt he could not let himself be discouraged by cold logic, because he sought perfection and had a 'romantic' outlook, which connected him to his Jewish ethnic identity.[73] This feeling of schism stemmed from growing up in a home characterized by limited communication (though not necessarily by indifference or lack of involvement) and from being exposed to two very different school systems. At the same time, a more general pattern is apparent—his mentality is marked by the sense of an unbridgeable gap between the reality of modernization and Jewish national aspirations which appear to have no relevance to this new reality.

Pesa, the daughter of a religious Jewish merchant, who provided her with economic stability but was unable to show her emotion or pass on his religious commitment, was attracted to a Zionist youth movement. She studied in a Jewish gymnasium but felt detached from Judaism, and her views even echo common antisemitic sentiments. In addition, she was repelled by the Jewish subjects taught in the lower classes of the gymnasium and encountered difficulties in learning Hebrew. Despite all her attempts to avoid confronting her Jewish identity, she had joined 'a Zionist movement' while in the ninth or tenth grade, initially without great enthusiasm, most probably Hashomer Hatsa'ir.[74] Belonging to this movement increased her interest in studying Hebrew and Jewish history, subjects she had considered up until then boring and even distasteful.[75] During the eleventh grade at the beginning of the 1930s she 'was [already] clinging to Zionism as a drowning person to a plank', probably because of pogroms and anti-Jewish riots at Polish universities, events she does not explicitly mention.[76] Nonetheless, she

---

[72] For a Galician intellectual from the previous generation undergoing similar processes, see E. Mendelsohn, 'From Assimilation to Zionism in Lvov: The Case of Alfred Nossig', *Slavonic and East European Review*, 49 (1971), 521–34. A similar characterization of the Jewish community to mine can be found in the recollections of Mordecai Ze'ev Braude ('Yemei kehunati bestanislav' [1952], in D. Sadan and M. Gelerter (eds.), *Stanislav*, Arim ve'imahot beyisra'el, 5 (Jerusalem, 1952), 98–165).

[73] YIVO Archives, RG 4: Autobiography 3844, 14–15.

[74] YIVO Archives, RG 4: Autobiography 3588, 28.   [75] Ibid. 24–5.

[76] Ibid. 29. From November 1931 anti-Jewish riots raged in the universities and other academic institutions, mainly at the beginning of the academic year. Their background was a demand (on the part of nationalistic circles) to limit the number of Jews in universities. Such riots took place in Warsaw,

continued to have a tormented relationship with Zionism. She was always sceptical about the abilities of the Jewish people in general, and her sympathy for 'Palestyna' was for her merely a symbolic expression of solidarity in the face of persecution. In her autobiography she describes her admiration for the *halutsim* but considered them 'martyrs', undertaking actions with no practical value, since, in her view, they could not succeed. She was especially doubtful whether a people of middle-men could become a proper nation with farmers, manual workers, merchants, and an intelligentsia. Only her sense that there was no 'hope for a better tomorrow' in Poland made her consider emigration to the Land of Israel, despite her belief that members of the intelligentsia would not be able to adapt to kibbutz life.[77]

Yehuda Freich from Tomaszów Mazowiecki was born in 1921 and was very religious until the age of 15 or 16. He had studied in *heder*s and yeshivas, but abandoned religion under the influence of a study partner in a *beit midrash*. At the age of 16 he was invited to the Hashomer Hatsa'ir *lokal* and, to his surprise, found his friends from the *heder* and *shtibl* (small hasidic prayer house) there. Being active in the organization led him to change his views about life, perhaps a change of deeper significance than that of abandoning religion.[78] In his words, the organization made him understand that 'a young man does not live for himself but for something higher, his people'. Spurred on by ideology, he became imbued with the 'pioneering ethos'.[79] Yet, although he was a local Hashomer Hatsa'ir leader, he was determined not to emigrate to the Land of Israel, since he had succeeded, with great effort, in getting a job in a factory.[80]

These autobiographers represent different spheres of Jewish society in central Poland. What they all had in common was that their fathers had become modernized as a result of their economic activity. The autobiographies reveal a 'conflict' response to their Jewish heritage, the outcome of deep scepticism about national renewal in its Zionist version. They opted for Zionism as the best response to the Jews' social and economic problems, but this did not result in the same enthusiastic support for it which was found in the autobiographies from Kresy or in the belief of the possibility of synthesis of the new and the old that can be encountered in the Galician autobiographies.[81]

Vilna, and the Jagiellonian University of Kraków and later in Lwów and Poznań. At the beginning of the academic year 1933/4 the first attempts to introduce 'ghetto benches', separate places for Jews in the lecture halls and laboratories, were made. See Melzer, *Ma'avak medini bemalkodet*, 111–12; S. Rudnicki, 'From "numerus clausus" to "numerus nullus"', *Polin*, 2 (1987), 246–68.

[77] YIVO Archives, RG 4: Autobiography 3588, 40–1.

[78] YIVO Archives, RG 4: Autobiography 3670, 49.   [79] Ibid. 50.   [80] Ibid. 63.

[81] On modernization in central Poland, see S. D. Corrsin, 'Progressive Judaism in Poland: Dilemmas of Modernity and Identity', *Harvard Ukrainian Studies*, 22 (1998), 89–99; for portraits of two prominent figures in the cultural life of the region, see B. J. Lipton, 'Janusz Korczak-Henryk Goldszmit: Pole or a Jew?', in J. Micgiel, R. Scott, and H. B. Segel (eds.), *Poles and Jews: Myth and Reality in the Historical Context* (New York, 1986), 262–74; K. Steffen, 'Das Eigene durch das Andere: Zur Konstruktion jüdischer Polonität 1918–1939', *Jahrbuch des Simon-Dubnow-Instituts*, 3 (2004), 89–111.

CONCLUSION

In the first part of this chapter, I showed how the autobiographies written by young Jews for the contests organized by YIVO in the 1930s illustrate the new currents of thought in their generation. These were the result both of the spiritual and religious split between these young people and their parents and of deep political and ideological fragmentation. The autobiographies reveal a spiritual and cultural reality in which the members of the various youth movements—mainly Zionist but also Bundist and communist—considered themselves to be the legitimate heirs of the *kehilot* which had characterized the premodern Jewish community. Jewish youth movements in Poland functioned, to a greater or lesser extent, as communal bodies taking over functions which the *kehilot* were increasingly unable to perform. These movements reinterpreted traditional ways of providing for the needs of the community. Their success in doing so enabled them to see themselves not as an alien and destructive element but as renewing traditions which had been undermined by the failures of the previous generations.

The autobiographies also shed new light on the relationships between the various movements, which are usually considered by historians to have been ideologically incompatible. All these movements—Zionism, which aspired to concentrate the people in the ancient homeland; Bundism, which considered itself as representing only the 'masses of the Jewish workers'; and communism, whose ideology did not include recognition of the existence of Jewish people at all—acted principally within the Jewish communal framework, on its behalf and that of its members.

The second part of the chapter attempted to provide a more detailed discussion of the continuity of youth movement activity with the traditional Jewish world, examining the different attitudes in Kresy, Galicia, and Congress Poland. Autobiographies from Kresy reveal the centrality of Hebrew in Zionist youth movements. Hebrew, which represented both the past (religious tradition) and the present (Zionism and the Land of Israel), was here an essential component of Zionist youth culture and was not simply a matter of ideology. Furthermore, the study and use of Hebrew did not divide the younger and older generations, and in some towns Hebrew was even used in daily life. In this region, even in explicitly non-religious movements, modern (political) Zionism was not understood in terms of a revolution but rather as a continuation, a realization of an 'ancestral dream'. By contrast, for the autobiographers from Galicia, who probably shared common ideas and modes of thinking with a large proportion of their generation, membership in a Zionist youth movement was a way to cling to their Jewish identity in a situation marked by a widespread use of Polish and a strong pull to integrate into Polish culture. In Galicia, Jewish culture was no longer felt to be central to the identity of many of the writers, but their alienation from it was not viewed as unbridgeable, and a synthesis between the two cultures was deemed attainable. Among the writers who lived in the former Congress Poland there was a stronger sense of fragmentation: more than in the other regions, the impact of modernization and secularization was keenly felt. They were seen as forces distancing young Jews not only from religion itself but also from the cultural and ethnic values that derive from religion. Reconnection with a Jewish identity, and above all with its Zionist incarnation, aroused inner conflicts and many uncertainties.

A Revolution in the Name of Tradition
Orthodoxy and Torah Study for Girls

NAOMI SEIDMAN

WHEN Sarah Schenirer, founder of the Bais Yaakov school system, died in 1935 at the age of 51, eulogists spoke of her enormous accomplishments in revitalizing Orthodox Jewish life through the education of young girls and women. Since 1917, when Schenirer accepted the first twenty-five students into her school, the movement she founded had become well established, with perhaps 200 schools and 38,000 students throughout Poland and beyond.[1] These students were enrolled in a wide range of programmes: a few of the institutions were full-time elementary or high schools in which Jewish as well as secular subjects were taught; the vast majority, however, were afternoon religious schools which supplemented public schools and at least in theory allowed students to avoid the religious instruction provided by those schools. The school system also included a number of vocational-training programmes, in which students could study Jewish subjects alongside dressmaking, secretarial skills, bookkeeping, or even nursing (the vocational school in Łódź established by Eliezer Gershon Friedenson was named Ohel Sarah, in Schenirer's honour). The crown jewels of the system were the teacher-training seminaries in Kraków, Vienna, and Czernovitz.[2] In 1926, along with Friedenson,

---

[1] A. Z. Friedman, 'Foreword', in H. Seidman, *Dos yidishe religyeze shul-vezn in di ramen fun der poylisher gezetzgebung* (Warsaw, 1937), 8. Joseph Carlebach documents a trip undertaken in July and August 1934 by the German Jewish leadership of Keren Hatorah, the educational foundation of Agudat Israel, to eastern Europe, and lists 187 Bais Yaakov schools, seminaries, and colonies (some still in the process of being formed) in Poland and another 23 in Austria (including the teachers' seminary in Vienna), Czechoslovakia, Romania, and Hungary ('Keren Hathora-Fahrt zu Jüdischen Kultur-Stätten des Ostens', in *Ausgewählte Schriften*, 3 vols. (New York, 1982–2002), ii. 1103–83). Such figures, as Joseph Friedenson acknowledges, are hard to establish with any certainty, given the number of schools (especially the afternoon schools in smaller towns) that opened and closed and the contradictory figures provided by the movement and contemporary scholars. Friedenson himself tentatively relies on internal Bais Yaakov figures from 1935: 225 schools with 27,119 students in Poland; 18 schools with 1,569 students in Czechoslovakia; 18 schools with 1,292 students in Romania; 16 schools with 2,000 students in Lithuania, and 11 schools with 950 students in Austria ('Batei hasefer levanot beit ya'akov bepolin', in T. Sharfstein (ed), *Haḥinukh vehatarbut ha'ivrit be'eiropah bein shetei milḥamot* (New York, 1957), 71).

[2] For more on the different categories of schools, see Friedenson, 'Batei hasefer levanot beit ya'akov', 69–71.

who served as editor of the *Beys-Yankev Zhurnal*, Schenirer also founded Bnos
Agudas Yisro'el, a youth movement for Bais Yaakov graduates and other Orthodox
girls, and helped establish the women's organization of the Orthodox political organization Agudat Israel.[3] Schenirer thus invented what supporters have described
as the single most important development of twentieth-century Orthodoxy: the
Bais Yaakov student, whose knowledge of and passion for Torah reinvigorated
Orthodoxy as a whole at a moment of great danger to Orthodox continuity.[4] While
the radical spirit of its origins had already diminished by the 1930s, the Bais Yaakov
movement saw a rebirth after the Holocaust and continues to flourish, with a loose
network of schools throughout the Jewish world, now no longer guided by a central
organization but continuing to keep alive the memory and myths of its origins.

The fascinating story of the founding of the Bais Yaakov movement in interwar
Poland has yet to receive sustained scholarly attention in the form of an academic
monograph. As with other complex or controversial issues within Orthodoxy, the
beginnings of Orthodox girls' education among east European Jews (German neo-
Orthodoxy began to educate girls formally in the Hirsch school system in the
1850s) are primarily remembered through hagiography, especially surrounding
the figure of Schenirer as founding 'mother' of the movement. Bais Yaakov girls
everywhere know the story of the pious seamstress who saw the need to teach girls
Torah lest they be swept away from Orthodoxy by the lures of modern life.
Orthodox texts often present these beginnings as a creation *ex nihilo*, in which a
simple woman had the unprecedented idea of bringing the 'garments of Torah' to
the 'naked' souls of Orthodox girls.[5] Yet Schenirer's modesty and simplicity hardly
explain the distinctive features of the movement or its astonishingly rapid success.
Bais Yaakov succeeded despite a formidable set of obstacles, including a 1903 rabbinic decision that rejected organized religious education for girls; active opposition from traditionalist elements in the Orthodox world; changing and unevenly
applied legislation and rulings by the Polish government concerning religious
schools; and, as Schenirer lamented, lack of interest in or hostility to religion
among the Jewish girls of her time.[6] As I will argue, the achievements of Bais

---

[3] Gershon Bacon provides figures that chart the growth of Bnos from 25 chapters with 750 members in 1926/7, the year of its founding, to 279 chapters in 1936/7, with 14,132 members (*The Politics of
Tradition: Agudat Yisrael in Poland, 1916–1939* (Jerusalem, 1996), 172).

[4] While Bais Yaakov is often described as the first Orthodox girls' school system in the *ḥaredi* world
and in fact referred to itself as such on graduation certificates in the 1920s, the description is not
entirely accurate, given the establishment of the Havatselet school in Warsaw at least a year earlier than
Schenirer's first class.

[5] Orthodox literature on Sarah Schenirer includes P. Beinisch, *Carry Me in your Heart: The Life and
Legacy of Sarah Schenirer, Founder and Visionary of the Bais Ya'akov Movement* (New York, 2003); D.
Rubin, *Daughters of Destiny: Women who Revolutionized Jewish Life and Torah Education* (New York,
1988).

[6] In 1903, at the Conference of Polish Rabbis held in Kraków, Menahem Mendl Landau, the rabbi
of Nowy Dwór, near Warsaw, called for the establishment of Jewish schools for girls, but the proposal
was rejected (see R. Manekin, 'Mashehu ḥadash legamrei: hitpatḥuto shel ra'ayon hadati levanot ba'et

Yaakov should be traced not to a rejection of these challenges, but rather to their dialectical incorporation: in revolutionizing Orthodoxy in the name of tradition, the movement brought together innovative and conservative impulses in an unprecedented and distinctive set of rhetorical and cultural practices.

When Schenirer assembled twenty-five girls in her seamstress's studio in the autumn of 1917 the Orthodox Jewish world lacked not only an established school system, curriculum, or philosophy of girls' education but, perhaps more importantly, a coherent rhetoric that could establish the legitimacy of girls' study of Torah and Judaism or place value on youth, women, and innovation. While Torah study—often understood as the cultural practices involved in learning the Talmud —is central to Jewish masculine identity, various rabbinic passages explicitly forbid or denigrate such study for girls.[7] Joseph Friedenson, an Agudah activist after the war and historian of the movement, sets the novelty of Schenirer's project, given these traditional constraints, in stark contrast to the modernization of religious education for boys:

What was the difference between the educational institutions of Agudat Israel for boys and those for girls? The educational institutions for boys were primarily nothing more than a continuation of the old traditional religious schools, even if these were modernized in some way. This was entirely different for the educational institutions for girls, which were organized by the Agudah under the name Bais Yaakov. This was an entirely novel phenomenon, and even a complete reversal in the approach of strictly traditionalist parents to the problem of the education of their daughters.[8]

Nevertheless, Friedenson continues (with perhaps some exaggeration), strictly traditional Jews, 'with their innate suspicion of any innovation, not only accepted this new movement to educate girls but even seized upon the idea with enthusiasm and dedication'.[9] The rapid success of the movement indeed demands explanation, especially given the 1903 rabbinic rejection of education for girls. Agnieszka Oleszak has recently argued that the success of the movement followed directly from a number of related critical developments in Poland: the granting of women's right to vote in 1918, the establishment of Agudat Israel as the representative political body of Orthodox Jewry in Poland and internationally, the Agudah's recruitment of Jewish voters, and 'the compulsory law of education introduced in February 1919'.[10] Political factors paved the way for the support of Bais Yaakov

haḥadashah', *Masekhet*, 2 (2004), 77–8; Y. Gutman (ed.), *Mekits nirdamim* (Piotrków, 1904), 54–5). For a detailed discussion of the juridical and legislative obstacles to legitimizing Bais Yaakov and the movement's response to these obstacles, see Seidman, *Dos yidishe religyeze shul-vezn in di ramen fun der poylisher gezetzgebung*, 28–33.

[7] On Torah study for girls, see S. P. Zolty, *'And all your children shall be learned': Women and the Study of Torah in Jewish Law and History* (Northvale, NJ, 1993), esp. 263–300.

[8] Friedenson, 'Batei hasefer levanot beit ya'akov', 61.   [9] Ibid.

[10] A. M. Oleszak 'The Beit Ya'akov School in Kraków as an Encounter between East and West', *Polin*, 23 (2010), 281. Support for Oleszak's argument that the Agudat Israel adoption of Bais Yaakov

by the Orthodox establishment in 1919 (and even more fundamentally in 1923), and Schenirer was helped nearly from the outset by Agudah activists and leaders. I would argue, however, that without Schenirer's rhetorical and organizational genius, the movement could hardly have taken off. Bais Yaakov functioned, in the early years, as a missionary movement in which graduates of the summer teacher-training course were immediately sent out 'into the field' to found new schools. The system required rabbinic authorization and the financial support of the Agudah, but only these young women could have founded and run the afternoon programmes that sprang up so quickly in the following decade, and only Schenirer could have energized them, drawing on their youth (in the first years some were as young as 15) as a mobilizing factor and finding Jewish resources for female empowerment rather than passivity or restriction.

The distinctive culture that Schenirer helped to create was a combination of often contradictory cultural influences. Her writings attest not only to her fierce and deep commitment to Orthodoxy but also to her cosmopolitan sensibility. According to her memoir, *Pages from my Life*, the vision of religious education for Jewish girls emerged from a fateful encounter she had in Vienna, where her family had fled at the outbreak of the First World War. Attending the Orthodox synagogue of Rabbi Moshe Flesch in the Schtumpfergasse, Schenirer was surprised to see the rabbi stand up before the Torah reading to deliver a sermon, 'a new thing for me'. But while Schenirer confessed that she had forgotten the details of the sermon, she remembered her own reactions at hearing the rabbi speak passionately about the figure of Judith, 'calling on contemporary women to follow the example of this historical heroine':

I felt immediately that the main thing missing is that our sisters know so little about their past and this alienates them from our people and their traditions. If they knew a little about the martyrs of our history, had some conception of the heroism of our great men and women, it would have been entirely different. . . . In my mind, at that moment, were born various grandiose plans.[11]

This debt to the cultural mores and thought of German neo-Orthodoxy, following the teachings of Samson Raphael Hirsch, is duly recorded as the very origin for the project of educating girls. This provenance also continued to guide the movement: requirements for all students entering the Kraków seminary, for instance, included not only seven years of schooling, two letters of recommendation, and modest clothing, but also possession of and familiarity with (in addition to the Pentateuch and a prayer book) Hirsch's *Nineteen Letters of Ben Uzziel*.[12]

was partly motivated by electoral concerns may be found in the many political advertisements in the *Beys-Yankev Zhurnal* urging readers to vote for Agudah in the elections of 1930.

[11] S. Schenirer, 'Bleter fun mayn lebn', in ead., *Gezamlte shriftn* (Łódź, 1933; 2nd edn. Brooklyn, 1955), 9.

[12] D. Weissman, 'Bais Yaakov: A Woman's Educational Movement in the Polish Jewish Community. A Case Study in Tradition and Modernity', MA thesis (New York University, 1977), 59.

The second influence was the growing phenomenon of Jewish girls' schools in Poland and throughout eastern Europe, including some that worked specifically for Jewish religious revival. Prior to the establishment of the Bais Yaakov movement, there was a semi-vocational high school for Jewish girls in Warsaw called Havatselet, which had been founded during the First World War by the German neo-Orthodox rabbis Emanuel Carlebach and Pinchas Kohn and led by Rabbi Moses Auerbach.[13] To these specifically Orthodox educational initiatives should be added the broader phenomenon of the modernization of Jewish schools for boys as well as girls beginning in the mid-nineteenth century under the influence of the Haskalah, which included specific attention to girls' education by leading figures such as Judah Leib Gordon.[14] During the years that Bais Yaakov was getting off the ground various efforts to modernize the traditional *ḥeder* were also under way, and the Agudah was involved with both efforts.[15]

The third influence was the contemporary world of cosmopolitan Kraków, with its public lectures, youth movements, and political activism. Schenirer records her interest in attending such lectures and meetings, although none of what she saw and heard conformed to her sense of what was appropriate for a religious Jewish woman. She began her educational work not by founding a school, but by establishing a library (stocked with books written by the leaders of German neo-Orthodoxy), offering lectures on Jewish topics (which were embraced as long as Schenirer did not insist on discussing the stringent requirements of Jewish law), and starting a youth movement for Orthodox girls (which Schenirer abandoned in favour of teaching younger and thus more malleable children). Schenirer readily acknowledged her attraction to many aspects of this youth culture, but just as often described herself as competing with it. In fact, she both resisted and liberally borrowed from an atmosphere that celebrated youth, self-education, and cultural engagement. This influence is particularly evident in the Bnos movement, which adapted a host of practices from socialist and Zionist youth movements: Bnos was established along principles of self-governance and, according to its own description, 'self-education and spiritual-cultural work' and included hiking and nature activities in its clubs, summer camps, and 'kibbutzim', some of which provided *hakhsharah*, training potential emigrants to the Land of Israel.[16]

The fourth influence was hasidism and the patterns of social and ritual engagement it provided for boys and men. Schenirer, who was raised in a Belzer hasidic family and proceeded with her plans only after receiving the blessing of the Belzer rebbe, Issachar Dov Rokeach, recreated some of the atmosphere of the hasidic

[13] On Havetselet and other informal or local efforts at girls' education, see Manekin, 'Mashehu ḥadash legamrey'.

[14] For a comprehensive history of Jewish girls' education in tsarist Russia, see E. R. Adler, *In her Hands: The Education of Jewish Girls in Tsarist Russia* (Detroit, 2011).

[15] See Bacon, *The Politics of Tradition*, 142–77.

[16] See the special issue of *Beys-Yankev Zhurnal* devoted to the newly founded Bnos (*Beys-Yankev Zhurnal*, 3/2 (1926)).

court in the ecstatic singing and dancing that were a part of Bais Yaakov. Yaffa
Gura, who attended the Kraków seminary and the summer teacher-training
courses in the mid-1920s, describes Schenirer as having instilled in her students
'the sensation of joy (I almost said, hasidic joy) and the fervour of mission'.[17] The
missionary character of the movement, which in this way mimicked early hasidism, manifested itself not only in the passionate commitment of its participants
but also, more practically, in the social networks created by and for graduating
teachers, who were sent to small towns to spread the Bais Yaakov word; in fact, the
Gerer rebbe, Abraham Mordecai Alter, was an earlier supporter, and his hasidim
were among the first to send their daughters to Bais Yaakov and to support the
establishment of schools in their various hometowns.

Perhaps the most salient model for Bais Yaakov was the yeshiva. The Bais
Yaakov movement followed, in accelerated fashion, the pattern of growth of the
yeshiva, from small study groups reliant on local community support to well-
endowed institutions in major cities that attracted students from throughout
Europe and even America. It is no surprise that the first Bais Yaakov high school
was established in Ponevezh (Panevėžys), site of the world-famous yeshiva, or that
the same 1923 Agudah conference that resolved to take on the financial support of
Bais Yaakov also founded the elite Yeshivat Hokhmei Lublin. While the yeshiva
system seems the closest counterpart to Bais Yaakov, Schenirer herself avoided
such comparisons, carefully maintaining the separation between girls' and boys'
education in the terminology and discourse of the movement and refraining from
teaching Talmud (as was also the case for the Hirsch *Realschule* in its curriculum
for girls), the emblem and centre of the male curriculum. Others were less cir-
cumspect: Joseph Friedenson describes the atmosphere at the professionalization
courses in its summer colonies, which Bais Yaakov teachers were required to
attend at least once every three years, as 'reminiscent of a yeshiva where students
were learning Torah for its own sake [*leshma*]'.[18]

While the Bais Yaakov movement borrowed freely from both traditionalizing
and modernizing currents, its discourse strategically left some of these currents
unstated. Schenirer framed her project as a traditionalist response to the lures of
the modern world, underplaying the degree to which modernization was both a
threat to Jewish culture and a resource for combating that threat. Bais Yaakov, as its
detractors rightly saw, was itself a product of Jewish modernity, beginning with
the spiritual and pedagogical influence of the neo-Orthodox slogan *torah im derekh*

[17] Y. Gura, '"Yemei habereishit" shel tnu'at beit ya'akov (pirkei zikhronot)', in A. Bauminger (ed.),
Em beyisra'el: sefer zikaron lesara shnirer (Benei Berak, 1983), 170.

[18] Friedenson, 'Batei hasefer levanot beit ya'akov', 74. Friedenson quotes from a description in
Beys-Yankev Zhurnal of the Rabka (Rabka-Zdrój) summer colony where the teacher-training course
was held from 1927 to 1929 ('Di grandiyoze khinekh-habones arbet in Rabka', *Beys-Yankev Zhurnal*,
45 (1929), 7). Learning Torah 'for its own sake' is often seen as the highest degree of commitment to
the Torah, and specifically not the form usually taken by women, who more normatively study the
Torah in order to understand the laws that apply to them.

erets, Torah with secular, practical education, a programme that found initial expression in the Hirsch school system: subjects such as Jewish ethics, law, history, and the Bible were taught as discrete courses; students were graded and examined regularly; physical education and critical and creative expression were encouraged; and pedagogy, psychology, and other secular subjects were taught, including Schenirer's favourites—Polish and German literature. In Deborah Weissman's summary, the innovations introduced by Bais Yaakov included:

Formal curriculum, teacher training, improved textbooks, the daily schedule of classes and the ringing of bells to mark the change of classes, the external, modern appearance of the schools, the emphasis on hygiene, an emphasis on the kindergarten as a unit, the introduction of secular studies and, particularly, of vocational training, the introduction of physical education as a part of the curriculum, the use of modern facilities such as gymnasia and laboratories, the exposure to world literature and art, and, lastly, the conceptualization of 'Judaism' as a subject area.[19]

The summer programmes for training Bais Yaakov teachers instituted in 1925 to meet the needs of the rapidly burgeoning movement were initially staffed by educators and administrators from Germany, Austria, and Switzerland, including most prominently Judith Rosenbaum (later Grunfeld). Rosenbaum was working on a doctorate in education at the University of Frankfurt when she was approached by the Agudah activist Leo Deutschländer and persuaded to abandon her plans to teach at the Hirsch school and devote her energies to training Bais Yaakov teachers.[20]

Perhaps ironically, the modern educational methods established in the early years may well have been accepted by the Orthodox community only because Bais Yaakov also reaffirmed the traditional principle of sexual segregation (by contrast, the Hirsch *Realschule* in Frankfurt taught boys and girls in the same building, although with slightly different curricula).[21] This phenomenon is a striking example of what Iris Parush has described, in a different context, as 'the benefits of marginality'.[22] As nineteenth-century Jewish girls and women were able to read secular literature because, as marginal participants of the traditional culture, they were beneath the notice of the rabbinic authorities, Sarah Schenirer could provide a 'modern' Orthodox education to early twentieth-century Jewish girls because their educational requirements, too, were outside the realm of male religious authority. As long as traditional sexual segregation was maintained and it made no inroads

[19] Weissman, 'Bais Yaakov: A Woman's Educational Movement', 69.

[20] See M. Dansky, *Rebetzin Grunfeld: The Life of Judith Grunfeld, Courageous Pioneer of the Bais Yaakov Movement and Jewish Rebirth* (New York, 2002).

[21] Shaul Stampfer notes, however, that sexual segregation was not necessarily the rule in nineteenth-century education, as it was not uncommon for girls 'to be sent to a *ḥeder* along with the boys. The mixing of sexes apparently was not considered worthy of note or reaction' (*Families, Rabbis, and Education: Traditional Jewish Society in Nineteenth-Century Eastern Europe* (Oxford, 2010), 169).

[22] I. Parush, *Reading Jewish Women: Marginality and Modernization in Nineteenth-Century Eastern European Jewish Society* (Waltham, Mass., 2004), 57–70.

into the male sphere, what went on in women's spheres need not concern the rabbis. In a 1927 article in the *Beys-Yankev Zhurnal*, 'Schoolbooks for Bais Yaakov Schools', Rabbi Tuvye Yehuda Gutentag made clear his support for the project of composing Bais Yaakov textbooks and other schoolbooks, which 'help gradually introduce students to a subject', providing textual support for his position by quoting Exodus 19: 3, 'Thus shall you say to the house of Jacob and relate to the people of Israel', the verse from which the name of the movement derived. Gutentag referred to the well-known midrashic interpretation of the doublet 'house of Jacob' and 'people of Israel', which maintains that 'the house of Jacob' means the women, while 'the people of Israel' means the men, taking this *midrash* as evidence that 'Moses spoke to the women first' and thus as a legitimating biblical proof text for girls' Torah study and even the production of textbooks for girls. Nevertheless, as useful as these books were for girls and as textually grounded as this Torah study could be shown to be, textbooks were 'not appropriate for a *heder*, where time-honoured methods prevail'.[23]

Bais Yaakov schools produced not female counterparts to their learned brothers but a distinct institutional culture of gendered learning practices. The denominational distinction between centrist and neo-Orthodoxy or the geographical distinction between German and east European Jewry thus reappeared as a gender distinction within east European Orthodoxy, with girls inhabiting a more 'modern' and 'central European' world than their male counterparts. As with the secularizing reading practices Parush charts, these innovations could spread from the female to the male realm. Shaul Stampfer, in documenting the spread of journals and newspapers among the hasidic yeshivas of Poland from 1913 to 1937, remarks:

One interesting fact that should be noted is that almost all of these journals were published after 1924, the year the *Beit Yaakov* (House of Jacob) journal published by the Orthodox Beit Yaakov school movement first appeared. Many of the sisters of yeshiva students attended these schools and, while I know of no way of checking whether the fact that young women had a journal was an incentive for young men to call for journals, the timing is thought-provoking.[24]

In one sense, sexual segregation marked the limits of the Bais Yaakov revolution, even if some of its practices were attractive enough to excite the interest of young men. In another sense, however, sexual segregation might be seen as a powerful tool of the movement, enabling Schenirer to harness the energy of a same-sex

---

[23] T. Y. Gutentag, 'Vegn ler-bikher far di beys ya'akov shuln', *Beys-Yankev Zhurnal*, 29 (1927), 5.

[24] Stampfer, *Families, Rabbis and Education*, 269. Stampfer does not note that the *Beys-Yankev Zhurnal* in fact published the journalism and creative writing of young men as well, thus serving as a literary mouthpiece for the younger generation more generally. Hasidic yeshiva students, then, could have been inspired by the journal more directly, as contributors, and not only as the brothers of female readers. Friedenson provides a list of male contributors, which includes rabbinic luminaries of Poland and Germany as well as young Agudah-affiliated men and women ('Batei sefer levanot beit ya'akov bepolin', 79).

community in clubs, summer courses, retreats, and camps. Memoirs of the early years attest to the ecstatic fervour of these girls' communities, vividly describing the strong connections forged among the Bais Yaakov and Bnos girls in the cere- monies, anthems, and dances that accompanied inaugurations and graduations.[25] As Deborah Weissman notes, 'the movement developed a complete system of slo- gans, mottoes, symbols, special holidays and celebrations, literature, songs, leader- ship roles, and other organizational techniques'.[26]

Schenirer played a central role in many of these areas: she not only was the founder of the movement but also wrote its first classroom curriculum, sewed lace collars for early classes as a kind of badge, composed plays to be performed on Jewish holidays, travelled around the network of schools to provide support for the young teachers, contributed articles to virtually every monthly or fortnightly issue of *Beys-Yankev Zhurnal*, and spoke at meetings and graduations. Schenirer was referred to, especially after her death, as 'the mother' of the movement, but she herself more frequently referred to her students as her 'sisters' (or 'sisters in spirit'), stressing not the maternal connection that might have located these rela- tionships within the traditional terrain of the Jewish family but rather the spirit that linked her project to the youth movements of her day. In one speech she delivered on the first anniversary of the founding of Bnos, Schenirer exhorted the assembled girls: 'Youth means happiness, courage, optimism, and faith in ancient ideals! Pessimism, doubt, sadness is anti-youth! Youth means enthusiasm, living, and striving! Our youth movement must have life!'[27] The radical elements in this discourse, which were drawn from Polish youth culture, also served to differen- tiate Bais Yaakov from the German Jewish neo-Orthodox discourse on femin- inity, which was strongly influenced by the surrounding bourgeois culture. Thus, in the 1850s Hirsch mobilized a discourse of women's special religious feelings and their responsibility to raise Jewish children as part of his own campaign for girls' education. Such family-oriented ideologies, with their emphasis on 'women's nature', were not entirely absent from the Bais Yaakov literature, which included Hirsch's and his students' writings prominently in textbooks, *Beys-Yankev Zhurnal*, and other movement publications.[28] However, equally prominent, including in Schenirer's own writings, were motifs that emphasized sisterly solidarity and the school as a replacement for, rather than a building block of, the Jewish family.

Such a discourse, focusing on youth, solidarity, and class equality, was espe- cially evident in the Bnos movement, with its summer colonies, theme songs, and orientation towards self-government by the young. Schenirer, despite being

[25] See Bauminger (ed.), *Em beyisra'el.*

[26] D. Weissman, 'Bais Yaakov: A Historical Model for Jewish Feminists', in E. Koltun (ed.), *The Jewish Woman: New Perspectives* (New York, 1976), 146.

[27] S. Schenirer, 'Der ershter yor-tog fun "bnos"', in ead., *Gezamlte shriftn*, 24.

[28] See e.g. M. Lehmann, 'Der moderner man un di frume froy (ertsaylung)', *Beys-Yankev Zhurnal*, 3/2 (1926), 26–8; S. R. Hirsch, 'Dos yudishe familyen-leben', *Beys-Yankev Zhurnal*, 19–21 (1925), 129–30.

considerably older than the Bnos activists she regularly addressed, consistently referred to them as her 'sisters', emphasizing the horizontal bond between participants in the movement. For all the radical dimensions of Bnos, Schenirer grounded its practices in traditional Jewish sources. The combination of innovation and tradition was perhaps most evident in the movement's celebration of 15 Av as its special holiday, promoted throughout the Orthodox world as a celebration of female solidarity. Talmudic sources describe 15 Av as a harvest holiday, a day of joy, with romantic and sexual associations, on which the unmarried girls of Jerusalem, dressed in borrowed white garments, went out to dance in the vineyards (*Ta'an*. 30*b*–31*a*). Schenirer's own writings on the subject make no reference to men—the holiday was apparently celebrated in the summer colonies of rural Poland as an entirely female dance ritual—stressing instead the homosocial *communitas* enabled by the levelling of differences between the female participants (another common theme in Bais Yaakov literature, which often includes descriptions of girls, 'many from well-off families', sleeping two to a bed). The attractions of the movement may in fact have been within these 'deprivations', rather than despite them.[29] Schenirer writes that the holiday, as celebrated in ancient times, has resonance for contemporary women:

Borrowed white dresses for each Jewish woman, without distinction between rich and poor—how beautiful that sounds! Today, when the young Jewish woman is drowning in a flood of different fashions and often forgets the fashion of modesty, this factor must teach us a great deal. Jewish women assemble for their special holiday not only in plain white but even borrowed dresses. No trace of luxury sparkles in their dress, there is nothing of the foolish pride that the rich feel towards the poor and encourages the poor to imitate the desires and pleasures of the rich. Everyone must wear a borrowed dress, which demonstrates clearly that everything we possess is not our own, but comes from God, and we must learn only what to do with what we have been given as a gift.[30]

In Schenirer's reading of the tradition, textual foundation is discovered for both a radically egalitarian youth culture and a traditionalist rejection of modern fashions. Such a reading of the holiday is echoed in *Beys-Yankev Zhurnal*, which published advertisements for material to be used in the Bnos movement's celebrations of 15 Av, describing the holiday as 'historically, a traditional Jewish holiday for religious girls'.[31]

Despite the apparently radical nature of Schenirer's revolution, she did in fact find support among the Orthodox leadership, many of whom urged their reluctant communities to recognize the value of religiously educating their daughters despite the well-known prohibitions against it. Such rabbinic opinions could rely on the distinction, by then canonical in the literature of Bais Yaakov, between the study of

[29] Friedenson, 'Batei hasefer levanot beit ya'akov bepolin', 67.

[30] S. Schenirer, 'Ḥamisha aser be'av', in ead., *Gezamlte shrifn*, 30.

[31] Central Secretariat of Bnos Agudath Israel in Poland, 'Greyt aykh tsu tsum yontev fun der yidisher tokhter: hamisha asar bav!', *Beys-Yankev Zhurnal*, 44 (1929), 1.

'written Torah', which is permissible for girls and women, and the study of 'oral Torah' (primarily the Talmud), which is forbidden to them with some minor exceptions.[32] It is striking then that, although such arguments were in principle available, the best-known responsa took an entirely different approach to the problem of Jewish girls' education. The exchange between rabbis Elijah Akiva Rabinowitz and Menahem Mendel Landau at the 1903 Kraków rabbinic conference where the question of Jewish girls' education was raised is instructive: Rabinowitz argued, predictably, that Torah study was forbidden according to the well-known ruling that 'anyone who teaches his daughter Torah teaches her frivolity [or lewdness]' (*Sot.* 21*b*). Landau began by drawing the familiar distinction between oral and written Torah, but continued, less predictably, by arguing:

I say that the times urgently demand of us that we teach girls Torah, so that they come to observe the commandments. After all, we see with our own eyes the decline especially in girls' observance, even ultra-Orthodox girls, because they have no conception of Judaism. And whoever says that teaching girls Torah is teaching them frivolity, I say that that refers to earlier times, when there was no wisdom in women except in the spindle [*Yom.* 66*b*], and they were locked inside their homes and knew nothing of the outside world . . . But now that they learn all sorts of actual frivolities why would the Torah be worse than any other studies?[33]

Landau was unsuccessful in arguing his case, but similar statements were issued by Rabbi Israel Meir (Hakohen) Kagan, first in 1918 and then in a letter dated 1933:

To the esteemed champions and lovers of Torah, the *haredim* of Pristik,

When I heard that *haredim* had volunteered to establish Bais Yaakov schools in the cities to teach Torah and piety, moral virtues and secular [or practical] studies and Torah to Jewish girls, I pronounced their enterprise praiseworthy and prayed that God would bring their efforts to fruition. Theirs is a great and necessary endeavour in these times, as the tide of heresy and all manners of miscreants are lurking and hunting for Jewish souls. Anyone who is concerned about piety should consider it a *mitsvah* to enrol his daughter in such a school. Those who have fears and doubts because of the prohibition against teaching their daughters Torah should not concern themselves with that in these times, and this is not the place to explain this at length, for our own times are not like those that have past, when there was a strong tradition of mothers and fathers to go in the path of Torah and religion, and to

---

[32] These exceptions include the rabbinic homiletic collection *The Sayings of the Fathers*, which was a favourite of Schenirer and others in the movement and the subject of her first public lecture. The basic distinction between oral Torah and written Torah nevertheless continues to shape Bais Yaakov culture. As Shoshanah Bechhofer reports: 'Often, a teacher wishes to use a Talmud text to explicate the Biblical text or philosophical concept he or she is teaching. Rather than photocopy the text, teachers copy the text in their own handwriting and photocopy the copy for distribution to students. No halachic source can be found for this practice; it is simply "the way it is done in Bais Yaakovs"' ('Ongoing Constitution of Identity and Educational Mission of Bais Yaakov Schools: The Structuration of an Organizational Field as the Unfolding of Discursive Logics', Ph.D. thesis (Northwestern University, 2004), 14–15).

[33] Quoted in Manekin, 'Mashehu hadash legamrei', 77; see Gutman (ed.), *Mekits nirdamim*, 51–7.

read the _Tse'ena ure'ena_ [Bible translation for women] every sabbath. Due to our many transgressions this is no longer the case. Therefore, every effort should be made to establish as many schools of this type as possible and to rescue what can still be rescued.[34]

Kagan had, in a comment on _Sotah_ 21_b_ published in 1911, relied on the distinction between oral Torah and written Torah to permit women's Torah study in places 'where the tradition of parents has become weakened'.[35] This letter, which was widely publicized in Bais Yaakov literature, is testimony not only to the principles by which Orthodox authorities overcame their doubts about the permissibility of teaching girls Torah but also to the factors that led them to advocate actively for the cause.

For Landau and Kagan, educating Jewish girls, despite being an innovation, was primarily justified by _hora'at sha'ah_, the needs of the moment: when long-established, family-oriented practices no longer served as a bulwark against the temptations of modernity, schools become an unfortunate necessity. As Weissman comments:

[Kagan's letter] legitimated an innovation within the Jewish tradition based on exclusively sociological grounds; for a historian of the Halachic process, the use of extra- or meta-Halachic considerations in making decisions is in itself a noteworthy occurrence. [Nevertheless] the innovation is of limited scope. It should be noted that he has not suggested that the girls be trained in the intricacies of Talmudic reasoning or traditional legal thought.[36]

Such a justification for girls' education has the benefit of implicitly answering the question of why previous generations did not educate Jewish girls if such education is indeed praiseworthy. However, it leaves open the question of whether modern innovations should be understood as temporary measures, a question that continues to exercise Bais Yaakov today.

By contrast with the rabbis, Schenirer only rarely described her accomplishments as a regrettably necessary response to contemporary conditions. Schenirer's

[34] Weissman, 'Bais Yaakov: A Woman's Educational Movement', 53; see Y. M. Kagan, 'A briv fun heylikn goen rabun shel kol bnei golah hakhofets hayyim zts"l' [19 Feb. 1933], _Beys-Yankev Zhurnal_, 107 (1933), 18; repr. in Schenirer, _Gezamlte shriftn_, 2nd edn., 1. In Schenirer's _Gezamlte shriftn_ the letter serves the secondary function of endorsing her writings, alongside the more institutional function of legitimating the movement.

[35] Y. M. Kagan, _Likutei halakhot_ (New York, 1957), 21; see B. Brown, 'Erekh talmud torah bemishnat hahafets hayim ufesikato be'inyan talmud torah lenashim', _Dine Israel_, 24 (2007), 110–18.

[36] These were not the only responsa issued in relation to Jewish girls' education. The new institution required a variety of rulings regarding men's participation. The Boyaner rebbe, Abraham Jakob Friedman, set the stage for the participation (often in leading roles) of men in a women's culture by ruling in 1924 that men could be present at the school registration and collect tuition fees, provided there were at least two of them present and neither was a bachelor. Married men were also permitted to lecture in the schools, though the regular teaching faculty was almost entirely female while men typically gave occasional special lectures. Elchanan Wasserman went further in ruling that men could be appointed to run a school, and give lectures to groups of women. Judah Leib Orlean was appointed principal of the Kraków seminary and de facto leader of the movement in 1935, a few months before Schenirer's death. See Weissman, 'Bais Yaakov: A Woman's Educational Movement', 59–61.

largest and most attentive audience were girls and women, who required not an apologetic on the legitimacy of their enterprise but rather a rousing call to arms. Thus, at the first International Congress of Orthodox Women, Schenirer began by speaking of modernity as a moment of awakening:

The Orthodox woman has awakened from her long, lethargic sleep and begun to organize. . . . Not long after we created the Bnos organization in Poland, the powerful voice of the religious Jewish woman rings out on the world stage. The intellectual Jewish woman is no longer isolated. In every corner of the world she is closely bound to her sisters.

I know well that many religious Jews will view this with suspicion. We hold sacred the ideal of women's modesty. 'She is in the tent' [Gen. 18: 9]. No doubt a portion of the Orthodox world views our congress as, God forbid, a transgression. But these Jews need to understand that this conference is an outgrowth of the dangers Jewish women face from various secularist directions. *Et la'asot lashem*, now is the time to act on behalf of God [i.e. Jewish values and observance are under threat and emergency measures are required]— from this perspective must our public efforts be understood.[37]

The tensions of Schenirer's project appear in unusually close proximity here. Schenirer began by celebrating the visibility and power of Jewish women, declaring an end to their cultural isolation. She then acknowledged that Jewish tradition prefers women to be modest and unseen, coded here in the biblical passage in which Abraham relays to the angels that Sarah is in the tent. Only in addressing these traditionalist doubts did Schenirer refer to the doctrine of *hora'at sha'ah*.

In speaking of girls' formal Torah study, especially to girls, Schenirer seems to have refrained almost entirely from the apologetic rhetoric of *hora'at sha'ah*, crafting instead a discourse that deemed girls' Torah study inherently valuable. This is evident even from the name of the movement, Bais Yaakov, which locates textual warrant for the project in Exodus 19, the very story of the revelation at Sinai that in Judith Plaskow's ground-breaking feminist manifesto provides painful evidence for women's exclusion from this revelation.[38] Bais Yaakov not only found in this midrashic reading evidence for God's giving the Torah to women first, as discussed above, but it also read its own history into the verse. A ubiquitous trope in the literature is the discovery of a reference to the first Bais Yaakov class, which numbered twenty-five pupils, embedded in the first word of the verse—*koh*, which adds up to 25. This intertextual play extends as well into the ritual realm: among the distinctive holidays of the movement, and the one that lacks the historical precedent claimed by the holiday of 15 Av, is the celebration of 3 Sivan (three days before the traditional date of the revelation at Mount Sinai and thus the date of God's message to Moses to teach Torah to women), which became for a time a Bais Yaakov holiday celebrating its own origins.[39] In such intertextual and ritual

---

[37] S. Schenirer, 'Arum unzer velt-kongres', in *Gezamlte shriftn*, 38.

[38] J. Plaskow, *Standing again at Sinai: Judaism from a Feminist Perspective* (New York, 1991).

[39] Yaffa Gura participated in the celebration of 3 Sivan in 1929, in which 'we danced for hours and hours, we girls and our spiritual mother, and sang without ceasing: "So shall you say to the House of

performances, the very innovations of the movement become occasions for discovering traditional precedent, just as the Torah is shown to foresee the rise of the
movement.

Another ubiquitous and particularly rich intertextual locus is the association
between Sarah Schenirer and her biblical forebear, the matriarch Sarah. Such a
connection is evident in the naming of the movement's Łódź vocational school
Ohel Sarah, a reference to the tent in which the biblical Sarah sat, traditionally a
sign of her modesty, and of Schenirer, whose own occupation as a seamstress was
among the courses of study at the school. In this name, the tensions between
modesty—with which Schenirer is also often associated, precisely through this
proof text—and economic self-sufficiency are resolved. (In other Bais Yaakov literature, traditional proof texts for the legitimacy of vocational training for girls
are found in the 'woman of valour' (Prov. 31).) Even more regularly, Schenirer is
connected with the biblical Sarah in her barrenness, a description that is regularly
qualified with the sentiment that although she 'unfortunately had no children of
her own', she nurtured thousands of daughters.[40] This rhetoric, too, conceals a
submerged tension, since unlike the biblical Sarah, who was indeed long barren,
Schenirer was not barren but rather unmarried during the formative years of the
movement. The trope of Schenirer as a modern-day Sarah thus not only grounds
her life in biblical precedent but also obscures her choices and circumstances, and
domesticates the radical social and cultural practices of the movement she founded
in the traditional Jewish language of reproduction, family, and lineage.[41]

While Bais Yaakov rhetoric provided the school and its founder with a powerful
textual precedent, the question of locating the students in the tradition was more
vexed. There was a range of attempts to answer it, none of which achieved canon-
icity. Schenirer most often described the students and teachers of Bais Yaakov as
incarnations of the priests who served the Jerusalem Temple in antiquity. Speaking to graduates of the summer teacher-training course, Schenirer exhorted them:
'You are going out and building temples! Like the priests your hearts must be
pure.'[42]

The analogy Schenirer finds for the new phenomenon of the Bais Yaakov girl is
a remarkable and somewhat exotic one. The priests were an all-male cadre, dedi-

---

Jacob | So shall you say to the House of Jacob"' ('The Earliest Days of the Bais Yaakov Movement',
144).

[40] 'Unfortunately and tragically, Sarah Schenirer was denied her own biological children. However,
she was granted the zechus [privilege] to be a mother not to one, ten, or twenty children, but to scores,
hundreds, thousands, generation after generation, of Jewish children' (Beinisch, *Carry Me in your
Heart*, 39).

[41] Strikingly in this context, the girls who are described as having sat *shiva* and torn their shirts at
her death (Friedenson, 'Batei hasefer levanot beit ya'akov bepolin', 62) are considered pious participants in Bais Yaakov culture, although this behaviour is not in accordance with Jewish law, since such
responses were restricted to close family members.

[42] S. Schenirer, 'Unzere piyonerns', in ead., *Gezamlte shriftn*, 33.

cated to religious life but separated from both learning and family. The priestly analogy is not entirely new: Chava Weissler has shown that it was popular in the women's supplicatory prayers, *tkhines*.[43] Schenirer's analogy, like that of the *tkhines*, imagined a high ritual function for what might be seen as women's worldly activities—whether cooking or founding schools for girls.

The analogy of priesthood provided Schenirer with another important association, purity: 'Before the High Priest would go out for the sacred service they would ask him, "Is there perhaps something alien in your heart?" You are going out into the great world, and pure, childlike souls will be entrusted to you. How terrible will be your sin if your heart is not, God forbid, pure.'[44] Schenirer transposes the language of idolatry from the Temple context to her own, finding Jewish terms for a distinctively modern concern, the necessity to guard against the influence of secularity and other 'alien' influences.

Schenirer's adoption of the priest as prototype also had another virtue: it avoided the more immediate models of the yeshiva and the hasidic court. Schenirer brought a hasidic spirit to girls' lives: her speeches traditionally ended with rapturous circle dances with her at the centre. Her teacher-training seminaries were elite academies along the lines of the Lithuanian yeshivas, recruiting ambitious adolescents from throughout the Jewish world. Such elitism was deliberately cultivated: in 1935 Judah Leib Orlean took over as sole director of the seminary in Kraków, which had had 80 students when it opened in 1931 and had in four years grown to nearly double that. Orlean deliberately reduced the student body from 150 to 120 and raised both entrance requirements and curricular standards. This move had the effect of expanding the geographical diversity of the student body, which was initially drawn primarily from Poland but after 1935 came from throughout eastern and central Europe as well as the United States, Canada, Switzerland, Belgium, and France.[45] The year 1930 also marked the opening of the Yeshivat Hokhmei Lublin, the most prestigious yeshiva in Poland. Unlike the Yeshivat Hokhmei Lublin, however, which revelled in the luxurious accommodation it provided for its students, Bais Yaakov took pride in the modesty of its infrastructure and the pioneering spirit that accompanied these values. Like earlier generations of yeshiva boys, Bais Yaakov girls (14- and 15-year-olds, though later the seminary generally taught girls who were 16 or 17) formed a network of scholars, which they could count on for professional introductions and a warm meal and a place to stay. Schenirer herself functioned as something of an itinerant *magid*, traversing the Jewish world in search of new students and financial support.

If the Bais Yaakov movement was almost but not quite a yeshiva system for girls, Schenirer's role was also difficult to categorize, given that her institutional function had no traditional Jewish equivalent. This was only partially resolved by

---

[43] C. Weissler, *Voices of the Matriarchs: Listening to the Prayers of Early Modern Jewish Women* (New York, 1999), 59–71.   [44] Schenirer, 'Unzere piyonerns', 34.
[45] See Friedenson, 'Batei hasefer levanot beit ya'akov bepolin', 74.

the rhetorical recourse to her role as mother of thousands, a perhaps ironic trope for a woman whose movement was praised for 'saving the Jewish family' and, in a messianic citation, 'restoring daughters to their mothers', in part by displacing the centrality of the Jewish family for young girls. Such a role could not describe every aspect of her work and was particularly difficult to reconcile with her function as chief ideologue and writer of the movement, who contributed to virtually every issue of the *Beys-Yankev Zhurnal* and other movement publications with learned discourses as well as memoiristic and institutional reflections. In its introduction, the 1933 collection of Schenirer's work by the Central Secretariat of the Bnos Agudas Yisro'el in Poland is described as 'a handbook for the Jewish daughter', which the Jewish woman 'should read and study regularly over and over again'.[46] While the word *sefer* is never used to describe Schenirer's writings, many terms associated with reading holy books are used to describe how they should be read, including the verb *lernen* (to learn), a term used to denote the practice of reading or studying sacred texts. In the 1955 American reprint, Vichna Kaplan, founder of Bais Yaakov in Brooklyn and one of Sarah Schenirer's students, repeats this earlier trope, describing the book as 'not just an adornment to a bookshelf'. The writings of Schenirer 'are not just to read and review but also to learn—to learn daily'.[47] The incongruence between a female-authored text and a prototypically male activity—the 'learning' of a text—seems to push this discourse in a number of conflicting directions: *Gezamlte shrifтn*, Kaplan writes, should also be read because it is 'a will—a holy will from a mother which must be read with attention to every word'. But what is important is to follow its instructions, Kaplan continues. Revising the first edition's categorization of the collection as a handbook, Kaplan describes it more strikingly as 'like a *Shulḥan arukh* . . . for every Jewish daughter'.[48] The descriptions of the collection as a book that should be 'read', a book that (like a *sefer*) should be 'learned', as a private family missive, and as an authoritative collective document suggest the challenges posed by female textual production to a religious culture that lacked categories by which to understand its import.

   That Schenirer was implicitly accepted as something of a *rosh yeshivah* may also be a function of her discursive work in situating her movement within the Jewish cultural and textual landscape. In speaking of the Bais Yaakov graduate as a latter-day priest, Schenirer may also have suggested a rabbinic model of understanding the movement by indirectly pointing to the traditional narrative that recognized the rabbis of late antiquity as replacing the priests. With sleight of hand, Schenirer displaced the rabbis who took up the mantle of priestly leadership and placed this mantle on the shoulders of her own students. The historical crisis described by Kagan, which required a change in the traditional pattern of teaching girls, is transposed into a heroic national key, with the new Council of Yavneh that rebuilt

[46] Central Secretariat of the Bnos Agudas Yisro'el in Poland, '[Foreword]', in Schenirer, *Gezamlte shrifтn*, n.p.   [47] V. Kaplan, 'Hakdome', in Schenirer, *Gezamlte shrifтn*, 2nd edn., 4.   [48] Ibid.

Jewish life after the destruction of the Temple arising in the form of Bais Yaakov.

After the Second World War the distinctive culture and discourse of Bais Yaakov gave way to different forms of collective memory. Shoshanah Bechhofer spells out a number of discursive developments in her analysis of the Bais Yaakov movement from the 1960s to the 1990s.[49] As she argues, the very charge of the movement, to educate Jewish girls, no longer seemed so obviously necessary—perhaps because a decision legitimated through the rubric of 'the needs of the moment' requires new validation in changing times. In 1995 the Orthodox journal *Jewish Observer* hosted a debate about the continuing value of and justification for a rigorous Bais Yaakov education. The challenge was raised in a article written under the pseudonym Uri Bergstein, 'Are Bais Yaakovs and Seminaries Doing their Job?', in which the writer, a male educator in the yeshiva system, argued that the strongly intellectual thrust of Bais Yaakov high schools and seminaries was not aligned with the ostensible goal of a Bais Yaakov education. According to the writer, that goal was to prepare girls to be 'effective wives and mothers'.[50] While a counter-argument was posed by a female Bais Yaakov educator,[51] Bechhofer suggests that the exchange is evidence for the growing conservatism of the movement, which had been compelled, in recent years, to distinguish itself from Orthodox feminist initiatives: for instance, the new institutions for Jewish women's Talmud study. In this new environment, it is Kagan's apologetic stance on the temporary necessity of Torah education for girls that reigns supreme, rather than Schenirer's far more forthright advocacy of the sacredness and value of such study.

These changes in the ideological direction of the Bais Yaakov movement have not meant an abandonment of earlier narratives of its history. On the contrary, the continuing mobilization of the figure of Sarah Schenirer and other aspects of the early years of Bais Yaakov serve contemporary purposes, among which, Bechhofer suggests, is the construction of a myth of origin. The image of

Sara Schenirer the Seamstress underscores the almost delightful element of surprise, the unlikelihood of this woman being an agent of change in Jewish history. It is the Cinderella fairy tale, a dressmaker turns overnight into teacher, dreams come true. Jews do not believe in fairy tales, however; her soul must therefore have come to her from afar, her success must be the work of Destiny. . . . She is thus the perfect vessel for Divine intervention in history. One could argue she is thus the perfect traditional heroine. [This image also] establishes, as a trope, Schenirer's rejection of external, materialistic beauty in favor of a different feminine ideal: the spiritually liberated woman. It thus draws on contemporary Orthodox

---

[49] See Bechhofer, 'Ongoing Constitution of Identity and Educational Mission of Bais Yaakov Schools'.

[50] U. Bergstein, 'Are Bais Yaakovs and Seminaries Doing their Job?', *Jewish Observer*, Apr. 1995, pp. 39–47; see Bechhofer, 'Ongoing Constitution of Identity and Educational Mission of Bais Yaakov Schools', 24–33.

[51] Z. Press, 'Bais Yaakovs and Seminaries: Doing their Job and then Some', *Jewish Observer*, Apr. 1995, pp. 45–7.

defenses of traditional Jewish womanhood in the face of feminism: that the restrictions of Jewish law emancipate women from their objectification by modern Western society.[52]

Obscured by the contemporary focus on Schenirer as a 'simple, pious seamstress' is 'the image of Sara Schenirer as a revolutionary, as an outspoken leader, and as an admirer of Western Orthodoxy'.[53] While the marriage of East and West, the 'professionalism' of German Jewry and the 'hasidic enthusiasm' of Polish Jewry, is a regular trope in the Bais Yaakov literature of the interwar years, these double origins of the movement are less often mobilized by American Jewry. Bechhofer suggests that this 'collective amnesia' is evidence of a new configuration of Orthodox Jewry:

A sociological explanation for this observation might focus on the changes in American Jewry during the second half of the twentieth century. The Eastern European Orthodox Jews who immigrated at that time quickly overwhelmed the Western European Jews who had immigrated earlier, and German Orthodoxy began to be perceived as inferior to the Lithuanian and Hasidic forms of Orthodoxy by the traditionalist Agudath Israel segment of American Orthodox Jews. Thus later sources, from 1964 on, de-emphasize the contribution of Western (German) Orthodoxy.[54]

Such evasion of the role of western Orthodox ideology has profound effects on Bais Yaakov's mission, given that its valuation not only of women's Torah study but also of secular studies (emblematized in Hirsch's slogan, *torah im derekh erets*) derives in major part from this ideology. Bechhofer continues:

With the collective memory diverted from the substantive influence of Western Orthodox ideology on Bais Yaakov, the schools no longer have an ideology that unapologetically supports the study of secular studies. Instead, they partake in the contemporary Haredi ideology, which views secular studies as a necessary tool for making a living, at best, and as a diversion from Torah study and the conveyor of values in conflict with Jewish values, at worst. What is different for Bais Yaakov, however, is that the value of uninterrupted Torah study does not apply to women in Jewish law. Thus, Bais Yaakov has no definitive positive ideological basis for either embracing or avoiding secular studies.[55]

Sarah Schenirer's role as 'mother' of the movement continues to do ideological work in this increasingly conservative cultural context. Unlike the issue of her marital history, which is simply left unmentioned in all but a stray comment in one of the memoirs Bechhofer reviewed, 'Schenirer's childlessness is acknowledged and turned on its metaphorical head in the commemorative texts by repeatedly referring to her as a mother figure'.[56] A memorial volume to Schenirer refers to her as a mother not only in the title ('A Mother in Israel') but also in a poem by Yehoshua Landau ('To Mama Sarah') and five of twenty-four chapters ('A Merciful Mother', 'Mother of Daughters', 'A Mother of Our Generation', 'The Mother that Arose', 'Mama').[57] An article by Joseph Friedenson, son of Eliezer

---

[52] Bechhofer, 'Ongoing Constitution of Identity and Educational Mission of Bais Yaakov Schools', 57–8.   [53] Ibid. 77.   [54] Ibid. 79.   [55] Ibid. 83.   [56] Ibid. 113–14
[57] Y. Rotenberg (ed.), *Em beyisra'el: sefer zikaron lesara shnirer* (Tel Aviv, 1960).

Gershon Friedenson, editor of *Beys-Yankev Zhurnal*, begins: 'She was not blessed with children of her own. And yet she was a mother. In fact, one could rightly say that no mother in our generation had as many children as she did.'[58] Finally, the memorial plaque on the former Bais Yaakov Seminary building in Kraków, erected in 2001, has the following inscription, ascribed to Eliezer Gershon Friedenson:

A woman who was a mother to thousands and tens of thousands, a caressing and a caring mother whose fervent words captured hearts: the fervour of a loving, caring mother. Favourable memories will accompany her great soul for hundreds of generations and years. May her name be remembered with praise and honour.

The image of Schenirer as mother, Bechhofer argues, 'is a comfortable, non-threatening symbol of feminine leadership'. Such an image overcomes the tension at the heart of the Bais Yaakov movement, of a female-led, female homosocial revolution in the name of a family-oriented tradition. As Bechhofer sees it:

The fact of Schenirer's childlessness—not to mention her having been divorced and later remarried—presents a challenge to holding her up as the personal embodiment of the message of Bais Yaakov, which is deeply rooted in visions of the ideal Jewish home. . . . Sara Schenirer's heroic persona serves to both embody the values of Bais Yaakov and to legitimize the movement despite the apparent contradiction between her leadership role and the traditional view of Jewish femininity. Imbuing her memory with this mother image serves to meet these challenges.[59]

Schenirer herself had drawn from a broader range of rhetorical and discursive semantic fields, and the selective modelling of her legacy and partial circulation of her work have produced a flatter image of its founder and a more constricted discursive field for describing the aims and goals of Bais Yaakov. In the post-Holocaust world, the charisma and revolutionary strands of the movement have given way to the traditionalizing tendencies that of course were always present. Nevertheless, as the debate in the *Jewish Observer* made clear, the movement cannot well function with a discourse that only partially legitimizes its work. Bechhofer is undoubtedly correct in pointing to the domesticating nature of Bais Yaakov rhetoric today; nevertheless, it is possible that Schenirer's image is kept alive not only as a way to resolve tensions—recasting the revolutionary figure as mother—but also to preserve some of the energy of the early movement.

Perhaps it is no surprise that Sarah Schenirer has multiple legacies, given the complexity of her project. Among Bais Yaakov students and former students throughout the world, Schenirer was a pious woman and beloved mother who, while she 'unfortunately had no children of her own', nurtured thousands of daughters. Feminist academics, among whom I include myself, are more likely to veer in the other direction, emphasizing the radical aspect of her work. The work

[58] J. Friedenson, 'Sara Schenirer, the Mother of Generations', *Jewish Observer*, Feb. 1964, p. 14.

[59] Bechhofer, 'Ongoing Constitution of Identity and Educational Mission of Bais Yaakov Schools', 111.

of Polish academics such as Oleszak is beginning to put the Bais Yaakov movement into a richer and more precise cultural and political context, the interwar years. That all these legacies should find support within one woman's biography and writings is the strongest testimony, perhaps, of the ambivalence, complexity, and tensions of Schenirer and her life's work.

'The children ceased to be children'

Day-Care Centres at Refugee Shelters in the Warsaw Ghetto

KATARZYNA PERSON

THE REPORTS prepared by care-givers from the Central Association for the Care of Orphans and Abandoned Children (Związek Towarzystw Opieki nad Dziećmi i Sierotami Żydowskimi; Farband fun Tsentrales far Yesoymim Farsorgung in Poyln; Centos) in December 1941 and copied for the collection of the Ringelblum Archive, the underground archive of the Warsaw ghetto, deal with education in the most extreme circumstances: the Warsaw ghetto.[1] Yet, while the institutional and clandestine schooling of the ghetto children has now been a subject of some research,[2] these reports reveal the attempts to educate those who still receive little attention in the scholarship: the young inhabitants of the Warsaw ghetto's refugee shelters (colloquially referred to as *punkty*, 'points') The reports answer the question of whether education was at all possible among the most impoverished children of the ghetto and, if so, what it looked like.

Centos was the main organization caring for Jewish children in interwar Poland, functioning from 1924 and involving in its activities in 1938 15,000 children, most of them in orphanages.[3] During the war Centos continued its work. In December 1941 it was the key body co-ordinating the care of children in the Warsaw ghetto, employing about 1,000 people involved in taking care of 25,000 children in over

[1] Archiwum Żydowskiego Instytutu Historycznego, Warsaw (hereafter AŻIH), Konspiracyjne Archiwum Getta Warszawy (Archiwum Ringelbluma) (hereafter ARG), II 228 (II/110): 'Zbiór sprawozdań świetliczanek z pracy z dziećmi ze schronisk dla uchodźców'; *Archiwum Ringelbluma: Konspiracyjne Archiwum Getta Warszawy*, ii: *Dzieci—tajne nauczanie w getcie warszawskim*, ed. R. Sakowska (Warsaw, 2000), 183–217.

[2] See, inter alia, M. Małowist, 'Three Essays on Jewish Education during the Nazi Occupation', *Polin*, 13 (2000), 147–65; S. Kardos, '"Not Bread Alone": Clandestine Schooling and Resistance in the Warsaw Ghetto during the Holocaust', *Harvard Educational Review*, 72/1 (2002), 33–66; A. Natanblut, 'Shuln in varshever geto', trans. P. Parsky, *YIVO Bleter*, 3/2 (Winter 1947), 173–87; R. Sakowska, 'O szkolnictwie i tajnym nauczaniu w getcie warszawskim', *Biuletyn Żydowskiego Instytutu Historycznego*, 55 (1965), 57–84.

[3] R. Żebrowski, 'Centos', in Z. Borzymińska and R. Żebrowski (eds.), *Polski słownik judaistyczny: Dzieje, kultura, religia, ludzie*, 2 vols. (Warsaw, 2003), i. 258.

100 establishments.[4] Financed by the Judenrat, collections in the community, and above all the American Jewish Joint Distribution Committee, it supervised care facilities, including orphanages, day-care centres, and 'children's corners' organized by house committees. The reports reflect on a particularly difficult part of its activities: the work of the Department of Day-Care Centres which at the beginning of 1942 oversaw more than thirty day-care centres in refugee shelters catering for over 5,000 children.[5]

As the reports illustrate, the work in the shelters was carried out in atrocious conditions. While the day-care centres described differ in terms of the degree of poverty—from that at Nowolipki 25, which was the headquarters of Żydowska Samopomoc Społeczna (Jewish Self Help), to a notorious shelter at Stawki 9, where lack of sanitation allegedly led to 228 deaths in three weeks in January 1942[6]—all of the shelters were constantly overcrowded with an extremely high mortality rate. Given the lack of space, centres were established in prayer rooms, theatres, and private homes, and it was rare for Centos care-givers to be able to organize a separate space to work with the children. In some shelters, rooms for day care became available only after their previous occupants had died of hunger or illness. One of the care-givers commented bitterly in her report: 'I am in "luck" as in apartment number 10 the whole family died of hunger and poverty; kind and tactful people who vacated a room for day care.'[7] As a result, children's corners could not be organized in all the shelters. In many of the most impoverished shelters, regular activities were replaced by visits from 'mobile care-givers' who would visit a few times a week and deal mainly with health and well-being, rather than education.

Aside from overcrowding, any attempt at schooling was also jeopardized by other aspects of refugee children's lives. Not all children were dressed adequately to attend school, even if something was organized for them and the funds for teaching resources were somehow obtained. In poorer shelters, almost all the children were dressed in rags, which they wore day and night, often for fear of them being stolen. It was uncommon for children to have shoes.[8] Many did not have any clothing and spent their days lying naked in bed. Others were simply too weak to attend classes. Taking care of children in such conditions also meant involvement with those who were sick with typhus, tuberculosis, or dysentery, whom sometimes even doctors refused to treat.[9] One of the care-givers, who took a position of a

---

[4] A. Berman, 'O losie dzieci żydowskich z zakładów opiekuńczych w getcie warszawskim (wspomnienia)', *Biuletyn Żydowskiego Instytutu Historycznego*, 28 (1958), 67.

[5] A. Berman, *Vos der goyrl hot mir bashert: mit yidn in varshe* (Tel Aviv, 1980), 114–15.

[6] AŻIH, 302/90, Henryk Bryskier, diary, 1943–4, 72–3.

[7] AŻIH, ARG II 228 (II/110): W. Hantowerówna, report on day-care centres at Zimna 3, 4; Zamenhofa 2, 6, 8, 9, 16; Pawia 12, 18; Nowolipki 5; Lubeckiego 12 (1 Dec. 1941).

[8] AŻIH, ARG II 228 (II/110): T. Boksenbaum-Nigelszporn, report on day-care centre at Dzika 3 (16 Dec. 1941).

[9] AŻIH, ARG II 228 (II/110): W. Hantowerówna, report on day-care centres at Zimna 3, 4; Zamenhofa 2, 6, 8, 9, 16; Pawia 12, 18; Nowolipki 5; Lubeckiego 12.

substitute teacher at Lubeckiego 12 to replace a colleague ill with typhus, wrote: 'I took over the feeding of twenty-four children, as a substitute, for the time being. Already in the first days three of them died, two of them in my arms.'[10]

Is it possible to speak of any form of education under these conditions? If it is, it is because, as the reports so clearly illustrate, what the organization lacked in money, it made up for in supportive teachers. While the organization was principally a broad social movement, relying on numerous and often very young staff for its everyday activities, it was supported by a number of key personalities from pre-war social and cultural life, among them experienced teachers and psychologists, such as geography teacher Stefania Halberstat, the author of the report from the refugee shelter at Nowolipki 25.[11] What the reports underline is that, even in the crushing poverty of the shelters, Centos teachers could still find children who were willing and able to study. These included, for example, children of marginally better-off refugees from western Poland who reached the ghetto relatively late.[12] A number of care-givers underlined the need to sort the children into those who could still participate in learning and those who, at best, could only participate in the activities of the day-care centre. While there were no attempts at organizing regular schooling, teachers still talked hopefully of 'removing the stigma of the shelter' from such children or incorporating them again into society.[13]

Unsurprisingly, the distribution of food played a key role in the educational efforts. Hunger provided the main and indeed often the only incentive for many children who frequented the shelters and who otherwise would be forced to eat food from refuse or to beg. As one of the care-givers wrote, 'a loaf of bread equals authority! Thanks to this prestige I managed to coerce children to wash and take baths on a regular basis throughout the whole summer.'[14] She explained: 'Initially we were surrounded by a group of half-wild children, stretching out their hands like beggars, and voraciously grabbing food as if in fear that it would be taken away from them. How much difficulty it cost before they were accustomed to a peaceful meal, to say: "thank you", "good morning", "goodbye".'[15]

Another incentive for refugee children proved to be the acquisition of skills which they could use to provide for their families, for whom they were often the only breadwinners.[16] As one of the care-givers explained: 'These children should be approached differently. They don't know how to play or be interested in

---

[10] Ibid. [11] AŻIH, 301/6094: Zdzisław Libera, testimony (10 Nov. 1964).

[12] AŻIH, ARG II 228 (II/110): B. Żychlińska, report on day-care centre at Żelazna 58a (Dec. 1941).

[13] AŻIH, ARG II 228 (II/110): J. Alfabet, report on day-care centre at Nowolipie 30 (Dec. 1941).

[14] AŻIH, ARG II 228 (II/110): W. Hantowerówna, report on day-care centres at Zimna 3, 4; Zamenhofa 2, 6, 8, 9, 16; Pawia 12, 18; Nowolipki 5; Lubeckiego 12.

[15] Ibid. Even such incentives were, however, not available to the 'mobile care-givers'. Children placed under their care were particularly vulnerable as carers could not spend enough time with them to protect them during eating hours and ensure that they were not forced to hand their food over to their guardians or other adults.

[16] AŻIH, ARG II 228 (II/110): B. Żychlińska, report on day-care centre at Żelazna 58a.

learning. They approach everything from the point of usefulness: "What will I have out of it?" They need to have constructive work; they want to earn; they seek an appropriate trade.'[17] As a result, the vast majority of care-givers stressed in their reports the need to enable the children to continue earning, usually by either providing them with time off during classes or by incorporating suitable training into the curriculum.

The four reports below form part of a collection of twenty which were placed in the second part of the underground archive of the Warsaw ghetto. According to Ruta Sakowska, they were most probably written as a result of the reorganization of the shelters in November 1941, as a consequence of which they were more closely subordinated to the Judenrat, while the influence of the underground aid organization over them was reduced.[18] As they were to provide an accurate picture of the current situation in the shelters and the role of Centos in their functioning, they are written in a very evocative, often self-reflective style, aiming to draw the attention of the reader to the plight of the centres. Unlike other surviving Centos reports, they not only quote data relating to operational functions but also document the experience of reaching the depths of ghetto poverty, providing a link to personal stories which would have otherwise been lost.

REPORT FROM A DAY-CARE CENTRE, NOWOLIPKI 25[19]

I have been in charge of the day-care centre at Nowolipki 25 since February 1940. The centre caters for children from the refugee shelters at Nowolipki 5, 25, and 27. The number of children peaked in June. Currently it is used by forty-eight children aged 2 to 15. Accommodation is quite good: a large room. Until August 1941, that is until the breakfasts began to be served, the centre was only open after lunch, currently it is open from 8:30 until 11:00 a.m. and from 4:00 until 6:30 p.m.

I begin my daily work with an inspection of cleanliness. I am helped by two older girls, 'hygiene nurses'. Dirty children are usually sent home, but sometimes, depending on the conditions, we wash them ourselves.

Between 9:00 and 9:30 a.m. the children receive breakfast. Two ladies on duty divide the orphans' bread and hand out plates with barley: 'bon appétit' and all children begin eating their meal. The care-giver on duty at the young children's table often has to feed 'her little ones'. I wait until all the children finish eating. 'Thank you' and the children take their plates back. A few of them go to lessons; a few go to pick up lunches for the grown-ups (a source of income: for bringing lunch from the kitchen a child receives 30 to 50 groszy. They bring a few lunches), I lead the rest in exercise and team games.

[17] AŻIH, ARG II 228 (II/110): Cajtagowa, report on day-care centre at Ogrodowa 27 (n.d.).

[18] See R. Sakowska, *Ludzie z dzielnicy zamkniętej: Żydzi w Warszawie w okresie hitlerowskiej okupacji, październik 1939 – marzec 1943* (Warsaw, 1993), 88.

[19] AŻIH, ARG II 228 (II/110): Stefania Halberstat, report on day-care centre at Nowolipki 25 (17 Dec. 1941).

Between 4:00 and 4:15 p.m. the children are back in day care. The room is tidied, tables cleaned. Depending on the weather and conditions, exercise with songs or team games and play.

On the table for the youngest ones, the care-givers on duty spread out bricks, toys, games: children build bridges, houses, towers, they play various games. At the table for the older ones 'studying' and 'work' take place. A few do their homework, a few read, sew (I taught them knitting and crocheting), the older ones also often whittle reeds for brushes. There are currently no volunteering duties for them due to a typhus epidemic. Both in the morning and after lunch my former students from neighbouring houses Nowolipki 19, 21, 23, 25, and 27 used to teach children and were happy to play with them. At the moment only four children benefit from their teaching, the rest of the children are taught by me.

Between 5:30 and 6:00 p.m. tea: bread and every now and again coffee with sugar. The spending of Centos [on other projects] has recently been very high and the house committee unfortunately gives very little. Once a week, on Saturday, sandwiches for tea.

Twice a week I try to organize talks. Once a week clothing repairs take place (I often manage to obtain spare pieces of cloth) and bathing. I received from the house committee a bathtub, constructed a drain, and wash children down with a garden watering can (in the summer children took baths every day and were washed with cold water).

Children eagerly participate in day care and are happy to spend time there, in the evenings I have to literally chase them out to their rooms. We constitute almost a family: their worries are my worries, their joy is my joy, and vice versa.

I have 500 kilogrammes of coal deposited with the house committee, and I received from the Jewish Social Welfare Association [Żydowskie Towarzystwo Opieki Społecznej] a large stove.

We are in constant contact with the supervisor of the shelter. He comes every day and knows all the children. I get in touch with the doctor once a week. Only the nurses are unfortunately not up to the task and in order to keep the children well taken care of I often fulfil their duties (only those relating to the children, however).

> 17 December 1941
> Stefania Halberstat

REPORT FROM A DAY-CARE CENTRE, NOWOLIPKI 76[20]

The day-care centre provides for one hundred children aged 1 to 14 years old. Some of them are children of refugees who arrived in Warsaw two years ago, forty are children of deportees from February 1941. There are sixteen orphans in the

[20] AŻIH, ARG II 228 (II/110): A. Motrolowa, report on day-care centre at Nowolipki 76 (Dec. 1941).

shelter, many half-orphans, and very few children whose parents earn anything at all. Forty per cent of the children have no shoes, hosiery, underwear, clothing. They are dressed in rags. The majority of them lie on wooden cots, and breakfast and other meals are brought to them in the hall. Smaller children are brought for their meals in the arms of their bare-footed mothers. The children are dirty, infected with scabies, gaunt, apathetic, and cannot be made interested in anything taking place in the day-care centre. The remaining 60 per cent crave work, they wish to study, crochet, draw. They happily listen to talks, readings, they like to read, they know many songs. For many months now they do not get a penny for any school aids—work or drawing materials, thread for sewing—without which I cannot lead systematic classes. I underline that some of the children are very keen on learning, but I have no books or notebooks. Some of them even had pencils and notebooks brought for them by their parents, so that their children would write and have some occupation. I cannot fill the whole work day only with singing, talks, and games as the children are too weak, and they also need to sit down and do something.

The work schedule is as follows:

• Cleanliness inspection

• Simple, not taxing, gymnastic patterns with games

• Breakfast

• After breakfast: talks, lessons, drawing, followed by the second meal.
  The so-called dinner, consisting of 8 kg of bread with some spread.
  Lunch is brought to the shelter very late, about 5: 00 p.m. It is not every day that the schedule can be adequately fulfilled, as the kitchen is not efficient at serving the early meal, sometimes the breakfast is an hour late, which takes away from the activities.

The breakfast has to be brought up by me, as otherwise it does not reach the shelter in its entirety.

Ever since we began feeding the children better, the death rate from hunger has decreased significantly. It is rare for one of them to die in my shelter; if they do, it is from cold or illness, but even then it is very few.

The children have no plates, spoons, or bowls; they eat out of broken containers, pans with holes in them, with scratched spoons, which looks very unappealing. They should be provided with eating utensils. The day-care room is very good as it has four windows. (The room has been recently taken over by the army boots workshop, supposedly for only a few days, as it belongs to the Judenrat. The day care is for now in the corridor and none of my interventions bring any result. The director explains that it is on the council's orders, the refugees have to live off something, and that it is only a temporary measure.)

As I underlined, there are good conditions for conducting day care: there is a room, a heater, coal, glassed windows, all that is needed is clothing, shoes, medications, ointments, learning aids.

We have a substantial influence on the children in terms of education. They know that I am bringing them a meal, which is exclusively for them, and they wait for me impatiently. Even gaunt orphans quickly spring up from their cots and run to the day-care room. They receive soap, a piece each, some sugar, barley, and that is why they follow all orders. Children clean the day-care room on their own, they scrub the barley and noodle buckets, they make sure that the convoy appears in time to pick up the breakfast, they pick up goods from the stores themselves, and bring them in their entirety to the shelter.

There are very few begging children in the shelter, only a few orphans go begging, saying that they have no money to buy rationed bread and other produce.

The shelter has no patronage which could provide funds for lunches for orphans and other needs, and in consequence the children are forced to beg. Other children, whose guardians send them begging, I have managed to keep away from it, as I warned them that their meals will be taken away from them. For the whole day those children remain with me and work. I take care of sick children, who are lying on their beds from exhaustion. I go to the room, take note of the cleanliness, and ensure that they eat their whole meal.

We provide them with additional soap and better nourishment in the form of additional sugar, barley, etc.

A. Motrolowa, Warsaw, in December 1941

REPORT FROM THE DAY-CARE CENTRE AT STAWKI 9[21]

The courtyard is drowning in mud and sewage. The corners are filled with faeces and rubbish. The house has no sewage system. Lack of running water. Impurities are poured out through the windows. Sanctions imposed by the director of the shelter do little. Stairs are slippery from mud. Banister is sticky from dirt. The director of the shelter a few weeks ago paid 300 zlotys to Cesa Society to take out the faeces and 700 zlotys to Heyman Company to take out the rubbish, but none of these materialized. The air is sickeningly intoxicating. The kitchen, where we prepare meals for the children, is smoky.

In those nightmarish conditions we take care of the children of refugees. We feed children in the day-care room. We provide, or rather send or take ourselves, meals to the room for sick children, but only after we are presented with a certificate from a doctor or nurse. Let us boast here that the mortality rate among them is negligible, almost non-existent.

We inspect the rooms. We are in constant contact with the parents. Through the parents we reach the children. We also take care of the parents so that the child has

[21] AŻIH, ARG II 228 (II/110): G. Konowa and S. Rydygerowa, report on day-care centre at Stawki 9 (16 Dec. 1941).

better conditions at home. In many cases we negotiated paid work for them. We petitioned the director of the shelter for a doctor and nurses for adequate care (I obtained for one child a loan of 20 zlotys to buy medications, in another case I obtained a place in the infirmary, etc.). We visit sick children. We raise their spirits and bodies. The youngest are placed in the orphanage, if possible. Among children frequenting the day-care centre, 20 per cent are orphaned.

For a few days now we have had a stove in our day-care room. Children, some even barefooted, eagerly come over to warm their feet and have fun. It is almost 4:00 p.m. and they are still sitting, warming themselves by the fire, baking frozen potatoes and singing bravely. It is difficult to induce them to leave this warm corner after day-care activities. There are 400 children. Not all of them come over: some guard their apartments and their last remaining belongings during the absence of their parents (there are frequent and almost unavoidable thefts). Quite a few children lie on beds, without any undergarments, in rags, bare-footed, feet frost-bitten, recently there were many cases of stomach bugs or even bloody dysentery. Last week we cooked rice for them ourselves, and we distributed it after discussing it with a doctor. Unfortunately the amount of rice was negligible. We are asking for fish oil for the weak and anaemic children. We cannot allow them to catch tuberculosis. In these nightmarish conditions we conduct socializing talks for children. They have improved significantly. They don't eat so hurriedly; they don't express their requests so rudely as before. The parents are well disposed towards us: I would even say that they express much gratitude and understanding.

Children count in their heads, eagerly listen to talks on nature and geography (I am speaking here of older children). They sing and play happily. Some children do some sewing repairs and repair bread sacks for the stores. There is a lack of material for repairing clothing. The threads are expensive and difficult to buy.

We don't draw and don't write. In the two day-care rooms there is not one chair or stool. Today an order of one (1) table and a bench arrived: but for whom? For the day-care room on the ground floor or the upper floor? We hope that we will soon receive more. There is a lack of learning aids and writing materials.

And now a few wishes. Some children have only a mother or a father, lying swollen with hunger. A naked bed, sheets long ago sold or stolen. Isn't such a child as hopeless as a full orphan? A sick mother or father are only a burden for the children. With sadness we should admit that such children are only waiting for matters to resolve themselves; they want to quickly become a full orphan to legally receive the additional meal for orphans. We cannot allow them to become demoralized. We are asking to ensure an additional meal for those very unhappy children while their mother or father is still alive. We are trying to show these children a lot of kindness.

Out of 400 children, some, as already mentioned, remain at home. A meal, even handed over to a child in person in their apartment, is not always eaten by them. Guardians, middlemen, and even parents force some barley or bread away from them. This takes place in particular among younger children up to 7 or 8 years old

(20 per cent of the orphans!) Older children are more self-sufficient. It would be highly desirable to have a mobile care-giver, who would not only hand out breakfasts but also be present when the child is eating it. They could also take care of children aged 14 to 16. They are often left to their own devices, lose their way, get demoralized. We could arrange for them a day club, find their talents and guide them appropriately, put them back on the right track. We do care a lot about these children. We propose that this section of work be entrusted to our colleague Rydygerowa. There is always so much that has to be resolved immediately: one returns home after work as if after a fight. Not everything can be mentioned: one has to be here with us to understand and alleviate the children's fate. For a few weeks now I have been writing and asking for a few bowls so children can be washed, but my request has not yet been fulfilled.

Among my wishes are: 4 bowls per day-care room, 2 buckets, 2 trays, 6 tables, 10 benches, coat hangers, shoes, hosiery, 2 shirts each, some garments, a cleaning brush, teaching aids, and writing materials.

We are aware that in today's times, it is difficult to equip the day-care centres adequately, but following the slogans 'Save our children', 'Our children have to live' reach out your hand to us, do not push us away, help us!

We are full of zeal and perseverance. In many cases we want to see results and an understanding of our sacrifice. Let our energy and effort become a stimulus for our supervising powers.

> Warsaw, 16 December 1941
> G. Konowa, S. Rydygerowa

REPORT ON THE WORK OF THE DAY-CARE CENTRE AT BAGNO 1[22]

When day-care centres were being set up in the shelters, the care-givers drew themselves a very comprehensive plan of work: the centre was to be in a warm, light-filled corner, in which a child would find all that they needed: toys; books; pencils; wise, good words; and a caring hand. The work was to centre around a clean, dressed, fed, learning, and playing child. And it seemed that reaching this goal would only be dependent on the talent and skill of a particular care-giver. Igniting an interest for play and study in a child depended only on a care-giver. A good educator should be able to fit the children into his programme, and that is why the care-givers were ordered: 'You have a group of children, teach and entertain them. Create for them a light-filled day-care centre, which for a few hours a day at least would tear them away from the street, from begging and theft; tear them out of fetid, over-crowded rooms, from the screams and fights of constantly screaming, hungry children.'

[22] AŻIH, ARG II 228 (II/110): E. Justmanówna, report on day-care centre at Bagno 1 (Dec. 1941).

The aim was not achieved. The day-care centre did not become what it was meant to be. Life played a joke on experienced educators and care-givers: what seemed easy turned out to be almost unobtainable. The new, specific, wartime conditions, in which the children found themselves, influenced their psyche so much that their interests and needs developed differently to how their care-givers would have desired. Those who did not understand that fact or did not want to understand it constantly called upon the care-givers to increase their efforts and energy in organizing day care. Since attendance in day-care centres was unsatisfactory, the care-givers were blamed for it. The care-givers were called to lead day-care activities with children and increase attendance.

What they did not appreciate was that if the same phenomenon repeats itself in a few dozen day-care centres, there must be one general, underlying cause, and that accusations against care-givers are pointless. The crucial reasons for difficulties in setting up day-care centres are psychological and social in nature.

The children underwent great psychological changes. The children ceased to be children. Burdened with tough conditions, they must attempt to earn not only for themselves but also for their families. They work, smuggle, or beg. Their main and dominating interest is bread. Everything else, which does not result in bread, cannot awaken their interest. They will come to the day-care centre for bread, after that they have to go and earn a dinner for themselves and their families. That which is a normal, natural interest of children and of high biological importance— a tendency to play—almost does not exist in the children of the shelter. Characteristic is an 8-year-old boy addressing his older brother playing in the day-care centre: 'Vi hostu a kop tsu azelkhe narishkaytn [How did you get such silly things into your head]?' He said it when looking at him with irony and contempt. Such is the stance of the vast part of our children. If they do play, they do it to please the care-giver not themselves.

Those who know the environment of the shelters, their sanitary conditions, constant diseases, lice infestations, nightmarish scenes created by poverty and hunger, know how extremely difficult it is to create in such conditions an atmosphere for day-care activities. It is a great misfortune that the day-care room is not adequately isolated from the shelter.

Children are without clothing, shoes. In almost two years of work in day-care centres I did not receive one pair of shoes for a child. [Without them] children are not able to come to the centre.

The day-care centre does not have any of the materials necessary for carrying out classes. There is none of the necessary equipment. Tables, benches: these are objects which can only be obtained with great effort. Glass was put in the windows in November, the stove was received in December. Many months pass during which you cannot do anything with children, as the day-care room is so cold. All this disorganizes work which has already begun, and stops and paralyses activities. Due to constant breaks it is difficult to impose on a child consistency and regularity in attending day care.

I have listed only the basic reasons for the difficulties faced by care-givers. There are many more of them. The fact that day-care activities are not carried out consistently and in some points not at all does not mean that the care-giver does not have an important place in the shelter and that her work there is not meaningful.

It is difficult to speak of the positive side of a care-giver's work, because the effects of her work are difficult to grasp for someone from the outside. In order to appreciate it, it has to be examined up close.

Clean, washed hands, scrubbed utensils, calm behaviour from hungry children during the distribution of meals, helping the care-giver in her work, responsibility in fulfilling a function entrusted to them, the manner of eating, speaking, these are seemingly small issues, but require so much arduous, painstaking effort and are impossible to carry out at once. The greatest educational opportunities are created by the distribution of meals. A meal is the starting point for all interests which one wants to lead the child into. This is the main point: books and play are secondary interests. Managing meals provides big opportunities for the care-givers: it allows for special care over particularly exhausted children, increasing in some cases breakfast rations. It provides educational opportunities: the care-giver gives children home-making duties, etc.

The duties of the teacher, home-carer, and nurse are all included in the work of the care-giver. Enormous work, difficult conditions, effects seemingly small, but in reality of great worth.

Conclusion

When planning the care-giver's work, we should expect the minimum rather than the maximum. If the day-care centre caters for 5 per cent of the children, we should consider it a success. If the care-giver teaches ten children to read and write, it should not be seen as an aim unworthy of the work. One child saved from beggary is significant. If we expect a lot—that is day-care provision for all children —that means that we don't take reality into consideration and we make the same old mistake. In some day-care centres there is a possibility of conducting classes (such is the situation in my shelter, Bagno 1). But even there it is necessary to introduce certain improvements, and certain conditions have to be met.

The most urgent needs of the day-care centre are:

1 clothing and shoes for children

2 teaching aids or a special funds for this purpose

3 improvement in providing meals to the shelter
   (some type of cart at our disposal, etc.)

4 constant control and help of economic bodies
   (various technical equipment, etc.)

I am certain that by fulfilling these wishes, at least partial realization of the day-care project will be enabled.

    E. Justamanówna
    Warsaw, in December 1941

The Survival of *Yidishkeyt*

The Impact of the American Jewish Joint Distribution Committee on Jewish Education in Poland, 1945–1989

ANNA SOMMER SCHNEIDER

THE END of the Second World War revealed the huge extent of the damage to Poland, damage which was not just physical. The country had lost nearly six million of its citizens, including almost its entire Jewish population. According to Albert Stankowski, only some 425,000 of the estimated pre-war Jewish population of 3,330,000 were still alive at the end of the war. Not all of them returned to Poland from the Soviet Union, where the largest proportion had survived. As a result, in the immediate post-war period the Jewish population of the country numbered between 220,000 and 350,000, including almost 160,000 Jews repatriated from the USSR.[1] The structures of Jewish life, including the local communities and the institutions that had regulated just about every aspect of daily life, had been entirely destroyed. Orthodox Jews, who before the war had been responsible for the religious education of many of the young, represented a huge percentage of the victims. People unconnected with the pre-war religious community made up the majority of those who survived, which had a real impact on the type of education envisaged for Jews in post-war Poland. Most were young or middle-aged. Barely a handful of children had survived the Holocaust: it is calculated that no

---

[1] A. Stankowski, 'How Many Polish Jews Survived the Holocaust?', in F. Tych and M. Adamczyk-Garbowska (eds.), *Jewish Presence in Absence: Aftermath of the Holocaust in Poland, 1945–2010* (Jerusalem, 2013), 205–16. According to Natalia Aleksiun quoting data prepared by David Engel, from mid-1944 to mid-1946 between 266,000 and 280,000 Jews were living in Poland (*Dokąd dalej? Ruch syjonistyczny w Polsce (1944–1950)* (Warsaw, 2002), 61–9). Leszek Olejnik states that 240,489 Jews were registered in Poland at the end of the first half of 1946 and that 157,420 of them had been repatriated from the USSR (*Polityka narodowościowa Polski w latach 1944–1960* (Łódź, 2003), 344; cf. M. Grynberg, *Żydowska spółdzielczość pracy w Polsce w latach 1945–1949* (Warsaw, 1986), 18–19). However, data prepared by employees of the JDC suggest that no more than 220,000 Jews were living in Poland at that time (A. Sommer Schneider, *Sze'erit Hapleta: Ocaleni z Zagłady. Działalność American Jewish Joint Distribution Committee w Polsce w latach 1945–1989* (Kraków, 2014), 83).

more than 5,000 of the youngest members of the pre-war Jewish community were still alive and most were orphans or semi-orphans. In July 1946 this figure increased to 25,000 as a result of the repatriation of Polish citizens from the USSR.[2] However, by September only 15,000 children remained—the result of the huge wave of Jewish emigration, especially intensified by the Kielce pogrom in July of that year.[3]

Representatives of the Central Committee of Jews in Poland (Centralny Komitet Żydów w Polsce; CKŻP), formed in Lublin in the autumn of 1944, knew that, as a result of Poland's disastrous condition, the new communist authorities did not have the appropriate resources to support everyone in need. Therefore, almost immediately after the liberation by the Red Army of Poland's eastern lands, the chairman of the CKŻP, Emil Sommerstein, contacted foreign Jewish organizations with an appeal for immediate aid for the surviving Jews in Poland.[4] The natural addressee was the American Jewish Joint Distribution Committee in New York (JDC or the Joint). The JDC had begun working in Poland after the First World War and from virtually the start of its activities it had tried to introduce a new form of aid, 'constructive aid'. The organization's representatives were intent from the outset on mobilizing Polish Jews to actively seek work or be trained in suitable trades which could lead to paid employment. Hence, the JDC focused its efforts on setting up professional training, creating loan organizations, and purchasing tools for artisan activity. Thanks to the pattern established long before the outbreak of the Second World War, immediately after the end of hostilities it was possible to begin rebuilding the foundations of life for the small handful of surviving Jews. The work begun by the JDC after the Second World War, both in investment in the development of the economy and in schooling, educational, and cultural work, had an enormous impact on the development and education of Jewish youth.

It was no accident that it was the JDC, of all the Jewish organizations founded in America, that functioned on the ground in liberated Poland. President Harry Truman authorized it to be one of the principal American organizations to operate in Europe after the war.[5] This decision was based mainly on the fact that from the start of its existence the JDC had been an apolitical organization whose work focused exclusively on providing charitable aid.[6] Hence, for Truman and his

[2] J. Adelson, 'W Polsce zwanej Ludową', in J. Tomaszewski (ed.), *Najnowsze dzieje Żydów w Polsce w zarysie (do 1950 roku)* (Warsaw, 1993), 398.

[3] American Jewish Joint Distribution Committee Archives, New York (hereafter JDC NY), 1945–54, 'Poland: Administration: General', folder 734: William Bein Report, 5 Feb. 1949.

[4] Y. Bauer, *Out of the Ashes: The Impact of American Jews on Post-Holocaust European Jewry* (Oxford, 1989), 2. David Guzik, the first post-war director of the JDC in Poland, made a similar appeal: 'We are ready to continue the work: 40,000 Jews need immediate assistance. Am awaiting instructions' (cited ibid. 76).

[5] United States Holocaust Memorial Museum, Washington DC, RG 68.059M Reel 62: JDC, press release, 28 Feb. 1946.

[6] The US government attached enormous importance to controlling the operations of American

administration, the JDC was the obvious choice. The representatives of the communist authorities in Lublin were guided by similar considerations. It was important for them to obtain foreign aid, but they feared foreign political influence. In addition, no other Jewish organization had more experience than the JDC in working in that part of Europe or had more people assigned to the continent.[7]

One of the JDC's operating principles from the very beginning of its existence had been to involve local leaders in its work. Accordingly, local bodies were made responsible for the distribution of funds and other supplies. After the war, the CKŻP was given the task of rebuilding the Jewish community. It soon tried to assume complete control of the money provided by the JDC, which led to constant conflicts between the CKŻP, Zionists, the religious community, and the JDC itself. Control over the funds would have allowed the CKŻP to control Jewish organizations' activities in Poland, including the upbringing and education of the youngest members of the Jewish community. This threatened Polish Jews with complete secularization. To a great extent this was also a consequence of the war. Orthodox Jews and hasidim represented the largest percentage of those killed, and the experiences of many survivors led them to turn away completely from religion and tradition.[8]

The new authorities' general policies, supported, it should be said, by a sizeable section of the CKŻP leadership, favoured secularization and assimilation. The situation began to deteriorate, especially after Jewish communists took control of the organization in 1947. Preserving the Jewish way of life, based above all on the appropriate education of children and young people, was one of the overriding aims of the JDC's New York leadership for post-war work in eastern Europe. Furthermore, this goal was also frequently advocated by donors, for whom preserving Jewish traditions in line with the demands of halakhah was a priority. The JDC therefore financed, in addition to the CKŻP, the operations of religious institutions and *hakhsharot* (agricultural institutes that trained potential emigrants to the Land of Israel) in Poland, which also provided their charges with education.

NGOs in different parts of the world. Starting in May 1946 all humanitarian NGOs from the USA, irrespective of where they were operating, were brought under the auspices of the Advisory Committee on Voluntary Foreign Aid, set up by Truman, and were obliged to follow its regulations. The committee continues to be the central organization regulating relations between the US government and charitable NGOs, and it defines areas of competence in providing aid and rebuilding various communities and ethnic groups outside the USA.

[7] In the first few months after the war the JDC had 266 employees in liberated Europe; the Jewish Agency had 92; the Hebrew Sheltering and Immigrant Aid Society had 34; and Va'ad Hatsalah, which was originally established to rescue rabbis and yeshiva students, had 12 (A. Grobman, *Battling for Souls: The Vaad Hatzala Rescue Committee in Post-War Europe* (New Jersey, 2004), 22).

[8] Sociological research by Irena Hurwic-Nowakowska in the spring of 1948 suggests that after the war unbelievers were in the majority. Among 817 respondents, 461 stated that they were unbelievers, 56 described themselves as practising believers, 121 as believers, 67 as non-practising believers, 38 as attached to tradition, and 26 as indifferent to tradition and religion (*Żydzi polscy (1947–1950): Analiza więzi społecznej ludności żydowskiej* (Warsaw, 1996), 184).

These funds supported instructional and educational centres, including Zionist professional training run by *hakhsharot* and not under the direct control of the CKŻP.

In addition to subventions for the development and running of the Jewish community, the JDC's direct post-war budget included special funds dedicated to searching for and recovering children who had survived the war years in the care of Poles in monasteries or convents. In many cases, such children were too young to remember their origins. Between January and September 1946 the JDC allocated 603,000 zlotys for this purpose, out of an overall budget of more than 743 million. Independently of the CKŻP, Zionist organizations helped to recover children and to provide essential assistance for the youngest survivors. To achieve this goal, the Zionist Co-ordinating Committee was formed, which set up care centres for children independently of the CKŻP. Most often children recovered by Zionist workers ended up in *hakhsharot* in Poland, which also soon became a new home for many survivors.

In 1949, after the CKŻP was disbanded and the JDC was forced by the communist authorities to terminate operations in Poland, Jewish education became a much more challenging issue. The Socio-Cultural Association of Jews in Poland (Towarzystwo Społeczno-Kulturalne Żydów w Polsce; TSKŻ), the new organization representing the Jewish community of Poland, followed the guidelines of the new regime and voluntarily relinquished responsibility for providing traditional Jewish education. When in the late 1950s the JDC resumed operations in Poland, the issue of Jewish education became contentious. Until the fall of communism, Jewish schooling remained an unresolved issue and discussion about it assumed various forms. This chapter explores some of the problems of Jewish education in communist Poland, from the end of the war until the fall of the communist regime in 1989, seeking in particular to analyse the involvement of the JDC.

CARE AND EDUCATIONAL CENTRES FOR JEWISH CHILDREN FOLLOWING THE WAR

Caring for children and providing for their education was the responsibility of the CKŻP. For this purpose it established a Department of Child Protection, headed by Szlomo Herszenhorn. Centres for childcare and education were set up in various parts of the country. The first of these was a children's home in Lublin, which was established as early as the summer of 1944. Over the next few months, similar centres were created in Otwock, Bielsko, and Zatrzebie near Warsaw, followed by Częstochowa, Kraków, and Przemyśl. During the first few months after the liberation of Poland, the centres' basic goal was to provide essential aid and medical care for all survivors, especially Jewish orphans. The issue of ideological instruction for Jewish children and adolescents arose only a year after the end of the war. At that time the CKŻP's General Assembly laid down new guidelines for the care and education centres which, according to Helena Datner, sought to inculcate human and national dignity as well as a positive attitude towards democratic Poland and the Soviet Union.[9] As revealed by the JDC's data, at the start of 1946 the CKŻP was running thirteen children's homes in Poland for a total of some 900 children. In August 1946 the JDC carried out a survey to which thirty-two children's homes throughout Poland responded.[10] The responses established that altogether there were 2,814 children in CKŻP homes and in centres run by religious and Zionist organizations including Ichud. Half of the children were orphans; most of the rest had just one living parent. Only 754 of them had survived the occupation in Poland. The remainder had come to Poland from the Soviet Union.

Of the 2,814 children, about 1,790 were attending school. Health problems kept the remainder away. As a result, children's homes were usually set up in places that provided medical treatment, such as Otwock, Śródborów, and Helenówek.[11] The most common illnesses were tuberculosis, mononucleosis, anaemia, and eyesight problems. By September 1948 the number of children's homes had fallen to eleven and the number of children to 782. The following month there were even fewer: 645 children in eight children's homes. This was the result of continuing emigration from Poland. Of all the remaining children, 243 were orphans, 334 semi-orphans, and 68 had parents who were unable to support them at home.[12] Yet another group of 290 children had been removed from the children's homes, since their families' situation had improved: the families now received a monthly subsidy of 2,000 zlotys. This allowed a limit to be imposed on the constantly rising costs of the children's homes. The monthly cost of supporting a single child rose from 8,700 to 10,950 zlotys over the course of just a few months. Administrative expenses, insurance, salaries, food, and other charges were subject to inflation. Around 3,300 children remained under the partial care of Jewish organizations. It is estimated that overall one-third of all Jewish children in Poland in February 1948 were orphans.[13]

Between January and September 1946 the JDC allocated 102,247,840 zlotys for children's aid organizations. However, it is difficult to calculate the real sum spent on aid for children, since financial reports only provide data on money transferred to the CKŻP through financial institutions controlled by the government. For instance, in September 1946 the JDC allocated almost 50 million zlotys for aid to Jews in Poland: out of this, nearly 15 million was spent on caring for children, of

[9] H. Datner-Śpiewak, 'Instytucje opieki nad dzieckiem i szkoły powszechne Centralnego Komitetu Żydów Polskich w latach 1945–1946', *Biuletyn Żydowskiego Instytutu Historycznego*, 119 (1981), 42.
[10] JDC NY, 1945–54, 'Poland: Administration: General', folder 734: William Bein, director of JDC, Poland, report, 5 Feb. 1949.
[11] American Jewish Joint Distribution Committee, Jerusalem (hereafter JDC Jerusalem), Bauer Collection, Box 1, 'Poland 1944–1948': William Bein, director of JDC, Poland, report, Jan.–Sept. 1946.
[12] JDC Jerusalem, Bauer Collection, Box 1: report on JDC activities in Poland, Dec. 1948.
[13] Jewish Telegraphic Agency, news release, 4 Feb. 1948.

which 635,000 zlotys were spent on education. However, it is not known how much was transferred directly to educational centres run by Zionist organizations out-side the regular budget.

According to data published by the Jewish Telegraphic Agency, in February 1948 there were a total of 773 children in eleven children's homes in Poland. These homes were for the most part financed by the CKŻP. Furthermore, fifty-six other organizations in Poland also supported young people and children financially, as well as helping the intellectual development of Jewish adolescents, who numbered around 3,300. More than 6,000 Jews below the age of 18 were receiving material assistance.[14]

Providing assistance for the youngest members of the Jewish community was always an operational priority for the JDC. The best evidence for this is the fact that every trip by the JDC's leadership to Poland included visits to children's homes, sanatoria, and summer camps. The interest shown by the children in these visits must have been gratifying, since many of the children in the homes, despite their youth, understood perfectly well where the numerous gifts they received—toys, sweets, clothes—came from. No doubt their care-givers saw to this, too, as is eloquently testified by the reaction of children who, during a visit by Joseph Hyman of the JDC to a sanatorium in Otwock, wished him farewell with the words 'Goodbye Papa Joint'.[15]

JEWISH SCHOOLING, 1944–1950

Schooling was organized wherever larger Jewish centres developed after the libera-tion of Poland. Elementary schools set up by the CKŻP came under the jurisdic-tion of its Department of Education.[16] In a few instances schools were established in towns that before the war had been centres of Jewish life and education. The first CKŻP primary school was operational in Białystok by 1944.[17] For the most part, the teachers worked without a defined curriculum, books, or essential teach-ing materials. Some were untrained, and so efforts were made wherever possible to organize help and support for those undertaking this difficult and responsible task.

On 1 November 1946 the first teachers' conference, attended by 150 Jewish teachers, was held at the instigation of the CKŻP's Department of Education. A representative of the Ministry of Education also took part.[18] One of the main

[14] In Poland there were also thirty-one Jewish cultural clubs; twenty-six drama clubs; thirteen libraries; a drama and music school; the Jewish Historical Institute; and the Cultural and Artistic Asso-ciation, which had 4,000 members (Jewish Telegraphic Agency, news release, 2 Apr. 1948).

[15] JDC Jerusalem, Bauer Collection, Box 2, folder 10: Joseph Hyman, account of trip abroad pre-sented at the meeting of the JDC Executive Committee, 17 Sept. 1947.

[16] H. Datner, 'Szkoły Centralnego Komitetu Żydów w Polsce w latach 1944–1949', *Biuletyn Żydowskiego Instytutu Historycznego*, 169–71 (1994), 104.   [17] Ibid.

[18] Y. Litvak, 'The American Joint Distribution Committee and Polish Jewry 1944–1949', in S. I. Troen and B. Pinkus (eds.), *Organizing Rescue: National Jewish Solidarity in the Modern Period* (London, 1992), 296.

topics of discussion was the language of instruction. Disagreement arose principally between the representatives of Zionist organizations and their opponents. As a compromise, it was resolved that during the first year of school children would learn Yiddish and in subsequent years Hebrew and Polish would be taught as well. Given the serious ideological differences between the various organizations, no overall curriculum for all schools was drawn up; however, a resolution was adopted, binding all organizations and stating: 'the aim of Jewish schooling is to transmit to the younger generation of Jews a national, democratic, and secular education appropriate to the progressive ideals of our time'. Only in CKŻP schools was an academic curriculum standardized and that was achieved as early as March 1946 by the organization's Department of Education.[19] By then Jewish schools were opening on a regular basis, as a result of the growing numbers of Jews returning from the USSR. In August 1946 the number of CKŻP educational centres for Jewish children had grown to thirty-six, with 3,300 pupils.[20] Despite increased emigration beginning in the summer of 1946, the number of children in school not only did not drop, it even grew.[21]

In Datner's view, the period before the conference in November 1946 marked the first stage in the development of an educational programme setting the ideological approach of the schools, which was followed by a period of relative stability until the fundamental change in the ideological character of CKŻP schools with the arrival of Stalinism.[22] Regarding the legal status of CKŻP schools, Datner distinguishes 'a phase of unregulated legal limbo starting at the end of 1947/beginning of 1948 when the educational authorities "tolerated" the schools and a phase in the legal existence of private schools lasting from early 1948 until April 1949, when these schools were nationalized on the instructions of the Ministry of Education'.[23] From 1 November 1945 a Department of Care for Young People operated within the CKŻP, its aim being to set up, as quickly as possible, centres where Jewish children and adolescents could begin their education. Within a short time, dormitories and trade schools appeared almost everywhere in Poland where Jewish life was re-emerging.[24] In 1945 schools and vocational courses existed in Warsaw, Łódź, Katowice, Kraków, Częstochowa, and Lower Silesia.[25] In Łódź alone, in 1945 and 1946 some 350 pupils attended Jewish schools thanks to the enormous dedication of the fifteen teachers working in them.[26] With the help of donations, mainly from the JDC, the Jewish Historical Commission managed to set up youth centres and a youth club.[27] In addition to boarding and day schools run by the CKŻP, a large group of young people was also being educated in *hakhsharot*

[19] Datner, 'Szkoły Centralnego Komitetu Żydów', 105. [20] Ibid. [21] Ibid. 107.
[22] Ibid. 103. [23] Ibid.; see also 110–12. [24] Ibid.
[25] Archiwum Akt Nowych, Warsaw, Ministerstwo Administracji Publicznej, sygn. 788, k. 25: 'Sprawozdanie z działalności CKŻP' [1945].
[26] Litvak, 'The American Joint Distribution Committee and Polish Jewry', 296.
[27] Archiwum Akt Nowych, Ministerstwo Administracji Publicznej, sygn. 788, k. 25: 'Sprawozdanie z działalności CKŻP'.

set up by Jewish political activists. In 1945, thanks to the financial support of the JDC, the number of schools was growing, as well as other educational and instructional centres on which in all $140,000 was spent (from the budgets of the JDC, 'associations of compatriots',[28] and that of the CKŻP). As a result, 4,350 children and young people were provided with education and care in children's homes and in boarding and day schools.[29]

The education of young Jews took place on various levels with different standards. Over time expectations changed. As before the outbreak of the Second World War, political organizations which ran schools based on their parties' ideological outlook had a considerable influence on educational policies. Separate schools were established by members of Zionist organizations. Data gathered by Joseph Schwartz show that in November 1946 ten Hebrew schools supported by the JDC were operating in Poland with 800 children.[30] Another JDC report reveals the existence of nine schools run by Zionist organizations, with 677 children who were not included in the official statistics.[31] It is possible that this information dates from the start of 1946. By 1948 there was one additional Zionist school but more than 200 more pupils—1,001 in all.[32] In 1946 the JDC allocated 3,050,000 zlotys for this type of school.

Instruction in the Zionist schools was mainly in Hebrew, as they were meant in principle to prepare children and young Jews for emigration to Israel, as well as to educate children whose parents supported Zionism.[33] The JDC pointed out that, unlike, for instance, the CKŻP schools, the schools run by Zionist organizations had far greater problems recruiting qualified teaching staff, a satisfactory knowledge of Hebrew being the key problem. However, it was emphasized that all these schools' teachers were distinguished by a high level of professional preparation, which was continually improved by on-the-job training.[34] The Zionist Co-ordinating Committee, and especially the branch responsible for educating

---

[28] *Landsmanshaftn, ziomkostwa*, which had developed in various parts of the globe before the war, played a key role in providing aid to surviving Jews in Poland. They united Jewish émigrés from Poland, who were trying to maintain contact with Jews remaining in their former homeland. The associations' principal activities were obtaining funds, clothing, and food. After the war, their operations were more or less rebuilt from scratch, since most of the pre-war centres of Jewish population had ceased to exist. The associations often shifted their aid to other parts of the country. Such *Landsmanshaftn* centres, linked with those abroad, appeared in Poland in both the provincial branches of the CKŻP and in county and urban centres. The JDC played an important part as liaison between the overseas associations and aid recipients in Poland. In January 1946 a special department for such associations was set up in the JDC. The associations' aid was for the most part sent to individuals or organizations, but assistance sent in this way was not part of the JDC's general budget.

[29] Bauer, *Out of the Ashes*, 77.

[30] JDC NY, 1945–54, 'Poland: 'Administration: Financial', folder 756: letter to J. Schwartz, JDC, Warsaw, 1 Nov. 1946.

[31] JDC Jerusalem, Bauer Collection, Box 1: William Bein, director of JDC in Poland, report, Jan.– Sept. 1946.

[32] JDC NY, 1945–54, 'Poland: Administration: General', folder 728: report prepared for the Polish Research and Information Service, Sept. 1949.   [33] Ibid.   [34] Ibid.

children and preparing them for emigration, played a crucial role in bringing up Jewish children below the age of 12 in the spirit of Zionism.

The committee's main task was to recover children from non-Jewish homes after the war and to place them in specially created centres. The costs of this operation were covered mainly by the JDC. In the first half of 1946 a total of 319 children arrived at these care centres, both homes and *hakhsharot*. By the end of September 1946 the JDC had provided 7.5 million zlotys for the committee's operations. Similar efforts by the Women's International Zionist Organization focused primarily on assistance for children in children's homes or *hakhsharot*, especially in the area of education and the teaching of Hebrew. This organization was also mainly funded by the JDC.

The greatest number of schools in post-war Poland were set up by the CKŻP. According to Datner, who quotes data prepared by the CKŻP in December 1946, after the great wave of emigration caused by the Kielce pogrom there were thirty CKŻP schools in twenty-nine locations with almost 3,000 pupils.[35] They had a definitely secular character, although an important element of the curriculum was Jewish tradition—in, it should be added, a watered-down and ideologized form— and Yiddish was the official language of instruction. Yiddish was also recognized as a key element in the formation of a Jewish spirit and character. It was the daily language of the older generation, and the CKŻP activists felt that it should have a major influence on the formation of Jewish consciousness among the younger generation. For many children who had survived the Holocaust, especially the youngest of those who had been hidden by Polish families, learning Yiddish presented a serious challenge, since most had had no previous contact with the language, and having been brought up completely removed from their familial environment led many to reject it. This was the principal factor which finally destroyed any chance of a rebirth of Yiddish culture or Yiddish as the national language of Polish Jews, despite the efforts of activists. Many years later Michał Fajersztajn, in conversation with Joanna Wiszniewicz, recalled:

We looked down on Yiddish. I never learnt Yiddish. . . . I always wanted to learn Hebrew, but they didn't teach Hebrew [in the Jewish school]. We made it clear to them that Hebrew was different from Yiddish, for Yiddish was ghetto speech (that's how we saw it, we were so immature!) and they told us that we couldn't learn Hebrew. Hebrew was banned as a Zionist, imperialist language . . . that Israel was imperialist—that's what they told us, and as late as 1960![36]

The authorities were not opposed to the creation of separate Jewish schools with Yiddish as the language of instruction and including the study of Jewish history; however, the curriculum in all Jewish schools had to follow the requirements of the Ministry of Education. Observers from the JDC emphasized that the

[35] H. Datner, 'Dziecko żydowskie (1944–1968)', in F. Tych and M. Adamczyk-Garbowska (eds.), *Następstwa zagłady Żydów: Polska 1944–2010* (Lublin, 2011), 261.

[36] J. Wiszniewicz, *Życie przecięte: Opowieści pokolenia Marca* (Wołowiec, 2009), 241.

study of Yiddish and Hebrew, of Jewish history and national traditions were at the educational heart of these schools: 'the study of Jewish customs, holidays and the Jewish way of life were the essential elements of the curriculum'.[37] JDC employees also praised the high professional competence of the teachers in CKŻP schools: 'Most of the instructors are very well trained. The state inspectors regulating schools were full of praise for the instructors and emphasized their achievements.'[38] After liberation, special classes were also set up for children requiring individual help and attention. Workers from the JDC stressed that 'these classes were essential during the first years after liberation, since a great many children had no educational background'.[39] However, within barely two years, thanks to appropriate instruction, their education was raised to a level which allowed them to continue their schooling with their peers.[40]

After the war *talmud torah*s, traditional religious schools, also functioned, organized by religious congregations. According to observers from the JDC, 'these schools are a link to the old traditional "Yavne" and "Yesodei Torah" schools'.[41] Special emphasis was laid on Torah study and other religion-based subjects. These schools ran a full school day, and the curriculum, apart from the study of religious subjects, included secular subjects in line with the requirements of the Ministry of Education. Afternoon classes solely in religious subjects were also run for children attending state or CKŻP schools. According to JDC reports, thirty-four small schools and religious schools, employing ninety-eight teachers with 1,100 pupils, were operating throughout the country in 1948.[42] There were *talmud torah* schools running regular all-day programmes in Wrocław, Kraków, Łódź, Wałbrzych, and Szczecin.[43] Despite the efforts of the JDC, which earmarked resources for this purpose, it was not possible to set up a proposed yeshiva in Łódź, and in June 1949 the JDC decided to withdraw the 250,000-zloty grant allocated for it.[44]

The number of Jewish pupils attending Polish state schools is, however, unknown. It could have totalled more than 1,500 in the larger enclaves such as Warsaw or Łódź,[45] and it seems that the number has usually been considerably understated.[46] A sizeable number were attending the schools of the Workers' Association of the Friends of Children, where religion was not taught. Until 1948 religion was a compulsory subject in Poland, and state schools became fully secular only in 1961.

Table 1 presents details about the Jewish schools supported by the JDC in September 1946. The sum of 900,000 zlotys spent in 1946 on education included 357,000 zlotys for teachers' salaries, 90,000 zlotys for other salaries, 108,000 zlotys

---

[37] JDC NY, 1945–54, 'Poland: Administration: General', folder 728: report prepared for the Polish Research and Information Service, Sept. 1949.   [38] Ibid.   [39] Ibid.

[40] Ibid.   [41] Ibid.   [42] Ibid.   [43] Ibid.

[44] American Jewish Joint Distribution Committee, Geneva (hereafter JDC Geneva), 1945–54, folder PL211: William Bein, letter to Judah Shapiro, 8 June 1949.

[45] JDC NY, 1945–54, 'Poland: Administration: General', folder 728: report prepared for the Polish Research and Information Service, Sept. 1949.   [46] Cf. Datner, 'Dziecko żydowskie', 263.

Table 1. Jewish schools supported by the JDC, September 1946

Location	Number of classes	Number of pupils	Number of teachers	Expenses (zlotys)
Łódź	6	130	8	183,000
Bytom	3	61	5	71,000
Bielawa	3	43	4	57,000
Wrocław	3	46	4	73,000
Wałbrzych	6	160	8	115,000
Legnica	3	50	4	68,000
Kraków	6	55	7	189,000
Rychbach (Dzierżoniów)	5	80	5	81,000
Szczecin	3	52	3	63,000
Totals	**38**	**677**	**48**	**900,000**

Source: JDC NY, 1945–54, 'Poland: Administration: General', folder 734: 'Zionist Kibbutzim Supported by the JDC', 30 Sept. 1946.

for food for pupils and staff, 68,000 zlotys for teaching materials, 26,000 zlotys for administrative costs, and 251,000 zlotys for running repairs.

Another type of education for young Jews was vocational training, usually administered by the Society for Trades and Agricultural Labour (Obshchestvo remeslennogo i zemledel'cheskogo truda; ORT),[47] which was also financed by the JDC. The JDC had no influence on the form or content of the curriculum but was kept informed of the results of ORT's work through periodic reports, usually summarizing a specific accounting period. There was no advance agreement on the type of education or classes,[48] but because these schools were intended only for Jews, they played a key educational role and, more importantly, were crucial in the psychological recovery of Holocaust survivors. In time groups of Jews who had been repatriated from the USSR also took advantage of this vocational training. ORT schools offered different levels of education: regular vocational classes, short-term courses for specific trades, and special courses organized for the Solidarity Centre of Manufacturing Co-operatives.[49] In 1949 almost 2,000 people were taking ORT courses, including 500 young people in children's homes. Vocational training brought quantifiable results: in most cases, graduates were hired by Jewish co-operatives, which in turn were obliged to give 10 per cent of

[47] ORT was founded in Russia in 1880. Its principal aim was to support the development of trades and agriculture among Jews through vocational training. ORT had played an important part in creating a network of schools in Poland even before the war. After the war it resumed operations in 1945 (receiving official approval in 1946) and set up educational centres in larger locations inhabited by Jews. Most of its financing came from the JDC, as well as from the Commissariat for the Productivization of the Jewish Population.

[48] JDC NY, 1945–54, 'Poland: Administration: General', folder 728: minutes of a board meeting of the JDC with its managers in Poland, 11 Oct. 1949.   [49] Ibid.

their income to the CKŻP. These funds were then used for the development of educational and cultural activities. Thanks to this, a number of investments were subsidized, including for education and the printing of books and newspapers in Yiddish, which Jewish activists who had survived the Holocaust continued to recognize as the Jewish national language.[50] The same was true at the end of the 1950s when the JDC resumed operations in Poland. At that time, the TSKŻ was receiving 20 per cent of the income of the Jewish co-operatives, which at that time were highly profitable, above all due to the machinery and raw materials that the JDC had helped import into Poland.

The leadership of the JDC believed that camps, summer courses, and youth clubs played an even more important role in the education and upbringing of Jewish youngsters in the spirit of *yidishkeyt* than traditional Jewish schools did. At times the goals behind such activities changed. At first, the priority was to ensure that children who had survived the Holocaust received the best conditions for their psychological and physical recovery. Summer camps were also suitable places for integrating children repatriated from the USSR, especially those who had never previously been to Poland and did not speak Polish. Over time, the summer camps run exclusively for Jewish children and adolescents began to play a growing role in the process of education and instruction in the spirit of the Jewish tradition and culture. This was particularly true before the end of the 1950s, when the JDC resumed operations in Poland.

In February 1948 the Jewish Telegraphic Agency published an article on Jewish schools in Poland. According to this, some 7,000 Jewish pupils were studying in high schools, with an additional 1,000 in vocational schools. It claimed that 'although Jews represent 0.4 percent of the overall population, 2 percent of all students in Poland are Jewish'.[51] Schools whose language of instruction was Yiddish (thirty-five in all) continued to operate, with 3,000 students, while there were around 1,000 students in thirteen Hebrew (Zionist) schools. Because of the decreasing number of Jewish students resulting from emigration, thirteen of these schools were to be closed by the end of the year.[52] By mid-1949 most of the Zionist schools had been closed not only because of the decreasing numbers of students but, above all, because of the decision by the Minister of Public Administration, Władysław Wolski, to nationalize Jewish schools in Poland. Paradoxically, that same year interest in Jewish education, especially in the study of Hebrew, grew substantially. However, this was a short-lived response to the possibility of emigration to Israel being legalized. By the end of the school year, six Zionist schools with 750 children still functioned. Two of these closed at the end of the year, depriving the 180 children who had continued to attend them of the chance of an education.

At the start of the 1949/50 school year, four schools in Poland offered courses

[50] JDC NY, 1945–54, 'Poland: Administration: General', folder 728: minutes of a board meeting of the JDC with its managers in Poland, 11 Oct. 1949.

[51] Jewish Telegraphic Agency, news release, 2 Apr. 1948.   [52] Ibid.

taught in Hebrew, which were attended by 850 children. There was also very great interest in learning Hebrew. The previous year had ended with a reasonable result given the circumstances: overall, such courses were available in ten cities, with 710 pupils. After the announcement of the government's decision to allow emigration to Israel, this number immediately grew to 1,200. None of the schools received government subsidies, and their only source of income was grants from the JDC and fees paid by parents.[53]

In April 1948 the authorities in Poland announced that they intended to nationalize education. The CKŻP held a plenary meeting on 25/6 February 1949 with Joseph Schwartz present as the JDC's representative. The nationalization of Jewish education was officially accepted and it was agreed that the operations of Jewish institutions would be adapted to the new official guidelines and 'legions of teachers' given appropriate preparation.[54] One of the most urgent tasks was to draw up new curricula. Special emphasis was laid on rekindling in the children patriotic feelings, and an 'attachment to the Polish and Jewish working-class revolutionary tradition and its heroes and martyrs'.[55]

The nationalization of schools sounded an alarm for the JDC's leadership in New York. In 1948, even before the official announcement, discussions were held on the subject by representatives of the JDC's offices in New York and Paris. The nationalization of Jewish schooling did not mean a complete abandonment of the study of Jewish subjects. The authorities agreed that some courses could continue, but there was a justified fear that teachers in Jewish schools, who earned much more than those in state schools, would not accept the new terms of employment and would simply emigrate. At this time, state-school teachers were earning between 7,000 and 8,000 zlotys per month, while those in private schools could make as much as 19,000 zlotys.[56] Therefore, efforts were made to find a way to improve their remuneration. The situation became much more complicated when, in November 1949, the Polish authorities forced the JDC to suspend operations in Poland from the end of the year.[57] Despite the educational changes, Jewish institutions, as well as a few schools, continued to offer at least some classes in Jewish history and languages. According to Datner, Jewish schools operated in Dzierżoniów, Bielawa, Wałbrzych, and Legnica after 1950: 'Despite the successive waves of emigration and internal migration, these towns would be the most important educational centres up to the end of Jewish schools in 1968. . . . Łódź would unfailingly retain

---

[53] JDC NY, 1945–54, 'Poland: Administration: General', folder 728: report prepared for the Polish Research and Information Service, Sept. 1949.

[54] JDC Geneva, 1945–54, folder PL211: William Bein, report, 3 June 1949.   [55] Ibid.

[56] JDC Geneva, 1945–54, folder PL211: Judah Shapiro, letter to Moses Leavitt, 17 Jan. 1949.

[57] The decision was dictated by the fact that the government was taking over all Jewish institutions, including children's homes and schools, which had previously been supported by the JDC and for which funds now had to be found out of the public purse. Given this situation, it would have been pointless for the JDC to maintain a base in Poland. As in other countries in the region, the JDC was forced to suspend operations.

its position as the most significant centre of schooling and one of the most important centres of Jewish life right up to 1968.'[58]

The nationalization of schools met with the approval of communist activists
within the CKŻP. The issue of the state assuming at least financial responsibility
for Jewish education had been a demand of Jewish leaders before the war. The state
takeover of Jewish schools involved the imposition of a curriculum reflecting the
growing Stalinization of the country. In one of his reports, William Bein of the
JDC described a statement made at the Second Plenary Meeting of the CKŻP on
16 May 1949 by the committee's secretary general Julian Łazebnik. Łazebnik
discussed the issue of nationalizing schools and also appealed for the creation of a
structure that would allow young Jews to be brought up in a patriotic spirit by
means of an increased number of summer (scout) camps. He also stressed the need
to nationalize Jewish institutions, including theatres.[59]

At the same time, plans for nationalization and a desire to take over the JDC's
leadership did not prevent the leaders of the CKŻP from turning to the organization to provide the lion's share of the budget for the second half of 1949 (300
million zlotys out of a total of 380 million), arguing that the nationalization of
Jewish institutions would not have any appreciable influence on reducing budgeted
operating costs.[60]

The policies of the communist authorities also had a very negative effect on
the operation of care facilities for Jewish children. At the beginning of 1950 the
government sought to 'integrate' Jewish and Polish facilities, leading to the closure
of Jewish children's homes and to Polish orphanages accepting their charges.
Śródborowianka was closed down, as were the children's homes in Chorzów and
Częstochowa. Some children from the poorest families, whose parents were unable
to bring them up, and semi-orphans went to legal guardians. Under-age and younger children requiring constant care were moved to other facilities in Poland.
Teenagers were sent to boarding schools or college.

THE 1950S AND 1960S: NEW CHALLENGES FOR
JEWISH EDUCATION

Faced with the events of the late 1940s, the president of the CKŻP, Grzegorz
(Hersz) Smolar, put forward a proposal to create a new Jewish institution to replace
the CKŻP, which was closed down at the end of 1949. His goal was to create an
organization representing Jews in Poland which would also allow them to maintain
contacts with Jewish communities throughout the world. Set up in 1950, the TSKŻ
was intended to fill these roles, and at the same time to be a 'conveyor belt' for the
ruling party's policies. Smolar became its head. A key element in the TSKŻ's

[58] Datner, 'Dziecko żydowskie', 261.

[59] JDC NY, 1945–54, 'Poland: Administration: General', folder 728: William Bein, report, 28 May
1949.   [60] Ibid.

activities was running primary schools with Yiddish as the language of instruction, despite the fact that the education of Jewish children was not one of the association's priorities, possibly because, as Joanna Nalewajko-Kulikov has observed, most of the leadership was over 50 and thus did not have any school-age children. At the same time, leaders of the TSKŻ assured the JDC of their interest in education. According to one of its reports, the TSKŻ was 'the sole legal representative [of the Jews] recognized by the Polish Government and its principal aim [was] the development of education and cultural activities in the Jewish community'.[61] The TSKŻ's publishing activities, through the publishing house Yidish Bukh, were also not insignificant for Jewish culture, especially in comparison to publishing houses in other European countries. Alongside the TSKŻ, another body, the Religious Association of the Mosaic Faith (Związek Religijny Wyznania Mojżeszowego; ZRWM), maintained twenty-three congregations throughout the country.[62]

One of the aims in nationalizing schools was to integrate all the national minorities into Polish society. As a result of emigration at the end of the 1940s, a number of Jewish schools were closed down because of low levels of enrolment. The remainder were usually merged with the schools of the Association of Friends of Children, which were strongly secular in nature. Parents often decided to send their children to these schools, which helped the process of integration and eliminated feelings of alienation. Since these schools did not offer classes in religious instruction, there was less danger of stigmatizing Jewish pupils. This also helped to combat what the communist authorities saw as the hostile force of Jewish nationalism. At the same time, in those schools that did teach Jewish subjects, the teaching of Hebrew was completely abandoned, while the teaching of Jewish history was brought into conformity with the ideological discourse prevailing in the country. As Datner points out, 'the Minister of Education's 1952 directive on teaching in Yiddish recommended that in the fifth grade, for example, "fighters for justice and freedom in antiquity, such as Isaiah, Amos, Bar Kokhba, Akiba, and others", be discussed'.[63]

The end of 1949 not only brought changes in how Jewish schools and institutions were run but also saw the end of the JDC's operations in Poland. As a result, until 1957 the committee almost completely lost contact with the Jewish community in Poland. This changed when Polish authorities once again renewed co-operation with the committee, although on different terms, including refusing to allow the JDC to open a permanent office in Poland. From 15 October 1957 the JDC operated through the Central Jewish Relief Committee, created exclusively for this purpose.[64] Since the authorities did agree to regular visits to Poland by representatives of the committee, for the next ten years until it was once again expelled the JDC was in constant touch with Polish Jewry and had an enormous

---

[61] JDC NY, 1955–64, 'Poland: Administration: General', folder 658: Zachariah Shuster, 'The Situation in Poland', memorandum to Foreign Affairs Department, 14 Aug. 1957. [62] Ibid.

[63] Datner, 'Dziecko żydowskie', 271. [64] Sommer Schneider, *Sze'erit Hapleta*, 220.

impact on rekindling and developing Jewish economic and cultural life, as well as contributing to the growth and meaning of Jewish education.

The direct and official reason for the communist authorities re-establishing co-operation with the JDC was the planned repatriation of thousands of Polish citizens from the USSR, including more than 19,000 Jews,[65] with which the Polish government hoped the JDC would help financially. For Polish Jews and those coming from the east, the JDC gave the hope that decent living conditions could be provided for them. However, for the overwhelming majority of those repatriated, Poland was simply a transit country, a temporary stop on a journey further west.

Even if their stay in Poland was temporary, the arrivals had to find means to support their families, which was not an easy task. Many had enormous problems finding work, often caused by their inability to speak Polish, inappropriate education, or lack of skills. As in the 1940s, ORT set up professional training programmes. The largest group (around 75 per cent) of those repatriated were workers and craftsmen. The remaining 25 per cent belonged to the working intelligentsia.[66] However, many of these workers had no specific trade. Efforts were therefore made to create training centres throughout the country, mainly through ORT. There were plans to use buildings that had belonged to Jewish communities before the war; however, repairs and remodelling were a problem. Professional training was also often undertaken by people who had been dismissed by Polish enterprises and who were hoping that such retraining would help them to find employment.

The children of repatriated families also faced difficulties. Torn from the environment in which they had been growing up, they now had to integrate into new surroundings. Like their parents, many did not speak Polish, which prevented them from attending school upon arrival. JDC workers reported that school lessons were held in Polish, Russian, and Yiddish, the latter because some pupils spoke it fluently.[67] It was also realized that summer camps were the best place outside school for younger members of the Jewish community to develop relationships with their peers. Unfortunately, camps were inaccessible to most of the repatriated children, as they were often organized by workplaces, and a large part of those returning to Poland were unemployed. Hence, the leadership of the TSKŻ and religious congregations appealed to the JDC to allocate additional funds for this purpose, which the JDC did immediately after its operations in Poland were sanctioned. The youngest representatives of the Jewish community, especially those who had been repatriated from the USSR, were afforded appropriate care and provided with special benefits. In November 1957 265 children in

[65] JDC NY, 1965–74, 'Poland, Administration, General', folder 322: Boris Sapir and Murray Kass, report, 5 July 1966.

[66] Archiwum Ministerstwa Spraw Zagranicznych, kol. 12 'Departament V, akta za lata 1955–1960', t. 344: report on emigration to Israel between 1951 and 1957, 14.

[67] JDC NY, 1955–64, 'Poland: Administration: General', folder 658: JDC New York, minutes of staff meeting, 3 Oct. 1957.

Szczecin were receiving regular aid from the JDC and by the end of December that number had grown to 1,800.

The JDC's return coincided with a rise of antisemitism and chauvinism in Poland. According to an anonymous informant who turned to the JDC for help in 1956, this problem affected Jewish children and representatives of other minorities. In a letter to Moses Leavitt, William Bein quoted a former JDC worker in Poland who emphasized that young people and schoolchildren, not just adults, were victims of antisemitism. He claimed that 'Jewish children are being ostracized. Polish children don't want to share a school bench with Jews, while daily beatings become more common. Many of them suffer so much that in the long run they won't be able to handle it.'[68] At the same time, the author of the letter emphasized that the problem was not simply antisemitism, as it also affected Ukrainian and German children and those of other minorities. In his view, the nationalist climate resulted more from 'the growing influence of the Catholic Church in the schools. The Church is above all fighting atheism . . . as a result of which children not wearing around their necks a cross or some other Catholic symbol are constantly jeered at for being Jews.'[69]

The JDC soon became involved—mainly financially—in organizing summer camps and courses. This certainly aided the process of integration. In 1959 almost 3,000 children took part in summer camps and courses co-funded by the JDC. Akiva Kohane,[70] who in 1959 travelled around Poland and visited summer camps, was greatly impressed by the way in which they were run:

I was very pleasantly surprised by the programme of summer camps, which, in my opinion, could be the most important element of our work in Poland. Three thousand Jewish children take part in summer camps with other Jews. I was pleasantly surprised visiting these camps to see that in principle they are in no way different from these types of camps organized elsewhere in Europe. Of course, there is no Israeli flag, which flutters over most camps in other European countries, nor can you hear Hebrew songs, there are also no *shlichim*[71] and no discussions about Israel. Despite this I was deeply moved when I saw the children singing in Yiddish and reading chapters from Peretz and Sholem Aleichem, replying to quiz questions such as 'What is the name of the Israeli parliament' or 'Which is the best theatre in Israel'.[72]

[68] JDC NY, 1955–64, 'Poland: Administration: General', folder 659: William Bein, letter to Moses Leavitt, 13 Dec. 1956.

[69] JDC NY, 1955–64, 'Poland: Administration: General', folder 659: translation of a letter by an unknown person, enclosed with William Bein, letter to Moses Leavitt, 13 Dec. 1956.

[70] Akiva Kohane came from Kraków. He had been associated with the JDC since the 1930s. After escaping from Poland in 1942, he spent the war years in Palestine and Teheran, where he also worked for the JDC. In the 1950s he lived in Geneva where he held the position of director of the Department of Reconstruction at the JDC's European head office.

[71] *Sheliḥim* were Israeli emissaries who conducted schooling for the Jewish community throughout the world with a view to building cultural and educational links between the local communities of the Diaspora and the State of Israel.

[72] JDC NY, 1955–64, 'Poland: Administration: General', folder 656: Akiva Kohane, report, 11 Aug. 1959.

At the same time, Polish educational policies were very clear, and no one strayed beyond the limits imposed by the state. However, for the JDC and some Jewish activists, especially those not associated with the TSKŻ, political indoctrination was not that important in the process of bringing up children. The issue was more one of explaining to the children what *yidishkeyt* was, what qualities were associated with being Jewish, that Jewishness was above all a way of life, and of the importance of coexistence with members of the community. For a great many young people, the time spent with Jewish peers helped them to establish links with the Jewish world. In a conversation with Joanna Wiszniewicz, Władek Poznański recalled:

I met Jewish children for the first time at Jewish [summer] camps. I discovered a new world at these camps! The atmosphere was different from that at Polish camps or scout camps (which I knew well); people behaved differently. There was a special bond between the children and the instructors. Everyone was on first-name terms; we even called Szmul Teneblatt, the camp leader, by his first name. At Polish camps and scout camps there was always a certain reserve, discipline, while here we had the discipline and everything else, but without the reserve. It felt like a family, not a camp. Honestly! We all felt ourselves to be one big family![73]

According to Regina Grol:

During that period of my development, Jewishness was becoming more important to me. . . . I was trying to understand the secret of this difference that led to me being sometimes not accepted in Polish circles. . . . TSKŻ camps (I went to one for the first time at the age of 15) provided me with an additional dose of Jewish culture. It was there that a number of instructors led us into the Jewish world. Marek Web was making up all sorts of Jewish tales and helping us to learn new things. We also sang songs in Yiddish. . . . They taught us the songs, which supposedly our grandparents had sung. But then of course none of us knew our grandparents![74]

All these factors were very important given the often negative attitude of Poles to Jews and the stigma attached to being Jewish. It was precisely society's dislike of Jews that often led a great number of Jewish children and adolescents to rebel and in many cases to reject their Jewish identity. In his memoirs, Michał Chęciński[75] describes the difficulties his family experienced because of their origins, diffi-

---

[73] Wiszniewicz, *Życie przecięte*, 210.   [74] Ibid. 131–2.

[75] Michał (Mosze) Chęciński survived the war first in the Łódź ghetto and then in Auschwitz. In January 1945 he escaped during the evacuation of the camp, the so-called 'death march'. After the war he was an officer in the Directorate of Information of the Polish Army and, after obtaining his doctorate in 1953, an instructor at the Polish Army's School of Information. Between 1959 and 1967 he was a researcher and then a lecturer in defence economics at the Military Political Academy. After March 1968, he migrated with his family to Israel, where he worked, among other places, at the Hebrew University of Jerusalem. After leaving for the USA he worked at Harvard University. After five years there, he worked for the Rand Corporation, and for the next thirteen years he was an instructor at the US Army Russian Institute as well as at the George C. Marshall European Center for Security Studies at Garmisch-Partenkirchen in Germany. He retired in 1997 and died in May 2011 in Haifa.

culties that would probably not have caused family conflict had it not been for the growing antisemitism of the 1950s. One of his daughters, Basia, then 6 years old, felt this especially painfully, announcing one day that she 'hated the Jews, because they had crucified Christ'. Chęciński's wife 'calmly explained to the child that her mummy and daddy were Jews and that Jesus had also been Jewish. At which [Basia] began to stamp her feet shouting, "You can be Jews if you want to, but not me."'[76] The scale of the problem was considerable, since Jacek Kuroń, not himself Jewish, felt it necessary to encourage young people to accept their Jewish identity, as another one of Wiszniewicz's interlocutors related:

I very clearly recall Jacek Kuroń from one of those camps. It was 1962 at Suche near Poronin. . . . Kuroń was a fascinating person. His laughter was very infectious; he had an amazing laugh! He spoke sense. We had an all-night discussion with him and he devoted the whole of it to the issue of the complex which many of us had about being Jewish. He told us to jettison this complex, to stifle it within ourselves, that we should not be ashamed of being Jewish, for this was an unnecessary shame, a false shame. If you're ashamed, all you are doing is humiliating yourself (he taught us Jewish pride, even though he was not Jewish himself, which we of course knew!).[77]

The end of the 1950s saw very high levels of Jewish migration from Poland, including, above all, Jews who had been repatriated. However, despite these greatly increased numbers, there was no noticeable drop in interest in summer camps on the part of young Jewish people. According to JDC reports, in the first session in the summer of 1960 some 1,500 young people attended, and the numbers increased during the second session in August.[78] The fears of Kohane and the board members of the TSKŻ that emigration would have a negative impact on the number of children taking part in summer camps were not realized: several hundred children could not be accepted due to lack of space. However, JDC employees were extremely unhappy at the role that the TSKŻ had assumed in selecting children to participate in the camps. It was a very common practice for the TSKŻ to ignore applications from religious congregations. This was unacceptable to the JDC. Kohane emphasized: 'whether people like it or not, in the eyes of the JDC the union—the Religious Association of the Mosaic Faith [the ZRWM]—is a full partner in the Relief Committee with the same powers and duties as those enjoyed by the TSKŻ'.[79] Accordingly, the JDC gave instructions to provide additional buses to enable children who had been denied a place in the camps to attend.[80]

Apart from summer camps, school remained the most important place to receive a Jewish education. The archives of the JDC indicate that in October 1957,

[76] M. Chęciński, *Jedenaste przykazanie: Nie zapomnij* (Toruń, 2004), 377.

[77] Wiszniewicz, *Życie przecięte*, 228.

[78] JDC NY, 1955–64, 'Poland: Administration: General', folder 674: Akiva Kohane, report, 28 Mar. 1960.

[79] JDC NY, 1955–64, 'Poland: Administration: General', folder 674: Akiva Kohane, report, 16 Aug. 1960.   [80] Wiszniewicz, *Życie przecięte*, 228.

Jewish history was taught in seven schools. Between 120 and 450 Jewish students attended these schools.[81] In all, some 1,500 pupils studied in them.[82] Smaller schools, popularly known as *talmud torah*s, continued to run alongside religious congregations. In April 1958 there were altogether 'ten such places in Poland—not quite *talmud torah*s, but still called that and where the children are at least learning Hebrew. We support them. But the number of students taking advantage of them is very small.'[83]

Table 2 shows the expenditure of the JDC on educational and cultural activities for Jewish children in Poland between 1961 and 1964. The cost of feeding children in Jewish schools was significant. The decision to introduce such food programmes was a direct consequence of the difficult financial situation of people who had been laid off en masse and unemployed repatriates. The additional food in schools was often an important factor in parental choices about sending their children to a Jewish school. The JDC did not provide this kind of aid to state schools attended by Jewish children. The Wrocław school district reported that 'a significant number of Jewish children have been going to school in their own local school districts and it is only the organized transport and relatively good food provided that has led some parents to send their children to schools with supplementary classes in Yiddish'.[84] This was also influential in the retention of Jewish schools in Poland in 1966. Food was also provided at TSKŻ clubs, which brought in a great many young people who also took advantage of the large number of courses.

Despite continuing emigration, the number of Jewish students significantly decreased only after 1960. According to Datner, 'in December 1962 147 pupils were going to school in Szczecin, while at the end of the 1964/5 school year this number had fallen to 78. In Dzierżoniów in 1960 there were 105 pupils, while at the end of the 1963/4 school year there were 48.'[85] The education and upbringing of Jewish children were undoubtedly among the TSKŻ's priorities. Ignacy Fehlender, a member of the TSKŻ board and head of its education and propaganda department, emphasized that young people were the future of the Jewish community in Poland and that the TSKŻ ought to focus on them. However, demographic data suggested the opposite. Although there was a population boom throughout Poland immediately after the war, the 1950s saw a huge decrease in births among Jews. Maciej Jakubowicz, who at the time was the president of the ZRWM in Kraków, claimed, for example, that in the ten years since he had assumed the leadership, only three children had been born. Emigration also caused a continual drop in the number of Jews in Poland. It was usually young people who decided to emigrate, since their age allowed them start a new life elsewhere. Available data for this period

---

[81] JDC NY, 1955–64, 'Poland: Administration: General', folder 658: JDC New York, minutes of staff meeting, 3 Oct. 1957.

[82] JDC NY, 1955–64, 'Poland: Administration: General', folder 658: Charles Jordan, report on visit to Poland between 20 Sept. and 1 Oct. 1957.

[83] JDC NY, 1955–64, 'Poland: Administration: General', folder 657: Charles Jordan, report to Moses Leavitt, 29 Apr. 1958.   [84] Cited in Datner, 'Dziecko żydowskie', 276.   [85] Ibid.

Table 2. JDC Expenditure on educational and cultural activities for Jewish children in Poland, 1961–1964 (zlotys)

Category	1961	1962	1963	1964
Feeding children at school	3,250,000	3,300,000	1,290,000	800,000
School equipment	200,000	100,000	0	0
ORT dormitories	5,400,000	4,000,000	2,700,000	2,500,000
TSKŻ	1,550,000	1,500,000	1,500,000	1,500,000
Children's holidays	150,000	1,500,000	0	0
Youth clubs	0	0	2,500,000	2,500,000
Summer camps	3,600,000	3,600,000	4,400,000	3,600,000
Total expenditure on educational and cultural activities	14,150,000	14,000,000	12,390,000	10,900,000
Total annual expenditure	36,400,000	41,350,000	29,660,000	29,660,000

Source: JDC NY, 1955–64, 'Poland: Administration: General', folder 674: Akiva Kohane, reports, 30 May 1962, 20 Mar. 1964.

are approximate and the basis under which they were collected is not clear (they were definitely prepared by TSKŻ field teams), but they do show the scale of the problem. In the first half of the 1960s, there were about 18,000 Jews living in Poland: 500 children below the age of 10; about 2,500 aged between 10 and 25; 2,000 between the ages of 25 and 50; and 13,000 over 50. Those between 50 and 60 were a clear minority in the top age range.[86]

Despite this, when Polish authorities proposed integrating Jewish children into Polish schools with the possibility of retaining lessons in Yiddish and Jewish history, the TSKŻ, as Datner indicates, 'did not agree, arguing that children deprived of their schools will emigrate, while "the opposition press will take advantage of this move to present the state's attitude to the nationalities issue in an inappropriate light"'.[87] It was eventually decided to retain the schools, but the idea of starting primary classes was abandoned. In 1966 only four Jewish schools remained in Poland—in Szczecin, Łódź, Legnica, and Wrocław—with classes in Yiddish and Jewish history.[88] In the following school year, even before the political crisis of March 1968, Jewish history was not considered a separate subject and was merged with general history.

To compensate for the closing down of Jewish schools, the TSKŻ set up youth clubs. Since those who were aware of their Jewishness were the most likely to leave Poland, an attractive network of clubs—not based, however, on Jewish values—

[86] Cf. D. Blatman, 'Polish Jewry, the Six-Day War and the Crisis of 1968', in E. Lederhendler (ed.), *The Six-Day War and World Jewry* (Bethesda, Md., 2001), 295.

[87] Datner, 'Dziecko żydowskie', 276. [88] Ibid.

became an important substitute for Jewish schools. It was only in 1963 that the JDC began to allocate funds for Jewish clubs, and these were intended for younger and more assimilated Polish Jews. This state of affairs did not last long. In 1967 the Ministry of the Interior called for clubs for Jewish children and adolescents to be closed on the grounds that 'retaining separate rules in this regard for the TSKŻ is unjustified, since the experience of recent years indicates that children and adolescents involved in the activities of child or youth clubs have in numerous cases been brought up in a Zionist spirit (e.g. exhibiting repeated Zionist excesses at summer courses and camps)'.[89] In this way, the authorities proceeded to eradicate Jewish education. The events of March 1968 were simply the culmination of these efforts which had started long before.

In August 1967, immediately after the Six Day War in the Middle East, the JDC was once again forced to terminate its work in Poland. The Central Jewish Relief Committee and all its field operations were shut down. ORT, too, was closed. As a result, organized Jewish life in Poland ceased to exist for the next dozen years or so.

THE 1980S: REBUILDING JEWISH IDENTITY

The absence of organized Jewish life in Poland lasted until the end of the 1970s. Although the JDC did not have a direct impact on subsequent changes within the Jewish community, the return of the Joint in January 1982 assisted in its rebuilding. In the 1980s Polish Jews' activities were limited for the most part to membership in one of the fourteen TSKŻ clubs located across Poland, most of which had sentimental appeal to the community's oldest members. These were actually the only places providing a substitute for Jewish cultural life while also attempting to maintain a link with the tradition. It was rare at this time for Jews to observe religious practices. Thanks to the JDC's aid, the clubs run by the TSKŻ received hundreds of films, as well as samples of Jewish music. Akiva Kohane recounted with satisfaction that during the lunch hour one could hear songs in Yiddish in every Jewish canteen. Separate funds were also allocated for actors from the Jewish theatre to go on tour, allowing them to perform in remote parts of Poland. For Kohane, work in Poland had undoubtedly sentimental significance, but his work was often challenging. The fact that he was born, raised, and educated in Poland definitely helped him to understand the situation of those Jews who remained in the country. His emotional involvement in what he was doing also shines through the documents describing the JDC's work in Poland. For him the hardest part was to visit Kraków, his family's home city. Even the passage of time was unable to erase the pain. In an interview in the 1980s, Kohane recalled that such visits 'are always emotionally draining'.[90] For him 'Poland is a vast cemetery of Jewish

---

[89] Cited in Datner, 'Dziecko żydowskie', 280.

[90] K. Friedman, 'Kohane: Custodian of Polish Jewry's "Lost Cause"', *Jewish World West Palm Beach*, 16 Jan. 1987, p. 161.

history. . . . For over 1,000 years [the Jews] shared with [the Poles] a splendid history, which no longer existed after the Second World War.' Kohane believed that 'within a few years there will be no Jewish community in Poland because there are no young people. . . . "Every week there are several funerals."' Furthermore, from his perspective, rebuilding the Jewish community in Poland was a lost cause: 'we won't be able to make this community self-sufficient'.[91] He therefore believed that the responsibility of the JDC and the Jewish community world-wide was to ensure that elderly representatives of the Jewish community in Poland spent their final years in dignity.[92]

It was soon apparent that these grim predictions were not being realized, and they were clearly at variance with what Kohane reported in the second half of the 1980s. In March 1987, for example, he described a meeting of sixty young people in December 1986 at the centre in Śródborów that had been organized by various TSKŻ branches. Although, as Kohane emphasized, only a few of the participants attending the meeting had grown up in Jewish homes, the gathering nevertheless served as proof of growing interest on the part of young people of Jewish descent in the culture and history of their ancestors.[93] In Kohane's words:

[The participants] expressed an interest in continuing these meetings and learning more about *yidishkeyt*. Therefore, smaller youth groups are meeting in Wrocław, Katowice, Wałbrzych, and Warsaw. They attend lectures on Jewish history, holidays and literature. . . . What is astonishing is that this group is making it a priority to do something about the phenomenon of marrying outside the faith. Consequently, *Folks shtime*, the organ of the TSKŻ, is soon to begin publishing matrimonial advertisements for this group. . . . The future will show if this is a real and serious attempt on the part of some of these young people to identify as Jews and whether they will become involved in Jewish life, or whether it will be a short-lived enthusiasm, partly the result of free vacations at Śródborów, and that some of them will lose interest in seeking their 'roots'. It is to be hoped that this interest will develop into a deeper involvement, to becoming a Jew. Whatever the future might bring, I believe that we must definitely support these activities. They can still bring results.[94]

This was undoubtedly the start of a new era for Jews in Poland. An important factor in the rebuilding of Jewish life was the discovery by young people of their Jewish ancestry. For many, this was the start of a struggle over their own identity, which often led to Jewishness growing in popularity.

Some younger Jews had grown up in assimilated, often communist, families. For them to recover their Jewish identity it was not enough to develop an awareness of their ancestry. In 1979 a group of mainly young intellectuals set up the informal Jewish Flying University. For the most part meetings were taken up with discussions of Jewish history, religion, and literature.[95] 'For some people', August

---

[91] Ibid.   [92] Ibid.

[93] JDC NY, 1975–89, 'Poland, General', folder PL#5: Akiva Kohane, report, 10 Mar. 1987.

[94] Ibid.

[95] A. Grabski, 'Współczesne życie religijne Żydów w Polsce', in A. Grabski, M. Pisarski, and

Grabski noted, 'this was the start of the road back to Judaism'.[96] Nonetheless, initial contacts with ZRWM members were somewhat discouraging.[97]

The JDC did not become involved in these kinds of activities, at least not as much as it had in the past. Its employees, including Akiva Kohane, did not share the opinions of members of the ZRWM presidium, such as Szymon Szurmiej, who saw in young people discovering their Jewish ancestry an opportunity for a Jewish future in Poland. Kohane was not convinced that people who had grown up outside the Jewish community, especially in Catholic families, would be able to remain committed to their Jewish heritage. From his perspective, the JDC should provide only limited financial support for programmes focused on additional training or on educational trips for young Poles to Śródborów and other places. He thus distinguished between people who were seriously involved with the life of the Jewish community and had integrated into it and were even considering conversion, and those who, motivated by curiosity, continued to be practising, mainly Catholic, Christians. Kohane wrote in one of his reports: 'We are ready to support these groups as long as *yidishkeyt*, the history of the Jewish people, Jewish literature, Jewish religion, and so on remain the focus of their attention. However, young people declaring Christianity [as their religion] and/or going to mass should be excluded, unless they wish to return to Judaism.'[98]

Soon the focus of reviving Jewish life again became Śródborowianka. For a number of years after the war it had served as a children's home and sanatorium for Jewish children. Towards the end of the 1950s its last owner offered to sell the site to the TSKŻ. Since the asking price was not high and the owner wanted to be paid in US dollars in instalments over ten years, the JDC allocated special funds to buy it. Also using JDC funds, with substantial support from the Polish government, the building was restored, thanks to which the centre continued to serve the Jewish community for both recreational and educational purposes.[99] It is there that meetings of young Jews have been held continually. However, neither the JDC nor the leaders of Jewish institutions in Poland were able to regain control of Jewish education until the start of the 1990s.

CONCLUSION

The detailed reports drawn up by employees of the JDC describe the projects for which the funds provided by American donors were used and how much they got. This reveals the committee's priorities. Certainly the care and education of young

---

A. Stankowski, *Studia z dziejów i kultury Żydów w Polsce po 1945 roku*, ed. J. Tomaszewski (Warsaw, 1997), 175.

[96] Ibid.

[97] See M. Niezabitowska and T. Tomaszewski, *Ostatni współcześni Żydzi polscy* (Warsaw, 1993).

[98] JDC NY, 1975–89, 'Poland, General', folder PL#5: Akiva Kohane, report, 6 May 1987.

[99] Ibid.

Jews were among their most important tasks. For instance, in the 1960s cultural and educational activities absorbed more than 30 per cent of the JDC's expenses in Poland. At the same time, the reports show changes in the JDC's attitudes, especially towards the future of the Jewish community in Poland.

Education and bringing up young Polish Jews in accordance with tradition was clearly one of the JDC's priorities. However, none of the extant sources suggest that the JDC interfered in the drawing up of curricula or had any direct influence on course content. The curricula in Jewish educational centres was defined, above all, by the people running them and the guidelines of the Ministry of Education. However, the fact that the surviving sources do not show JDC employees exerting direct influence on education does not mean that such issues were not raised with the leaders of Jewish institutions in Poland. That a curriculum covering history, literature, and Jewish culture was systematically developed for special courses and camps, as reported by Akiva Kohane, suggests that this was the case. Certainly the fact that the JDC was responsible for financing educational institutions would have had an influence on the inclusion of certain elements in the curriculum. Without the JDC's support after the war, there would have been no aid centres or Zionist educational organizations. Similarly, without aid from the JDC, there would probably have been no religious schools run by congregations, as they received no funding from the state, the CKŻP, or the TSKŻ.

The JDC also played an important indirect role in educational development. The committee helped to set up and subsidize Jewish manufacturing co-operatives. Thanks to its influence, high-quality machinery and raw materials unavailable in Poland were brought in, and consequently Jewish co-operatives were extremely competitive and brought in high profits. The co-operatives usually gave 10 to 20 per cent of their income to the CKŻP, and these revenues were used to expand educational and cultural activities.

In the first few years after the war the JDC had an enormous influence on the Jewish community, including in education and the upbringing of children according to Jewish tradition and in a spirit of *yidishkeyt*. In the following decades the JDC's work was equally important; however, due to the political conditions, it had limited access to Polish Jewry and those who were responsible for distributing its funds. Because of the paucity of records in Poland it is impossible to describe fully the impact of the JDC after 1949, although the lack of information can partly be corrected through examination of the JDC's own archives. It is also clear that the JDC's representatives, particularly Akiva Kohane, made a tremendous impression on Jewish cultural, intellectual, and educational life in communist Poland.

PART II

New Views

PART II

Everyday Life and the Shtetl
A Historiography

JEFFREY VEIDLINGER

THE IDEA of the shtetl has become so romanticized in the Jewish imagination of today that it is difficult to separate fact from fiction. The shtetl first emerged as a popular setting for fiction in the late nineteenth century, at a time when romantics and populists throughout Europe were valorizing the peasantry and common folk for their alleged purity and for sustaining the national values that were supposedly being corrupted in the urban metropolis, while enlightened reformers used the simple folk as a foil to demonstrate where the nation had gone wrong. Jewish writers had few Jewish peasants and farmers to lionize or satirize and so turned instead to the small-town folk, the shtetl Jews, as an archetype.

It was in the small town that 'common folk' were imagined to lead 'everyday lives', whereas in the city everything was 'extraordinary'. While extraordinary events did occur in small towns, and Jewish luminaries did live in small towns (albeit usually only before leaving for the city), studies of the shtetl have tended to focus on the routine rather than the exceptional and on ordinary folks rather than luminaries. Whether from an economic, social, or cultural perspective, the study of the shtetl is often about what Fernand Braudel termed the 'realm of the routine'.[1] Although the study of everyday life is often associated with the Annales school in France or Robert Lynd and Helen Lynd's 1929 study of 'Middletown' in America,[2] in the Russian context its origins can also be seen in the type of ethnographic work done in the provinces in the late nineteenth century. In the aftermath of the Great Reforms of the 1860s, scholars and writers across Russia became fascinated with provincial life: some in order to learn about the environment they were seeking to change; others in order to preserve and record a lifestyle that they believed was about to disappear.[3] The turn to the shtetl coincided with the mid-nineteenth-century Russian literary emphasis on the provinces and daily life, epitomized by Mikhail Saltykov-Shchedrin's 'Provincial Sketches'.[4]

---

[1] F. Braudel, *Civilisation matérielle, économie et capitalisme, XVe–XVIIIe siècle* (Paris, 1993).

[2] R. Lynd, *Middletown: A Study in American Culture* (New York, 1956).

[3] C. Evtuhov, *Portrait of a Russian Province: Economy, Society and Civilisation in Nineteenth-Century Nizhnii Novgorod* (Pittsburgh, Pa., 2011).

[4] M. Saltykov-Shchedrin, 'Provincial Sketches', *Russkii vestnik*, 1856–7.

The shtetl as a concept and as a source of Jewish life owes much of its popularity today to its role in fiction. Small-town Jews figured largely in the stories of Israel Aksenfeld, Sholem Aleichem (Shalom Rabinovitz), Mendele Moykher Sforim (Sholem Yankev Abramovitsh), S. Y. Agnon, and Y. L. Peretz, and the fictional shtetls of Kasrilevke, Kabtsansk, and Tuneyadevke entered the geography of the Jewish world, along with the existing but highly fictionalized town of Chelm. 'Anyone who is familiar with our Russian Poland knows what a little shtetl is', wrote Aksenfeld. 'A little shtetl consists of several small houses. Every second Sunday there is a fair, and the Jews trade in liquor, grain, cloth, and tar.'[5] Russian Jewish writers, as well, wrote of the shtetl: N. Naumov-Kogan's 'In a Remote Shtetl', for instance, appeared in the 'thick' journal *Vestnik Evropy* in 1892 and told of an assimilated Jewish student who returns to his native town as a teacher.[6] In these stories, the shtetl is filled with well-meaning but naïve folk, whose simple charm and old ways challenge the modern readership to reflect on the nature of progress.

At the same time, the shtetl (*mestechko* in Russian; *miasteczko* in Polish) was beginning to enter the vocabulary of non-Jewish Russian and Polish writers as a Jewish space. Vladimir Korolenko wrote of the '*mestechko* in which we lived' with its 'Jewish businesses (*gesheftn*)' in *In Bad Company*, and Gogol set *The Fair at Sorochyntsi* in a *mestechko*, where Jews and Gypsies intermingled with Ukrainians.[7] But the shtetl was not only a literary invention, it was also a reality of life for millions of Jews, a fact recognized by historians, demographers, sociologists, and ethnographers for generations.

The first historians to write about the Jews of eastern Europe from the Wissenschaft des Judentums school did not view the shtetl as a category of analysis. In the relatively little space Heinrich Graetz gave Russia and Poland in his *History of the Jews*,[8] he wrote about governmental policy towards the Jews and Jewish intellectual greats of the era—most of whom, even if born and bred in a shtetl, achieved their fame in a city—but little about the daily social, cultural, or economic life of ordinary Jews in eastern Europe. The shtetl was also not a source of interest for the earliest historians of Russian Jewry writing from within the Russian empire. They tended to shy away from the small-town Jews of the western provinces and instead looked to the Jews of Central Asia and the Crimea in an effort to prove the existence of Jewish settlement in Russia since antiquity. The Karaite scholar Avraam Firkovich, for instance, wrote about the Karaites of the

[5] Y. Aksenfeld, *Dos Shterntikhl* (Moscow, 1938), 51.

[6] N. Naumov-Kogan, 'V glukhom mestechke', *Vestnik Evropy*, 6 (1892), 36–92.

[7] V. Korolenko, *V durnom obshchestve* (Moscow, 1894), 3; N. V. Gogol, *Sorochinskaya yarmarka* (Moscow, 1947); see A. Glaser, *Jews and Ukrainians in Russia's Literary Borderlands: From the Shtetl Fair to the Petersburg Bookshop* (Evanston, Ill., 2012).

[8] H. Graetz, *Geschichte der Juden von den ältesten Zeiten bis auf die Gegenwart*, 11 vols. (Leipzig, 1853–75).

Crimea, who he argued were descended from Jewish migrants who had arrived before the Christian era.[9] His opponent Avraham Harkavy, who demonstrated that Firkovich's documents were fabricated, also wrote primarily about the Khazars and the Karaites rather than the Jews of the shtetl.[10] He too sought to demonstrate the antiquity of Jewish settlement in the lands of Russia, even arguing that Jews in Russia had spoken Slavic dialects prior to the German migrations of the seventeenth century, a position eventually refuted by Simon Dubnow.[11] The realities of contemporary Jewish life in the Pale of Settlement, and particularly the small towns of the Pale, were of little concern to these early historians of Russian Jewry.

The only major scholar of Russian Jewry who did write about everyday life in small towns was Sergei Bershadsky, a Russian Orthodox historian who collected thousands of archival documents dealing with Jewish life in Lithuania. Although his analytical focus was on the relations between Jews and the state and he did not know the Jewish languages, some of the documents he collected shed important light on the everyday activities of small-town Jews in the early modern period.[12]

It was actually not professional historians but the maskilim who first addressed the shtetl, but then only as a foil to represent the 'traditional' Jewish life they hoped to reform. They tended to regard small-town Jewish life, in all its manifestations, as backward and undesirable. They portrayed Jewish education in the shtetl as antiquated, the practice of Jewish religion that dominated there—particularly hasidism—as superstitious, and the occupations that flourished there as harmful. These attitudes came out primarily in their memoirs, which, beginning with Salomon Maimon's autobiography, became one of the primary means by which maskilim expressed themselves. Whether writing in German (Maimon),[13] Hebrew (Moses Leib Lilienblum),[14] Yiddish (Yekhezkel Kotik),[15] or Russian (Abram Paperna),[16] Jewish proponents of the Haskalah portrayed their hometowns as backwater prisons out of which they had managed to free themselves. Despite their polemical tone, these memoirs contain useful ethnographic descriptions of daily life in small towns.

The first scholars to investigate the shtetl as a concept and to question the prejudices that permeated shtetl life were actually legal scholars who were combing through collections of Russian laws and edicts in order to ascertain the true legal

[9] A. Firkovich, *Sefer avnei zikaron* (Vilna, 1872).

[10] A. Harkavy, *Altjüdische Denkmäler aus dem Krim mitgetheilt von Abraham Firkowitsch (1839–1872)* (St Petersburg, 1876).

[11] S. M. Dubnow, 'Razgovornyi yazyk i narodnaya literatura pol'sko-litovskikh evreev v XVI i pervoi polovine XVII veka', *Evreiskaya starina*, 1909, no. 1, pp. 7–40.

[12] S. A. Bershadsky, *Litovskie evrei: Istoriya ikh yuridicheskogo i obshchestvennogo polozheniya v Litve ot Vintovta do Lyublinskoi unii, 1388–1569* (St Petersburg, 1883).

[13] S. Maimon, *Lebensgeschichte* (Berlin, 1792–3); Eng. trans.: *Salomon Maimon: An Autobiography*, trans. J. Clark Murray (Urbana, Ill., 2001).   [14] M. Leib Lilienblum, *Ḥatot ne'urim* (Tel Aviv, 1966).

[15] Y. Kotik, *Mayne zikhroynes* (Warsaw, 1913); Eng. trans.: *Journey to a Nineteenth-Century Shtetl: The Memoirs of Yekhezkel Kotik*, ed. and trans. D. Assaf (Detroit, 2008).

[16] A. I. Paperna, 'Iz nikolaevskoi epokhi', in id., *Perezhitoe*, 4 vols. (1908–13), ii. 1–53.

situation of Russia's Jewish population. In the absence of any legal guide-book, Jews and local officials were often unsure of what laws applied to Jews and what edicts had been issued in reference to Jews. This situation created constant confusion and made any Jewish dealings with the law deeply problematic. The most important of these publications were those by Ilya Orshansky and Mikhail Mysh.[17] Mysh, in particular, played an important role in pointing out the problems the state had in defining a shtetl.[18]

The definition of a shtetl had become a crucial matter when the May Laws of 1882 prohibited Jews from residing in villages but did allow them to reside in shtetls. Thus, whether a settlement was classified as a shtetl or a village was the difference between staying or losing one's home. Mysh noted that the law had 'not made a distinction between shtetls either according to their social structure or according to their origin'.[19] The Russian senate subsequently changed its view on several occasions about what constituted a shtetl. The senate, Mysh demonstrated, was bombarded by requests from provincial officials to decide whether individual towns should be classified as shtetls or merely as settlements. As a guide, the senate suggested using the Ministry of Internal Affairs' collection, *Urban Settlements in the Russian Empire*,[20] but also showed itself willing to ignore it in cases where it could be shown that the population of a 'shtetl' was entirely rural. This established the principle that one official recognition of a settlement as a shtetl was insufficient to determine the legal right of Jewish residency there.[21] Mysh's chapter on the limitations of Jewish settlement in the Pale of Settlement was designed as a legal handbook, but it also constituted one of the first historical studies of the shtetl as a distinct entity.

Other scholars focused their attention on the *kahal*s, the Jewish governing boards that functioned in most towns. Indeed, until the official abolition of the *kahal* in 1844, they were the official administrative units of most shtetls. In their emphasis on the *kahal*, though, these scholars were primarily studying the political structure of the shtetl rather than its social, economic, or cultural life. Simon Dubnow, in particular, romanticized the *kahal*, seeing it during its sixteenth-century heyday as the lynchpin of what he called a 'firmly knit organization of communal self-government' that helped foster 'a spirit of discipline and obedience to the law' and 'provided the stateless nation with a substitute for national and political self-expression, keeping public spirit and civic virtue alive in it, and up-

---

[17] I. G. Orshansky, *Russkoe zakonodatel'stvo o evreyakh: Ocherki i issledovaniya* (St Petersburg, 1877); M. Mysh, *Rukovodstvo k russkim zakonam o evreyakh* (St Petersburg, 1914).

[18] On the origins of Russian Jewish historiography and the law, see B. Nathans, 'On Russian-Jewish Historiography', in T. Sanders (ed.), *Historiography of Imperial Russia: The Profession and Writing of History in a Multinational State* (Armonk, NY, 1999), 397–432.

[19] Mysh, *Rukovodstvo k russkim zakonam o evreyakh*, 121.

[20] Ministerstvo vnutrennikh del, *Gorodskie poseleniya v Rossiiskoi imperii*, 7 vols. (St Petersburg, 1860–5).   [21] Ibid. 122–3.

holding and unfolding its genuine culture'.[22] In the period of enlightened absolut-ism, Dubnow continued, the authority of the *kahal* declined, eventually becoming restricted to fiscal and spiritual matters. Despite his inclinations to popularize Jewish history and write the history of the common Jew, Dubnow's analysis of the role of the *kahal* remains a political one that does little to shed light on the lives of ordinary small-town folk.

But Dubnow was adamant in his desire to collect and study the documents that would shed light on everyday life. In his 1891 booklet *On the Study of Russian Jewry* he urged the collection and study of communal minute books, such as those of the *kahal* and the burial society, as well as popular folk sayings and stories and gravestone etchings, all of which, he wrote, would reveal what he called the 'folk customs' (*narodnye obychai*) of the Jews in the cities and shtetls of the Pale of Settlement. 'We ought to hurry to collect information about all these old local customs that are so important for our history', he wrote.[23]

It was not until the early twentieth century that a critical mass of such infor-mation had been collected and became available to scholars to allow for detailed studies of the shtetl. These studies were made possible, in large part, by a growing number of statistical data collected by organizations such as the Jewish Coloniz-ation Association and the Society for the Promotion of Enlightenment among the Jews of Russia (Obshchestvo dlya rasprostraneniya prosveshcheniya mezhdu evreyami v Rossii; OPE). Most importantly, the 1897 census, the first all-Russian census ever conducted, facilitated the study of the economic and social life of Jews in small towns. Soon thereafter, the establishment of the Jewish Historical Ethno-graphic Society (Evreiskoe istoriko–etnograficheskoe obshchestvo) in 1908 and the foundation of its scholarly journal, *Evreiskaya starina*, the following year provided a forum for professional work in the field of history.

On the basis of the 1897 census and scattered local census data, economists such as Boris Brutskus argued that Jews had no racial aversion to agrarian pursuits, but rather were encouraged by the structure of the local economy to gravitate towards specialized trades in small towns instead of rural colonization.[24] Arthur Ruppin's Berlin-based journal, *Zeitschrift für Demographie und Statistik der Juden*, estab-lished in 1905, also included some of the first data-based demographic studies of the Jewish community in the Pale of Settlement, making extensive use of the 1897 census materials.[25]

Between 1899 and 1913 the St Petersburg OPE published a collection of his-torical documents, *Registers and Inscriptions: Collection of Materials for the Jews of*

---

[22] S. M. Dubnow, *History of the Jews in Russia and Poland from the Earliest Times until the Present Day*, trans. I. Friedlander, 3 vols. (Philadelphia, 1920), i. 113.

[23] S. M. Dubnow, *Ob izuchenii istorii russkikh evreev i ob uchrezhdenii russko-evreiskogo istoricheskogo obshchestva* (St Petersburg, 1891), 15.

[24] B. Brutskus, *Professional'nyi sostav evreiskogo naseleniya Rossii* (St Petersburg, 1908).

[25] See esp. A. Ruppin, 'Die russischen Juden nach der Volkzählung von 1897', *Zeitschrift für Demographie und Statistik der Juden*, 1906, no. 1, pp. 1–6; no. 2, pp. 17–22; no. 3, pp. 39–45.

Russia (80–1800),[26] which included 1,111 documents from 212 sources, including travel accounts, diaries, and legal edicts, all of which could serve as the basis for
more in-depth investigations into the history of the Jews of the Polish–Lithuanian
Commonwealth in general and their daily life in particular. In an extended essay
based on materials from the volume, Mikhail Kulisher wrote about the integral
role that Jews played in the economic development of Poland from the sixteenth to
the eighteenth century, focusing on small-town economics. He showed that Jews
dominated, and in certain regions monopolized, petty trade and played an important role in larger international trade as well. Jews were important industrialists
and producers in small towns, contributing greatly to the wealth of Polish urban
centres. Jews, he showed, also engaged in handicrafts, particularly as tailors, jewel-
lers, furriers, cobblers, hat-makers, and metalworkers.[27]

Rather than just shun small-town Jewish life as the maskilim had done, a new
generation of scholars, informed by the Wissenschaft des Judentums tradition,
began to investigate the historical reasons why Jews tended to remain in small
towns. Again the publication of collections of source materials made possible by
intellectual interest in provincial life facilitated detailed studies. K. Korobkov
wrote an economic history of the Jews based on the *Archive of South-Western Russia*,
a collection of archival materials that the Temporary Commission to Investigate
Historical Decrees had been publishing since 1859.[28] Korobkov agreed that the
Jewish economic role in small towns was a major contributor to antisemitism, but
he showed that late eighteenth-century governmental measures to entice Jews into
farming were ineffective because of countervailing governmental measures that
made a change of residency difficult: the *kahal*, for instance, had to testify that all
taxes had been paid in order for an individual to enrol in a different *kehilah*.[29]
Ignacy Schipper was interested in demonstrating that the shtetl and its economy
had not always been the primary form of Jewish existence in Poland. In his 'Agricultural Colonization of the Jews in Poland', he argued that early Jewish settlements in Poland were often agricultural in nature, basing his arguments on the
names of various Polish villages.[30] Similarly, in an article on Jewish credit in Poland
in the fourteenth century, Schipper used court documents to argue that Jews were
engaged in landholding in the early modern Polish–Lithuanian Commonwealth.[31]

In addition to these large-scale assessments of the economic and social standing of Jews in the Russian empire, another movement, influenced by a parallel de-

---

[26] Obshchestvo dlya rasprostraneniya prosveshcheniya mezhdu evreyami v Rossii, *Regesty i nadpisi: svod materialov dlya istorii evreev v Rossii (80g–1800g)*, 3 vols. (St Petersburg, 1899–1913).

[27] M. Kulisher, 'Pol'sha s evreyam i Rus' bez evreev', *Evreiskaya starina*, 1910, no. 2, pp. 214–34.

[28] Vremennaya komissiya dlya razbora drevnikh aktov, *Arkhiv Yugo-zapadnoi Rossii*, 37 vols. (Kiev, 1859–1914).

[29] K. Korobkov, 'Ekonomicheskaya rol' evreev v kontse XVIII v.', *Evreiskaya starina*, 1910, no. 3, pp. 346–77.

[30] I. Schipper, 'Agrakolonisation der Juden in Polen', in *Jüdische fragen* (Vienna, n.d.), 64–78).

[31] I. Schipper, 'Evreiskii kredit v Pol'she v XIV v.', *Evreiskaya starina*, 1910, no. 4, pp. 542–68.

velopment in Russian historiography, began to study provincial life at a local level, facilitated by the late nineteenth-century interest in statistics and data. Many of the practitioners of local studies were intellectuals sent to the provinces in conjunction with the *zemstvo*s, the local self-governing boards established by the Great Reforms of the 1860s. Teachers, lawyers, land surveyors, doctors, statisticians, and other professionals were dispatched to the provinces. Some of them took it upon themselves to study the regions in which they were working, publishing statistical and ethnographic materials about provincial life.[32] Although *zemstvo*s were not established in most of the western provinces that constituted the Pale of Settlement, a parallel process took place there, as Jewish and non-Jewish researchers turned their attention to daily life in provincial small towns.

In 1909 Lazar Rokhlin, who spent two years working as a doctor and communal rabbi in Krasnopole, published a study of the town under the title *The Shtetl of Krasnopole: An Attempt at a Statistical-Economic Sketch of a Typical Shtetl in the Pale of Jewish Settlement*. Rokhlin was probably the first to portray his study of one individual shtetl as typical of shtetl life as a whole, a claim that—with appropriate caveats—was probably fairly accurate. His work begins with the disclaimer:

The current investigation concerns only one shtetl in the Pale of Settlement. But, as can be seen from the following account, this shtetl is not distinguished by any type of exclusive peculiarity in its economic condition. The economic life of its population developed under the influence of the same factors that operate in the life of the Jewish shtetl population in the great part of the territory of the Pale of Settlement. Therefore, the economic and daily life that the author establishes in this shtetl, can be considered typical, if not for all the settlements of this type, than at least for the majority of shtetls in the north-western regions.[33]

Like many of the amateur enthusiasts who published local histories, Rokhlin combined his own observations with the growing amount of statistical data at his disposal. Most importantly, Rokhlin used the 1897 census data and combined it with data collected by the Jewish Colonization Association in order to provide an in-depth socio-economic structure of the shtetl, full of charts and figures on topics related to education and literacy, handicrafts, philanthropy, emigration, property, and other aspects of shtetl life. The book is richly documented and stands as a valuable work of local research.

In 1912 the Jewish Historical Ethnographic Society initiated a new section in its flagship journal, 'Episodes from the Life of the Jews'. This section would come to include materials relating to daily life, such as personal letters from the past and extracts from diaries and memoirs. Oral history and ethnography played an important part in the journal's attempts to illustrate the everyday life of Russian and Polish Jews. One of the chief proponents of this approach was S. An-sky (Shloyme Zaynvl Rapoport), whose ethnographic expeditions to the shtetls of Podolia and

[32] See Evtuhov, *Portrait of a Russian Province*.
[33] L. Rokhlin, *Mestechko Krasnopol'e Mogilevskoi gubernii: Opyt statistiko-ekonomicheskogo opisaniya tipichnogo mestechka cherty evreiskoi osedlosti* (St Petersburg, 1909), 1.

Volhynia between 1912 and 1914 represent a major turning point in the study of the shtetl. An-sky played an important role in reorienting Jewish historiography away from economics towards cultural studies and in reorienting Jewish ethnographic work away from racial anthropology towards what we would term today 'cultural anthropology'.[34] An-sky's emphasis on culture in many ways presaged the 'cultural turn' in history that would take place nearly a century later.

By fusing together history and ethnography, the Jewish Historical Ethnographic Society set a precedent that would remain relevant for years to come. History was regarded as part of ethnography. In the words of Lev Shternberg, the renowned ethnographer who would succeed Dubnow as director of the society, 'an ethnographer is also a historian. The sole difference is that historians study more or less the distant past, whereas ethnographers study the recent past and the present, both of which will become subjects of history in the future.'[35]

After the Bolshevik revolution, Shternberg was instrumental in continuing An-sky's tradition of Jewish ethnography. At the same time, he helped reorient shtetl studies away from the romanticized salvage ethnography that An-sky pioneered towards what he called 'a new ethnography of the present'.[36] The next generation of Soviet scholars would focus less on preserving old traditions and more on examining the impact of change in the shtetl. In the 1920s and 1930s, Soviet scholarship revived interest in the shtetl, particularly its economic aspects. Soviet statisticians associated with the Society for Trades and Agricultural Labour (Obshchestvo remeslennogo i zemledel'cheskogo truda; ORT) began collecting data on selected shtetls in an effort to guide small-town Jews towards agricultural and industrial pursuits.[37] The most important such collection was probably Vladimir Bogoraz-Tan's *Jewish Shtetl in Revolution*, a collection of articles written by student ethnographers based on their expeditions to various shtetls. In this collection, the shtetl was portrayed as a bygone phenomenon—plagued by parasitism and violence—whose salvation lay in the ongoing processes of Soviet modernization and industrialization.[38]

The theme of supersessionism—that Soviet modes of industrialization and labour organization were superseding Jewish ways of life—was repeated in numerous other Soviet works. The party official Motl Kiper, for instance, published one of the most detailed demographic and historical studies of the Soviet shtetl in 1929, and the following year Ilya Veitsblit published his study of the old and new

---

[34] See G. Safran, *Wandering Soul: The Dybbuk's Creator, S. An-sky* (Cambridge, Mass., 2010); G. Safran et al., *The Worlds of S. An-sky* (Stanford, Calif., 2006); N. Deutsch *The Jewish Dark Continent: Life and Death in the Russian Pale of Settlement* (Cambridge, Mass., 2011).

[35] L. Shternberg, 'Problemy evreiskoi etnografii', *Evreiskaya starina*, 1928, no. 12, pp. 12–13.

[36] Ibid.

[37] See *Materialy po demografii i ekonomicheskomu polozheniyu evreiskogo naseleniya SSSR*; I. Osherevich (ed.), *Di shtetlekh fun VSSR in rekonstruktivn period* (Minsk, 1932).

[38] V. G. Bogoraz-Tan (ed.), *Evreiskoe mestechko v revolyutsii: Ocherki* (Leningrad, 1926), 8; see also D. Yalen, 'Documenting the New Red Kasrilevke', *East European Jewish Affairs*, 37/3 (2007), 353–75.

shtetl, both of which followed the supersessionist narrative.[39] Lev Zinger's *The Renewed People*, published on the eve of the Second World War, also contained relevant information on the shtetl, and again celebrated its decline in favour of industrial settlements: 'The old shtetl with its *ḥeder*, with the *besmedresh* as the "communal centre" of the Jewish population has been left in the past', he crooned. 'Today's shtetl is truly an advanced cultural-economic settlement.'[40] The same themes can be discerned in Y. Yakhinson's sourcebook on the social and economic history of Jews in Russia, which presents a variety of primary source material on Jewish daily life in small towns.[41]

In Poland, professional historians tended to shy away from the study of ordinary folk in small towns, with most studies focusing on the grand cultural achievements of the Jews of Warsaw, Lublin, Łódź, and other large urban centres. One notable exception was Isaiah Trunk's work on Plotsk.[42] But amateur *zamlers*—who collected local materials—and those who engaged in *landkentenish*—informed tourism of the countryside—produced many useful investigations into their own local history.[43] The best of these were conducted under the auspices of YIVO, and particularly its Ethnographic Commission. But even the Ethnographic Commission tended towards folklore more than ethnography and history, as signified by its 1930 name change to the Folklore Commission. Some of its publications, though, were oriented towards history, like N. Vaynig's 'Historical Motifs in Yiddish Folksong'.[44] The type of folkloric and philological studies conducted by YIVO in the interwar period can shed important light on the history of daily life in the shtetl.[45] Polish scholarship on Jewish daily life, though, was forestalled by the onset of the Second World War and the Holocaust.

After the war, the shtetls as they had existed before the war were decimated and most small-town communities in eastern Europe completely destroyed. The loss of this mode of Jewish life led to a newfound nostalgia for the shtetl and a desire to preserve the memory of these small towns and their former inhabitants. The

---

[39] M. Kiper, *Dos yidishe shtetl in ukrayne* (Kharkov, 1929); I. Veitsblit, *Vegn altn un nayem shtetl* (Moscow, 1930).

[40] L. Zinger, *Dos banayte folk (tsifern un faktn vegn di yidn in FSSR)* (Moscow, 1941), 119.

[41] Y. Yakhinson, *Sotsyal-ekonomisher shteyger ba yidn in rusland in XIX y'h* (Kharkov, 1929). On Soviet conceptions of the shtetl, see D. Yalen, 'Red Kasrilevke: Ethnographies of Economic Transformation in the Soviet Shtetl: 1917–1939', Ph.D. thesis (University of California, 2007).

[42] I. Trunk, *Di geshikhte fun yidn in plotsk, 1237–1567* (Warsaw, 1939).

[43] On *zamlers*, see I. Gottesman, *Defining the Yiddish Nation* (Detroit, 2003); on the *landkentenish* movement, see D. G. Roskies, 'Landkentenish: Yiddish Belles Lettres in the Warsaw Ghetto', in R. M. Shapiro (ed.), *Holocaust Chronicles: Individualizing the Holocaust through Diaries and Other Contemporaneous Personal Accounts* (Hoboken, NJ, 1998), 11–30; S. Kassow, 'Travel and Local History as a National Mission: Polish Jews and the Landkentenish Movement in the 1920s and 1930s', in J. Brauch, A. Lipphardt, and A. Nocke, *Jewish Topographies: Visions of Space, Traditions of Place* (Aldershot, Hants., 2008), 241–64.

[44] N. Vaynig, 'Historishe motivn in yidishn folkslid', *Fun noentn over*, 2 (1939), 79–83.

[45] See also Gottesman, *Defining the Yiddish Nation*.

immediate aftermath of the war saw an enormous proliferation of *yizker bikher* (memorial books), a genre that includes a wide range of texts that memorialize individual towns or regions. Many were published and written by ad hoc committees of former residents and survivors and distributed free or by subscription through personal networks to others with connections to the town. Typically, these books included short pieces on the various political, philanthropic, cultural, and social organizations and clubs that had existed in the town, usually written by former members; biographical sketches of famous people and rabbis; brief descriptions of major communal buildings; personal reminiscences; and a history of the town, sometimes written on the basis of communal memory and sometimes after consultation with primary sources. The books also almost always included a martyrology, listing the names of those murdered during the war.[46] A similar genre of single-authored works by survivors or former residents of individual towns with the purpose of memorializing their hometown through local history and personal reminiscences appeared at the same time. The best of them represent disciplined scholarship and are often colourfully written; many others have the literary quality of a high-school yearbook or quarterly report. But even the latter have historical value.[47]

Other scholars continued to conduct extensive research on the history of Polish and Russian Jewry on the basis of census data, which provided insights into the daily life of small-town Jews. In Poland, Raphael Mahler examined Jewish economic history, including some analysis of small-town life in the early modern period,[48] and, in Israel, Jacob Lestchinsky studied the demographic history of Soviet Jewry in great detail.[49]

Mark Zborowski and Elizabeth Herzog's 1952 publication of *Life Is with People* represented a major turning point in the way Americans thought about the shtetl. The book was produced in conjunction with the Columbia University Research in Contemporary Cultures Project headed by Margaret Mead and Ruth Benedict.[50]

---

[46] The New York Public Library has digitized many *yizker bikher*, which can be viewed online at <https://www.nypl.org/collections/nypl-recommendations/guides/yizkorbooks#books> (accessed 1 Feb. 2017); see also Z. Baker, 'Appendix I: Bibliography of Eastern European (Yizkor) Memorial Books', in *From a Ruined Garden: The Memorial Books of Polish Jewry*, ed. and trans. J. Kugelmass and J. Boyarin (New York, 1983), 273–340.

[47] For some examples, see P. Granatshteyn, *Mayn horev shtetl sokolov: shilderungen, bilder un portretn fun a shtot umgekumene yidn* (Buenos Aires, 1946); V. Tshernovetski, *Teplik, mayn shtetele: kapitaln fun fuftsik yor lebn* (Buenos Aires, 1946–50); M. Kuper, *Di yidn fun mayn benkshaft: zikhroynes fun mayn heymshtot sharhorod* (Buenos Aires, 1968).

[48] R. Mahler, *Yidn in amolikn poyln in likht fun tsifern* (Warsaw, 1958); see also B. Mark, *Di geshikhte fun yidn in poyln* (Warsaw, 1958).

[49] J. Lestchinsky, *Dos sovetishe yidntum: zayn fargangenhayt un kegnvart* (New York, 1941).

[50] On the fascinating story of Zborowski and his involvement with the Research in Contemporary Cultures Project, see S. J. Zipperstein, 'Underground Man: The Curious Case of Mark Zborowski and the Writing of a Modern Jewish Classic', *Jewish Review of Books*, 2 (Summer 2010), available at <https://jewishreviewofbooks.com/articles/275/underground-man-the-curious-case-of-mark-zborowski-and-the-writing-of-a-modern-jewish-classic/> (accessed 1 Feb. 2017).

Zborowski and Herzog imagined a lost home in the midst of the Diaspora. 'The small-town Jewish community of Eastern Europe—the *shtetl*—traces its line of march directly back to Creation', they wrote in the prologue to the book, before speaking of 'the road from Mount Sinai to the *shtetl*'.[51] The book was immediately panned by some critics: 'Such a synthetic shtetl is not only bad anthropology; it is also poor fiction', wrote the *Jewish Frontier*, before going on to compare the work unfavourably with *Middletown*: 'There everything was concrete; here one wallows in uncertainties.'[52] Zborowski and Herzog often confused fact and fantasy, litera-ture and social science. Notably, Zborowski had published some of his findings about the Jewish family in the journal *Psychiatry*, which tested his 'hypotheses' not only against the Research in Contemporary Cultures data but also 'against facts in literature, against our own scattered interviews, and against Eastern European Jewish films'. Footnotes and references overwhelmingly led the reader to rabbinic codes, or to sayings, proverbs, and fiction, as though these were true reflections of lived life.[53]

This romanticized version of the shtetl was largely a post-war invention, a nostalgic attempt to recreate and reimagine a life that was perceived to be no longer accessible. Steven Zipperstein wrote of the expansion of American interest in eastern Europe in the 1950s as a result of the 'greater distance separating Amer-ican Jews from Eastern Europe, which encouraged, among other responses, a heightened sentimentality' in the aftermath of the Holocaust.[54] Similarly, Jeffrey Shandler noted that 'postwar attraction to the shtetl paradigm suggests a desire for a vestigial, premodern model of East European Jewish life that is both integral and intimate in scale'.[55]

It was during this period that the shtetl became a metonym for Jewish life in eastern Europe and was imagined as a wholly Jewish space. Maurice Samuel, who did much to bring the idea of the shtetl to American audiences, wrote in 1963 of the shtetl as an 'impregnable citadel of Jewishness'.[56] In one of the first academic articles published on the shtetl as a sociological phenomenon, Natalie Joffe referred to it as 'a culture island'.[57] To Elie Wiesel, the shtetl (always spelled in his writings with a capital 'S') is a 'small colorful Jewish kingdom so rich in memories'.[58] In Wiesel's imagination, 'no matter where it is located on the map, the Shtetl has few geographical frontiers. . . . In its broad outlines, the Shtetl is one

---

[51] M. Zborowski and E. Herzog, *Life is with People: The Culture of the Shtetl*, 5th rev. edn. (New York, 1995), 29. [52] *Jewish Frontier*, 19 (27 June 1952).
[53] R. Landes and M. Zborowski, 'Hypotheses concerning the Eastern European Jewish Family', *Psychiatry*, 13 (1950), 447–64.
[54] S. Zipperstein, *Imagining Russian Jewry: Memory, History, Identity* (Seattle, 1999), 29.
[55] J. Shandler, *Shtetl: A Vernacular Intellectual History* (New Brunswick, NJ, 2014), 73.
[56] M. Samuel, *Little did I Know: Recollections and Reflections* (New York, 1963), 137–8.
[57] N. F. Joffe, 'The Dynamics of Benefice Among East European Jews', *Social Forces*, 27 (1949), 238.
[58] E. Wiesel, 'The World of the Shtetl', in S. T. Katz (ed.), *The Shtetl: New Evaluations* (New York, 2007), 290.

and the same everywhere.'[59] It had become customary to write about the shtetl as an ur-space located outside any particular time or place.

Although these sentimental images of the shtetl persisted in literature and popular memory, new scholarly works by professional historians with training in both Polish and Jewish history started to provide detailed studies of individual towns in the late Polish–Lithuanian Commonwealth. The works of Gershon Hundert and Murray Rosman are exemplary in this regard: both used Polish archival materials to present case studies of specific communities in order to analyse Jewish–magnate relations, in Rosman's case, or Jewish communal structures in Hundert's.[60] By focusing on the turbulent eighteenth century, when hasidism threatened rabbinic oligarchies and the Polish state itself was crumbling, these works challenged the notion of the shtetl as an unchanging island of Jewish life. Yohanan Petrovsky-Shtern's more recent *The Golden Age Shtetl* challenges the perception of the shtetl as perpetually in decline by looking at the vibrancy of life in the late eighteenth- and early nineteenth-century small market town.[61]

Rosman's and Hundert's works were both written on the eve of the collapse of communism in eastern Europe. The beginning of a new world order in eastern Europe helped facilitate a new round of interest in the shtetl. As Hillel Halkin noted, this interest came about as the children of east European immigrants started to become interested in their parents' early lives, when travel to eastern Europe became possible, and as 'proponents of a new Diasporism' looked to the shtetl as a source of Jewish cultural revival.[62] These tendencies produced what Halkin termed a new genre of literature, the 'shtetlogue'. Theo Richmond, Eva Hoffman, Yaffa Eliach, Shimon Redlich, and others wrote well-researched books about their ancestral homes, modelled on the *yizker bikher* of the previous generation but informed with more rigorous scholarly traditions.[63] In this connection, Mayer Kirshenblatt and Barbara Kirshenblatt-Gimblett's excellent *They Called Me Mayer July*, which uses paintings and narratives to evoke the history of Mayer's native shtetl, is also noteworthy.[64]

Still another genre of historical work on the shtetl takes the form of micro-

[59] Wiesel, 'The World of the Shtetl', 293.

[60] M. J. Rosman, *The Lords' Jews: Magnate–Jewish Relations in the Polish–Lithuanian Commonwealth during the Eighteenth Century* (Cambridge, Mass., 1990); G. D. Hundert, *The Jews in a Polish Private Town: The Case of Opatów in the Eighteenth Century* (Baltimore, 1992).

[61] Y. Petrovsky-Shtern, *The Golden Age Shtetl: A New History of Jewish Life in East Europe* (Princeton, NJ, 2014).

[62] H. Halkin, 'The Road to Naybikhov', *Commentary* (1 Nov. 1998), <https://www.commentary-magazine.com/articles/the-road-to-naybikhov/> (accessed 19 Jan. 2017).

[63] T. Richmond, *Konin: A Quest* (London, 1995); E. Hoffman, *Shtetl: The Life and Death of a Small Town and the World of Polish Jews* (Boston, 1997); Y. Eliach, *There Once was a World: A 900-Year Chronicle of the Shtetl of Eishyshok* (Boston, 1998); S. Redlich, *Together and Apart in Brzezany: Poles, Jews, and Ukrainians 1919–1945* (Bloomington, Ind., 2002).

[64] M. Kirshenblatt and B. Kirshenblatt-Gimblett, *They Called Me Mayer July: Painted Memories of a Jewish Childhood in Poland before the Holocaust* (Berkeley, Calif., 2007).

histories of individual communities, many of which complicate our understanding of the relationships between Jews and Christians. Rose Lehmann seeks to deal with 'ordinary people and not with the public discourse' in her study of 'Poles and Jews in a small Galician town'.[65] In his 2009 *Death of the Shtetl*, Yehuda Bauer seeks to understand 'how Jews lived before they were murdered, what their reactions were in the face of the sudden, unexpected, and, for them, inexplicable assault on their lives by a power whose policies they did not and could not understand'.[66] Jan Gross's highly influential study of Jedwabne, where, as he put it, 'one day, in July 1941, half of the population of a small East European town murdered the other half', has also spawned an extensive debate about the relations between Jews and Christians in Poland.[67]

Three recent collections of English-language essays, edited by Steve T. Katz, Gennady Estraikh and Mikhail Krutikov, and Antony Polonsky, have brought together a variety of perspectives on the shtetl.[68] John Klier's 'What Exactly was a Shtetl?' demonstrates the complexities of defining the shtetl.[69] Samuel Kassow, who has written several key articles on the shtetl, including the entry in the *YIVO Encyclopedia of Jews in Eastern Europe*,[70] defines it as a settlement 'big enough to support the basic network of institutions that was essential to Jewish communal life' and yet small enough to be 'a face-to-face community'.[71] Adam Teller, looking for a definition of the eighteenth-century shtetl, settles upon 'a small settlement of less than 300 houses, which dealt mostly in agricultural produce, and at least 40 per cent of whose total urban population was Jewish'.[72]

Much of the scholarship in these collections has sought to differentiate the historical shtetl from the literary image of the shtetl. Dan Miron wrote of the influential tradition that set up a straw shtetl to 'be satirized, exposed as benighted and reactionary, soporific, resistant to initiative and innovation, or, alternatively, portrayed nostalgically and romantically as the quintessence of spirituality and communal intimacy, the nucleus of a besieged civilization that nevertheless enjoyed internal harmony and perfect internal communication'.[73] The notion of a compact community of Jews, living largely according to their own time-honoured laws, customs, and values, with only occasional—often hostile—relations with the

---

[65] R. Lehmann, *Symbiosis and Ambivalence: Poles and Jews in a Small Galician Town* (New York, 2001), xi.   [66] Y. Bauer, *The Death of the Shtetl* (New Haven, Conn., 2009), 2.

[67] J. T. Gross, *Neighbors: The Destruction of the Jewish Community in Jedwabne* (Princeton, NJ, 2001), 7.

[68] Katz (ed.), *The Shtetl*; G. Estraikh and M. Krutikov (eds.), *The Shtetl: Image and Reality* (Oxford, 2000); A. Polonsky (ed.), *The Shtetl: Myth and Reality* (*Polin*, 17 (2004)).

[69] J. D. Klier, 'What Exactly was a Shtetl?', in Estraikh and Krutikov (eds.), *The Shtetl*, 23–35.

[70] S. Kassow, 'Shtetl', in G. D. Hundert (ed.), *YIVO Encyclopedia of Jews in Eastern Europe*, <http://www.yivoencyclopedia.org/article.aspx/Shtetl> (accessed 19 Jan. 2017).

[71] S. Kassow, 'The Shtetl in Interwar Poland', in Katz (ed.), *The Shtetl*, 125.

[72] A. Teller, 'The Shtetl as an Arena for Integration in the Eighteenth Century', *Polin*, 17 (2004), 39.

[73] D. Miron, *The Image of the Shtetl and Other Studies of Modern Jewish Literary Imagination* (Syracuse, NY, 2000), 4.

outside world, has appealed to fiction writers for generations. Most scholars now recognize that the shtetl has entered public consciousness not as a historical or sociological entity but rather, in Arnold Band's terms, as 'an imagined construct based on literary descriptions'.[74] David Roskies writes that 'the Shtetl, or Jewish market town of Eastern Europe, is arguably the greatest single invention of Yiddish literature'.[75] Israel Bartal agrees, noting that 'the literary image of the shtetl obliterated the historical facts and distorted the geographical maps'.[76]

The shtetl was not always portrayed as an unchanging and pristine homeland, however. Much of the fiction of Sholem Aleichem is precisely about the impact of modernity on the shtetl, and Mendele Moykher Sforim's *Travels of Benjamin III* is also about what happens when new ideas and prospects for adventure infiltrate the town.[77] As Mikhail Krutikov noted, 'it was not until the beginning of the twentieth century that Yiddish literature reinvented the shtetl as a lost paradise and transformed it into a full-scale fantasy of social harmony'.[78] The key text in this transformation was Sholem Asch's *The Shtetl*, which, written on the eve of the 1905 revolution, painted a romantic picture of the shtetl as a peaceful haven.[79] I. M. Weissenberg mocked the distance between Asch's portrait and the reality of the revolutionary era.[80]

Among the chief components alleged to have been missing from the literary shtetl are non-Jews. As Dan Miron pointed out, 'the literary Kasrilevke was depicted as an exclusively Jewish enclave, an unalloyed entity. Of course, it was a tiny Jewish island in a vast non-Jewish sea.'[81] Bartal agrees that the exclusion of non-Jews from the literary landscape of the shtetl eviscerated the 'complex ethnic mosaic' from the historical shtetl.[82] Ben Cion Pinchuk largely concurs, writing that the shtetl 'became in the narrative of the Jewish people one of the more lasting symbols of life in the Diaspora'[83] and that 'the place of the *shtetl* in the dominant Jewish narrative was determined principally by those who left it, and frequently turned the small town into cliché, stereotype, and symbol'.[84]

However, Pinchuk is unwilling to see the shtetl solely as an invented landscape: 'the shtetl was a real Jewish town, not a mythical Jewish world. There was nothing mythical about its portrayal as such in literature and in Jewish cultural and political discourse.'[85] Rather, he points out that in contrast to the perpetual image of the

---

[74] A. J. Band, 'Agnon's Synthetic Shtetl', in Katz (ed.), *The Shtetl*, 234; see also B. C. Pinchuk, 'Jewish Discourse and the Shtetl', *Jewish History*, 15/2 (2001), 169–79.

[75] D. Roskies, *The Jewish Search for a Usable Past* (Bloomington, Ind., 1999), 41.

[76] I. Bartal, 'Imagined Geography: The Shtetl, Myth and Reality', in Katz (ed.), *The Shtetl*, 183.

[77] Mendele Moykher Sforim, *Kitser masoes binyomin hashlishi* (Vilna, 1878).

[78] M. Krutikov, *Yiddish Fiction and the Crisis of Modernity, 1905–1914* (Stanford, Calif., 2001), 26–7.

[79] S. Asch, *A shtetl* (Warsaw, 1928).   [80] I. M. Weissenberg, *A shtetl* (Warsaw, 1911).

[81] Miron, *The Image of the Shtetl*, 3.   [82] Bartal, 'Imagined Geography', 190.

[83] B. C. Pinchuk, 'The East European Shtetl and its Place in Jewish History', *Revue des études juives*, 164/1–2 (Jan.–June 2005), 187.

[84] Ibid. 189.   [85] B. C. Pinchuk, 'How Jewish was the Shtetl?', *Polin*, 17 (2004), 118.

shtetl in decline, the accelerated growth of the Jewish populations in small towns towards the end of the nineteenth century 'stands in stark contrast to the image of a dwindling Jewish shtetl as it has been presented'.[86] Using data from the 1897 census of the Russian empire, Pinchuk identified 462 shtetls with Jewish majorities and 116 in which Jews constituted over 80 per cent of the total population.[87] 'The single most important feature or characteristic of that settlement, the one that made it distinctive and unique', he argues, 'was its being a Jewish town, a Jewish island and enclave, a world of its own. This basic fact, true for hundreds of towns, has to be emphasized, because, while obvious to contemporaries who were familiar with life in the *shtetl*, it was treated as a literary concoction by later generations.'[88] The fact of Jewish majorities in many shtetls was a significant attribute of the town. Gershon Hundert has even questioned whether Jews of eighteenth-century Poland should be considered a minority, since they tended to constitute a majority within their own communities and lived primarily among other Jews.[89] Of course, there was constant interaction between the Jewish community of the shtetl and Christian peasants, as well as Christian officials. In recognition of the complex networks linking Jewish and non-Jewish communities around the shtetl, John Klier has proposed that 'the shtetl might better be envisioned as the centre of an economic-cultural zone, linking Jews to Christians and Jews to Jews'.[90] Indeed, attempts to 'demythologize' the shtetl have been ongoing since at least the early 1980s.[91]

Most work on the shtetl, ever since An-sky's expeditions between 1912 and 1914, regarded it as a remnant of the past. With the Bolshevik revolution it was largely imagined that the shtetl ceased to exist in the Soviet Union, while the Holocaust destroyed the remnants of shtetl life elsewhere in eastern Europe. Some recent scholarship, though, has sought to question the extent to which the shtetl persisted as a space of Jewish life in the Soviet period. Binyomin Lukin, Alla Sokolova, and B. Khaimovich compiled a scholarly travelogue in 2000 that traces the history of many shtetls in the Podolian region based on newly available archival evidence, primarily from local Ukrainian archives.[92] Similarly, the collection of articles on the twenty-first-century shtetl edited by Valery Dymshits and based on the ethnographic expeditions he has been leading to the small towns of eastern Europe over the last decade also attest to both the perseverance of Jewish tradi-tions in small towns and the many ways traditions have changed and continue to change in the twenty-first century.[93] Charles Hoffman's study of Shargorod, while rooted

---

[86] Pinchuk, 'Jewish Discourse and the Shtetl', 177.

[87] Pinchuk, 'The East European Shtetl and its Place in Jewish History', 199. [88] Ibid. 205.

[89] G. D. Hundert, *Jews in Poland–Lithuania in the Eighteenth-Century: A Genealogy of Modernity* (Berkeley, Calif., 2004). [90] Klier, 'What Exactly was a Shtetl?', 26.

[91] See e.g. J. Rothenberg, 'Demythologizing the Shtetl', *Midstream*, Mar. 1981, pp. 25–31.

[92] V. M. Lukin, A. Sokolova, and B. Khaimovich, *100 evreiskikh mestechek Ukrainy: Istoricheskii putevoditel'*, 2nd edn. (St Petersburg, 2000).

[93] V. Dymshits, *Shtetl, XXI vek: Polevye issledovaniya* (St Petersburg, 2008).

in his own personal experiences as a representative for the American Jewish Joint Distribution Committee in the town, also revealed the persistence of shtetl life into the post-war period.[94] A monograph by Arkady Zeltser used extensive primary source materials, including newly available archives, to demonstrate both the continuities and radical changes that Soviet power brought to Vitebsk province, and, using oral histories and written primary source documentation, I have written on similar developments in Vinnytsya province.[95]

It goes without saying that everyday Jewish life in eastern Europe took place in rural villages, big cities, small towns, and everything in between. Historiographically, however, studies of the everyday and of Jewish history from below have tended to focus on small towns, where it was imagined that life was somehow simpler. Two recent books, though, help put this association in perspective: in *Shtetl: A Vernacular Intellectual History*, Jeffrey Shandler looks at how the term 'shtetl' has migrated from everyday 'vernacular' usage to what he terms 'post-vernacularity': '"the shtetl" exemplifies a dynamic relationship with vernacularity', he writes. 'This relationship entails shifts not only in how scholars study the lives of "ordinary" Jews but also in how scholars understand scholarly activity in relation to vernacular practices, past and present.'[96] The documentary collection *Everyday Jewish Life in Imperial Russia*, edited by ChaeRan Y. Freeze and Jay M. Harris, provides the most varied selection of documents on Jewish life in eastern Europe in a century. For Jews living in tsarist Russia, they write, 'the everyday meant interaction with an emerging modernity: the quotidian confronted them with a new world and drove them to seek creative, strategic ways to negotiate their place in it'. In other words, Russian Jewry became 'modern; not only by confrontation with "crisis" but through ordinary life'.[97] Historians should continue to see the shtetl not only as a fountain from which Jewish life emerged only to flow elsewhere but also as an ordinary space in and of itself. Small town life is an important part of the Jewish historical experience in eastern Europe, but the everyday was everywhere.

[94] C. Hoffman, *Red Shtetl: The Survival of a Jewish Town under Soviet Communism* (New York, 2002).

[95] A. Zeltser, *Evrei sovetskoi provintsii: Vitebsk i mestechki 1917–1941* (Moscow, 2006); J. Veidlinger, *In the Shadow of the Shtetl: Small-Town Jewish Life in Soviet Ukraine* (Bloomington, Ind., 2013).

[96] Shandler, *Shtetl*, 138.

[97] C. Y. Freeze and J. M. Harris (eds.), *Everyday Jewish Life in Imperial Russia: Select Documents, 1772–1918* (Waltham, Mass., 2013), p. xvii.

Economic Struggle or Antisemitism?

SZYMON RUDNICKI

IN RECENT times all kinds of 'judaeo-sceptics', as well as some historians, have attempted to prove that there was no antisemitism in Poland before the Second World War; rather, there was simply an economic struggle. This serves to hide the fact that the aim of this struggle was not to 'Polonize' the economy but was against the Jews as such: the economic war was an important aspect, but only an aspect, of a wider phenomenon. While collecting material for this chapter, I came to the conclusion that this apologetic point of view was also upheld by the radical nationalists. *Ruch Młodych*, the paper shaping the political thought of the National Radical Movement (Ruch Narodowo-Radykalny; RNR), included writings about 'antisemitism, and particularly economic antisemitism'.[1] Initially I wanted to focus on the RNR propaganda. It turned out, however, that the entire nationalist press spoke with one voice. The Catholic press was no different in this respect.

There is no doubt that the Endecja (National Democrats) were the leaders in spreading antisemitism in Poland. It became a permanent element of their propaganda, and its intensity grew as the years went by and it became increasingly aggressive.[2] As Stanisław Cat-Mackiewicz wrote, 'when using the word "minorities", the average nationalist was only seeing Jews, only thinking about Jews'.[3] The advantage of the anti-Jewish programme was its concreteness and immediacy. In the process the Endecja exploited the Catholic Church's anti-Judaism, which over the centuries had grown to be a significant element of its culture. In addition, the Polish lands were particularly susceptible to antisemitic slogans because of the large Jewish population and its role in economic life. Antisemitism led the nationalists to perceive reality through the prism of the Jewish question.

Endecja was supported in the spread of antisemitism by the church, which led to an increase in resentment and hostility towards Jews. Father Mateusz Jeż wrote that in villages, where clerical influence was stronger, there were fewer Jews, while

---

[1] T. Wojnar, 'Etapy rozwiązania kwestii żydowskiej', *Ruch Młodych*, 1937, no. 6, p. 28.

[2] The Christian Democratic press was no less active in this respect, 'being equally aware of the Jewish danger and of the need to combat that danger' (S.J.K. [S. Kaczorowski], 'Na froncie walki', *Pro Christo*, 1933, no. 5, p. 307).

[3] S. Cat-Mackiewicz, *Historia Polski od 11 listopada 1918 r. do września 1939 r.* (London 1985), 206.

in the cities 'those Catholics who are the better, practising Catholics, who listen regularly to masses and sermons, tend to be more antisemitic'.[4]

Endecja was also the first party in Polish political life to use antisemitism on a larger scale as a weapon in the fight for influence and power. The adoption of an anti-Jewish programme had obvious advantages. It exploited existing sentiments, exaggerated the role of Jews, and incited the masses against them. In 1905 Endecja exploited antisemitism to fight against the revolution. By promoting slogans of national solidarity, it started identifying socialism with Jews, which would lead to the concept of *żydokomuna*, 'judaeo-communism'. As a result of losing the elections in 1912, Roman Dmowski, the leading ideologist of Polish ethno-nationalism, developed an obsession with antisemitism,[5] and his followers—trying to make up for the failure—announced an economic boycott of Jewish businesses. This was organized by Rozwój, the Society for the Development of Trade, Industry and Crafts, founded in mid-1913 and responsible for publishing the first Polish edition of the *Protocols of the Elders of Zion*. During the 'Second Conference on Jewish Studies' organized by Rozwój, a unanimous resolution was passed demanding the unconditional separation of Polish society from the Jews.[6] Rozwój was active until 1933, when its role was taken over by the apparatus of the National Party (Stronnictwo Narodowe). The National Party advanced the thesis that the Jews had created both communism and capitalism in order to gain control of the world. The Jews became richer by exploiting the Poles. The issue of Jewish wealth presented in these terms further justified the necessity to eradicate it.

The economic crises of the 1930s gave a new dimension to the issue. It was not difficult to convince a society struck by disaster of who was to blame for all the negative aspects of social, political, and economic life, and to use antisemitism as an integrating element. On 6 December 1931 *Gazeta Warszawska*, a xenophobic daily newspaper published by the Endecja, wrote that the separation into different political groupings in Poland was often purely accidental, while the real division between them concerned their attitude towards the 'Jewish question'. However, the economic battle reached its peak not during the crisis but afterwards. Leadership of the boycott was taken over directly by the economic department of the

---

[4] M. Jeż, 'Duchowieństwo polskie a żydostwo', *Rozwój*, 18 Dec. 1925.

[5] 'The Masonic-Jewish obsession in the interwar period was the decisive factor in Dmowski's views' (A. Micewski, *Roman Dmowski* (Warsaw, 1971), 363); 'a separate place in the process of the formation of Dmowski's obsession was occupied by the Jewish issue' (R. Wapiński, *Roman Dmowski* (Lublin, 1988), 200); the reader of Dmowski's writings 'could bridle at the simplifications, the demagoguery, the attempted conspiracy theories with regard to various phenomena, and finally at his—verging on obsessive—emphasizing of the role of the Jews, whom he saw literally everywhere' (K. Kawalec, *Roman Dmowski* (Wrocław, 2002), 303). The Jewish question occupies increasingly greater space in Dmowski's thinking, leading to what was dubbed, probably by Zdzisław Stahl, 'judaeo-centrism'. It has even been suggested that his position on this matter acquired 'the characteristics of mania' (W. Wasiutyński, *Źródła niepodległości* (London, 1977), 20).

[6] 'Minutes and resolutions of the Second Conference on Jewish Studies', *Rozwój*, 23 Dec. 1923.

National Party. It organized weeks of boycotting Jewish trade, divided markets into Polish and Jewish sections, moved farmers' markets to Saturdays, and kept Jewish traders out of the farmers' markets. There were also deliberate actions—blocking access to Jewish shops, tipping over stalls, assaulting individuals—which sometimes turned into mass demonstrations. The real goal of the boycott was revealed by the weekly *Falanga*: 'For small towns and villages the boycott is exceptionally significant. Firstly, it is sometimes very effective at expelling the Jews. Secondly, it constitutes a certain shock for the sleepy, often passive population. . . . Conscious antisemitism is often the first step towards adopting the full national radical programme.'[7]

The organ of the RNR noted correctly that 'a massive, bursting wave of antisemitism is passing through Poland'.[8] Jan Korolec, the chief journalist and ideologue of the National Radical Camp (Obóz Narodowo-Radykalny; ONR), noted with satisfaction that 'antisemitism in Poland has spread over the last few years at a rate terrifying to the Jews'.[9] According to Korolec, Poland was taking its part in the fight with world Jewry, and in Poland one could 'observe the joyful phenomenon whereby—with increasing clarity—two fronts are being formed: the front of the entire normal Polish society and the Jewish front, supported by Poles who are moral cripples or sadly even traitors to the national cause'.[10]

In 1921 Father Kazimierz Lutosławski claimed: 'We have to enlighten the widest masses that letting a Jew into the family, society, the company, the business, the officer corps, the office, the teaching profession, the school, the club—into any form of Polish life—is a kind of high treason.'[11] Ten years later Wojciech Wasiutyński wrote: 'Not only did National Party supporters sever all links with them, excluding them from the youth groups, but they created such a mood that today friendship between a young Pole and a Jew is something almost unthinkable.'[12] This expressed itself in the transition from the universities' programme of *numerus clausus* to *numerus nullus*. Increasingly student and professional organizations adopted so called 'Aryan clauses', stating that membership was closed to Jews and people ranked as Jews. This was not limited to words. Antisemitic brawls took place every year in the universities: 'autumn manoeuvres', as they were dubbed by Maria Dąbrowska. In 1937 'ghetto benches' (compulsory separate seating for Jews) were introduced.

In the course of time, antisemitism grew into an obsession for nationalists. Regardless of the subject, it always began or ended with the Jewish question. From occupying a peripheral position in social and political life, the Jewish question was steadily moving into the centre. While Karol Stefan Frycz had written about 'the

---

[7] 'Zwycięska fala antyżydowska ogarnęła całą Polskę', *Falanga*, 14 Sept. 1937.

[8] 'Powódź', *Ruch Młodych*, 1936, no. 2, p. 4.   [9] 'Zwycięska fala żydowska ogarnęła całą Polskę'.

[10] J.K. [J. Korolec], 'Komu wolno być antysemitą', *ABC*, 19 Dec. 1936, p. 1.

[11] K. Lutosławski, 'Ostatnia walka o niepodległość', *Myśl Narodowa*, 11 Jan. 1922, pp. 3–4.

[12] W. Wasiutyński, 'Najmłodsze pokolenie przez pryzmat "Myśli nowoczesnego Polaka"', *Myśl Narodowa*, 23 Aug. 1931, p. 112.

overwhelming, huge burden of the Jewish issue, which for us is simply the problem of paving the way to other possibilities of development',[13] Witold Rościszewski wrote: 'In Poland there is no other problem spoken and written about more loudly than the Jewish question', concluding his article by claiming that antisemitism was essentially a 'racial conflict'.[14] Some argued against biological racism, but in fact such an approach was reflected in Cat-Mackiewicz's observation: 'The only logical, clear criterion is Hitler's criterion. A Jew is anyone of Jewish descent.'[15]

What followed was, as defined by Joanna Kurczewska, the 'monsterization' of the Jewish question.[16] It became the main point of reference for every other issue.[17] As Ksawery Pruszyński put it, as years went by 'it was not so much that antisemitism was part of the nationalist world-view, but just the opposite: the nationalist world-view evolved out of antisemitism'.[18] The isolation of the Jews was pursued not just in the economy but also in the areas of law and the state. Antisemitism was exploited in the political struggle—the most extreme example being the campaign against Gabriel Narutowicz during the presidential elections of November 1922—and then became a weapon in fighting Józef Piłsudski. After Piłsudski's death, all these phenomena intensified. Antisemitic propaganda and actions against the Jews served to maintain tension within the country and created an atmosphere of fear. It was also a useful tool for disqualifying rivals, including the Sanacja, which was accused of supporting the Jews.

From the very beginning Dmowski considered economic war an additional element of the political struggle. He wrote in 1902: 'An important manifestation of the active social elements emerging in the Kingdom [of Poland] is the economic movement which is challenging the Jews to a battle of small businesses.'[19] The fact that antisemitism was much more than merely a tool in the economic struggle with the Jews is shown in a diary entry by one of the most intelligent members of the National Camp, Juliusz Zdanowski, who noted, 'at the popular level, the most simple understanding of nationalism and even the political goal of the Catholic political movement was and still is antisemitism. Making use of this slogan we create for ourselves the means for winning votes and support among the masses.'[20]

---

[13] K. S. Frycz, 'Zagadnienie ukraińskie', *Prosto z Mostu*, 9 Jan. 1938, p. 1.

[14] W. Rościszewski, 'Kwestia żydowska', *Falanga*, 15 July 1936.

[15] S. Cat-Mackiewicz, *Słowo*, 5 Mar. 1938.

[16] J. Kurczewska, *Patriotyzm(y) polskich polityków: Z badań nad świadomością liderów partyjnych lat dziewięćdziesiątych* (Warsaw, 2002), 194.

[17] 'For many years we were absorbed as a matter of our programme by the Jewish question, the most burning and the closest to the heart' (W. Wasiutyński, 'List do Ukraińca', *Prosto z Mostu*, 24 Feb. 1935, p. 7).

[18] K. Pruszyński, 'Kampanja młodych 1926–1934: Przyczyny klęski rządów pomajowych', *Prosto z Mostu*, 24 Nov. 1935, pp. 1–2.

[19] R. Dmowski, *Myśli nowoczesnego Polaka*, 3rd edn. (Lwów, 1907), 92.

[20] J. Zdanowski, *Sprawa żydowska: Fragmenty dziennika i notatki różne z lat 1914–1928*, ed. M. Sobczak (Wrocław, 1998), 110; cited in E. Maj, *Związek Ludowo-Narodowy 1919–1929* (Lublin, 2000), 242.

In 1936 Jędrzej Giertych developed this idea in the pages of *Myśl Narodowa* in an article titled 'Seriously or Seemingly': 'The economic boycott; ridding small towns like Przytyk of Jews; tightening the boundaries of the Łódź ghetto; removing Jews from the universities—this is all positive, creative activity, leading in a direct way to the liquidation of the Jewish question in Poland.'[21] Similarly *Ruch Młodych* wrote that 'dealing with the Jewish question in Poland by means of extremism, strength and depth of work, stimulates the energy of the nation'[22] and that 'the current apathy of the nation . . . demands a shake-up of the Polish soul'.[23] These statements by people from different generations and organizations indicate what purposes the Jewish question was meant to serve. *Ruch Młodych* thought it wrong to see the Jewish question solely as an economic problem. To them the Jewish question was predominantly an ethical question. A nationalist leaflet of 26 January 1937 aimed at the younger generation also indicates the point of the anti-Jewish activity: 'Progress, science, democracy: it sounds beautiful. But what is behind it? The revolting Jewish spirit.' It ends with a shocking sentence advising what to do if you meet a Jew: 'Slam him straight in the teeth with an iron bar. Just don't hold back, you mummy's boy!'[24]

The nationalists went from a defensive position, worried about what Jews might do to Poles, to considering what they could do to Jews. There were reassurances: 'We have them in the palm of our hand, and it's up to us whether they leave the country without any further harm or like a fleeing mob, disorganised and demoralised.' By not underestimating them, 'we are becoming an utterly deadly danger to them'.[25]

There was increasing support for the stereotype of the Jew as dangerous, immoral, exploitative, and intent on destroying Poland. The image was created in such a way as to evoke moral and aesthetic aversion.[26] This language was not only typical of the nationalist press: according to the most important Catholic cultural magazine:

The Jews are parasites. In fact our emotional attitude to them is very similar to the attitude towards a flea or a louse. I do not care about a parasite as long as it does not bother me. . . . The thing is, however, that a Jew is something very different from a flea. Finding a solution to the Jewish question is not the same as sanitising your home. The Jewish problem may still persist even when not a single Jew remains.[27]

[21] J.G. [J. Giertych], 'Serio czy dla pozoru?', *Myśl Narodowa*, 25 Oct. 1936, no. 44, pp. 685–6.

[22] J.G. [J. Giertych], 'Brześć', *Ruch Młodych*, 1937, no. 6, p. 2

[23] J.G. [J. Giertych], '*Bunt Młodych* o kwestii żydowskiej', *Ruch Młodych*, 1937, no. 3, p. 13–16.

[24] Biblioteka Narodowa, Warsaw, III 6480/2: nationalist leaflet, 26 Jan. 1937, included with B. Chrzanowski, 'Wspomnienia'.

[25] 'Tylko dynamiczny i agresywny nacjonalizm uwolni Polskę od Żydów', *Falanga*, 14 June 1938.

[26] See E. Maj, *Komunikowanie polityczne Narodowej Demokracji 1918–1939* (Lublin, 2010), 527; D. Libionka, 'Obcy, wrodzy, niebezpieczni: Obraz Żydów i "kwestii żydowskiej" w prasie inteligencji katolickiej lat trzydziestych w Polsce', *Kwartalnik Historii Żydów*, 2002, no. 3, pp. 326–33.

[27] E. Januszkiewicz, 'Wstęp do części dalszych', *Kultura*, 1936, no. 19, cited in Libionka, 'Obcy, wrodzy, niebezpieczni', 327.

Such images of the Jew were defined by Dariusz Stola as 'a cohesive diversity of abomination'.[28] There is no mention of an economic struggle, which remained somewhere beyond the horizon. Equally frequent was the conviction that as the result of their contact with Jews, Poles were losing their national character, becoming spiritually stunted, materially weakened.

It was constantly stressed that Jews were spiritually different from Poles. In the view of the nationalists their danger lay mainly in the fact that they constituted an obstacle to building the psychological unity of the nation, a threat to its morality. Therefore, as Bolesław Piasecki put it in his pamphlet *Przełom narodowy*, it was necessary to destroy them as well as communism and masonry. Maria Rzętkowska, chief columnist of *Falanga* and *Ruch Młodych*, wrote: 'There is no doubt today that the coexistence of the Poles and the Jews in its current form is impossible in the long term. The only difference is in the views on the means and possibility of solving the question.'[29] Starting from 1931, the nationalists instituted a programme of total mutual isolation of the two communities. This was to be the first stage of solving the problem. The second was the complete removal of Jews from Polish territory. It was believed that they were Poland's primary enemy and that the right moment to solve the Jewish question had come.[30] There was appreciation for what the Nazi government was doing and the world's reaction to its actions was closely observed.

To realize the second stage, it was anticipated that a statutory differentiation between Poles and Jews would be introduced. Witold Rościszewski saw the justification of antisemitism in 'the fight of the races, which is a natural outcome of the human condition'.[31] Alfred Łaszowski claimed: 'We don't care whether Jews are a race or not. To us it is sufficient they are Jewish, and the anthropological arguments can be easily left to learned specialists.'[32] Denials of racism and claims to being a 'spiritual' rather than a 'biological' racist were contradicted by the use of racist terminology. Despite Łaszowski's claims, only Jews were considered to be racially alien: the racist terminology was used only with reference to them, and they were clearly juxtaposed to the 'Aryan' race.[33] In this situation it is no surprise that the three leading nationalist journalists—Tadeusz Gluziński, Wojciech Wasiutyński, and Stanisław Piasecki—defended themselves from accusations that they had Jewish blood. They went through the courts not because they were fighting an economic battle, but because to them it was a dishonour to be a Jew. Assimilation was not an option. Baptism did not change nature or nationality: there were calls for a separate parish to be set up for converts.

The proposed solutions to the Jewish question became increasingly radical. There was a popular quote from the writer Karol Hubert Rostworowski, who was a

[28] D. Stola, *Kampania antysyjonistyczna w Polsce 1967–1968* (Warsaw, 2000), 152–3.

[29] M. Rzętkowska, 'Hierarchia przeciw Żydom i lożom', *Ruch Młodych*, 1936, no. 1, p. 33.

[30] Ibid.   [31] W. Rościszewski, 'Kwestia żydowska', *Falanga*, 15 July 1936.

[32] A. Łaszowski, 'Majaczenia filosemickie', *Falanga*, 27 Sept. 1938.

[33] H. Swinarski, 'Poznajmy żydów', *Falanga*, 23 Jan. 1938.

member of the League of Nations and also a leading member of the Camp of Great Poland (Obóz Wielkiej Polski) and the National Party: 'For there can be no agreement where two nations live in one country. You can't reduce their needs, you can't give them more land. One of them must give way: the guest or the host.'[34]

Even the Catholic periodical *Odrodzenie*, which was critical of solving the problem by force, wrote that 'the Jewish question can be non-existent only for those who close their eyes to racial, national or religious differences'.[35] Wasiutyński outlined the political, cultural and economic aspects of the Jewish question.[36] The first and last have already been discussed: the nationalist press also devoted considerable space to the 'Jewish infestation' of culture. *Prosto z Mostu* wrote: 'The issue of the role of Jewry in Poland is first and foremost the issue of ethics and culture',[37] while, according to *Rozwój*, 'culture and Christianity face complete extinction should Jewry realize its plan'. Aryan self-defence should be coordinated.[38] To this effect *Gazeta Warszawska* published lists of the writers they considered to be Jewish.

Falanga published an article by Onufry Kopczyński, the leader of the Polish Organization for Cultural Action (Polska Organizacja Akcji Kulturalnej; POAK), which claimed that 'artistic creativity is—next to the school—one of the most important social organizations and structures for educating the national masses and that is why it is sometimes necessary for the political authorities to intervene in art when it is demoralizing; and that is why it is right and necessary to interfere in this way today'. Therefore next to the political and economic changes there had to be—in his view—a cultural revival: 'International, materialistic art, international materialistic science, must give way to national art and science, Polish art and science, the art and science emerging from a world-view which puts spiritual values above all material ones.'[39]

According to the nationalists, great culture could be created only by ethnic Poles: 'The artist must have an awareness of his ethnic belonging.'[40] A writer's adherence to the 'national idea' was set above the artistic and cognitive values of literature and art. The advocates of such a position proposed the introduction of means of control as a method for fighting for national culture. Works that did not fulfil set criteria should be dealt with by the method favoured by the Nazis: burning.[41] Mieczysław Biegański came to the conclusion that an artist must be 'in

---

[34] K. H. Rostworowski, *Antychryst, Tragedia w trzech aktach* (Lwów, 1925), 135.

[35] T. Wojciechowski, 'Kwestia żydowska', *Odrodzenie*, Apr. 1936, cited in D. Libionka, '"Kwestia żydowska": myślenie za pomocą clichés. Przypadek "Odrodzenia" 1935–1939. Przyczynek do historii antysemityzmu w Polsce', *Dzieje Najnowsze*, 1995, no. 3, pp. 31–46.

[36] W. Wasiutyński, 'Wnioski z zakończonej kampanji', *Prosto z Mostu*, 1 Dec. 1935, p. 3.

[37] 'Na marginesie', *Prosto z Mostu*, 17 Jan. 1937, p. 1.

[38] S. Zakrzewski, 'Aryjczycy wszystkich krajów łączcie się', *Rozwój*, 1 Jan. 1928.

[39] O. B. Kopczyński, 'Uzdrowimy sztukę rewolucją', *Falanga*, 29 June 1937.

[40] T.D. [T. Dowiat], 'O nową treść kulturalną', *Falanga*, 15 Nov. 1938.

[41] 'So despite all the reservations one could and should have towards Hitlerism, it is hard to deny that the National Socialists did the right thing burning this vile literature, although a few outstanding

the first instance of Slavic, Polish origin'. To avoid all doubt, he wrote further that understanding Polish national art was 'never within [the Jews'] scope due to their non-Aryan origins'.[42] In the pages of the Jesuit *Przegląd Powszechny*, Józef Kruszyński wrote that 'a Jew breaking into the territory of literature . . . poisons our spirit and kills in us the Aryan way of thinking'.[43]

The arts also had to be purged of Negro influences, but the greatest threat remained the Jews. However, cultural life at the time was very strongly influenced by Jews, and the cleansing of Polish culture required 'excluding them from all Polish social associations, from schools of any kind and level, from any public and teaching position, from the army, theatre, cinema, radio, trade unions and publishing unions, from the Polish press',[44] and externally isolating the Jewish press and books by Jewish authors. On 21 November 1937, at a general meeting of POAK, Jerzy Pietrkiewicz put forward a proposal which was passed in the form of a resolution setting out the chief tasks of POAK:

1 A strictly nationalist conduct must be imposed on Polish cultural life.

2 The first stage in the realization of the task must be the introduction of a categorical demarcation line into artistic and cultural life: in terms of accepting or not accepting the Jewish element as a culturally harmful element. Those not accepting the harmfulness of Jews or those refraining to make the decision should be treated on a par with the Jews, as harmful and hostile.[45]

Similar proposals were made by Łaszowski during the session of the Związek Zawodowy Literatów Polskich (Union of Polish Authors) on 30 April 1938. He suggested changing the organization's name to Związek Zawodowych Literatów w Polsce (Union of Authors in Poland), because it had too many Jewish members. He claimed that Jewish writers should not be allowed to translate foreign works because they made too many errors in Polish, citing as an example Aleksander Wat, although the journalist who reported his speech did not say whether any specific example of wrong translation by Wat was provided. Next he attacked Antoni Słonimski, the well-known poet and publicist of Jewish origin.[46]

A common claim among the Polish ethno-nationalists was that Jews were incapable of original creative work. All their cultural achievements were merely imitative. They did not create any value independently. They were attacked for alleged cosmopolitism and literary formalism. The main targets of these passion-

---

literary works might have fallen victim to the flames' (Z. Zimorowicz, 'O reglamentacji w kulturze umysłowej', *Pro Christo*, 1938, no. 3, pp. 22–6).

[42] M. Biegański, 'Problemy sztuki narodowej', *POAK: Biblioteka Ruchu Kulturalnego* (n.p., n.d.), 15–16.

[43] J. Kruszyński, 'W sprawie żydowskiej', cited in Libionka, 'Obcy, wrodzy, niebezpieczni', 332.

[44] B. Płachecki, 'Podstawy programu kulturalnego', *Ruch Młodych*, 1936 no. 3, p. 20.

[45] 'Młodzi artyści w służbie Przełomu Narodowego', *Falanga*, 30 Nov. 1937.

[46] B. Płachecki, 'Podstawy programu kulturalnego', *Ruch Młodych*, 1936, no. 3, p. 20. Łaszowski also proposed expelling communists to the USSR (*Falanga*, 10 May 1938).

ate accusations were Słonimski, Julian Tuwim, and the non-Jewish Tadeusz Boy-Żeleński, who was seen as a 'Jewish stooge'. Right-wing intellectuals denounced Tuwim for 'debasing' the Polish language and for his 'semitic' sensuality. Thus Józef Mackiewicz, the Vilna journalist, asserted bluntly that Tuwim was not a Polish poet, while the Kraków writer and critic Karol Hubert Rostworowski described him as a 'Jewish poet writing in Polish'. The right-wing literary weekly *Prosto z mostu* abounded in headlines such as 'Tuwim and Słonimski are One Hundred Per Cent Jews', 'A New Centre of Masonry has been Established in Warsaw', 'The Literary Ghetto', and 'Jewish Poetry in the Polish Language'.[47]

The film industry was claimed to be completely riddled with Jews and described as the most 'putrefied part of the economy': 'Jewish cinema owners constituted the most disgusting wheeler-dealers'.[48] In September 1938 POAK organized a 'Week without Jewish Cinema'. They boasted of distributing a quarter of a million leaflets in the streets of Warsaw and published a pamphlet: *W natarciu*. There were continuous press releases. It was indicated that, apart from the economic aims, the action also had a political character.[49]

The Union of Polish Authors finally agreed that writers of Jewish origin such as Tuwim, Słonimski, Wittlin, Hemar, and Leśmian could write in Polish but only under specific restrictions: 'Since there are so many Jews with such an antisemitic disposition that they do not wish to use any of their own languages, we are liberal enough to allow them the use of the Polish language.' But their writings must be visibly marked. The most appropriate mark would be a yellow patch. However, the organization was prepared to accept any other distinguishing mark and even organized a competition for Jewish artists to design one. *Dziennik Popularny*, a left-of-centre daily, would be marked with a yellow patch, as would several articles in the conservative daily *Czas*, while *Wiadomości Literackie*, the liberal literary weekly, would be printed entirely in yellow ink. The yellow patch would mark the works of Jewish poets such as Tuwim, Słonimski or Wittlin.[50] The light tone of this feature should not mislead anyone: there is here a clear rapprochement with the Nuremberg Laws, which had already been passed. In the words of Konstanty Ildefons Gałczyński, affiliated at the time with *Prosto z Mostu*:

> Onto all those who remain mute,
> onto the readers of uncle Proust,
> the Skamandrites, the hypocrites,
> the word-twisting makers of puns,
> Angel of God, send down from the skies
> The night of long knives.[51]

---

[47] See J. Ratajczyk, *Julian Tuwim* (Poznań, 1995), 102–3.

[48] 'Sutenerzy i oszuści wyścigowi, rządzą polskim kinem', *Falanga*, 25 Oct. 1938.

[49] 'Polacy chodzą tylko do polskich kin', *Falanga*, 6 July 1938; 'Sutenerzy i oszuści wyścigowi rządzą "polskim" kinem', *Falanga*, 25 Oct. 1938; 'Tydzień bez żydowskiego kina', *Falanga*, 25 Oct. 1938, 1 Nov. 1938.   [50] J.K. [J. Korolec], 'O żółtą łatę', *ABC*, 8 Dec. 1936, no. 351, pp. 1–2.

[51] K. I. Gałczyński, 'Polska wybuchła w roku 1937', *Prosto z Mostu*, 21 Feb. 1937, p. 1. The

Antisemitism was an all-encompassing phenomenon. Jews were blamed for all the evils of contemporary reality. It is of course possible to examine particular elements of the phenomenon, including the impact of the economic struggle on its popular appeal, but while doing so the full picture must not be overlooked. Indeed though economic antisemitism was an important part of the anti-Jewish campaign it was far from being its most important element.

Skamandrites were the dominant literary clique in Poland in the 1920s; a number of them, such as Julian Tuwim and Antoni Słonimski, were Jews.

Gender Perspectives on the Rescue of Jews in Poland

Preliminary Observations

JOANNA B. MICHLIC

INTRODUCTION

HISTORIANS have only recently begun to rectify the neglect of the study of women's experiences in eastern Europe during the Second World War.[1] One area in which there have been very few analytical studies is the role of women in both the rescue and the betrayal of Jewish fugitives during the Holocaust. Little work has been done on the relationships between female rescuers and their Jewish charges,[2] on Polish women who denounced Jews and their rescuers, or on Polish women who rescued Jews 'for profit'. In 'The Contribution of Gender to the Study of the Holocaust', Dalia Ofer, one of the pioneering scholars of women and the Holocaust, called for gender analysis to be applied to topics such as 'cooperation with or resistance to the Final Solution, responses to the plunder of Jewish assets, and rescue efforts'.[3] In historical studies, gender perspectives typically complicate and nuance understandings of events.[4] Can they complicate and nuance understandings of the rescue of Jews in Nazi-occupied Poland? Is gender a useful lens

---

[1] See N. M. Wingfield and M. Bucur, 'Introduction', in eaed. (eds.), *Gender and War in Twentieth-Century Eastern Europe* (Bloomington, Ind., 2006), 1–20; K. R. Jolluck, *Exile and Identity: Polish Women in the Soviet Union during World War II* (Pittsburgh, Pa., 2002), 1–24.

[2] See J. L. Marlow, 'Polish Catholic Maids and Nannies: Female Aid and the Domestic Realm in Nazi-Occupied Poland', Ph.D. thesis (Michigan State University, 2014). Phillip Friedman was the first to discuss the loyalty, dedication, and altruism of female Polish housekeepers employed by Jews (*Their Brothers' Keepers* (New York, 1957)).

[3] D. Ofer, 'The Contribution of Gender to the Study of the Holocaust', in M. A. Kaplan and D. Dash Moore, *Gender and the Jewish History* (Bloomington, Ind., 2011), 12–135; see also D. Ofer and L. J. Weitzman, *Women in the Holocaust* (New Haven, Conn., 1998).

[4] M. Kaplan, 'Revealing and Concealing: Memoirs in German-Jewish History', in E. Lederhendler and J. Wertheimer (eds.), *Text and Context: Essays in Modern Jewish History and Historiography in Honor of Ismar Schorsch* (New York, 2005), 383–410. I would like to thank Marion Kaplan for drawing my attention to this article.

through which to view rescue activities? How does gender relate to other characteristics of rescuers, such as socio-economic background, religion, and age?

This chapter follows on from my earlier work on the rescue of Jews during the
Holocaust in Poland.[5] It is not a gender analysis of the subject, but a discussion of
the difficulties of studying it from a gender perspective. It focuses on 'dedicated
rescuers', those individuals who went above and beyond the call of duty to save
Jews without profiting from their actions or taking advantage of their charges.
Were male and female rescuers treated differently by their communities during
and after the war, and, if so, what does this reveal about wider Polish social and
cultural norms, especially towards Jews?

I aim to answer these questions through a careful examination of 500 personal
letters written shortly after the end of the war, when memories were still raw, by
rescuers and rescued Jews, and sent to the Central Committee of Polish Jews
(Centralny Komitet Żydów w Polsce; CKŻP) and its various local branches and to
the American Jewish Joint Distribution Committee.

THE LETTERS

A small number of the letters were written by people searching for former rescuers
or charges. One male rescuer wrote asking for help in locating his Jewish wife. He
had rescued her and married her, but once the war was over she had suddenly left
him.[6] Another small number were written by Polish widows of Jewish men who
had been killed in the Holocaust, asking Jewish organizations for assistance in
raising their half-Jewish children. The widows were uncertain of their status and
that of their children in the Jewish community, and their letters are very self-
effacing. The majority of the correspondence, however, consists of letters from
Poles who had been involved in rescuing Jews, often requesting material or medical
assistance. Many were accompanied by testimonies from their charges or local
Jewish organizations confirming the claims of the rescuer. Both the rescuers'
letters and the testimonies of the rescued provide insights into their emotions and
personal recollections of their wartime experiences, especially which aspects of the
rescue were important and remained clear in their memories. They disclose the
human depth and texture of their experiences. They also challenge the myths and
memories of Polish rescue of Jews that developed during the communist period
(1945–89) and which have continued in the post-communist debate on Polish–

---

[5] J. B. Michlic, '"I will never forget what you did for me during the war": Representations of Res-
cuers and Relationships between Rescuers and Jewish Survivors in the Light of Correspondence to the
Central Committee of Polish Jews and the Joint, 1945–1949', *Yad Vashem Studies*, 39/2 (2011), 169–
207; ead., 'Daily Life of Polish Women, Dedicated Rescuers of Jews during and after the Second World
War', in C. S. Gould, S. Gigliotti, and J. Golomb (eds.), *Ethics, Art and Representations of the Holocaust
Essays in Honour of Berel Lang* (Lanham, Md., 2013), 215–34.

[6] Such intimate relations formed under the extreme conditions of the time deserve separate treatment.

Jewish relations during the war despite the fact that recent research in Poland and abroad has contributed to the dismantling of the hegemonic narratives of Polish solidarity with the Jews and demonstrated the incongruence of these themes with historical reality,[7] mainly by uncovering previously suppressed dark aspects of the relationships.[8] As a result, the emphasis has shifted to the study of rescuers for profit[9] and those who abused their Jewish charges or denounced them later.[10] These new studies are generally descriptive and focused on a particular region.

The correspondence alone cannot provide a comprehensive picture of the rescue of Jews during the Holocaust and needs to be viewed alongside other historical documents and placed within a broader context. However, these letters and testimonies, written by rescuers, Jewish survivors, members of survivors' families, and representatives of Jewish organizations recounting rescue activities, corroborating rescuers' accounts, or asking for assistance on their behalf, constitute a multi-voiced description of rescue. They constitute rare and barely examined

[7] On communist memory of Polish–Jewish relations during the war, see e.g. J. B. Michlic and M. Melchior, 'The Memory of the Holocaust in Postcommunist Poland', in J.-P. Himka and J. B. Michlic (eds.), *Bringing the Dark to Light: The Memory of the Holocaust in Postcommunist Europe* (Lincoln, Neb., 2013), 412–20; for pre-1989 attitudes in contemporary debate and historical writing, see e.g. P. Lisicki, *Krew na naszych rękach?* (Lublin, 2016); D. Walusiak, *Winni: Holokaust i fałszowanie historii* (Kraków, 2016); for Jan Żaryn's claim that perhaps a million Poles had engaged in the rescue of Jews, see 'Prof. Żaryn w "Bliżej": Polaków, którzy w bardzo różnorodny sposób pomagali Żydom, mogło być nawet 1 milion', *Polityka*, 6 Dec. 2013, <http://wpolityce.pl/polityka/172799-prof-zaryn-w-blizej-polakow-ktorzy-w-bardzo-roznorodny-sposob-pomagali-zydom-moglo-byc-nawet-1-milion> (accessed 11 Nov. 2016); see also A. Poray-Wybranowska, 'Naród bohaterów', *Nasz Dziennik*, 9 Oct. 2004; D. Baliszewski, 'Czy jesteśmy nacjonalistami?', *Wprost*, 2 Apr. 2006, <http://www.wprost.pl/ar/88353/Czy-jestesmy-nacjonalistami/> (accessed 18 Dec. 2009). For a recent questioning of the alleged large number of Poles helping Jews, see J. Leociak, 'Cały naród ratuje swoich Żydów', *Krytyka Polityczna*, 18 Aug. 2016, <http://www.krytykapolityczna.pl/artykuly/kraj/20160818/caly-narod-ratuje-swoich-zydow> (accessed 22 Aug. 2016). The claim that large numbers of Poles assisted Jews has been promoted in various popular media. For a critical evaluation of the television series *Sprawiedliwi*, see A. Haska, 'Na marginesie serialu "Sprawiedliwi", czyli (prawie) cała Polska ratuje Żydów', *Zagłada Żydów: Studia i Materiały*, 6 (2010), 405–10.

[8] See e.g. E. Rączy, 'Stosunki polsko-żydowskie w latach drugiej wojny światowej na Rzeszowszczyźnie', in A. Żbikowski (ed.), *Polacy i Żydzi pod okupacją niemiecką 1939–1945: Studia i materiały* (Warsaw, 2006), 891–940; ead., *Pomoc Polaków dla ludności żydowskiej na Rzeszowszczyźnie, 1939–1945* (Rzeszów, 2008); A. Pyżewska, 'Pomoc dla ludności żydowskiej w Okręgu Białystok w latach okupacji niemieckiej', in Żbikowski (ed.), *Polacy i Żydzi pod okupacją niemiecką 1939–1945*, 941–79; J. Leociak, *Ratowanie: Opowieści Polaków i Żydów* (Kraków, 2010); *Zagłada Żydów: Studia i Materiały*, 4 (2008).

[9] See e.g. *Zagłada Żydów: Studia i Materiały*, 4 (2008); J. Grabowski, *Rescue for Money: Paid Helpers in Poland, 1939–1945*, Search and Research: Lectures and Papers, 13 (Jerusalem, 2008); id., *Judenjagd: Polowanie na Żydów 1942–1945. Studium dziejów pewnego powiatu* (Warsaw, 2011); for the first sociological study of the rescue of Jews for ideological and financial reasons, see N. Tec, *When Light Pierced the Darkness: Christian Rescuers of Jews in Nazi-Occupied Poland* (New York, 1986).

[10] See e.g. J. Tokarska-Bakir, 'Sprawiedliwi niesprawiedliwi, niesprawiedliwi sprawiedliwi', *Zagłada Żydów: Studia i Materiały*, 4 (2008), 170–217; Eng. trans.: 'The Unrighteous Righteous and the Righteous Unrighteous', trans. A. Greenberg, *Dapim*, 24 (2010), 11–63; B. Engelking, *Jest taki piękny słoneczny dzień . . . Losy Żydów szukających ratunku na wsi polskiej 1942–1945* (Warsaw, 2011).

documentation of the relationships between the rescuers and the rescued Jews and the rescuers and members of their local communities.

Rescuers, both male and female, were of all ages, marital status, socio-economic background, and educational level. They mainly operated in four regions: Warsaw and its province, the Kielce region, Małopolska, and Kresy. The educational level of rescuers from the countryside was very low. Some of their letters were written by someone else and signed by the rescuer with one or three crosses, indicating complete illiteracy. Yet some of their accounts, especially the women's, are intensely emotional. A few letters by working-class men who declared an affiliation with the Polish Socialist Party or other left-wing organizations emphatically stated that they rescued Jews for ideological reasons. However, it is impossible to discern the ideological affiliations of most of the letter writers. Their politics seem irrelevant, as the majority declare that they saw rescue as an ordinary human action, as an act of decency to help needy and endangered people. Only a few writers make positive references to the political transformations which took place in Poland immediately after the war. Their statements are uniform, careful, and vague, and speak about the endorsement of democracy and equal civic rights for every citizen of the new Poland.

Of the writers discussed here, none—except for the recently publicly recognized Irena Sendlerowa (1910–2008)[11]—wrote or spoke about their wartime rescue efforts elsewhere, and nothing else is known about them apart from what can be deduced from their letters. The great majority of them were ordinary men and women. In their requests for assistance, both female and male rescuers explain in an almost uniform fashion that the harshness of their current situation has forced them to turn to Jewish organizations for help. They stress, in a less or more sophisticated manner, depending on their educational level, that they do not seek repayment for their actions and that their assistance was of a purely humanitarian nature. They show an awareness that their fellow countrymen abused and took advantage of Jewish fugitives, and it was important to them to dissociate themselves especially from 'rescuers for profit', who also wrote to Jewish organizations for help. Some rescuers from the intelligentsia, both female and male, appear embarrassed to be making requests for assistance: some of them refused financial help, accepting only food, toiletries, and clothes and shoes for their families. Under the harsh economic conditions immediately after the war, such necessities were expensive

[11] See e.g. *Irena Sendler: In the Name of their Mothers* [documentary], dir. M. Skinner (PBS, 2011); *Dzieci Ireny Sendlerowej* [documentary], dir. J. K. Harrison (TiM Film Studio, 2009); based on A. Mieszkowska, *Matka dzieci Holokaustu: Historia Ireny Sendlerowej* (Warsaw, 2004); for the elderly Sendlerowa's meeting with American schoolgirls in Warsaw, see *Lista Sendlerowej* [documentary], dir. M. J. Dudziewicz (TVP, 2002); see also *Irena Sendlerowa* [DVD] (Narodowe Centrum Kultury, Multimedialne Wydawnictwo Edukacyjne, 2009); J. Mayer, *Życie w słoiku: Ocalenie Ireny Sendler* (Warsaw, 2013); A. Mieszkowska, *Prawdziwa historia Ireny Sendlerowej* (Warsaw, 2014); H. Grubowska, *Ta, która ratowała Żydów: Rzecz o Irenie Sendlerowej* (Warsaw, 2014).

and hard to find.[12] The refusal to accept money for saving a human life reflects a particular attitude towards honour within the Polish intelligentsia. The testimonies of their former Jewish charges typically confirm the deteriorating material circumstances, severe medical problems, and poverty of their wartime benefactors.

GENDER PERSPECTIVES ON THE RESCUE OF JEWS DURING THE WAR

Micro-historical studies can illuminate the gender division and its relationship to rescue in different geographical regions, and the related method of prosopography can shed light on the collective experience of the rescuers and the environment and social structures in which they functioned. However, there are no such studies for Poland. A 2008 study of the rescue of Jews in France and Belgium revealed that men and women were equally involved.[13] Although in absolute numbers women's participation was slightly higher than men's in both countries, this is explained by the wartime shortage of men.[14] There is no comprehensive statistical information about the number of Polish men and women involved in rescue activities.

Nachum Bogner, the pioneering scholar of the rescue of Jewish children in wartime Poland, and himself a child Holocaust survivor from Galicia, claims that women constituted the majority of rescuers in Poland.[15] Of over 6,350 Polish rescuers recognized by the Yad Vashem Institute in Jerusalem, most are female.[16] The letters and testimonies of rescuers and their charges also suggest that there were more female rescuers than male ones. As in France and Belgium, this was probably the result of the shortage of men caused by the war and the Nazi and Soviet occupations. The shortage of men led to what could be characterized as a gender revolution in Polish society and the emergence of a matriarchy.[17] On the one hand, there were large numbers of lonely women; on the other, they enjoyed much greater economic and sexual independence than they had ever had.[18]

---

[12] On the social, economic, and mental conditions of Polish society after the war, see e.g. M. Zaremba, *Wielka Trwoga. Polska 1944–1947: Ludowa reakcja na kryzys* (Kraków, 2012); on the political transformations, see A. Paczkowski, *Pół wieku* (Warsaw, 1996).

[13] J. [L.] Frenk, *Righteous among the Nations in France and Belgium: A Silent Resistance* (Jerusalem, 2008), 40–1.   [14] Ibid.

[15] See N. Bogner, *Beḥasidei zarim: hatsalat yeladim bizehut she'ulah bepolin* (Jerusalem, 2000); Eng. trans.: *At the Mercy of Strangers: The Rescue of Hidden Jewish Children in Poland*, trans. R. Mandel (Jerusalem, 2009); J. B. Michlic, interview with N. Bogner, Kibbutz Netiv Halamed-He, 9 May 2014.

[16] I would like to thank Bozenna Rotman, from the Polish Desk at the Department of Righteous Among the Gentiles at Yad Vashem, Jerusalem, for helpful observations on the subject.

[17] M. Fidelis, 'Czy "nowy matriarchat?" Kobiety bez mężczyzn w Polsce po II wojnie światowej', in A. Żarnowska and A. Szwarc (eds.), *Kobieta i rewolucja obyczajowa*, Społeczno-kulturowe aspekty seksualności: Wiek XIX i XX, 9 (Warsaw, 2006), 421–36.

[18] See H. Jędruszczak, 'Miasta i przemysł w okresie odbudowy', in F. Ryszka (ed.), *Polska Ludowa 1944–50: Przemiany społeczne* (Wrocław, 1974), 339–40; D. Jarosz, 'Kobiety a praca zawodowa w Polsce w latach 1944–1956 (główne problemy w świetle nowych badań źródłowych)', in A. Żarnowska and

Polish women of all ages lost husbands, fiancés, and boyfriends, as well as fathers and brothers. According to the available statistics, in 1939 there were 104.9 women for every 100.0 men, in 1946 there were 115.5, and in 1947 there were 113.1. The highest deficit of men was in large cities: in Warsaw in 1931 there were 119.4 women for every 100.0 men, in 1946 there were 140.8; in Łódź in 1931 there were 117.2 women for every 100.0 men, in 1946 there were 134.2.[19] In 1950 the percentage of single women between the age of 20 and 49 was 46 per cent, whereas in 1931 it had been only 34 per cent.[20]

The war forced Polish women to take up roles inside and outside their homes that had generally been the exclusive preserve of men prior to 1939. During the five-year Nazi occupation they became the heads of household and chief breadwinners for their families. Did playing these new roles prompt Polish women to rescue Jews? Did it enable them to make practical decisions about saving Jews? Was the loss of or fear of losing a male family member a contributing factor in the decision to rescue Jews? These are important gender-related questions that need to be thoroughly investigated.

A close examination of their letters and the testimonies of their charges suggests that this increase in responsibility and freedom did inspire the majority of female rescuers, even those whose wartime professions were somewhat murky. Shmuel Ron (Rozencwajg), a member of an underground Jewish youth movement in Zagłębie who lived openly on the Aryan side, recalls that one of his main rescuers, Sofia, was the caretaker of a building in a prestigious neighbourhood of Katowice and a prostitute. Her particular beliefs inspired her to rescue Jews and her occupation gave her the freedom to do so, despite her tiny apartment. According to Ron:

Sofia believed in the Creator and in Jesus. She would speak to Jesus as to some distinguished man sitting by her side, and she told me she had made a deal with him: if she saved me, Jesus would save her son, who was about my age and serving with the German army on the eastern front. Sophia had a husband, who was also posted in the east. Sophia would introduce me as her nephew when I went along to help with her cleaning and maintenance job at the NSDAP offices, and the people working there sometimes asked me to do odd jobs for them. At home, Sophia treated me like an adopted son and even called me that.[21]

A. Szwarc (eds.), *Kobieta i praca*, Społeczno-kulturowe aspekty seksualności: Wiek XIX i XX, 6 (Warsaw, 2000), 217–44. On standards of living, see B. Brodziński, *Stopa życiowa w Polsce w latach 1945–1963* (London, 1965).

[19] M. Krasocki, 'U źródeł siły żywej', *Praca i opieka społeczna*, 22/1 (1948), 35; Główny Urząd Statystyczny Polskiej, *Powszechny sumaryczny spis ludności z dn. 14 II 1946 r.* (Warsaw, 1947).

[20] Fidelis, 'Czy "nowy matriarchat?"', 426.

[21] S. Ron, 'And you shall tell your children' [unpublished memoir] (1995), 117–18. Ron kept in touch with Sofia, even after he had moved to Israel, often referring to her as 'his mother'. See also N. Zvuluni, 'Hanotsriyah sofiyah klemens mikatovits bepolin unekhadeihah hayehudiyim biyerushalayim', *Herut*, 18 Sept. 1963, <http://www.ranaz.co.il/articles/article1790_19630918.asp> (accessed 12 May 2014). I would like to thank Amos Ron, Shmuel's son, for allowing me access to his father's memoir.

Female rescuers also included nuns. In contrast to the directives from religious leaders in France and Belgium to assist Jews,[22] the Catholic Church in Poland did not issue any statement on behalf of Jews nor urge Christians to protect them.[23] Therefore, in Poland, those Roman Catholic priests and nuns involved in the rescue of Jews were acting of their own accord. Often the attitude of the mother superior or abbot in each nunnery, monastery, or mission was decisive in whether Jews were helped or not. The comprehensive history of their operations, motivations, achievements, and limits remains to be written, as scholars do not have full access to church archives in Poland.[24] However, the involvement of nuns in the rescue of Jewish children was significant. According to the statement of Sister Teresa Antonietta Frącek, the Franciscan Missionaries of Mary alone rescued approximately 500 Jewish children.[25] Because of the nature and isolation of religious organizations, it was easier to hide Jewish children among non-Jewish children in nunneries and monasteries than with families. Were the nuns motivated by *agape*—selfless love—or was this sometimes mixed with the desire to save the individual by having him or her convert to Christianity? Were they more inclined to rescue Jews because their charitable nature overrode official edicts? Did suppressed maternal and nurturing instincts urge them to rescue Jewish children? These are also important gender-related questions that need further investigation.

[22] See e.g. W. D. Halls, *Politics, Society and Christianity in Vichy France* (Oxford, 1995), 97–106; F. R. Nicosia (ed.), *Archives of the Holocaust*, iv: *Central Zionist Archives 1939–1945* (New York, 1990), 161–6; L. Gevers and J. Bank (eds.), *Religion under Siege: The Roman Catholic Church in Occupied Europe (1939–1950)* (Leuven, 2007), 222; M. van den Wijngaert, 'Les Catholiques Belges et les Juifs durant l'occupation Allemande 1940–1944', in R. van Doorslaer and D. Dratwa (eds.), *Les Juifs de Belgique: De l'immigration au génocide, 1925–1945* (Brussels, 1994), 121.

[23] On the Catholic Church in Poland under German occupation, see F. Stopniak (ed.), *Kościół katolicki na ziemiach Polski w czasie II wojny światowej: Materiały i studia*, x/5 (Warsaw, 1981); Z. Zieliński (ed.), *Życie religijne w Polsce pod okupacją hitlerowską 1939–1945* (Warsaw, 1982); id., *Życie religijne w Polsce pod okupacją 1939–1945: Metropolie wileńska i lwowska, zakony* (Katowice, 1992).

[24] The works published on the subject are descriptive rather than analytical (see e.g. J. Kłoczowski, 'The Religious Orders and the Jews in Nazi-Occupied Poland', *Polin*, 3 (1988), 238–43; E. Kurek-Lesik, *Gdy klasztor znaczył życie: Udział żeńskich zgromadzeń zakonnych w akcji ratowania dzieci żydowskich w Polsce w latach 1939–1945* (Kraków, 1992); ead., *Your Life is Worth Mine: How Polish Nuns Saved Hundreds of Jewish Children in German Occupied Poland, 1939–1945* (New York, 1997); F. Stopniak, 'Katolickie duchowieństwo w Polsce i Żydzi w okresie niemieckiej okupacji', in K. Dunin-Wąsowicz (ed.), *Społeczeństwo polskie wobec martyrologii i walki Żydów w latach II wojny światowej: Materiały z sesji w Instytucie Historii PAN w dniu 11.III.1993 r.* (Warsaw, 1996), 19–55).

[25] Archiwum Główne Zgromadzenia Sióstr Franciszkanek Rodziny Maryi (hereafter ZSFRM), Warsaw: Teresa Antonietta Frącek, director of the Central Archives of the Franciscan Missionaries of Mary, statement, 23 Oct. 2013, citing a questionnaire conducted in Poland in 1962. The statement is included in documentation about the rescue actions of Czesława Strąg. I would like to thank Nachum Bogner for drawing my attention to this item. Ewa Kurek identifies fifty-three orders of nuns who rescued no fewer than 1,200 Jewish children in almost 200 convents and institutions (*Dzieci żydowskie w klasztorach: Udział żeńskich zgromadzeń zakonnych w akcji ratowania dzieci żydowskich w Polsce w latach 1939–1945* (Lublin, 2001), 139–204). However, some of her interpretations of the data are flawed.

Of course, the larger number of female rescuers represented in the letters and testimonies does not necessarily mean that all Polish women were unsung heroines of the war. In their interactions with Jewish fugitives, Polish women, like Polish men, behaved in a variety of ways. Some displayed narrow ethno-nationalism, antisemitism, greed, curiosity, suspicion, indifference, and personal interest, while others reflected sympathy, humanitarian attitudes, and a belief that Jewish fugitives were deserving of assistance and care. Were women more likely to spot rescuers behaving differently, such as purchasing and delivering food to hidden Jews? Were they more alert to suspicious sounds and movements in neighbouring apartments and houses? Were they more likely to hear rumours about their neighbours' suspicious activities? Were they more disposed to betray neighbours hiding Jews? Did they disapprove of rescue activities for different reasons than men? Were they responsible for the social exclusion of rescuers, which often led to and enabled physical violence during and after the war? Were they as likely as men to blackmail rescuers?[26] These gender-related questions also need to be investigated.

In his important study of the rescue of Jews in France, Jacques Semelin discussed in depth the small gestures of protection made by ordinary French people during the mass deportations of Jews between 1942 and 1944.[27] Semelin divided rescuers into four categories: the 'host', the 'guardian angel', the 'forger', and the 'smuggler'. These categories are useful in understanding the mechanics of rescue on a daily basis. In my work on the rescue of Jewish children in wartime Poland, alongside the categories of long-term and short-term rescuers, I introduced that of the 'sudden helper'.[28] Both men and women played the role of sudden helper on the streets and in railway stations, offices, and shops, saving Jewish fugitives from encounters with Germans, Polish blackmailers, and police. Some members of the *granatowa policja*[29] acted as sudden helpers by refusing to accept that the person stopped was a Jew in hiding and letting them go.

The letters and testimonies reveal that both female and male rescuers often

---

[26] For blackmailers in Warsaw, see J. Grabowski, *'Ja tego Żyda znam!': Szantażowanie Żydów w Warszawie, 1939–1943* (Warsaw, 2004); for organized searches for Jews by groups of peasants, see the journal of Stanisław Żemiński written in October 1942: S. Żemiński, 'Kartki dziennika nauczyciela w Łukowie z okresu okupacji hitlerowskiej', *Biuletyn Żydowskiego Instytutu Historycznego*, 27 (1958), 105–12.

[27] J. Semelin, *Persécutions et entraides dans la France occupée: Comment 75 % des Juifs en France ont échappé à la mort* (Paris, 2013).

[28] J. B. Michlic, *Jewish Children in Nazi-Occupied Poland: Survival and Polish–Jewish Relations during the Holocaust as Reflected in Early Postwar Recollections*, Search and Research: Lectures and Papers, 14 (Jerusalem, 2008).

[29] The 'blue police', the Polish police force in German-occupied Poland (see A. Hempel, *Pogrobowcy klęski: Rzecz o policji 'granatowej' w Generalnym Gubernatorstwie, 1939–1945* (Warsaw, 1990)). In *The Condemnation of Franciszek Kłos* the renowned Polish filmmaker Andrzej Wajda addressed the problem of members of the *granatowa policja* collaborating with the Nazis in the annihilation of Jews (*Wyrok na Franciszka Kłosa* (TVP, 2000)).

played multiple roles. Czesława Strąg (née Kisielewicz) was a 19-year-old Polish woman who rescued 7-year-old Róża Kateganer, whom she met in the summer of 1942 in her hometown of Brzeżany, Galicia, despite her own parents' fear that she might endanger the whole family.[30] With the agreement of Kateganer's father, she brought Róża to her home and managed to organize a 'good' birth certificate for her in the name of Maria Szkolnicka, one of Strąg's cousins who had been sent to Siberia by the Soviets in 1940. She also approached a friendly priest to obtain a baptism certificate for her. Strąg decided to leave her hometown with her Jewish charge and moved to Sambor and then to Lviv in order to protect the girl and herself from denunciation. However, it became clear that Maria had a better chance of survival with the Franciscan Missionaries of Mary in Podhajce, near Brzeżany. Strąg kept in touch with her through a trusted nun and telephoned and visited regularly. In the spring of 1944 the Franciscan Missionaries of Mary had to move to a safer location first in Lviv and then near Kraków, because Ukrainian military units were killing Poles and Jews indiscriminately in the area. Strąg thus lost contact with Maria. Nonetheless, after the war they were reunited in western Poland and both settled in Wrocław. They remained close after Maria Szkolnicka (now Damaszek) left for the United States of America in 1963 to be reunited with her father's family.

A few of the letters were from Polish women whose husbands had been killed by the Germans for sheltering and assisting Jews. They speak of their husbands as the driving force behind the rescue efforts and depict themselves as emotionally and physically detached from them. The majority of them seem to be overwhelmed by the loss of their husbands and unsure about the future of their families.

Letters written by local representatives of the Polish community, such as village heads, or representatives of Jewish organizations often included requests for the support of Polish children whose parents had been killed by the Germans for helping Jews. However, these letters seldom provide information about the rescue activities or which of the parents was the driving force behind them. Testimonies of Jewish survivors throw more light on the issue, indicating that in general both spouses co-operated and their rescue activities were complementary, although one of them was usually the initiator. In many cases, survivors mention the wife's role in the daily care of the fugitives. It seems that traditional gender divisions shaped the daily routine. In the countryside, mature peasant women sometimes had to protect Jewish fugitives from violence or sexual harassment by drunken, male members of their families. But some of the testimonies mention men who were more caring and compassionate than their wives.[31] Some child survivors' testimonies speak of

---

[30] ZSFRM: Czesława Strąg, 'Wspomnienia Czesławy Strąg z Holocaustu i o uratowaniu Marii Szkolnickiej, Róża Rozalia Kateganer' [interview], 27 Sept. 1993; ZSFRM: Maria Damaszek [née Róża Rozalia Kateganer], testimony, 21 Dec. 2013). I would like to thank Nachum Bogner for drawing my attention to these items. On the history of wartime Brzeżany, see S. Redlich, *Together and Apart in Brzezany: Poles, Jews and Ukrainians, 1919–1945* (Bloomington, Ind., 2002).

[31] See e.g. E. Turzyńska, *Sądzonym mi było żyć…* (Warsaw, 2009), 168–73.

compassionate and nurturing male rescuers whom they regarded as trusted family members, referring to them as 'uncle' or 'father'.[32] One of the most moving testimonies, showing the total dedication of an illiterate, religious, male peasant to his adult Jewish charge, is that of Dawid Nassan. The testimony was given in Kraków, Nassan's pre-war hometown and enclosed with his request for assistance for his rescuer, Józef Biesiada of Smardzowice, near Kraków.[33]

When the last Jews of Skała were killed in the local cemetery in November 1942, Nassan lost his 22-year-old wife, 6-month-old daughter, and his parents-in-law. However, he managed to escape, running and hiding between graves. Half-naked and traumatized by witnessing the death of his relations, Nassan needed clothes and shoes to try to get to the Kraków ghetto but was too afraid to visit the peasant in Smardzowice who already possessed all of his family's belongings, Cieślik, as he suspected that Cieślik might kill him. Therefore, he decided to approach an unknown peasant family, the Biesiadas. In the dark, through the window, Nassan saw Józef Biesiada praying and his wife and four children already in bed. Nassan knocked on the door and asked for clothes and shoes, but they did not have any spare trousers or shoes to give him. They were shocked at his appearance and his account of escaping from the cemetery. At first Biesiada's wife was afraid to shelter Nassan, as she feared that the entire family would be killed if the Germans found out. But, according to Nassan, Biesiada knelt in front of his wife and begged her to let him shelter him, arguing that Nassan's miraculous survival in the cemetery must have been God's will, and he was obliged to help him.[34] Biesiada built a special hiding place in his barn, and Nassan hid there for twenty-seven months. Despite the family's dire poverty, Biesiada brought him food, water, and homemade cigarettes. Nassan remained with the Biesiada family for three weeks after the Soviets took over the region in February 1945. Finally, Biesiada drove him, hidden in his cart, to Kraków where he received medical care. Before they separated, Biesiada begged Nassan not to disclose his name publicly, as he feared that his neighbours might take violent action against him and his family for rescuing a Jew.

To what extent was Józef Biesiada's caring and nurturing behaviour towards a Jewish stranger the norm among male rescuers? Were traditional gender roles within families a major factor in determining how couples shared the daily responsibilities of looking after their Jewish charges? Were more complicated combinations of factors, such as gender, personality, individual values and beliefs, family dynamics, and personal relations with the Jewish fugitives involved? These are more important gender-related questions that need to be thoroughly investigated.

There is also the question of the role that the romantic and sexual desires of

---

[32] See Michlic, 'Jewish Children in Nazi-Occupied Poland', 5–7.

[33] Archiwum Żydowskiego Instytutu Historycznego, Warsaw (hereafter AŻIH), 303/VIII 'Centralny Komitet Żydów w Polsce: Wydział Opieki Społecznej, 1944–1950', j. 222: Dawid Nassan, testimony, 25 June 1947, 20–8; id., letter to the Committee to Aid Poles Assisting Jews during the War, Warsaw, sent care of the Jewish Committee, Kraków, 7 July 1947, 18–19.

[34] AŻIH, 303/VIII, j. 222: Dawid Nassan, testimony, 25 June 1947, 26.

both male and female rescuers played in their assisting of Jewish fugitives. The social history of Polish women in general during the war suggests that many women whose husbands were away engaged in informal sexual and intimate relations with new, short-term partners.[35] The testimonies of survivors reveal that it was not only male but also female rescuers whose husbands were absent who engaged in romantic and sexual relations with hidden Jews.[36] Was this the norm? This gender-oriented question needs to be further investigated.

Of course there were also certain roles that women could not play. Some skills, such as producing forged documents for Jewish fugitives, were the preserve of men because of their professional backgrounds. Managers of welfare, legal, and medical institutions and members of the *granatowa policja* were also in a position to perform rescue tasks that were not possible for women.

GENDER PERSPECTIVES ON THE STIGMATIZATION OF RESCUERS AFTER THE WAR

The letters reveal that both during and after the war rescuers were stigmatized by members of their local communities who disapproved of their actions on ideological grounds. This was not a new phenomenon: before the war ethnonationalists of various shades, headed by the National Democrats (Endecja) and the Catholic Church, launched a propaganda war against Poles who were sympathetic towards Jews, distinguishing between good Poles serving the Polish cause and bad, impure, and corrupt Poles serving the interests of Jews and other minorities.[37] At the centre of what could be called symbolic boundary-making was the myth of the Jew as the great internal enemy of Poland.[38] Between 1918 and 1939 this myth reached its apogee and had a pernicious impact on political culture and society: liberal politicians, academics, public intellectuals, artists, and ordinary people who defended the rights of Jews were labelled 'Jews', 'shabbes goys', 'Jewish uncles and aunts', 'Jew protectors', or 'Jew saviours'. This was intended to undermine their national belonging, symbolically excluding them from the pure ethnic Christian Polish community, the 'true Poles', as traitors transgressing social and cultural boundaries. The importance of protecting the true Polish nation and

[35] Fidelis, 'Czy "nowy matriarchat?"', 430–3.

[36] Some of these female rescuers expected the relationship to continue after the war, and some of their male charges—who might be in hiding with their wives and other members of their families—gave them the impression that they would leave their wives when the war was over. See, for example, Shimon Redlich's account of the affair between Vovo, the handsome husband of his mother's younger sister, Malcia, and Tanka Kontsevych, their Ukrainian rescuer (*Together and Apart in Brzezany*, 96–8).

[37] See e.g. J. B. Michlic, *Poland's Threatening Other: The Image of the Jew from 1880 to the Present* (Lincoln, Neb., 2006); on Roman Dmowski, the founder and intellectual leader of Endecja, see G. Krzywiec, *Szowinizm po polsku: Przypadek Romana Dmowskiego (1886–1905)* (Warsaw, 2010).

[38] On boundary-making, see P. Kolstø (ed.), *Myths and Boundaries in South-Eastern Europe* (London, 2005).

stigmatizing those who betrayed it was disseminated in the ethno-nationalist press, slogans, books, pamphlets, posters, at public events, and in sermons. Thus, even prior to the war, ordinary people were exposed to the idea that those who were sympathetic towards the Jews were traitors.

During the Nazi occupation, violence against those sympathetic towards the Jews reached a level unknown in the Polish state, which had strived, albeit not always successfully, to contain civil discord. The Nazis' punitive measures against those who helped Jews transformed the homemade hate language of the 1920s and 1930s into vicious deeds.[39] The letters and testimonies of rescuers and their charges reveal that rescuers were often perceived as traitors to the Poland of the ethno-nationalist vision and deserved to be punished for their actions. Neighbours and acquaintances subjected both male and female rescuers to condemnations, threats, robberies, and denunciation to the occupying forces. In the early post-war period of ideological civil war, poverty, and high levels of uncertainty and volatility, rescuers continued to be persecuted. In a bitter letter of 15 January 1948 to the CKŻP complaining about the lack of assistance from his former Jewish charges, Jan Kulpa of Biała Krakowska wrote: 'Today those who know about my actions laugh at me that I have gained nothing [from rescuing Jews]. They laugh at me that I was a "Jewish father" but I do not take this to heart. In fact I am proud of it.'[40] As during the war, underground military units, who saw themselves as 'moral police' acting on behalf of the Polish nation, continued to mete out punishment against those who had assisted Jews. In their letters and testimonies, rescuers and their charges referred to these military units as the chief threat, describing them as 'bandits', 'night-time military bands', or 'forest bands'. Historical research conducted in the last decade confirms that the Polish right-wing nationalistic military units, especially the National Armed Forces, were involved in killing rescuers and Jewish fugitives on a significant scale that is difficult to establish in precise figures.[41] No doubt, these 'forest bands' had family and other connections in the local communities through which they could learn who had sheltered Jews. The letters and testimonies do not provide any precise information about who tipped the bands off, nor do they mention any female members, but this is not to say that women did not play a role in stigmatizing rescuers or organizing violence or robbery.

[39] See Grabowski, *Judenjagd*; Engelking, *Jest taki piękny słoneczny dzień…* .

[40] AŻIH, 303/VIII, j. 230: Jan Kulpa, letter to the CKŻP, 15 Jan. 1948, 80.

[41] See e.g. M. Tryczyk, *Miasta śmierci: Sąsiedzkie pogromy Żydów* (Warsaw, 2015); for a critical review of the book, see N. Aleksiun, 'Zmarnowana szansa: O "Miastach śmierci" Mirosława Tryczyka', *Kultura Liberalna*, 19 Jan. 2016, <http://kulturaliberalna.pl/2016/01/19/zmarnowana-szansa-o-miastach-smierci-miroslawa-traczyka/> (accessed 22 Aug. 2016); for the crimes committed by Józef Kuraś ('Orzeł', 'Ogień'), an anticommunist partisan in the Podhale region of southern Poland, see L. Konarski, '"Ogień" był bandytą', *Przegląd*, 4 Mar. 2012, <http://www.tygodnikprzeglad.pl/ogien-byl-bandyta-o/> (accessed 22 Aug. 2016); K. Panz, '"Dlaczego oni, którzy tyle przecierpieli i przetrzymali, musieli zginąć": Żydowskie ofiary zbrojnej przemocy na Podhalu w latach 1945–1947', *Zagłada Żydów: Studia i materiały*, 11 (2015), 33–89.

In cities and in the countryside rescuers saw their neighbours, whom they often referred to in their letters without mentioning names, genders, or occupations, as a major threat to their Jewish charges and themselves. Maria Jakubowska, who sheltered eight Jews in her modest apartment in Warsaw, recalls: 'Honestly, I am not capable of describing what we really went through. It was important to manipulate neighbours in such a way, so they would be totally clueless about the presence of Jews nearby. Neighbours always were the worst to deal with.'[42]

After the war, some rescuers had to abandon their homes, villages, or towns because of death threats. Antoni Misiejski, from Bubel-Granna in Biała Podlaska county, had to flee the Lublin voivodeship to escape bandits.[43] He endured physical violence many times as a punishment for rescuing three Jewish men.

Antonina Wyrzykowska, from Janczewko near Jedwabne, is the best-known female rescuer. She had to endure physical violence as punishment for her activities.[44] Wyrzykowska struggled with selective memory, repression, and visceral fear during her recounting of wartime events, as a result of the suffering she had undergone during and after the war. She and her first husband, Aleksander, sheltered seven Jewish men and women who had survived anti-Jewish violence in the summer of 1941 on their farm from November 1942 until the Germans were driven out of the area in January 1945. After the Germans had gone they were harassed and physically abused by their neighbours: Wyrzykowska was severely beaten and had to move from her home three times. Even after the state authorities officially recognized her deeds during commemorative ceremonies in July 2001, and after a peaceful life between Łomża region and the United States, she refused to speak about the behaviour of her local townspeople.

Some rescuers did not mention the stigmatization they had incurred in their letters. Information about it comes from Jewish organizations. For example, the Jewish Committee of Jasło wrote to the CKŻP in February 1947 requesting clothes and shoes for a peasant named Adolf Jachym from Sowina and his family, and also some cash. In the letter Jachym is described as a brave man who had sheltered eleven members of two Jewish families, the Korzeniks and the Krigers, for over two years on his small farm. He had managed to get forged identity cards for two of the female Jewish fugitives, allowing them to pose as Christian Polish women and do forced labour in Germany, where they survived the war. During the two years in which he sheltered the Jewish fugitives, he risked the lives of his family—his wife, four children, and elderly mother. Just after the entry of the Red Army into the region, bandits beat him up and robbed him and his family of their belongings,

---

[42] AŻIH, 303/VIII, j. 227: Maria Jakubowska, letter to the CKŻP, n.d., 45.

[43] AŻIH, 303/VIII, j. 232: Antoni Misiejuk, letter to the CKŻP, Social Welfare Department, 8 Oct. 1947, 82; Jewish Committee of Biała Podlaska, testimony, 14 Mar. 1946, 85.

[44] See A. Bikont, *My z Jedwabnego* (Warsaw, 2004); *Sąsiedzi* [documentary], dir. A. Arnold (TVP, 2001); *Legacies of Jedwabne* [documentary], dir. S. Grünberg (LOGTV, 2005).

including their clothes. An economic element featured in this crime, but the robbery and beating were in part a punishment for rescuing Jews.[45]

Other rescuers saw writing to Jewish organizations as an opportunity to unburden themselves of secret and traumatic wartime experiences which they could not share with their compatriots for fear of retribution. Katarzyna Dzieżyńska, a 70-year-old widow, who was a lonely repatriate to Przemyśl from the village of Radochońce in the Kresy, wrote about losing her husband and all her possessions as punishment for sheltering three brothers, Jankiel, Chaim, and Majorko Echstein. In her statement, Dzieżyńska said she did not let the warnings and threats stop her from assisting the brothers:

All three brothers had to hide in the forest, because in the village their lives were constantly threatened. They used to visit me in my home during night-time, and I provided them with everything I could: bread, milk, eggs, and cheese. They would put everything in a sack and run back to the forest. I helped them in this manner for two years and they managed to survive. When the bandits began to suspect I was helping the poor brothers, I received death threats. But I did not pay attention to those threats and continued to help.

In 1945, when the Russian army entered our village, all three brothers survived and were free. Unfortunately the bandits did not forget about me. One night they paid us a visit and robbed us of everything, including the boots that we wore on our feet. A few weeks after this incident, my husband passed away out of fear. I am a 70-year-old woman left without anything.[46]

Letters from members of the intelligentsia express embarrassment and anger that rescuers were subjected to stigmatization. Cecylia Piotrowska, an upper-middle-class woman, describes the stigmatization of her sister, who like herself sheltered Jews:

I never expected any reward. Many of my acquaintances, particularly observant Catholics, did the same and for the same reasons. During the Nazi terror, someone painted a Star of David on the door of my sister's apartment. This was a warning directed at her so that she would cease hiding Jews. I could say many things about those who saved Jews because of their convictions. They put their lives in danger and paid for their actions with their lives, freedom, and wealth. They expected neither payment nor glory. But I have no right to write about them. Nevertheless, after a long hesitation I finally decided to write about my life and the lives of my dearest, so the truth will be known: Only great love, love of God and people can save humanity from bestiality and hatred.[47]

Iwo Trunk, one of Piotrowska's charges, corroborated her statement and described her as an ideal rescuer:

[45] AŻIH, 303/VIII, j. 227: Jewish Committee and Jewish Religious Congregation in Jasło, letter to the CKŻP, 12 Feb. 1947.
[46] AŻIH, 303/VIII, j. 224: Katarzyna Dzieżyńska, letter to the Jewish community in Przemyśl, 24 Mar. 1947, 110–11.
[47] AŻIH, 303/VIII, j. 235(5–6): Cecylia Piotrowska, letter to the CKŻP, 8 Aug. 1947, 74–5.

During the time of the greatest adversity during the war, I myself experienced a lot of good in her home. I received not only moral but also material support. This was not an unusual action on her part. Many Jews passed through her home, and they owed their lives to her. If there were more Poles like her, certainly more Jews would have been saved. I emphasize that she did it all for purely selfless reasons.[48]

The letters and testimonies reveal the feelings of rescuers after the war: feelings of social isolation, frustration, despair, and anger. Female rescuers were generally much more emotionally expressive than male rescuers. However, both male and female rescuers were aware that not everyone in their local communities perceived their actions as heroic or patriotic. Many kept their deeds secret from neighbours, colleagues, and even family, out of fear of being identified as a rescuer of Jews and becoming the victim of stigmatization and physical violence. J. Ciechocińska, who had rescued a young Jewish man, wrote: 'God only help me if this reaches the ears of the antisemites and their tongues start wagging.'[49] In some cases, there seemed to be no end to the violence, as a letter from Helena Sadowska from Miastkowo, near Łomża, reveals:

Because I sheltered Jews, forest bands destroyed my farm and took away my two horses, a cart, and pigs. They 'visited' me nine times. [Therefore,] I ask you [the Jewish community in Warsaw] for a positive attitude towards my request and to offer me financial aid, so that I will be able to buy a horse. Without a horse, I cannot run my farm.[50]

Sadowska was a typical middle-aged peasant woman, head of the household, and chief breadwinner struggling for physical survival and economic independence. Immediately after the war Polish women of all ages and socioeconomic back-grounds were called upon to play the role of head of the household, as there were few healthy Polish men between the ages of 18 and 40. Newspapers and magazines of the period directed at female audiences suggested that women should not give up the economic independence they had achieved during the war. Some female journalists stated that a man was 'an expensive piece of furniture' without which a woman could easily manage.[51]

The letters and testimonies provide anecdotal reports about the stigmatization of rescuers, its nature, and its practical effects, but no statistical data about the extent of stigmatization are available. Stigmatization is difficult to research because for decades the subject was taboo for its victims, the perpetrators, and their fami-lies. However, there were some punishments meted out by male members of the ethno-nationalistic 'moral' police against women that had a distinctly gendered

[48] AŻIH, 303/VIII, j. 235(7): Iwo Trunk, testimony, 8 May 1947, 76–7.

[49] AŻIH, 303/VIII, j. 223: J. Ciechocińska, letter to the Jewish community of Warsaw, 1 Mar. 1948, 4.

[50] AŻIH, 303/VIII, j. 238: Helena Sadowska, letter to the *kehilah* of Warsaw, 29 May 1947, 848. Sadowska's letter was accompanied by the testimonies of Leon Kofler and Pinkas Gruszniewski. Gruszniewski, whom she took to the Jewish children's home in Bytom at Smoleńska 16, was the youngest of the six Jewish charges under her care.   [51] Fidelis, 'Czy "nowy matriarchat?"', 429–33.

component. This is perhaps the most difficult aspect of stigmatization to research. Were these cases an exception, or were they the norm but extremely hard to detect because of the high level of taboo?

The most common gendered violence against female rescuers involved shaving their heads. Stanisław Chęcia, a peasant from Bełżyce, described how he, his wife, and their two daughters were 'disciplined' for having saved a Jewish baby. After the war, Chęcia returned the child to its biological uncle and the newly reunited Jewish family left for Paris. According to Chęcia, when the news reached his neighbours: 'homegrown fascist bands invaded our home, demolished all our furniture, beat up everybody, and cut off my wife's and my daughters' hair, shouting that this is punishment for [sheltering] a Jewish child'.[52] During the war, local women throughout Nazi-occupied Europe who had sexual relations with Germans were viewed as collaborators and also had their heads shaved.[53] Those who shaved the heads of female rescuers in Poland treated them as traitors in the same way. Polish women, who were employed by Jewish children's homes in Podhale in south Poland in the immediate post-war period, also received threats from the underground anti-communist and antisemitic military units threatening that if they did not stop working for the Jewish organizations their heads would be shaved, and that they could expect punishment for helping 'the enemy'.[54] Immediately after the war, Polish women, especially unmarried ones, were portrayed not as victims but as heroines in the press;[55] however, female rescuers were denied the status of war heroines.

Only one letter mentions the attempted rape of a female rescuer or female charges. The perpetrators did not necessarily consider rape a punishment, but were merely taking advantage of the women's vulnerability. Mrs Jastrzębska, a mature, lower-middle-class woman who ran a kiosk selling cigarettes and drinks near Poniatowski Bridge in Warsaw, provided shelter to two young Jewish women, Regina and Ewa Greiss, aged 15 and 24, from Drohobycz near Lviv. Hieronim Duda, her husband's nephew, brought them to her apartment in April 1943. They had been robbed of everything by their previous rescuers.[56] Jastrzębska provided them with clothing, hid them in various family apartments and at her place of work, and organized forged identity cards for them as Maria and Krystyna

[52] AŻIH, 303/VIII, j. 223: Stanisław Chęcia, letter to the CKŻP, n.d., 13; see also AŻIH, 303/VIII, j. 223: Jewish Committee in Lublin, testimony, 29 Mar. 1947, 14.
[53] See e.g. B. Frommer, 'Denouncers and Fraternizers: Gender, Collaboration, and Retribution in Bohemia and Moravia during World War II and After', in Wingfield and Bucur (eds.), *Gender and War in Twentieth-Century Eastern Europe*, 111–32; F. Virgili, *Shorn Women: Gender and Punishment in Liberation France* (Oxford, 2002).
[54] See Panz, '"Dlaczego oni, którzy tyle przecierpieli i przetrzymali, musieli zginąć"'.
[55] Fidelis, 'Czy "nowy matriarchat?"', 435.
[56] AŻIH, 303/VIII, j. 243: Mrs Jastrzębska, letter to CKŻP, Social Welfare Department, n.d., 6. According to Jastrzębska, Hieronim Duda was murdered at the request of the previous rescuers, 'because of his assistance and sympathy towards Jewish fugitives' (ibid.).

Kaweckie. They remained with her until the end of the Warsaw uprising of August 1944 and were reunited with her in July 1945 in the ruined city. They then spent five weeks with her, preparing to depart for the United States. Jastrzębska recollected how she struggled with blackmailers and potential rapists:

We were afraid of our own shadows, of each neighbour, of each acquaintance, and of each stranger. Thanks to my level-headedness, I saved [Maria] by creating a safe exit for her from a tram that she had to jump off. I stopped the [blackmailer] with my body, shouting at him that due to his aggressive behaviour, people were crowded in the tram. . . . We experienced continuous blackmail by the construction workers on Poniatowski Bridge. They recognized [Maria's] semitic features and attempted to take advantage of the situation in every way they could. They blackmailed her and they blackmailed me in a disgusting way. Once they paid us a visit in my kiosk and began to shout at us. They not only wanted to blackmail us again but attempted to rape us. We were in an oppressive situation then, women on their own facing beast-like men. I defended her honour as if she was my daughter. My bravery was my best weapon. Knowing what was about to happen, I took out Maria's coat and hat without the men noticing and whispered to her: 'Maria, run away to the apartment and hide where you can.' Then I was left alone with the men. I did not give up and defended myself to the end. They called me horrible names.[57]

How many such cases of rape or attempted rape as sexual blackmail were conducted by civilian Polish men? How many of these cases resulted in the murder of the female victims? Further research is needed to establish the scope of this phenomenon.

Recent research has shown that the rape and murder of female Jewish fugitives was practised during the war by sections of the military and male Polish civilians, especially in the countryside. Rape emerged as a brutal weapon against Jewish women: typically they were murdered afterwards.[58] The nature and goals of rape in Poland do not appear to differ from those in other parts of Nazi-occupied Europe. During the Second World War, rape was used as a weapon to humiliate national and ethnic groups regarded as enemies and lower races.[59] The rape of

---

[57] Ibid. 7–8.

[58] The brutal rape and murder, in the summer of 1941, of twenty young Jewish women from the Szczuczyn ghetto by Polish men from Bzury where the women worked as forced labour in the fields is one of such cases that has been publicized recently in the Polish press (A. Domanowska, 'Mord Żydówek w Bzurach: IPN po 71 latach wszczyna śledztwo', *Gazeta Wyborcza*, 6 Mar. 2012, available at <http://wyborcza.pl/1,75248,11289917,Mord_Zydowek_w_Bzurach__IPN_po_71_latach_wszczy na.html?utm_source=rozne#ixzz10M7Acv70> (accessed 12 May 2014); see also Gross and Grudzińska-Gross, *Golden Harvest*; 'Zbrodnie NSZ', *Żołnierze przeklęci: Nacjonalizm zabija*, available at <http://zolnierzeprzekleci.wordpress.com/zbrodnie/> (accessed 9 May 2014)).

[59] N. M. Naimark, *Fires of Hatred: Ethnic Cleansing in Twentieth-Century Europe* (Cambridge, Mass., 2001); J. Burds, 'Sexual Violence in Europe in World War II, 1939–1945', *Politics and Society*, 37 (2009), 35–74; D. Herzog (ed.), *Brutality and Desire: War and Sexuality in Europe's Twentieth Century* (Basingstoke, Hants., 2009). For comparison with rape during the Armenian genocide of 1915 to 1917, see L. Shirinian, *Survivor Memoirs of the Armenian Genocide* (Reading, Berks., 1999); D. E. Miller and L. Touryan Miller, *Survivors: An Oral History of the Armenian Genocide* (Berkeley, Calif., 1999).

German women as revenge for what the Nazis did to Soviet men, women, and children during the war also constitutes a special case.[60]

Was rape a part of the stigmatization of female Polish rescuers? Was it a typical punishment for rescuing Jews? The letters and testimonies provide few details about it, but this can be explained by the extremely humiliating nature of the act and the lack of social protest against it. The growing literature on rape as a weapon of war and genocide in the twentieth century demonstrates that speaking about the experience is a brave act for victims of both genders: many keep the memory of these painful, dishonouring, and humiliating events to themselves for various social and cultural reasons.[61]

Humiliation and dishonour could explain the lack of evidence about the rape of female Polish rescuers. Interviews with the children of female rescuers can provide evidence of rape as part of the stigmatization of female rescuers in Poland. For example, in a chilling account recorded in 2010, Kazimierz and Stanisław from the village of Zucielec, near Trzcianne, the sons of the rescuer Anna Wasilewska, spoke about how they became orphans because their mother was punished for rescuing Jews. Before the official end of the war on 18 April 1945, an unnamed military unit invaded their home and raped and killed Wasilewska in front of her sons.[62] Was this case an exception rather than a non-reported norm? The subject deserves further investigation.

---

[60] See N. M. Naimark, *The Russians in Germany: The History of the Soviet Zone of Occupation, 1945–1949* (Cambridge, Mass. 1995). On gendered violence against Polish women deported to the Soviet Union during the Second World War, see K. R. Jolluck, 'The Nation's Pain and Women's Shame: Polish Women and Wartime Violence', in Wingfield and Bucur (eds.), *Gender and War in Twentieth-Century Eastern Europe*, 193–219.

[61] See e.g. African Rights, *Rwanda: Broken Bodies, Torn Spirits: Living with Genocide, Rape and HIV/AIDS* (Kigali, 2004); R. Ali and L. Lifschitz (eds.), *Why Bosnia? Writing on the Bosnian War* (Stony Creek, Conn., 1993); M. Cherif Bassiouni and M. McCormick, *Sexual Violence: An Invisible Weapon of War in Former Yugoslavia* (Chicago, 1996); A. Stiglmayr (ed.), *Mass Rape: The War against Women in Bosnia-Herzegovina* (Lincoln, Neb., 1994); M. Bjornlund, '"A Fate Worse Than Dying": Sexual Violence during the Armenian Genocide', in Herzog (ed.), *Brutality and Desire*, 16–58; T. Iacobelli, 'The "Sum of Such Actions": Investigating Mass Rape in Bosnia-Herzegovina through a Case Study of Foča', in Herzog (ed.), *Brutality and Desire*, 261–83; P. R. Bos, 'Feminists Interpreting the Politics of Wartime Rape: Berlin, 1945; Yugoslavia, 1992–1993', *Signs*, 31/4 (2006), 995–1025; P. A. Weitsman, 'The Politics of Identity and Sexual Violence: A Review of Bosnia and Rwanda', *Human Rights Quarterly*, 30 (2008), 561–78; L. Sharlach, 'Rape as Genocide: Bangladesh, the Former Yugoslavia, and Rwanda', *New Political Science*, 22/1 (2010), 89–102.

[62] See *Ukryci* [documentary], dir. Ł. Konopa (Ethnographic Archives of Warsaw University, 2010). In 1988 Yad Vashem honoured Jan and Anna Wasilewscy and their three sons, Kazimierz, Stanisław, and Jerzy, as Righteous Among the Nations. According to Kazimierz and Stanisław, one of three Jewish survivors, a young woman was also killed by Poles after she left the shelter of their family home and moved back to Białystok. I would like to thank Joanna Tokarska-Bakir for making the film available to me.

CONCLUSION

Although this chapter is not a gender analysis of the rescue of Jews in Nazi-occupied Poland, it shows how gender categories can contribute depth and richness of texture and detail to analysis of what was involved in rescue on a daily basis and the danger of betrayal faced by rescuers. This chapter argues that gender should be explored not only in relation to objective factors, such as the age, socio-economic background, and religiosity of rescuers, but also in relation to more subjective factors such as family practices, individual beliefs, and the sexual desires of married, widowed, and single male and female rescuers.

At this point, the total number of men and women involved in rescue activities in Nazi-occupied Poland is unknown. Some scholars insist that Polish women made up the majority of rescuers precisely because of their gender, whereas others wonder if the apparent over-representation of Polish women rescuers can be explained by the shortage of men during and after the war that also plagued other European countries. Is this a Polish variant of European-wide trends? This important problem can be illuminated by micro-historical and prosopographical studies of rescue.

The analysis of the letters from rescuers and the accompanying testimonies of their charges, their families, and members of Jewish organizations demonstrates that much remains unknown about the rescue of Jews in Poland. Gender-related aspects in particular deserve further investigation.

Relations between the gender of the rescuer and their stigmatization by their community are complex and disturbing and need to be further examined using less conventional historical sources such as oral history and ethnography. Immediately after the war members of the Jewish Historical Commission who interviewed both female and male rescuers reported that many did not wish their names to be publicly known. In her introduction to the collection of testimonies, *The Children Accuse*, Maria Hochberg-Mariańska, a survivor and former member of the Jewish underground, pondered the reasons for the need among rescuers, even those who had saved penniless orphaned Jewish children, to keep their rescue activities secret.[63] Fear of being insulted and robbed was no doubt one reason, but this fear cannot be understood in cultural isolation. People who robbed and ransacked rescuers' properties did not do so solely for economic reasons, though they may have stolen in the belief that rescuers had acquired Jewish wealth. Economic reasons and benefits were important, but the rationale and motivation was to stigmatize, ridicule, and punish rescuers for saving Jews.

The pre-1939 ethno-nationalistic intention in labelling an individual a 'Jewish saviour' was to isolate them from the community for betraying Polish social and

---

[63] M. Hochberg-Mariańska, 'Introduction', in M. Hochberg-Mariańska and N. Grüss (eds.), *The Children Accuse* (London, 1996), 24; Pol. orig.: M. Hochberg-Mariańska and N. Grüss (eds.), *Dzieci żydowskie oskarżają* (Kraków, 1946).

cultural norms. Pre-war stigmatization of Poles who spoke out against anti-semitism took on much more violent and aggressive forms under the Nazi occupation. Verbal abuse easily turned into actual violence against those who rescued Jews, and this continued after the war, when Jewish survivors began to come out of their shelters and leave their rescuers.

The rescuers' letters reveal a great deal about the mechanism of stigmatization and its devastating impact. Ridicule, beatings, and robberies were typical punishments for rescuers, both male and female; however, the punishment of female rescuers took on, in some cases, a specific gendered form through cutting their hair off and rape. Given the extremely humiliating nature of such treatment and the fear of continuing repercussions, the victims of these crimes were reluctant to speak out about it, even in their letters to Jewish organizations. Was gendered violence against female rescuers an exception in Poland during and shortly after the war? Or was it a large-scale phenomenon? Was the rape of women who rescued Jews during the Second World War a special case of gender violence? Are there any similar cases of gender violence in the wars and genocides after 1945? These questions deserve full investigation.

Julian Tuwim's Strategy for Survival as a Polish Jewish Poet

GIOVANNA TOMASSUCCI

Christian selling trousers: 38 Krucza Street
.   .   .   .

Jew buying trousers: 38 Krucza Street

ANTONI SŁONIMSKI and JULIAN TUWIM,
W oparach absurdu

THE POET WHO WANDERS

From the very start of his poetic career, Tuwim presented his literary alter ego as wandering about the city in search of spontaneous adventures, a twentieth-century flâneur with spare, aimless time on his hands.[1] Sometimes his 'idyllic walk' or brisk, Whitmanesque pace changed into a 'sad and crazy' meandering, leaving sluggish footprints behind. This inventive part poet, part vagrant, part rogue—like Socrates or the demonic Feliks struggling in the cellars of the Vatican[2]—was also known to creep about stealthily, 'on the diagonal' or 'at a hound's pace'. Thanks to the visit of a certain 'unpleasant guest', his way of walking underwent another change, and then he plodded about the world 'with steps on the edge of the abyss'.

Tuwim's alter ego was often a man of the streets, not belonging to any specific environment but alone and free, observing urban life, sometimes delighted by his surroundings, sometimes critical of them. Tuwim, however, had another mask: he sometimes took on the role of the clown and buffoon, which allowed him to highlight his personal attitude to his surroundings and at the same time provide a satirical image of the era. Tuwim performed a voluntary balancing act, living his life 'in between': in between the Polish literary tradition and the world of the European avant-garde; in between the sublime and the ridiculous; and in between

This chapter first appeared as Giovanna Tomassucci, '"Klin" Tuwima: strategie przeżycia polsko-żydowskiego poety', *Acta Universitatis Lodziensis: Folia Litteraria Polonica*, 2014, no. 4, pp. 55–73.

[1] J. Tuwim, 'Symfonia o sobie', in id., *Wiersze I*, Dzieła, 1/I (Warsaw, 1955), 64.

[2] J. Tuwim, 'Skrzydlaty złoczyńca', in id., *Wiersze II*, Dzieła, 1/II (Warsaw, 1955), 79–80.

428   *Giovanna Tomassucci*

Polish and Jewish society (with neither of them regarding him as theirs, because he refused to belong exclusively to either of them).

SELF-FASHIONING

All members of Polish society of Jewish origin struggled with their identity as a result of strong social pressures which refused them the right to define themselves as multi-ethnic (what Janusz Korczak called 'being chequered'). The advantages of multi-ethnicity were not appreciated in the Second Polish Republic: the contributions of ethnic minorities—especially Jews—to Polish culture were generally regarded as dangerously contaminating. Korczak was one of the few Poles who promoted cultural and linguistic pluralism and a sense of solidarity and community among the ethnic groups living in the Polish lands. His 'bold plan to rebuild the world' aimed from the start at the acceptance of cultures and languages and the creation of a new, pluralistic way to be a Pole.[3]

Korczak's interesting, but unfortunately little-known, novella 'Pieśń wiosenna' ('Spring Song'), first published in *Herold Polski* in 1906, anticipates the sort of provocative remarks made by Witold Gombrowicz's characters. One fine spring day, the narrator accosts a series of people who sit down on his bench 'in the avenues', making rhetorical appeals to them for love within the family and within society. When one of them asks whether he is 'white or red', he unexpectedly answers that he is 'chequered', prompting his interlocutor to admit that he is afraid of 'chequered people'.[4]

The man 'from outside' is the same sort of anti-conventional hero. The art of being 'chequered' that Korczak promoted, harmonizing in oneself the disparate elements of one's identity (ethnic, cultural, and sometimes linguistic), was extremely difficult and thus very rare in twentieth-century Poland. Writers of Jewish origin in particular were expected to be totally Polonized and to reject their Jewish identity, but, in the interests of 'cultural healing', were refused a place among 'Polish artists' because of their ethnicity or for stylistic or linguistic reasons.

According to the extremely deeply rooted convictions of a large part of Polish society, being Jewish was a handicap which should not be acknowledged, not even to oneself. Thus Polish writers of Jewish origin seeking a reconciliation between the Jewish and Polish worlds were obliged to create a particular public reputation for themselves, an example of so-called 'self-fashioning'. However, this does not mean they renounced important aspects of their dual personality. In 'a homeland [where] to a foreign faith | God does not descend',[5] where antisemites enjoyed denouncing 'literary bastardizations' that were ethnically Jewish,[6] and where nation-

---

[3] J. Korczak, *Pamiętnik* (Poznań, 1984), 5.

[4] J. Korczak, 'Pieśń wiosenna', in id., *Koszałki opałki: Humoreski i felietony*, Dzieła, 2 (Warsaw, 1998), 19.   [5] A. Słonimski, 'Dwie ojczyzny', in id., *Poezje zebrane* (Warsaw, 1964), 381.

[6] K. H. Rostworowski, cited in S. Imber, 'Rekapitulacja, czy kapitulacja?', in id., *Asy czystej rasy* (Kraków, 1934), 53.

alists from the Jewish camp found 'fault with those who disavow "membership of the Jewish race"',[7] any effort to 'highlight one's own identity'[8] or merely to show an interest in Jewish culture could be the focus of a hate campaign or of manipulation (Korczak was a notable example of going against the grain). Besides that, each person adopted their own 'survival strategy' and applied their own self-censorship, because the situation of the Polish Jewish writer who did not belong with the Jewish nationalists or did not sympathize with Yiddish culture entailed coming to terms with one's own identity on an entirely individual basis, never a collective one (hence Jewish writers who wrote in Polish rarely used the first person plural).

One of the reactions was a radical cosmopolitanism and a defiant attitude to any sort of nationalist rhetoric. As Antoni Słonimski declared in 1932:

The law and the constitution allow one to be non-denominational. Should lack of denomination also be banned in ethnic matters? Should one necessarily have to love only one of the two chosen nations, either the Poles or the Jews? That's too limited a choice, gentlemen![9]

Tuwim's attitude was very different: he stressed his Polishness and his Jewishness as important parts of his personal identity. However, like Słonimski, he did not just see reasons for pride in being a Polish Jew. He also saw reasons for censure: for ignoring the opinions of Poles but also for passive imitation of them.

From statements he made in interviews between the wars and in 'My, Żydzi polscy' ('We Polish Jews'), it appears that Tuwim often associated being Jewish with blood and suffering. At first, as an elemental component of his nature, the blood running in his veins connected him with Israel thanks to its 'mystic reflexes',[10] and then later it signified 'the bloody, burning, martyred brotherhood of Jews'.[11] Another metaphor he used was the ambivalent and self-ironical image of a 'wedge': 'In my case . . . the Jewish question is in my blood, it is a component of my psyche. It forms a sort of powerful wedge that cuts into my view of the world and my deepest personal experiences.'[12] Maybe some of his poems have a connection with this wedge, although they appear to have nothing to do with discrimination. One of Tuwim's favourite poems comes to mind, 'Garbus' ('The Hunchback'), published in *Skamander* in 1922 and written in the jocular tone of a cabaret song:

---

[7] S. Imber, 'Co nam i tobie, Tuwimie…?', *Nowy Dziennik*, 22–5 Dec. 1929; repr. in id., *Asy czystej rasy* (Kraków, 1934), 40.

[8] J. Tuwim, in S. Leben, 'Luminarze literatury i nauki polskiej o kwestii żydowskiej', *Nasz Przegląd*, 6 Jan. 1924, no. 6; repr. in T. Januszewski (ed.), *Rozmowy z Tuwimem* (Warsaw, 1994), 15.

[9] A. Słonimski, *Moje walki nad Bzdurą* (Warsaw, 1932), 141.

[10] J. Tuwim, in D. Silberberg, 'Godzina z Julianem Tuwimem', *Nasz Przegląd*, 15 Feb. 1935, no. 46; repr. in Januszewski (ed.), *Rozmowy z Tuwimem*, 54.

[11] J. Tuwim, 'My, Żydzi polscy', in *Nowa Polska*, 1944, no. 8, p. 491; Eng. trans.: 'We Polish Jews', trans. R. Langer, in Organization of Former Brody Residents in Israel (ed.), *Ner tamid: yizkor lebrody / An Eternal Light: Brody, in Memoriam* (Jerusalem, 1994), 55.

[12] Tuwim, in Leben, 'Luminarze literatury i nauki polskiej o kwestii żydowskiej', 14.

Such beautiful neckties,
But what do I, the hunchback, care?
This one, with silver stripes,
Would suit me very well.
But all in vain:
Nobody will ever notice.

Even if it's rainbow-patterned,
Even with parrot-like colours,
No one will say: 'What a lovely tie!'
Everyone will say: 'What a horrid hump!'

I need a nice long ribbon,
The most gorgeous tie of all!
I'll knot it so very finely
That you simply won't recognize me!
'Ooh!' and 'Aah!' you'll whisper,
'What a hump that is!
But . . . why are you hanging by your tie?'[13]

Is this an allusion to the birthmark on the poet's cheek? Or to Jewishness felt as a handicap, as a brand marking him out as dramatically different? It is probably both.

Marian Hemar wrote, more openly and unambiguously, about the same thing:

I seem to go about with grace,
But sadly I remember:
I'm a Jew.
What can I do? My heart bleeds,
How can I look the National Democrats in the eye
Without shame?
I pretend I'm one of the Aryans
        .   .   .   .

I'm no Aryan at all! How could you, Marian!
Srul!!![14]

Tuwim could not erase the memory of his Jewishness or of his nation's tragedy. He openly declared that he never stopped considering the Jewish question.[15] Further evidence of this is provided by the fine poem 'Żydek' ('Jewboy'), in which his inner dilemma takes on a double incarnation as a 'gentleman from the first floor'

[13] J. Tuwim, 'Garbus', in id., *Wiersze I*, 25. Tuwim mentioned other favourite poems: 'Dzieciństwo', 'W Barwistanie', and 'My ludzie' in Znamor [Roman Zrębowicz], 'U Juliana Tuwima', *Wiadomości Literackie*, 1926, no. 5, p. 1; repr. in Januszewski (ed.), *Rozmowy z Tuwimem*, 19.

[14] M. Hemar, 'Ból serdeczny, rozwagi wstrzymywany siłą', *Wiadomości Literackie*, 1935, no. 44, p. 8. *Srul* is a diminutive form of the popular Jewish name Israel and a rather contemptuous way of referring to a Jew.

[15] Tuwim, in Leben, 'Luminarze literatury i nauki polskiej o kwestii żydowskiej', 14. In an interview given to D. Silberberg, Tuwim stated that his opinions about Jews and Zionism had undergone change over time (ibid. 54).

(a rather well-off man, comfortably sitting in the window of his apartment) and a young *meshugene* beggar;[16] by the comic verse polemics aimed at Pieńkowski and Wasilewski;[17] by the 'catalogue' of antisemitic nonsense in 'Anonimowe mocarstwo' ('The Anonymous Power');[18] by some poems that were not published in his lifetime, from his juvenilia to those in the collection of Tomasz Niewodniczański;[19] and by his nonsense advertisements which reveal the absurdity of Polish politics.[20] This has far more significance than that Tuwim 'knew very little' about the whole complicated constellation of Polish Jewry,[21] did not know Yiddish well,[22] and was not particularly interested in any of it.

Polish Jewish writers and artists not only generally refused to exhibit their Jewishness but also renounced their own—both remote and recent—Orthodox ancestors. Family memories only went back to the point when their forebears had assimilated (or even when they had themselves, as in the case of Adolf Rudnicki, who hid his hasidic roots all his life). Significant exceptions were Janusz Korczak, who wrote fabulous descriptions of the past fortunes of his grandfather, Hersz Goldszmit, in his novellas *Herszele* and *Trzy wyprawy Herszka*, and Aleksander Wat. For others, everything that took place before the date of their departure from the so-called ghetto was almost always ignored and by implication deprecated. In Polish society, where the nobility were obsessed with lineage, a person with no genealogy was automatically suspect. In Polish literature the prototype was Pankracy in Zygmunt Krasiński's *Nie Boska komedia*, a revolutionary and ally of the Jewish converts to Christianity, who came from nowhere, had 'no name, no ancestors . . . no guardian angel, faith, nor God'.[23] Having no roots also had a notable effect on one's sense of emptiness. The condition of the contemporary Jew was that of an outsider, an alienated parvenu: in Kafka's diaries there is a reference to being 'without forebears, without marriage, without heirs, with a fierce longing for forebears, marriage, and heirs. They all of them stretch out their hands to me: forebears, marriage, and heirs, but too far away for me.'[24] Paradoxically this feeling could be enhanced by the sight of Jews, looking glaringly different in their gabardines, reminders of undesirable, 'disowned' ancestors. This may also explain Tuwim's merciless satirizing of long-tailed caftans and side-locks, of a 'Hebrew—

---

[16] J. Tuwim, 'Żydek', in id., *Wiersze I*, 282.

[17] J. Tuwim, 'Z Heinego', *Wiadomości Literackie*, 1934, no. 42, p. 6.

[18] J. Tuwim, 'Anonimowe mocarstwo', in id., *Jarmark rymów*, Dzieła, 3 (Warsaw, 1958), 50.

[19] See J. Tuwim, *Utwory nieznane. Ze zbiorów Tomasza Niewodniczańskiego w Bitburgu: wiersze, kabaret, artykuły, listy*, ed. T. Januszewski (Łódź, 1999), 83–90.

[20] 'Seat on the Number Eighteen on the front platform to be given up immediately. Pocielski, Zbawiciela Square. For Christians only' (A. Słonimski and J. Tuwim, *W oparach absurdu* (Warsaw, 2006), 115). [21] A. Hertz, *Żydzi w kulturze polskiej* (Warsaw, 1988), 257.

[22] A. Sandauer, *O sytuacji pisarza polskiego pochodzenia żydowskiego w XX wieku: Rzecz, którą nie ja powinienem był napisa* (Warsaw, 1982), 15 n.

[23] Z. Krasiński, 'The Undivine Comedy', III, in *The Undivine Comedy and Other Poems*, trans. J. Walter Cook (Philadelphia, 1875), 239.

[24] F. Kafka, *The Diaries*, trans. M. Greenberg (London, 1982), 402 (21 Jan. 1922).

German stew', of 'the black hasidic rabble',[25] and of mispronounced Polish speech.

But Tuwim did not find all of the Jewish tradition repugnant. Antoni Słonimski, who came from Hrubieszów, the same shtetl as the Goldszmidts, Janusz Korczak's family, only discovered the poetry of the shtetl after it had been annihilated (partly thanks to meeting the famous Jewish poet Itzik Manger in London[26]), but Tuwim extolled it in 'Miasteczko Będzin' ('The Shtetl of Będzin'), the tale of the fiddler Jankiel Wasserstein, 'the number one rogue' from the Będzin marketplace, who moved to Warsaw, then New York, and metamorphosed into the 'king of the jazz band' and the Charleston. Wasserstein (who shares some features with the wonderful musician Menuchim from Joseph Roth's novel *Job*, which was published in the same year) changes his name, first to Jan Wodnicki and then to John Waterstone, but despite his brilliant career he never forgets what links him with his ancestors. As he shows his son the family fiddle, he says:

> Never fear!
> As long as the Jew knows how to play, he'll never disappear,
> You will have this self-same fiddle
> And you'll play it for your children.
> The strains of an ancient song
> Will follow you into the world,
> You'll take the fiddle in your hands
> And play the same tune as your granddad.
> Whether it's Rothschild or whether it's me,
> Every Jew has tears in his eyes,
> On hearing songs from days gone by.[27]

But this sort of content is only incidental, just as Tuwim's mockery—which tended towards the absurd—of antisemitic campaigns remained on the margins of his work.

It was better to believe in the future, and in the possibility of reforming the world in some way. Thus Tuwim, as 'an imitator of the world's voices', 'a conjuror',[28] and 'an alert and intent . . . word catcher',[29] also, like Korczak, hatched his own 'bold plan to rebuild the world'.[30] He dreamed of a new poetic language that would be a common home and motherland for all readers, promoted Esperanto, and often resorted to acrobatic plurilingualism, using quotes and phrases from all the European languages familiar to him.

In 1905 the creator of Esperanto, Ludwik Zamenhof, remarked: 'If I had not been a Jew from the ghetto, the idea of uniting humanity either would never have entered my head or it would never have gripped me so tenaciously throughout my

[25] J. Tuwim, 'Wspomnienia o Łodzi', *Wiadomości Literackie*, 1934, no. 33, p. 11.

[26] Manger had lived in Warsaw before the war but had never met any members of the literary clique Skamander.

[27] J. Tuwim, 'Stara piosenka [Miasteczko Będzin]', in id., *Utwory nieznane*, 168–9.

[28] J. Tuwim, 'Hokus-pokus', in id., *Wiersze I*, 288.

[29] J. Tuwim, 'Słowo i ciało', ibid. 267.   [30] J. Korczak, *Pamiętnik* (Poznań, 1984), 5.

entire life. No one can feel more strongly than a ghetto Jew the sadness of dissension among peoples.'[31] According to George Steiner, 'the artificial languages proposed since J.-M. Schleyer's Volapük (1879) and the Esperanto of L. L. Zamenhof (1887) are auxiliary *interlinguae* . . . meant to counteract the threats of chauvinism or isolation in a tensely nationalist world.'[32]

Throughout its long history the Jewish nation survived by remaining faithful to the language of the Bible, but everywhere it went it also absorbed linguistic elements from the people it encountered. After they had become assimilated, Jewish linguists, journalists, poets, and philosophers of language continued to give almost religious significance to spoken and written language, either through their great concern for correct form or by making it the object of deformation and destruction. Tuwim was one of them. As he wrote about Esperanto, 'the construction of this language is, in my view, brilliant, and admiration for its merits has not weakened—in fact affection for it has been so ardent and sincere, that one day I shall devote a special article to the topic of an international language, focusing on Esperanto.'[33]

It is a great pity that he never wrote that article. All his poetry, not just the bold experiments, such as 'Słopiewnie' or 'Atuli mirohłady', aspired to create an unrestricted area, something like a poetic, universal *interlingua*.

TALKING ABOUT ASSIMILATED JEWS WITHOUT TALKING ABOUT JEWS

Korczak's 'Pieśń wiosenna' and Tuwim's 'Garbus' highlight a particular way of making a metaphor out of a sense of being racially different. Many Jewish authors writing in Polish used a similar tactic, especially during the interwar period. They placed allusions in their texts that testified to a sense of discrimination, and also coded demands for universalism, in the hope that some of their readers would be capable of deciphering them. Several of Tuwim's poems can be interpreted in this way, and, though disguised by 'self-fashioning', the 'wedge cutting into his view of the world' and into his 'deepest personal experiences' let itself be felt painfully in his poetry.

Tuwim's 'Psy' ('Dogs') was attacked many times in the interwar period for blasphemy.

> Growling, I loped along at a hound's pace,
> Hackles up, taciturn and angry,
> Until I came outside the house, barked with despair,
> And was answered by my dogs.
> .   .   .   .

---

[31] L. Zamenhof, letter to Michaux, 1905, cited in A. Korzhenkov, *The Life of Zamenhof*, trans. I. M. Richmond (New York, 2010), 5.

[32] G. Steiner, *After Babel: Aspects of Language and Translation* (Oxford, 1975), 201–2.

[33] J. Tuwim, *Tam zostałem: Wspomnienia młodości* (Warsaw, 2003), 56.

It is only man who cries for help,
Man who is bent on awful wonder.

.   .   .   .

And so let us sleep, worn out by weeping,
Maybe we'll find relief in sleep,
Seeing poor mongrel dreams,
The grey phantom of our canine death.

There a flat, low heaven will appear,
We shall sniff at the doorstep of God,
And as He once came to the poor and the anxious,
To the dogs will come the saviour God.[34]

The poem is often cited as a sign of the poet's solidarity with the animal world, but it can be interpreted in a totally different way by calling to mind another 'awful wonder', the 'canine metamorphosis' in the first of Heinrich Heine's beautiful *Hebräische Melodien* 'Prinzessin Sabbat', about the fortunes of an enchanted prince who has been changed into a dog by an evil witch. Every Friday evening he regains his original shape and returns to the wise and beautiful Princess Sabbath, but soon he has to change back into a monster and return to life's filthy mire:

As a dog, with dog's ideas,
All the week, a cur, he noses
Through life's filthy mire and sweepings,
Butt of mocking city Arabs;

But on every Friday evening,
On a sudden, in the twilight,
The enchantment weakens, ceases,
And the dog once more is human.

And his father's halls he enters
As a man, with man's emotions,
Head and heart alike uplifted,
Clad in pure and festal raiment.[35]

In a jocular tone Heine describes the discord, also discussed by Sandauer and Hertz, between the vision of the Jews as a sacred race and their image as an accursed nation, between pride and shame, between the Jew's sense of himself as being chosen, 'a member of a charismatic group', and the pariah role assigned to him in Christian society.[36] Tuwim rated Heine highly from the very start of his

---

[34] J. Tuwim, 'Psy', in id., *Wiersze II*, 42.

[35] H. Heine, 'Princess Sabbath', trans. M. Armour, in *The Standard Book of Jewish Verse*, ed. J. Friedlander and G. A. Kohut (New York, 1917), 254.

[36] Hertz, *Żydzi w kulturze polskiej*, 123–4; Sandauer, *O sytuacji pisarza polskiego pochodzenia żydowskiego w XX wieku*, 5. On antisemitic attacks on Tuwim and his ambivalent attitude to Jews, see A. Polonsky, 'Why Did They Hate Tuwim and Boy so Much? Jews and "Artificial Jews" in the Literary Polemics in the Second Polish Republic', in R. Blobaum (ed.), *Antisemitism and its Opponents in Modern*

writing career, and they had similar dramatic experiences, including surviving a pogrom in childhood. Tuwim owed a lot to Heine, was often compared to him, and referred to him in his satirical poems about Pieńkowski and Wasilewski,[37] but he never quoted the cycle of witty yet sad *Hebräische Melodien*, which had been translated into Polish by Maria Konopnicka.

Under the 'barrage of schoolboy mockery', of which Heine complained and which unfortunately was still very present in twentieth-century Europe, it was impossible to object openly. In fact, Tuwim himself tells us about it:

> On all fours on my doorstep
> I cry to the stars, as you dogs do, just like you,
> That there's nobody to tell, to inform
> How we suffer, nocturnal people, mournful dogs.
>
> Not because of the cold or hunger do we howl,
> But since the moon has laid its lifeless sheet upon us,
> And in despair for this silver corner of the garden,
> For this incredible silence, for this world.
>
> Ah, to whom in our yearning, to whom
> Did we raise our terrified heads?
> The lousy [*parszywe*] dogs cannot answer,
> No more can I, my brother dogs![38]

Tuwim expressed a sense of solidarity with the suffering Jews in other places as well.

It is not entirely true that Tuwim refused to take an interest in Jewish culture. For example, 'Żydek' features a positive character taken straight from Jewish folklore: the young *meshugene* of the title. (The only other place in his work where Tuwim provides an equally favourable image of a typical Jew is in *Kwiaty polskie* ('Polish Flowers').) Tuwim took the pejorative Polish diminutive *Żydek* (Jewboy) and gave it its primary meaning (a little Jewish boy) and imbued it with much warmer feelings. In the final verse Tuwim makes his first reference to the Jews in the first person plural (apart from in 'Psy', Tuwim only used this form during the war, in 'My, Żydzi polscy'):

Poland (Ithaca, NY, 2005), 189–209; P. Matywiecki, 'Narody Tuwima', in *Twarz Tuwima* (Warsaw, 2007), 254–330; J. B. Michlic, 'Culture of Ethno-Nationalism and the Identity of Jews in Inter-War Poland', in R. I. Cohen, J. Frankel, and S. Hoffman (eds.), *Insiders and Outsiders: Dilemmas of East European Jewry* (Oxford, 2010), 131–47; 'Julian Tuwim: Dyskusja z udziałem Aliny Molisak, Belli Szwarcman-Czarnoty, Michała Głowińskiego i Piotra Matywieckiego', *Midrasz*, 2013, no 5, pp. 12–20.

[37] 'Wasilewski and Pieńkowski | Poles from the National Democratic Party | Curse me for my Jewish blood | But mainly for my b[alls]' (Tuwim, 'Z Heinego', 6).

[38] Tuwim, 'Psy'. *Parszywy* was frequently used as derogatory adjective for Jews. Tuwim used a similar canine metaphor in his earlier poem, 'Groteska': 'I get to know dogs, who are Jews' (*Wiersze I*, 166).

And we will both go on our way
A path sad and crazed
And we will never find peace or rest
Singing Jews, lost Jews.[39]

This could perhaps be a polemic echo of the symbolic singing and dancing of the hasidim in Act One of Y. L. Peretz's masterpiece *Di goldene keyt* ('The Golden Chain'). According to Chone Shmeruk, from the very first version (entitled *Khurbn beyt tsadik* ('The Fall of the Tsadik's Court')), Peretz never stopped working on the play: his aim was to show the calamities suffered by the three main nineteenth-century currents of east European Judaism: the hasidim, the Orthodox mitna-gedim, and the maskilim. In the final version, Peretz introduced the mystical *tsadik* Reb Shloyme, who attempts to have time annulled. Peretz contrasted the fall of the *tsadik*'s court with the cultural advances of the younger generation (in the figure of the *tsadik*'s grandson), advances that were tied to the past by a golden chain, because they drew on the old, poetic tradition of hasidism.[40] Tuwim once said in an interview that he 'knew and appreciated' the typical 'old Jew in a gabardine, not yet infected by European culture', who represents 'certain original values'.[41]

Reb Shloyme encourages dancing and singing:

To him! With singing and dancing we go to him.
Come sing, come dance with me (*he dances while singing*).
And so we go, singing and dancing . . .
We, the great Jews . . . and we do not ask,
nor do we beg, we are great, proud Jews.[42]

Peretz was exceedingly popular among the Jews, and the Poles valued him too, as an author who was strongly under the influence of Stanisław Wyspiański: his plays were performed either in part or in their entirety in Łódź, Warsaw, and other Polish cities,[43] and in 1928 Tadeusz Boy-Żeleński gave Peretz's *Bay nakht afn altn*

[39] Tuwim, 'Żydek'.

[40] In his review of Yiddish drama, Shmeruk wrote: 'The play was written and published in Hebrew in 1903. Peretz was not satisfied with the first edition, in which only the ruin of hasidism fully corre-sponded with his intentions. . . . In 1906 he made a translation into Yiddish . . . and struggled to pro-duce a final version of the play until the day he died' ('Przegląd literatury dramatycznej w języku jidysz do I wojny światowej', in A. Kuligowska-Korzeniewska and M. Leyko (eds.), *Teatr żydowski w Polsce: Materiały z międzynarodowej konferencji naukowej, Warszawa, 18–21 października 1993 roku* (Łódź, 1998), 49). It was the only one of Peretz's plays to be staged in his lifetime, but only the premiere took place: 'the main reason for abandoning further performances were threats by Warsaw hasidim, for whom the appearance on stage of a *tsadik* as a character in a play was a profanation of the memory of a greatly revered *tsadik* from Kock' (ibid.).

[41] J. Tuwim, in 'Wywiady z pisarzami polskimi pochodzenia żydowskiego, Rozmowa z Julianem Tuwimem', *Dziennik Warszawski*, 6–7 Feb. 1927; repr. in Januszewski (ed.), *Rozmowy z Tuwimem*, 25.

[42] Y. L. Peretz, *Di goldene keyt*, I. A talk on Peretz at Korczak's orphanage in the Warsaw ghetto also included readings from his works (M. Zylberberg, 'Na Chłodnej 33', in L. Barszczewska and B. Milewicz (eds.), *Wspomnienia o Januszu Korczaku* (Warsaw, 1981), 266–7).

[43] See R. Węgrzyniak, 'Hebrajskie Studio Dramatyczne w Łodzi (1928–1932)', in M. Leyko (ed.),

mark an enthusiastic review:

The man who said that travel shapes people was right. Yesterday evening I came back from a journey of this very kind: I went to Karowa Street to see the Jewish theatre, and I wasn't sorry I went. . . . And one thing struck me. Does it make any sense for people who live side by side to know so little about each other, to be so completely ignorant of one another? Plays from all over the world are performed in our city, often trite and of poor quality, but we do absolutely nothing to get to know the spirit of the nation with which we are destined to cohabit.[44]

The words of Reb Shloyme were carved on Peretz's tomb in the mausoleum where S. An-sky and Jakub Dinezon were also laid to rest in the cemetery on Okopowa Street in Warsaw. Thus this play may possibly have been known to Tuwim, and, if he heard a text read out in Yiddish, he was capable of 'working it out on the basis of knowing German'.[45]

Of course Tuwim, who did not recognize the old hasidic traditions, could not agree with Peretz's vision of Jewish pride. Despite this, 'Żydek' was a coded dialogue with the recently deceased father of contemporary Yiddish literature: leaving Peretz's personal pronoun 'we', Tuwim converted the hasidic dance of 'great and . . . proud Jews' into a solitary dance of two very different eternally wandering Jews, an assimilated poet and a small Orthodox madman, who symbolize two separate factions of twentieth-century Polish Jewry.

BOTANICAL ETHNOGRAPHY: *KWIATY POLSKIE*

One of the central themes of *Kwiaty polskie*, written during and after the war, is national prejudices and racial misunderstandings. Ignacy Dziewierski is prejudiced against the Russians; his granddaughter Aniela against the Bolshevik Jews; Wicek Jałowiecki against Jewish Bolshevik art; and young Kazik hates Aniela, whom he doesn't actually know, for being a Russian officer's daughter. The epilogue alone confirms the pointlessness of this attitude, as it results in the murder of the innocent Aniela. It is a satire on being obsessed with racial purity, as testified by the telling name of Folblut ('full blood'), the plutocrat with Jewish origins. Tuwim dreamed of tolerance and peaceful coexistence between different denominations and traditions, at a moment when it seemed quite impossible. In *Kwiaty polskie* he did not abandon his dream but showed how a sense of tolerance was integral to the Christian tradition and also part of the culture of pre-partition

Łódzkie sceny żydowskie: Studia i materiały (Łódź, 2000), 75; M. Bułat, 'Źródła do badania dziejów scen żydowskich w Łodzi', in Leyko (ed.), *Łódzkie sceny żydowskie*, 194.

[44] T. Boy-Żeleński, review of Peretz, *A Night in the Old Marketplace*, *Kurjer Poranny*, 24 Oct. 1928; *Nowy Dziennik*, 26 Oct. 1928, p. 3; repr. in *Pisma*, xxii: *Flirt z Melpomeną: Wieczór siódmy i ósmy* (Warsaw, 1964), 518–20.

[45] Tuwim, in 'Wywiady z pisarzami polskimi pochodzenia żydowskiego', in Januszewski (ed.), *Rozmowy z Tuwimem*, 26.

Poland–Lithuania. He cited authorities that both Jews and Poles could accept as authoritative. In 'Modlitwa' ('A Prayer') he wrote: 'There is neither Greek nor Jew', a reference to St Paul's Letter to the Galatians: 'There is neither Jew nor Greek, there is neither bond nor free, there is neither male nor female: for ye are all one in Christ Jesus. And if ye be Christ's, then are ye Abraham's seed, and heirs according to the promise' (Gal. 3: 28–9).[46]

Many of Tuwim's Polish contemporaries preferred to forget about the universalist message of the Gospels ('Excellent "Catholics" by now | But not yet Christians', as he defined them[47]), just as they preferred not to know that they were 'Abraham's seed'. It was much easier for them to resort to stereotypes:

> The Jew eats onions. I, a Catholic,
> Am fond of cabbage. Each to his own.
> (The Jews have one lack, one drawback.
> They haven't any saints in their church.)[48]

Whereas Tuwim urges:

> Whether you're a Tatar or a Greek, my man,
> Or whether you're black, it's irrelevant.
> Just be human. Don't amass wealth
> By harming your neighbour. Just be human.[49]

Another text to which *Kwiaty polskie* makes reference is Adam Mickiewicz's epic poem *Pan Tadeusz*, which is deeply rooted in Polish tradition (though its aims to unify were not understood either: by comparing Tuwim to the old Jew Jankiel in *Pan Tadeusz*, Nowaczyński was patronizingly mocking him).[50] Instead of a noble-man's farm there is an orchard ('miserable, sparse and shrivelled | with a poor Jewish gardener'[51]) instead of Jankiel's inn (in *Pan Tadeusz* resembling 'a Jew, who is nodding at prayer'[52]), there is the poor Jewish house:

> There the tradesman in black gabardine
> with stern and focused gaze
> Inspected old breeches held to the light
>
> .   .   .   .
>
> like the cantor during worship, when
> He raises the Torah from the altar.[53]

From the 1930s onwards Tuwim had stopped sticking 'large, small, and baby needles' into those who wore gabardines, aiming his weapons at the 'converts'

[46] J. Tuwim, *Kwiaty polskie*, Dzieła, 2 (Warsaw, 1955), 105.   [47] Ibid. 110.
[48] Ibid. 260   [49] Ibid.
[50] Apparently Nowaczyński made a toast to Tuwim: 'There is no Polish literature without Mick-iewicz, there is no Mickiewicz without *Pan Tadeusz*, there is no *Pan Tadeusz* without Jankiel. Long live Tuwim!' (cited in M. Urbaniak, *Tuwim: Wylękniony bluźnierca* (Warsaw, 2013), 126).
[51] Tuwim, *Kwiaty polskie*, 39.   [52] A. Mickiewicz, *Pan Tadeusz*, Dzieła, 4 (Warsaw, 1958), 107–8.
[53] Tuwim, *Kwiaty polskie*, 246–7.

instead.[54] In *Kwiaty polskie* he regarded the lumpenproletariat of Łódź with a deeply spiritual, almost Chagallian eye, completely differently from earlier on. He cast his mind back to a woman he knew, a 'rag-and-bone man's widow' desperately trying to protect her seven children from disease and antisemitic violence. He also recreated the figure of the fruit-farmer and cobbler who 'somehow in the course of the year | patched his poverty with patches'.[55] At first glance naturalistic, this image immediately acquires a metaphysical note, by evoking (even metrically) characters out of Bolesław Leśmian: the mad crippled shoemaker who makes 'shoes to fit the foot of God' and the hunchback who 'even in a sunny, Indian summer . . . dies a real hunchback's death'.[56]

Tuwim counters intolerance and racism with the universalism and metaphorical vision of *Kwiaty polskie*. It is no coincidence that several figures in the poem have botanical nicknames. This 'botanical ethnography' reflects the ethnic abundance of the Second Polish Republic. The poet composes an idea bouquet out of three races, which in reality were incapable of peaceful coexistence, but to which he felt attached. (The poem's first title was *Bukiet* ('The Bouquet').) The significance of the botanical symbolism is further confirmed by the recurring references to the Song of Songs. The 'self-taught artist' Dziewierski writes it out in fine calligraphy; his granddaughter Aniela recites it in church as a counterblast to the messianic sermon of a nationalist priest, provoking a scandal; and echoes of it can be heard in the description of the Jewish fruit-farmer and his family. The Song of Songs is part of the Hebrew as well as the Christian Bible, and it includes the motif of the world as a garden, which is also present in Tuwim's poem (Dziewierski the gardener, the Jewish fruit-farmer, and so on). Thus it symbolizes unity and reconciliation, because the love of the man and the woman in the Song of Songs was interpreted in Jewish tradition as an allegory for the union of Israel and God, and in the Christian one for the union of the Church and Christ. There was no lack of racist references to the Song of Songs in the antisemitic campaign against Tuwim or in the debate it provoked. In his *Asy czystej rasy*, Samuel Jakub Imber, who defended Tuwim against Rostworowski, claimed:

> Mr R[ostworowski]'s 'frankness' in rehabilitating the Song of Songs is evidenced by the fact that he cannot resist the temptation to stress involuntarily that the element of nature in the Song of Songs is 'a commercial fruit-farming element'. And thus the *numerus clausus* has been introduced into nature too! A vegetable garden is Christian–Aryan 'nature', whereas an orchard is second-class nature, of an inferior kind, because an orchard brings the lease-holding Jew to mind. . . . It is certainly going to be necessary to extend nature's *numerus clausus*, Count![57]

Sandauer interpreted Tuwim's attitude to the Jewish question using the concepts of self-hatred and self-demonization, declaring that he 'took care of himself with

---

[54] J. Tuwim, 'Rym', in id., *Utwory nieznane*, 100.   [55] Tuwim, *Kwiaty polskie*, 39.
[56] B. Leśmian 'Szewczyk', in id., *Poezje wybrane* (Wrocław, 1983), 97–8; id, 'Garbus', in id., *Poezje wybrane*, 98–9.   [57] S. J. Imber, 'Rekapitulacja, czy kapitulacja?', in *Asy czystej rasy*, 58.

humour'.[58] Tuwim opposed the antisemitic madness with his Heine-like humour, drawing inspiration from racist stereotypes for his demonic masks. Jewish writers writing in Polish lacked the strength and determination to speak openly about their condition; however, in the coded dialogue that Tuwim conducted with his readers, the poet's masks did not express self-loathing but, on the contrary, exalted the brilliantly creative Polish Jewish diversity.

Translated from the Polish by Antonia Lloyd-Jones

[58] Sandauer, *O sytuacji pisarza polskiego pochodzenia żydowskiego w XX wieku*, 14, 49.

A Church Report from Poland for June and Half of July 1941

TOMASZ SZAROTA

IN 2004 I was honoured to be invited by Father Julian Warzecha to contribute to the Festschrift for Father Michał Czajkowski.[1] The book was partly intended to serve the cause of 'rapprochement between various Christian denominations as well as between Poles and Jews'. In my opinion this cause is best served by speaking the truth—even if this truth is painful, bitter, and shameful. The national debate around the mass murder of Jews in Jedwabne in the summer of 1941 has shown that Poles have the courage to discuss the crimes committed by their compatriots. Faced with the sins of their forefathers, they asked for forgiveness, but the discussion of Polish–Jewish relations did not end there—in fact this was only the beginning.

'Sprawozdanie kościelne z Polski za czerwiec i połowę lipca 1941 roku' ('Church Report from Poland for June and Half of July 1941') was discovered by Krzysztof Jasiewicz in the archives of the Polish Underground Movement Study Trust,[2] and a facsimile of it was included in his book *Pierwsi po diable* (The First After the Devil).[3] There is a copy in the Yad Vashem archive in Jerusalem,[4] which was probably the version used by the first scholar to study the document, the Dutch historian Hans Jansen, who quoted large parts of it.[5] Feliks Tych quoted from the Jerusalem copy in an essay published in 2002 in the bilingual Berlin magazine *Dialog*.[6]

---

[1] T. Szarota, '"Sprawozdanie kościelne z Polski za czerwiec i połowę lipca 1941go roku": Próba analizy dokumentu', in J. Warzecha (ed.), *Słowo pojednania* (Warsaw, 2004), 669–82; repr. in id., *Karuzela na placu Krasińskich: Studia i szkice z lat wojny i okupacji*, 2nd edn. (Warsaw, 2007), 200–18. In preparing this English version, I have made some necessary additions.

[2] Studium Polski Podziemnej, London, Ministerstwo Spraw Wewnętrznych, teczka 46: 'Sprawozdanie kościelne z Polski za czerwiec i połowę lipca 1941 roku'.

[3] K. Jasiewicz, *Pierwsi po diable: Elity sowieckie w okupowanej Polsce 1939–1941 (Białostocczyzna, Nowogródczyzna, Polesie, Wileńszczyzna)* (Warsaw, 2002), 1195–1203.

[4] Yad Vashem, Jerusalem, 0-25/89: 'Sprawozdanie kościelne z Polski za czerwiec i połowę lipca 1941 roku' [copy]. The copy has a note saying: 'from the archive of the Polish Underground Movement Study Trust'. It has a few minor copying errors. I am grateful to Ewa Łazoryk for photocopying it and sending it to me.

[5] H. Jansen, *Der Madagaskar-Plan: Die beabsichtigte Deportation der europäischen Juden nach Madagaskar* (Munich, 1997), 167–8, 464.

[6] F. Tych, 'Świadkowie Zagłady: Polacy wobec Holocaustu', *Dialog*, 60 (2002), 47.

The report originally consisted of nine and a half typed pages, but page 4 is missing. About one and a half pages, less than 20 per cent of the text, concern the 'Jewish question':

We need an urgent solution to the Jewish question which is more acute in Poland than anywhere else in the world, as about 4 million of this highly harmful and in all respects dangerous element live or rather parasitize here. As for the Jewish question—it has to be seen as a special decree of divine providence that the Germans, alongside the many injuries they have been inflicting on our country, in this one respect have made a good start: they have demonstrated the possibility of liberating Polish society from the Jewish plague and shown the way which—even if less cruelly and brutally—we should follow consistently. It is a clear divine decree that the occupiers themselves have aided in solving this burning question, since the Polish nation, soft and unsystematic, would never be able to take such energetic and necessary steps. It is quite clear that the matter is of the greatest urgency, since Jews cause untold harm to all our religious and national life. Not only do they suck the nation dry economically, prevent the development of Polish trade and the participation in it of those in the countryside who can no longer earn their living in agriculture, and deprive our cities and small towns of their Catholic character, but they are the source of all kinds of demoralization of the whole society. They promote corruption and graft, deform our public life through their secret influence on government and administration; they run bawdy houses and engage in human trafficking and inflame the people through pornographic literature; they corrupt the young, infiltrate literature, the arts, and public opinion with immoral and un-Catholic ideas; and finally they always support anything that would harm, weaken, and humiliate the church and Poland. Strangely enough even today, when they are being so ruthlessly persecuted by the Germans, through some peculiar psychological reaction, they hate the Poles more than the Germans and are hoping to take revenge on them for the injuries suffered.

According to the most serious people in the country, when Poland is reborn the Jewish question will have to be handled quite differently. The long-term goal—which must be pursued unwaveringly also in the international forum—is Jewish emigration to some overseas country of their own. As long as this cannot be achieved, it is necessary to isolate the Jews as much as possible from our society. They must unconditionally leave villages and small towns and in larger towns have their own closed settlement areas; they must have their own primary and secondary religious schools, but in higher education must be limited by a strict *numerus clausus*; they must be excluded from the army, from public office, and from teaching young Catholics; and finally, through various means, their participation must be restricted in legislature, in free professions relating to Christians, and in some types of trade and industry. All this will be very difficult and will probably lead to tensions between the government-in-exile—which is greatly exposed to masonic and Jewish influences—and the country, which is organizing itself already now, yet on this depends largely the health of our, God willing, reborn motherland.[7]

Although I will concentrate mainly on this particular section, an outline of the rest of the text will be useful.

[7] 'Sprawozdanie kościelne z Polski za czerwiec i połowę lipca 1941 roku', 6–8.

The report opens with a discussion of attempts by the German occupying forces to gain the support of the Polish Catholic Church for the anti-communist propaganda campaign which started with the beginning of the German–Soviet war. The author mentions two 'surreptitious attempts to win over the higher church hierarchy in particular':

First they tried to persuade one of the bishops to come out with a pastoral letter against the Bolsheviks and thus give the church's blessing to German actions in the East. Then, quite recently, a well-known 'confidential agent' for church matters, Father Odillo (OFM), was dispatched to the episcopate with the proposal that the bishops should establish a kind of regency in German-occupied Poland over not only spiritual but also civilian and public matters.[8]

Both these proposals were rejected. I assume that it was the archbishop of Warsaw, Stanisław Gall, who was asked to write the 'pastoral letter'.[9] Father Odillo Gerhard was a German monk who came to Kraków from Fulda in 1938. The following year he moved to Stopnica and—suspected even before the war of spying for the Third Reich—was subsequently jailed in Bereza Kartuska and later liberated by the Germans. In 1940 he set up a German parish in Kraków and illegally imported surgical instruments from Germany. He was arrested by the Gestapo in 1942 and sent to a concentration camp. After the war he apparently settled in Hamburg.[10] The attempt to create some form of regency meant that the Germans were trying to establish a collaborationist authority consisting not of politicians, but of Catholic clergy. However, the attempt was unsuccessful because the Polish clergy categorically refused.

The next section of the report deals with incidents of persecution and reprisals against Polish priests and monks both in the Generalgouvernement and in the territories annexed by the Reich. It mentions, among other things, the martyrdom of Archbishop Antoni Julian Nowowiejski, but provides neither place nor date,[11] and 'the fate of his suffragan, Bishop Wetmański'.[12]

Undoubtedly, one of the main aims of the report was to create a vision of the future, post-war Poland:

We can be confident that the new Poland, which will emerge from the wartime chaos after the German defeat, will be truly and profoundly Catholic. Initially great difficulties are to

---

[8] Ibid. 1.

[9] I base this assumption on the fact that the governor of Warsaw, Ludwig Fischer, requested a similar pastoral letter from Gall's successor, Antoni Władysław Szlagowski, on 6 April 1943, shortly before the propaganda campaign around Katyń. I am grateful to Dariusz Libionka for this information.

[10] Archiwum Franciszkanów-Reformatów, Kraków: Fr Ryszard Sakiewicz and Fr Tomasz Kon, testimonies, transcribed by Fr Modest Jan Pasiecznik, 1975. I would like to thank Jan Żaryn for this information.

[11] Archbishop Nowowiejski (born 1858) died in the concentration camp in Działdowo on 28 May or 20 June 1941 (A. K. Kunert, *Rzeczpospolita Walcząca: Styczeń-grudzień 1941. Kalendarium* (Warsaw, 2002), 186).

[12] Bishop Leon Wetmański (born 1886) died in Działdowo on 10 October 1941 (ibid. 343).

be expected, due to the still unresolved differences of opinions and methods within organizations struggling for independence, as well as possible clashes between the home country and the London government. Preparations are being made, however, so that as soon as Germany collapses the country will have at its helm a brave and wise man, who is also an outstanding Catholic.[13]

I will return to the issue of possible clashes between the underground in Poland and the government-in-exile, as it also concerns the treatment of Jews as citizens of the Polish state.

A substantial part of the report is taken up by critical remarks about the Catholic clergy. In the writer's opinion, '[the] people have not had sufficiently good pastors' and the clergy 'often discourage the faithful by a somewhat materialistic approach to ministry and lack of courteous and sincere kindness to their flock'. He wrote with apprehension:

Even before the war, as well as now, our good poor people have been receptive to communist or pro-communist or at least very leftist slogans: they have started forming unions without the participation of the intelligentsia and searching by themselves for ways to improve their lot and for passionately desired social advancement. Despite all their affection for the church and religion, they have begun to dislike their pastors, including unfortunately also the head of the church [Pope Pius XII] about whom the most outrageous slanders were being spread in the villages.[14]

The writer was convinced that in order to 'remedy the harm' caused by 'popular movements' and to rebuild the authority of the Catholic Church in Poland it would be necessary to take certain steps:

What is needed first of all is a sensible and truly Catholic government, which would really understand the people's needs and implement the necessary economic and educational reforms—not for immediate party-political or demagogical purposes but for the real good of the country. Next, a great effort is needed to improve the level of the clergy. We need many more priests with a vocation who would truly seek only God's kingdom. Thirdly, there is an urgent need to solve the Jewish question.[15]

Before turning to the solution to this question, the author devoted more than half a page to the problem of church property.

It would be beneficial if the Polish church returned the considerable lands owned by some Latin and Russian bishoprics, chapters, monasteries, and numerous parishes to the state—naturally with proper compensation—for the purpose of distribution among smallholders. . . . I believe that it would be sufficient for the church to retain one farm [to supply] a bishop's table and one farm for a seminary . . . while parish priests could retain—as is customary in the territories formerly in the Russian partition—six *morgas* [three hectares] each.[16]

---

[13] 'Sprawozdanie kościelne z Polski za czerwiec i połowę lipca 1941 roku', 3.
[14] Ibid. 5.   [15] Ibid. 5–6.   [16] Ibid. 6.

This is followed by the previously quoted section dealing with the 'Jewish question'. The last section concerns Poland's mission in the east: 'the spreading of . . . Catholic culture, which it received a thousand years ago from Rome, as its most precious religious and national treasure'.[17] The mission was to consist, among other things, in converting the Russians, in doing which the author believed that 'the Latin rite', that of western Catholicism, would be more successful than 'the Uniate rite' of eastern Catholicism.[18]

The report is not signed and the writer's identity remains unknown, but some details can be gleaned from the text. Undoubtedly, he had access to the Polish episcopate: probably he was a layman, but he might have been a priest or a monk. It is very likely that he was charged with gathering information on the persecution of the Catholic Church in occupied Poland, possibly by the Government Delegation for Poland, an agency of the Polish government-in-exile. He was a deeply religious man with the interests of the church close to his heart, but he was also aware of the faults which weakened its authority, and he had the courage to write about them. He did not belong to the extreme right, although there is no doubt he was anti-communist. He felt the need for social and educational reform in post-war Poland. He saw himself as a Polish patriot and was probably pleased to write that the church hierarchy rejected the invitation to participate in the German propaganda exercises and political games. He adds with pride that 'among lay personalities there wasn't a Darlan or a Kissling [*sic*] to be found in Poland'.[19]

All this has to be squared with the picture of a rabid antisemite that also emerges from the document. Some of his pronouncements about Jews (always written *żydzi* with a lower-case *ż*) and the phrases he uses are simply mind-boggling. He would appear to be following in the footsteps of Father Stanisław Trzeciak, who was notorious in interwar Poland for his radically antisemitic views and wrote many articles and books on Jews and Judaism.[20] Jews were the cause of all of the country's misfortunes—political, economic, cultural, even moral. Jews not only turned Poles into drunkards (the old stereotype of the Jewish innkeeper) but also controlled brothels. This type of nonsense is very frequent in the document—though it is not its most shocking part for the modern reader.

The truly appalling fragment of the report concerns 'the special decree of divine providence' made manifest in the 'good start' the Germans had made in 'liberating Polish society from the Jewish plague . . . which—even if less cruelly and brutally [Poles] should follow'. As the report was written in July 1941, it is unlikely the author was talking about the physical annihilation of the Jews. Perhaps

[17] Ibid. 8.   [18] Ibid. 8–10.

[19] Ibid. 1. Admiral Jean François Darlan was a member of the French collaborationist government in Vichy. Vidkun Quisling was the leader of the Nazi puppet government in Norway.

[20] See T. Szarota, *On the Threshold of the Holocaust. Anti-Jewish Riots and Pogroms in Occupied Europe: Warsaw—Paris—The Hague—Amsterdam—Antwerp—Kaunas*, trans. T. Korecki (Frankfurt am Main, 2015), 43–5.

even in the Third Reich itself the decision had not yet been taken as to 'the final solution of the Jewish question'.[21] The idea of sending the Jews to Madagascar was still entertained in some circles.[22]

What, then, did it mean for the Poles to follow the path shown by the Germans? The scheme for resolving the 'Jewish question' in post-war Poland presented in the report entailed discriminatory legislation against the Jews that would lead to their elimination from the political, economic, social, and cultural life of the country and gradually deprive them of their rights as citizens. The legislation would be temporary, lasting until the Jews left the country.

The report does not give any information about the persecution of the Jews, although it had begun in the first days of the German occupation. There is no mention of the ill-treatment, humiliation, or robbery of Jews, the organized pogroms, such as the incidents in Warsaw at Easter 1940,[23] or the murders.[24] There is no mention of anti-Jewish laws, such as the requirement to wear the Star of David in the Generalgouvernement from 1 December 1939.[25] Perhaps the omission is intentional, or perhaps the author's hostility to the Jews prevented him from noticing the beginnings of the tragedy that was about to be played out. It is not certain whether he was familiar with the underground press, which truthfully reported the worsening situation of the Jews, for example, in the Warsaw ghetto. I will return to this later.

Before proceeding any further, let us compare a fragment of the report with another text, also dealing with 'Polish–Jewish relations':

Strangely enough even today, when [the Jews] are being so ruthlessly persecuted by the

---

[21] The exact point at which Hitler made the decision is still a matter of contention. The German historian Christian Gerlach maintains that it took place as late as December 1941 and was connected with the entry of the United States into the war (see 'Die Wannsee-Konferenz, das Schicksal der deutschen Juden und Hitlers politische Grundlagsatzentscheidung alle Juden Europas zu ermorden', in *Krieg, Ernahrung, Volkermord: Forschungen zur deutschen Vernichtungspolitik im Zweiten Weltkrieg* (Hamburg, 1998), 85–166). Personally, I am not convinced by Gerlach's argument. The police order of 1 September 1941 introducing the Star of David for Jews in the Third Reich, among others, indicates that the decision had been taken earlier. For Hitler's 'order' concerning the extermination of the Jews, see P. Longerich, *Der ungeschriebene Befehl: Hitler und der Weg zur 'Endlösung'* (Munich, 2001).

[22] See Jansen, *Der Madagaskar-Plan*; M. Brechtken, *'Madagaskar fur die Juden': Antisemitische Idee und politisches Praxis 1885–1945* (Munich, 1997). According to Brechtken, in February 1940 in occupied Warsaw Alfred Nossig was working on sending the Jews to Madagascar (223–4). Nossig was shot as a Gestapo agent by Jewish resistance fighters in the Warsaw ghetto on 22 February 1943. He deserves a thorough scholarly biography.

[23] See Szarota, *On the Threshold of the Holocaust*, ch. 1.

[24] The Germans began killing Jews during the military operations in September 1939. Fifty-three Jews who lived at 9 Nalewki Street in Warsaw were arrested on 13 November in reprisal for the killing of a Polish policeman by a criminal released from prison. They were probably shot in the Żerań area on 22 November. See W. Bartoszewski, *1859 dni Warszawy*, 3rd edn. (Kraków, 2008), 94, 98–9.

[25] Cf. T. Szarota, 'The Reaction of Occupied Europe to the Stigmatization of the Jews with the Star of David', *Acta Poloniae Historica*, 90 (2004), 97–111.

Germans, through some peculiar psychological reaction, they hate the Poles more than the Germans and are hoping to take revenge on them for the injuries suffered.[26]

We are aware that [the Jews] hate us more than the Germans and make us responsible for their misfortunes. Why? On what grounds? That remains a mystery of the Jewish soul, but it is an incontrovertible fact.[27]

Although the report mentions the 'ruthless persecution' of the Jews by the Germans, it only talks about it in general terms. Much more can be gleaned from the underground press. On 28 November 1940, after the sealing of the Warsaw ghetto, the *Biuletyn Informacyjny*, produced by the Union for Armed Struggle, precursor of the Home Army, reported:

This is how the Nazis carried out their mad plan to lock up 400,000 people in a tiny, isolated area, completely devoid of free space and soil. Systematic robbery of the Jews continues. Moreover, the rounding up of the Jews used for work outside the ghetto is becoming more frequent. They are taken off the streets, out of their beds at night. The Warsaw ghetto is becoming a gigantic crime: over 400,000 people have been condemned to suffer from the inevitable epidemics and slow death from starvation.[28]

A few months earlier the editors of the *Biuletyn Informacyjny* unequivocally condemned the already mentioned pogrom of March 1940 in Warsaw:

This is a typical work of German agents. By exploiting Polish antisemitism and the low moral level of the Polish masses, this action aims at: (a) diverting the attention of the masses from the occupation, (b) 'sublimating' the accumulated hatred of Germans by transferring it onto Jews, (c) undermining pro-Polish sentiments among the Allies and in the USA, (d) breaking up the anti-German front within the country into competing groups.[29]

This was also the stance of *Polska Żyje!*, the most popular underground paper in Warsaw at the time:

All pogroms must be categorically condemned by the whole of Polish society. Such incidents are harmful both from the ethical and Christian point of view as well as the national interest. . . . We must not copy the Germans. We must not do anything that they would support and aid. We are not allowed to adopt their principles, methods and ideas.[30]

[26] 'Sprawozdanie kościelne z Polski za czerwiec i połowę lipca 1941 roku', 8–9.

[27] Z. Kossak-Szczucka, *Protest!* [pamphlet] (Aug. 1942); facsimile in *Polacy—Żydzi, 1939–1945: Wybor źrodeł. Polen—Juden, 1939–1945: Quellenauswahl. Poles—Jews, 1939–1945: Selection of Documents*, ed. A. K. Kunert (Warsaw, 2001), 213.

[28] *Biuletyn Informacyjny*, 28 Nov. 1940; repr. in *Biuletyn Informacyjny, 1940–1941*, special issue of *Przegląd Historyczno-Wojskowy*, 190 (2001), p. 328. Thanks to the initiative of Grzegorz Nowik, *Biuletyn Informacyjny* has been reprinted in four special issues of *Przegląd Historyczno-Wojskowy*: *Biuletyn Informacyjny, 1940–1941*, special issue of *Przegląd Historyczno-Wojskowy*, 190 (2001); *Biuletyn Informacyjny, 1942–1943*, special issue of *Przegląd Historyczno-Wojskowy*, 195 (2002); *Biuletyn Informacyjny, 1944*, special issue of *Przegląd Historyczno-Wojskowy*, 200 (2003); *Biuletyn Informacyjny, 1945*, special issue of *Przegląd Historyczno-Wojskowy*, 205 (2004).

[29] 'Prowokowanie pogromów—Nie naśladować Niemców', *Biuletyn Informacyjny*, 29 Mar. 1940; repr. in *Biuletyn Informacyjny, 1940–1941*, 114–15.

[30] Biblioteka Narodowa, Warsaw, microfilm 52898: 'Nie naśladować Niemców!', *Polska Żyje!*, nos. 41–2 (n.d.); facsimile in Szarota, *On the Threshold of the Holocaust*, 38.

The Polish underground press differed from the church report in its perception of the situation of the Jews, as a description of the Warsaw ghetto, whose existence is not even mentioned in the report, published in the *Biuletyn Informacyjny* on 23 May 1941 clearly demonstrates.

In the crowded streets wander, mostly aimlessly, groups of pale, thin people, beggars sit and lie under the walls, often you can see people dying of hunger. Every day the orphanage increases with a dozen of babies, every day some people die in the streets. Contagious diseases are spreading, especially tuberculosis. . . . The treatment of the Jews by the Germans shows extraordinary bestiality and barbarity. . . . The Jewish question has been pushed into a blind alley without a solution. Or rather one solution: a slow death from poverty, hunger, and contagious diseases.[31]

Unlike the church report, the underground press was not silent about negative aspects of Polish behaviour and attitudes which were considered shameful. A good example is an article entitled 'Drops of Poison' in *Nowe Drogi*, published by the Alliance of Democrats:

German propaganda in various ways reaches the least resistant social groups. It dazzles the young with brutal power, attracts by flattering the lowest inclinations, attacks on the ideological front. . . . Unfortunately there exists an understanding between certain parts of our society and the invaders. The so-called 'Jewish question' provides a platform where we side with the enemy, adopt his methods and are infected by his sick psyche.[32]

The church report was probably sent to the Polish government-in-exile in the second half of July 1941, a few weeks after the start of the German–Soviet war. Surprisingly, it does not contain any information about the Polish territories which were under Soviet occupation. If the author had had such knowledge he would certainly have made use of it, especially in view of the accusations that many Jews collaborated with the Soviet occupying forces, as it would strengthen his arguments. However, in this respect the underground press could not supply much information either. The events taking place in Białystok, Vilnius, and Lwów were not widely known and hardly mentioned.[33] The article in *Polska Żyje!* about the Easter pogrom in Warsaw continues: 'We are aware of the Jewish danger. We know how Jews behaved towards Poles under Soviet occupation. We know and we remember.'[34] However, there exists no proper scholarly treatment of this topic. Obviously the authorities of the emerging Polish Underground State had some knowledge of the situation and, after June 1941, more information was coming from eyewitnesses arriving from the east to German-occupied Poland. General

---

[31] *Biuletyn Informacyjny*, 23 May 1941; repr. in *Biuletyn Informacyjny, 1940–1941*, 488–90.

[32] 'Krople trucizny', *Nowe Drogi*, 5 Aug. 1941; cited in Kunert, *Rzeczpospolita Walcząca*, 273.

[33] Research is urgently needed on the state of knowledge in the Warsaw centre of the Polish underground about the situation in the Soviet-occupied territories. Only a few articles on the subject appeared in the underground press. In mid-July 1941 it was not known in Warsaw that Jews were being killed in those territories after the outbreak of the German–Soviet war.

[34] 'Nie naśladować Niemców!'

Stefan Rowecki of the Union for Armed Struggle telegraphed to General Władysław Sikorski in London:

Please accept it as given that the overwhelming majority of the country is antisemitic. Even
socialists are no exception. The only differences are tactical. Hardly anyone advocates imitating the German methods. Such methods awakened sympathy [for the Jews], but it
diminished after the two occupations united and the general public learned about the
behaviour of the Jews in the East.[35]

Evidently Rowecki unjustly blamed all the Jews under Soviet occupation. Also he
was probably mistaken in claiming that 'the general public' in Poland was aware of
what was going on there in the years 1939 to 1941.

Controversies around Jewish attitudes towards the Soviet invaders appeared
in London émigré circles as early as the end of 1940 and the beginning of 1941. On
15 December 1940 the London-based *Wiadomości Polskie: Polityczne i Literackie*
published an article by Jan Hulewicz entitled 'Untimely Overcoming', in which
he wrote: 'We, who in the days of the September catastrophe witnessed the joy
of Jewish crowds in the streets of Lwów, Stanisławów, Kołomyja, and Kosów, we
saw and felt acutely the prophetic intuition of Żeromski.'[36] The same paper on
12 January 1941 published a letter to the editor signed by Dr Marceli Dogilewski
on behalf of the Council of Polish Jews in Great Britain. Its most significant
fragment read:

This sentence may easily give a wrong impression, which we suppose was not intended by
the author. We also know about the behaviour of the Jewish public at that time: if a small
part of that community showed joy, it was a negative joy due to the removal of the cruel
Nazi invaders, who were particularly brutal towards the Jewish population—and not a positive joy because of the arrival of the Bolsheviks. . . . We are concerned that Jewish–Polish
relations are not presented in a distorted mirror, as, in a certain measure, is done by the
honourable author in the sentence quoted above.[37]

In his telegraph to General Władysław Sikorski of 25 September 1941, Rowecki
wrote:

I report that all actions and pronouncements of the government and members of the
National Council regarding the situation of the Jews in Poland make the worst possible
impression in the country and greatly facilitate negative and hostile anti-government propaganda. . . . I do not know the reasons which make the government do this, but here [in
Poland] this rapidly lowers its popularity and is exploited by the 'Sanacja' organizations.[38]

---

[35] General Stefan Rowecki, telegraph to General Władysław Sikorski, 25 Sept. 1941, facsimile in
Polacy—Żydzi, 197.

[36] A. Ordęga [J. Hulewicz], 'Przezwyciężanie nie na czasie', *Wiadomości Polskie: Polityczne i Literackie*, 15 Dec. 1940, p. 2. It is not clear what 'the prophetic intuition of Żeromski' refers to.

[37] M. Dogilewski, letter to the editor, *Wiadomości Polskie: Polityczne i Literackie*, 12 Jan. 1941, p. 6;
cited in Kunert, *Rzeczpospolita Walcząca*, 42; facsimile in illustration section (n.p.).

[38] General Stefan Rowecki, telegraph to General Władysław Sikorski, 25 Sept. 1941.

This raises the question of the significant differences of opinion on the Jewish question between the Polish underground and the government-in-exile. The author of the church report wrote about tension and conflict 'between the government-in-exile—which is greatly exposed to masonic and Jewish influences—and the country, which is organizing itself already'. The vision of post-war Poland in the pronouncements of Sikorski's collaborators was at odds with the conjectures and proposals put forward in the report. These pronouncements are still not widely known.

In a speech on 3 October 1940, at a ceremony arranged by the Organization of Polish Jews in London, the Minister for Labour and Welfare of the Polish government-in-exile, Jan Stańczyk, said: 'the pernicious slogans of totalitarianism, racism and antisemitism' had reached Poland and added that he 'would like to emphasize with pride that those slogans have never become the slogans of Polish society, they were always alien to its psyche. The current government in accord with the national psyche and its previous declarations is against such slogans'. Then followed the statement:

In liberated Poland, Jews, as Polish citizens, will have equal duties and rights with the rest of Polish society. They will be able to develop their culture, religion, and customs freely. This will be guaranteed not only by state legislation but also by their shared sacrifices for the sake of Poland's liberation and shared sufferings in this most tragic period of oppression.[39]

On 20 April 1941 Stańczyk, representing the Polish Socialist Party in the government-in-exile, made a speech at the Anglo-Palestinian Club in London. He began by calling antisemitism 'the shame of humanity in our times' and admitted that 'in Poland as a result of its defective economic structure and the large concentration of Jews, mostly in commerce, there have existed groupings which, by propagating antisemitic slogans, attempted to explain mass poverty and to draw supporters from among uncritical lower middle classes'. He hastened to add: 'As Germany's next-door neighbour, Poland was unable to protect its territory from the germs of totalitarianism and racism.' He said the Jewish masses lived in the same poverty as the Polish population, but 'Polish antisemites simplified . . . antisemitic propaganda by trying to persuade the poor that if only the Jews left Poland, they would take their place and find work and prosperity.' He argued further: 'I know that the world Jewry fears that anti-Semitism might come to the fore in the liberated Poland. I am deeply convinced that it will not.'

Stańczyk did not hesitate to deal with the very sensitive question of Jewish emigration from Poland after the war. His views on the subject differ widely from those of the author of the Church report:

Are there too many Jews in Poland and will they have to emigrate after the war? The answer to this question is: 'Yes' and 'No'. In the economically underdeveloped Poland there are too

---

[39] J. Stańczyk, speech at the Organization of Polish Jews, London, 3 Oct. 1940, *Dziennik Polski*, 5 Nov. 1940, cited in *Polacy—Żydzi*, 41–2.

many Jews, since hundred of thousands of Poles were unemployed and lived in poverty. Had there been countries with no immigration restrictions, not only Jews but also Poles would have willingly emigrated when they could not find employment and secured means of existence. But in the Poland which will develop its industry and change its structure from purely agricultural to industrialized economy, everybody—Poles, Jews and Ukraini-ans—will find employment. The question of emigration will become outdated. But let us not forget that the Poland to which we will return will not only have devastated villages and towns, with industry in ruins, but will also be deprived of its intelligentsia. In order to reconstruct the country we will need not only many hands but also brains. Poland will need engineers, doctors, lawyers, scholars—be they Polish or Jewish.

At the end of his speech Stańczyk wondered what should be done if, despite every-thing, the question of Jewish emigration became topical in liberated Poland. He concluded:

Should the problem of Jewish emigration come to the fore, it would have to be solved by Poles in the closest co-operation not only with Polish Jews but with world Jewish organiza-tions. In that case Poland would have to strive together with Jews to secure lands suitable for the development of Jewish national, economic, and cultural life from states who have such areas at their disposal. Only harmonious co-operation of Poles and Jews can solve the Jew-ish problem in a way satisfactory for both sides. All antisemitism must be condemned not only because it is contrary to human feelings, an ignoble barbarity promoting hate instead of love, but also because it precludes any harmonious Jewish coexistence with the rest of Polish society.[40]

Five days after Stańczyk's speech in London, Prime Minister Sikorski met the representatives of the World Jewish Congress in New York. He heard their com-plaints and their claims of Polish antisemitism and pogroms. In reply he presented the liberal and democratic principles of his own government and stated that 'in post-war Poland all citizens of the republic, irrespective of their nationality, race and religion, will be bound by the principle of "equal responsibilities, equal rights"'.[41] On 4 June 1941 Sikorski informed members of the National Council in London (and a week later members of the government) about this declaration. The cabinet of the National Council adopted the declaration as its own resolution, 'Concerning Jewish Policy'. According to the press statement, 'this is the posi-tion of the Polish government, which considers any kind of antisemitic policy damaging'.[42]

According to the 'Directive for the Country no. 2', signed by General Sikorski on 23 June 1941, the day after the outbreak of the German–Soviet war, 'the gov-ernment strongly stresses the need to warn the people not to succumb to the

[40] J. Stańczyk, speech at the Anglo-Palestinian Club, London, 20 Apr. 1941, cited in *Polacy—Żydzi*, 46–9.
[41] Sikorski, speech to the World Jewish Congress, New York, 4 June 1941, cited in *Polacy—Żydzi*, 56.
[42] Government of the Republic of Poland, declaration concerning policy towards Jews, 11 June 1941, cited in *Polacy—Żydzi*, 57.

German incitement to anti-Jewish actions in the areas released from Soviet occupation'.[43] This document has not been given sufficient consideration in the debate concerning Jedwabne. It is important since it shows that the government-in-exile foresaw that the Nazis would organize pogroms in the territory they occupied.

In 1941 the problem of post-war Jewish emigration exercised Polish minds both in the country and in exile. This was not only their preoccupation. The Federation of Polish Jews in Great Britain met in London on 20 July 1941, as reported by the émigré paper *Dziennik Polski*:

Commander Olivier Locker-Lampson, a Conservative MP, well-versed in national relations in Eastern Europe since his days in Poland and Russia at the time of the Great War as well as a long-standing friend to the Jews, emphasized in his speech the right of the Jewish people to their own sovereign state. An enthusiastic applause greeted his statement that the only true improvement in the situation of the Jews can be achieved by their mass emigration from Eastern Europe to Palestine—and that from Poland alone two million Jews should go to their national Jewish home.[44]

Neither the commander nor his audience was aware of the fact that with the outbreak of the German–Soviet war four operational groups of the Sicherheitspolizei and Sicherheitsdienst had began to carry out the 'final solution of the Jewish question'. It did not entail emigration but extermination.

A few months later, on 18 December, an article entitled 'The Jewish Question' appeared in the *Wiadomości Polskie*, an underground bi-weekly published in Warsaw by the Union for Armed Struggle:

No matter which political camp organizes social and economic life in the new Poland, whether it is called 'nationalization', 'socialization', or 'syndicalization', there is no doubt that it will involve far-reaching socialization of trade, credit, and means of production, making it impossible for the Jewish masses to return to their former economic role in Poland. Such a return would be further impeded by the fact that vast numbers of Poles were pushed by the circumstances of war into areas of economic activity which until now had been almost exclusively in Jewish hands. Many Poles will probably remain in their new occupations, and nothing will force them to give up voluntarily or under duress their life and work plans. These circumstances make the radical solution to the Jewish question in Poland urgent and inevitable. The Jewish masses in Poland are condemned to look for places to emigrate to. We are writing this not out of hatred of the Jews but because it is in the interests of both communities, Polish and Jewish, to look for solutions in accordance with the evolution of the Jewish question in Poland.

This evolution concerns both economic and political life. The current war in the Polish lands has demonstrated better than any other period of our history that the Jewish masses are alien to the political and historical aims of the Polish nation. We will not dwell here on the situation in the areas of former Soviet occupation, where Jewish citizens of the republic mobilized to co-operate with the enemy against Poland and Polish culture. . . .

[43] General Sikorski, 'Directive for the Country no. 2', 23 June 1941, cited in *Armia Krajowa w dokumentach*, ii: *June 1941–April 1943*, ed. H. Czarnocka et al. (London, 1973), ii. 8.

[44] *Dziennik Polski*, 25 July 1941; cited in Kunert, *Rzeczpospolita Walcząca*, 249.

Having noted facts of this kind, we do not want to increase antisemitic feelings in Polish society. The Jewish position may be justified from the Jewish point of view by the difficulties of the Jewish situation in pre-war Poland as well as in today's and future Poland. This is not a question of mutual grudges and grievances. It has to be acknowledged that there is a serious and systematically deepening rift between the evolving Polish and Jewish political tendencies. It is not a temporary or accidental phenomenon. Its roots reach deeply into the ever stronger and fuller development of national-political consciousness and separateness of the Jewish masses. It is increasingly difficult to be a Jewish Pole and the necessity to choose between being either a Pole or a Jew—as two separate national positions—becomes more and more clear.[45]

The author of the article could not have known that exactly ten days before its publication by the Warsaw underground, on 8 December 1941, the Nazis had opened the first of the extermination camps in Poland in Chełmno on Ner (Kulmhof).

I have long hesitated before confronting texts written in 1941 with a document on the Jewish question written two years later. It is a long paper entitled 'Remarks on our International Politics, No. 1', most likely prepared by the director of the Foreign Affairs Section of the Government Delegation for Poland, Roman Knoll,[46] and sent to London on 23 July 1943. In the margins of the ten-page closely typed document a number of questions are highlighted, among them 'the Jewish question':

The mass murders of Jews in Poland perpetrated by the Germans will decrease the Jewish problem but not remove it entirely. There is no question that a large number of Jews will survive, and their re-immigration after the war may lead to a Jewish population of one to two million. In view of the horrific persecution of the Jews in Europe, world public opinion will be even more sensitive to their fate and will look after their interests better. In Poland at the moment Christian sympathy for the maltreated Jews prevails. In eastern Poland, however, there is a very strong feeling of irritation towards them from the time of the Bolshevik occupation. In the country as a whole, independently of psychological moments, there is no question of the return of the Jews to their positions and workshops, even in greatly reduced numbers. The non-Jewish population has taken over their places in cities and small towns and this profound change in most of the country is irreversible. The return of the Jews en masse would be perceived not as restitution but as an invasion, to be resisted by all means, even physically.

It would be tragic for our policy if—at the moment of defining our borders, securing credits, entering alliances or federations—Poland were to be pilloried by the world opinion as an antisemitic country. . . . The government is right in assuring the world that there will be no antisemitism in Poland, provided that the Jewish survivors of the pogrom will not try

---

[45] 'Zagadnienie żydowskie', *Wiadomości Polskie*, 18 Dec. 1941; see also G. Mazur, *Biuro Informacji i Propagandy SZP-ZWZ-AK 1939–1945* (Warsaw, 1987), 30). Andrzej Leśniewski, who had worked for the paper, suggested that Stanisław Herbst could have written the article. According to Mazur, he headed the national minorities section of the Biuro Informacji i Propagandy from 1941 onward (ibid. 82).

[46] 'Knoll Roman (1888–1946)', in *Polski Słownik Biograficzny* (Wrocław, 1967–8), xiii. 130–1; cf. W. Grabowski, *Delegatura Rządu Rzeczypospolitej Polskiej na Kraj* (Warsaw, 1995), 116.

to return en masse to Polish cities and towns. There is only one possible solution: the Polish government has to take initiative in advance, preferably immediately, in order to create for the Jews of eastern Europe their own national hearth. . . .

It is too early to specify the locality in question. Our position in this matter must be pro-Jewish and not anti-Jewish. Jews are a nation with the right to have their own territory and their own social structure and classes. Diaspora is their curse and they deserve compensation for the current monstrous persecution, to be secured above all by those nations which for centuries hosted the Jews and after a peaceful separation would be ready to offer the new state economic aid and military defence.[47]

The number of Holocaust survivors was much smaller than anticipated by the author of this text. According to the estimate by Lucjan Dobroszycki, quoted by Natalia Aleksiun, the number of Jews in post-war Poland never exceeded 250,000.[48] The fate of those people, the majority of whom left for Israel and other places, is a completely different subject.

[47] Archiwum Akt Nowych, Warsaw, Delegatura Rządu RP na Kraj, 202/I-34, pp. 54–63: 'Uwagi o naszej polityce międzynarodowej, Nr 1' (22 July 1943), 61–2 (I am grateful to Robert Spałek for photocopying the document). Another copy of the same document, dated August 1943 (202/XIV-9, pp. 134–45), was published in *Polacy i Żydzi pod okupacją niemiecką 1939–1945: Studia i materiały*, ed. A. Żbikowski (Warsaw, 2006), 173–4.

[48] N. Aleksiun, 'O konstruowaniu historii Żydów polskich', in D. Stola and M. Zaremba (eds.), *PRL: Trwanie i zmiana* (Warsaw, 2003), 335.

'I am in no hurry to close the canon'
An Interview with Professor David G. Roskies

PAWEŁ WOLSKI

PW: I would like to centre this conversation on your book *Holocaust Literature: A History and Guide*.[1] The book presents a very interesting vision of a Holocaust canon, mainly because of the 'Guide to the First Hundred Books' included at the end. But before we focus on the list, could you comment on one of the initial statements, in which you argue against a 'one model fits all' canon of Holocaust literature and postulate that it ought to be read 'in all languages. From the beginning: before time, in time and against time'?[2] Does such an approach allow us to conceive of a Holocaust literary canon as a coherent entity? If so, what could its selection mechanism be based on? Doesn't such a concept dissolve any possibility of construing a canon?

DGR: I don't think the operative term is 'coherent'. I would rather use 'evolving'. That is where my concept of approaching Holocaust literature before time, in time, and after time comes from. In other words, my solution to the problem is to posit a periodization. The key issue for me is to look at Holocaust literature over the course of time.

The periodization I present in the book is different from the one in my earlier article.[3] I keep fine-tuning the time-span and number of distinct phases. Even though I know that periodization is an artificial construct, I still believe in its explanatory power. Chronology, I believe, lies at the bedrock of literary research. When you are dealing with a literature that is event-based, it is all the more obvious that you have to start at the beginning. I could never understand

This interview was conducted in English. It was then translated into Polish by Paweł Wolski and published as '"Nie spieszy mi się domykać kanon": Rozmowa z Profesorem Davidem G. Roskiesem, współautorem książki *Holocaust Literature: A History and Guide*', *Narracje o Zagładzie*, 1 (2015), 15–30. The version published here is based on the original interview with corrections by David Roskies.

[1] D. G. Roskies and N. Diamant, *Holocaust Literature: A History and Guide* (Waltham, Mass., 2013).

[2] Ibid. 19.

[3] See ibid., ch. 1, based on D. Roskies, 'What is Holocaust Literature?', *Studies in Contemporary Jewry*, 21 (2005), 157–212.

why most studies of Holocaust literature started somewhere in the middle, as if there were no beginning. So wartime writing for me is the beginning of the story: only here, in fact, can one speak of a closed canon. Why? Because you're looking at books written in a discrete period of time: between 1 September 1939 and whenever the war ended, wherever it ended—let's say: in 1945. It's closed —insofar as one knows when the works were written. That to me is the point of departure. But it is an evolving canon—we keep on discovering new things: manuscripts keep coming to light, such as *Suite française*, Némirowsky's novel.

What happens is that there are multiple beginnings. What's so interesting about our subject is that it is not a continuous, unfolding story. It's very jagged; every few years the clock stops and restarts. I would say that one of the unique features of Holocaust literature is that amnesia sets in: whatever was written during wartime is forgotten, neglected, rejected. On the day of liberation, there's a new outburst of writing. I call this second period 'communal memory', because it is very much rooted in a language, in a culture, and in a particular political environment. 'Communal' is another way of saying 'political', because Holocaust memory in the immediate post-war period is highly politicized. I don't mean only behind the Iron Curtain—the same is true for Italy, France, and certainly Israel, where all publications were in the hands of political parties. Maybe this was less true in the USA: in fact there are relatively few Holocaust texts written in this period in America. So the years 1945 and 1960 are tremendously important because Holocaust literature is reinvented in this period —mostly in total ignorance of what came before. In 1960/1 the Eichmann trial turns the Holocaust into a matter of global concern and gives it its name, 'the Holocaust'. I call this third phase—1960 to 1985—'provisional memory'. Here at last I turn my attention to the United States. The fact that the Library of Congress adopts the category of 'Holocaust, Jewish (1939–1945)' as a catalogue label in 1968 is highly significant. It's not merely a symbolic marker but is really a turning point. There has been such a vast accumulation of writing on the subject that the cataloguers at the Library of Congress cried: 'Wait, wait, we can't keep using the old categories, we can't catalogue everything on the same shelf; it has to have a special name and number, section, subsection.' In 1985 there comes another turning point, driven by a variety of political and cultural events, the period I call 'authorized memory'. By this point in time everyone needs to stake a claim to the Holocaust. You cannot be a self-respecting culture without that. Note what happened in Latin America, where hundreds and hundreds of books were published on the Holocaust and the events leading up to it, but they were all written in Yiddish. By the 1980s and 1990s, with the rapid decline of Yiddish as the lingua franca of Ashkenazi Jews, it was felt that if something is not written in Spanish or Portuguese, it is not authentically Latin American. So with exception of Zvi Kolitz's *Yosl Rakover Talks to God* and Elie Wiesel's *And the World Remained Silent*, the first version of *Night*, the legacy of

Yiddish literary creativity goes underground—the entirety of this diverse and formative body of writing just vanishes. Since there must be a Latin American Holocaust literature, it must at first be based on the translation of a now-recognized international canon. 'Local production', so to speak, will take time to develop. This is why periodization is so important to me. In order to maintain a comparative and global perspective, I keep the First World War in the back of my mind, for the genesis of my work was Paul Fussell's *The Great War and Modern Memory*. This was the first global war, and the body of writing that it produced, both during and after the war, is *sui generis*. Fussell's book is not about 'modern memory' writ large: its sole concern is Great Britain. But that's fine. Thanks to Fussell, we have a template of how to track the development of war literature in a single national culture. Following his lead, others have adapted his template to France, Germany, and other countries. In fact my own research began with Yiddish and Hebrew literature about the First World War. It was a subject that no one dealt with at the time for one simple reason: the Holocaust eclipsed the memory of the First World War. So if you go back to the memory of the First World War you can understand how the comparison between the literatures of the First and Second World Wars can be drawn and where it breaks down. There is so clearly a canon of First World War literature, at the core of which lies the anti-war novel. Why should this be so? Because it was an evolutionary process and the turning point was, of course, Erich Maria Remarque's *All Quiet on the Western Front*, although there were dozens of other anti-war books. Even though the fund of First World War literature is vast, one book or one kind of writing eventually stands in for the whole. For me as a cultural historian the task is to track the evolutionary process in the literatures of catastrophe and war, a process that is anything but smooth, and the second is to look back in time and to ask: is the body of writing that goes by the name 'Holocaust literature' comparable to any other? I would say that the closest analogy to the literature of the Holocaust is the multilingual literature of and on the First World War.

PW: Before I read your *What is Holocaust Literature?* I never thought that some-one from within Holocaust studies—considered by me a separate, autonomous genre—would be able to say that Holocaust literature is comparable to any other kind of writing. The main topos within the discipline is to say that the Holocaust as an event and Holocaust writing as a genre constitute a whole new chapter, 'something else'. But you are saying—if I understand you well—that, if there's anything particular in that kind of writing, it's that it 'eclipses', in your own words, any other kind of writing. Which does not mean it does not have any pre-figurations but that it has become such an immense event in our imagination that we cannot conceive of anything preceding it. Still, we do reach deeper and deeper trying to find Holocaust writing as early as possible. After all, it goes against the decision of the Library of Congress to situate the beginning and the end of the canonical period between 1939 and 1945. Now if that is true, then is there an end of going back in search of precedents?

DGR: The answer is 'Yes' and 'No'. I reject categorically the idea of pre-Holocaust literature. There are no direct precursors, no predictions of the Holocaust which should be considered a part of the Holocaust canon. Such ideas may arise from the fact that catastrophe is strongly inscribed in the Jewish imaginary, especially in such apocalyptic expressionist poets as Uri Zvi Greenberg, akin to expressionist Polish poetry between the wars. Greenberg became an important voice in Holocaust literature with the publication of *Streets of the River* in 1951, but what comes before has to be dealt with separately. That being said, the major thrust of my own research has been on the Jewish response to catastrophe. In Jewish culture there is a cumulative ongoing process where what comes later builds on what is remembered from before and is inscribed into the cultural DNA. This became clear to me when I began to read wartime writing and was so amazed by the prevalence and density of intertextuality. There were so many references! Not necessarily to the First World War, but going back to the Khmelnytsky massacres of 1648–9, to the Middle Ages, or to antiquity. That is the main focus of my *Against the Apocalypse*;[4] and is then instantiated in a companion volume,[5] an anthology which allowed the reader to judge whether what I have described actually exists or not. So my first understanding of the Holocaust as a corpus was wartime writing, which to me was separate, almost sacred in its separateness, but at the same time was an amalgam of everything that came before. The power of this literature derived from its embrace of everything that came before, which was then transformed in a vortex of total destruction and mass murder. Even when a writer says: 'This experience is incomparable, something like this has never happened before', he or she inevitably draws an analogy, and in that comparison they inevitably create a link. Although Holocaust literature is discontinuous and does not necessarily come into conversation with what has been before, there is always some link. And this is what is so fascinating to me. And the third thing—something that became clear to me writing my latest book—is that I reject the idea of a centre of evil: that Auschwitz is the ultimate reference point of Holocaust literature.[6] This is unacceptable to me. There are multiple points on the Holocaust compass. The death camps were indeed unprecedented killing factories, but Holocaust literature cannot be reduced to Auschwitz. I understand why this was so appealing to the Western imagination: trench warfare in the First World War became what Auschwitz became for the Second, a terrible metonymy.

[4] D. G. Roskies, *Against the Apocalypse: Responses to Catastrophe in Modern Jewish Culture* (Cambridge, Mass.), 1984.

[5] D. G. Roskies (ed.), *The Literature of Destruction: Jewish Responses to Catastrophe* (Philadelphia, 1989).

[6] 'For Western intellectuals, Auschwitz became the *telos*, the sum and substance of the Holocaust, the ultimate and exclusive reference point' (Roskies and Diamant, *Holocaust Literature*, 4).

Now the trench was a First World War experience, but it was different for eastern and western fronts: the war was not necessarily fought in trenches in the east. But it became a universal trope nonetheless. There's an expression in English, I don't know whether it exists in Polish: 'over the top'. It means going over the trench to a certain death. That entered into English and has now become a slang expression. Young people say: 'Oh my God, that's really over the top', without any historical memory of where it came from. So my answer is that in war literature—in Yiddish and Hebrew literature in particular—there is a very keen sense of pasthood, of collective memory. Most of Elie Wiesel's writing . . . well, all of Wiesel's writing, is informed by that. It goes for Uri Zvi Greenberg, for Abraham Sutzkever's ghetto poetry, and even for Ka-Tzetnik. The example that I give in *Against the Apocalypse* is *The Diary of the Vilna Ghetto* by Yitskhok Rudashevski, who was a young pioneer,[7] a member of a communist youth movement. What can be more secular than that? In his diary he writes: 'We were rounded up, it was like a scene out of the Middle Ages; we were reliving the Middle Ages.' How does a 15-year-old know that he is reliving the Middle Ages? This is not a religious child who prays three times a day. It was in his DNA, that there was such a thing as a ghetto and there were ghettos in the Middle Ages and that once upon a time Jews were locked up inside the walls of a ghetto. Rudashevski has a sense of déjà vu, we've been here before. So there are precedents, definitely, but the war itself creates its own precedent. And what is also unique about reading Holocaust literature is that you can vicariously experience the birth of a new archetype: when, where, and how the archetype of the Holocaust was created. It did not happen all at once or everywhere to the same degree: the Final Solution did not become apparent in occupied Poland until October–November 1942, while Operation Barbarossa, the genocide of Soviet Jewry, began in the summer of 1941. But globally the awareness that we have never been here before, that this is unprecedented, begins to take shape all over the world, both inside the 'Jew Zone' and outside the Jew Zone, by late 1942.[8] And I would say that Holocaust literature as a separate, discernible genre was born no later than 1943. That's amazing. We don't have another historical event which is so richly documented, where we have so much cross-cultural data and is so richly documented that we can say: 'This is where the archetype was born'. So the Holocaust becomes its own archetype at a certain point in time. And that is another reason why wartime writing is so important.

[7] 'After November 1940 everyone became a historian, from forty-year-old Ringelblum to fourteen-year old Yitskhok Rudashevski of Vilna, both of whom recognized the ghetto as "a return to the Middle Ages"' (ibid. 202).

[8] 'Geography was destiny, and to render that objective and subjective reality, one needs a simple, brutal demarcation of space. What is needed is a new term of art, something so in-your-face and unsettling that it cannot be spoken of in polite company. What is needed is to restore the division of the globe in the years 1939–45 into two zones: a Free Zone and a Jew-Zone. Without such a Holocaust-specific map, it is impossible to imagine what it was like to live in that real time and space' (ibid. 22).

PW: Is there a master trope of Holocaust literature?

DGR: There isn't one, there are many. Auschwitz, of course, is one of them. The idea of *anus mundi*, of another planet, as Ka-Tzetnik describes it (and Borowski; Levi; Wiesel; or even Weiss in *The Investigation*, taking the transcripts of the Auschwitz trial and turning them into a modernist play; Rolf Hochhuth in *The Deputy*; Paul Celan in *Death Fugue*). The texts that occupy the centre of the canon describe the inner circle of hell. But it's only one trope. Another one is what I call Marrano children.[9] 'Marrano' is a reference to the forced conversion of Jews in Spain from the late fourteenth century onwards. I could have adopted the more common term 'hidden children', but I made a conscious choice to call them Marrano children in order to underscore the fact that there were other examples in Jewish history of children forced to hide their identity and pretend to be non-Jews. This aspect of Holocaust literature—children hiding on the other side—came into its own late in the day. One of the earliest texts I found is Uri Orlev's *Lead Soldiers*, which came out in Hebrew in 1956. I would also include Henryk Grynberg's writing in this category. Then we skip to 1990 and Louis Beagley's *Wartime Lies*. And of course Michał Głowiński's *Dark Seasons* is a prime example. But it is obviously going to take a while for this literature to emerge. The children have to be old enough to become writers: 1956 is astonishingly early for this literature. The first edition of *Lead Soldiers* was written in faulty Hebrew. Orlev had not yet mastered the language: he was still thinking in Polish. He only came to Palestine in 1946–7. But it was his first work: describing him and his brother hiding on the Aryan side of Warsaw. So Marrano children is a separate trope. Another is the idea of pilgrimage, going back to the killing fields. This is a trope that will go on forever, as every generation has to go back. Not only survivors: their children, grandchildren, and great-grandchildren. On my list there is a novel by Yehuda Amichai, *Not of this Time, Not of this Place*. It is a story of an imaginary trip back to Germany published in 1963. So the first novel of return—a pilgrimage—is from 1963! It's not even twenty years after the war!

PW: Well, Rachela Auerbach's reportage, written almost immediately after the war, is also, in a way, a story of 'going back' to Treblinka.

DGR: Yes, you are right. It is a very rich topic. In fact there is a travelogue literature in Yiddish written right after the war, 1946, 1947. My colleague and fellow Canadian, Jack Kugelmass, has written a short book on this topic.[10] So travel literature is a very rich topic. The last book on our list of the first hundred books, in fact, is *The Lost* by Daniel Mendelsohn, which belongs to the

---

[9] Roskies and Diamant, *Holocaust Literature*, 175–7.

[10] J. Kugelmass, *Sifting the Ruins: Emigre Jewish Journalists' Return Visits to the Old Country, 1946–1948* (Chicago, 2014).

same genre. That's another reason why the last period begins in 1985: only with the fall of the Iron Curtain do people from the West begin to go back. Arnold Zable's *Jewels and Ashes* came out in 1991, but his trip back to Białystok to revisit the scene of the crime took place in 1986. For someone like me who grew up after the war, going back to Poland was simply inconceivable. It was a cognitive impossibility.

PW: Yes, this is how Levi describes it. And in fact the head of Centro Culturale Primo Levi in Genoa, Piero Dello Strologo, once confessed to me that as a child of survivors he first came to Poland in 2011 when the centre awarded Andrzej Wajda with the Premio Internazionale Primo Levi in Kraków. But apart from this one you made several fascinating points. I'll go back to just one of them: we do not have, as far as I know, an equivalent of 'over the top'. But we do have 'iść na druty', which an informed reader knows the meaning of: to commit suicide.[11] I mention this example because along with the fact that the Holocaust is very deeply rooted in the cultural imaginary, it also creates its own tropes. Do you think we can say that most of them are a completely new, Holocaust-centred formation?

DGR: Some of them are very new. I think Marrano children is new. We didn't have the Aryan side before, we didn't have thousands of people trying to stay alive by hiding outside the ghetto. And the Aryan side created the *szmalcownik* [blackmailer who profited by threatening to expose the Jewish identity of those hiding on the Aryan side] and a whole array of historical possibilities which then became symbolic and finally developed into literary tropes. Another example which I think is unprecedented is 'second generation'. The concept of a generation goes back to the First World War, the idea that the generation of 1914 constituted 'the lost generation'. Our modern generational consciousness has been shaped by the First World War, but the children of those who survived the First World War don't self-identify as a generation of survivors. However, because of the centrality of the Holocaust, we now have second-generation survivors of the Armenian massacre—a growing literature by the children and grandchildren of those who survived the Armenian massacre, as well as the second-generation Roma who are now organizing commemorations outside Kraków. The Holocaust created a new trope; there never was such a thing as 'second generation' before. The idea that generations after the war will carry the psychic scars of the war is new and has to do with the psychological orientation of the twentieth century: post-traumatic stress disorder, the concept of trauma —that the deepest scars are not the battle wounds, not an amputated leg, or the loss of sight or hearing, but something much deeper. And that is trauma, a

---

[11] 'Iść na druty' means literally 'to go to the wires'. It refers to committing suicide in the concentration camps, either by running towards the perimeter fence and provoking gunfire from the guards or reaching the fence and being electrocuted (P. W.).

trauma so deep that it is passed on to your children and to the generations to come.

PW: You very diplomatically mentioned the 'Armenian massacre', but we do from time to time hear of the 'Armenian Holocaust'. So the mechanism of Holocaust trope-making is evidently strong enough to define events preceding it by many decades. I hope this fact allows me to insist on the question about tropes. As you show, we can list both tropes adapted by the Holocaust discourse and those which are apparently new, different, Holocaust-specific. But maybe there is something not about the tropes themselves but about the mechanism of their creation. I would see one: usually archetypes evolve from tropes over long periods of time: centuries, generations, cultures. Nowadays, however, we have tropes evolving into archetypes almost during our lifetimes, certainly within mere decades; the Holocaust speeds things up. It is strongly connected to the dawn of the capitalist culture (which is also linked, according to some, such as Zygmunt Bauman, to the Holocaust): things are supposed to get more and more efficient —and quick. The whole culture speeds up after the Holocaust: from celebrities lasting a few days to archetypes evolving within couple of decades.

DGR: I'll answer with a couple of examples. In Yiddish of course one does not use the word *shoah*. In Yiddish the word is *khurbn*—the same word that is used to describe the destruction of the Temple in Jerusalem. We now know that the word 'Shoah' as a separate term was first used by the poet Saul Tchernichowsky in 1942. Intellectuals writing in Hebrew but actually thinking in Yiddish found the word *khurbn* insufficient and they needed something more terrible. So they went back to the biblical prophets where they found the word *shoah,* and its use as a term for the ongoing mass murders became operative from 1943 onwards. Another example is *Zagłada*. Thanks to Monika Garbowska's work, I know that in all of the historical studies written in the 1940s *zagłada* is written with a lower-case 'Z'. In her studies she says that it's not until maybe the 1990s that *Zagłada* with a capital 'Z' appears. Now it's the 'Catastrophe'. That's fascinating. With the changing of the lower case to the upper case the language makes an extraordinary statement. That's Exhibit B. Exhibit C: in Russian they now use the term *kholokost,* which is obviously a foreign loanword. Why is it foreign? You could have found some Russian-language equivalent, or pronounced the word *golocost*. The reason I think they chose to render the 'H' as 'Kh' is that it is characteristic of the Jewish language: e.g. *Khanuka*. What's more, there are no diphthongs in Russian: you cannot say 'Holoc*au*st'. All of these things need to be studied.

PW: We do use the word *Zagłada*, but more often than not it's *Zagłada Żydów,* 'the destruction of the Jews' (as in the title of the journal edited by Dariusz Libionka, Barbara Engelking, and Jacek Leociak). Do you think that the Jewish experience is a condition *sine qua non* to speak of Holocaust literature as a genre?

I do not necessarily mean the author has to be Jewish: many authors are not (such as Tadeusz Borowski).

DGR: Yes. I do. And that's why I think the Library of Congress did the right thing. The category is 'Holocaust, Jewish (1939–1945)'.

PW: Well then, what about post-trauma as a Holocaust-specific trope? Passing on the experience means that eventually it can also be inherited by non-Jews. Does the 'Jewishness' dissolve eventually? Is that possible?

DGR: Of course it is possible. It is inevitable. In my book I stop in 2008 because I don't want to deal with the turn towards postmodernism. I didn't want to end the book on a polemical note. You know, I do have some critical things to say about Lillian Kremer's encyclopedia.[12] I wrote a book without footnotes in order to create a fairly seamless narrative that would be of interest to a general, non-specialized reader. I also made a conscious decision not to include the term 'post-memory'. Marianne Hirsch, who is a friend and colleague—she teaches at Columbia University—is a very fine scholar; but I refuse to adopt the term 'post-memory', to give equal credence and attention to remembrances of atrocities and traumas that one has never experienced. I am not ready to go there. I am not prepared to mortgage the past in favour of the present.

PW: I know that's not what you mean to tell me, but one could say that in such a case we can now close the Holocaust canon. I am sure you do not mean that —you do include Mendelsohn on your list after all—but if there is no post-memory, then Holocaust literature ends with the last living survivor.

DGR: I suppose what I polemicize with is the following: I think that there are three groups that now sustain a very uneasy coexistence. The first is the Holocaust historians who are excavating the origins, the unfolding, and the aftermath of the Holocaust. The second is the literary scholars, who comprise the smallest group. They are trained as readers of texts. And the third group, which is growing exponentially, are the people in the field of memory. Memory is becoming a separate field. It is both anthropological and psychological and partly sociological. And if you look at most course offerings on the Holocaust, you'll see what they are really about: this amorphous and all-inclusive area of memory. This to me is a matter of a great concern. I believe that in order to do Holocaust studies, one first has to be trained and grounded in a classical discipline. And knowing English is not enough.

PW: But the first two disciplines mix together. Hayden White for example deals with the Holocaust, and more often than not he does it somewhere on the verge

---

[12] 'S. Lillian Kremer's two-volume *Holocaust Literature: An Encyclopedia of Writers and Their Work* (2003) was supposed to be that kind of disinterested summation. Instead, the selection of authors and the allocation of space to each were based on celebrity, current fashion, and political correctness' (Roskies and Diamant, *Holocaust Literature*, 6).

between literary and historical studies. He somehow manages to go back and forth between the historical–ethical and literary–aesthetic fields. But many scholars who deal with the Holocaust merge those two: ethical means for them aesthetic in the sense that ethics, the postulate to speak of the Holocaust, is more important than aesthetics: that is, how we speak of it. And in effect, differently from any other canon in the case of the Holocaust, the 'popular canon' entangles with the 'academic canon': apart from the denial literature, the Holocaust literary canon does not seem to make a clear-cut distinction between 'high-brow' and 'low-brow' writing. It also dissolves the clear-cut distinction between disciplines: historians and literary critics sometimes do the same thing. Do you agree with such a statement? If so, what is the reason for that peculiar state of affairs?

DGR: That's a good question: how come we lost the distinction between high and low literature? The truth is that in our 'Guide to the First Hundred Books' we included some really bad books.

PW: Which ones do you mean?

DGR: I think that Ka-Tzetnik is pulp fiction. Leslie Epstein, borderline kitsch. . . . And then you have this phenomenon of works that fall between the cracks, that defy easy categorization. The prime example is Curzio Malaparte's *Kaputt*. The first mass-market paperback edition in English was sold in the USA as pornography. The cover art shows American GIs looking at a scantily dressed woman sitting under a decapitated statue somewhere in Italy.[13] Now *Kaputt* is a problematical and extremely hybrid work: Proustian, pretentious perhaps, preoccupied with sexual violence, and extremely provocative. But it cannot be catalogued as pornography! So the boundaries have become permeable. Maybe the best example is Art Spiegelman's *Maus*, the first Holocaust comic book. It's read by pre-teens and teenagers who have never read anything else on the Holocaust. There are only two books that my undergraduate students at the Jewish Theological Seminary have read before they enter my class: Wiesel's *Night*, because it's required reading in many American high schools, and *Maus*, which they read on their own because it looks like a comic book. After Art Spiegelman the concept of what is high and what is low is completely blurred because now graphic novels are considered high art. (I should add that while I am a great admirer of Spiegelman, my co-author, Naomi Diamant, is not. Both our views on *Maus* are inscribed in our volume.) So you are right to heed the historians who expose the ethical valence of a text. But I would invoke an earlier group of literary critics and scholars for whom Holocaust literature became a sacred object. I am referring to Alvin Rosenfeld's *A Double Dying*, Sidra Ezrahi's *By Words Alone*, and even, if I may say so, to my own *Against the*

[13] *Kaputt* was first published in the USA in 1946. The cover described here is from a 1966 edition.

Apocalypse. In some of my own writing I speak of a closed canon as a euphemism or a synonym for the word 'sacred', but, once the literature is read as sacred, it is impossible to judge it by any aesthetic standard. And this I find to be extremely problematical. Then there is an opposite problem, namely, that Holocaust literature is inherently anti-aesthetic, pornographic. Everything about it is obscene. And so *Kaputt*'s cover is not entirely wrong. According to Omer Bartov, if you were a teenager growing up in the 1950s in Israel, there was no Hebrew pornography for you to read. If all you could read was Hebrew, the only titillating thing available was Ka-Tzetnik. So teenagers would buy Ka-Tzetnik 'under the counter'. These are two opposite features of the same literature: because it's considered sacred it cannot be judged on aesthetic grounds, but the underlying core of the Holocaust is pornographic; how an entire people was reduced to living in subhuman conditions on the eve of their total destruction. How can such an obscene subject be judged on aesthetic grounds, if it is inherently anti-aesthetic? This is very challenging for people who devote their lives to making aesthetic judgements. What I believe, what I believe in my heart of hearts, is that fifty years from now, a century from now, the only works that will be still be read are the works of literary merit. At the end of the day, the aesthetic judgement will prevail.

PW: Is this why you advise your readers to read Holocaust literature as literature?[14]

DGR: That is correct.

PW: You mentioned books taught in the USA. So how about the teaching canon in the USA?

DGR: Well, the North American (including the Canadian) university has become very PC. A few things have happened. First of all, students are no longer willing to read long texts: they prefer to read in soundbites. So the canon consists of works that are getting shorter and shorter. That is why Wiesel's *Night* and Cynthia Ozick's *The Shawl* are so popular in the classroom. Feminism is a second factor. The self-representation of women is a major feature of Holocaust writing, from the diary of Anne Frank until the present. So short texts written by women are tailor-made for any syllabus of Holocaust literature. Now Ida Fink is among the handful of writers who will still be read a century from now, and not only because she is a woman who perfected the genre of the short story. She is a great writer who exemplifies the principle, as I put it, 'to the extent that women were victims, they were also Jews. To the extent that all Jews were victims, all Jews figuratively were also women.'[15] Such underlying assumptions remain largely unexamined, however, when teachers decide on the weekly reading assignment. No one will admit that the reading list of Holocaust literature was chosen on the basis of brevity and feminism.

[14] Roskies and Diamant, *Holocaust Literature*, 5.   [15] Ibid. 188.

I, too, must be highly selective—I can't assign all of *Kaputt* because it's too complicated and too long. I must think twice about assigning epic poetry, a major Holocaust genre that our students are simply not trained to read. That means I cannot assign Sutzkever's epic verse, only his lyric poetry. For the same reason, Uri Zvi Greenberg is unassimilable, and Yitshak Katzenelson's *Song of the Murdered Jewish People.* Diaries, by contrast, are eminently readable. Holocaust diaries are emotionally accessible: they may be read ironically, because we know how the story ends and the diarist doesn't. We are fortunate to have the new definitive edition of the diary of Anne Frank, in which the censored material has been restored, the record of her emerging sexuality, etc. Diaries are an obvious place to begin because readers can identify with the first-person narrator. But try teaching Chaim Kaplan's diary and see how far you get! Its mental curriculum is much too demanding, even for Israeli students who are reading it in the Hebrew original.

Holocaust Literature: A History and Guide was written for what I would call the curious undergraduate. But even as I tried to simplify the prose, I created a new critical vocabulary. I invented the term 'Jew Zone' because I needed a Holocaust-specific term that did not yet exist, a non-PC term that is hardly acceptable in a classroom setting. I can use the term Jew Zone without fear, in an effort to be provocative. Indeed, one of the most versatile terms I came up with is 'scandalous memory'. The surest way to track the evolutionary course of Holocaust literature is to retrieve the scandals, the public controversies: the controversy about Yosl Rakover, Schwarz-Bart's *The Last of the Just*, Jean-François Steiner's *Treblinka*, *The Deputy*, and so on. What this means is that there are works that violate the reader's horizon of expectations—a concept derived from reception theory. My feeling is that so long as there are works that scandalize us for whatever reason, the Holocaust will always be alive. Once everything becomes sacred, it's a dead subject. What are some of the things that can scandalize us? Calek Perechodnik's diary is arguably the most scandalous work that was rescued from the Jew Zone.[16] That is why it couldn't be published until 1993 in Polish. It's a horrifying work to read. For decades, Yad Vashem refused to publish anything by Jewish policemen. This goes back to 1943, when the Jewish Fighting Organization decided to assassinate the head of

[16] This was published by Karta in a bowdlerized form: C. Perechodnik, *Czy ja jestem mordercą?*, edited with notes and afterword by Paweł Szapiro (Warsaw, 1993). This formed the basis for an English translation by Frank Fox, *Am I a Murderer? Testament of a Jewish Ghetto Policeman*, which was published by Westview Press (Boulder, Colo., 1996). The bowdlerization was exposed by David Engel ('On the Bowdlerization of a Holocaust Testimony: The Wartime Journal of Calek Perechodnik', *Polin*, 12 (1999), 316–29). As a result, Karta withdrew their version and published a new edition with a less provocative title, *Spowiedź: Dzieje rodziny żydowskiej podczas okupacji hitlerowskiej w Polsce* ('Confession: The History of a Jewish Family during the Nazi Occupation in Poland'), and notes and an afterword by David Engel (Warsaw, 2004). Westview Press have not seen fit to withdraw the text they have published.

Jewish police in the Warsaw ghetto. Ever since then, the subject of Jewish police has been taboo. The Hebrew translation of Perechodnik's diary was published by his family. Yad Vashem had the manuscript and would not go near it. So Calek Perechodnik will always be a scandalous work. Reading it for the first time is a shattering, unforgettable experience. And that's what makes it such a timeless work. It challenges your whole outlook on life.

PW: Could you explain the place Binjamin Wilkomirski's *Fragments* occupies in your 'Guide to the First Hundred Books' (a somewhat similar—*toutes proportions gardées*—example is Kosiński's *Painted Bird*)? The fact that the narrative has been denounced as fiction ('autofiction' according to some, a 'scam' according to others) puts the book's right to be on the list under question. However, its position on this list is justified by the fact that it treats one of the central figures of the Holocaust genre: the survivor.

DGR: We included them precisely because they're fake. First of all, they were not immediately understood to be forgeries. In Kosiński's case it took quite a while. In Poland it became an immediate subject of controversy, but in America, even after he was exposed by the *Village Voice*, many influential people continued to believe that what he wrote was based on his own experiences. The acclaim with which he was met tells us about the horizon of expectations at that moment in time. When Kosiński's novel came out, I was in college. I read it in one night. I thought: this is the real thing. A tale of absolute moral extremity, that is allegorical at one and the same time Of course, we all thought that it was true, that it was a species of autobiography, written by an actual survivor. And the same goes for Wilkomirski, whose proper subject is PTSD. Fifty years later, we thought that Holocaust literature should be concerned with one subject alone: individual, indelible trauma. When it turned out that it was fabricated, that we were all taken in, it turned the mirror back on ourselves. So what is considered scandalous at a given point in time is an important signifier. Holocaust literature should scandalize us. So maybe that is my ultimate answer to your question on canon-formation. I am in no hurry to close the canon. I think, quite to the contrary, that so long as there are works we cannot assimilate, that don't fit, that we consider outrageous, that arouse fierce controversy—it's a very positive sign. It means that the subject of the Holocaust is alive and well.

PART III

Obituaries

Władysław Bartoszewski

19 February 1922 – 24 April 2015

WŁADYSŁAW BARTOSZEWSKI, who died of a heart attack in Warsaw in April 2015 at the age of 93, was one of the great figures in Polish public life in recent times. Born into a Catholic family, he grew up next to Warsaw's Jewish district and had many Jewish friends. He became active in the Polish resistance to Nazi occupation and was imprisoned for a period in the Auschwitz concentration camp from which he was released in the spring of 1941 as a result of the intervention of the Red Cross, for which he had been working. He returned to underground activity and was one of the founders and principal organizers of the Council for Aid to Jews, code named Żegota, which provided material and moral support for Jews persecuted by the Nazis. For this activity, he was designated by Yad Vashem as one of the 'Righteous among the Nations'. When asked by the journalist Michał Komar why he had risked his life on behalf of Jews, he replied: 'Because I could not have done otherwise.'

Bartoszewski strongly opposed the communist takeover of Poland and was an active member of Mikołajczyk's Polish Peasant Party. He was also a founding member in 1946 of the All-Polish Anti-Racist League. His activity aroused the ire of the communist authorities, and he was accused of spying and imprisoned for nearly seven years before being released in 1954 on grounds of ill-health. He continued his oppositional activity and also wrote extensively on Polish Jewish topics and on the Second World War. In all he wrote more than forty books. His writing was not to the taste of the rulers of the Polish People's Republic, and in 1970 he was not permitted to publish his work in Poland for four years. An active supporter of Solidarity he was again briefly imprisoned after the imposition of martial law in December 1981. He took an active part in the conferences in the 1980s which led to a major breakthrough in Polish–Jewish relations and the understanding of the Jewish past in Poland. He was one of the founders of *Polin: Studies in Polish Jewry* and contributed to it on a number of occasions.

After the negotiated end of communism in Poland in 1989 Bartoszewski became the country's ambassador to Austria between 1990 and 1995 and subsequently foreign minister from March to December 1995 and again from June 2000 to October 2001. A fluent German speaker, he made a major contribution to the Polish–German reconciliation that has been a central pillar of the new Europe which has emerged since the collapse of communism. This was a role which came to him as somewhat of a surprise. In an interview in 2009 he observed: 'If someone had told me, 60 years ago, when I was standing on the assembly square in Auschwitz, that I was going to be friends with Germans, citizens of a democratic and friendly nation, I would have said they were cuckoo crazy.'

He also played a major role in Polish–Israeli and Polish–Jewish reconciliations and often remarked how proud he was to have been made an honorary Israeli citizen. He was a member of the council of the Polin Museum of the History of Polish Jews and always played a positive role in its discussions. An eloquent speaker, his rapid-fire delivery led him to be dubbed 'Uzi'. He was a great moral authority, whose lifelong motto was 'Be decent.' At the commemoration of his ninetieth birthday, he was awarded a medal by President Bronisław Komorowski inscribed: 'To the one who dared to be disobedient.' In a speech a few days before his death, he remarked:

We need to keep our dignity and values, such as tolerance, friendship and the ability to make sacrifices across ethnic or religious boundaries. We can dream that one day this will become the norm for our children. Because future generations of Jews, future generations of Christians, and future generations of Muslims—hopefully not extremists—will have to live together on this planet whether they want it today or not.

He will be sorely missed. We extend our sympathy to his wife Zofia and his son Władysław Teofil Bartoszewski, the reviews editor of *Polin*.

Antony Polonsky

Ezra Mendelsohn

26 October 1940 – 13 May 2015

EZRA MENDELSOHN, who, sadly, died of cancer in May 2015, was one of the pioneers of the rediscovery of the Polish Jewish past. For many years he was a professor at the Institute of Contemporary Jewry at the Hebrew University of Jerusalem and after his retirement became Rachel and Michael Edelman Professor Emeritus of European Jewry and Holocaust Studies at the Hebrew University. He completed his doctorate at Columbia University in 1966 and subsequently moved to Israel where he spent his entire academic career. A highly creative thinker, he wrote widely on many topics, including the Jewish labour movement, the history of Jews in eastern Europe, modern Jewish politics, and modern Jewish art and music. At the time of his death, he was working on a volume of articles dealing with universalism among Jews. He also served as co-editor for many years of *Studies in Contemporary Jewry* and more recently as an editor of *Zion*. He was also an editor of the monograph series of the Center for Research on the History and Culture of Polish Jews.

His books included *Class Struggle in the Pale* (1970), a pioneering study of the Jewish labour movement; *Zionism in Poland: The Formative Years 1915–26* (1981), which is still the standard work on the topic and awaits a sequel dealing with the period from 1927 to 1938; and *Jews of East Central Europe between the World Wars* (1983), a remarkable work of synthesis which has also been translated into Polish. Also worthy of note are his brilliant synthesis *On Modern Jewish Politics* (1993) and his remarkable account of one of the first Polish Jewish artists, *Painting a People: Maurycy Gottlieb and Jewish Art* (2002). His interest in Jewish art derived partly from his family background which included a number of artists and scholars, including the painter Raphael Soyer. As he wrote in the preface to *Painting a People*, 'three of my uncles, the Soyer brothers, were artists in New York, and while I admit that I took little interest in their work when I was a child, I see now that they had a profound influence upon me. I was extremely fortunate to grow up in a family that honoured learning and was imbued with Jewish idealism.'

His work received considerable recognition. In 2003 *Painting a People* was awarded the Orbis Prize of the American Association for the Advancement of Slavic Studies for the best book in Polish studies that year. In 2005 he was granted a Lifetime Achievement Award in Jewish Scholarship by the National Foundation for Jewish Culture, and in 2008 he received the Bialik Prize of the Shazar Centre in Jerusalem also for *Painting a People*.

Mendelsohn was an active participant in the series of academic conferences which took place in the 1980s and which led to the revival of Polish Jewish studies. One of the highpoints of the Oxford conference in September 1984 was his lecture 'Interwar Poland: Good for the Jews or Bad for the Jews?' Brilliantly delivered, it sparked off an extensive and heated debate and was subsequently published in *The Jews in Poland* (edited by Chimen Abramsky, Maciej Jachimczyk, and Antony Polonsky, 1986) and frequently repeated. Ezra was a member of the editorial board of *Polin* and contributed an important article to volume 8 on the historiography of Jews in interwar Poland.

To our regret, he was unable to attend the International Conference held in Warsaw at the Polin Museum of the History of Polish Jews. One of the sad obligations of the organizers was to mark his death on the second day of the conference. We will long remember his scholarship and striking personality. He was deeply dedicated to a socialist and humanist understanding of Zionism and at the 2012 conference at YIVO on 'Jews and the Left' made a moving plea for an Israel organized on these principles. We extend our deepest condolences to his wife and family.

Antony Polonsky

Jerzy Tomaszewski
8 October 1930 – 4 November 2014

JERZY TOMASZEWSKI, who died on 4 November 2014 at the age of 84, was one of the principal figures in the revival of the study of the history of the Jews in Poland. He was born in Radomsko, a town between Łódź and Częstochowa which, before the war, was the home of a large Jewish community and the court of the Radomsker rebbe. Tomaszewski often remarked that it was the constant presence during his childhood years of hasidim in traditional Jewish dress which made him aware of the multi-ethnic and multi-confessional character of Poland. He was for many years professor and director of the Mordechai Anielewicz Centre for the Study and Teaching of the History and Culture of the Jews in Poland at Warsaw University. After his retirement in 2002 he took the post of professor at the Academy of National Economy in Kutno.

Tomaszewski was one of the pioneers in the study of national minorities in Poland in the twentieth century, above all the Jews, and a great expert on the history of central Europe, particularly that of the Czechs and Slovaks. He was present at all the conferences which transformed Polish Jewish studies. As one of the founders of *Polin*, he was a member of its editorial collegium and contributed frequently to its volumes. For many years, he was connected with the Jewish Historical Institute in Warsaw. A member of its Scientific Council since 1970, he was also elected in 1985 to serve on the institute's board of directors and, in addition, served as deputy chairman of the Jewish Historical Institute Association. He was also a member of the editorial board of *Biuletyn Żydowskiego Instytutu Historycznego* and its successor *Kwartalnik Historii Żydów*, as well as *Polin*. In 2005 he was one of the signatories, along with the Minister of Culture and National Heritage and the mayor of Warsaw, of the agreement establishing the Polin Museum of the History of Polish Jews. In 1998 he was the recipient of YIVO's Jan Karski and Pola Nireńska Award and thereafter served on the Karski Award Committee.

His many publications include *Z dziejów Polesia 1921–1939: Zarys stosunków społeczno-ekonomicznych* ('On the History of Polesie 1921–1939: An Outline of Social and Economic Conditions', 1963), *Rzeczpospolita wielu narodów* ('A Republic of Many Nations', 1985), *Ojczyzna nie tylko Polaków: Mniejszości narodowe w Polsce w latach 1918–1939* ('A Fatherland not only for Poles: National Minorities in

Poland in the Years 1918–1939', 1985), and *Preludium Zagłady: Wygnanie Żydow polskich z Niemiec w 1938 r.* ('Prelude to Destruction: The Expulsion of Polish Jews from Germany in 1938', 1998). His latest book *Czechy i Słowacja* ('The Czech Lands and Slovakia') was published only a few months before his death. The conference held in London on 15 January to launch volume 27 of *Polin* was dedicated to his memory. He will be sorely missed. We express our condolences to his wife Zofia, his daughter Agata, and his family.

Antony Polonsky

Feliks Tych

31 July 1929 – 17 February 2015

FELIKS TYCH, who died on 17 February 2015, was a leading figure in Jewish life in Poland and was, from 1996 to 2007, director of the Jewish Historical Institute in Warsaw. Born in Warsaw, he grew up in Radomsko in central Poland, the ninth child of the owner of a metal works. The town was the site of the first ghetto to be established in the General Government after the German invasion of Poland in 1939. In the summer of 1942, his parents entrusted him to a non-Jewish friend who brought him secretly to Warsaw, where he survived on false documents as the 'orphaned' nephew of a Polish high-school teacher. His parents and siblings were murdered in Treblinka.

He studied history at the University of Warsaw and received his habilitation with a study of the left wing of the Polish Socialist Party during the First World War which was published as *PPS-Lewica w latach wojny 1914–1918* ('The Polish Socialist Party—Left in the War Years, 1914–1918', 1960). He had already become a researcher at the archive of the Institute of the Polish Labour Movement and succeeded in convincing the Historical Institute of the Central Committee of the Polish Communist Party to publish a journal on social and labour history, the quarterly *Z Pola Walki* of which he became editor-in-chief. He was also subsequently employed by the Institute of History at the Polish Academy of Science. In 1966 he published a biographical study of the Polish revolutionary Julian Marchlewski co-authored with Horst Schumacher under the title *Julian Marchlewski: Szkic biograficzny* ('Julian Marchlewski: A Biographical Sketch').

He was dismissed from this post in the 'anti-Zionist' campaign of 1968 and also 'purged' from all other scholarly bodies, losing his position at *Z Pola Walki*. His wife, Lucyna, daughter of Jakub Berman, a key figure in the establishment of communist rule in Poland after 1944, lost her position as stage director. Tych continued his scholarly research as an 'independent writer', publishing three volumes of the letters from Rosa Luxemburg to Leon Jogiches under the title *Listy do Leona Jogiches-Tyszki 1893–1914* ('Letters to Leon Jogiches-Tyszka', 1968–71). These made him well known outside Poland, and he became an honorary member of the International Conference of Labour and Social History, playing an active role in the conferences it organized in Linz in Austria. In the early 1970s he was again hired as a researcher at the archive of the Central Committee of the Polish

Communist Party. Here he became editor of the periodical *Archiwum Ruchu Robotniczego*. In 1970 he was granted the title of associate professor and in 1982 full professor.

As he grew older Tych became more interested in his Jewish background. This led him to take the position of director of the Jewish Historical Institute (Żydowski Instytut Historyczny; ŻIH). Here his expertise in the publishing of document collections gave a new impetus to publishing the rich archives of the ŻIH, above all the archive organized in the Warsaw ghetto by Emanuel Ringelblum. He also wrote a major study of the Holocaust, *Długi cień Zagłady: Szkice historyczne* ('The Long Shadow of the Holocaust: Historical Sketches', 1999). Among the other books on this topic which he wrote, edited, or co-edited are *Facing the Nazi Genocide: Non-Jews and Jews in Europe* (co-edited with Beate Kosmala, 2004), *Pamięć: Historia Żydów polskich przed, w czasie i po Zagładzie* (2004; published in English as *Memory: History of Polish Jews Before, During and After the Holocaust*, 2008), *Widziałem Anioła Śmierci. Losy deportowanych Żydów polskich w ZSRR w latach II wojny światowej* ('I Saw the Angel of Death: Experiences of Polish Jews deported to the USSR during the Second World War', co-edited with Maciej Siekierski, Magdalena Prokopowicz, and Adam Rok, 2006), and *Kinder über den Holocaust: Fruhe Zeugnisse 1944–1948* ('Children on the Holocaust: Early Testimonies 1944–1948', co-edited with Alfons Kenkmann et al., 2008). Most recently he co-edited an extensive study of the history of the Jews in Poland since the Second World War with Monika Adamczyk-Garbowska, published by Yad Vashem in 2013 as *Jewish Presence in Absence: The Aftermath of the Holocaust in Poland, 1945–2010*.

On Holocaust Memorial Day, 27 January 2010, he was asked to address the German Bundestag and gave a moving account of his family's fate under the Nazi occupation. He concluded his speech as follows:

The internalization of the meaning of the Holocaust requires a quantitative change in our ethical understanding. It will remain distorted and incomplete as long as the complicity of other European governments and peoples in the German state in organized criminality, planned and executed from here in Berlin, does not become a part of the European historical consciousness.

Cheerful and outgoing, Tych was a born raconteur and congenial companion. He will be sorely missed. Our condolences go to his wife and family.

Antony Polonsky

Notes on the Contributors

ELIYANA R. ADLER is an associate professor in history and Jewish studies at Pennsylvania State University. She is the author of *In her Hands: The Education of Jewish Girls in Tsarist Russia* (Detroit, 2011) and articles on the history of Jewish education. Currently she is preparing a manuscript on the experiences of Polish Jewish refugees in the Soviet Union during the Second World War.

IDO BASSOK is a poet, translator, and researcher of Hebrew literature and modern Jewish history in eastern Europe. His doctorate addressed Jewish family structure and children's education during the interwar period in Poland. Two books related to his doctoral project have been published in Hebrew: the anthology *Alilot ne'urim: otobiyografyot shel benei no'ar yehudim mipolin bein shetei milḥamot olam* (Tel Aviv, 2011) and *Teḥiyat hane'urim: mishpaḥah veḥinukh beyahadut polin bein milḥamot ha'olam* (Jerusalem, 2015). He has recently completed a comprehensive biography of the Hebrew poet Shaul Tchernichovsky.

GEOFFREY CLAUSSEN is the Lori and Eric Sklut Emerging Scholar in Jewish Studies, assistant professor of religious studies, and the Jewish Studies Program co-ordinator at Elon University. He holds a BA (summa cum laude) from Carleton College and an MA, rabbinic ordination, and Ph.D. from the Jewish Theological Seminary of America. He is current president of the Society of Jewish Ethics and is the author of *Sharing the Burden: Rabbi Simḥah Zissel Ziv and the Path of Musar* (Albany, NY, 2015).

LEVI COOPER undertakes research on legal history in the late modern period and the interplay between Jewish legal writing and broader legal, intellectual, and cultural contexts. He teaches at the Pardes Institute of Jewish Studies, Jerusalem. After completing his doctorate at Bar-Ilan University Faculty of Law, he was awarded postdoctoral fellowships in Bar-Ilan University Faculty of Law (2012–14), Tel Aviv University Faculty of Law (2014–15), and the Israeli Inter-University Academic Partnership in Russian and Eastern European Studies (2015–16).

JORDANA DE BLOEME is a doctoral candidate in the Centre for Jewish Studies of the Department of Humanities at York University, Toronto. Her dissertation, 'Creating Yiddishist Youth: The Vilna Educational Society in Interwar Vilna', looks at Polish–Jewish acculturation through secular Yiddish schooling and informal education in interwar Vilna. She is a former visiting research fellow at the Hebrew University of Jerusalem and a former Melezin Fellow at the YIVO Institute for Jewish Research. Her research interests include east European Jewish history, Yiddish studies, and nationalism of stateless cultures.

AGNIESZKA FRIEDRICH is an assistant professor working in the Institute of Polish Philology at the University of Gdańsk. She is the author of *Bolesław Prus wobec kwestii żydowskiej* (Gdańsk 2008). Currently she is undertaking research on Polish antisemitic journalism in the weekly *Rola* from 1883 to 1912.

BRIAN HOROWITZ is the Sizeler Family Chair Professor at Tulane University. He is the author of numerous monographs on Russian Jewry, including *Empire Jews: Jewish Nationalism and Acculturation in 19th- and early 20th-Century Russia* (Bloomington, Ind., 2009), *Jewish Philanthropy and Enlightenment in Late-Tsarist Russia* (Seattle, 2009), *Russian Idea—Jewish Presence: Essays on Russian-Jewish Intellectual Life* (Brighton, Mass., 2013), and most recently he edited the first English translation of Vladimir Jabotinsky's *Story of my Life* (Detroit, 2016).

VICTORIA KHITERER is an associate professor of history and director of the Conference on the Holocaust and Genocide at Millersville University, Pennsylvania. She holds a Ph.D. in Russian Jewish history from the Russian State University for the Humanities, Moscow (1996) and a Ph.D. in Near Eastern and Judaic studies from Brandeis University (2008). She is author and editor of five books and over eighty articles on Russian and east European Jewish history. Among her books are *Jewish Pogroms in Kiev during the Russian Civil War, 1918–1920* (Lewiston, NY, 2015) and *Jewish City or Inferno of Russian Israel? A History of the Jews in Kiev before February 1917* (Boston, 2016).

KAMIL KIJEK received his Ph.D. from the Institute of History at the Polish Academy of Science in Warsaw. He is assistant professor in the Jewish Studies Department at the University of Wrocław and a former Prins Foundation Post-doctoral Fellow at the Center for Jewish History and Sosland Fellow at the United States Holocaust Memorial Museum.

ANDREW N. KOSS is the associate editor of *Mosaic*. He received his doctorate from Stanford University in 2010 and is currently writing a book tentatively titled *The Jews of Vilna during the First World War*.

SEAN MARTIN is associate curator for Jewish history at Western Reserve Historical Society in Cleveland, Ohio. He is the author of *Jewish Life in Cracow, 1918–1939* (London, 2004). His research interests include the history of Jewish child welfare in Poland.

JOANNA B. MICHLIC is a member of the Centre for Collective Violence, Holocaust and Genocide Studies at University College, London. She is also a member of the International History Initiative, the Historical Commissions Project of the Carnegie Council for Ethics in International Affairs, set up by Elazar Barkan of Columbia University. Her publications include *The Neighbors Respond: The Controversy about Jedwabne* (co-edited with Antony Polonsky; Princeton, NJ, 2004) and *Poland's Threatening Other: The Image of the Jew from 1880 to the Present* (Lincoln,

Neb., 2006). She is currently working on a monograph, *The Social History of Jewish Children in Poland: Survival and Identity, 1945–1949*. She has written articles for *East European Jewish Studies*, *Holocaust and Genocide Studies*, *Jewish Social Studies*, and *Polin*. Her research interests include the history and culture of east European Jewry, childhood in eastern Europe, the Holocaust and its memory in eastern Europe, and nationalism and minorities in Europe.

KATARZYNA PERSON is an assistant professor at the Jewish Historical Institute in Warsaw. She is a historian of east European Jewish history and has written on the Holocaust and its aftermath in occupied Europe. She also edited five volumes of documents from the Underground Archive of the Warsaw Ghetto.

ANTONY POLONSKY is emeritus professor of Holocaust studies at Brandeis University and chief historian of the Museum of the History of Polish Jews, Warsaw. Until 1991 he was Professor of International History at the London School of Economics and Political Science. He is co-chair of the editorial board of *Polin*; author of *Politics in Independent Poland* (1972), *The Little Dictators* (1975), and *The Great Powers and the Polish Question* (1976); co-author of *A History of Modern Poland* (1980) and *The Beginnings of Communist Rule in Poland* (1981), and co-editor of *Contemporary Jewish Writing in Poland: An Anthology* (2001) and *The Neighbors Respond: The Controversy Over the Jedwabne Massacre in Poland* (2004). His most recent work is the three-volume *Jews in Poland and Russia* (Littman Library, 2010, 2012), published in 2013 in a single-volume abridged version as *The Jews in Poland and Russia: A Short History*.

SZYMON RUDNICKI is professor emeritus of Polish contemporary history at Warsaw University and specializes in the history of Poland. He is the author of several monographs and many articles about Polish nationalistic and right-wing political movements and Polish–Jewish relations. Among his most important books are *Obóz Narodowo-Radykalny: geneza i działalność* (Warsaw, 1985), *Żydzi w parlamencie II Rzeczypospolitej* (Warsaw, 2004), and *Równi, ale niezupełnie* (Warsaw, 2008).

VASSILI SCHEDRIN is Alfred and Isabel Bader Postdoctoral Fellow in the Department of History at Queen's University in Kingston, Canada. He earned his Ph.D. in modern Jewish history at Brandeis University and has taught Jewish history at many campuses in North America and overseas, including Virginia Tech, Ohio University, Franklin and Marshall College, University of Florida, and St Petersburg State University in Russia. Schedrin has recently finished his first book, examining the political and social aspects of the official Jewish policies in the late Russian empire, and is currently researching new book projects on the history of the Yiddish theatre in the Soviet Union and on Jewish history writing in nineteenth-century Russia.

NAOMI SEIDMAN is Koret Professor of Jewish Culture and director of the Richard S. Dinner Center for Jewish Studies at the Graduate Theological Union. She is the author of *A Marriage Made in Heaven: The Sexual Politics of Hebrew and Yiddish* (Berkeley, Calif., 1997), *Faithful Renderings: Jewish–Christian Difference and the Politics of Translation* (Chicago, 2006), and *The Marriage Plot: Or, How Jews Fell in Love with Love, and with Literature* (Stanford, Calif., 2016). She is presently working on a translation of Sarah Schenirer's collected writings and a study of the emergence of Orthodox Jewish girls' education in interwar Poland for the Littman Library.

ADVA SELZER is a historian and educator. She develops and writes educational programmes in history, political science, and critical thinking for high-school teachers and teaches history and critical thinking in high school in Tel Aviv.

ANNA SOMMER SCHNEIDER received her Ph.D. from the Department of Jewish Studies at the Jagiellonian University in Kraków. Currently she is an adjunct professor at the Program for Jewish Civilization, Georgetown University. She is the author of *Sze'erit Hapleta: Ocaleni z Zagłady. Działalność American Jewish Joint Distribution Committee w Polsce w latach 1945–1989* (Kraków, 2014) and co-author of *Ratunek, pomoc i odbudowa: 100 lat Jointu w Polsce* (Kraków, 2014). She is also the author of scholarly and critical articles on Holocaust memory and the history of the Jews in post-war Poland.

TOMASZ SZAROTA is a professor in the Institute of History of the Polish Academy of Sciences in Warsaw. He is the author of *Stefan Rowecki 'Grot'* (Warsaw, 1993), a biography of the commander of the Armia Krajowa; of *Okupowanej Warszawy dzień powszedni* (Warsaw, 1972), which has gone through four editions; and of *Życie codzienne w stolicach okupowanej Europy* (Warsaw, 1995). His *U progu Zagłady. Zajścia antyżydowskie i pogromy w okupowanej Europie: Warszawa, Paryż, Antwerpia, Kowno* (Warsaw, 2000) has appeared in English as *On the Threshold of the Holocaust. Anti-Jewish Riots and Pogroms in Occupied Europe: Warsaw—Paris—The Hague—Amsterdam—Antwerp—Kaunas* (Frankfurt am Main, 2015).

GIOVANNA TOMASSUCCI is an associate professor of Polish literature and language at the University of Pisa. In 1987 she completed her Ph.D. thesis on Polish Baroque poetry. She has translated the work of Polish writers and poets, including Anatol Stern, Julian Tuwim, Kazimierz Brandys, Tadeusz Borowski, and Hanna Krall, into Italian and published on the Polish renaissance; Baroque, Romantic, and contemporary Polish literature; and Polish–Italian cultural relations. Her most recent research focuses on twentieth-century Polish poetry (Polish Futurism, Julian Tuwim, Czesław Miłosz, Wisława Szymborska) and links between the Jewish tradition and Polish twentieth-century culture. She is a member of the editorial staff of *Pl.it: Rassegna italiana di argomenti polacchi* and *Przestrzenie teorii*.

JEFFREY VEIDLINGER is Joseph Brodsky Collegiate Professor of History and Judaic Studies and director of the Frankel Center for Judaic Studies at the University of Michigan. He is the author of the award-winning books *The Moscow State Yiddish Theater: Jewish Culture on the Soviet Stage* (Bloomington, Ind., 2000), *Jewish Public Culture in the Late Russian Empire* (Bloomington, Ind., 2009), and *In the Shadow of the Shtetl: Small-Town Jewish Life in Soviet Ukraine* (Bloomington, Ind., 2013).

DANIEL VIRAGH recently submitted his dissertation on Hungarian Jewish identity to the University of California, Berkeley. He is currently researching the effects of industrialization on religious Jews in eastern Hungary at the beginning of the twentieth century.

PAWEŁ WOLSKI is an assistant professor at the University of Szczecin. He holds an MA in comparative literature from the University of Genoa and a Ph.D. in human studies from the University of Szczecin. His main academic interests are literary theory and Holocaust studies, especially the representation of sport as a bodily experience in Holocaust literature. His doctoral dissertation was awarded second prize in the fifth Majer Bałaban competition organized by the Jewish Historical Institute and was published as *Tadeusz Borowski i Primo Levi: Przepisywanie literatury Holocaustu* (Warsaw, 2013).

Index